IN ESSENTIALS UNITY

REFLECTIONS ON THE NATURE
AND PURPOSE OF THE CHURCH

In Honor of Frederick R. Trost

M. Douglas Meeks & Robert D. Mutton, Editors

Kirk House Publishers
Minneapolis, Minnesota

IN ESSENTIALS UNITY
REFLECTIONS ON THE NATURE
AND PURPOSE OF THE CHURCH

Library of Congress Cataloging-in-Publication Data

In Essentials Unity : reflections on the nature and purpose of the church : in
honor of Frederick R. Trost / M. Douglas Meeks & Robert D. Mutton, editors.
    p.cm.
   Includes bibliographical references
   ISBN 1-886513-13-9
   1. Church. I. Trost, Frederick R. II. Meeks, M. Douglas. III. Mutton, Robert
D.
  BV600.3 .I62 2001
  262--dc21

                  2001029673

Kirk House Publishers, PO Box 390759, Minneapolis, MN 55439
Manufactured in the United States of America

In necessariis unitas,

in dubiis liberatas,

in omnibus caritas

Table of Contents

Section I

The Nature of the Church

Section II

The Centrality of Christ, the Word

Art

Section III

The Vocation of the Pastor

Section IV

The Mission of the Community

Section V

Remembrances

Foreword

The contributions of this volume honor the life and ministry of Frederick Richard Trost. The wide range and variety of the pieces reflect the scope and multiple facets of his ministry. He has been a pastor, author, editor, judicatory officer, denominational and ecumenical leader, theological educator, prophetic witness in national and international politics, and quickener of the conscience of a generation. His friendship and compassion have touched people in all dimensions of the life of the church and society. The sweet partnership through which Fred and Louise have testified to God's steadfast love and the gift of family has lifted our spirits in the uncertainty around us. It is no wonder, then, that there should be such a variety of responses to what God has wrought in the ministry of Frederick Trost. Moreover, it should be no surprise that in a book celebrating his forty-year ministry various genres appear side by side: essays of a more scholarly bent, sermons on several occasions, prayers of God's people, and, in the closing section, personal narratives of Frederick's ministry.

The reader will discover pulsing through these literary offerings a deep sense of gratitude to Frederick for his uncommon steadfastness in discipleship, and, in not a few places, the stimulation of the inimitable Trost spirit itself will be delightfully discovered. For the witnesses congregated under the covers of this book are, one and all, recipients of the encouragement that has flowed from the largeness of his heart.

The themes that emerge in this book have been the daily passions of Frederick Trost: The church's faithful worship, sound theology, fellowship of love, and mission of justice to a divided and violent world. It has always seemed to me appropriate to call Frederick Trost "Bishop," if the term is rightly understood. The title "Bishop" is, of course, foreign to the United Church of Christ lexicon, but according to ecumenical theology every church has the *episkopē*; the only question being where it is located. The Greek word means literally the one who overlooks or supervises, but the word can also mean the one who looks around or goes around a region. Bishop Augustine maintained that if a bishop only rules, he or she is no bishop, and agreed with earlier teachers of the church that the two most important functions of the bishop are: to teach the faith and thus seek the unity of the church in Jesus Christ, and, secondly, to look around the region for the poor and unite the congregations in their ministry to the poor and their ministry of reconciliation and peacemaking in the world. In these ways Frederick Trost has manifestly performed the ancient offices of the *episkopē*.

In a time of theological confusion he has cried out for a faithful theology that is the church's self-examination according to the truth it confesses in the living Christ attested by scripture. It may be that he has been the chief theological teacher of the United Church of Christ in his generation, tirelessly studying the scripture with pastors and lay people in his own Conference and throughout the church. He has given leadership to the UCC in remembering its theological traditions. He has brought into the present the richness of his beloved Reformation traditions, Luther and Calvin, Bonhoeffer and Barth, and yet he has understood that all theology has to be profoundly ecumenical and thus has led a life of communion with the other churches of Christ.

And in the midst of all of this Fred has been a pastor to a multitude of pastors and laypersons. We go to Fred when we are in pain and in joy because we know he is neither an optimist nor a pessimist. Rather he lives in the Christian dialectic of hope and despair. He can fall into despair because the church he loves so much can so easily fail its Lord. But because in the end he counts on nothing but the resurrection power of God over death, he is an amazing fountain of hope. Nothing but this hope could possibly explain his contagious humor about the human condition.

And because of this tested hope he has been a bishop in the second sense. He has been in the trouble spots. He has stood with the poor in Central America and in this country, been in jail because of his protest for peace and justice, and refused to pay taxes for the support of unjust wars and the militarization of our lives. To sense the secret of this bishop's passion, his perseverance, his courage, his sense of humor, you have to know about his love of the gospel.

And so the authors hope that our contributions celebrating the witness of Frederick Trost may point to this gospel and serve the church's life in the grace of God.

The editors would like to thank three persons who served as an editorial committee with us. Jacki Mitchell, Blair Gilmer Meeks, and Catherine Rasmussen did the job of manuscript editing. Theirs was a task so mammoth that we marvel at the good nature and sound judgment with which they did their work.

On behalf of all the contributors and readers of this volume we also express a deep gratitude to those who have given generously to make it possible: Theodore Tetzlaff, Chicago, Illinois; James and Deborah Fellowes, Wheaton, Illinois; St. Pauls United Church of Christ, Chicago, Illinois; William and Dolores Wenzler, Milwaukee, Wisconsin; Betty and Corkey Custer, Madison, Wisconsin; John Reed, Oregon, Wisconsin; David and Valerie Black, Radnor, Pennsylvania.

M. Douglas Meeks

SECTION I

THE NATURE
OF THE CHURCH

No Other Foundation

Hans-Jürgen Abromeit

The nature of the church is not immediately apparent, in contrast, to other communities whose nature is quite obvious. Common sense allows us to understand why families, marriages, independent organizations, or the state exist. The family primarily provides a general framework for a new generation, where children experience a sense of closeness and affection and where they learn to deal with challenges and responsibilities. Marriage provides security, where a husband and wife complement, respect, and love each other. It is a life-long relationship that forms the foundations of the family across generations. Independent organizations, movements, and non-governmental organizations (NGOs) provide us with a means of achieving objectives and bringing about changes in a civil society. Parties seek to gain majority approval for certain policies, manifestos, and members. It is the responsibility of the state to provide a framework within which its citizens can live together peacefully and in a just manner.

But what purpose does the church serve? Is its nature distinct from that of the state or NGOs? The church has constantly found itself being drawn into forming ties with other communities, particularly with the state. Throughout history, since the days of Constantine the Great, Charles the Great, the Prussians, and right up to the present day, there are many examples of the unholy alliance between the throne and the altar. In most cases, the church hoped to gain power by forming these alliances. However, only when it was too late did the church realize that its credibility was suffering as a result. Today's trend towards closer links between the church and NGOs is also not without its problems. The church of Jesus Christ is not an environmental organization, a freedom movement, nor is it an organization for providing social welfare. While it is true that the nature of Christian life is certainly sympathetic towards such movements, and indeed often shares their goals, the origins of the church lie somewhere very different. So what makes the church unique?

Born of the Spirit

The church, wherever it may be, cannot be driven by humanity, nor can it be invoked by spiritual means. The confessional writings from the Reformation period express biblical theology succinctly: "That we may obtain this faith, the Ministry of Teaching the Gospel and administering the Sacraments was instituted. For through the Word and Sacraments, as through instruments, the Holy Ghost is given, who works faith; where and when it pleases God, in them that hear the Gospel, to wit, that God, not for our own merits but for Christ's sake, justifies those who believe that they are received into grace for Christ's sake" (*Confessio Augustana* = CA V). The church is born out of God's indeterminable Word (*creatura verbi*). Through the doctrine of the gospel and the administration of sacraments, God bestows the Holy Ghost. The Holy Ghost is indeterminable, bestowing faith "where and when it pleases God." The church of Jesus Christ on earth is born of the Spirit and depends on God alone.

The church is a communion of the faithful. CA VII emphasizes that the church is "the congregation of saints, in which the Gospel is rightly taught, and the Sacraments are rightly administered" (CA VII). The phrase "the congregation of saints" suggests that the church exists within a clear and tangible framework. One can enter this congregation, feel angered by it, or derive pleasure from it. It is a communion of people, on whom God has acted, congregating at a particular place at a particular time. The concept of time and place is the basis of realistic theology. Yet the Christian church does not exist in an entirely pure form, "since in this life many hypocrites and evil persons are mingled therewith" (CA VIII). This is why the Reformers draw a distinction between a visible and an invisible church (*ecclesia visibilis et invisibilis*). Indeed, it cannot be any other way, since the church owes its very existence to the word and sacrament. The voice of the preacher can be heard by all. The water of baptism is visible to all. The bread and wine can be tasted by all. Whether the Spirit of God is acting through the doctrine of the gospel and the administration of sacraments, however, is not directly visible.

The fundamental declarations of the Reformation period are beautifully depicted in the paintings at the Reformation altar by Lukas Cranach the Elder in the *Stadtkirche* of St. Mary in the Luther city of Wittenberg. The altar, with its four paintings, is a vivid portrayal of the articles of the Augsburg confession of 1530. The church flourishes wherever the gospel of God's love is preached and the sacraments are administered. Everything depends on the "Word of the Cross"—God's life-giving self-sacrifice through the death of Jesus Christ. Above the altar are the words: "There can be no other foundation beyond that which is already laid; I mean Jesus Christ himself" (1 Cor 3:11).

The three main images of the altar, which portray baptism, communion, and confession, are based on another, smaller painting that illustrates the "Word of the Cross." On the right-hand side of this painting, in a very simple nave, is Luther preaching from the pulpit. Opposite him are the parishioners of Wittenberg, some standing, others sitting, among them the painter Lukas Cranach, Luther's wife Käthe and his son Hans. The center of the painting—between the preacher and the congregation—is dominated by an image of Jesus on the cross. The crucifixion is the focus of the painting. It is in the image of Jesus on the cross that the church finds its roots, boundaries, and strength. The focus of Christianity is a man who willingly suffered and died for others. "He who knew no sin was abandoned, condemned, tortured, and killed in the name of religion, in the name of politics, in the name of Jewish and Roman law, and in the name of public morality and opinion" (M. Welker, *Kirche im Pluralismus* [Gütersloh, 1995], 108).

Those who place their faith in Jesus Christ must be prepared, if necessary, to find themselves at odds with religious authorities, politics, law, morality, and public opinion. The church of the Crucified does not seek to distance itself from these institutions at all costs, but rather work with them where it can. However, it needs the courage to place its trust in Him only, and not other institutions, and be prepared to draw strength from Him, for Jesus lives on. The shroud blowing in the wind shows imminent power of resurrection in this dying figure.

Recalling the origins of the Reformation shows us three things:

1. The church cannot be made by human beings. The church of Jesus Christ is a gift from God. But humans are capable of hindering its growth.
2. The church owes its nature to its relationship with Jesus Christ. The more his message becomes clear within it, the more it must be prepared to become the church of the Crucified.
3. The church of God is a real congregation. If it is not to be fictitious, it must be a community church.

One Mission and Many Consequences

The church would not be the church of Jesus Christ if it failed to fulfill the one mission bestowed upon it by Jesus after his resurrection, namely to preach and teach the gospel. This was summed up succinctly by St. Paul the Apostle: "We come therefore as Christ's ambassadors. It is as if God were appealing to you through us: in Christ's name, we implore you be reconciled to God!" (2 Cor 5:20). The church is able to do a lot of things. It can seek new ways, or cling to conservative ideas. The one thing it must not do if it is to remain the church of Jesus Christ is deny its mission—for its mission is to proclaim the gospel. If it does so, the promised consequences are great (see Mk 4:8-20). Below, I have set out some examples of the effects of the gospel. The list is not intended to be comprehensive, nor do any of the examples attempt to reflect the gospel in its entirety. And yet a proclamation that does not bear fruit in one sense or another would be tantamount to sowing seeds without a harvest.

- Christians seek to open up the world to heaven. They oppose the self-absorption of human beings, and seek to free them from their superficial pleasure-seeking ways. They question why life has been reduced to nothing more than pleasure, and they open up the horizon of human existence for eternity. Christians know how to quench humanity's metaphysical thirst. They seek to combat spiritual neglect.

- Christians strengthen democratic structures. They recognize diversity from the co-existence of different traditions and denominations within Christianity. They have known pluralism as an enriching force, not just as a destructive one. They understand the connection between human rights and the law of God.

- Christians strive for education for all. Because Christians believe that God created human beings in God's own image, they believe that education is an integral part of human nature. Without creativity and the capacity for critical thought, education is impossible.

- Christians contribute towards a dynamic culture. They value history, and think globally.

- Christians believe in justice and the integrity of creation. For this reason, social work is a vital expression of their faith. Justice, peace, and the integrity of creation represent the essence of Christian ethics.

- Christians play an active part in shaping economic structures that are socially just. A social market economy is thus one of their main aims.

A church that had lost itself in many respects and forgotten its very essence prompted Dietrich Bonhoeffer in the middle of the last century to formulate the following considerations on reshaping its direction: "Encounter with Jesus Christ. The experience that a transformation of all human life is given in the fact that 'Jesus is there only for others'. . . The Church is the Church only when it exists for others." (*Letters and Papers from Prison*, enlarged edition, ed. Eberhard Bethge, [New York: Collier Books, Macmillan Publishers, 1972], 381f).

Viewing the Church in Stereoscope

Lee C. Barrett III

It is old news that the mainline Protestant churches have been experiencing a profound identity crisis. Accusations of infidelity and threats of schisms are heard at national denominational meetings with alarming regularity. The diagnoses of the roots of this ecclesial malaise vary according to the factions doing the analysis. According to some, various sectors of the mainline have over-identified with quite specific political agendas, treating the church as a chaplaincy corps for the political left in the current round of culture wars. The fear is not only that this identification will subordinate the unique values of Christianity to ideologies of questionable ultimacy but also that it may reduce Christianity without remainder to political activism. In this scenario the church will merely function as a task force for those who, by accident of upbringing or aesthetic taste, harbor a quaint nostalgia for religious ceremonies. Christianity will degenerate into politics tinged with emotion. Eventually the church will become redundant as people discover that they can derive the same emotional benefit from a political rally without the inconvenience of getting up early on Sunday.

A very different faction locates the problem in the blandishments of the privatistic piety that has lured many ex-mainliners to non-denominational worship centers. Here the often-voiced suspicion is that the high-tech mega-churches water the faith down to nothing more than cheap comfort and emotional adrenaline for self-absorbed individuals vexed by the anxieties of upward (or downward) mobility, family life, and physical health. God, it is feared, is transformed into a cosmic buddy who gives support in the struggle to hold family and career together in an increasingly complicated and inhospitable society. Here the church is reduced without remainder to a support group and pep club spiced with an innocuous smidgen of evangelical language. Both of these divergent diagnoses agree on at least one thing: the distinctiveness of the church is jeopardized as it degenerates into a duplication of functions provided, often more powerfully, by secular channels.

Although both critiques trade in polemical stereotypes, each one has some truth. At the very least, they suggest that the mainline churches are indeed in trouble. In fact, their maladies are so many and so deep-rooted that health, including Christianly healthy types of political involvement and care of souls, will not come through further institutional restructurings or committee resolutions. Genuine health can only come about through a renewed appreciation of the basic nature and purpose of the church, which in turn requires a renewed appreciation of Jesus Christ its Lord.

The true contours of the church can only be discerned from the perspective of the paradox of the Incarnation. The story of Jesus Christ is both the story of the descent of God in solidarity with humanity and the story of the exaltation of human nature in fidelity to God. Divinity descends to be with us just as we are, and humanity ascends to become that which it has failed to be. This incarnational paradox is reflected in the Christian life in the paradox of justification, the bestowal of fellowship with God to sinners as unmerited gift, and sanctification, the sinner's growth in faith, hope, and love. The corporate dimension of this counterpoint of descent and ascent, of justification and sanctification, is the dual nature of the church as both gift to be received and ideal to be approximated. Misunderstandings of the church have arisen when one of these two poles has been neglected, leading to a one dimensional ecclesiology. The church must be viewed stereoscopically, holding two different images together in order to generate the perception of depth.

Of these two images, the church as "gift" has a certain priority. The very existence of communities of Christians who gather to praise God and hear the gospel is a gift of grace; it is a fruit of God's coming into this sinful and suffering world in order to be with humanity. The church is established by God's work, not by human efforts. It is called into being by its Risen Lord, not by human initiatives. While this conviction is the common heritage of ecumenical Christianity, the historic Reformed confessional documents are particularly clear about it. The Heidelberg Catechism (1563) declares that "from the beginning to the end of the world, and from among the whole human race, the Son of God, by his Spirit and his Word, gathers, protects, and preserves for himself, in the unity of the true faith, a congregation chosen for eternal life." Similarly, according to the Belgic (1561) and Scottish (1560) Confessions it is God who calls and preserves the church. No amount of institutional reforms can guarantee the oneness, holiness, catholicity, and apostolicity of the church. Only God's gracious activity can unite Christians of all times and places in one community. Consequently, the cohesion and vitality of the church are not based on ideological like-mindedness, shared class interests, or ethnic loyalties. Political parties and country clubs may root their corporate identities in the commonalities of blood and culture, but the church cannot trust in such tribalisms. The confessions' extravagant claims about the divine grounding of the church have a definite rhetorical purpose: they function as encouragements to trust in and be grateful for the reality of God's ecclesial gift.

The church as God's gift to humanity confers a very distinctive benefit: a context in which God's gracious presence can be received. Of course, as John Calvin warned, Christ is not imprisoned by the church or trapped within the "outward" means of grace. Nevertheless, the church's ministries are the ordinary ways in which God makes God's own self present to Christians. The Second Helvetic Confession (1566) asserts, "Because God from the beginning would have men to be saved, and to come to the knowledge of the truth (1 Tim 2:4), it is altogether necessary that there always should have been, and should be now, and to the end of the world, a church." The church is an extension of the gift of the availability of God in Jesus Christ. Christians have expressed this aspect of the church variously, some describing the church as the body of Christ, even as a continuation of the Incarnation, and some describing it as a Spirit-infused community following the Risen Lord. The understanding of the exact way in which Christ is present varies according to doctrinal heritage. Some traditions tend to stress Christ available as the eternal Word mysteriously mediated by the fallible human words of kerygmatic proclamation. For them the church is a herald, enabling an encounter with the Risen Lord through the telling of the gospel story. Other traditions locate the presence of Christ in the church's corporate praise and supplication, and particularly in the sacraments. For them the church is a sacramental community, experiencing Christ as a real presence, not just as a memory or a hope. In spite of these differences, the traditions agree that God is typically available to us through a special community, in all the messy details of its practices, rituals, and structures. Along with Cyprian, these traditions all celebrate the gift of the church as our mother, whose nourishment we require.

The "gift" aspect of the church requires an emphasis of the objectivity of God's gracious presence, apart from any human response. Accordingly, both Luther and Calvin locate the essential marks of the church in the objectivities of the preaching of the gospel and the proper administration of the sacraments, not in their faithful reception. The objectivities of word and sacrament ground the validity of the church. The reality of Christ's gracious availability in word and sacrament parallels the objectivity of Christ's work of justification; it does not depend on our feeble and sinful responses but upon God's ordination of the ordinary means of grace.

This focus on the objectivity of the gift leads to a realistic appraisal of the failures and foibles of the church as a collection of human beings. Again the paradox of the Incarnation is reflected in the nature of the church: the body of Christ is a body of ordinary people. Even worse, this assembly of believers remains lamentably sinful. Fortunately the holiness of the church is not rooted in any moral excellence it has attained but in the availability of the holy means of grace. The church is more like a school for sinners rather than a club for saints. A trajectory leading from Augustine's controversy with Donatists through Luther's quarrels with the Spiritualists points to the church as a "mixed body" inclusive of sinners and saints, with most of the saints remaining manifestly deficient in sanctity. The wheat and the tares will only be separated eschatologically. According to Calvin the "invisible" church will be revealed in its purity only at the end of time. Any effort to make the validity of the church dependent upon the faithfulness or righteousness of its members would jeopardize the objectivity of God's gift and undermine trust and confidence.

But the church as God's objective gift is not the only image to be viewed. Jesus Christ is exalted humanity as well as descended God. God's grace includes sanctification as well as justification. In the language of many traditions, the Holy Spirit enables the exalted humanity of Jesus to take form as the body of Christ on earth. Consequently, the vitality of the church is our task as well as our gift; it is our challenge as well as our comfort. The church is called not only to receive grace but also to become an agent of grace. The story of Jesus is not only told but also enacted. This image of the church does require it to become a transformed community, characterized by genuine piety, trust in God's promises, obedience to God's will, heart-felt care for others, and service to neighbors. Koinonia and diaconia, the church as community and as servant, are emphasized. In this context the matter of corporate subjectivity cannot be avoided. The church must visibly, palpably exhibit faith, hope, and love. Accordingly, some Protestants added more visible marks to the definition of the church, besides the proclamation of the gospel and the administration of the sacraments. The Geneva Confession adds that the word must not only be proclaimed but also heard and kept. Martin Bucer, the Scots Confession, and the Belgic Confession include discipline as a mark of the church. The Anabaptists pushed the theme of visible purity to its logical conclusion, defining the church as the assembly of the righteous separated from the world.

More recently some Reformed theologians, continuing this trajectory, have even proposed adding the active struggle for justice for the world as a fourth mark of the church. The church is partly defined by its function of being a corporate instrument of Christ's activity in the world. The church's liberating mission to the world is rooted in the Divine going-forth into the created order. The eschatological vision of the rule of the ascended Lord should fuel the church's hopes and commitments. In the words of the Barmen Declaration, "God's mighty claim upon the whole of life" has very visible affective and behavioral implications for the church. Institutional arrangements, the administration of finances, the power dynamics within the ministerial staff and the congregation, and, of course, intentional projects of social ameliorization are all aspects of the church's fidelity to its Lord.

These two images of the church are very different. One foregrounds the objectivity of grace apart from any human response, and the other highlights demonstrable growth in Christian virtues. Attempts to integrate them on paper in a grand theological system generally fail, usually by swallowing one up into the other. Either the objectivity of grace is so emphasized that the church's response in active faith, hope, and love becomes nothing more than an optional by-product, or the church's active response is so stressed that grace is eclipsed by the church's corporate self-justification through political good deeds. In the first case there is very little impetus toward growth, and in the second there is little to be thankful for. The mystery of the church as both gift and task is as recalcitrant to theoretic resolutions as are the mysteries of the union of the Divine and human natures in Christ and the co-agency of God's grace and human freedom. Like these other mysteries, the two contrapuntal themes of the church as gift and the church as task are not contradictory, but rather complementary. Truth resides in both of them. In much the same way there is truth in both the "wave" and "particle" theories of light. Although the two cannot be synthesized in a grand meta-theory, each one makes sense for particular purposes in particular contexts. The behavior of light cannot be grasped in its complexity without recourse to both conceptualities. Similarly, the two images of the church must be held in dialectical tension in order to avoid one-dimensional truncations. Their integration does not occur in the pages of a theological treatise but in the lives of ordinary Christians as they struggle together to understand the promises and commands of God. Pastoral skill requires discernment concerning when and where to stress which theme. In some situations the emphasis must fall on reverent gratitude for the reality of God's embrace of sinners in order to comfort the contrite heart. In other situations the stress must fall on the passion for transformation into Christ-likeness, in order to destabilize the devotees of cheap grace. It takes the kind of pastoral sensitivity evident in the sermons and writings of Frederick Trost to tell when to sound loudly which note.

Of course, the interaction of these two images of the church does establish limits for the proper use of each one. If the church is the gift of

God's presence, some ways of understanding its task are misleading. For example, if the church claims to possess sufficient wisdom and virtue to establish the reign of God through its own efforts, it has so ignored the "gift" character of grace that it has fallen into a kind of corporate Pelagianism (and probably into self-idolatry). The image of the church as gift warns us: we are not Christ; we cannot save the world. Or, if the church draws the boundaries of its political commitments too narrowly, tying its vision of justice too tightly to a particular political ideology, it has failed to appreciate the extent of its own sinfulness and ignorance. The church cannot claim to have a comprehensive grasp of the logistical details of the implementation of the Reign of God. On the other hand, if the church is also our task, called to enact the mind of Christ, some ways of thinking about it as gift are infelicitous. A church that totally ignores the systemic economic and political dynamics that hurt ourselves and our neighbors, claiming that the gift of God's grace to the poor and victimized makes oppression of no consequence, has denied the enfleshment of Christian love.

Within these boundaries there is much latitude for Christians who struggle to negotiate the tension of the church as both gift and task. Perhaps our final reflection should be a meditation upon the motto of the old Evangelical Synod: In the essentials unity; in the non-essentials toleration; in all things charity. In our present polemical context we should be rather generous concerning the non-essentials.

Recognizing Unity

John E. Burkhart

Sunday after Sunday, in congregations around the world, millions of Christians, whether Orthodox, Protestant, or Roman Catholic, recite the so-called Nicene Creed of 381 C.E. And, whatever they may make of some of the creed's ancient terminology and arcane concepts, they continue, as have many faithful generations before them, to profess a shared belief in "one holy catholic and apostolic church." These words may often seem churchly and mesmerizing, as they roll off the lips. But they can conceal as much as they articulate. After all, "holy" and "catholic" and "apostolic" are fairly uncommon words. They are seldom uttered in the shopping mall. Furthermore, after all these long centuries of liturgical and theological usage, precise definitions of such terms remain somewhat elusive. Hence, it is no surprise that professional theologians have argued, and still do argue, over the proper meanings of these familiar but ambiguous words.

Nevertheless, at first glance, despite what we may understand of holy, catholic, and apostolic, the word "one," at least, has the look of a somewhat obvious simplicity. But, when it is applied to the church, it ever so quickly begins to look arguable and even questionable. After all, we all know that there are several groups that can and do lay claim to the name "church." To start with, close at hand, there are the Baptists and the Lutherans, with distinct and competing brands of each, as well as the Methodists, the Episcopalians, and the Presbyterians, to say nothing of the RCs and the UCCs. And, insofar as we know the intricate histories and the contrasting characters of these storied groups, we are aware of the countless tensions and conflicts within and between them. Hence, the happy notion that they are all somehow "one" does not immediately come to mind. They are, instead, both severally and together, quite diverse; and they live their days in behavioral regions somewhere between friendship and competition, amicable congeniality and mutual deterrence, truce and hostility.

I

For other Christians, the affirmation of the church as "one" is predicated upon a somewhat nebulous and overarching "spiritual" unity. For such, whether in mind or heart, the warm glow of some ecumenical dusk or dawn seems to haze the differences and to suffuse everything with good feeling. Whether dreaming or hoping or imagining that all the differences are only peripheral or superficial or unreal, they would have us all awaken to acknowledge a meaningful, albeit somewhat fuzzy, "oneness" that already permeates the churches and/or some of their members.

For still other Christians, oneness is a task. It is a goal. It is an opportunity. It is a worthy achievement still to be achieved. It is a call to participate in Jesus' prayer "that they may all be one" (Jn 17:21). Of course, the vision of what it actually means to "be one" may need to be opened to adjustment and arrangement. Quite obviously, some do and will express a fear of a so-called "super" church. And they may have their reasons. Not all of them good! For, some may fear a united church that could speak persuasively on issues of social justice. And others may worry that they might lose their privileges and perquisites. Nevertheless, some genuine measure of unity, approaching that of the unity of the Father and the Son, is surely called for by the gospel.

In any event, however it should be understood, the ecumenical landscape is confused and confusing. Furthermore, the fact of our continuing divisions is not only patent and undeniable. It is scandalous. It impedes our witness to the world. And it is a matter of profound and ongoing distress to many who have been so close, and yet so distant, with and from, those who shared so much of the same faith. Yes, and the agony, which now, for so many, simply will not go away, makes ever more inexplicable the outlook and attitudes of those who claim to be Christian but evidence little or no care for unity.

II

Nevertheless, despite all the confusion that now marks the present ecumenical situation, there are some genuine signs of hope. Some good things are happening, here and there, as many Christians now seek and find one another in common causes and shared efforts.

Among the most significant and fruitful of these efforts, surely, has been the patient and ongoing work of the Faith and Order Commission of the World Council of Churches. That work was formally begun in 1927 with the first Faith and Order Conference, and it has continued through the years. Those engaged in it have been a veritable who's who of notable ecclesiastics, of biblical, historical, and theological scholars, and of ecumenical theologians, representing various traditions and persuasions. In more recent years, since the Second Vatican Council, the group has included several distinguished Roman Catholic theologians. The simple fact of their presence, as well as their active participation, may have served to enhance the breadth and credibility of the whole enterprise.

The enterprise has been a focused one. Through the years, since the first World Conference on Faith and Order in Lausanne (1927), the second in Edinburgh (1937), the third in Lund (1952), and the fourth in Montreal

(1963), there has been a growing focus. Initially, the emphasis had been upon comparative ecclesiologies; but, providentially, it came to focus upon the recognizably pivotal ecclesiastical issues of baptism, Eucharist, and ministry. These three topics, each in its own way, have been at issue in the ongoing separation and tensions between the churches. Moreover, from the very beginnings of the modern ecumenical conversations, these three matters have been perceived as more or less interrelated. Furthermore, along the way, as some "agreements" have been reached, not the least of these has been the general recognition that these three topics of baptism, Eucharist, and ministry are crucial to any meaningful discussions towards unity. And, now, even as something of a "convergence" has begun to be achieved in the matters of baptism and Eucharist, it is widely recognized that a common understanding of "ministry" is still the hardest ecumenical nut to crack.

Something of the continuing difficulty over "ministry" was signaled, whether intentionally or not, in the report of the "agreed statements" that resulted from the Faith and Order conference at Accra (1974). Published in 1975, as Faith and Order Paper No. 73, it was titled, *One Baptism, One Eucharist, and a Mutually Recognized Ministry*. At its best, the title suggests a work in progress; but, at its worst, the title suggests that, while baptism and Eucharist unite, ministry divides. In a word, ministry still lacks the oneness which mark baptism and Eucharist. What is more, if only to complicate matters, and to indicate the complexity of the agreements, it should be noted that the agreed statement on ministry is more than three times as long as either of the other two statements.

Nevertheless, perhaps some of the hidden strength of these "agreed statements" from Accra lies in the simple fact that their sequence works from baptism, through Eucharist, to ministry. For, in this, as in other matters, sequence itself matters. Yes, and one may easily surmise the vast ecumenical impasses that might have been erected had the movement come from the other direction! But, by wisely charting the proper move as from baptism to ministry, the Accra document is able to call for "a serious recognition that through baptism we are one people serving the one Lord in each place; for baptism, once performed and never repeated, leads into the continuous worshiping life of the royal priesthood (1 Pet 2:9), the people of God."

In many ways, the discussions of the "agreed statements" of Accra (1974) opened the way for the "convergences" of Lima (1982). There, as a result of the earlier work and discussion, and with the helpful steering of Max Thurian, the Faith and Order conference discerned and formulated a new document. Published as Faith and Order Paper No. 111, it is titled *Baptism, Eucharist and Ministry*. Known as BEM, it is a watershed document, for it rightly stands as something of a culmination of all the earlier processes, and also as a basis for ongoing ecumenical discussion. Indeed, by 1989, it had already "become the most widely distributed, translated, and discussed ecumenical text in modem times." In BEM, admittedly, many would have wished for a little more of this or a little less of that; but the ongoing discussions of it have, if the official responses of the churches may be taken as a fair indication, been generally affirmative. And, arguably, it may be that some serious and careful work still needs to be done to enhance the convergence between the themes of baptism, Eucharist, and ministry. Nevertheless, in what may offer a clue to the future of ecumenism, BEM does, by its sequence of topics, suggest the foundational and unitive significance of baptism.

III

BEM gives primacy of place to the statement on baptism. This is as it should be, for baptism is the beginning. It is foundational, so that Eucharist and ministry follow after and from it. It has a certain ineluctable primacy. After all, it should be noted, it is the only sacrament mentioned in the so-called Nicene Creed. Thus, "We believe in one holy catholic and apostolic church. We acknowledge one baptism for the forgiveness of sins." Indeed, in its own way, baptism represents the ultimate means of grace. Here, in this primal event, we can, ultimately, do nothing for ourselves. What we need needs to be done to us. We can only receive it. We cannot baptize ourselves. It comes only as a gift. And as a gift, like grace itself, it is properly "indiscriminate," since it takes no actual notice of race, gender, or class. Furthermore, as we are united with Christ in baptism, our baptism unites us with all those who have been united to him in baptism. Therefore, as *BEM* puts it, "our one baptism into Christ constitutes a call to the churches to overcome their divisions and visibly manifest their fellowship." *BEM* is right. But the wording is still slightly hesitant. There is a hesitancy to confess that baptism, once acknowledged as "one," is actually unitive. But baptism is itself ecclesiological. Therefore, because of the "one baptism," the truly decisive unity already exists, and waits only to be acted upon.

When this unity is recognized, baptism suffices to open the way to eucharistic sharing and hospitality. The ecumenical consequences are immense. Because of the unity intrinsic to baptism, the ecclesiological burden has shifted. It is no longer properly the burden, and never should have been the burden, of the baptized to establish their rights to share in their Lord's Table. Rather, it is incumbent upon all those who hold ministerial office to find such welcoming ways that all of the baptized may hear and receive the gracious welcome of him who alone is their true host. And those who fail in this, no matter their rank or ecclesiastical pedigree, fail in everything, since they thereby make their own ministry questionable. By failing to recognize the unitive and therefore ecclesiological reality of the baptism of others, they betray their own. Only at the peril of risking any valid claim to "ministry" dare they, for whatever reason, interpose themselves between the baptized and their Lord. Ministry, as evangelical ministry, does not rule at the Lord's Table. It can only serve the host, the shepherd who always knows his own. As ministry, as servant of the servants of God, it serves only insofar as it recognizes the unity already established, once and for all, by the "one baptism."

"What a Gift You Have Given Us"

What a gift you have given us Creator of our souls: the body of your beloved Son, the church. Here there is: singing and serving, praying and praising, feasting and fumbling, weeping and wandering. Here there are: words and wonder, mission and ministry. Here there is: welcoming and worshiping, seeking and signs, covenant and commitment, and hope for the hurting. Your gift to us, the church, where we dance and where we feast, where we search for justice and peace, where we listen, where we learn and where we love. This body, where we work side by side with each other to love and glorify you and to serve all people in your name.

Mary Gafner

The Church in the Shadow of the Cross or the Grand Irony

James D. Eckblad

The grand illusion from which "the church" (as we call it) perpetually suffers is that the church has any "nature" at all. When we speak of the "nature" of anything, such as human nature, or the nature of what it means to be truly a horse (in itself and so distinct from a lion), or the nature of sound, light, or color, or the nature of a community, we speak about that which constitutes quintessentially what makes the thing about which we speak essentially what it is. That is to say, when we speak about the genuine nature of something, be it material or immaterial in nature, we speak about what the thing is in itself, whether *in re* or *in se*. We speak about that which is the *sine qua non* of a thing, about "that without which" the thing could not be what it is—indeed, without which the thing truly could not *be* whatsoever.

To speak about a thing in any way in which its nature is not referenced, at least by assumption or implication, is to fail to speak about the thing at all, to speak only nonsense or what Wittgenstein calls "language on a holiday."

To speak about "the nature of the church," however, is in a very real way, to speak nonsense or language on a holiday from the very first. We can speak all we want about the nature of the church being the gathered body of believers: that group which throughout time has confessed Christ as Lord and manifests the traditional "notes of the church," such as unity, holiness, catholicity and apostolicity, that gathering where the word of God is preached and the sacraments are rightly administered, etc. But the reality, both *in re* and *in se*, both in fact and in principle, is that the church has no nature. There is nothing about the church that one can reference or imply, without which the church would not be the church. The church as church is the one "thing," the one purely intra-mundane reality that is not in itself, that is quintessentially nothing in itself. Nothing else in the world but the church is (or can be) "nothing in itself." Only in this way, and along this line of discourse from the first, can one speak at all meaningfully about the church and not fall into babble or "language on a holiday."

According to Jesus, the church, against which even the gates of hell could never prevail, would be built on Peter the Rock (Mt 16:18-19). But it was not as if by virtue of that quality one could identify the church, or point it out, or in detectable lines of demarcation that separate the church as something distinct from the rest of things. By imperfect analogy, it is the case that we can encounter and know and so speak meaningfully about the extra-mundane reality called "the Kingdom of God" which is among us. But once we say "the Kingdom of God is here" or "the Kingdom of God is there" as an intra-mundane reality that we can supposedly identify, we are no longer speaking about "the Kingdom of God" at all but about something of our own creation (Mk 4; Mt 13). The Kingdom of God is only where it is not. Consistent with the logic and language of speaking about the Kingdom of God, one must say "the church is only where and when it is not."

It is the grand illusion of the church that it thinks it can ever be the church, and its "grand sin" is that it tries to be the church. It is the grand illusion of the church that it can be and so attempts to be the body of Christ. It is its grand illusion that the church believes it can be faithful or just or humble or peaceful. And its grand sin is that it tries to be faithful and just and humble and peaceful. It is the church's grand illusion that it possesses—even by grace, *even by grace*—[and so can exercise] a natural, inherent capacity for love or hope or perseverance as the church of Jesus Christ. Part of the church's grand illusion is that it can appeal to the presence and power of Christ as the church's center or core nature and, thus, in its very appeal be the church and speak meaningfully about the church as the church.

But one can never say "the church as church is here in this place or gathering of people" or "the church as church is there in that place or action." One can never say the church as the church is now in this moment or will be in a later moment, or even that the church was in a moment in the past. It is only the church's grand illusion and so its grand sin of hubris to believe at any moment that it can be, and so try to become, the church of Jesus Christ. Then, and always then, at those places where the church believes it is the church, the church most certainly is not the church. Then, and always then, in those moments when the church believes, even and especially in the fullness of piety and Christian virtue, that it is the church, the church *most certainly is not*—committing in those moments the grand sin, the worst of sins, which is the sin of self-satisfaction and even self-admiration.

The "grand (and divine) irony," however, is that the church of Jesus Christ can be the church of Jesus Christ only when it is not the church and knows it is not the church and so confesses itself not to be the church. Only when the church confesses that it is not the church, and can never be the church, is it possible for the church to be (i.e., exist) at all.

Only when the church confesses that it is not loving, can the loving church exist. Only when the church confesses that it is not hopeful, and not capable of being hopeful, and never is hopeful, can the hopeful church exist. Only when the church confesses that it is not faithful or persevering or just or peaceful or humble, can there exist the church that is faithful and persevering and just and peaceful and humble. Only when the church confesses that it has no "nature" as the church—even and especially by the grace of Jesus Christ—may it truly be said that the church of Jesus Christ can exist.

If to be the church of Jesus Christ is to be the body of Christ, then the church can exist only when it confesses that it most certainly is not the body of Christ. If the church to be the church is truly the gathered body of believers, or that group throughout time that has confessed Christ as Lord and manifests the identifying qualities of unity, holiness, catholicity, and apostolicity, or that gathering where the word of God is preached and the sacraments are rightly administered, then the church can exist only when it confesses that it is none of those.

Only then, but truly then, like tracers that do not show where electrons are but only that they are, can there be "tracers" that show the church exists. Ironically, only by confessing that it does not, and never can, exist, can the church become and so exist as the church—and thereby leave tracers of its existence that we call the "fruits of the Spirit," (Mt 3:8, 7:15-20; Gal 5:22; Eph 5:9) such as the manifestation of Jesus' love, or the witness of faith or of hope or of genuine forgiveness or of utter selflessness. There, in the fruits of the Spirit that are noted in the world, is there witnessed that the church of Jesus Christ is. There, in the fruits of the Spirit that are witnessed in the world can one discern the existence of the church of Jesus Christ, not here in that fruit of the Spirit or there in that fruit of the Spirit but simply by virtue of the fruits of the Spirit that "trace" the church's existence in the world.

Accordingly, if the church of Jesus Christ can exist (note, I have said not "does exist" but "can exist") only where the church confesses that it is not (and can never be), the church of Jesus Christ, the church—to be the church of Jesus Christ at any moment—must in all moments assume a posture of confession, a continual, unbroken and unending posture of confession, where the church confesses that it is, and always will be, although it does not ever want to be, like the thief on the cross, a miscreant, one who is forever guilty and deserving of the punishment of death that is "the just reward of its own existence" (Lk 23:41). The church—to be the church of Jesus Christ at any moment—must in all moments assume a posture of confession where the church admits continually and unbrokenly and unendingly, even to its continual death in this world, that "it does not do the things that the church wants to do and does the things that church does not want to do" (see Rom 7:14-20); that it is the one who is "unworthy to untie the thong of Jesus' sandal" (Lk 3:16); the "one who is unfit to be in Jesus' presence" (Mt 8:8; Lk 5:8).

And so, if the church is to be the church of Jesus Christ at any moment, it must in all moments be the penitent church on its knees, it must in all moments be the humble church at Jesus' feet, the entirely self-effacing church that dies to (it)self, always the sinful church that has nothing good whatsoever to say about itself, in all moments the son who believed wrongfully that he was deserving of his father's blessing for being a good child.

Then, in all such moments, and in every such moment, the Judicious One, Jesus Christ, will say to the church at every moment of its death to self—as he said to the penitent thief at the moment of his death—the words of exoneration and liberation: "Today [in this moment] you will be with me in paradise" (Lk 23:43). "Today, in this moment, you are cleared of the charge against you, for you are forgiven, and you shall rise from death. Today, in this moment, you are no longer the selfish and sinful one, no longer the one who is not and can never be the church, but the one who can be the church, the one who, by my imputation, is the church, and, therefore, the one who, at specific moments known only to me, and by my infusion, will be the church of Jesus Christ."

Ambassadors of Reconciliation

Christa Grengel

Only once in my professional life have I experienced a whole synod reacting as one emotionally. The reason for this singular response was the word of greetings in the name of the United Church of Christ by Frederick Trost during the Synod of the Evangelical Church of the Union, GDR Region, in 1980, in which full communion between the EKU and UCC was officially declared. Frederick Trost ended with a stanza from a German hymn his grandmother had taught him. The Synod rose spontaneously and sang the stanza that followed. I have never forgotten the unexpected emotional outpouring of our synod, caused by the deep and convincing faithfulness of Frederick Trost which came through the words he had spoken to us.

I have experienced Fred's presence in later meetings again and again in the same way. I have therefore decided to greet him at this leave-taking with some of my own faith experiences as an expression of gratitude to him and also to the many friends I have through the EKU-UCC *Kirchengemeinschaft*. There are many traces or "footprints" of God in our world and our history. I will choose only a few in which I experienced what God's reconciliation could mean today.

Mendoza, Argentina, 1964

After the Central Committee of the World Student Christian Federation in Rio Tercero, I was the only participant who stayed in Argentina. The students who had served us during the conference were happy to have at least one of the guests join them in their local surroundings. They brought me to Mendoza near the Andes mountains. We had a few language problems. They spoke Spanish or Portuguese; I had learned Russian and French in school. English was weak on both sides, so we asked a Swiss professor to help us translate in a meeting at the university. These students were enthusiastic socialists, looking with great hope towards the developments in Chile. They were very interested in learning how concrete life was taking shape in the German Democratic Republic, a state where socialism already existed. I wanted to give the students a differentiated picture and answered their question in detail. Unfortunately, the Swiss professor was very conservative and corrected all my sentences in a way that had to be corrected then by me also.

After a while we came to feel that this kind of discussion made no sense, and we decided to go to a private house to continue the discussion there with our weak English. It worked better than we had expected. We came into a deep and intensive debate about their hopes, the realities in Eastern Europe, and the possibilities for the future. A wonderful atmosphere arose.

The students finally asked me if I had a wish, and I did. During our conference I had watched the Argentine students again and again drinking *maté* from a small gourd. I also had heard that the function of *maté* drinking is similar to that of smoking a peace pipe. I had the impression that drinking *maté* now would be appropriate to our new friendship. One of the students then left the room. The others explained to me that in a private home the woman of the house always celebrates the *maté* ceremony. The student had gone to find his mother to do that.

He stayed away for a long time, and he came back with both parents, who spoke to me in perfect German and explained why it had taken them so long to join us. They were Jews who had emigrated from Germany in the thirties. All their relatives had died in German concentration camps, and they had sworn never again to use the German language and never to receive a German in their house. Now their son had not only brought a German home with him but one who also wanted to drink *maté*, a ritual that means making peace. This request had brought them into consternation. They needed to think about it. But finally they decided to fulfill this wish and truly make peace. The consternation was now with me. If I had known what a difficult thing I was asking them to do, I would never have pronounced that wish. But then I was able to accept their gift of peace and reconciliation. We explained the situation to the other students, who didn't understand our German conversation, and then drank *maté* together. It was a deeply moving celebration of reconciliation. We spoke with each other for a long time. For me it was the most beautiful "Holy Communion" I have ever experienced—and that in a Jewish home.

Berlin, GDR, 1979

The setting was the Sunday morning service in St. Mary's Church near Alexander Place. In a corner of the church I translated the prayers and sermon for some American students. We had met the evening before for an intensive and sometimes contentious discussion. The students were visiting behind the Iron Curtain for the first time, and they knew only what they had learned from U.S. newspapers about the situation in Eastern Europe. They were therefore already astonished to find Christians like themselves worshiping in a church building. The liturgy was very similar to that of their own church.

At last we went forward for Communion. We stood in a circle around the altar, received bread and wine, and clasped hands as a sign of our community in Christ. After the service a further round of talks was planned. But the lively students of the evening before were remarkably silent and seemed disturbed. Then one of them burst out with the troubling admission: "They are Christians like us—we were together at the Lord's table—how can we ever shoot at them? Maybe I will never be able to shoot!"

We all had felt during the eucharist that something had happened to us, and this student was only expressing what we all had experienced. The message of Holy Communion had changed us and it gone deep into our hearts. Reconciliation had happened here too.

Kaluga, Soviet Union, 1988

I was a participant in the observance of the thousand years of the "baptism of the Ru's." The Russian Orthodox Church was celebrating the millennium of its existence and had invited many guests from the world-wide ecumené. After the official opening, the Russian Church first held its National Council. During that time the ecumenical guests were sent in groups to smaller places around Moscow to celebrate the millennium with local congregations. Many places had never before been allowed to receive guests from foreign countries. I was in a group that visited Kaluga, a town on the route between Warsaw and Moscow. We were warmly greeted by the town officials and given a tour of the principal sites of the town, which was newly built. We also learned the reason for the rebuilding: Kaluga was nearly completely destroyed by the German troops on their way to Moscow during World War II. There were almost no remains of the old Kaluga; for this German visitor the information was distressing.

After the tour we went to the liturgy in the Russian Orthodox Church. The members of the congregation greeted us warmly. The church was so full that we could not move. We stood for about four hours, tightly packed, in the festive service. Beside me was another German, and since we were at times whispering with each other, the elderly women around us knew that there were Germans among the guests. It suddenly came to me: What were they thinking and feeling when they realized we were Germans, people from the country that destroyed their town? This could have been the first time since the War that they heard German words. Again I was overtaken by the past, by the guilt of my people. I had four hours to think about that.

At the end of the service the priest turned toward us, the ecumenical guests, and greeted us heartily. In his hands he held a small icon, the Godmother of Kaluga. He announced that each of the guests would receive such an icon to take home in remembrance of the festivity on this day in Kaluga, which had opened the gate to world-wide Christianity for this congregation. Then he handed over the icons to be passed towards us. I had already seen the small icon which was intended for me. But where was it? In the thick crowd it had quickly disappeared. I confess that at first I had bad thoughts. On a few previous occasions, presents meant for us had not reached us because some of the state escorts had taken them, and I thought that perhaps this had happened again. But this was a totally different situation, and soon I felt ashamed that I'd been suspicious. The women around us had taken the icons reverentially in their hands, kissed them, and started to weep, moistening the icons with their tears. Finally they took us in their arms, kissed us, and made us quite wet with their tears: We found reconciliation in Russia. I haven't dried the tears on the icon. They belong to it. The small icon was handled and hallowed by these old women. Ever since then it has hung over my bed and reminds me of those unforgettable hours in Kaluga.

Volgograd, Russia, 1999

On May 11, 1999, about 900 people from Germany and Austria flew far away to a city named Volgograd. All the travelers had a relation to that place, formerly known as Stalingrad. Do you know that name? Do you know what it meant to all those people? In December 1942-January 1943. Stalingrad was the site of the most terrible battle in World War II. In a way it was *the* turning point in the war because the Germans lost that battle and from that time had to retreat or flee back to Germany.

The Soviet army had surrounded the German army. Some figures: 300,000 German soldiers were in Stalingrad. One hundred thousand were killed, more than 100,000 were missing, and 100,000 (exactly 96,000) were sent to prisoner-of-war camps after a cruel fight of six weeks. From the last group less than 6,000 survived and returned after some years to Germany (the last of them 10 years after the battle). The losses on the Soviet side were even higher. Between the armies were civilians who also died in great numbers. Stalin had not evacuated the city because he did not want to tell his people how serious the situation was. When I went to Volgograd for the first time in 1993—50 years after the battle—I met a woman who lived as a 17-year-old girl in Stalingrad during that battle.

My father was among the missing. He was a simple soldier, but as a radio-operator he always had to be in the first lines. After the death of my mother, I read his letters, written in December 1942 in Stalingrad. The battle was terrible. The place where those masses of soldiers (600,000 to 700,000) fought was a narrow valley; the space was no more than the length of a 10-to-15-minute walk, between the railway and Volga River. In some houses the Germans occupied the first and third floor and the Russians the second. The soldiers fought in close combat that bitter winter (-25° Celsius). Perhaps 400,000 or 500,000 people were killed in that small area. Nobody knows the exact figures, and most were never buried. The new city after the war was built up over the bones, and in 1993, I found still unburied bones on the hill.

Stalingrad was the great shadow in my childhood because it had taken my father. I always asked myself and my mother: What in the world was my father—what was the German Army—doing there, 8,000 kilometers away from my hometown? It was the aggressive war policy of German National Socialism. Not only my childhood but my whole life was in its shadow—that horrific battle, the cruelty, that great evil, the guilt of the German people, the guilt of my own father.

The shadow was deepened because of our situation in the GDR. Our fathers had been part of the Nazi system, and we were not allowed to mourn them. We had to celebrate the victory of the Russians and visit their memorials. Intellectually we could follow that line because the Soviet Army really had ended that terrible war for us, but emotionally we also needed to mourn our own killed relatives. Only after 40 years, on May 8, 1985, were we allowed for the first time to have a public worship at a German soldiers' cemetery.

What happened last year (May 11-17, 1999)? After the change in the Soviet Union, the German institution that is concerned with soldiers' graves (*Volksbund Deutsche Kriegsgräberfürsorge*) asked the Russian government if they would be allowed to bury the German soldiers from World War II. Permission was granted for the burial, including the bodies in Volgograd. First, an old Russian soldiers' cemetery and an old German soldiers' cemetery were restored, side by side, on the steppe near Volgograd, and then they built besides these two, a new graveyard, collecting bones and bodies of soldiers found in common graves and elsewhere, putting them into the new resting place. Since then 20,000 bodies have been buried; 8,000 of them could be accurately identified. And the process will go on.

In 1999 it was proposed that the cemetery be dedicated in a major official event with the president of our Parliament in attendance. Relatives of the dead were invited. About 900 wanted to come. But then the Kosovo War started, and for the first time since World War II, German soldiers were involved again in a war outside Germany. The Russians' fear (and also the hate) escalated again. The governor of Volgograd therefore prohibited the official dedication. The German government and embassy withdrew. But the leadership of the *Kriegsgräberfürsorge* decided to go to Volgograd anyway, for three reasons: 1) The city of Volgograd wrote that they were still ready to welcome the 900 relatives as tourists. 2) More importantly, the Russian veterans of World War II (including soldiers who had fought in Stalingrad) wrote: "Please come; we have to come together; we have to clasp each other's hands over the graves; we have to make peace." 3) A youth camp, organized by the *Kriegsgräberfürsorge* with Russian and German young people, working on both cemeteries, was not prohibited from taking place—also an urgent reason to go.

But how to proceed in that situation? The danger that the Russian population would feel provoked had to be taken seriously. The president of the *Kriegsgräberfürsorge* had discovered my name and profession in the list of relatives and asked me in advance if I was willing to offer a short prayer at the cemetery. Of course, I was. He also invited me to be part of the group of leaders during that visit. When we arrived in Volgograd at midnight, the leaders met and decided to do something more than a short prayer. They asked me to prepare a worship service, not to provoke the Russian population or the governor, but nevertheless to truly dedicate the cemetery. They also decided to bring the 900 relatives in small groups (two or three buses) rather than all at once to the cemetery over two days. In the first group were the Russian veterans and the Russian young people. I prepared a liturgy, therefore, partly in Russian, partly in German. (How good, that in my GDR schools Russian had been the first foreign language!)

The next morning we went to Rossoschka, the location of the cemeteries on the steppe near Volgograd. First, we went to the old Russian and German cemeteries, and then we worshiped at the new one. It was a very moving event: not long, not provocative. In addition to the president of the *Kriegsgräberfürsorge* and me, a Catholic priest from Poland was with us, singing the Roman Catholic liturgy for the dead. We were not only people from different countries but also from different confessions. Veterans from both sides who had survived that terrible battle 56 years before; relatives who had never heard anything about their husbands, fathers, friends; young people full of hope for the future because of the beginning of friendship between them. After that first worship we celebrated similar small services for the other groups, and in this way we dedicated the cemetery over a two-day period. It was much better than any official event would have been.

Because I was involved in the worship leadership, many people came and wanted to speak to me. They told me their stories, sharing in many cases for the first time in their lives deep feelings about their loss. All the stories were very similar and also similar to my own: they had never heard what had happened to their relatives, if, when, where, and how they had died. For all of them, Stalingrad had always been the great shadow and symbol of the evil. And that changed in those days in Russia in 1999. Was it really meaningful to construct a cemetery after more than 50 years? (In our other cemeteries the time limit is 25 years). Was it meaningful to bring the relatives of those cruelly killed soldiers to that place? Yes, it was! We all experienced a real transformation, a coming of peace and reconciliation. It was peace for those soldiers, but it was more: peace for us and also peace between Russians and Germans who had fought against each other. And there was now the opportunity to speak about it, to speak about the past as many had never done before. There was a possibility for peaceful encounters between young and old, Russians and Germans. Yes, the whole situation changed: the shadow we called "Stalingrad" disappeared. We went home as changed people.

During those days many smaller events happened in the spirit of reconciliation. God moved hearts—not only those of the veterans from both sides and the relatives of the dead. It had a much wider effect:

- The governor, who had forbidden the official dedication, received our leaders and said: "I have learned during the last days that you mustn't allow current problems like the Kosovo War to get in the way of reconciliation. I thank you for coming for this purpose."

- On Sunday some of us participated in the Russian Orthodox service. The archbishop, whom we knew because he had worked with us for some years in Berlin, prayed at the close of the service, in Russian (to be heard by his own people) and in German, for the Russian and the German soldiers killed in Stalingrad and their peace in the Russian earth.

- And the most moving little sign of reconciliation happened when we visited the huge memorial of the Russian victory in Volgograd. On the bus I was sitting beside an old man, a Stalingrad soldier on the Soviet side. That terrible battle had also stamped his whole life. We told each other our life stories. Because he was very old (87), he rode on the bus to the top of the memorial hill. I got out and climbed the steps (maybe more than 200). When I arrived at the top, he stood there with flowers, yellow flowers, buttercups. He had picked them for me from the grass on the hill as a sign of his feelings and his wish to be at peace with me.

The whole event, the whole story, was for many others and for me a gift of God to us: shadows of the past disappeared; the memory of our dead or missing relatives came to peace. And Stalingrad as the symbol of the great evil became now for us the place of reconciliation.

Reconciliation in Biblical Texts

"Reconciliation" is a keyword for our Christian faith, for our Christian life. Let me now reflect for a moment on what it really means. When I looked into the Bible, I was astonished because the word "reconciliation" is used infrequently. There are other words, that express the meaning too: peace, forgiveness, covenant, mercifulness, shalom. But there are two texts that I found especially significant:

Matthew 5:23-24 (from the Sermon on the Mount):

> So when you are offering your gift at the altar, if you remember that your brother or sister has something against you, leave your gift there before the altar and go; first be reconciled to your brother or sister, and then come and offer your gift.

2 Corinthians 5:17-20:

> So if any one is in Christ, there is a new creation; everything old has passed away; see, everything has become new! All this is from God, who reconciled us to himself through Christ and has given us the ministry of reconciliation; that is, in Christ God was reconciling the world to himself, not counting their trespasses against them, and entrusting the message of reconciliation to us. So we are ambassadors for Christ, since God is making his appeal through us; we entreat you on behalf of Christ, be reconciled to God.

These texts are very important to all of us, especially the text from St. Paul. They speak about our deepest existence: We are messengers of reconciliation, ambassadors for Christ.

I cannot explore the entire strength and depth of the text in this context. I only will speak about some aspects that point to the meaning of reconciliation:

1. In 2 Corinthians it is quite clear: *the subject is God. God* is reconciling the guilty man and woman. *God* accepts him/her again; *God* accepts him/her fully. *God* is doing this because of Jesus Christ. That means: the possibility for reconciliation is given by God in Christ. Also, *God* makes it possible for us to reconcile with each other; the possibility comes from God. On our own we are not able to bring about human reconciliation because our natural response to an act that we perceive as aggression would be revenge (an eye for an eye, and a tooth for a tooth). Therefore *God* must stand behind us; *God* enables us. *God* is the subject. (In

Russian this is much easier to understand because *primirenie* always means that reconciliation comes from above; this is similar, by the way, to the meaning in the Old Testament: the covenant is always concluded by God).

2.   *Reconciliation is not a superficial kindness but a total change of thinking.* "Metanoia," repentance, re-turn, is a true change. Reconciliation has to do with guilt, with the confessing of guilt. It is not an easy matter; sometimes it is painful. It is Jesus Christ's contradiction of and resistance against "an eye for an eye, a tooth for a tooth." Jesus Christ wanted to stop that automatic reaction. *He* says: No, the world will be healed only when we stop that and start anew, accepting each other, taking each other as friends. This doesn't mean that the past is only forgotten or swept under the carpet. No, the truth is possible with Christ; you can now say very openly, what your guilt is. You can confess it because there is a new beginning in God's love. Perhaps it is painful: Christ was indeed crucified for it.

3.   *Reconciliation is the only possibility of stopping the process of violence and counter-violence.* It can happen that as reconcilers we will get into trouble too. Maybe people will laugh at us, will fight against us. But again: it is the only possibility of stopping violence, hate, and war in our world. It is the only way that the world can be healed. It is Christ's way in our world.

4.   *Christ is asking us to go with him.* "We entreat you on behalf of Christ, be reconciled to God." I am not a linguist, but I think the German version is better and more correct: *Lasset euch versöhnen mit Gott.* The Greek language has a form that is neither active nor passive. With this form you can express more clearly that the main activity comes from God. *God* is acting, but we are not passive. We are asked to be open, so that *God* can act with us and through us. Let yourself be reconciled to God—and then go and do the same with your brother and sister.

On Being the Church after Christendom

Douglas John Hall

To be a serious Christian at the beginning of the twenty-first century is to know that the churches exist in a state of prolonged crisis. The crisis lies in their effective, though not necessarily conspicuous, disestablishment; but not so much in the fact of their disestablishment as in their refusal to acknowledge this fact. As long as they can manage it, the churches continue attempting to function as though nothing had changed. There are exceptions but too few of them.

When human beings and institutions postpone for some indefinite future the problems of the present, they only increase the problematic nature of the latter, and leave for future generations a situation that may well have become, by then, irresolvable. Worse, they miss the *opportunities* that are present today and may by tomorrow have disappeared. One does not have to agree with everything that Bishop John Spong writes to feel the rightness of his dictum that "Christianity must change or die." Hope depends upon that kind of truth orientation.

What is needed if such hope is to take root, however, is some glimmering of what is possible *on the other side of the present crisis*. Crises not only signal endings, they also contain opportunities for new beginnings. What are the opportunities divine Providence might be holding out to the Christian movement in the midst of its "humiliation" (A. Van den Heuvel)?

A Movement of Responsible Prophetic Witness

The life and witness of the man being honoured by this volume suggests four such opportunities. *First, the church after Christendom is free to become a movement of responsible prophetic witness.* One does not say that prophetic witness is impossible under the conditions of establishment. Christianity, like our parental faith of Judaism, is by nature and calling a prophetic faith. It would have been strange indeed if all those centuries of biblical story and symbol had not produced at least a few who did not bow the knee to Baal! All the same, the very fact and character of religious establishment has meant, and means, that the prophetic calling of faith has been terribly difficult to sustain. Especially in our so-called New World, where Christian establishment was not of the legal variety but one of identification at the level of ideology, Christian churches have been under social pressure to conform to the values, moral codes, and general lifestyle approved by the policy-making majority. It is expected even today, for example, that Christians will uphold the same sexual morality as the dominant culture; and part of the difficulty that many denominations are experiencing over questions of ordination stem not from biblical or theological considerations but from the (rhetorical!) moral assumptions of the classes that have been the chief supporters of the churches—assumptions that are rarely inspired by doctrinal or scriptural knowledge and reflection.

Establishment not only limits the extent of Christian freedom *from* society, however; it also greatly impedes the church's freedom *for* society. This was the point with which Reinhold Niebuhr began his 1935 (!) work, *The Interpretation of Christian Ethics*,[1] the remarkable opening sentence of which reads: "Protestant Christianity in America is, unfortunately, unduly dependent upon the very culture of modernity, the disintegration of which would offer a more independent religion a unique opportunity." The freedom that accompanies disestablishment, if and insofar as it is appropriated, is not for the purpose of becoming a separate entity, an enclave of religious purity. It is, rather, the necessary condition for the exercise of social and worldly responsibility. We can only be in the world as disciples of the Christ if we are not simply of the world but find the source of our life beyond the world's own ways and possibilities. If, as I argue, the church should embrace its disestablishment and seek to give it a positive direction, the reason lies, not in pious disdain for this world but in the kind of worldliness that Dietrich Bonhoeffer intended in his letters from prison. Perhaps, since the churches have been so reluctant to pursue a course distinct from their host cultures, their present rejection by those cultures is the divine Spirit's way of ensuring a sufficient distance from the world to enable the churches to be of some worldly use! Rather than waiting for the waves of disestablishment to wash over us, therefore, like some irreversible fate, we are being invited to participate in them actively.

To represent the divine love for creation, Christ's church must not be "conformed to" this world but must maintain a spiritual though not a physical, distance from it. Its gospel must not be a stained-glass version of the values and goals of the society that it wants to address, but "good news" that names the "bad news" that the world is very apt to call good. For fifteen or sixteen centuries, with a few notable exceptions. Christianity has been busy *reflecting* its worldly context. The point however is to *engage* it. And to engage its socio-historical context the Christian community must disengage itself from that context. It *dis*-engages in order to *re*-engage, namely, to address its context from a different perspective and motivation. Such a process is in my view the principal opportunity that God is presenting to Christendom in its extremity.

A Community of Alternative Memory and Hope

The *second* opportunity is an extension of the first: The church that emerges out of the ruins of Christendom can be (and here and there is already being) a community of alternative memory and hope. There is no point trying to live in the past, but there is a point—and a vital one—in remembering the past. Indeed, if the past is *not* remembered, not only are its worst aspects regularly repeated, but there is a concomitant loss of hope for the future. For the building blocks of hope are always salvaged from the ruins of history; and when we forget the slow and painful evolution of our hopes as a civilization (think, for example, of the painfully gradual emergence of the idea of democracy!), we lose the capacity to renew our hope and to inculcate it in others, notably the young.

Some of the keenest observers of modern mass culture—a culture celebrating, with a certain desperation, the present and immediate future—feel that our society is already very far along the path to historical and cultural amnesia. Still deceived by the shabby myth of progress, titillated by technology, and "entertained to death" (N. Postman), many of our contemporaries are so ignorant of the past that they possess no standards of comparison for assessing present and future realities. Those who are affluent and content are apt to imagine, pathetically, that ours is the best of all possible worlds; those who are the victims of global trends, on the other hand, are left without dreams. The church that makes its way through the ending of Christendom to a new beginning as the disciple community of the Christ bears within itself the possibility—indeed, the necessity!—of being a zone both of memory and hope.

Even humanly speaking, memory and hope are inseparable. In theological terms they are of the essence of discipleship. That is why the central liturgical act of the *koinonia* gives them such prominence: "Do this in remembrance of me." "Inasmuch as you do these things, you show forth the Lord's death until he comes." To remember what, as Christians, we remember (the cross), and to hope, accordingly, for what we await (the consummation already anticipated by Christ's resurrection)—this is to be set down in the world as an enduring alternative to what the world regularly offers—which the Bible, with great consistency, calls death. If Christians earnestly considered the cross and our own continuing baptism into Christ's sacrificial death, we would know—more knowingly than we seem to—that a great deal of what our world remembers and hopes for is vain and illusory.

Contrary to the gospel of acquisition, none of the "things" that people spend their lifetimes accumulating or lamenting because they have failed to accumulate them will lend us either security or meaning. Contrary to the gospel of information technology, none of the data that the Internet makes available will ever add up to wisdom. And if we took the resurrection of Jesus Christ as seriously as we say we do, we could certainly not be satisfied with the bourgeois hopes that are enacted on Easter Sunday, hopes founded on the shifting sands of repression and secular optimism.

A Community That Opts for an Ethic of Resistance

To observe this, however, already verges on a *third* opportunity awaiting a Christian movement that has surpassed Christendom; *for to be in truth a community of alternative memory and hope is to opt for an ethic of resistance.* In the situation of Christian establishment, the church was under constant pressure to conform. That, after all, was part of the bargain. But in the post-establishment situation, this kind of pressure, while it most certainly will always and everywhere be present, is at least not as intense; for the basic agreement—the spoken or unspoken, legal or sociologically assumed, covenant between church and culture—no longer pertains.

This is not just a piece of naive idealism! Those who have been alive to the course of history in the 20th century know that wherever Christian communities have achieved (or been onto!) an "independent" (Niebuhr) identity, they have had a definite foretaste of the potentiality of this faith for creative resistance. The church in the former German Democratic Republic (a church with which Frederick Trost and others among us were in rapt dialogue) is only one instance of this reality; and the role of the East-German church in 1989-90 demonstrates in the most concrete terms the fact that such independent resistance, far from being motivated by separatist religion, can and should lead to a greater and more explicit worldly concern.

Recently, I asked a good friend, "What do you consider the most important 20th-century lesson for us to carry over into the new century?" He responded at once: "Resistance!" My friend is a natural scientist, and he knows well enough the propensity of the scientific community to serve political and economic masters. He is also a German who, as a youth, though he voted against Adolf Hitler, joined the German army and fought in World War II. Through bitter experience, he learned, as did many of his contemporaries, how important it is to be discerning, vigilant, and ready to resist what may seem, on the surface of it, beneficent, true, and liberating.

The forces that call for Christian resistance today are, of course, more subtle than those that evoked *Protest*-ant responses in either the Reformation or the Modern periods. What threatens life on the planet today has more to do with economics than it does with the crass political posturing of the likes of Hitler, Mussolini, and Stalin. Moreover, as the richest of earth's peoples, we North Americans, collectively speaking, are most of us on the receiving end of the material "benefits" of the reigning economic system. It is therefore doubly hard for us to name and to resist that system, even when significant numbers of our own people are victimized by it. Yet, as, for example, one saw with Christian participation in the protests against the World Trade Organization meetings in Seattle, there is a clear opening in that direction. The more the Christian community recognizes that it exists now *on the edge* of empire, the more frequently will it find itself at home in the role of resistance. One can envision a Christian future in which it will no longer be thought unusual or shocking when Christians stand for something really "different." It may become the norm—as it was in the beginning.

Existing in a Religiously Pluralistic Worldly Context

Fourth, *post-Christendom, Christianity will know itself as existing in a religiously pluralistic worldly context, and therefore to be a religion of choice rather than one of convention.* This must be considered "opportunity" by all who recognize the dialectic of election and decision in the foundational traditions of biblical faith. The sheer reality of religious plurality constitutes a vital dimension of the breakdown of Christendom. Even in areas of North America (and elsewhere) where Christianity is clearly, perhaps even exclusively, present, the reality of other religious and quasi-religious alternatives is felt by virtually everyone. Most of us, to be sure, are late in recognizing what the late Wilfred Cantwell Smith saw plainly half a century ago:

> The religious life of mankind from now on, if it is to be lived at all, will be lived in a context of religious pluralism . . . it will become increasingly apparent, and is already essentially true, that to be a Christian in the modern world, or a Jew, or an agnostic, is to be so in a society in which other [people], intelligent, devout, and righteous, are Buddhists, Muslims, Hindus.[2]

Christians who have made the transition to the post-Christendom reality need neither repress nor fear this new religious situation. For one thing, they will realize that it is by no means new. All along, planet earth has been the scene of countless faiths; and if, in the West, we have not been very conscious of all these "others," it is only because, prior to the 19th century, there was relatively little intermingling of peoples, or even widespread dissemination of information.

More significantly, however, the pluralistic religious situation could hold no novelty or surprise for biblically and historically informed Christians. Until Constantine and his successors made Christianity the favored—and finally the exclusive—religion of the Roman imperium, Christianity existed in a religiously pluralistic context of the most conspicuous sort, and it did so *as a religious minority*. Every word of the newer Testament, as well as most of the writings of classical or primitive Christianity, presuppose the presence, strength, and (in at least some cases) appeal of other religions, religious philosophies, superstitions, and the like. If we take the Bible as our norm and guide—that is, if the *sola scriptura* of the Reformers applies also to ecclesiology—then religious plurality must be regarded as the normal situation of the Christian movement in the world. From the scriptural point of view, what is abnormal is Christian hegemony, monopoly, or majority status. That is, biblically speaking, as Kierkegaard famously maintained, what is abnormal is precisely—Christendom!

Yet it is not enough to legitimize, in this way, religious plurality. It should be seen, rather, as positive gain. For it means the end of Christianity as a byproduct of human habit and mere convention. It is perhaps natural for Christian parents to lament (as many of us must do) the failure of their children to gravitate "naturally" towards the church, their tendency to "shop around," or their preference for religious alternatives that seem visibly simplistic. But who—with the Bible in one hand and the newspaper in the other—could wish for a return to the era in which every Brown or Smith was an Episcopalian or a Methodist, every O'Reily Roman Catholic, every Schmidt Lutheran? Christianity from now on, where it is real, will assume choice and not once-for-all choice, but ongoing decision-making in the face of much evidence to the contrary. Very few of those who will be Christians at the end of the century that has just begun will be so unless they have good reasons for the hope that is in them.

The end of automatic Christianity means that, already now, the church is under obligation to become (what it has said about itself all along but rarely practiced imaginatively) a teaching faith. People will need to know what Christian belief actually entails—what sort of deity Christians believe in, what is meant when Jesus is called "the Christ," what the church is and does, what ethic is involved in Christian discipleship, how Christians regard the relation between the human species and the rest of nature, and so on.

In short, *theology*, which throughout most of Christian history has been nearly superfluous so far as the daily working of Christendom was concerned; theology, which has been indeed a veritable nuisance to the authorities of both church and state, becomes in the post-Christendom situation the daily bread of Christian thought and life. The very presence of other religious choices, in other words, has laid upon the churches a whole new obligation. They must become articulate! And as they become newly articulate about their own faith, Christians will begin to manifest greater understanding of and sympathy for the faiths of others. They will begin to perceive these others not as rivals and competitors but as communities of "ultimate concern" (Tillich) that are in many cases the greatest allies that Christians are likely to find as the world moves towards ever more mechanistic and dehumanizing alternatives to civilization.

The faith of the early Christians prior to the Constantinian establishment was not less explicit because it was practiced in the midst of religious plurality; if anything, it was more finely honed, more christologically focused. Churches able to absorb, despite the illiteracy of many of their members, the complex letters of St. Paul, must indeed have been wonderfully concentrated on their own "scandal of particularity." Evidently they did not feel constrained to downplay their christological specificity in order to have dialogue (as Paul did on Mars Hill) with the worshipers of other gods.

Nor do we! Christianity is not made "inclusive" by relativizing the place of Jesus in it. Real as distinct from rhetorical inclusivity only happens when Christians go deeply enough into what they mean when they confess that Jesus is the Christ to realize that, precisely as such, he is *not* the exclusive possession of Christians but the focal point of a love for the whole that is broad enough to be found in every part of the whole.

To conclude: These four opportunities do not, of course, exhaust the possibilities for new life of a disciple community that has passed through the death of Christendom. Their only function is to suggest an ecclesiology and a missiology that have never been far from the thoughts of men and women throughout the ages who have tried to follow the way of Jesus Christ. Such a person is the one for whom these simple observations have been penned—with the gratitude of the writer.

Notes

1. Reinhold Niebuhr, *The Interpretation of Christian Ethics* (New York and London: Harper & Brothers Publishers, 1935), 3.

2. Wilfred Cantwell Smith, *The Faith of Other Men* (Toronto: CBC, 1962), 2-3.

"Salt and Light"

Our Lord and Savior Jesus Christ,
you have called your church
to be the salt of the earth
and the light of the world.
We ask you:
Rouse us out of all inertia;
move and enable us to act and to speak as messengers
of God's all embracing love.
Renew our churches to become living letters,
communicating your great invitation.
May they become places where people
who have not yet felt God's love
come to know that they are loved by God
and be encouraged to believe in God.
We ask you who, with the Father and the Holy Spirit,
lives and reigns, one God, for ever and ever.

Gerhard Linn

Love Thy Niebuhr's Brother:
Church as Polar Reality

John C. Helt

It is a commonplace: the middle of the twentieth century (1925-1975) was an age of theological giants in German American Protestantism. Frederick Trost has helped to keep the names of two of the "big four" alive for the church of the twenty-first century: Karl Barth and Dietrich Bonhoeffer. Paul Tillich and Reinhold Niebuhr, often unnamed foils of the first two giants, nevertheless share responsibility with Barth and Bonhoeffer in shaping the church we know today. For half a century seminarians and other theological students read the "big four" as leaders of a roughly homogeneous movement widely known as neo-orthodoxy. We also read them as paired representatives of a distinct polarity, different if not antithetical approaches to theological work whose outcomes would bring either the deliverance or the demise of the Christian church.[1]

Barth-Bonhoeffer stood for a confessing church, sometimes accused of being too conservative, evangelical, apolitical, isolationist, christocentric, biblicist, theologically aloof or just too theological and otherworldly. Tillich-Niebuhr stood for the apologetic church, sometimes accused of being too accommodated to the world, ideological, political (in Niebuhr's case) or psychological (in Tillich's), liberal, and anthropocentric.

Both poles of so-called neo-orthodoxy were eclipsed by liberation and other theologies by the late 1970s. Before long, contextual and constructive theology would replace systematics in seminary curricula, and where systematic theology did survive, it would pay little or no attention to Barth or Tillich. Similarly, Bonhoeffer and Niebuhr dropped out of vogue among ethicists well before the end of the century. But that is not to say that the considerable influence of the "big four" no longer lingers in the hearts and minds of middle-aged and older pastors and teachers of church and academy in the year 2000. Under the rocks of many fifty-somethings you will find to this day Barthians, Tillichians, Niebuhrians, and fans of Bonhoeffer, in every imaginable combination of alliance and enmity.

I daresay Reinhold Niebuhr has been the most influential of the four, like it or not. He has shaped our thinking in oldline Protestantism in general, and the United Church of Christ in particular. Niebuhr's anthropocentric starting point, so very clear in his mid-career *magnum opus,* the two-volume *The Nature and Destiny of Man,* remains more methodologically typical among us than Barth's many-many-volume

Church Dogmatics. Niebuhr's political interests and activist example made "realism" and "relevance" our watchwords. Martin Luther King, Jr., paired Mahatma Gandhi with Reinhold Niebuhr in describing the roots of his commitment to non-violent resistance and social justice. Camelot's Arthur Schlesinger, Jr., called Niebuhr "the greatest man I knew." Reinhold Niebuhr graced the cover of *Time* magazine's silver anniversary edition in 1948 as a national spiritual force. In the same year, at the founding assembly of the World Council of Churches in Amsterdam, the quip of British seminarians first circulated more widely: "Love the Lord thy Dodd with all thy heart, and thy Niebuhr as thyself."[2]

Niebuhr's calls for justice in *Moral Man and Immoral Society* still drive some of our political judgments and ecclesiastical attempts to find a prophetic voice. I would suggest that his disinterest in ecclesiology also continues to influence us. Reinhold Niebuhr's chief theological concern was in the title of his first book, *Does Civilization Need Religion?* (1927) The church's role in answering that question was never very clearly developed in Reinhold Niebuhr's thought. That was his younger brother's concern, however.[3]

Another Niebuhr Heard From

In the pantheon of theological giants we find Helmut Richard Niebuhr next in line. I will argue that the younger Niebuhr brother, for whom polarity and dualism are central theological motifs, offers a transitional, mediating alternative as we recover from the Barth-Bonhoeffer/Tillich-Niebuhr neo-orthodox impasse of the twentieth century.

H. Richard Niebuhr was a fan of Jonathan Edwards and the sovereignty of God. In an unpublished paper, "The Idea of the Church in Theological Education," he indicates the context and perspective of his concern as a teacher of the church and a researcher of its academic situation:

> Jonathan Edwards once said that the trouble with [people] was not that they had no ideas of God or that they were atheists, but that their ideas of God were too little and too small. This is doubtless the most important problem in theological education—this problem of helping [people] to understand the greatness of God. But in connection with it, it is important that they should understand the greatness of the church in its complexity but also in its marvelous unity, its present modern existence but also its existence in all times, its distinction from Israel but also its unity with Israel. *Let us try to give [people] a big idea of the church* in everything that we do in theological education.[4]

This was Helmut Richard Niebuhr's agenda: helping people to

understand the greatness of God and the church. From 1919 until his death in 1962, theological education was the center of his life, his churchly vocation. His concern for his students and their vocations in the church was his first academic priority. His biographer, Jon Diefenthaler, says, "As a faculty member, Niebuhr scrupulously observed the counseling duties assigned to him and never stopped revising his annual course in 'Christian Ethics' This commitment to the church set him apart from his brother Reinhold. Looking back on the decade of the Great Depression, the younger Niebuhr recalled that, whereas his brother had assumed the responsibility to reform his culture, the 'special task' to which he felt called was the reformation of the church."[5]

H. Richard Niebuhr devoted his life to theological reflections on the church and the world. Wrote Diefenthaler, "Richard Niebuhr was a man for whom the vocation of churchman remained central throughout his life." The youngest of five children, Helmut grew up in Missouri and Illinois parsonages of the German Evangelical Synod of North America. His German mother was the daughter of an immigrant Evangelical Synod missionary pastor. His German father was an immigrant who became a pastor and promoter of home mission in the Evangelical Synod. His sister was a church educator. His aunt was a consecrated parish deaconess. Other aunts were pastor's wives and uncles were pastors in the Evangelical church.[6]

Like brother Reinhold, Helmut was ordained in the Evangelical Synod and served a parish after being educated at the Synod's schools, Elmhurst Preseminary (near Chicago) and Eden Seminary (near St. Louis), and at Yale Divinity School. Helmut returned to teach at Eden in 1919, received a Ph.D. from Yale in 1924, and then, at the age of thirty, returned to Elmhurst as president. After three difficult but important years at Elmhurst, he returned again to Eden to teach and serve as academic dean for four more years. Helmut chaired the Evangelical Synod Committee on Relations with Other Churches, exploring union with the German Reformed Church and the Evangelical United Brethren. Had this three-way ecumenical venture succeeded, it would have created a United Church in America twenty-five years before there was a United Church of Christ. Beginning in their student days at Elmhurst and Eden (1910-1915), both Niebuhr brothers championed the cause of Americanization in the Synod and its schools. Symbolic of this interest, Helmut became Richard when he left the Midwest for a teaching post at Yale in 1931.[7]

At the peak of his career, following the publication of his two most important books (*The Meaning of Revelation*, 1941; and *Christ and Culture*,

1951), H. Richard Niebuhr postponed all other scholarly research in order to direct an intensive study of theological education in North America. One of the three published results of this investigation was the book, *The Purpose of the Church and Its Ministry* (1956). Most often remembered from that work are his summary of the church's purpose and his re-imagining of the pastoral office. Reflecting his ongoing though critical appreciation for the Social Gospel, he defined the mission of the church as the "increase among [people] of the love of God and neighbor." He re-imagined the task and title of the pastoral office as one who ministers to a ministering community, calling it "pastoral director." Less frequently remembered but more helpful in mediating between the given neo-orthodox polarities that have shaped us are the six polarities between which, Niebuhr says, the responsible church moves.[8]

The Church as Polar Reality

• *Subject and Object*

Niebuhr says the church is "the subjective pole of the objective rule of God." Negatively, this means that the church cannot simply identify itself with the reign of God on earth. Positively, this means that the church is the subject which directs its attention and worship beyond itself to the *object* of its life and faith who is God. The importance of this polarity, Niebuhr says, "is the distinction of the Church from the realm and rule of God; the recognition of the primacy and independence of the divine reality which can and does act without, beyond and often despite the Church; and the acceptance of the relativity yet indispensability of the church in human relations to that reality." Nearly half a century since Niebuhr wrote those words, the church remains tempted to blur Kierkegaard's "infinite qualitative distinction" between God and humanity. We either identify with the *object* in pseudo-propheticism or we dismiss the *object* in our devotion to subjectivity. The language of much new hymnody and liturgy, for example, lacks a transcendent referent: we sing and pray to ourselves. "Where there is apprehension of, and participation in this Object, there the Church exists," Niebuhr declared.

• *Community and Institution*

A second polar feature affirms that the church is both a community of divine and human interaction and the embodiment of its shared memories and hopes in certain institutional forms. It is both the flawed but necessary institution which a younger H. Richard Niebuhr condemned in *The Social Sources of Denominationalism* (his first book, 1929) and it is the dynamic movement which he praised in *The Kingdom of God in America* (1937).

Young Helmut and his brother Reinhold struggled with the ethnic and conservative institution of the German Evangelical Synod, even as they were fed by the vital, heartfelt piety of this community of faith. Today, the United Church of Christ is at its best in maintaining a healthy balance between these poles. Widespread indifference to national restructuring at the turn of this new century, for example, is offset by renewed vitality among Conferences, Associations and congregations.

• *Unity and Plurality*

"The Church is one, yet also many," Niebuhr writes, reflecting the Pauline metaphor of the body of Christ. "It is a pluralism moving toward unity and a unity diversifying and specifying itself." Every setting of the church is the church of Jesus Christ only by virtue of its participation in the whole. The United Church of Christ falls down at the altar of the gods named pluralism, diversity and autonomy when it forgets the pole of unity. The Johannine motto of the UCC was the motto of the Evangelical Synod of the Niebuhrs' birth as well: "That they may all be one." The longing in that prayer demands movement to unity in our day, just as in Niebuhr's day the situation called for movement in the other direction.

• *Locality and Universality*

The church exists wherever radical faith is incarnate. That means the church is always local. But a localized church also always implies a universal church of which it is a part. When remembered here and now, Jesus Christ is present and brings along with him the whole company of the saints who have been and will be reconciled to God and neighbor through him, then and there. The United Church of Christ, like much of oldline Protestantism, suffers a deep divide between congregations and wider settings of the church, within and beyond the denomination. In the heretical geography of autonomy we have learned that the distance between us and Cleveland is about the same as that between us and New York. As an Association Minister once put it, "Autonomy means we all are free to ignore one another." For the church to be fully catholic and united, we must stop referring to local churches as if they were public school districts or states invoking a right to local control.

• *Protestant and Catholic*

Neither word is capitalized. Niebuhr means that the church needs both principles, protestant iconoclasm and catholic incarnation. The infinite must always be represented in finite symbols. This is the catholic principle. Yet the symbols must not displace the infinite, nor confuse the subject with the object. This is the protestant principle. Much of the inclusive language struggle of the last twenty-five years failed to recognize this polarity. Deconstructionists reversed the direction of the symbolic. Words did not represent another reality but created reality. The iconoclasm of feminist ideology became rigid, traditionalistic, and catholic as it precluded the use of "Lord" and "kingdom of God."

• *Church and World*

A sixth and final pair of polar features may be Niebuhr's most important. Here, as in the first pair of subject and object, the church itself is one pole. The other is the world, both the community of the unfaithful but called into the church and the context of the faithful sent out of the church. The relations between church and world vary constantly, as Niebuhr showed in his classic work, *Christ and Culture*. But the two poles are inseparable as well. The church is in the world and the world is in the church. "The world is sometime enemy, sometimes partner of the Church, often antagonist, always one to be befriended." In John's Gospel, after all, Jesus is not the light of the church but the light of the world. The church lives and defines itself over against two "others," both God and the world. In his early, more radical perspective, Niebuhr identified the ideal as "the church against the world." Later, he preferred the conversionist option, "the church transforming culture." In both instances, Niebuhr maintained that this polar reality of the church in relation to the world helps to keep the community centered in God and concerned for the world. Both must be present to be the church. Sensitivity to these poles keeps the church involved in what Niebuhr called, "a permanent revolution of the heart and mind," beginning in repentance as accountability to God and ending in responsibility for God's world.

In the brief history of the United Church of Christ we have prided ourselves in our worldliness as an expression of our catholic commitment to incarnation. We have placed the cross of Jesus Christ on an orb, symbolizing the world of human need and responsibility. We have emphasized our calling to be the church in the world. But as Niebuhr said in the 1930s, the problem of the church is not the church in the world but the world in the church. H. Richard Niebuhr reminds us that the crown rests atop the cross, not the world.[9]

Notes

1. See, for example, Alasdair I. C. Heron, *A Century of Protestant Theology* (The Westminster Press, 1980).

2. Reinhold Niebuhr biographies are many and varied. The most recent and

reliable are Charles C. Brown, *Niebuhr and His Age* (Trinity Press International, 1992) and Ronald H. Stone, *Professor Reinhold Niebuhr: A Mentor to the Twentieth Century* (Westminster/John Knox Press, 1992).

3. William J. Wolf argues that Reinhold Niebuhr lacked a doctrine of the church as a redemptive instrument in the world but sees the seeds of one in the last chapter of Niebuhr's *Faith and History* (1949): The church is a community of believers "persuaded that the whole of life and all historical vicissitudes stand under the sovereignty of a holy, yet merciful God," a community where the grace of Christ is known through sacraments and preaching, and pride is pierced through transformed lives. Wolf was a contributor in the definitive Kegley and Bretall, eds., *Reinhold Niebuhr: His Religious, Social, and Political Thought* (Macmillan, 1961). See also Charles C. Brown, 155.

4. H. Richard Niebuhr, "The Idea of the Church in Theological Education" (unpublished paper), quoted in Libertus A. Hoedemaker, *The Theology of H. Richard Niebuhr* (The Pilgrim Press, 1970), 138.

5. Jonathan Diefenthaler, *H. Richard Niebuhr: A Lifetime of Reflections on the Church and the World* (Mercer University Press, 1986), xi.

6. Diefenthaler, p. 93. For Niebuhr family material see William G. Chrystal, *A Father's Mantle: The Legacy of Gustav Niebuhr* (The Pilgrim Press, 1982) and John Clifford Helt, *Lydia Hosto Niebuhr: "The Queen Bee of American Theologians"* in *On the Way* (Wisconsin Conference, United Church of Christ, 1993).

7. For HRN's Elmhurst years see Stephen Crocco, "President H. Richard Niebuhr: The Elmhurst Years," (Unpublished paper, 1987). For the Eden years see Walter Brueggemann, *Ethos and Ecumenism, an Ecumenical Blend: a History of Eden Theology Seminary, 1925-1975* (Eden Publishing House, 1975). For the role in union conversations see Diefenthaler, pp. 17-18, and David Nussmann, *Helmut Richard Niebuhr and the Evangelical Synod: A Conversation* (Unpublished presentation for the Eden Seminary centennial celebration of HRN's birth, September 1994). Of course, the union conversations did result in the formation of the Evangelical and Reformed Church in 1934, but HRN no longer chaired or cared as much about the process after 1930.

8. Good bibliographical reviews may be found in Diefenthaler, Hoedemaker and Lonnie D. Kliever, *H. Richard Niebuhr* (Word Books, 1977). HRN's *The Purpose of the Church and Its Ministry* may be found in paperback beginning in 1977 (Harper and Row).

9. HRN, 17-27.

Three Protestant Identities:
The Ecclesiological Study of the
Leuenberg Church Fellowship

Wilhelm Hüffmeier

In a commemorative speech on the occasion of the 50th anniversary of the death of Jochen Klepper, the greatest Protestant hymn writer and novelist of the 20th century in the German language, Joachim Mehlhausen formulated the following theses to the Protestant identity:

"Protestant identity has three facets wherever it is represented in its entirety. It comprises personal, political, and ecclesiastical identities."[1] A "well-balanced formation in all these three identities," said Mehlhausen, is "very rare."[2] In the German Confessing Church during the period of National Socialism, the main stress was laid on the "ecclesiastical identity," which was described as the "ecclesiasticalization of the German Protestantism." Since 1945 the same Protestantism has been striving intensely for "a new political identity."[3] The personal Protestant identity which Jochen Klepper found, proved, and kept under difficult circumstances "is missed nowadays in the awareness of Protestant Christians."[4] Mehlhausen could have added that nobody in Germany has embodied all these three identities in equal proportions better than Dietrich Bonhoeffer.

What is then meant by the ecclesiastical, political, and personal Protestant identities in terms of their contents? I would like to broach this question by referring to a paper which was adopted unanimously in Vienna at the General Assembly of the Leuenberg Church Fellowship in May 1994. With this paper the Protestant churches in Europe agreed on a common understanding of the church for the first time since the Reformation. The paper entitled "The Church of Jesus Christ: The Contribution of the Reformation towards Ecumenical Dialogue on Church Unity"[5] is acclaimed as the ecclesiology of the Leuenberg Agreement. The nature and the shape of the church (I), its mission in the present-day world (II), its understanding of ecumenism (III) and the guideline of its relationship to Judaism and non-Christian religions and world-views (II.3) are succinctly formulated therein. The paper expresses in some fifty pages what the Second Vatican Council dealt with in four papers, "Lumen Gentium," "Gaudium et Spes," "Unitats Redintegratio" and "Nostra Aetate." It seems to me meaningful to draw the attention of North American readers to the fundamental statements of this Leuenberg ecclesiastical study because in the United States, Presbyterian, Reformed, United and Lutheran churches have also reached a comparable concord with "A Formula of Agreement" (1997).

To speak of identity has a double function: Whoever talks about identity intends to reveal to those who are standing outside that this is who we are, and at the same time it has to be conveyed to the affiliated what they can expect as a home in the end. Identity is therefore to be understood as a reliable self-determination and recognizable profile. In this sense we raise a question as to what the study "The church of Jesus Christ" says about the particular profile of the European Protestantism.

The Ecclesiastical Protestant Identity

Protestantism cannot determine its ecclesiastical identity in the same way as did the Second Vatican Council, according to which "the one church of Christ which in the Creed is professed as one, holy, catholic and apostolic . . . subsists in the Catholic Church, which is governed by the successor of Peter and by the Bishops in communion with him" ("Lumen Gentium," 8). According to the Protestant Creed, the church of Jesus Christ is not the sum of all Christian churches and church traditions nor does it float over the others like an idea still to be realized ("Civitas Platonica"). Rather, the Protestant faith confesses that each church must live in the distinction between the church of faith and the visible church, in such a way that it is the task of the visible and concrete individual church to examine constantly its shape, whether and how it corresponds to its "essential attributes and nature given in its origin": unity, holiness, catholicity (universality), and apostolicity (cf. I.2.4 and I.2.5.4). In constant recurrence to the apostolic witness, the church confesses its unity, its holiness, and its catholicity as gifts of God given in Christ, and gives expression to its nature in the community of churches (cf. I.2.3 and I.2.5.4).

Therefore, a certain degree of fundamental self-relativization belongs to the Protestant identity, which necessitates a constant distinction between the foundation and the concrete shape of the church. This self-relativization permits the churches the freedom of shaping (I.1.4) and commits them "to do justice to the scope of their mission without sacrificing the clarity of their witnessing" (I.3.2). The church has the mission "to be an instrument of God for the actualization of God's universal will to salvation as a witness to the gospel in the world" (I.3.2). To quote the Barmen Theological Declaration, that one Word of God which is called Jesus Christ is a message for all people (Barmen I and VI). The Protestant ecumenical approach is also founded on such a self-relativization. He who can distinguish himself from the basis of the church, i.e. Jesus Christ himself, also has the force to see the living Christ in other churches as being ecclesiastically effective. This enables a church fellowship in which no one concrete existing church becomes the norm of all the others.

Self-relativization of one's own church does not mean any indifference to the mission of shaping the church. As regards the clarity of the shape of Protestant churches, the Reformers identified the marks of the church (I.2.4) as "those fundamental features of the visible life of the church through which the origin of the church presents itself and through which a church holds fast to its origin" (I.2.4.1). According to the conviction of the Leuenberg Agreement and the confessional writings of the Reformation, these are the "appropriate proclamation of the gospel and the administration of the sacraments according to the gospel" (I.2.4.3).

In determining the identity of the church, two additional notions are of fundamental significance in the tradition of K. Barth and D. Bonhoeffer, namely witness and service. These notions are also of substantial importance for the Leuenberg Agreement. The study greatly contributes to the elucidation of these two key notions. First and foremost it points to the self-evidence that both witness and service are the marks of the church (LA 29 and 36) and those of Christian life (LA 11 and 13). In its service of witness, the church needs concrete ministries of proclamation and leadership (*Episkopē*) regardless of the priesthood of all believers (cf. I.2.5.1).

At the same time it is made clear in the study that both the aspects, witness and service, belong so closely together that they cannot be divided into two domains or organizations of the church: church and congregation with witness on the one hand and diaconia with service in the other hand. Rather, the implementation of God's will is in both tables of the Ten Commandments "always 'witness and service' together" (I.2.5). This principle applies to church's ways as well as individual Christian life.

Personal Protestant Identity

How to recognize a Protestant Christian? In the last century, Albrecht Ritschl answered this question with the following distinction:

- Self-discipline and conscientiousness: they find the "independence and uprightness of character."
- Wisdom, contemplation, determination, perseverance: they find the "lucidity and energy of character."
- Goodness, gratefulness, righteousness: they find the "disposition or warmth of character."[6]

It is not difficult to recognize a good Prussian mind in such a listing as described by Fontane in his novels. Is it also the personal identity of a Protestant as described in the light of the New Testament and the Reformation? According to the ecclesiological study of the Leuenberg Church Fellowship, the accent should be shifted away from it. We find the following answer in section I.3.3:

- A Protestant Christian is unthinkable without the knowledge of the "fundamental and permanent" character of worship. It is an unequivocal mark of a Protestant Christian to follow this knowledge. I call it the mark of liturgical or vertical spirituality (cf. I.3.3.1). This includes saying grace and personal prayers.

- A Protestant Christian accepts the message of Christ as the "guide-line and criterion for interpreting and shaping of the reality of life" in daily, familial, and professional lives and at leisure time. He/she should bring this message of Christ home to self and others without turning it into law (cf. I.3.3.2). Christianity is freedom (Ph. Melanchthon). I call this the mark of daily claim through Christ.

- The Protestant Christian appreciates the professional and independent character of the worldly responsibility. Precisely for this reason one should remain aware that also in one's professional life witness and service belong inseparably together (cf. I.3.3.3). I call this the mark of practicality of Christian mold.

- The Protestant Christian knows of a community which "encompasses, relativizes, and transcends" all natural, social, and national forms of community (I.3.3.4). He/she knows of the human unity and understands the church in the community of churches as an interim presentation of this unity. At the same time he/she is aware of the dangers of this community caused by ideologies and utopias which play down the dangers resulting from human sins. For Christ's sake the Protestant Christian cherishes the boundless hope for the unity of churches and the one humanity. I call this the mark of ecumenical passion for the unity of churches and the solidarity of societies (cf. I.3.3.4).

Political Protestant Identity

The political Protestant identity is formed through the common awareness of the commission of living up to the scope of the church's mission without sacrificing the clarity of its witness. In doing so the churches of the Reformation know that they must put across their witness and service in open pluralistic societies. They come up to their foundation and the hopes and expectations of humans by remaining recognizable and profiled.

Talking of the political witness of the church, many Protestants instantly think of the commission of the "prophetic criticism." The study recognizes the identification mark of political Protestantism also in the sense of "warning and admonition, everywhere where human dignity, human life and the integrity of creation is being infringed upon and violated" (II.2.4). It mentions this identification mark, however, only in the fourth place. It makes clear that the church has to fulfil its commissions as "confessing," "pastoral," and "helping" churches (II.2.1. to II.2.3) before taking a stance with prophetic criticism. No prophetic criticism on politics and economy is possible without the will to pastoral care for those who are active in politics and business world. The fifth thesis of the Barmen Theological Declaration expresses a similar view. Reminding the political leaders of God's kingdom, God's commandment, and God's righteousness is linked—at least in the early version of the fifth Barmen thesis—not only with gratitude but also with intercession for them.[7]

In doing so, it is crucial that Protestantism makes itself clearly understood with the fact that its confession, pastoral care, and help come from the gospel. Making the gospel recognizable is the central mission of the Protestant churches. Therefore, the churches ought not to go off course getting into their particular ethical commissions, but first and foremost they should persevere in pointing to the origin of their mission.

I would like to conclude with a picture to which Frederick Trost drew my attention and of which Karl Barth made use in his lecture entitled "The Real Church" given in various places in Hungary in 1948. After depicting the affiliation and common bond in the real church in which each one recognizes, loves, and helps the other, Barth condenses all said in the following image: "Behold and listen—a truly edifying spectacle which I cannot admire enough here in Hungary—as each single person in the gypsy band has his eyes and ears entirely on the primary violin and tries to play his own instrument according to its melody, so it is essential to play with all the others in a natural and joyful harmony. . . . So we stand side by side in the real church, facing a common commission under a common mission."[8] In the real church, all three facets of Protestant identity are forged in a perfect balance, including the political identity, because the church is a political entity merely through the fact that it is there.

Notes

1. Joachim Mehlhausen, Jochen Klepper. "Eine Gedenkrede und Anmerkungen zum Forschungsstand," in: *Zeitschrift für Kirchengeschichte*, 104 (1993): 369.

2. Ibid.

3. Ibid.

4. Ibid.

5. The study has been published by W. Hüffmeier in German and English as Volume 1 of the Leuenberg Documents through Otto Lembeck Publishing House, Frankfurt/Main. The Roman and Arabic numbers in quotations refer to the corresponding chapters and sections respectively.

6. A. Ritschl *Unterricht in der christlichen Religion,* republication of the first edition of 1875 = *Texte zur Kirchen- und Theologiegeschichte*, ed. G. Ruhbach, 1966, 56ff.

7. Cf. W. Hüffmeier (ed.) *Für Recht und Frieden sorgen. Auftrag der Kirche und Aufgabe des Staates nach Barmen V. Theologisches Votum der Evangelischen Kirche der Union*, 1986, 93ff.

8. K. Barth "Die wirkliche Kirche," in *Evangelische Theologie* 8 (1948/49): 136.

The Gifts of Benedictine Monasticism to the Church

Joanne Kollasch, Lynne Smith, and Mary David Walgenbach

Monasticism is a cell within the church. Its life flows from the bosom of the Triune God into a particular time and place. Like the church, it holds the memories of graced and decisive events in its history.

A vital tension between memories, tradition, and the movement of the Spirit brings new life to the church and the monastery. This creative relationship causes the church and the monastery to live in the context of their founding events and to articulate and realize the work of the Holy Spirit for the present and future generations. The church and the monastery are always in the process of becoming who they are called to be in a particular time and place. Rooted in their identities, they become fertile ground for the growth of new life.

In the church's journey and in the 1500-year history of monasticism there have been and there will be significant events and individuals particularly marked with the true power of the Spirit. Their experience and their teaching form a reservoir of wisdom which constitutes the great spiritual heritage of the church.

The Second Vatican Council was one such event. It called the Roman Catholic Church in general and religious communities in particular to touch the roots of their origins and to listen to the present voice and gifts of the Holy Spirit. Fidelity to a tradition means a willingness to change, modify, and adapt that tradition.

Worship and Liturgical Reform

Knowledge of history liberates people, for it frees them from the tyranny of the present and allows them to forge a new future. Like the scribe instructed in the reign of heaven, they can bring forth from the storeroom both the new and the old (Mt 13:51-52). This has been particularly true of the history of Christian worship and the key role of the Benedictine community in the nineteenth and twentieth centuries, first of all as a gift to the Roman Catholic tradition but also to all the Christian churches in this age of ecumenism.

The Benedictine tradition was well equipped for this task. The monks possessed a continuity of monastic worship extending back to the sixth-century *Rule of Benedict*. They had trained scholars and developed libraries of manuscripts enabling them to go back before the Reformation and the Council of Trent, through the accretions of medieval worship, to simpler lines of worship in the age of the Fathers of the Church. There was found evidence of a more authentic worship in terms of proclamation of the Word of God and community participation, providing a more sure basis for renewal of worship in the last half of the twentieth century and astonishing ecumenical consensus (the Lima document *Baptism, Eucharist and Ministry,* for instance).

Benedictine scholars rediscovered some of the worship gifts of the Reformation, such as worshiping in the language of the people and the importance of proclaiming and hearing the Word. But there were other gifts: the new Roman Lectionary and the Revised Common Lectionary, the resurgence of the Eucharist Prayer as authentic praise and thanks, and increased frequency of the celebration of the Eucharist. As all the major Christian churches have found more commonality in the grand outlines of their orders of worship, they have also rediscovered their authentic particularity, for unity in plurality was also a hallmark of Patristic liturgy. These are all gifts of our time to which Benedictine scholars, among others, contributed in a major way.

Nor was this merely an academic project. Beginning in the great Benedictine monasteries of France, Belgium, and Germany, spreading eventually to St. John's Abbey in Collegeville, Minnesota, this research was not history for history's sake but knowledge brought to bear on a renewed and enriched theology of worship and a more informed and conscious practice of worship. For the Benedictine men and women lived liturgy; it was the framework of their lives. They could not help but carry their knowledge into practice. The church makes the liturgy; in turn, the liturgy makes the church. All of this came to partial fruition in the liturgical reforms and renewal of the Second Vatican Council. Protestant observers not only contributed to the Council but brought back insights gained to their own constituencies and ecumenical discussions.

There are special gifts that the monastic Benedictine tradition still offers to all the Christian churches as part of a marvelous Christian pluralism. The Benedictine tradition has always lived the liturgical year very deeply and authentically through the celebration of both Eucharist and Liturgy of the Hours. The mystery of salvation at work comes to the fore, resistant to all the secular characterizations of time in our age.

Benedictines are schooled in the art of listening to the word of God, a listening that comes first in the individual heart, ahead of any other voices of our times. Morning and evening prayer consecrate the day, in the sense of acknowledging that each day comes as a gift from God. Benedictine liturgy is steadfastly communal, guarding against the kind of individualism that is destructive of community.

Throughout history there has been a steady contribution from the Benedictine monastic community in providing places of worship and patterns of worship true to their original tradition yet adapted to contemporary life. That all is holy and the gift of God needs to be expressed regularly: hence the daily pattern of prayer.

Stewardship

A spirit of reverence for all creation permeates the *Rule of Benedict,* a sense of oneness with the land, the days, the seasons. "Regard all utensils and goods of the monastery as sacred vessels of the altar."[1] This is interpreted to apply not only to tools, books, buildings, and other tangibles but also to the use of time, care of the self, and care of the earth.

Benedictine spirituality asks for harmony, awareness, balance. The church and the community are reminded by Saint Benedict that creation belongs to God, that we have been put here as its keepers. We are to care for the small piece of the planet entrusted to us, recognizing that our actions, however insignificant they may seem, are global in scope and meaning. We are to act in moderation as "stewards of God" rather than being wasteful, greedy, or extravagant. "Benedictine spirituality sees the care of the earth and the integration of prayer and work, body and soul, as essential parts of the journey to wholeness that answers the emptiness in each of us."[2]

A Model of Leadership

Benedictines offer the church a particular style of leadership. In the monastery, the abbot or prioress "is believed to hold the place of Christ" (RB 2:2). The monastery, like the church, is christocentric. Church leaders are to follow Christ's example as they guide the community of faith. Standing in the place of Christ, the abbot or prioress is a trustee of the community's vision. He or she articulates the monastic tradition and provides direction and focus for the community. The abbot or prioress is to lead both by teaching and by example but "more by example than by words" (RB 2:24). "He [She] must so accommodate and adapt himself [herself] to each one's character and intelligence that he [she] will not only keep the flock entrusted to his [her] care from dwindling, but will rejoice in the increase of a good flock" (RB 2:32). Such advice is beneficial and appropriate for any church leader.

Dialogical listening leads to discernment and obedience in the community. Monastic leaders do not exercise their office in isolation. They are guided by Scripture, by the monastic tradition, and the Rule of Benedict. In addition, Benedict advises the abbot or prioress to seek the council of the community members on important matters. Each member, young and old, is heard because "the Lord often reveals what is better to the younger" (RB 3:3). In the consultation process, the monks "are to express their opinions with all humility, and not presume to defend their own views obstinately" (RB 3:4). The abbot or prioress is responsible for the final decision, but all members have the responsibility to offer their wisdom to the community. Leadership is exercised for the building up of both the community and the individual monk in their quest for God. Both the leader and the community are obedient to what they hear as they seek to do the will of God.

Hospitality

Benedictine monasteries are known for their hospitality. Saint Benedict said, "All guests who present themselves are to be welcomed as Christ, for he himself will say: I was a stranger and you welcomed me" (Mt 25:35) (RB 53:1). "Great care and concern are to be shown in receiving poor people and pilgrims, because in them more particularly Christ is received" (RB 53:15). The monastery provides a place where people can come and be welcomed as Christ. Guests can find a quiet place apart from the noise and busyness of their lives to be nourished in body and soul for their journey. They may join in the prayer of the community and listen deeply to the word in the Liturgy of Hours. They may walk the grounds of the monastery and behold the glory of God in creation. They may spend time in silent reflection and experience the movement of the Spirit in their hearts or seek spiritual guidance from a member of the community who listens and helps them hear their own wisdom. They may enjoy a simple, nourishing meal and be strengthened for their continuing journey.

In the monastery, members show hospitality to one another as well, treating all persons with love and respect. This mutual service becomes an occasion for one's continuing formation in the Christian life. This might also be true in the local church, where receiving one another as Christ can go a long way toward helping the church remain a vital, growing Christian community.

In conclusion, monasticism, as a cell within the church, offers rich gifts to the Christian community. Out of its treasure house of scholarship, daily worship, and listening to the word in the Liturgy of Hours, Benedictine monasticism provides resources for the renewal of worship in the contemporary church. With its spirit of reverence for all creation and its balanced way of life, monasticism calls the church to practice stewardship of the earth, a holy use of time, and care for the self. The monastery offers a model of leadership that listens deeply to the word, to the individual, and to the needs of the community and acts for the personal development of the individual as well as the building of community in the search for God. Finally, as it continues Christ's ministry in the world, the monastery offers guests and all seekers hospitality where they may step apart for a time and be renewed for their continuing journey.

Notes

1. *The Rule of Benedict in Latin and English with Notes*, ed. Timothy Fry (Collegeville, Minn.: The Liturgical Press, 1981), 31:10. Hereafter abbreviated as RB.

2. Joan O. Chittister, OSB, *The Rule of Benedict: Insights for the Ages* (New York: Crossroad, 1992), 107.

"Gathered Together"

John W. Lynes, Jr.

Let the peace of God reign in your hearts, because it is for this purpose that you were gathered together as one body (Col 3:15).

Paul writes these stirring words to the Christians at Colossae, and while he certainly did not intend them as a definition of the church of Jesus Christ, one might suggest that it is as elegantly succinct a definition as one might ever need, especially when coupled with his equally eloquent blessing to the Philippians: "May the peace of God, which lies beyond all human comprehension, keep your hearts and minds in Christ Jesus" (4:7). We are, indeed, gathered together by God as the church of Jesus Christ, as one body, to help everyone experience the peace of God reigning in their hearts.

And yet, as elegantly succinct as these verses may be when construed as a definition of the church, Paul would be the first to admit their shortcoming. Indeed, he would likely counsel against any attempt to define the church on the grounds that all such attempts would be self-defeating because incomplete. Of course, in the nearly two millennia since Paul, few have been deterred from proffering such definitions, and I confess I shall suggest yet another.

Perhaps this is as it should be for one writing out of the Reformed tradition of the church, whose very commitment is *ecclesia semper reformanda*. But there is a more personal reason. In a variety of ways, the ministry of Frederick Trost is and has been continually informed by his vision of and passion for what the church is, ought, and can be. It is imperative, therefore, that some definition of the church of Jesus Christ be in the forefront of this *Festschrift,* honoring Frederick Trost as pastor and teacher, prophet, and priest.

The church of Jesus Christ might be described as a worship-centered, prayer-based, learning-inspired, spirit-guided, faith-developing, love-flowing, mission-engaging, peace-promoting, justice-seeking, grace-incarnating, multi-racial, multi-cultural covenanted communion of disciples of Christ, accessible to all.[1] Grounded in faith, covenanted in love, sustained by grace, and nurtured by hope, as covenanted disciples, its members seek to live sacramentally in faithful response to the ever-faithful God who gathers them together into being as a church, choosing them as covenantal friends in the service of God's created world. As covenantal friends and disciples of Christ, they seek to live in the majestic mystery of

God's abiding presence and, thus, to live in the sacredness of God's continual creation, the holiness of God's covenantal friendship, the faithfulness of God's steadfast love, the integrity of God's boundless grace, and the ecstasy of God's joy-filled hope. In whatever they do, they seek to live out of the sacramental mystery of God's Eucharist.

The Covenantal (*Agape*) Friendship of God

It may seem odd to describe our relationship with God and one another as one of covenantal friendship. And yet, this may be one of the richest ways in which to conceive of these relationships. By God's own creative action, deliberately and intentionally, lovingly and graciously, God has chosen to create us in God's own image and has entered into a special covenant relationship with us, both equipping and calling us to be God's friends in maintaining, sustaining, and nurturing the relationships in which we humans stand to God and the created beings in God's world and to preserve the integrity of these basic relationships. As covenanted partners, we are to live as agape friends to one another in response to the *agape* friendship in which God has created us.[2]

Living in the Majestic Mystery of God's Abiding Presence

To live in covenantal (*agape*) friendship with God and one another is, I suggest, to live continually in the majestic mystery of God's abiding presence. Abraham Heschel[3] has repeatedly pointed out that as mysterious and incomprehensible as it may seem, God continually seeks us out where we are, long before we seek to find God. This has the consequence that everyone and everyplace is a person and a place where God is present and in which God's love and grace are at work. God's self-revealed name, "I Will Be Present Howsoever I Will Be Present," serves to remind us of this awesome characteristic of God.[4]

I am suggesting we think of living in the mystery of God's abiding presence as including five dimensions, namely, living in (1) the *sacredness* of God's continual creation, (2) the *holiness* of God's covenantal friendship, (3) the *faithfulness* of God's steadfast love, (4) the *integrity* of God's boundless grace, and (5) the *ecstasy* of God's joy-filled hope. And I suggest that the church of Jesus Christ lives as the church as I have sought to define it by living in these ways.

Living in the Sacredness of God's Continual Creation

Christ's disciples view life as *sacred*. Not part of it—say, the human part—but all of it. They see the world in all its diversity of being and complexity of living as the arena in which God faithfully reaches out to be in relation and in which, therefore, God's love and grace are at work. They believe, accordingly, that there is a kind of interconnectedness and interdependence of all created beings in God's world and that they are called to be servants (stewards) of the relationships God creates and seeks to sustain, nurture, and bring to maturity in God's world. They confess that their human sinfulness will seek to dissuade them from recognizing and affirming this interconnectedness and interdependence, because it prefers they think of human life as somehow "privileged" and "set apart" from everything else in God's world that is not human. But their Christian discipleship bids them say farewell to this narrow and pride-full perspective and invites them instead to make a habit of the heart the affirmation of this interconnectedness and interdependence. Christ's disciples thus see life as a sacred gift, not a possession, and their role as servant, not as privileged dominator.

Living in the Holiness of God's Covenantal (*Agape*) Friendship

Christ's disciples understand that by God's own choice, intentional and deliberate, loving and gracious, God and they are covenantal friends. To be a faithful covenantal friend to God, the ever-faithful one, is to strive to live a *holy* life. Now, this does not mean that one aspires to be God nor even perfect. It means, rather, that one seeks to be human and thus live life in the way God intended we humans could. The gathering together and creation of a special people, Israel, and the revelation by God of a special teaching (Torah) to provide them with a way for living that would be a blessing for all the peoples of the created world is but one of God's faithful revelations to us about what this holiness in covenantal friendship includes. For those gathered together by God as disciples of Christ, Jesus the Christ reveals in yet more poignant ways what forms this holiness in covenantal friendship is to take. And the apostle Paul provides several litanies of the "virtues and vices" of such living (Rom 12:9-21; Gal 5:19-26; Col 3:11-17; Eph 4:22-32; and 2 Tim 2:20-25).[5]

This holiness in covenantal friendship requires, accordingly, that we be servants of economic, social, and political justice for all God's children, since its very purpose is that all should participate in the fullness of life as God intends it. The church, of course, needs to confess that it has not been faithful here—often racist and sexist, often culturally insensitive and imperialistic, often indifferent at best to those on the margin, the oppressed, the exploited, and the disenfranchised. But such sinful shortcomings do not eviscerate its mission and purpose in the world.

Living in the Faithfulness of God's Steadfast Love

The experience disciples of Christ cherish, the experience they seek to share with others, is the experience of the *faithfulness* of God's steadfast love. The relationship in which humans stand to God—all, not simply those in the church—is, by God's choice, eternal. Again and again in God's revelations as recorded in scripture and as attested by clouds of witnesses, we see God's faithful commitment to that choice and that relationship. The self-emptying of God as suffering servant attests to this commitment. The birth, life, death, and resurrection of Jesus Christ as the incarnation of this suffering-servant God attest to this commitment and beckon Christ's disciples to live in the faithfulness of this suffering-servant love.

Living in the Integrity of God's Boundless Grace

The transforming experience of God's love, however, is the experience of God's grace, which liberates and sets us free to reconcile and be reconciled, to heal and to move toward maturity. As Karl Barth[6] sought desperately to point out, the response of the church and Christ's disciples to the integrity and affirmations of God's grace in Christ (the "Nevertheless" of God's grace) can only be one of thankful response. Out of the self-emptying of this God, we have been forgiven and redeemed. As the incarnation of this self-emptying of God, Christ Jesus does not make the reconciliation possible; he is that reconciliation.[7] And our life as a Christian community of faith proclaims that good news and seeks to help others to experience its power to liberate and transform.

Living in the Ecstasy of God's Joy-Filled Hope

There is no question, therefore, that a singular mark of the Christian church is its hope. Its hope is not grounded in itself, or in its own accomplishments. Its hope is grounded in the hope-filled grace of its head, Jesus Christ. Its hope is grounded in the reconciling love and transforming grace of the continually creating God. And this is cause for ecstasy in the highest degree among its members, an ecstasy that informs all they do. There can be nothing they do that is not infused with this hope. There can be nothing they seek to accomplish that is not infused with this hope. There can be nothing they can be that is not infused with this hope. And the church's worship and prayer-life are grounded and centered precisely in this hope-filled ecstasy.

Living Out of the Sacramental Mystery of God's Holy Eucharist

To live in the majestic mystery of God's abiding presence is, then, to live in the sacredness of God's continual creation, the holiness of God's covenantal friendship, the faithfulness of God's steadfast love, the integrity of God's boundless grace, and the ecstasy of God's joy-filled hope. Seeking to live out its faith in this way, the church of Jesus Christ can be that worship-centered, prayer-based, learning-inspired, spirit-guided, faith-developing, love-flowing, mission-engaging, peace-promoting, justice-seeking, grace-incarnating, multi-racial, multi-cultural covenanted communion of disciples of Christ, accessible to all, God gathers it together to be!

A poignant model for integrating all of these dimensions of the ministry of the church is to envision that its members, individually and corporately, seek continually to live in the mystery of God's Eucharist. If all Christ's disciples in the church lived as if everyone shared Christ's table and were consequently part of the circle of life that it represents, if they all lived as if all of life's decisions and the consequences of those decisions were made and lived out at this table, where no one is excluded, then the church of Jesus Christ might more faithfully approximate what it can be.

The life-long ministry in the United Church of Christ of Pastor Frederick Trost is a ministry lived out at this table and as such constitutes a faithful witness to the power of this definition of Christ's church suggested here and to the sacramental living it proclaims. "In steadfast love, my God will meet me" the psalmist exclaims (59:10a). In Frederick Trost's ministry, as with Moses before him, one must add "face to face as with a friend" (Ex 33:11). What a legacy!

Notes

1. This definition of the church reflects the tradition of the United Church of Christ, as it seeks to be a multi-racial, multi-cultural church, accessible to all. However, this seems to be a worthy goal for any particular communion in whatever tradition.

2. I develop this notion of "covenantal friendship" more fully in my *Themes in the Current Reformation in Religious Thinking: The Covenantal Friendship of God*, Studies in Religion and Society, vol. 36 (Lewiston, New York: Edwin Mellen Press, Ltd., 1997). I link the term *agape*, traditionally associated with the love of God has for us humans with *friendship* to lift up the special character of this covenantal relationship, emphasizing that it is rooted in God's love and takes the form of this special kind of friendship. See also Sally McFague, *Models of God* (Philadelphia: Fortress Press), 164ff.

3. Abraham Joshua Heschel, *Man is Not Alone* (New York: Farrar, Strauss, and Young, 1952) and *God in Search of Man* (New York: Farrar, Strauss, and Young, 1955).

4. Everett Fox, *The Five Books of Moses* (New York: Schocken Books, 1983), 170ff., who bases this translation of the self-revelation of God's name (Exodus 3:14) on the translation of Martin Buber and Franz Rosenzweig, *Die fuenf Buecher der Weisung* (Heidelberg, 1976).

5. Paul's use of phrases like "In Christ," "Into Christ," "Through Christ," "With Christ," and "Of Christ," as well as his notion of "Maturing into Christ" suggest that participation in Christ is a central motif in his theology. See James Dunn, *The Theology of Paul, the Apostle* (Grand Rapids, Michigan: William Eerdmans, 1998), 390ff.

6. Karl Barth, *Church Dogmatics,* Vol. IV, Part I (Edinburgh: T. & T. Clark, 1951), 173ff.

7. See George Hendry, *The Gospel of Incarnation* (Philadelphia: Fortress Press, 1958), 132-34, 139, 142-43, 147.

"Lord of the Church and of All the World"

Lord of the church and of all the world, you call us into your church and we are astonished and fearful. For even though we know you are the Lord, we are ever conscious of our own weakness and of our inclination to abandon your way for us.

Remind us that your grace is sufficient for those who are called, and that life without your Word is no life at all. Remind us that even as you suffered you revealed your grace to the thief next to you on the cross. Remind us that your grace is inexhaustible and that your judgment restores the church and the world to the true path.

Strengthen your church that it might be a sign of compassion and hope in the world, especially in those places where great pain and despair seem to have the upper hand.

We ask you, gracious One, to make yourself known to us in such a way that no bitterness of experience can overcome the reality of our faith, so that the church everywhere and in all circumstances might boldly declare your love in word and in deed. All this we ask because we belong to you, Lord, forever.

Richard L. Christensen

Proclaiming the Gospel:
From Gutenberg to Cyberspace

M. Douglas Meeks

Frederick Trost's life has been devoted to the church's work of communicating the gospel. The striking poetry of his existence has made him an uncommon preacher. But the faithfulness of the church is never just a question of communicating the gospel. It is also a question of the freedom to speak the gospel.

In the early 1930s Dietrich Bonhoeffer raised serious questions about the American churches. They lacked, he said, "both the cutting edge of the Reformation and the 'confession of faith' that could challenge their *prideful pretentiousness*."[1] " Whether the churches of God are free can only be decided by the actual preaching of the Word of God. Only where this word can be preached concretely, in the midst of historical reality, in judgment, command, forgiveness of sinners and liberation from all human institutions is there freedom of the church. But where thanks for institutional freedom must be rendered by the sacrifice of freedom of preaching, the *church is in chains* even if it believes itself to be free."[2]

Frederick Trost has been among us as one open to the freedom God gives for the gospel and as one ready for the struggles necessary to free the church from its pretension and blindness to the gospel. We thank God for the freedom for the gospel we have seen in Frederick's life. From him we have learned that the gospel requires both communication and communion and that both depend on the grace of God.

The Ministry of the Gospel

It belongs to the self-understanding of Christianity that it is a missionary movement, that is, that it is not an end in itself but exists for the sake of God's passion for and redemption of the world. Therefore the church has assumed that it can communicate the gospel across cultural and social boundaries. This has always required translation into different languages and social contexts. The ever present threat is that the translation will swallow up the gospel and change it into the coin of the receiver culture. And yet the gospel cannot be communicated except through the words of a culture. Preachers whose knees are not shaking as they enter the pulpit are probably not clued into their severe predicament: The church is asking them to utter the Word of God, but all they have are the words mediated to them by their own culture.

The ministry of the church is to communicate the gospel about the rescue of human beings from false communication and distorted relationships. In announcing God's deliverance from the bondage that people live under, the church shows the world what is possible for its relation to God. The good news is that human community is possible because God intervenes to make communion with God possible.

Communication without Communion

In preparation for the turn of the millennium it was a popular occupation of historians to make lists of the hundred most important this or that in the last thousand years. A number of historians put down as the most important historical event of the last millennium the invention of the moveable type printing press by Johannes Gutenberg in the 1450s in Mainz, Germany. From its inception printing was a phenomenal force for uniting and yet, not unlike many advances in techné, it was "the physical instrument that tore the West asunder."[3] The Reformation, the development of the middle class, the modern university, and the dissemination of scientific and technological information would have been inconceivable without the printing press. Nor would the steady drive toward possessive individualism have been conceivable without it.

But the printing press was only the first step of the communication revolution. The eighteenth century saw the introduction of print media and with it a new definition of the "public." The nineteenth and twentieth centuries greeted the telegraph, teletype, typewriter, telephone, radio, recording and copying machines, television, and at the end of the twentieth century fax machines, cell phones, modems, broadband, the Internet, and the World Wide Web have set off a new communication revolution and a new economy. The way we communicate has come to define our culture. We have become creatures of our communication systems. Because it is widely believed to be the primary reason for the longest run of a bull market in history, communication technology and the gigantic conglomerates that control its uses are given a wide berth.

Recent developments of the communication revolution have made it possible for the market logic to occupy the last sphere we thought could be free from commodity exchange, culture itself.[4] The invasion of culture by commercial values produces "cultural capitalism."[5] Industrial production is replaced by cultural production. Of all the possible meanings of "postmodernism," perhaps the most acute is that postmodernism is the "cultural logic" of advanced capitalism.

Intellectual property is the guiding force of the new era. Concepts, images, ideas, and experiences, not things, are the real items of value in the new economy. Culture becomes the means of transaction as well as what is transacted. Those who have control over the "pipes" (broadband) are able to control the content of what is communicated. Add to this the fact that people are increasingly purchasing their lived experiences and we have a situation in which the communication of the gospel becomes an enormous challenge. Our plight is that we have tremendously sophisticated communication that does not lead to communion.

Communication of Grace

The ministry of communicating the gospel must begin with the assumption that the gospel is God's proclamation to the world and as such it is not at the disposal of the world or the church. We cannot change the gospel, even if we all agreed to do so democratically. The gospel is God's own word. How else can we speak about God if God Godself has not already spoken? The gospel as God's uttered Word effects its own claims; it illuminates through its own being. Proclamation or preaching, on the other hand, is our attempt to say this gospel in the church and to the world. The Word of God will endure, but the proclamation of the gospel is an extraordinarily fragile thing because it partakes of our signs with all their capacity to communicate as well as their faculty for false communication. The living Word Jesus Christ is constant, but the written word must always be interpreted afresh and proclaimed faithfully in a changing culture.

In the new millennium, as at all other times, the gospel has to be proclaimed in two senses. First, we must preach the gospel that *Jesus himself preached*: The kingdom of God is at hand. This is the promise in Israel from the beginning that God will reign and not the others. It is the proclamation of freedom from Pharaoh's slavery and every other urge to domination that crushes God's creatures. That everything in the gospel depends on the at-handness of the reign of God's righteousness means the church's ministry has to recognize the timing of the gospel. The preaching of the gospel is not possible at all times and places but belongs to the messianic times. If the kingdom is not imminent, then Jesus came too soon. If the reign of God is not beginning in our midst, then it is too early to preach the gospel. The gospel initiates the future in which God's creative righteousness will become manifest and God will be all in all. In this sense the gospel creates time for itself. It is time to utter the gospel when the signs of the messianic age are expected as matters of course: the poor have good news preached to them, the blind see, the captives are set free, and the Jubilee year of the Lord is announced (Lk 4:18ff.). Those who live by *fate* will not see the signs. The signs of the kingdom do not appear in the virtual world of the global economy.

The second aspect of the good news is the gospel *about* Jesus. The good news is that the righteousness of God has the shape of Jesus Christ, that the judgment of God's righteousness is *grace*. The gospel the church proclaims *is* the life, death, resurrection, and future of Jesus the Christ, the Son of God. The Gospel proclaims: The reign of God has already dawned in Jesus' death and resurrection. It has already become accessible to everyone.

The gospel announces grace as the abundance of God's self-giving and thus undermines the primary assumption of the global economy, namely, scarcity. From the manna in the desert, to the feeding of the five thousand, to the elevation of the Eucharistic Host, the gospel creates an economy that begins with the assumption that there is not only enough but more than enough. "He who did not withhold his own Son, but gave him up for all of us, will he not with him also give us everything else?" (Rom 8:32).

The intention of the gospel is to make disciples for God's redemption of the world by delivering them from various forms of slavery. How can we keep the command of God when we are slaves to sin and the fear of death? For this purpose the gospel has its own language. It is a language that sets free, a language that does not define or determine. It is composed of lived, enacted, performative words that free us from the debilitation of our guilt and our fear of death. The gospel speaks the first-person language of Jesus: "I forgive you." God's justification of the godless stands at the center of every proclamation of the gospel. It is a forgiveness that liberates us from guilt's compulsion to evil, from the dread by which principalities and powers control us, and from the apathy of the isolated life, turned in on itself. It gives courage for a new life in fellowship with Christ. The gospel also speaks the first-person language, "I love you." God's excessive gift of God's own life is the surety grounding the amazing gospel command, "Do not be afraid." Nothing can separate us, not even death or the fear of death, from the love of God (Rom 8:38-39).

The Ministry of Communion

Every language lives in a community and creates one. The church is the community that corresponds to and embodies its primary language, the gospel. The gospel is not just the spoken word; it is the experienced and lived new being of grace. The gospel has to have a context, a framework, a culture into which it is spoken, that is, a time and space in which the gospel is being lived at the same time it is spoken in order for faith to be nourished. Thus the proclamation of the gospel enlists the life and practice of the whole church. The church narrates the story of Christ by the way it lives. It shows the grace of God by mutual self-giving in the congregation and by the giving of its life to God's redemption of the world.

The deepest challenge to Christian discipleship in the new millennium may be that we have forgotten how to conceive grace, for its reality of gifting has become arcane and perplexing to us. So used to the logic of commodity exchange are we that the logic of grace seems foreign. We have forgotten how to be gifted and to gift.

Everyone is suspicious of gifts, for gifts make one "much obliged." Gifts destroy the freedom to follow one's whim. We restrict gifts to private, sentimental occasions. This is why public policies assume that all solutions to all social problems should be market and contractual solutions. This is also why the stewardship of the church is often governed by Andrew Carnegie's rules of philanthropy. Is gifting possible in the postmodern conditions of the global market society? Can a gift be given? Has our culture become so saturated by commodity exchange that there can be no such thing as a gift anymore?[6]

If there is no such thing as a gift, if a gift cannot be given, then there is no content to Christian faith and no possibility of the church of Jesus Christ. For our faith, our hope, and our love depend utterly on the gift (*charis*) God has given and on the gifting God enables us to do. If there is no real space and time for gifting, what chance is there for human life?

The New Community of Gifting

If we ask how the gospel creates new time and space for life in the power of the Spirit, we have to turn to the Eucharist. "Thanks (*charis*) be to God for God's gift beyond words" (2 Cor 9:15). Charis leads to Eucharist.[7] The Eucharist provides the foundation for the upbuilding of the church and its social practices. In this meal one is invited to a physical communion, not merely a spiritual experience. Bodies matter in the Eucharist.[8] God gives Godself in what is accessible to general experience. To eat with the Host and all those whom the Host has invited provides a disconnection with the way things are. It causes one to become "unwired" in the confrontation with a global order that refuses access to those without knowledge or something to exchange.

The Eucharist as the community meal in which the reconciliation with God and each other is celebrated creates home for the homeless. The acts at the Eucharistic table conform to all the meals Jesus celebrated with the lost: He takes bread as gift from God, blesses it, breaks it, and gives it to the other. This mode of distribution follows a radically different logic from the exchange of commodities. The Eucharist is the mutual building up of Christian persons in the likeness of Jesus by giving them gifts so that, having been gifted, they can gift others. The church lives as a feast that is the present memory of Jesus broken for us and the present celebration of God's coming peace of the new creation.

God's hyperbolic giving initiates all our giving and thus points to a certain surplus of unilateral giving over reciprocity. God always gives without the guarantee of return. But God's love should not be depicted as so transcendent and idealized that God's gratuity excludes human giving in return. Response to God's giving should not be the logic of commodity exchange, but God's giving does create more than gratitude (that is, gratitude narrowly construed as less than a real return of the gift). God's grace creates human mutuality and further giving.

God aims at a community that responds to giving with further giving, creating relationships of obligation and responsibility. The perfect sacrifice of our worship, our gratitude to God, opens up the possibility of our giving "like" God's giving, though the gift God gives us is a "crucified" gift that qualifies all the possibilities of our giving under the conditions of suffering, deceit, and violence in history. But even under these conditions giving is the way in which God is received.

In giving the Son, God gives God's own life (Jn 3:16). The Father's gift is infinitely great, so great that we are in infinite debt.[9]

Notes

"Protestantism Without Reformation," in *A Testament to Freedom*, ed. Geffrey B. Kelly and F. Burton Nelson (San Francisco: HarperSanFrancisco, 1990), 524.

2. Ibid.

3. Jacques Barzun, *From Dawn to Decadence: 500 Years of Western Cultural Life* (New York: HarperCollins, 2000), 4.

4. See Frederic Jameson, *Postmodernism: Or, the Cultural Logic of Late Capitalism* (Durham: Duke University press, 1991) and David Harvey, *The Condition of Postmodernity* (Oxford: Blackwell, 1990).

5. For the following, see Jeremy Rifkin, *The Age of Access* (New York: Tarcher/Putnam, 2000).

6. Postmodern philosophy, especially in the work of Jacques Derrida, has taken up the ancient paradox of gift as the thorniest question in the global market society: The gift in order to be gift must not be returned, and, yet, by obligating a return gift, the gift always becomes a form of exchange. See

God, the Gift, and Postmodernism, ed. John D. Caputo and Michael J. Scanlon (Bloomington: Indiana University Press, 2000).

7. This is the primary structure of Calvin's *Institutes of the Christian Religion*.

8. William T. Cavanaugh, *Torture And Eucharist: Theology, Politics, and the Body of Christ* (Oxford: Blackwell,1998).

9. For the following see M. Douglas Meeks, "Trinity, Community and Power," in *Trinity, Community and Power* (Nashville: Abingdon/ Kingswood, 2000).

Extravagant Love! Amazing Grace!

Dorothy Heckner Mendonca

Do not fear, for I have redeemed you; I have called you by name, you are mine. (Isaiah 43:1b)

In the middle of the sixth century B.C.E.—with Jerusalem totally destroyed, the temple in ruins, the royal line of David ended, and Israel in Babylonian exile—the prophet of Second Isaiah discerns God's presence in history and boldly proclaims God's will to be the salvation and redemption of God's people. His message speaks of God's single act of redemption and a continuing relationship of grace initiated by God's call and ownership. It is addressed to the nation, but it is amazingly individual. The prophet's message is true for all time in a profoundly personal way.

God tells us not to fear. But we live in a fearful world. Meaninglessness, despair, and hopelessness abound. Workplace downsizing, biopsies, insurance coverage, and retirement costs create fear. Our drug culture, the worldwide AIDS epidemic, constant war and violence, abuse of children, and natural flood and fire disasters make us afraid.

A new fear in modern society is credit card fraud, one of the fastest growing crimes today. Easy Internet access to credit card and social security numbers, the explosion in credit card use for purchases of every kind, selling names and statistics from retailer to retailer, contribute to this rapid rise. Those involved in this newest criminal activity brag about how easy it is to gain access to another person's identity and lines of credit.

Thousands of dollars can be charged to our bank accounts by persons we don't know, without our knowledge or consent, and with amazing swiftness! Victims of this new style crime say that what truly devastates them is the theft of their identity: their person has been violated because someone else has stolen and used who they are—what identifies them as a unique person in the world—their special name.

For who are we if we are nameless, if we don't possess a name that is uniquely ours? That was one of the great crimes of the holocaust: elimination of identity, erasing of names. Everything that identified people in a family unit or geographical community was destroyed. Numbers were tattooed across prisoner's forearms and they became known by that number and no longer by a name.

One college summer I worked as an aide at Arizona State Hospital. There was a designated ritual at bath time in the large women's dormitory.

The women formed a line past several aides, the first of whom removed each identical plain gray dress. They passed on to a second aide who had a bucket filled with warm, soapy water. She washed each body as the women filed past. The line continued into the shower room where another aide washed hair and helped rinse off soap in the shower. Afterward the women were dried and clean gray dresses were placed on them. It became automatic. We became task-oriented, relating to the women as bodies—as if they had no identity and no name.

Why is a name important?

When a baby is born into a family, much deliberation occurs. What shall this child be named? The name chosen must not be too unusual, so odd that it will cause jokes and taunting. It must not be an ordinary name that everyone has. Will the nickname be acceptable? Shall the child be named after her grandmother? Which one?

Scandinavians named the father "Lars" or "Peder" and the son "Larson" or "Pederson." Germans were named according to their occupation. Thus Bauermann was a farmer and Fleischmann owned a meat market.

Shall the child be named for a personality trait, such as Faith or Joy, that you hope she will possess? Shall a name be chosen because of its traditional meaning? Thus John is Hebrew for "God is merciful" and Frederick is German for "peaceful," while Louise is Teutonic for "female soldier" and Marni is Hebrew for "to rejoice." Shall the child be named after some famous person like Lincoln or Martin Luther King?

Why all this deliberation? Is a name really that important? Yes, it is!

In biblical thought a name is not merely a label that identifies you. Your name is an expression of your essential nature, the essence of personality, the expression of your innermost being. Your name reveals your character. A name change necessitates a personality change. Thus Saul became Paul with a total turnabout of character and personal mission.

In Hebrew thought your name is bound up with your existence. Nothing exists that doesn't have a name. In Genesis, creation is not completed until each creature is given a name.

There are many nameless people in the Bible: the boy who gave his lunch of five loaves and two fish to Jesus, the man who was let down through the roof opening to the pool to be healed by Jesus, the woman who was bent-over for eighteen years, and many more.

There are also times when individuals are called by name by God or by the Christ:

"Moses, Moses!" God calls from the burning bush.

"Samuel, Samuel!" God calls the young temple boy.

"Saul, Saul! Why do you persecute me?"

And after the resurrection, in the garden, simply "Mary!"

To be called by our name by God! Can we even begin to imagine what that means? Can we even begin to fathom the intimacy and power of such a personal relationship with God?

Walter Brueggemann, theologian of our time, told a group of Christian educators, "The most important question you have to answer is not 'Who are you?' but, rather, 'Who called you?'" Do we really understand that by our baptism it is God who calls us? Do we understand the power of being named and claimed by God? Do we ever take God's call seriously enough?

I remember choosing teams for baseball games in grade school. Those with long legs, great swinging arms, the ability to catch fast balls, or to throw swift and straight, were chosen immediately! Then picking slowed down to almost a standstill while choosers weighed the abilities of the remaining lineup. Those waiting in line begged to be called by name.

God's call is different from any other call. God's call is not based on our ability to play baseball. It's not based on our qualifications for discipleship. God does not call us because we are able, but God calls us and makes us able. God calls us because God created us and wills to redeem us. God's call is never abstract. It is always a call to respond, to be more than we have ever been before, to grow in faithful discipleship and discernment of God's will for our lives.

The world is forever telling us who we ought to be. God's cross on our forehead at baptism tells us who we are.

God not only calls us by name, God also claims us as God's own. "To be owned" has bad vibrations! We equate ownership with loss of freedom to be ourselves.

It used to be traditional in weddings to have the bride's father "give her away" to the groom with the words, "Who gives this woman to be married to this man?" No longer! Today it's very rare. It hints of ownership, and modern women do not choose to be owned. Likewise the promise "to obey" is gone from our marriage vows. We won't be owned by anyone.

But many things in our culture really do own us. We are a nation of buyers and collectors who are rarely satiated. We always want more, bigger, newer, better. "Shop till you drop!" is our lifestyle. Yet the more things we own the more we feel owned. Cars must be tuned and the oil changed regularly. Lawns need mowing. Flower beds need weeding. Computers need repairing. Clothes need washing. Faucets need fixing. Something always needs replacing, dusting, oiling, scrubbing. Closets need cleaning again so we have space to put all we own/all that owns us.

Closets may be our problem. Before there were closets, people hung their clothing on wall pegs. My mother, who grew up on a Wisconsin farm, spoke of having one everyday dress and one Sunday dress. You wore one and the other was either in the wash or hanging on the wall peg. Then came that marvelous invention—*closets*. Now we can have more possessions for we have a place to keep them. Now our primary consideration in a house is how many closets does it have? Sometimes I think we will be judged in the hereafter by the number of closets we had.

We forget who it is who owns us! God calls us to release whatever owns us and become God's own people, claimed and owned by God! In early baptismal liturgies the bishop would dip his finger into oil and draw the sign of the cross on the new Christian's forehead to mark the Christian as chosen and owned by God forever. I belong to God not because of who I am or what I have done but because God chose me, called me, and claimed me as God's own.

This is the truth of our lives: it is God who redeems us, calls us by name, and claims us as God's own. What do we have to fear? Isaiah 43:1*b* is the powerful promise of God's everlasting covenant relationship with us.

Extravagant Grace! Thanks be to God!

Churchly Metaphor in These Times

Gaylord Noyce

They were good sermons, occasionally moving. In my practice preaching course that year the students chose their own texts as their turns came. At semester's end we made a collective discovery: Without exception, the African Americans had selected their texts from the Hebrew Scriptures. The white students had used only the New Testament. The episode of itself is of little import, but one can wonder, if it were found to be typical on a much wider basis, what it might mean about our cultural quirks—or blinders—across the whole people of God. The subtle differences in viewpoint arising from such habits of mind are one interest of this essay.

A second interest, unrelated as it may appear, is a hope that in coming decades the church will take serious account of the ghastly violence that made the last century the bloodiest of all time. Was this, as someone asked, the end of true humanity itself? How do we properly take account in order to remain human?

Yet a third concern, seemingly even further afield, is the church's language about itself, language that reflects and shapes church action in the world. And this of course relates to such matters as the texts we emphasize in preaching or even the woodwork decor of the sanctuary. We want reflective depth to play out in real world witness, the kind of concern to which Frederick Trost has dedicated such magnificent energies over the years.

The Jewish Origins of our Faith

A recent book *In Abraham's Bosom* by the German scholar Manfred Gorg suggests that because of its limited usage of Hebrew Scriptures, early twentieth century New Testament study was a contributing factor to the Holocaust. The scholarly Christian world denied the Old Testament its right to speak independently. It was not allowed space of its own because it was always read with a sidelong glance at its reception in the "New."

W. D. Davies echoes the same sentiment as he introduces his essays on Jewish roots of the New Testament. The case is put most strongly, perhaps, by Johann Baptist Metz in *Hope against Hope* (p. 16):

> What happened in the *Shoah* does not just require that we revise the way Christians and Jews have related to one another down through history; rather it calls for a revision of Christian theology. Should not the Dead Sea Scrolls, so heatedly discussed of late, bring home to us how deeply the origins of Christianity are woven into Jewish history?

The recent spate of books on Jesus' Jewishness underlines the point. It may be part of a solution as time goes on. The theological change Metz calls for will be unnerving to those whose lives are framed around a triumphalist missiology, but it need not be so. And if exclusivist christology played even a small part in the Holocaust and the preceding two-thousand-year history of anti-Semitism, then some kind of change is an overdue part of Christian witness in the present age. It does us no credit to be preaching Jesus Christ in an unchristian way

Such a movement could conceivably match in significance other turning points in Christian history, like the Reformation or the Constantinian shift. The goals of mission agencies are already changing from conversion to dialogue. The substance of world religions is regularly studied now by evangelicals. Triumphalism in the institution and its preaching are on the wane.

What are our attitudes to be as we renew our scriptural roots in a non-exclusivist christology? The problem is not new, immense as it may seem. St. Paul, in those crucial Romans chapters 9 through 11, expresses anguish over the issue. He begins by saying that he would sacrifice his very life in Christ if he could heal the breach. He rehearses the glory that is the tradition, but he hastens to assure his Roman readers that it is not that the word of God has failed in the case of the Jews.

In Paul's theological reasoning, these kin in Israel are not a clear-cut demographic group. Not all who are descended from Israel belong to Israel (9:6). As to who does belong, it is absolutely up to God in the divine freedom. God says to Moses, " I will have mercy upon whom I will have mercy" (9:15). That mercy even extends to the Gentiles. Acceptance by God has always been a matter of faith. And Gentiles, thanks to Christ, can also know God in faith. God has not rejected the Israelites. "I myself am an Israelite" (11:1). Rather in God s own wisdom, some of the Israelites remain behind. But Paul has confidence that they too will be grafted back into the root.

In amazement at the strategy of God, who has "imprisoned all in disobedience so that he may be merciful to all" (11:32). Paul closes with a doxology. "How unsearchable are his judgements and how inscrutable his ways!" (11:33)

Karl Barth interprets this section of Romans, with its insistence that Christians cannot boast over branches broken off so that they might be grafted in, as a profound appeal to every believer to let faith remain centered on the grace of God. There is no ground for arrogance.

God's People Are a Light to the Nations

Could our sacred story be told in the following manner then? In the beginning, God created the natural universe. God also peopled it—earth, at least. These people were made in a holy "image" in and for human community. One group, Israel, was given the law. God called Israel to live aware of all this in gratitude and loyalty and in an obedient, intentional life. God struggled long with this people, over and again redeeming them from exile and from their own waywardness.

In the history of that relationship there arose those rich metaphors of the religious culture into which Jesus was born, and in which our own lives are rooted—the garden, the flood, the sacrifices, the covenant, Egypt and the exodus, the conquest, Davidic kingship, the Babylonian captivity and the return. This history fed into a profound literature—the Psalms, the prophets, Job, and the other Wisdom texts. More basically yet, it formed a people, Israel, gathered around that history, that literature and, institutionally, around the temple and the synagogue.

Finally, in the Christian view, God fulfilled the Messianic hopes that had also developed among the Israelites. This fulfillment was in the life, death, and resurrection of Jesus Christ. Ambiguity remained. The world was still a place both of crucifixion and of hope. Some saw the Messiah as yet to come, and others explained that he who had already come would come again. Both groups acknowledged the yes and no of the present and, in spite of large cultural differences, both in their best moments strove to keep central the holiness of God.

This is a Bible story of a particular chosen people. The purpose of God's choice is emphasized repeatedly. This people is to be a light and a witness to the nations. The narrative paints us no pretty picture. It involves suffering by the elected ones, often interpreted as chastisement at God's own hand. It also involves the violent defeat of many alien clans and peoples whom the Israelites, in their historical understanding of election, displaced—the Canaanites, the Hittites, the Amorites, the Peruzzites and countless others whose sonorous names roll so comfortably off our tongues.

As Jews, the first Christians were steeped in this history. The denials of that rootage came later. As the movement grew among the Gentiles, the Jewish law made little sense, and a sense of discontinuity set in. Factions also arose within the movement. The rootage was forgotten in the energizing experience of growth among the Gentiles. Forgotten too was the gospel within the law, the redemptive God of Hosea and Second Isaiah and the Psalms working the divine will in the midst of the Old Testament story. (Conversely, some of Paul's most radical antinomian followers were blind to the law within the gospel, the "law of Christ.")

In the end, the people God had formed broke apart. As an aside it may be noted that some commentators, such as rabbi theologian Pinchas Lapide, call this schism providential. Echoing Paul in Romans 11, they say that owing to the split, the people-of-God movement bursts its restricted Israelite context, thereby reaching the much wider gentile world.

We know this is not the only way to read the long story. Another portrayal uses imagery of revision and displacement, of error and correction, of failure in the first covenant and of another one truer to God's way. We are coming, however, to comprehend the importance of seeing this story as a single Jewish-Christian reality, to use Paul van Buren's term. This approach is urgent not only for rightly understanding the origins of the Christian movement but for the sake of shalom. The histories of anti-Semitism and the Holocaust demonstrate the eventual danger of letting the story fall apart. Our world has been sobered by Holocaust and cries out in its third millennium for a deeper unity than commercial globalization of itself can provide. Anything less mocks the six million and the Holy One of Israel.

Metaphors of the Church

So we come finally to reflect on how we envision church. We have been blessed in the past half century with helpful studies of metaphor and image for doing this. Paul Minear found ninety-six images of the church in the New Testament, the bulk of them, of course, derived from their Jewish milieu. James Gustafson, gave us a sociological perspective—helping us see our on-going identity as a community of interpretation, of memory, of language, of human cohesion. Avery Dulles summarized in five figures of speech the options for theological self-understanding—institution, servant, herald, spiritual community, sacrament.

For these authors, the merely institutional image of the church is least satisfactory. We can observe that institutional perspectives tend to be the more competitive and arrogant.

The richness of the images Minear cites should prevent our settling upon any single correct scriptural definition of church. Certain images may be more appropriate at particular times. At present we need less the clarity of differentiating theological precision than the strong sense communicated by organic metaphors, for a subterranean spiritual rhizome unites us all.

We must emphasize the continuities. The pope speaks for us all when he visits Jerusalem. And so too did the cluster in a preaching class that discovered an unconscious cultural bias that separated white from black.

This is not a time for aggressive proselytism. The light to the Gentiles was an offering of faithfulness, not a military campaign. Ours is not a time for eschatological visions that heighten triumphalism. This is a time of quiet witness to what we have seen and heard as one people living in the midst of others.

And what does this thinking suggest for church policy and practice? First, we will continue to emphasize the collective nature of the church and our continuity with Israel. Far more than a mere aggregation of individuals, we are leaven, branches of the vine, vineyard, God's people. For the present, laying aside the issue of other world religions, we begin with an awareness of God's people in two kinds—Jews and Christians.

Second we will be cautious about stark in-or-out expressions of salvation in Christ. These fly in the face of St. Paul's more subtle arguments that Abraham also believed. They also suffer from human measure that does not rejoice in the wideness of God's grace, implicit in parables like the wheat and tares (Mt 13). Paul does not boast as he agonizes over the schism in Israel.

Again, we will be more alert to opportunities that build oneness with the Jews. If white, we probably do neglect the Old Testament in rehearsing our religious identity. In our driving energy we may fail to appreciate the humbler organic metaphors.

In its decor, one church I know of put a star of David in a coordinate position with the cross. We can add more Jewish liturgical materials to our repertoire, going well beyond our present use of the Psalms and readings. One pastor suggests that the congregation stand not only for the Gospel but occasionally for the law or the prophetic reading. It is a good time for more inter-faith sewing circles or study groups and for ending the vestiges of Jesus marches with their boisterous detours past the community synagogue.

Fourth, in our secular time, we may want to accelerate the re-claiming of what the Jews gave the world in the Sabbath. For younger couples who seek help in shaping their lives, this heritage of home-centered ritual and the weekly change of pace may be a (literal) godsend.

Finally, in social witness, social service, and social action we will cooperate in freedom from much of the weight in doctrinal difference. Our social service and social action do not derive from a theocratic nostalgia, yearning for secular power. They are proleptic signs of the coming shalom time, and they are grateful witness to God's caring compassion.

Jew and Christian alike yearn for that time when "earth shall be full of the knowledge of the Lord as the waters cover the sea."

Selected Bibliography

Barth, Karl. *The Epistle to the Romans,* 6th ed. Trans. Edwyn C. Hoskyns. London: Oxford University Press, 1933.

Davies, W. D. *Christian Engagement with Judaism.* Harrisburg, Penn.: Trinity Press International, 1999.

Dulles, Avery, S. J. *Models of the Church.* Garden City, N.Y.: Doubleday & Company, Image Books, 1978 .

Gorg, Manfred. *In Abraham's Bosom: Christianity Without the New Testament.* Trans. Linda Maloney. Collegeville, Minn: The Liturgical Press, 1999.

Gustafson, James. *Treasure in Earthen Vessels: The Church as a Human Community.* New York: Harper & Brothers, 1961.

Lapide, Pinchas, *The Resurrection of Jesus.* Minneapolis: Augsburg, 1983.

Lapide, Pinchas, and Jürgen Moltmann. *Jewish Monotheism and Christian Trinitarian Doctrine.* Philadelphia: Fortress Press, 1981.

Metz, Johann Baptist and Elie Wiesel. *Hope Against Hope.* Ed. Ekkehard Schuster and Reinhold Boschert-Kimmig, trans. J. Matthew Asley. Mahwah, N.J.: Paulist Press, 1999.

Minear, Paul. *Images of the Church in the New Testament.* Philadelphia: The Westminster Press, 1960.

VanBuren, Paul. *A Theology of the Jewish-Christian Reality, Part Three.* San Francisco: Harper & Row, 1988.

Relying on God's Choice:
A Theology for Church Life

Richard H. Olmsted

In our individual Christian lives and in the life of the church, we place our trust in God's choice of us rather than in our choice of God. This insight, I have found in my ministry, is a key to faithful, fruitful, and spiritually healthy church life. In what follows I will commend it by indicating some of its intrinsic strengths and by showing how it can help us to avoid some common theological and spiritual dangers. The first half of the paper will sketch this theology of the radical priority of God's gracious choice and the second half will suggest some of the benefits derived and some of the dangers avoided.[1]

I

As I hope to show, the key to much that goes wrong in individual and congregational Christian life is making our religious life depend on our choice of God. Yet, to the minds of many, this is the way things must be. As they see it, our freedom and dignity as human beings depend upon it. Indeed, the touchstone of human freedom, it is commonly thought, is our freedom to accept or reject God.

But regarding our choice for or against God as the paradigm of human freedom is really a very odd thing to do. For this choice itself would be a choice between freedom and slavery. Our true freedom is actually to live as God's grateful, loving, and obedient children. Rejection of God, on the other hand, could only mean bondage to evil, sin, and death.

Since the idea is so widely held that the only true freedom is freedom of choice, the ability to do whatever we want, it is worth pausing for a moment to show that there is good reason for thinking that this is not the case. Freedom of choice is compatible with perfect slavery. You may be in a position to do whatever you want, but your wants themselves may be enslaving—as they often are, for example, if one is a heroin addict. True freedom, I suggest, is the freedom to be what we are, and this is a freedom that is fully compatible in particular circumstances with not having any choice at all. You may, for example, be in a department store which has such a good security system that you could not possibly steal anything. If you are not the kind of person who would steal anyway, this would not be a restriction of your freedom.

These considerations are of heightened importance as far as our freedom to choose or reject God is concerned. Many are inclined to think of this freedom as not being significantly different from the kind of freedom we would have in relation to someone or something at our level or beneath us. Though it may indeed feel this way, this is never the way it is. We are choosing the One who is so far above us that it is only by his grace moving our will that we could in fact choose God. More importantly, we are choosing the One who in Jesus Christ has already chosen us. This means that the truth about who we are, whether we know it or not, is that we belong to him. And, therefore, our true freedom is to know that we belong to God and to live as those who belong to God.

There is, in other words, something that stands between determinism and decisionism, between our being puppets pulled this way or that against our will and our deciding in sovereign, neutral freedom to opt for or against God. What stands between is God, his decision for us to rescue us in the life, death, and resurrection of Jesus Christ, and God's Spirit moving our will freely but dependently to choose God.

God's choice of us is a *rescue* operation. Our situation before God is never one of mere neutrality but one of lostness, enmity, and mortal peril. The assumption of our neutrality is an underestimation of our bondage to sin; indeed, the blindness involved in this assumption is indicative of that bondage. "Truly, truly, I say to you, everyone who commits sin is a slave of sin (Jn 8:34). Furthermore, if our true freedom is to know that we belong to our gracious Lord and to live as those who belong to God, it is important to recognize that this knowing and this living are themselves not things which are in our competence (especially not as fallen creatures) but are gifts of God's grace. They are never our secure possession which we could take for granted and dispose of as we see fit. They are always gifts that come to us again and again from our risen Lord and from the eschatological future we have in him. "What do you have that you did not receive?" (1 Cor 4:7)

Everything we have covered thus far may be summed up by saying that faith, both in its origin and in its continued existence, is a miracle. It is not a miracle that happens without us or against us. It is not the destruction of our freedom but its highest realization—"Where the Spirit of the Lord is, there is freedom" (2 Cor 3:17). But it is a miracle, nonetheless; it is not our achievement in the sense of a claim we have on God's favor, something that makes us deserving of that favor in distinction from those who do not have faith and are therefore undeserving of it. No one is deserving. God's favor is pure grace. "You did not choose me but I chose you" (Jn 15:16). Nor can we say with finality that anyone is ultimately excluded. Christ died for the sins of the whole world and his will to save is great and resourceful beyond our imagining. "For God has imprisoned all in disobedience so that he may be merciful to all" (Rom 11:32).

So having faith is not something we do to save ourselves. Strictly speaking, it is not faith that saves us. We do not have faith in faith but in Christ. Faith places us in communion with Christ and with the salvation that is ours in him. It rests on the blessed exchange centered in the cross of Christ that is ours and the world's salvation, the exchange by which he takes our sin upon himself and clothes us in his righteousness and holiness instead. He is our saving justification and sanctification before God. Whatever traces of righteousness and holiness may be found in our own lives are the fruits of the justification and sanctification we have in him. They are the work of the Holy Spirit in us but they are imperfect, they wax and wane, and they certainly are not that upon which we place our reliance in life and in death.

This is not by any means to say that what we do is unimportant. While we never outgrow the need to confess our sins, and, as far as our ability to stand before God is concerned, we must ever rely on Christ's atoning death and must ever say that "all our righteousness is as filthy rags" (Isa 64:6), nevertheless, we are summoned to that freedom for which "Christ has set us free" (Gal 5:1). This is our freedom for life with God; the freedom we have in spite of our sin and only by grace to live in obedience to God's commandments. In our freedom in Christ, his commandments do not confront us as the coercion of an externally imposed law. They are descriptive of, and invitations to, "the glorious liberty of the children of God"(Rom 8:21); they say "you may" rather than "you must"; they are "written not with ink but with the Spirit of the living God, not on tablets of stone but on tablets of human hearts" (2 Cor 3:3). This freedom includes "love, joy, peace, patience, kindness, generosity, faithfulness, gentleness, self-control" (Gal 5:22-23), walking humbly with God in doing justice and loving kindness (cf. Mic 6:8). Ultimately, it is the freedom we have in obeying the double commandment of love, by which we become conformed to the image of Christ in self-giving love and are drawn toward the eschatological fulfillment of our participation in the triune life of God. If all of this sounds a bit grandiose in relation to our actual lives in the Christian community of faith, there is good reason for that. Our progress in Christian freedom in this life is fragmentary, inchoate, and rarely untroubled. We are never far from the edge of the abyss of unfaith, disobedience and utter bondage to evil, sin and death. Thus, in our efforts to obey Christ as teacher and follow him as example, we are again and again driven back to our reliance on him as Savior and living Lord. In joy, repentance and thanksgiving, we place our trust in God's choice of us rather than our choice of God.

II

The problems connected with placing the emphasis on our choice of God have been radicalized in our time, for that choice has become a matter of choosing who God is. A serious theological problem for the church today is that of making-up God. Cafeteria-style religion is the order of the day. In whatever form—"post-modernist," "inclusivist," "pluralist," "liberationist," "expressivist"—the temptation to create a concept of God that meets our perceived needs and desires is one that is widespread. The obvious difficulty that it would be impossible to worship or entrust ourselves in life and death to a god who is so clearly the work of our own hands does not make the difference one would expect it to make. It does not seem to override the short term "real world" advantages to be derived from an instrumentalist use of theology for other ends that are deemed desirable: self-realization, empowerment, tolerance, overcoming oppression. This essentially atheistical situation, whether it is recognized or not, requires renewed theological clarity about the fact that we are in the hands of the living God and not he in ours.

It is God who puts an end to the making-up-God project by revealing himself. We do not and cannot determine who God is. In sovereign freedom God determines who God is, a self-sufficient trinitarian communion of love. And in a distinct but related way, God also determines who we are. God's self-determination in relation to us, which God reveals to us by bearing witness to himself through the primary witness of scripture and the secondary witness of the church's proclamation and life, is God's free and purely gracious decision not to be God alone but to be God with us. In light of our bondage to evil, sin and death, this is also God's decision "from the foundation of the world" (Rev 17:8), through the life, death, and resurrection of God's Son, to be God for us. This "with us" and "for us" by the self-determination of the living God is the touchstone of reality. It is God who determines what counts as the real world, and it is in the light of God's doing this that our concerns, desires and felt needs need to be assessed, that is, need to be understood, rejected or corrected, and pursued. The meaning and goal of our existence are to be found in God. "He chose us in Christ before the foundation of the world to be holy and blameless before him in love" (Eph 1:4).

It is only by forgetting the living God who acts and chooses that the making-up-God project gets off the ground. Very often today, at the heart of the idea that we could make-up God lies an experiential-expressivist understanding of revelation. From this perspective, our understanding of who God is and who we are in relation to God is based on and circumscribed by our experiences and feelings. But if salvation means what the gospel proclaims it to mean (forgiveness of sins and the promise of eternal life in communion with God), then the inadequacy of experiential-expressivism becomes clear. For no matter how bad we may feel about ourselves, we cannot really feel the depth of our sinfulness before the holiness of God. And no matter how good we may feel about ourselves, we cannot really feel the perfection of the righteousness we have in Christ. The depth of our plight and the wonder of its resolution can only be revealed to us from outside ourselves by what God has done for us in the life, passion, death, and resurrection of our Lord. It is as at the foot of the cross and not by introspection that we begin to grasp this depth and this wonder. Important as our feelings and experiences may be, placing the emphasis on God's acting and choosing puts them in their appropriate place; it dethrones them as sources of revelation.

Overestimating the religious significance of feelings can easily lead to a tyranny of feelings in church life. Since this can be a significant spiritual hazard for Christian fellowship, I want to pause to offer a couple of helpful hints: 1) It is sometimes thought that feelings must be accepted and accredited simply because someone has them. While people's feelings should always be treated with respect and compassion, there is an important distinction between feelings which are justified by the circumstances that gave rise to them and feelings which are not so justified. This distinction should have an important bearing on how we respond. 2) The tyranny of feelings becomes especially burdensome when it takes the form of emotional blackmail. "You should not say or do what seems to you true or right because it will hurt my feelings if you do." Of course, this kind of confusion is not always so blatant. We need to be alert to the many subtle ways in which it can arise in church life and to be compassionate but firm in our response.

Let me conclude with some reflections on the non-instrumental heart of the church's life. God chooses us for full fellowship with him. What God gives us in Jesus Christ is himself and what he promises us through our union with Christ is creaturely participation in eternal life, the trinitarian communion of the love of God. This communion is an end in itself. It is the supreme good. There is no good for us to be sought outside of it. "He who spared not his own Son, but delivered him up for us all, how shall he not with him also freely give us all things?" (Rom 8:32)

All this our gracious God gives us by choosing us. Our response can only be to love, revere and glorify him. This too is something for which we are freed by grace, and it too, as the high priestly prayer of John 17 makes clear, is a participation in the self-glorifying of the Father and the Son in the Spirit:

"Father, the hour has come; glorify your Son so that the Son may glorify you. . . . So now, Father, glorify me in your own presence with the glory that I had in your presence before the world existed. . . . All mine are yours, and yours are mine, and I have been glorified in them. . . . The glory that you have given me I have given them, so that they may be one, as we are one" (1, 5, 10, 22).

All this is to say that the essential structure of the church's life is doxological. This is true not just of its worship but of its teaching, its mutual service in the body of Christ and its outreach to the world in evangelical mission, social service and social action. The church is in all of these things first and foremost the fellowship of those who praise God's holy name and who thus bear witness to the great salvation and glorious future that has been prepared for us, for all people and the whole creation in Christ. By holding on to this doxological center, the church is preserved from the blasphemy of a merely instrumental use of God, of its own life and of its action in the world.

There is no one I know whose ministry better exemplifies holding on to the doxological center than Frederick Trost. I am grateful to God for his service to the United Church of Christ and to the holy catholic church.[3]

Notes

1. For the sake of conserving space, I am presenting my theological convictions without indicating the sources which have influenced me in arriving at them. My chief indebtedness is to the writings of Martin Luther and Karl Barth. Those interested in tracing their influence may consult my paper "Staking All On Faith's Object: The Art of Christian Assurance According to Martin Luther and Karl Barth," *Pro Ecclesia*, forthcoming.

2. Some of the key ideas in this paragraph are more fully developed in my paper "Speaking the Triune God, An Impossible Possibility," published by the Confessing Christ Movement of the United Church of Christ. It may be obtained through writing to Confessing Christ, P.O. Box 435, DeForest, WI 53532, or it may be accessed from the Confessing Christ web page: www.execpc.com/~confess/

3. I thank Wallace Alston and the Center of Theological Inquiry in Princeton for the opportunity to spend a month there in the summer of 2000 during which I wrote this paper. I thank Robert Jenson for his insightful criticism, advice and encouragement. Finally, I thank George Hunsinger for numerous discussions and several classes over the last few years which have deepened my theological thinking and enriched my ministry.

"Most Gracious Heavenly Father, We Thank Thee"

Most gracious Heavenly Father, we thank Thee and praise Thee for the gift of the Holy Spirit and for the church which the Spirit has brought into being. We thank Thee and praise Thee for the work of the Spirit in bringing us into mystical communion with our Lord and Savior Jesus Christ, for building us up in the body of Christ. We pray for the renewal of the church as the Spirit convicts us of sin and leads us into repentance and obedience to the law and to the gospel. We pray for the triumph of the church over the principalities and powers of the world. We pray for the unity of the church as a witness to the world concerning the truth of Jesus Christ and his gospel. May the Holy Spirit endow us as members of the church with a passion for truth and for a willingness to serve under the cross of our Lord Jesus Christ. May we reaffirm through the power of the Spirit the evangelical truth that animates the church and the catholic faith that gives the church its direction and goal. We ask all of these things in the name of the Father and of the Son and of the Holy Spirit.

Donald G. Bloesch

The Church and Theological Education: An Essay to Honor Frederick Trost

Jack Stotts

Faith seeking understanding. That ancient phrase is one that may seem overly familiar. It reeks of overuse and may well defy the possibility of freshness. But as with many tired truisms, it is nevertheless true. For it points beyond itself to an ongoing practice of the church's life. It invites participation in an essential and enduring dimension of the church's life, the love of God with the mind. It affirms that the life of the mind is a friend, not an enemy, of believing and acting. It is an invitation to join in the ongoing search by the faithful follower of Jesus Christ to understand more fully the faith which by grace has been given to him or her.

Faith seeking understanding is a short hand way of saying theological education. It is an enterprise conducted sometimes more and sometimes less formally. It takes place formally in theological seminaries, where the church's pastoral leadership is prepared and faculty attend to rigorous reflection, research, and sharing of their findings with scholars, students and the church which they serve. Less formally it occurs when an individual member of the church or a church school class seeks more adequately to understand the gospel for themselves, for the church and for the world. It occurs when people, individually or together, explore the meaning of the holy Trinity and when they try to make sense of what they are to do with their lives.

Faith seeking understanding. It is a self-conscious undertaking embraced more by some churches than others. But it defies exile from the life of any church. For its source lies both in the great commandment and in the common human experiences of trying to make sense of our lives, both individually and together. No one is exempt from questions like these: why did a beloved, or for that matter, any child die; what shall I do with my life; why do the good suffer and the evil prosper; how do we decide about complex issues like cloning human beings; and what about the sexuality of our lives? And as we try to make sense of our lives, we try to make sense of the God who reigns as the lord of our lives. So in the midst of our faith we try to understand more adequately ourselves, our neighbors and our God. We reject easy formulae in favor of a restless search for a deeper comprehension of what we know is finally beyond our full understanding. Those traditions tagged Reformed and Lutheran—as well as others—are not content with a fideism that calls for the setting aside of our reason and simple acceptance on blind faith what the church says or has said in the past.

We do not tuck our reason away when it comes to understanding what we are to believe and how we are to act. We are blessed, or cursed some would say, with reason and reasoning as necessary servants of, not antithetical to, faith. We seek lives integrated around loving God and our neighbors with all our heart, mind, soul, and strength. We seek to think with the mind of Christ.

Faith seeking understanding. It is one way of saying what we call theology. This theology is dynamic and ongoing because God is dynamic and dwells finally in mystery, not controlled by human categories. Its dynamic resides as well in the changing situation of the human enterprise. This theological undertaking is not dogma, unquestioned assent to formulae or beliefs thought first by others. It is thinking with the help of companions in the communion of saints who have thought before us about these issues of God's relationship with us and with the whole creation.

The scope of theological education suggested above frees such education from particular institutional settings. Theological education is not limited to seminary education. Indeed seminary or divinity school education is one species of the more inclusive genre. Seminary education is one necessary dimension of theological education. That is not to suggest that the education of pastoral leaders for the church is unimportant. What it does do is to affirm that the context of theological education is one mandated by the church's self understanding of its own nature and identity. Theological education as practiced in the theological schools called seminaries is necessarily linked with preaching and teaching in all the manifestations of the church as a teaching and learning community. So understood, Frederick Trost is as pastor a theological educator by training and commitment. Theological education at all levels was defining for his ministry as I knew it in Chicago when he was pastor of St. Pauls Church and when I was on the faculty of McCormick Theological Seminary (Presbyterian), located about two blocks from that congregation.

Let me illustrate by way of incidents how Frederick Trost functioned as a theological educator. These are representative, not exclusive, of the rich and varied ministry of St. Pauls Church as given leadership and formed by its pastor. I will focus on three theological strands that are essential for theological education. They are knowing and transmitting the tradition, relating the tradition to the current context, and making theological judgments concrete.

First, theological education involves a respect for the tradition of the church. This tradition is not static. It is dynamic. Professor Jaroslav Pelikan of Yale University is reported to have said, "Traditionalism is the dead faith of the past; tradition is the living faith of the dead." So understood, a task of theological education is to be faithful to the past while relating that past constructively to the present and the future. The great reformer, John Calvin, in a work entitled *A Defense Against Pighuis*, wrote: "Our constant endeavor, day and night, is not just to transmit the tradition but also to put it in the form we think will prove best" (cited in B. A. Gerrish, *Tradition and the Modern World*).

Theology involves respect for and transmittal of the tradition. Really one should say traditions. In a simple way, the legitimacy of that conviction was illustrated each Sunday when Frederick Trost preached both at an early morning service and at an 11:00 o'clock service. What distinguished one from the other was not the time. It was the language of the worship. The early service was conducted in German. And Fred preached I was told in true German. That practice derived from the tradition of that particular congregation, practiced from the early days of its establishment. Fred honored it, though the numbers in attendance declined slowly over the years. And some in the church scoffed at the attempt to hold on to a distant past, calling it archaic or only nostalgic. But it could be seen another way. The tradition was being honored. And that tradition was not just linguistic. It was a sign that diverse traditions in diverse languages are able to carry the intrinsic message of God's love in Jesus Christ.

"We have this treasure in clay jars, so that it may be made clear that this extraordinary power belongs to God and does not come from us" (2 Cor 4:7). Whether in German or English or Spanish or Russian, truth flows through diverse channels; all can carry the gospel. The essential question is not what language is used but what truth is conveyed. To have a worship service conducted in German was a reminder of the power of the tradition to speak in a variety of tongues to a variety of people. The tradition of preaching and worshiping in German could have become what Pelikan was quoted earlier as calling traditionalism. But it was saved from that by a pastor and a people who sought the living word of God. We have many traditions and one lively faith. In the case of St. Pauls Church in Chicago and its pastor, it was the worship and the preaching in a "foreign" language that conveyed the gospel into the contemporary world.

At 11:00 a.m. Frederick Trost conducted the worship service and preached in English. Another tradition was honored. And the two services illustrated the validity of multiple traditions; one not superior to the other but both relativising the other, while each pointed to the accommodation God makes to humans, no matter what their background, language, national origin, race, or gender. We didn't have the favored terminology of multi-culturalism in the 1960s, but that was being affirmed in the two services. The theology being practiced was that of critically honoring the traditions and the tradition of faith.

Second, to honor and to be instructed by the tradition occurs as one learns from those who manifest by their lives and their thought the human reality of the faith. These "saints" put a human face on what we believe and what we are to do as followers of Christ. That is important to those whose specific vocation is studying and learning theology and to those who are not academic theologians. Fred Trost made those heroes of the faith visible and accessible to the congregation. He did so by his preaching and by initiating and sponsoring special "saints'" days. But to learn about these figures was to examine how what we learned from them was applicable to a contemporary context.

One example. In my copy of the mammoth biography of Dietrich Bonhoeffer by Eberhard Bethge, a bookmark peaks out of the pages. It is red and white and wrinkled with use. It carries the dates November 14th and 15th, 1970. Large white letters proclaim the occasion for its distribution: The Bonhoeffer Festival. The event was a two day affair sponsored by St. Pauls Church, with McCormick Seminary participating. The occasion was the 25th anniversary of the martyrdom of Dietrich Bonhoeffer, born, 1906, died 1945. Agonizing over how he should respond to the Nazi horrors, Bonhoeffer, a pastor and theologian, moved from a position of pacifism to one of active opposition to the regime. He was executed in a German concentration camp just days before the end of the European sector of the 2nd World War. He was put to death as a traitor because of his participation in the attempt to assassinate Adolph Hitler. Bonhoeffer agreed to assist in this failed plot out of his sincere theological convictions that the follower of Christ must participate in the full life of the world with all its ambiguities and clash of values.

Under Frederick Trost's leadership, the local churches and the seminaries of the area came together to celebrate the life and thought of this religious and political martyr. Lectures by noted scholars were given. Individual Christian men and women who had lived in Germany in that terrible time spoke of the "cost of discipleship." In a book by that name, Bohnoeffer had written that "when Christ called a man, he bade him come and die." The death referred to was not only the physical death of a person but also a dying to the ways that were a scandal to the gospel. But physical death was included as the last event of faithfulness.

During the days, discussions abounded about the contours of Bonhoeffer's faithfulness. They moved to the issue of what Bonhoeffer's life meant for those living in these times; prayers were offered, prayers of thanksgiving for those who had indeed given the full last measure for what they had believed in and prayers seeking guidance for all peoples of all times who were called to follow Christ.

It was a marvelous event, stirring and instructive. And note the date. It was 1970. The Vietnam war was raging. The church, along with the public in general, were deeply divided over what was "right" and what one's responsibility as a Christian and citizen was with reference to the ongoing struggle. Debates over the proper use of violence and the place of non-violence were every day conversations for many. Families were divided. Some young men were fleeing to Canada to escape participation in a war they believed to be unjust. Other young men went to Vietnam out of a sense of duty to their country. But no matter one's perspective, the issue was important to all citizens, regardless of age. In that context, to attend to Bonhoeffer as one who struggled with his own participation in a war was to gear into the contemporary struggle over what ought a Christian to do when faced with similar questions. Theology came alive through understanding a Christian "saint" seeking and expressing faithfulness. His struggle became our struggle, his thinking challenged our thinking. Bonhoeffer became a conversation partner for us, a midwife for our reflections about what we were to think and to do now. These conversations did not yield unanimous agreement about the continuities and differences in the contemporary situation. Theology that began with a person seeking faithfulness led to personal explorations about what God is calling us to do and to be. We experienced tradition in its most positive state. It was a living tradition. It was to bring the tradition home.

These first two elements of theological education took place under Frederick Trost's leadership. The tradition of faith came alive and was honored in its own integrity. Second, when tradition and a contemporary situation came together, theology took on a human face and confronted our too small convictions. Tradition became integral to our context. Theological education took place. "Faith seeking understanding," drawing from the past to assist the present, these are gifts Frederick Trost brings to his ministry. He is involved in theological education whether he called it that or not.

Third, Fred Trost fulfilled the claims of theological education by helping to make the faith concrete. His own understanding of the faith challenged and stretched the people to think, individually and corporately, what the consequences of their own understandings were.

One example. The days were those around and during the Democratic Party's political convention in Chicago, 1968. It had been a tragic and volcanic year. Martin Luther King, Jr,. had been assassinated in April. Bobby Kennedy was killed two months later. The sitting president, Lyndon B. Johnson, had been forced by the waves of dissent to his foreign policy to refuse re-nomination. A cultural revolution affecting young and old stretched fragile ties that bound together different generations. Rioting in the streets and neighborhoods over issues of civil rights had been rampant.

The culmination was in Chicago, in August. The yippies, a conglomerate of young and somewhat older folk, converged on the city. Many camped out in Lincoln Park, a lovely green space on Lake Michigan. Planned and spontaneous demonstrations popped up in the park and in the city streets. It was political theater on the big screen. Supporters of those politicians who carried the banner of opposition to the Vietnam War marched in the downtown area and in Grant Park, another green sward, this lying between the Lake and the downtown area.

There was a curfew—11 p.m.—on occupancy of the parks. At that hour the Chicago police moved in to clear Lincoln Park of all occupants, mostly consisting of young and often idealistic and naive younger people. In what later would be called a police riot the park was cleared. In the process many were beaten, some were arrested, and hundreds ran through the streets seeking some shelter.

What was to be done? Fred Trost and St. Pauls church did what they could. Located just a few short blocks from "the war zone," they opened the doors to the fellowship hall and invited those who would to come in and find a safe place. The strangers were welcomed. A sanctuary from the fire storms of violence was provided. Some snacks and water. No drugs. No alcohol. Only space and a welcome.

Theology as understanding a God who cared for the homeless, the hungry, the lost, was made concrete when the church's doors were open to those who had need. No longer was the belief about welcoming strangers abstract. It was concrete. It had to do with real life situations, with people stretching out hands to care for those who were in need, including many with whom one disagreed.

As one could imagine, not every one in the church or in the neighborhood welcomed this kind of activity. But its grounds were articulated by Pastor Trost and others as clearly theological. Theological education, teaching and learning about God, ourselves and our neighbors, took place. Theology became practical theology, shaping the practices of the church and helping to form the conscience of its members and friends.

One could say or write much more about Frederick Trost as a theological educator. One could acclaim his forthright support for seminaries as essential for the education of pastoral leadership. One could affirm his own theological teaching, which took many forms. He could be applauded for his keeping the scriptures as the tradition without peer. But I want to emphasize in this brief essay that Frederick Trost embodies theological education in all aspects of his ministry. He not only applauds theological education. He lives it. In doing so he helps to make theology an authentic servant of the church and, through the church, of service to the world. For Fred Trost theological education in its broadest sense has been and is a defining characteristic of the church of Jesus Christ. Wherever it occurs—whether in a seminary, a local church, a synod—theological education involves a people of faith seeking richer and fuller understandings and becoming willing and able to integrate tradition, current context, and concreteness, and all to the glory of God. That is, where faith seeks understanding, there is theological education.

Confessional Identity: An Early Exchange

Theodore Louis Trost

The First World War marked a time of crisis for Americans of German descent. Formerly happy to maintain a comfortable distance from the majority culture—from "the English," as Anglo-Americans were often called—German-Americans were suddenly viewed as the enemy. Students in the college town of Ann Arbor, Michigan, for example, were known to parade across Division Street on a war-era evening, fortified by drink. Once in the neighborhoods on the old West Side, the young scholars would proceed to hurl vegetables and invectives at the homes of the predominantly German residents.[1] Actions such as this, repeated in countless communities in the midwest and across the nation, caused many German-Americans to reassess the desirability of their distinctiveness in relation to the majority culture. With their loyalty to the United States coming under corporate scrutiny, many in the German-American community were asking had the time arrived finally to assimilate and assimilate boldly?

This question, I believe, lurked behind debates about "church union" within the German Evangelical Synod of North America (and later, for that matter, the Evangelical and Reformed Church). As a proponent of assimilation, Reinhold Niebuhr argued that his denomination could escape obscurity through merger and thereby become a powerful voice within the culture. Others felt that the denomination could best make a distinctive contribution to American culture by remaining small and relatively "insignificant." This essay examines the earliest stage of the debate as it was carried out in the *Magazin für Evangelische Theologie und Kirche*, the theological journal of the German Evangelical Synod of North America. Ultimately, of course, the Niebuhr position won out. The union of the Evangelical and Reformed in 1934 was followed by another war against Germany and then the United Church of Christ merger in 1957. But in the late teens and early twenties, Niebuhr met strong opposition from some of his co-religionists. The call to be "ecumenical," despite the recent war in Europe, was not necessarily equated with an appeal to church union. Niebuhr's opponents felt that there was more to lose through merger than the stain of "Germanness." They hoped to preserve a particular, much-cherished confessional identity. For a time they did.

"Where Shall We Go?" appeared in the March 1919 issue of the *Magazin für Evangelische Theologie und Kirche*. The article was written by "R. Niebuhr," a signature that may at first cause confusion for 21st century readers—for there were two well-known Niebuhr brothers in the 20th century, both of them "R," Reinhold and Richard. But in 1919, Reinhold's brother was addressed by his first name, "Helmut." It was not until the 1930s, after he went east to Yale University, that this Germanic "Helmut" was transformed into the less ethnic "H. Richard." The author of "Where Shall We Go?" then, was Reinhold Niebuhr, pastor of the Bethel Evangelical Church in Detroit, Michigan. Already a leading figure within the denomination, Niebuhr had received national attention for two articles he had written recently in the *Atlantic Monthly*, one of them bearing the revealing title "The Failure of German-Americanism."[2] This epitaph was perhaps premature—at least within Niebuhr's own denominational circle. Of the ten articles that constituted the March issue of the Evangelical Synod's *Magazin*, Niebuhr's was one of only three written in English.

"Where Shall We Go?" argued that the German Evangelical Synod should join the emerging movement to unite the Protestant churches in America. The urgency to do so arose in the aftermath of two significant events. One was the merger conference that brought into being the United Lutheran Church in America. Representing a union of "three of the more liberal Lutheran synods," Niebuhr speculated that the new denomination might one day "present a united Lutheranism in America."[3] The other event was the "Conference on Organic Union" which took place in Philadelphia on December 4 and 5, 1918. Initiated by the Presbyterian General Assembly, this conference brought together representatives from the nation's leading denominations to discuss the prospect of "uniting American protestantism into an 'organic union.'"[4] Although no plan for a pan-Protestant union emerged from the gathering, one specific development did merit great attention, according to Niebuhr, namely "the new attempt to unite all Calvinistic churches in America even before a general union is undertaken."

It was obvious to Niebuhr that the German Evangelical Synod needed to sign on with one or the other of these plans. As it stood, his denomination faced extinction as an irrelevance—left in the lurch by both of these plans somewhere between a united Lutherdom and a united Calvinism. The pressing question for Niebuhr thus became to what family should the Evangelical Synod belong? As the title of his article put it "Where Shall We Go?" Niebuhr allowed that some within the denomination might object to the implications of the question. After all, he conceded, the German Evangelical Synod had a distinctive religious identity that would inevitably suffer through merger. The ministers of the Synod had "served our Lord faithfully and have labored in the part of the Kingdom entrusted to [them]." But in the aftermath of World War I, that was neither the most significant nor the most comfortable part of the Kingdom to be in. Indeed, the Synod "failed to make any distinctive contribution to American life." To continue in isolation, to hide from the larger culture would be "unchristian," according to Niebuhr.

Meanwhile, he rejected the suggestion that, since the German Evangelical Synod was historically a union church, other denominations should come to the Synod and seek to be absorbed into it. First of all, the non-Missouri Synod Lutherans most closely resembled the Evangelical Synod both theologically and culturally; but they showed no interest whatsoever in uniting with unionists. Probing deeper into his denomination's confessional convictions, Niebuhr offered that the Synod was not really a "union" church anyhow; it remained "far more Lutheran than Reformed in polity and tradition." But as he had already established, the move toward Lutheranism was a dead end. This meant that the German Evangelical Synod must "accommodate [itself] to the positions of other denominations than those with which our tradition is connected." In order to survive, the denomination needed to surrender its Lutheran leanings and embrace another tradition.

Casting his lot in favor of the "Calvinists," Niebuhr discounted the various objections some in the Synod might have toward them. He argued that the Reformed were irenic in nature as opposed to the bellicose Luther. Niebuhr considered the historical difference between the Lutheran and the Reformed on the doctrine of the Lord's Supper to be "non-essential"; after all, this was already the position of the German Evangelical Synod —which maintained allegiance to both the Augsburg Confession and the Heidelberg Catechism. Besides, Niebuhr noted, most laypeople and the younger members of the clergy held to a position that was more Zwinglian than Lutheran. As far as the doctrine of grace was concerned, Niebuhr argued that Calvinism led to moral action in the social sphere; Lutheranism, on the other hand, tended toward quietism and detachment from the social and political problems of the day. Niebuhr deemed polity issues inconsequential; they were mere human traditions that needed to be sacrificed for the sake of Christian unity. What was urgently needed, Niebuhr argued in conclusion, was a denominational policy to pursue church union.

The very next issue of the *Magazin* carried "Why Go At All?"—a systematic refutation of Niebuhr's position, written by W. F. Henninger. Henninger, a scientist and layperson in the Synod, began with an analogy from the political realm. Just as it was in line with American thinking to assert the importance of independence for "Esths, Letts, Finns,

Lithuanians. . . etc.," so too must one support the independence of the small denominations: "To contradict this would mean to be disloyal, unjust, un-American." Besides, Henninger argued, simply because a denomination was small did not mean that it lacked quality. The presence of "modest Brother Niebuhr" in the Evangelical Synod suggested that the denomination might be sufficiently significant to make "a distinctive contribution to American religious life." Perhaps the "problem" was not smallness or lack of distinction at all, Henninger speculated. After all, whose standards was Niebuhr adopting here? Henninger postulated that since the German Evangelical Synod had its origins in the Middle West instead of the East, anything the Synod might accomplish inevitably would appear insignificant to those of a certain cultural orientation. "Everybody knows," Henninger remarked, "that the East claims, often with very poor proof, to be superior in all things, all the way from theology down to the pigeon-fanciers' association." To appeal for legitimation to the cultured elites on the East coast seemed a most dubious enterprise.[5]

Henninger went on to dispute the various theological points Niebuhr put forward. The assertion that the German Evangelical Synod did not represent a true union of Lutheranism and Calvinism, for example, was contradicted. Henninger refuted the suggestion that Calvinism was "irenic" with a rhetorical catalogue of crimes. Was it irenic when Calvin had seventy-six men banished and fifty-eight executed out of a population of 20,000 at Geneva? Was it irenic when the Scotch Presbyterians murdered the archbishop of St. Andrews? Was it irenic when Cromwell slaughtered thousands of Catholics in Ireland? Was it irenic when the New England Puritans drove out Roger Williams?

In the end, Henninger insisted that the Evangelical Synod did represent a unique contribution to religious life in America. There were indeed significant differences between Lutherans and Calvinists and "only where you have the bond of love and peace, as in [the German Evangelical] Synod, can these great differences be bridged over, softened, and brought to a happy union." Henninger wrote off the whole unification movement, at least as Niebuhr presented it, as nothing more than "a grand and united effort to get into the limelight." Of Reinhold Niebuhr, Henninger said (quoting "the prophet of old") "Ephraim hath turned to idols, let him alone." And to the question "Where Shall We Go?" he replied with the counter-question "Why Go At All?"

Reinhold Niebuhr lost this early battle over cultural and denominational identity. Henninger had attacked the underlying call for assimilation with the argument that maintaining difference was an essential element of "Americanness." He perceptively pointed out that the inferiority of the Middle West was, in effect, a cultural construct (and perhaps a psychological problem); it was not a natural law. And he argued that the German Evangelical Synod's confessional stance represented an essential contribution to the life of the church writ large. Although Reinhold Niebuhr was allowed the favor of a response in the next edition of the *Magazin*,[6] his position regarding church union was not an immediately popular one within the denomination. It would be another decade before the leaders of the Evangelical Synod would seriously contemplate church merger. And while they did look to the East, they also looked for a partner who shared their cultural background and their confessional convictions.

Notes

1. This story, repeated on numerous occasions, was first related to me by Theodore L. Trost, Sr., Frederick Trost's father, during the summer of 1965 at Wasaga Beach, Ontario.

2. The two articles were "The Failure of German-Americanism," *Atlantic* (July 1916): 16-18, and "The Nation's Crime Against the Individual," *Atlantic* (November 1916): 614.

3. This and subsequent quotations from the same article by R[einhold] Niebuhr, "Where Shall We Go?" in the *Magazin für Evangelische Theologie und Kirche*, 47/2 (1919): 125-126.

4. George W. Richards, "The Historical Significance of Denominationalism: A Paper Read Before the Conference on Organic Union Held at the Invitation of the General Assembly of the Presbyterian Church in the U.S.A." (Philadelphia ,1918): 18-19.

5. This and subsequent quotations from the same article by W. F. Henninger, "Why Go At All?" in the *Magazin für Evangelische Theologie und Kirche*, 47/3 (1919): 194-197.

6. Reinhold Niebuhr, "In Rebuttal, by the Author of 'Where Shall We Go?'" in the *Magazin für Evangelische Theologie und Kirche*, 47/4 (1919): 270-271.

The Banner of the Heidelberg Catechism

Reinhard Ulrich

In the great debate over Mercersburg, which divided the German Reformed Church for the better part of the nineteenth century, historians have always assumed that the Sheboygan Classis (and later the German language synods) supported the so-called "Old Reformed" party (centered in the Ohio Synod) against Mercersburg. The pietistic background of many of the German immigrant pastors and the fact that the Mission House was modeled after the pietistic missionary schools of the old country seemed sufficient reason to do so. Taking exception to this view, I shall argue here that the German immigrant part of the church whose institutional centers were the Mission House, the Sheboygan Classis, and later the German language Northwest Synod, established and understood itself as a separate "confessional" party within the church. They were pietists, yet they were churchly pietists who had fought for a confessional church against theological rationalism. So, hoisting the banner of the Heidelberg Catechism, the German missionaries and lay people saw themselves as the faithful remnant affirming the hallowed traditions of the Reformed faith against both "Dr. Nevin's controversies" and what they perceived to be the excessive subjectivism of "New Measures."

Herman August Muehlmeier was the first to arrive on the field. He and Herman August Winter were native Lipper who had come to the United States by way of New Orleans in 1847. They eventually made their way to Mercersburg where they received their theological education. In 1852 they had joined other German students protesting to the seminary's Board of Visitors against the "Romanizing tendencies" of John Williamson Nevin. Characteristically, Muehlmeier accepted the mediating efforts of the Board and remained at the school while Winter joined four other German students who left Mercersburg. Muehlmeier refers to his experience at Mercersburg as follows: "The first preachers of the Sheboygan Classis . . . with one exception, received their theological training in the seminary at Mercersburg at a time when our church was put to the test. Here it had to be determined, whether it would remain a truly Reformed church, i.e. a church of the Word. Those were the times when the Reformed Church in this country had not yet developed a proper identity. It did not really know where it came from. Many people were looking backwards, became confused, and even returned to the fleshpots of Egypt (i.e. Rome) precisely because of their confusion."

It does not follow from Muehlmeier's opposition to Nevin's extreme views, however, that the German students had thrown in with the old Reformed party sympathetic to New Measures. For Muehlmeier continues with what amounts to approval of Nevin and Philip Schaff's basic critique of the effects of Americanization on the older Lutheran and Reformed Churches in the East:

The High Church tendencies, to which we have alluded, were not the only sting of the wasp our church had to suffer. No lesser danger threatened from the opposite side and this danger was first, bringing forth in due course the other extreme. Dr. Nevin hastened to meet this danger; he wrote against unbiblical conversion, and thus helped to overcome the machine-like fashion of "doing" revivals. This however caused him to embark upon studies which later nearly gave the death blow to him and the whole church. The labyrinth, in which he almost was lost, was Moehler's *Symboli*, a proud work which certainly makes quite an impression upon reason. If a servant of Christ cannot humble himself completely under the Word, let him . . . stay away from the books of the Roman Church.

In those days, for almost thirty years, our church had fallen on bad times. The Reformed and Lutheran churches were virtually asleep. Many a stout heart felt the need for an awakening. Yet, instead of looking for help in God's Word, where alone help may be found, help was sought from human beings . . . . They even brought the anxious bench into the Reformed Church of the Word. Thus, they tried to force by mechanical means what only the Spirit of God can rightfully accomplish. It can truly be said, "In those days there was no prophecy in the land." Our preachers were like watchmen who had fallen asleep.

Oh, everything was so empty and cold. Then the wild flames of enthusiasm were kindled. Some people recognized this and tried to douse the flames. Naturally, they used whatever seemed the handiest and best. No wonder that our dear Dr. Nevin found himself on a slippery road. Wouldn't anyone be bewildered if all of a sudden fire broke out at night? It's not surprising; especially if one discovers the fire burning brightly on opposite sides and cannot decide which of the two fires is more dangerous: the fire of high church tendencies or the system of New Measures.

The contrast between Muehlmeier's reference to "our dear Dr. Nevin" and the polemical spirit of J. I. Good's treatment of the same subject clearly shows that the Germans in the West took an independent position between Mercersburg and the Old Reformed parties. As an aside, none of the German students voiced objections against Nevinism until after the publication of "Cyprian" and "Early Christianity" in which Nevin expressed views which even Philip Schaff considered of questionable Protestant orthodoxy.

An endorsement of the "ancient Reformed doctrine" by the Sheboygan Classis therefore would be directed against both the New Measurism in the "Old Reformed" party and the extreme forms of Nevin's theology after 1852. Here we have a deliberate attempt to reaffirm the church's confessional tradition as expressed in the Heidelberg Catechism. In this respect, the Sheboygan Classis was moved by a concern quite similar to that of Nevin and Schaff in the formative period of the Mercersburg Theology, 1840-51, when both professors used their considerable literary skill to remind the church of its confessional heritage. There is no evidence of a basic disagreement between the Germans in the West and the more moderate theology of Philip Schaff. Rather, there are indications to the contrary. Schaff himself visited the Mission House in 1867 and assisted with donations of books. Scattered references indicate that his *Church History* was used in instruction at the school. Yet, while Mercersburg's concern for the Heidelberg Catechism served primarily to support "scientific" (read *Hegelian*) theology, the Sheboygan Classis in more orthodox fashion considered the catechism constitutive of the church.

The very nature of the catechism as a mediating confession encouraged latitude in interpretation. The Mercersburg party, with Schaff and Nevin as its principal spokespeople, emphasized the historic character of the document in an attempt to reconcile Lutheran/Reformed differences and in deference to their own Hegelian view of church history which tended to seek "agreement" of the Heidelberg position with that of Rome, Wittenberg, and Geneva.

The Old Reformed party loudly acclaimed its orthodoxy on the basis of the Catechism but in effect denied its spirit. Resonating the Arminian temper of American religion at the time, the Old Reformed party carried on a vigorous polemic with Mercersburg which was characterized by a Zwinglian view of the sacraments and a Lockian doctrine of the church. In view of this, it is a bit ironic that the Old Reformed faction called its own theological school, founded in 1870, Ursinus College.

The Sheboygan Classis shared and possibly exceeded the general enthusiasm for the Heidelberg Catechism. Yet, where Mercersburg stressed the historical and catholic spirit of the catechism and viewed it as a bridge toward the Melanchthonian wing of Lutheranism, the Germans in the West, with greater awareness of the confessional role of the document in the Reformed Church of Germany, emphasized its "difference" from Rome and Wittenberg. Consequently, the Sheboygan Classis rejected the Mercersburg notion of Protestant catholicity and used the catechism to shore up the ramparts of Reformed particularity. In striking contrast with

Schaff's view of the Prussian Union, Muehlmeier and Stienecker in a brief review of the Reformed regions of Germany are talking about an erosion of the Reformed Church caused by the union. In each instance, they are citing as a cause the abandonment of the Heidelberg Catechism in favor of other confessions. On the other hand, the principality of Teklenburg, Westphalia, is held up as a shining example: "For centuries, the *Heidelberger* has been firmly established there. *So far, the Union has not been able to eradicate it*" (italics mine). They deplore that in Hesse-Nassau "the union has wiped out much of the Reformed consciousness but not all." With evident satisfaction they note that "in America, many a Hessian has returned to the precious *Heidelberger*."

For the Sheboygan Classis and all the other German Reformed immigrant churches in the West, the Heidelberg Catechism constitutes the church, i.e. it is the *distinguishing* mark of their church. One could argue that in this respect the German immigrant faction was closer to the spirit of continental confessional Protestantism than either Mercersburg or the Old Reformed party. While Ohio Synod affirmed the letter of confessional allegiance, it was so thoroughly immersed in the mainstream of nineteenth century American religion that it denied its spirit. Mercersburg took its cue not from the confessional as such but from a developmental concept of the church as a divine human organism which may have been closer to Hegel than Heidelberg. While Schaff's great developmental scheme towards catholic unity may well have justified giving special recognition to the Palatinate symbol for its irenic and synthetic qualities, Schaff seems to ignore the historical role played by the catechism in the development of the Reformed Church in Germany, where it became the benchmark of the German Reformed identity. The deliberate attempt of the Sheboygan and the other German classes to establish churches on the basis of the Heidelberg Catechism leads to the conclusion that the immigrant church in the West more closely resembled the Reformed confessional tradition of Germany than either Mercersburg or the Old Reformed. It reinforces the thesis that the Germans in the Northwest constituted a third theological party in the German Reformed Church. In fact, the Sheboygan Classis was well aware of its calling to lead the whole German Reformed Church back to the faith of its fathers:

> By the efforts of pious and faithful laborers in the vineyard of the Lord, our church has slowly awakened to remember that it is the Church of the Word. . . . Slowly but ever more clearly it is rediscovering the treasure we have in the confession of the fathers (i.e. the Catechism).

Not unlike Schaff, the founders of the Sheboygan Classis considered it their theological mission to call the Reformed Church back to its traditional heritage in the "German Charisma." But lacking Schaff's sweeping, ecumenical vision, they planted the banner of the Heidelberg Catechism in their forest clearings as a rallying point for the weary of both sides in the controversy which had divided the church. Their churchly, German Pietism enabled them to sympathize with Nevin's earlier position on revivals expressed in the *Anxious Bench* and a number of shorter articles which held that legitimate conversion had a place in the church but that New Measures constituted a self-centered deviation from true conversion. With Mercersburg, they deplored the conjunction of "Pietism and separation" in American religion, its "one-sided subjectivity" with Arminian undertones, an odious notion even to a moderate Calvinist. Also, with Mercersburg they shared a "high" concept of the church and its unity, a mute witness to their traditional Reformed belief in the "firm old discipline."

Unlike Schaff, whose fertile mind trained in the Hegelian dialectic saw visions of reconciliation between Rome, Geneva, and Wittenberg, the Germans in the West staked out a lesser claim. They hoped for renewal of the church by way of a return to confessional identity and traditional piety.

The Sheboygan Classis and its theological school, the Mission House, founded in 1862, had a large part not only in the geographical expansion of the church but also in the shaping of its tradition. Frederick Herzog, who served as professor of systematic theology at Mission House Seminary from 1953 to 1960, talked about this as late as 1959 in the school's publication, the *Bulletin*:

There is, however, one badge of distinction which the school can deny only at its peril. It is responsible for that strand of the Reformation heritage summed up in the Heidelberg Catechism. The school is not its guardian but its debtor. It never sought to establish a Heidelberg Catechism orthodoxy but did try to witness to the basic teachings of the catechism: God's free grace, the election of the sinner without any merit of his own, and the life of thankfulness for God's grace. It dare never forget the continuing need for this kind of witness (Fall 1959, 2-3).

Herzog's words are still true: the United Church of Christ and its institutions dare never forget the continuing need for this kind of witness.

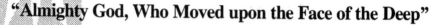

"Almighty God, Who Moved upon the Face of the Deep"

Almighty God,
who moved upon the face of the deep,
who moves the stars in the heavens and overcomes all darkness with light,
whose unfathomable love was revealed in our Lord Jesus Christ,
we pray for the church in the world today.
We need your love, the love that breaks forth into every human soul,
thirsting for you in a land where there is no water.
Grant that the church may not be obscure.
Let the church carry a real sense of your power and glory into the world.
Remind us that we are but dust without you,
and that the world needs more of what you alone can give.
Keep us from knowing too much and risking too little.
Grant, O Gracious God, that the church may witness and celebrate your
power and presence through Christ and the Holy Spirit.
Grant that we may be sustained by your peace that passes all understanding
and empowered by your knowledge that has no earthly dimensions.
Keep us from discouragement and despair, for we are lost too often,
fulfilling our own needs, forgetting that you have taken care of them
already.
Your grace and mercy are our only hope.
We give thanks for the wonders of your love,
for the three-fold cord that binds our hearts together,
and for the glimpses of your glory to come.
In Christ we pray.

*Dedicated to Frederick R. Trost whose loving encouragement and example
in the word has given hope for the church today.*

Barbara Kline Seamon

The Way of Faithfulness

Richard S. Williams

Hans Küng writes that the church is "the eschatological community of salvation."[1] Above this statement by a Roman Catholic theologian hovers, for the Protestant, a comfortable Barthian haze. After all, Küng wrote his doctoral dissertation on Barth. At the same time, this understanding of the nature of the church makes us early Third Millennium Protestants squirm in a most uncomfortable way. For the mainline church in America is caught in a curious mishmash of understandings, many a church exhibiting a self-perception of itself as some kind of civic club with a unique role as stand-by chaplain in times of transition or stress. Samuel McCrae Cavert (an ecumenical "war-horse" of the '50s) told a group of us about his being at a village gathering where representatives brought in candles for each of their organizations, setting them all one by one on a table: one for the Grange, one for the Boy Scouts, one for Rotary, one for the Church, and so forth!

The awakening to the crisis of the church was slow to become evident. Those of us theologically educated immediately post World War II in America were still, even after wrestling with the "realism" of Reinhold Niebuhr, at heart "liberal," and confident of the prospect that with good preaching and effective Christian education, justice and goodness would prevail, especially since America was the hope of democracy and freedom as over against Soviet communism. Civil religion reigned without significant challenge. Church attendance and Sunday School enrollments "spiked" upward on all the graphs.

Looking back, one sees this period almost as an "age of innocence," at least on the North American continent. Nonetheless, there were some noteworthy occasions of faithful witness. Vatican II and the *aggiornamento* of Pope John XXIII opened up amazingly rich dialogues between Protestants and Roman Catholics. The Civil Rights' witness led by Martin Luther King, Jr., was one of the church's finest hours, of course not without pain and sin. But there was reaction. The National Council of Churches became a target for Joe McCarthy-type right-wingers. And this writer-pastor, under siege by such political operatives, found himself resorting to the Barmen Declaration in sermons that were reported in the local weekly newspapers. Ecclesiology was once again taking shape out of crisis.

But the '60s provided other realities that together with general societal upheavals shattered the elitism and smugness at the base of the "we have the answers" mentality of the collection of faith-community patricians. Most prominent among these land-mines along the road to supposed settlement on an agreed-on standard spirituality were the Vietnam War and the hippy culture of protest, joined by an increasingly purposeful and articulate feminism. Then, too, the new musical idioms of rock musicians in all their manifestations plus the introduction of psychedelic drugs into more widespread usage changed the landscape of common culture and its values and assumptions.

For the churches this all turned out to be a Tillichian "shaking of the foundations." The "hermeneutic of acceptance" was superseded by a "hermeneutic of suspicion." One reaction by the church to all this is to try to speak the language of the new culture. This leads to many attempts on the part of the church to be primarily a therapeutic operation, seeking to "hear the pain" of those bruised by the contemporary scene and in various ways to offer healing. Surely, there is much that is admirable about such ministry. But the distinctive message of hope and new life from the Word of God is lost in the effort to be so fashionably relevant and so narrowly engaged.

The other widespread reaction to this changed cultural scene is found in the resurgence of those who see themselves as evangelicals. The phenomenon of the arrival of mega-churches and the proliferation of evangelically oriented books, videos, and musical groups all seem to speak to some deeply felt needs of many for certitude and a felt salvation. But in all fairness there are varieties of evangelical witness. Some are deeply concerned with social issues and bring a degree of sophistication to their perception of these issues and possible approaches.

Rampant among early Third Millennium North Americans are a super preoccupation with the self, often to the point of narcissism and the breakdown of any convincing allegiance to authority in morals and in faith. Robert Bellah's "Sheila-ism" has become the state church.[2] Unfortunately the church as it now exists is in large part poorly positioned to speak effectively to this social scene and to be able to proclaim and incarnate the redeeming and saving love of the Lord Jesus Christ. Individualism is so strong that its presence is not even noticed. As Robert Jenson points out, current participation in the Eucharist in either Protestant or Roman Catholic churches engenders little community. One sees individuals receiving the elements; faith is all an individual-to-God transaction.[3]

The church then today is called out to proclaim the *transcendence and otherness of God in judgment and saving grace on behalf of the world; and to unite people in a communio, a participation in the community of the Holy Trinity; or, to put the proposition in a kind of theological shorthand: to unite kerygmatic and communio ecclesiologies, with an identification of ministry with the servanthood of Jesus Christ to the human family and all the world.*

Protestantism, especially in the Reformed tradition, finds the focus on God's transcendence in judgment on the world along with offering saving grace set forth in the proclamation of this Word congenially in line with its Calvinist heritage. Note that here I use the word, "heritage," for in many churches of Reformed lineage there has been so far as faithfulness to the Calvinist tradition is concerned a backsliding of mammoth proportions. The "church of therapy" has frequently transformed the church of Jonathan Edwards with the message proclaiming "sinners in the hands of an angry God" to a community the message of which is "sinners we feel your pain and want you to know you're O.K." No doubt this is a caricature of the situation in North America, but the authority of the pulpit with a message in faithfulness to the Word, proclaiming saving truth to contemporary self-absorption is noteworthy more by its absence then by its presence. The market is for hope *now*, and to live in anticipation of the fullness of hope is unacceptable to current generations, so that not only the term "eschatology" but the reality that God's future is still to come, informing the "nowness" of our living, is off the monitor screen of perceived pictures of life.

There can be no question that the witness of Karl Barth remains crucial to confronting this apostasy. Avery Dulles, in his *Models of the Church,* includes the view of the church by Barth under the heading, "The Church as Herald": "It sees the Church as gathered and formed by the word of God. . . .This model is kergymatic, for it looks upon the Church as a herald." And Dulles quotes Richard McBrien: "The community itself happens wherever the Spirit breathes, wherever the Word is proclaimed and accepted in faith. The Church is event, a point of encounter with God."[4]

The Barmen Declaration spoke to a church in deep crisis as to the nature of its being and mission, a crisis occasioned by the claims of the German State under Nazism. In many ways the current situation in Western Europe and North America does not exhibit such a stark contrast between faithful church and pagan hegemony. However, in some ways the current situation is even more inimical to the integrity and faithfulness of the church. For we are confronting an amorphous and seductive mass of prideful self-absorption along with a state of hypnosis over modern technology and communication, with the reality of globalization calling the tune in regard to who we are one with the other.

The very dazzling glitzyness of such a scene simply crowds God out. We all live along a Las Vegas Strip, the lights of which make us blind to the desert that surrounds us, the desert that continues to ask the questions as to who we are and who is our God. The call then is for the church to heed Barth in praying that once again we have the eyes and heart to see with grace that the church is an *event,* the work of the Holy Spirit. Faithfulness to the Word in the midst of the world is of the very essence of the being and mission of the church. And the church always continues to be judged by the Word. Biblical preaching in the pastoral context and addressing the challenge to the gospel in each age, preaching that by grace can proclaim the full dimensions of hope in Christ, by the gift of the Holy Spirit, such preaching is central to bringing into being the church as the people of God.

Having said that, however, we need to be open to being made to feel at home in and to draw strength from what is called *communio ecclesiology.* Lutheran theologian Robert Jenson states: "The communion of the church is grounded in the communion of the triune God." And he adds the following quotation from the Orthodox-Roman Catholic Dialogue, *The Mystery of the Church and the Holy Eucharist in the Light of the Mystery of the Holy Trinity,* 11.2. "The church finds its model and its end in the mystery of the one God in three persons . . . [The] mystery of the unity in love of plural persons constitutes the trinitarian *koinonia* which is communicated to human persons in the church."[5] At first glance this seems far removed from the kerygmatic model of the church as espoused by Barth. But the thesis of this paper is precisely that this dynamism of the mystery of the body of Christ as present in the church and in baptism/eucharist is faithful to the call of the church to be Christ's body and gives today's church a coherence of inner life that can establish hope and empower discipleship. At the same time this *communio* ecclesiology needs to be in tension with kerygmatic ecclesiology in order for God's judgment and grace to be active in a continuous reformation that witnesses to the eternal dialectic between sin and salvation, between human fallibility and God's otherness.

Jenson writes that *communio* ecclesiology has two parts: one is a doctrine of the church's ontological foundation and the other is a doctrine of the church's structure, namely that the one church consists *in et ex* the many churches.[6] For the purpose of this paper attention will be given to the former part, "the church's ontological foundation."

In *The Catholicity of the Reformation*, Jenson asserts:

The church is founded in the triune life of God because the church anticipates being taken into that life, and because, as the gospel interprets reality, it is precisely what creatures may *anticipate* from God that as their deepest being the church is the people of God, the church is the body of Christ, and the church is the temple of the Spirit. In all these cases, the church exists only by anticipation. God's one people will not gather until the last day; therefore the church can now be the people of God only in anticipation of that gathering of the church as the body of Christ whose return in like fashion we must still await. The church is the temple of the Spirit whose very reality among us is "down payment," *arrabon*. . . . Our end is not participation in an abstract essence of Godhead, but in the life that Father, Son, and Spirit have among themselves; all *koinonia* is founded and defined in the *koinonia* that, under the traditional label *perichoresis*, is the life of the triune God.[7]

What we have in *communio* ecclesiology is the mystical reality of the community of the Trinity intersecting with the fleshy reality of human striving and living, so that through grace and love humans are being continually formed and reformed into the shape of their being as persons in the community of God's creation and rule (kingdom, *basilea*). And the heart of perceiving the truth of this mystery is to be found in the worship of the church. In the faithful church there is to be found an interplay between church doctrine and church worship, echoing the old rule: *lex orandi vis a vis lex credendi*. Often, this has meant that the "law of prayer establishes the law of belief." But as Geoffrey Wainwright has pointed out the more salutary understanding lies in the sense of interplay between the two.[8] This is all by way of saying that sacramentology as regards our understandings of baptism and eucharist is united with ecclesiology in a continuing relationship of conversational dialogue and reformation of practices. For example, when baptism is understood primarily as *invitation into membership in the body of Christ and the people of God*, then baptism "is to be understood as a *total* reorientation and redirection of the individual away from the essentially noncommittal, alienating and dying world (establishment) toward the communal, bonding, resurrecting Church of Christ." (See Philip J. Lee, *Against the Protestant Gnostics*).[9]

Immediately such a view of baptism affirms the church as "the eschatological community of salvation." In eloquent language Lee asserts that: "Within the context of Christ's community, acceptance of *myself* has been replaced by acceptance of my *humanity*. Having been accepted by Christ and his people, self-acceptance becomes irrelevant. The important question rather becomes: How can I offer myself, such as I am, with my special talents and my personal limitations, to the Person and people who have already accepted me?"[10] Thus, we are in a very special perceptual field so far as the church is concerned, exalting its nature as the eschatological community of salvation, led by the Spirit, and discovering new life every day in a continual dance with the Holy Trinity, participating in the servanthood to the world constantly modeled by Jesus on the cross. This perceptual field gives the lie to the revivalist mode with its self-centered claims of being born again, no matter how modishly contemporary the trappings may be. And at the same time it cuts the ground out from under any "liberal" dilution of the church through being enamored of domesticating Jesus to be a peasant teacher with enlightened social views or as someone uniquely gifted in showing us therapies to make us feel good. In either of those cases the probability is strong that the church will degenerate into "civic clubs for socially compatible families."[11]

It remains to be emphasized that the source of continual nourishment for the church as the eschatological community of salvation is to be found in the Eucharist conjoined with preaching the Word, proclaiming judgment and grace, and giving openness to the work of the Spirit to direct the church both in its inner life and in its ministry as Christ the Servant, bringing healing and redemption to the world. In words that do justice to the nineteenth century witness of John Williamson Nevin, Jenson states "the church's communion with Christ, actual as the Eucharist, is with the living person, and so must be participation in his own present action before the Father."[12]

Kerygmatic ecclesiology and *communio* ecclesiology offer, *when in a constant dialectical relationship one with the other*, a perceptual field of seeing the church that best expresses for our day the reality of the church as "the eschatological community of salvation." There are dangers in *communio* ecclesiology: the possibility of a too easy identification with one expression of the institutional church and also (noted by Nicholas M. Healy of St. John's University, Staten Island) a leaning in the direction of "baptizing" uncritically a wide variety of human communities. As Healy reminds us: "the implications of an eschatological 'not yet' should not be relegated to a secondary concern."[13]

Tillich wrote of the need for "the Protestant principle" to maintain dynamic connection with "Catholic substance." And "justification by grace" was seen as the heart of the Protestant principle. Braaten and Jenson summarize Tillich at this point by noting: "Protestant principle without its Catholic substance would be 'empty': Catholic substance without the Protestant principle would be 'blind.'"[13] So we can conclude that Evangelical Catholicism, wherein flourishes the Reformed witness to the eternal distance between the creator and the created while confessing God's sovereign grace given through Jesus Christ in the power of the Spirit, shows us the way of faithfulness to God the Father, Son, and Holy Spirit, in our life together in the church, members of the body of Christ, the Suffering Servant on behalf of the world.

Notes

1. Hans Küng, *The Church* (New York: Sheed and Ward, 1967), 77.

2. Robert Bellah et al., eds., *Habits of the Heart: Individualism and Commitment in American Life* (Berkeley: University of California Press, 1985), 221.

3. Robert W. Jenson, "The Church and the Sacraments," in *The Cambridge Companion to Christian Doctrine*, ed. Colin E. Gunton (Cambridge University Press, 1997), 219.

4. Avery Dulles, S.J., *Models of the Church* (New York: Doubleday, 1974), 71.

5. Robert W. Jenson, "The Church as *Communio*," in *The Catholicity of the Reformation*, ed. Carl E. Braaten and Robert W. Jenson (Grand Rapids: Eerdmans, 1996), 1.

6. Ibid., 4.

7. Jenson, in Gunton, ed., *Christian Doctrine*, 215.

8. Geoffrey Wainwright, *Doxology: The Praise of God in Worship, Doctrine, and Life* (New York: Oxford University Press, 1980), 218.

9. Philip J. Lee, *Against the Protestant Gnostics* (New York: Oxford University Press, 1987), 254.

10. Ibid., 252.

11. Eric Voeglin in *Order and History* (Baton Rouge: Louisiana University Press: 1964), 111, 278 in Lee, *Against the Protestant Gnostics,* 166.

12. Jenson in Gunton, ed., *Christian Doctrine*, 223.

13. Nicholas M. Healy, "Communion Ecclesiology: A Cautionary Note," *Pro Ecclesia*, Vol. 4, No. 4 (Fall 1995): 451.

14. Carl E. Braaten and Robert W. Jenson in *The Catholicity of the Reformation*, x.

Challenges Facing Tomorrow's Church

Barbara Brown Zikmund

Frederick Trost is a churchman. His entire ministry has been devoted to pastoring and empowering the church. Unlike some liberals who may spend a lot of energy critiquing the church, he embraces the church as a given. The question in his ministry is not "Why the church?" but rather "Whither the church?" He continually calls the church of Jesus Christ into account.

Over the years Frederick has both chided and supported the church. I first came to know Fred during his ministry in Chicago in the late 1970s. In recent years we have worked together on the *Living Theological Heritage* project. As I look at his life and reflect about how his ministry is "of" the United Church of Christ, I wish to lift up three themes which permeate the church he loves and the ministry he exercises. These three themes highlight the UCC at its best and call it into a challenging future.

I begin with a theme that is seen most clearly in the life and work of Reinhold Niebuhr, favorite son of the Evangelical Synod of North America. Niebuhr was a product of the unique blend of piety and intellectual rigor that informed the German Evangelical Synod. His theology was grounded in the daily challenges facing local pastors. And his theology was highly critical of the naive optimism of social gospel liberals.

In the 1930s, as Hilter's evil spread across Europe, Niebuhr pointed out that liberalism seemed to be unconscious of the basic difference between the morality of individuals and the morality of collectives. He launched a critique of the liberal assumption that the egotism of individuals might be progressively checked by the development of rationality. In his classic book *Moral Man and Immoral Society*, Niebuhr argued that a sharp distinction needed to be drawn between the moral and social behavior of individuals and social groups. Although individuals may be moral in the sense that they can consider interests other than their own, human societies and social groups rarely have the capacity to overcome the natural impulses by which society achieves its cohesion. As a consequence there are always certain elements in the collective behavior of human societies which belong to the order of nature and can never be brought completely under the dominion of reason and conscience. [1]

The United Church of Christ at its best has been greatly influenced by Niebuhr's understanding of human nature. Although the UCC has attracted many social liberals and become well known for its cutting edge statements and courageous witness against social injustice, when it is true to its roots the UCC knows that ultimately human societies can never be tamed by human reason and conscience. Indeed, the UCC takes issues of social and political injustice seriously *precisely* because it is convinced that only faithful communities humbled by divine grace can bring about justice and peace. Authentic UCC activism is never driven by an idealism that Christians can save the world; rather it is chastened by an awareness that justice is possible only because God loves the world. As we move into the future, I believe that only when Christian leaders rediscover the chastened liberalism of Niebuhr will the Christian Church avoid the arrogance of misplaced moralism and fanaticism.

The ministry of Frederick Trost invites us to reclaim this legacy. Throughout his career Fred has taken ecclesiology seriously. He has recognized that collective entities must repeatedly be called into account. He has worked to keep the church of Jesus Christ faithful to the gospel. And in keeping with the unique strength of the United Church of Christ he has taken risks for justice—always knowing that the collective sins of the church are just as dangerous as those on the public square.

Second, Frederick Trost has been deeply influenced by the progressive and serious biblical scholarship that has shaped and reshaped the church's ministry during the past one hundred and fifty years. All the denominational traditions that have come together to create the United Church of Christ were grounded in biblical truth. However, unlike some denominations that did not take the Bible seriously enough to become disturbed by its demands, or other denominations that became embroiled in divisive controversies about biblical authority, the historic traditions that came together to create the UCC were always open to new biblical insights and interpretations. Congregationalists quoted the words of Pastor John Robinson to the Mayflower Pilgrims: "There is yet more truth and light to break forth from God's Holy Word." Christians upheld liberty of conscience and insisted that although the Bible was their guide to faith and practice, texts were never as important as how believers lived out their faith in context. The German Reformed Church was more biblically flexible than many Reformed immigrant communities grounded in Dutch theology and practice.

Within the Evangelical Synod of North America there is the story of Karl Emil Otto, professor and one-time president of Eden Theological Seminary. Otto was a biblical scholar who grew up in Europe in the Church of the Prussian Union and attended the University of Marburg. During his studies he was influenced by three progressive faculty members: Professors Tholuck, Mueller, and Hupfeld, especially Hupfeld's critical philological approach to Near Eastern languages.

In 1865 Otto came to America, working first with Lutherans in Wisconsin. Very quickly Otto determined that Wisconsin Lutherans were too strident for him, and he found himself more at home among the German Evangelicals. In 1870 he became a professor of biblical studies at the Evangelical seminary in Marthasville, Missouri. (This institution later moved to St. Louis and became Eden Theological Seminary.) Soon thereafter, with the death of Andreas Irion, and after the short intervening presidency of Johann Bank, at age 38 Otto became president of the seminary in 1873.

Otto was on the cutting edge of biblical scholarship and was teaching the critical theology of the German universities to ministerial students raised on the American frontier. His students loved his exegesis, but the longstanding pietistic leadership of the Evangelical Synod became alarmed. In 1880, when Otto published a progressive symbolic analysis of the Genesis temptation story, the General Conference of the Synod felt called to investigate his work to determine if it deviated from synodical doctrinal positions. Although he defended himself eloquently, in the end the General Conference rendered a vote of no confidence (47 to 9). Suddenly the highest denominational body had censured the president of its flagship seminary. This could have been the end of Otto, but the important part of this story is that it was not the end. Although Otto resigned as professor and briefly left the Evangelical Synod, serving for five years as a pastor in a non-Synodical church, he was not repudiated as a person, and the capacity of the denomination to embrace diverse biblical perspectives was not thwarted. In fact a few years later he became a professor at the denomination's Elmhurst College.

In the end, the German Evangelical Synod of North America, unlike many Protestant denominations in the late nineteenth century, was not torn apart by arguments over new biblical critical scholarship. And as the years went by, according to historian Lowell Zuck, Otto's approach to scriptural authority, learning, individual conscience, and willingness to allow missionary-like accommodation to American life prevailed. Although the German Evangelicals stumbled for a moment when they censured Otto, they went on to maintain a balanced progressive stance which allowed sound biblical criticism and flexible churchly pietism to live together.[2]

When I read the story of Karl Emil Otto, I find myself thinking of Frederick Trost. He stands firmly in this Evangelical tradition, committed to progressive scientific scholarship, without the naivete of liberalism. To be a Christian does not mean leaving your best intellectual self at the door.

For many years his ministry has consistently promoted critical theological scholarship and serious doctrinal conversation in the United Church of Christ. At the same time his respect for the holiness of scripture is deep. He wants others to agree with him, but he is also willing to accept the fact that the Holy Spirit works in many ways. The Craigville Colloquies and the Confessing Christ movement are ongoing expressions of his style. Through them and various other efforts, he has encouraged church leaders of considerable diversity to live together into God s future.

Third, Frederick Trost is above all committed to the unity of the church, not as a social construct to overcome past divisions, but because Christians are called to one faith, one baptism and *are* already "One" in Christ Jesus through the grace of God. His theology has been influenced by European and Latin American thinkers, but it is also very North American. In that sense he is part of the midwestern heartland where most of his ministry has taken place.

I grew up in the midwest, went to college in Wisconsin, and although I have lived on both coasts, I believe that the churches scattered across the middle of the United States have a special approach to Christian discipleship which is worthy. There is a grass-roots mind which thrives in the midwest. New Yorkers, Bostonians, and Californians may scorn its apparent simplicity, but the grass-roots mind in America deals with the unity of the human family and the givens of daily life in a manner which has integrity. It does not put on airs.

A quotation from a book that I read over twenty years ago entitled, *The Grass-Roots Mind in America: The American Sense of Absolutes* is helpful:

[There is] a basic and winning vitality [which] is reflected in the grass-roots mind's optimism that somehow things will work out. It is reflected in the ability to roll with the punches life delivers, adjusting expectations to fit concrete possibilities and personal limitations. It is reflected in the intuitive rejection of life-denying preachments by those who too far surrender to theorizing. Most of all it is reflected in an unpretentious self- respect, a quality most accessible to those who with courage have engaged life fully and sometimes failingly across a wide spectrum.[3]

If one gives so much that a similar gift cannot be returned, then the receiver thereby becomes enslaved. This violates the duty to receive, namely the duty to give in such a fashion that one expects to receive in turn. God would then look like the "strong man" of archaic and modern economies who gives in order to subjugate the receiver. Why is not this the case with the gift of the Triune God?

The reason that the immensity of this gift does not destroy us is that in giving the Son, God forgives us our debt. The gift of the crucified, risen Son is appropriate; it may not be what we desire but it is the one thing needful for life. The power of God's love freely given us is the only power that is stronger than death, evil, and sin. This, then, is the freedom in obedience which we know in justifying grace.

But if we do not go beyond justifying grace, we are not yet living in the fulness of God's grace, for we have not yet returned the gift. Holiness means the practice of love in justice as the return of the gift of God's love. We have been forgiven our debt, and yet in the life of grace we receive a new command: "Owe no one anything except to love one another" (Rom. 13:8). Love is not the effect of our will and yet, for all that, it is the subject of a strange command: "Love one another even as I have loved you" (Jn 13:34). Sanctification is our return of God's gift. God the Holy Spirit gives us the power to return the gift of God. God the Holy Spirit makes it possible for us to serve the life-giving grace of God in the world.

That something will come back to the giver is not the condition of the gift, though the character of gifting is that something does come back. The sacrificial gift of ourselves will not come back in the same form. And therein is the surprise and joy of the sanctifying gospel. In order to retain the character of gift, gifts are transformed in their circulation. They are changed by the character of the person or the community that receives. The joy of the gift, if it succeeds in establishing an understanding too deep for words, is the mutuality of peace. When we receive a reciprocal gift (even if it is only gratitude) we receive the same gift of mutuality that we had first offered. But now gifter, giftee, and the gift are all transformed into the mutuality of the new creation.

In commodity exchange there is neither motion nor emotion; the whole point is to keep the balance, to make sure that the exchange doesn't consume anything or involve one person with another. In gift-giving, however, an imbalance is created that causes momentum and creates new relationships. We give because God has first given to us. We give back what God has given us: our lives. This is the power of gifting that creates communion in which lies the power for reconciliation in a world of enmity.

Frederick Trost is grounded in middle America and he understands the attributes of the grass-roots mind. At its core it informs his deep commitment to the ecumenical agenda and the unity of the church.

There are many "challenges facing tomorrow's church." We need to remember that the church is both a gift from God and a self-serving human organization. Only by constantly reminding ourselves of our ecclesiological limitations will there be room enough for God's grace. We need to remember that critical biblical scholarship and serious theological conversation, even disagreement, is actually a way to nurture Christian faithfulness. We need to remember that unity and ecumenical energy are alive and well at the grass roots. The life and ministry of Frederick R. Trost have reminded us of all of these things. And to God be the glory.

Notes

1. Reinhold Niebuhr, *Moral Man and Immoral Society* (New York: Scribners, 1932, rev. ed., 1960), xi-xii.

2. Lowell Zuck, "Evangelical Pietism and Biblical Criticism: The Story of Karl Emil Otto," *Hidden Histories in the United Church of Christ*, vol. 2 (New York: United Church Press, 1987), 66-79.

3. Conal Furay, *The Grass-Roots Mind in America: The American Sense of Absolutes* (New York: New Viewpoints, 1977), 25.

THE CENTRALITY OF CHRIST, THE WORD

"Come My Way, My Truth, My Life"

Come my Way, my Truth, my Life:
Such a way as gives us breath;
Such a truth as ends all strife;
Such a life as conquers death. *

O transforming radiance, new dawn from heaven,
your wisdom exceeds the limits of our minds.
How is it, with a universe to govern,
you dwell with us, your Spirit stirring in our midst?

Awakened by such truth, whose heart shall not be lifted up in awe?

Each day signs of your presence unfold before us:
in the laughter of little children,
the unexpected smile on a stranger's face.
Floral hues in sunset and garden enchant our eyes.

Awakened by such signs, whose voice shall not be lifted up in praise?

Yet suffering abounds, cherished relationships sag or go awry.
There is illness; there is pain.
Though our grief will not subside, no despair of ours
shall ever alter our trust, for your love is equal
to the pathos of our troubled lives.
Even when we falter we are raised up, for you live among us
and console us through the presence of our risen Lord.

*Awakened by such knowledge, whose life shall not be lived in gratitude
and joy?*

Come my Way, my Truth, my Life:
Such a way as gives us breath;
Such a truth as ends all strife;
Such a life as conquers death. *

*George Herbert, 1633

Edwin E. Beers

Prayers from a Children's Hospital Chapel

Joseph Alden Bassett

In the Children's Hospital Chapel there is pencil and paper beside a box for prayers. Numerous prayer requests are left after Thursday. So many, in fact the chaplain asked if I would go to the chapel sometime on Sunday with one or two members of our church and say those prayers. So it is that two of us gather in the out-of-the-way chapel on Sunday afternoons at 3:00 to do just that. But what sort of liturgical setting do these prayer slips require? At Mass the priest places the slips on the altar in a stack and "offers them up." But that is a eucharistic liturgy. We, at the hour once called *none*, say a pastoral office and read the slips of paper aloud.

A congregation might include an Orthodox mother from Greece for whom this Sunday is Easter or a Methodist minister heartily singing "What Wondrous Love Is This." Or there may be no one in the pews. Only the prayers they have left for us to say mark their presence.

We begin the service with a sung doxology, followed by a prayer of confession. The first hymn is then sung with a collect for the day. We say a psalm antiphonally followed by a collect. The Sunday scriptures are read from the *Revised Common Lectionary*, making manifest the liturgical year. A homily is preached. That Word creates the liturgical space in which to say the prayers and gives shape to the prayers we say as well.

Following the versicles and a moment of silence, we read responsively the prayers left in the box. Each prayer is concluded with "Lord in your mercy," accompanied by the response, "Hear our prayer." A time of silence follows for people's spoken or unspoken prayers as the Lord may lead them. There is a short prayer of thanksgiving for the ministry of a particular nurse. Their names can be found in anniversary histories of the hospital, on forgotten plaques, in yearbooks of the nursing school, or in the living memory of the staff. We conclude our prayers with the Lord's Prayer. We sing a final hymn. Following the benediction we greet one another asking who is in the hospital and what is their home church. After this brief exchange, we scatter into the corridors, rarely if ever to meet again.

One Lord's Day in the winter, a grandparent left a slip to say her daughter had been told "some abnormalities [were] present" in her first pregnancy. The arguments for abortion were certainly presented to the pregnant woman in the grandparent's family. The argument will have been made that while men and women may not be responsible for germs, they can be responsible for genes. "Responsible reproducers" should be allowed to "cleanse" their family gene pool.

At times like these we miss the Lutheran "First Use of the Law" as Bonhoeffer described it in March of 1943. Pondering the commandment "Thou shalt not kill," Bonhoeffer defined "The First Use of the Law" as providing "a worldly order that protects persons from disorder and arbitrariness."[1] This Christian family, however, having rejected abortion, went to pray in the chapel. In the words of Micah (6:7) they refused to give their first born for their "transgressions"; namely, bearing a child outside the parameters some would term "normal." As the people of God they were created "to do justice, love kindness and walk humbly with their God." The slip they left in the prayer box invites us to join them.

"What language shall we borrow?" said Pastor Gerhardt in his hymn, and I ask the same question when we share this grandparent's prayer. Origen directs us to 1 Timothy 2:1 and presents four choices. They are: "supplications," an entreaty for the obtaining of something the person lacks; "prayers," offered in a dignified manner with ascription of praise by someone concerning matters of importance; "intercessions," a request to God for certain things made by one who possesses more than usual confidence; and "thanksgivings," an acknowledgment with prayer that blessings have been obtained from God.[2] There aren't many intercessions in a hospital chapel. The news and stress of that place overwhelms people's extraordinary, as well as ordinary, confidence. What intercessions there are can be found among supplications, prayers, and thanksgivings.

The words we speak rest upon a eucharistic prayer and the Lord's Prayer. The communion prayer is the primary form of Christian liturgical prayer because the Lord's Supper nurtures our vocation as Christian people in the world communicating a sense of thanksgiving for the life, death and resurrection of Christ. Out of that sense of thanksgiving we are bold to say "Our Father. . . ." The phrases of the Lord's Prayer, "Thy will be done," and "Thine is the kingdom, and the power, and the glory," speak in the hospital with uncommon authority.

Given those prayers and the Word on the Fourth Sunday after Epiphany we pray:
Blessed are you, Ruler of the Universe.
    We praise you as the source of our creation,
        as the Word of our life,
        as the Spirit of our patience.
    We recognize so much that we cannot know;
        despite our inventions,
        our curiosity,
        and our worries.

We know that we are a statistic;
        but we know not on which side of the line,
            in what part of the equation,
            in what column we are entered.
Thus, we can only humbly pray;
        Be with us in these times of unknowing,
        as you were with Jesus in Gethsemane,
        as you were with Judas in his calculus,
        as you were with Peter in his confusion,
        as you were with the Magdalene in her watching,
        as you were with the other Mary in her waiting.
Know, Almighty God, that we are grateful:
        for the sustaining gifts freely given in the past,
        for the ancient promises that have not failed,
        for the call to move through this world following Jesus
            with the words of the psalms on our lips
            and David's melody in our heart.

We make a supplication:

Blessed are you
        who created the world out of nothing,
        who speaks to your people generation to generation,
        who moves with surprising and unseen force.
We come before you wondering, what is "healthy?"
        Mary Magdalene was cured, but of what, O Lord?
        Jesus healed many but no definitive list of maladies is
            given;
So what is the wholeness we are called to enjoy?
Teach us, Lord, to embody that health which:
        embraces children that others would banish;
        surprises parents with good news of healing;
        answers desperate pleas for help.
We thank you for that health
        we are given by that "one Physician
            of flesh yet spiritual,
            born yet unbegotten,
            genuine life in the midst of death,
            sprung from Mary as well as God—
            Jesus Christ our Lord."

And finally we give thanks:
God, who keeps covenant with your People
    and recalls the sacrifices of humanity;
        God of Abraham, God of Jesus,
        God of Sarah, God of Mary Magdalene,
make us confident
    that Christ's arms
        stretched out on the cross to
        embrace all of humanity
            will reach this family;
    that your Holy Spirit
        will seal your promises of new life
            in their minds and on their hearts;
    that you will feed them,
        when they come to your table
        and meet them,
        when they bring their child to the font.
Know that these signs of your presence
    make a crucial difference for the holy people
        who remember with thanksgiving Christ's
            victory
            in a blasphemous world that passes by
            and forgets you.
Not of our worthiness,
    but of your tender mercy,
        Hear our prayer.

Notes

1. Dietrich Bonhoeffer, *Ethics* (New York: Collier, 1955), 312.

2. Origen, "On Prayer," XIV:2, in *Alexandrian Christianity,* The Library of Christian Classics, vol. II (Philadelphia: Westminster, 1954), 267.

Christian Faith and Church in the Multi-Religious Marketplace

Hans Berthold

Christian churches in Germany have demanded and practiced a monopoly status among religions for more than a thousand years. Because of this, they have pretty much shaped the life of the individual, family, and society. Christianity lost this apparently preeminent status at the beginning of last century even though it had up to then been boosted by tradition. The Christian faith and the church of today have to face competition in the multi-religious marketplace.

The changes that confront us follow the formula: theology and churches are losing in significance, the demand for religion and religious experience is rising. Magazines like *Time* and *Newsweek* as well as *Der Spiegel* and *Psychologie heute* confirm this trend for the United States and Germany. According to *Newsweek*, a third of the adult population in the United States say they have had religious and mystical experiences; a fifth is convinced that they have experienced a personal revelation of God; an eighth regularly senses the presence of angels. Every seventh German believes in magic and witchcraft, every third believes that the future is predictable, and, if *Der Spiegel* is correct, more clairvoyants and sooth sayers offer their services than Protestant and Catholic pastors combined. It is not that religion and religious experience have lost their appeal but theology and church have lost their power to convince and bind people to the faith.

These developments are driven by irreversible changes in societal trends. While the freedom of conduct and choice is steadily increasing, firm social bonds such as class, religious convictions, loyalty to authorities, and obligations are losing in significance at the same rate. As a result, a new form of religiosity which reflects the wishes and needs of the individual is gaining in importance. Faith becomes a private matter in the sense that it becomes a matter of choice between one option or another. A kind of patchwork religion evolves.

Social scientific studies have shown that religious change in Germany often moves through three phases. First, a person makes the effort to get in contact with congregations and is quickly disappointed by the spiritual emptiness he/she encounters there. As a second step, seekers enter the world of therapy and psychology. There they make emotional discoveries, gain in self-knowledge, and find intense human contact, but there is still no link to the transcendent. This leads us to the third phase where many seek out esoteric groups which make that which is merely talked about in congregations tangible and open the experiences made in the psychological sphere toward the transcendent.

The critique of the spiritual emptiness of many congregations is unfortunately valid. In normal congregations one rarely encounters Dietrich Bonhoeffer's fascinating combination of prayer and faithfulness to the earth, or of prayer and work as with the Benedictines, or of spiritual experience and fellowship lived out in evangelical groups. I often ask myself: how many pastors view their vocation as the calling to guide people toward prayer and a deeper understanding of the biblical message? In his final lecture 1961/62, Karl Barth defined our vocation using the key words "prayer" - "study" - "service" - "love" and emphasized: Prayer without study would be empty. Study without prayer would be blind. Bonhoeffer's distinction between three uses of the Bible points us in a similar direction: the Bible lies *kerygmatically* "on the pulpit," *theologically* "on the writing desk," and *meditatively* "on the prayer bench." In this way, Bonhoeffer, following Luther, taught and practiced spirituality as *lectio, meditatio, oratio,* and *tentatio.* He could be our teacher and model today, and this would help us represent Christian faith authentically in the multi-religious market place.

Christian faith is, however, biblically grounded and attractive only when we confess/profess Jesus Christ as the messiah of Israel, the reconciler of peoples and redeemer of the cosmos (Col 1:15-20). In the New Testament, the word "confess/profess" always refers to persons. One confesses/professes someone to whom one belongs and thereby takes one's stand publically with that person through word and deed (Rom 10:9; Mt 16:16; Jn 11:27). Jürgen Moltmann has precisely formulated the heart of the problem for us pastors: Whoever limits christology to the historical Jesus, whoever reduces the eschatological person of Christ to the private individual Jesus and whoever limits his presence to his lifetime should not be surprised when christology is then no longer a relevant topic because who should be interested in a historical, private, and dead Jesus of Nazareth 2000 years later?

That internal and external reform of the church is necessary is undisputed in Germany. That is why there are many proposals for the improvement of the communication of the Christian message. With all due respect for such efforts, I regard it as realistic and theologically appropriate for today to grant the theological declaration of Barmen a key position in our attempt to define the mission of the church. Only in this way can the church remain true to the gospel of Jesus Christ and survive in the multi-religious market place.

Against the *totalitarian* claim of the Nazis to power, Barmen professes Jesus Christ as the "one Word of God that we have to hear, to trust in our living and dying and to obey" (Barmen I). Beyond this, Barmen offers a clear orientation in the face of a loss of tradition. This is also stated clearly in the *missionary* call: "It is the mission of the church, in which her freedom is grounded, in Christ's stead and also in the service of his own word and deed to proclaim the message of the free grace of God to all people through word and sacrament" (Barmen VI). Barmen has rightly been called the mark/goal/aim of the confessional statements of 1934 in my opinion and the EKU has gained a great deal in the last decades by arguing for and elaborating on this thesis in detail.

It has of course come into fashion to criticize vehemently Barmen I and VI. People speak of a Christian "totalitarianism" (M. Honecker), of "Christian *intolerance* toward other paths to salvation" (P. Lapide) and demand the willingness toward a "*christological* renunciation of ownership" (P. Von der Osten-Sacken) as if Barmen was a new version of the Christian claim to sovereignty from the time of imperialism and colonialism. Yet, Christ and the confession of Jesus as the Christ could not be more misunderstood because God does not declare absolute/exclusive sovereignty in either the New or the Old Testament. Rather, God grants a mutual covenant in the Old Testament with the covenantal people Israel (Ex 5:2; 7:9) in which Christians, according to the New Testament, participate through Christ (Rom 9-11). The content of this covenant is defined by the triad "true worship, justice, and compassion," as Paul D. Hanson pointed out in an extensive study. We speak with Jesus of the double commandment of love, that is, toward God and toward neighbor (Lk 10:27; compare Deut 6:5; Num 19:18).

In terms of how we live out our confession of Jesus Christ, we are faced with two dangers in the multi-religious market place. These dangers can be defined clearly with the words "neglect" and "patronism." We neglect our task of confessing Christ when we "hide our lamp under a bushel" (Mt 5:15) out of fear that we could railroad people. Conversely, we do railroad people when we act toward them like know-it-alls and arrogant guardians/bearers of the truth. In this case, 1 Corinthians 13:13 holds true: "So faith, hope, love abide, these three; but the greatest of these is love."

translated from the German by Ute Molitor

A Defining Utterance on the Lips of the Tishbite: Pondering "The Centrality of the Word"

Walter Brueggemann

Karl Barth has provided the definitive statement concerning the Word of God—preached, written, revealed.[1] None has shown so closely as Barth what it means that "the Word is central." An Old Testament teacher, however, may have a much more modest sense of the theme of "the Word," before it is overlaid with all of the christological freight that it has come to carry. In the Old Testament, the "word of the LORD" is characteristically taken to mean *direct utterance* that is efficacious and performative, that causes to be by the authority of the one who utters. When one moves in a christological direction, the one who *utters* becomes the *utterance*.[2] Here, however, I shall consider the utterance of Elijah the Tishbite who did indeed, according to the tradition, give utterance from God that made all things new. There is no doubt that his utterance is understood as central to every episode of his narrative and to the larger narrative of Israel in which his stories are embedded. The narrative account of Elijah attests to the conviction that in the horizon of faith, the Word is indeed central in redefining and transforming the world of death into an arena for life.

I

The word is central to the widow of Zarephath who has no other resource for life (1 Kings 17:8-24). Indeed the life-giving, life-restoring Word is a perfect counterpoint precisely for those who have no other hope in the world. The Tishbite is sent by "the word of the LORD" to this woman about to die of starvation (vv. 8-16). By his utterance, Elijah asserts a supply of plenty in a world of scarcity, declaring the economics of scarcity to be null and void:

> For thus says the LORD the God of Israel: The jar of meal will not be emptied and the jug of oil will not fail until the day that the LORD sends rain on the earth. (v. 14)

Elijah's greater utterance, however, is in his second encounter with the widow, whereby he restores her dead son to life (vv. 17-24). In this case his utterance is a powerful prayer addressed to the God of all life. We are told that "the LORD listened to the voice of Elijah." His utterance evokes a response from God as God impinges upon the world of deathliness. Elijah has summoned YHWH to action in that world of death. In both episodes, the concluding formula acknowledges the centrality of the word:

The jar of meal was not emptied, neither did the jug of oil fail, according to the word of the LORD that he spoke by Elijah (v. 16).

Now I know that you are a man of God, and that the word of the LORD in your mouth is true (v. 24).

The narrative knows that we are in the presence of an utterance and an utterer who decisively reshapes the world.

II

The word is central to the memory and identity of Naboth (1 Kings 21:1-24). In the first sixteen verses of the narrative, Naboth, Jezebel, and Ahab manage without the word. Life managed without the word, so the narrative makes clear, is short, brutish, and ugly, filled with rapaciousness, mendacity, and finally death. This real-life episode features the big ones eating the little ones, characteristically manipulating the powers of governance and the law for the sake of land advantage. Long before Karl Marx, this narrator knows that the powerful will manage the processes of governance for their ruthless advantage.

As we have it, however, the narrative does not end—as it otherwise would—with the execution of Naboth and the new royal success. It would have ended there if the Word were not central. But in verse 17 comes the Word, insisting that no earthly transaction is finished or proper if it is void of the relentless utterance that keeps the story of the world from shriveling into death. So speaks Elijah. First he utters a speech of judgment with its characteristic indictment and sentence of the king (vv. 17-19). Elijah is properly and correctly acknowledged by the king as "troubler," for the Word that is central is always a trouble for the shut-down royal world that wants to operate without the disruption of transformative utterance. In this account, however, the royal shut-down is not finally permitted.

Second, in verses 20-24 Elijah offers a long, formal, devastating utterance against the house of Omri. As in 14:7-14 and 16:2-4, this narrative specializes in prophetic oracles that terminate royal dynasties. What an odd portrayal of public power: *oracles* terminating *dynasties*, speech upsetting power! That is what Elijah does in this encounter with Ahab, threatening every heir of the royal family, with a special notice of the much despised queen. The oracle makes clear that royal power is at best pen-ultimate, is always at the behest of what is ultimate, namely, the uncompromising will of the one who authorizes the utterer.[3] This word from Elijah has two identifiable features. First in verses 27-28, even Ahab accepts the prophetic verdict and repents, willing to accept the demanding conditions whereby he retains power for a little while. But second, the repentance gives only a deferral of the Word, not its nullification. For in 2 Kings 9:36-37, the Word that causes powers to "rise and fall" comes to fruition in the termination of the dynasty (see also 1 Samuel 2:6-8).

These two utterances, in turn to a powerless widow and to a powerful king, are surely twinned. Together they exhibit the capacity of this God-sent utterer to intervene decisively in closed power arrangements that pertain to both economics and politics. This is the utterance that brings fullness midst scarcity, life midst death, and death midst life. Elijah's utterance is his own; it comes from his lips in understandable human coding. Nobody has trouble understanding him. At the same time, however, the narrative insists that the formula "the Word of the LORD" makes clear to all parties that this utterance so central to the deployment of economic, political power is not "merely" a Tishbite utterance. The narrator displays no curiosity about this odd juxtaposition of the Word so central that belongs to the Tishbite and yet belongs beyond the Tishbite to the central Utterer of life in the world.

III

The Word is central to the dynasty of Omri. The house of Omri featured four kings, Omri its founder (1 Kings 16:23-28), Ahab its star performer (1 Kings 16:29—22:40), and his two relatively inconsequential sons, Ahaziah (1 Kings 22:51) and Jehoram (2 Kings 3:1-3). We know from ancient Near Eastern records that the house of Omri was a major political-military force to be noticed and reckoned with in the world of international posturing. What interests us, however, is that the narrative of the books of Kings pauses over the House of Omri so long. We may be astonished by that fact because, in the ideology of the narrator, all Northern kings are in principle condemned and dismissed out of hand, precisely because they are non-Davidic or anti-Davidic.

Given that angle of assessment, the coverage given the Omri dynasty amazes. The reason, of course, is that the Omri dynasty that lasted thirty-four years, is the launching pad and arena for the utterance of Elijah and his disciple Elisha. This extended narrative is precisely a study in the centrality of the Word, a meditation on how it is that something as elusive, "non-substantive," and fleeting as utterance can impinge decisively upon the royal world of ideology, management, technology, and ruthlessness. One would know beforehand that the Word stands no chance in such a managed environment. And yet it does! That is the purpose of the narrative that cannot turn its attention away from this inexplicable wonder. As a consequence, we are offered an exposé of Niebuhrian proportion about the penultimate character of worldly power in the face of such utterance. Indeed, the dynasty is, in the end, defined by this utterance that it can neither withstand nor administer.

The presenting problem for the dynasty is a drought. The dynasty lives in an arid climate where water is always a preoccupation. Like every government, this one is in the end legitimated and consented to by its capacity to provide adequate resources for viable life and a viable economy. Obviously, if the royal government cannot supply water, it cannot endure. What the royal house may know but cannot acknowledge is instigated, beyond royal control, by the Holy Utterer who operates on the lips of Elijah. Indeed, in 1 Kings 17:1 when Elijah first abruptly appears in the narrative, the very first utterance, not even framed by a conventional "messenger formula," is a declaration of drought. This is a divine resolve to threaten the government in Samaria by withholding rain:

> As the LORD the God of Israel lives, before whom I stand, there shall be neither dew nor rain these years, except by my word (1 Kings 17:1).[4]

It is the drought that creates disaster for the widow. It is, moreover, the drought that generates the decisive confrontation at Mt. Carmel in chapters 18—19. In 18:1-6, we are offered a sketch of the pitiful, helpless Ahab traversing the land in a "research and development" venture to find water. But of course he will not find water, because water has been denied at a "higher level" of government to which the king has no access.

That sketch of royal impotence at the beginning of the narrative report on the drought is matched in the conclusion with a report of heavy rain (1 Kings 18:41-46). The drought ends, not by any royal maneuver, but by the Word of Elijah, who has secured public allegiance to YHWH and who now prays for rain as he prayed for the life of the boy. The narrator adds laconically:

> But the hand of the LORD was on Elijah; he girded up his loins and ran in front of Ahab to the entrance of Jezreel (1 Kings 18:46).

The power of YHWH is upon Elijah. He precedes the king in triumphant royal procession. There is no doubt that this utterer and his utterance—his own, yet not his own—is the decisive, concrete reality of the Omride house. Characteristically, these kings who hold the appearance of power are slow to notice that the realities of power lie beyond them. These kings, who mange the levers of government, late if ever notice that which is central is utterance and not their royal appearance.[5]

IV

The word is central to the royal narrative of 1 and 2 Kings. Gerhard von Rad has perceptively noticed that the editors of 1 and 2 Kings juxtaposed *prophetic utterance* and *narrative fulfillment* as a central organizing principle of the narrative.[6] By this arrangement, von Rad nicely understood that prophetic utterance is not incidental to the narrative; it is rather the decisive constitutive feature of this theory of public power.[7] Von Rad's exquisite exposition, however, could leave the impression that such a narrative device is an editorial imposition upon the royal narrative.

But that, of course, is not the case. For the fact is that kings in Israel and Judah are characteristically confronted with prophetic utterance that judges and condemns, that summons to repentance or that legitimates in office. Kings in Israel and Judah characteristically must exercise their royal authority in a context of confrontive utterance that stands outside royal legitimacy and that has of itself no visible authorization beyond its self-proclaimed "messenger formula." That utterance, however, is, in the horizon of the narrative, recognized to be a valid utterance that cannot be safely disregarded. That is, the management of earthly power, so this material attests, always takes place in the presence of inconvenient, disruptive, unaccommodating utterance. If we consider this claim "from above," it is to be concluded through the "messenger formula" that such inescapable utterance is a recurrent vehicle for the will of the Holy God who stands outside royal orbit and addresses royal power. This is the intent of the narrative that by the messenger formula makes a Yahwistic claim. If, however, we consider the matter "from below," it is characteristically the case, as this regime learned and as every self-contained concentration of power learns, that the human yearning for well-being is irreducible and finally not silencable, not by ideological manipulation nor even by the use of techniques of intimidation or torture.[8] Human voices of protest and hope will sound and have social force.[9] Thus when we say "the Word is central," we are able to see a convergence: Elijah is *sent by* YHWH with a word; Elijah arises midst a population of *deprivation* and will speak with and for that population. There is no contradiction in the narrative, for the theological claim and the sociological reality completely converge. His is a word bestowed "from above," arising "from below."

That is, the speech-fulfillment pattern offered in the narrative and discerned by von Rad is indeed intrinsic to the human process when that process is known to be more than the manipulation of images and the arrangements of power. That fragile, vulnerable reality of human entitlement, entitlement God-given in creation, will come to speech. And when it speaks, it is offered, in this case as in other cases, as the Word of the LORD.

The Word is central to this narrative because the LORD of covenant is committed to the raw reality of human life. The books of Kings are introduced by a cunning report on Solomon (1 Kings 1—11) and conclude with a celebrative but sobered recognition of the reforms of Hezekiah (2 Kings 18—20) and Josiah (2 Kings 22—23). Between Solomon and the belated royal reforms sit the Elijah-Elisha materials, with 1 Kings 12—15 and 2 Kings 11—17 as materials that connect these accent points. Solomon is "top down," interrupted only belatedly by Ahijah (1 Kings 11:29-39); in parallel Hezekiah and Josiah deal respectively with Isaiah and Hulda. Both the long introduction and the extended conclusion are royal accounts that are only interrupted by prophetic voices. In our long central section, however, the kings are bit-players and the drama is completely concerned for prophetic utterance. This central section shows the Word to be so central that kings count for very little. Indeed the books of Kings are arranged for radical subversion of royal power, a subversion that suggests that where Holy intention and human vulnerability converge, there is the truth of the matter.[10]

V

It is no wonder that this Elijah who did not die but "ascended" continued to haunt Israel (2 Kings 2:9-12). Utterance authorized by YHWH has staying power. It keeps uttering. It is not finished in its "original," historical-critical context. It keeps reuttering, so that the face-to-face utterances of Elijah to the woman and to the king become a force vis-à-vis the dynasty. Beyond the dynasty this Word stays central to the larger narrative and to an entire theory of power expressed in the narrative, a theory that depends upon remembered utterance made in quite locatable, concrete circumstance.

Beyond all of that in the books of Kings, however, this odd utterer continues to loom very large in the imagination, hope, and therefore text of Israel. Thus in the Christian Old Testament, Elijah has the last word in the book of Malachi, as we witness not a remembered Elijah but an expected Elijah:

> Lo, I will send you the prophet Elijah before the great and terrible day of the LORD comes. He will turn the hearts of parents to their children and the hearts of children to their parents, so that I will not come and strike the land with a curse (Mal 4:5-6).

The Elijah that ascended into heaven will, at the right time, descend into the earth again. And when he comes again, he will enact "family values," reconciling children and parents, in order to avoid the curse, the sort of curse Elijah found inevitable upon the house of Omri.

The concrete, uttered Word—its precise cadences known, treasured, and reiterated in Israel—keeps ringing in the ears of the faithful, keeps reassuring widows (see Lk 4:25-26), keeps terminating kings (see Lk 3:18-20), keeps supplying water in many lands of drought (see Jn 4:14). It is this utterer, with utterances that have inexplicable futures, who remains engaged in the imagination and expectation of the faithful. It is precisely because the Word is central, because this particular concrete utterance is durable and keeps respeaking, that the Gospel narrative surrounds its account of Jesus with Elijah references:

- John is drawn into the orbit of Elijah (Mt 14:14);
- Jesus is seen to be not unlike Elijah (Mt 16:14; 17:10-12);
- Elijah is one of the "old ones" who comes to legitimate and identify Jesus (Mt 17:3-4);
- The cry of Jesus on the cross is taken to be a petition for the coming again of Elijah (Mt 27:47-49).

It is clear that this remembered utterer is central to the Jesus narrative and to the imagination of the earliest circles of his followers. While there is no doubt that Elijah is engaged precisely to attest to Jesus as the Word, it is equally clear that the Jesus narrative could not be fully told and that Jesus as the Word could not be adequately recognized except in the world of Elijah's utterance that persists.

VI

The narrative in Kings spends little time pondering how it is that this human utterer could offer a Word so central that is Holy Utterance. We may, however, notice the way in which the Elijah narrative is framed. At the outset Elijah is commanded to the wilderness, outside the royal aegis, where he lives on the food of the land apart from royal offers of food that would soften his utterance (1 Kings 17:3-6; see Dan 1, Mk 8:15). From the outset Elijah is an utterer who is unencumbered by the gifts of those who would like to undermine the power, authority, and force of his utterance. He is nurtured in a way to protect the force and credibility of his unfettered utterance.

At the conclusion of his narrative when he is "taken up," Elisha asks for a "double share of your spirit" (2 Kings 2:9). Nowhere have we been told that the spirit had come upon Elijah. That reality, however, may be inferred from Elisha's petition as from Elijah's own performance. He is indeed a man beyond himself in authority. He is seen to have such unencumbered power precisely because he is powered singularly by the spirit of God that made him bold, fearless, and fully capable of transformative action. This framing of an introduction in *unencumbered nurture* (1 Kings17:3-6) and this conclusion in *underived power* (2 Kings 2:9) provides context and definition for the narratives of utterance in between. The narrative is deftly arranged in order to show that this utterer is fully engaged in the life of the world with all its risks, but he is not of that royal world. It his "in, but not of" that makes his word so central.

VII

No doubt this notion of the word as central does not fully come up to Karl Barth's christological notion of the centrality of the Word, nor does the narrative intend such a claim for the utterance of Elijah. It is correct, nonetheless, to see that the utterance on the lips of Elijah, in Barth's categories:

a) is indeed "Word preached":

It is the miracle of revelation and faith . . . when proclamation is for us not just human willing and doing characterised in some way but also and primarily and decisively God's own act, when human talk about God is for us not just that, but also and primarily and decisively God's own speech;[11]

b) is indeed "Word written":

This consists in the fact that in Holy Scripture, too, the writing is obviously not primary, but secondary. It is itself the deposit of what was once proclamation by human lips. In its form as Scripture, however, it does not seek to be a historical monument but rather a Church document, written proclamation;[12]

c) is indeed "Word of God revealed":

The Bible is God's Word as it really bears witness to revelation, and proclamation is God's Word as it really promises revelation. The promise in proclamation, however, rests on the attestation in the Bible. The hope of future revelation rests on faith in that which has taken place once and for all. Thus the decisive relation of the church to revelation is its attestation by the Bible. Its attestation![13]

I have no wish to push Elijah in an excessively christological direction; that, moreover, is not necessary in order to see in this lingering text that the concrete Word of the Tishbite is and remains central. Rather my concern, as it was early on with Barth, is not to make a christological connection, but to notice, with and for other preachers, that words faithfully uttered from these words have long time, enduring, transformative potential. Entrusted as we are with such remembered, expected utterance, it matters what and how we say words that are more than our own. It matters acutely, moreover, because in the world of technological consumerism, there is immense pressure to silence serious, revelatory, subversive utterance. A purpose of our technology of imagery, as Jacques Ellul has seen so clearly, is to preclude utterance wherein the irreducibly human and the irresistibly Holy converge.[14] It belongs to the heirs and children of this text to stand outside such killing of the human and such trivializing of the Holy. To stand outside for the sake of utterance depends, in some way, on refusing royal junk food (as in 1 Kings 17:3-6), and being powered by the Spirit (as in 2 Kings 2:9). Where such refusal and empowerment happen, there is a chance that widows will live, that powers will notice, and that water will abound.

It is a deep delight to salute Frederick Trost who has understood so well and worked so tenaciously that the Word be central in all its life-giving freedom in the ministry of the church. Would that his mantle were to be thrown over a host of his followers who know him to be a "chariot of Israel."

Notes

1. Karl Barth, *Church Dogmatics*, I.1 (Edinburgh: T. & T. Clark, 1975) 88-124.

2. By such formulation I allude to the dictum of Rudolf Bultmann, *Theology of the New Testament,* I (New York: Charles Scribner's Sons, 1954) 33, "The proclaimer became the proclaimed." I am grateful to my colleague, Charles Cousar, for helping me locate this formula. Cousar notes, moreover, that in English translation Bultmann did not use capital letters on "proclaimer" and "proclaimed," thus making the parallel with Elijah more accessible.

3. Reference might usefully be made to Dan 4:25, 32, "until you have learned that the Most High has sovereignty over the kingdom of mortals, and gives it to whom he will." The same learning is so urgent and difficult for the House of Omri.

4. The drought is readily understood in that ancient world as a curse authorized by YHWH who will brook no disobedience (see Deut 28:23-24; Lev 26:19-20).

5. The same interface is nicely narrated in Lk 3:1-2. There the full pedigree

of kings and priests is offered, only to be tersely contrasted with "the Word of God."

6. Gerhard von Rad, *Studies in Deuteronomy* (SBT 9; Chicago: Henry Regnery, 1953) 74-91.

7. This theory of history is nicely phrased by Klaus Koch, *The Prophets: The Assyrian Period* (Philadelphia: Fortress Press, 1982) 5, 73, 8, 99, 121, 155, and especially his schematic presentation on 156.

8. On the remarkable juxtaposition of speech and torture, see Elaine Scarry, *The Body in Pain: The Making and Unmaking of the World* (New York: Oxford University Press, 1985).

9. Robert R. Wilson, *Prophecy and Society in Ancient Israel* (Philadelphia: Fortress Press, 1980) has provided a suggestive analysis of the way in which social forces generate speech that turns out to be the prophetic word of the LORD. See especially 192-206.

10. On such subversion that undermines established power, see Paul Lehmann, *The Transfiguration of Politics: The Presence and Power of Jesus of Nazareth in and over Human Affairs* (New York: Harper and Row, 1975) 48-70 and *passim*.

11. Barth, *Church Dogmatics,* I.1, 93.

12. Ibid., 102.

13. Ibid., 111.

14. Jacques Ellul, *The Humiliation of the Word* (Grand Rapids: Eerdmans, 1985).

The Smell of Flesh

Herbert R. Davis

Grace to you and peace from God the Father and our Lord Jesus Christ.

And the Word became flesh and lived among us, and we have seen his glory, the glory as of a father's only son, full of grace and truth (John 1:14).

The prologue to the Gospel of John is both an introduction and summary of the Gospel. There is no doubt in the reader's mind concerning the identity of Jesus. You can't confuse Jesus with a prophetic teacher or a wandering cynic or a rebel hero. Jesus is the *Logos*, the Word who "was in the beginning with God." The Word "through whom all things were created." The Word is "life, and the life was the light of all people." As we read the prologue one soars to the heavens and smells the divine nature of Jesus. But John does not allow us to linger in heavenly bliss. He does not allow us to confuse the Word with a spirited person. John abruptly shifts from eternal Word to vulnerable human, from life and light to cross and death. John does not allow us to gently stumble upon the Incarnation, he shouts it from the rooftops, "and the Word became flesh and lived among us."

I am always surprised and embarrassed when I read this text. Surprised, because I always expect the Word to become Spirit and hover above us. John and spirituality seem so to go together. Surprised, because it is so unfriendly to the Greeks who could not imagine the Word becoming flesh. Surprised, because it raises questions about any spirituality that does not smell of flesh. Yet John is right. The Word does not become spirit; it becomes flesh.

Maybe I should not be too surprised. The Incarnation is about redemption and redemption is really about the flesh. The biblical story never turns its back on the flesh. The hope is that "the glory of God shall be revealed, and all flesh shall see it together" (Isa 40:5*a*). The prophetic hope is not just that human flesh shall be redeemed but: "The wolf shall live with the lamb, the leopard shall lie down with the kid, the calf and the lion and the fatling together, and a little child shall lead them" (Isa 11:6). So the Word becomes flesh and in so doing lifts all flesh from darkness to light, from death to life. The flesh is not a prison from which we are to escape but the creation, which was redeemed when "the Word became flesh." It is the fulfillment of the messianic hope.

So when the "Word becomes flesh," we can never again see humans simply as workers, or parents, genes, enemies, or friends. Now all flesh is more than flesh. All flesh is colored with eternity. All flesh now smells of everlasting life. We can never again see creation, all things bright and beautiful, as destined to a cold and dark and dead universe. "The light shines in the darkness and the darkness did not overcome it."

Not only am I surprised but embarrassed by this text. "The Word became flesh and dwelt among us."

We adorn flesh with beautiful colors and jewelry. We mold our flesh with diet and exercise and surgery. We struggle against the wrinkles and the aches. We may believe, "all flesh shall see the glory of God," but we know all flesh dies. The psalmist had it right, "For he knows how we are made, he remembers that we are dust. As for mortals, their days are like grass; they flourish like a flower of the field for the wind passes over it and it is gone" (Ps 103:14-16a). The glorious *Logos* becomes vulnerable to all the corruption of the flesh. The Word became death for us. That's more than we asked for. Maybe we can accept "the Word became friendly" or "the Word became supportive," but "the Word became flesh"—that is an embarrassment. We can never see the eternal, the almighty God as a two-fisted bully who threatens the faithful, tramples on the disobedient and destroys the enemy. The Word becomes flesh, the eternal is marked by death, Jesus Christ became sin for us. "For our sakes he made him to be sin, who knew no sin" (2 Cor 5:21a). That's embarrassing.

"The Word became flesh and lived among us." That's embarrassing. We are really more comfortable with a friendly visitor who drops in at special holidays or festivals or maybe at Holy Communion and baptism, but to live among us, that is more than we expect. Living among us is a little too close for comfort. That is a little more intimate than we want. That's embarrassing.

John keeps pushing all the right buttons. It is as if he is writing to us, for our time. He won't leave us any leeway. He continues, "and we have seen his glory, the glory as of a father's only son, full of grace and truth." It is fashionable in our time of inclusivity to glorify our ignorance of God. We like to claim God knows us but we don't really know God. We like to be modest in our confession and limited in our affirmations. It is a time when we glory in our openness to other wisdom. But John has a holy boldness. He has seen the glory of the Son and witnesses to that glory. What an embarrassment for John to proclaim. Unless we see God's glory in the suffering and death, the vulnerability and the powerless and humiliation of the Son, we will never see God. The glory "of the father's only son, full of grace and truth," is revealed in the face of Jesus Christ hanging on the cross. There is no room for a victorious cross. The king we crown is the lamb upon the tree. That's embarrassing in an age that loves success, longs for acceptance and denies death.

We believe this surprising and embarrassing text. Frederick Trost believes "the Word became flesh." He believes and lives it. In the summer of 1968, a time when our nation was deeply divided over the war in Vietnam, the Democratic Party held its national convention in the city of Chicago where I was serving along with Frederick at St. Pauls United Church of Christ. Along with the party delegates who came to nominate Hubert Humphrey for president, came thousands of youths who wanted to disrupt the convention and stop the war. The members of the Democratic Party were welcomed in our city as responsible Americans; the youth were pictured as arrogant, violent disrupters of the democratic process. They were the enemy of the good people of Chicago, and they were treated as an enemy. They were hounded from parks, to streets, to alleys. They were rejected, beaten, and abandoned. Youth who knew loving, caring families and communities were shocked and defeated by a brutal showing of police power. Most institutions and people in the city closed their doors, locked their gates, and turned their backs on the army of youth.

Pastor Trost witnessed the hounding, the beating, and the rejection. Yet he saw not enemy but the suffering flesh, the suffering Lord Jesus. Without counting the cost or planning the act, he opened the doors of St. Pauls Church to the youth. The word went out, "welcome in the name of Jesus Christ the one who suffers with you." The word went out to youth who seldom came to church in those days. The word spread without any help from the media. The youth came. They came by the hundreds; they came and were welcome. They came and slept in the gym, the classrooms, and the halls. The showers and the toilets never stopped running.

Frederick, who was not into planning in those days, decided we ought to offer some bread to the multitude of youth. So we went to the local restaurants on the north side of Chicago and asked for leftovers to feed the youth. The response was generous. Then the German Women's Society of St. Pauls was called to help serve. The breakfast menu was weird: gourmet soup and desserts, day-old salad and bread. The hospitably was warm, the women saw their grandchildren in the faces of the youth. They worried about the bruises, the bandages. You could hear loving words of concern, "How are you feeling today?" "Did you call your parents last night?" "You ought to have someone look at that cut."

For Frederick, who believes "the Word became flesh," ministry has a fleshy smell. Word and sacrament are mingled with breaking bread and binding wounds, flushing toilets, and running showers, with justice and peace. Yet if he remembers the good works, all the ministries of justice and peace he has accomplished in Wisconsin and Europe and Latin America, the "tempter" will come to him at night in his retirement community and say, "What a good job you did Fred, but you could have done more." The "tempter" will be so caring and understanding, "You did all you could Fred, but look: the poor and oppressed still suffer. Is there really a God who loves the world?"

But if Frederick Trost can see his good works as filthy rags before the glory of God, if he, and we, can remember that the world has been redeemed not though our good deeds but because the "Word became flesh and lived among us," then he, and maybe we, will stab the "tempter" in the heart with the words of this surprising and embarrassing text and witness with joy to the "Word become flesh," and declare with boldness "we have seen his glory, the glory as of a father's only son, full of grace and truth."

Pass Along the Faith

Deborah Rahn Clemens

In 1995, a working group of United Church of Christ pastors serving in Pennsylvania accepted the challenge of asking questions about the faith professed by Christians and attempted to refine their answers in contemporary language. Since, for centuries, primers or catechisms have been used to help teach newcomers to Christianity the meaning of such articles of faith as the Apostles' Creed, the Ten Commandments, and the Lord's Prayer, this challenge was undertaken with resolve and joy. The project is nearing completion. Several of the questions and responses included in this project follow as an illustration of the efforts of the working group. Encouraging pastors with such experiments has consistently been one of the marks of Frederick Trost's ministry, for which our working group is grateful.

What is the faith by which we live and die?

(A) The Christian faith into which we are baptized, the faith of the one holy catholic and apostolic church: that God came in Jesus Christ to save us from sin, evil, and death, so that by the Holy Spirit we might love the Lord and serve the world.

Why is this faith necessary for life and for death?

(A) Because in both life and in death we are comforted in knowing that we do not belong to ourselves, but to Jesus Christ.

Where do we meet this Jesus Christ?

(A) We meet Christ in the Holy Scriptures of the Old and New Testament; in the sacraments and traditions of the holy catholic church expressed in the ecumenical creeds and confessed by the Protestant Reformers; and in worship, where the community of the faithful strives to make the faith its own.

How do we affirm God in Jesus Christ?

(A) We believe that Jesus is God's Son, perfectly one with the Father and with the Holy Spirit. We believe that Jesus is God incarnate, which means that at a particular moment in time God came to us as a human being, a Jewish man. We worship Christ. We pray in Jesus' name. We baptize into his life, death, and resurrection, and we are fed by him in communion.

Who is the person we call Jesus Christ?

(A) Peter boldly proclaimed to Jesus: "You are the Messiah, the Son of the Living God." With Peter we affirm Jesus as the Christ, the one who comes to save. Jesus came to the sinner and the outcast, the despised and abandoned in order to show that no one is beyond the love and saving power of God.

How do we affirm the unity of Christ?

(A) We affirm the unity of Christ by saying he is fully human and fully divine. Just as a parent is fully parent but also fully a child, these aspects are distinguishable but not divisible.

What did Jesus accomplish?

(A) Through his life and ministry, Jesus announced in word and deed the new reality of God's rule in the world and showed God's love. Through his death and resurrection, Christ saved the world from sin and death thus making us one with him. By ascending into heaven, our Lord reigns with God eternally.

What does it mean to be God's only Son?

(A) Christ is one with God, the Word of God, like none other. This describes his relationship to the Father from eternity.

What does it mean to say Jesus is our Lord?

(A) The confession that Jesus is our Lord is central to what it means to be Christian. He is the one in charge. Our Messiah is both commander and liberator. Our Sovereign is possessor, protector, and servant of all. We, whose very lives have been preserved through his life, owe our allegiance to him.

Over whom or what is Jesus Lord?

(A) Christ is Lord over the church, the human race, the world, the universe. He is Lord whether we know it or not, like it or not, accept it or not. To call him Lord is to give to him our trust, submission, obedience, love and hope. When we call Jesus Lord, we are freed from all earthly powers and are freed to serve as Jesus served.

Discipleship and the Church's Struggle for Justice and Peace

Richard D. Crane

The United Church of Christ Statement of Faith affirms that God has promised to all who trust him courage in the struggle for justice and peace. This statement also upholds the centrality of Christ in its identification of God as the God of our Savior Jesus Christ.[1] How are these two affirmations related? How is the struggle for justice and peace authorized by Jesus Christ?

The scholars associated with the most recent quest for the historical Jesus suggest that we must get behind the text in order to discover the Jesus with significance for matters of social and political justice. For example, Marcus Borg contends that it is historical scholarship that keeps alive Jesus' liberating memory as one who provocatively and courageously opposed the systems of domination and injustice of his day. This quest to discover the Jesus behind the text, however, is often accompanied by the theological judgment that the identification of Jesus as the divine Son of God by the canonical Gospels is a fundamental betrayal of the message and vision of the "historical" Jesus, a teacher of subversive wisdom who challenged the existing social order, based upon an *ethos* of holiness, and advocated an alternative one based on compassion. These scholars would have us believe that there are only two alternatives. One must either jettison the church's historic confession that Jesus Christ is the divine Son of God or one must embrace the naive but "popular image" of Jesus of Nazareth as an a-political, docetic figure whose message was about himself, the saving purposes of his death, and the importance of believing in him. In this brief essay, I cannot offer a thorough evaluation of the methods, assumptions, and agenda of the most recent quest for the historical Jesus. My point of departure will be that of challenging the rhetorical strategy represented by this stark either/or.[2]

Themes within Hans Frei's theology provide resources for the development of an ethic of discipleship which displays passionate concern for the poor and the vulnerable of this world while simultaneously embracing the church's historic confession that Jesus Christ is fully human and fully divine. This proposal can only be presented in a suggestive rather than comprehensive fashion. My goal is simply to present the outlines of a theology of discipleship that is based upon the canonical Gospels' witness to and identification of Jesus Christ.[3]

In *The Identity of Jesus Christ*, Hans Frei repudiates the liberal theological tradition's anthropological starting point for christology. In Frei's judgment, this leads to a construal of the Gospel narratives as religious myths and symbols which re-present and evoke an existential stance or possibility for authentic existence that is discernible by reason alone. On this approach, the subject matter of these texts is not Jesus Christ in his particularity as savior but rather a general anthropological possibility that Jesus instantiates in an exemplary fashion.[4]

Frei insisted that the literary genre of the Gospels most resembles that of realistic narrative, which depicts the inextricable mutual involvement of specific, unsubstitutable chains of events with equally specific individuals and renders personal identity in its unsubstitutability. Frei's central theological claim is that "what may be categorized as a high christology" is the logical implication of coming to terms with the Gospels' character as narratives. Their literary structure is sufficiently novel-like, he argued, that Jesus' universal redemptive significance is indissolubly connected with his own unsubstitutable personal identity. According to Frei's formal statement of the identity of Jesus Christ, "he is the man from Nazareth who redeemed humanity by his helplessness, in perfect obedience to God, enacting their good on their behalf. As that same one, he was raised from the dead and manifested to be the redeemer." Jesus' identity is most fully depicted in his resurrection appearances, where the unity of the unsubstitutable individuality of Jesus with the presence and action of God is made manifest.[5]

A second theme is Frei's affirmation that the church, through the Holy Spirit, is the public and communal form taken by the indirect presence of the risen Christ in the world. On this basis, he maintains that the identity-description of Jesus Christ applies, in an analogous fashion, to the church as the collective disciple of Christ. The church can never be a complete reiteration of Christ's identity since the enactment of the good of humanity on their behalf has already been done once and for all by Jesus on the cross. The church's task is to follow, albeit imperfectly and in different historical and cultural contexts, the identifiable patterns of behavior, such as innocent suffering and "serving rather than being served," embodied by Jesus Christ.[6]

A third consideration is Frei's account of the relation between doctrinal formulations and theological statements, on the one hand, and the biblical narratives on the other. For example, Frei endorsed the Chalcedonian definition of Jesus Christ as a faithful conceptual re-description of the logic implicit within the Gospel narratives and other New Testament writings. However, he insisted that the doctrine is not the meaning of the story but rather should function as a heuristic aid that thrusts the reader back into the stories themselves.[7] The same principle is applicable to Frei's formal statement of the identity of Jesus Christ that we encountered earlier. This statement would be a rather thin abstraction if it did not function to encourage a meticulous reading of each Gospel's storied sequence on the premise that all of Jesus' narrated words and deeds are ingredients in the cumulative rendering of his identity for the Christian community. For example, the Gospel of Matthew identifies Jesus as the Son of God who enacts his Father's intention to save his people from their sins (1:21). But it is also crucial to attend to his teachings (e.g., the Sermon on the Mount), proclamation of the dawning of the Kingdom of Heaven, healings and demon expulsions, fellowship meals with social outcasts, and prophetic denunciations of the religious leaders for their greed, injustice, and neglect of mercy (chap. 23) as ingredients in the identification of Jesus as God's Son who saves his people.

Though it is not possible to survey current New Testament scholarship or to present the careful exegetical analysis needed to make the case that the identification and characterization of Jesus Christ on the level of the narratives themselves[8] provide a theological rationale for a practice of ecclesial discipleship that is concerned with social justice for the poor, the marginalized, and the mistreated of our world, we can make some tentative suggestions. The crucial assumption is not that these narratives are, in every instance, accurate factual reports but rather that these stories provide a faithful depiction of Jesus' identity and character.[9]

1. Jesus displays extraordinary concern and compassion for the outcast and marginalized. Examples include his table fellowship with tax collectors and sinners, and his violation of purity regulations in order to touch and heal those considered to be ritually impure (1:40-42; 5:21-43).

2. The point of Jesus' mighty acts of power was to deliver human persons from bondage and suffering. Edward Schillebeeckx contends that Jesus' mighty acts should be interpreted in relation to the field of understanding centered in the power of the "evil one" as over against the power of God. In Jesus' culture, illness and suffering were indications that the world is in the stranglehold of the "evil one." Jesus' ministry of healing illness and expelling unclean or evil spirits is interpreted as an assault upon the stronghold of the evil one (Mt 12:22-29; Mk 1:23-24; Lk 11:14-23). The dawning of God's kingdom or the messianic age becomes visible in Jesus' person through his deliverance of human persons (Mt 11:2-6) and victory over the powers of evil that oppress and damage human lives. Jesus is on the side of human wholeness.[10]

3. Jesus opposed the authorities in his society when their practices were antithetical to human wholeness. His repudiation of the dominant *ethos* of purity, which functioned to exclude most of the common people from the circle of those considered to be righteous, in favor of the priority of compassion, which is so important to Marcus Borg's reconstruction of the Jesus of history,[11] is evident on the level of the narratives themselves. This is exemplified in his healings on the Sabbath (Mk 3:1-6; Lk 13:10-17) and the parable of the Good Samaritan (Lk 10:25-37). His opposition to injustice is evident in his critique of the Pharisees and scribes for their status-driven behavior, their greed, and their economic exploitation of widows, who were the vulnerable in that society (Mt 23; Mk 12:38-40). One might also point to the cleansing of the Temple, which is interpreted by most New Testament scholars as a prophetic denunciation of the Sadducean establishment.

This ethic of ecclesial discipleship would maintain that the church's mission and identity are derived from and should display continuity with Jesus' own ministry of delivering human persons from bondage and suffering, of including those who are excluded and marginalized, and opposing unjust social, political, and economic arrangements when these exercise a destructive impact upon human lives. Many voices contend that the doctrinal attribution of divinity to Jesus leads either to a fundamentalism in which the Christian life consists primarily of believing that Jesus is one's personal savior or to a portrayal of Jesus as the cosmic *pantocrator* who is patron and protector of the empire or some other unjust *status quo*. I would argue, however, that the traditional Christian assertion that Jesus is God's Word incarnate, combined with careful attention to these themes within the synoptic narratives, provides the theological rationale for the church's commitment to the struggle to break chains of bondage, meet human need, and challenge economic and political arrangements that condemn millions of human beings to lives of devastating poverty and dehumanizing conditions.

John Milbank contends that the doctrinal attribution of a final perfection to Jesus is meant to re-direct our attention to, rather than away from, these narratives, which display the shape of Jesus' life and death as a pattern to be imitated within the context of our communal life as the body of Christ. The implication of the church's confession that Jesus Christ is the risen Lord and incarnate Word of God is that his teachings, practices, and the characteristic patterns of his life, as depicted in the New Testament, have supreme authority for the life of the Christian community.

Of course, an adequate ethic of discipleship can only be fully developed in connection with a comprehensive theological vision. In these final paragraphs, I will demonstrate the importance of such connections. First, an ethic of discipleship should not be understood in a Pelagian fashion as an ethic of heroic human moral achievement that would undercut the church's proclamation that a right relationship with God is a gift of divine grace. One corrective resource is Glen Stassen's exegetical analysis of the Sermon on the Mount. Stassen insists that an ethic of discipleship based upon Matthew 5–7 is not about human striving for high moral ideals but is about the gracious deliverance that God is accomplishing through Jesus Christ and God's invitation to us to participate in God's gracious processes of deliverance from every form of bondage.[12]

Secondly, it is urgent that an ethic of discipleship avoid a "Constantinian" identification of God's cause with any particular political agenda, party, or movement. In opposition to the notion that the church is charged with the task of constructing the Kingdom of God on earth, Frei encouraged a genuine modesty by reminding us that it is God who is actively governing the course of human history, which is providentially ordered in the life, death, and resurrection of Jesus Christ. Frei maintained that there is a mysterious unity between Christ's presence in the Holy Spirit to the church in Word and sacrament, and Christ's presence in and to the events of human history, which is moving toward consummation in Christ.

God's providence is ultimately mysterious and coexistent with the contingency of events. There is no mathematical formula to calculate how God is at work in human events. Frei believed, however, that we can discern faint traces of God's action when the Bible's identification of Jesus Christ provides the church with an interpretive framework for making sense of human events. For example, Frei spoke of the pattern supremely embodied by Jesus' suffering and death on the cross as that of the innocent suffering on behalf of the guilty in order to bring about reconciliation.[13] Though Jesus' death was a once-for-all unsubstitutable event, Frei argued that God's presence can be discerned in those historical events in which analogous performances of this pattern lead us to long for an as-yet-unfulfilled hope for reconciliation, redemption, and resurrection. As an example, Frei claimed that this pattern was discernible in the sufferings of persons struggling for racial justice in the American Civil Rights movement. One might add that Jesus' identification with the marginalized, the vulnerable, those who were desperate, poor, and sick provides a particularly powerful clue about those persons for whom the church should be most concerned in its ministries of service and political advocacy. Such discernment can allow us to catch a faint glimpse of God's activity in our world and to guide Christian judgments about participation in particular struggles for social change.

M.A. Higton points out that Frei believed that the church's involvement in the world should take the form of a tentative discernment of the movements of God's Spirit in human events and a responding co-operation with those movements. The church searches for the presence of Christ prevenient in the world and on that basis, hopes for a temporary design of fitness between God's action and the church's action in the world. He described the church's style of political engagement as pragmatic and provisional, involving the making of temporary, *ad hoc* alliances between Christians and others in order to promote the greatest imperfect good, with the least possible bloodshed and violence, within particular social and political contexts.[14]

The ethic of discipleship we have suggested is one that affirms, with the Barmen Declaration, that *"Jesus Christ, as he is attested in Holy Scripture*, is the one Word of God."[15]

Notes

1. "United Church of Christ Statement of Faith," in *Book of Worship: United Church of Christ* (New York: United Church of Christ Office for Church Life and Leadership, 1986), 512.

2. Like Luke Timothy Johnson, I am not sympathetic to the claim that the historical reconstructions offered by Marcus Borg, John Dominic Crossan, and others, provide such a fundamental critique of Christian faith that the church must reexamine its creeds. Luke Timothy Johnson, *The Real Jesus: The Misguided Quest for the Historical Jesus and the Truth of the Traditional Gospels* (San Francisco: HarperCollins, 1996); Marcus J. Borg, *Jesus: A New Vision: Spirit, Culture, and the Life of Discipleship* (San Francisco: Harper & Row, Publishers, 1987; idem., *Jesus in Contemporary Scholarship* (Valley Forge, Penn.: Trinity Press International, 1994), 193-96; Robert W. Funk, *Honest to Jesus: Jesus for a New Millennium* (San Francisco: HarperSanFrancisco).

3. The case to be made in this essay is developed in much further detail in my as yet unpublished dissertation, "The Public and Political Character of Postliberal Theology." M.A. Higton has also written on Hans Frei's incipient political theology. I discovered Higton's essay after I had completed the penultimate draft of my dissertation. M. A. Higton, "'A Carefully Circumscribed Progressive Politics': Hans Frei's Political Theology," *Modern Theology* 15:1 (January 1999): 55-83.

4. One example of the position criticized by Frei is David Tracy's appropriation of Paul Ricoeur's phenomenological hermeneutics. Tracy identifies the principle referent disclosed by the Gospel stories and their limit-language as the disclosure of a certain limit-mode-of-being-in-the world, a new and agapic, self-sacrificing righteousness. Frei contends that for Tracy, Jesus is not the primary referent, nor he is construed as the subject of his own predicates. His status in the texts is reduced to that of exemplification of a generalized set of attitudes or an existential stance that is re-presented as a life possibility for the reader to appropriate for himself or herself. It is important to point out that Frei's critique was based upon *Blessed Rage for Order* and therefore, has not taken into account his later christological reflections. David Tracy, *Blessed Rage for Order: The New Pluralism in Theology* (New York: Seabury Press, 1975), 221; Hans W. Frei, "The 'Literal Reading' of Biblical Narrative in the Christian Tradition," in *Theology and Narrative: Selected Essays*, eds., George Hunsinger and William C. Placher, (Oxford and New York: Oxford University Press, 1993), 127-28. Hans W. Frei, *The Identity of Jesus Christ: The Hermeneutical Bases of Dogmatic Theology*, (Philadelphia: Fortress Press, 1975), 126, 136-40.

5. Frei, *The Identity of Jesus Christ*, viii.-ix., 12, 41-45, 49, 60, 87-94, 102-103, 114, 140-54.

6. Ibid., 157-60; John Milbank, *Theology and Social Theory: Beyond Secular Reason* (Oxford: Basil Blackwell, 1990), 396.

7. Frei, *Types of Christian Theology*, 126.

8. This claim does not entail a denial of the importance of historical-critical scholarship, as well as other tools of analysis, for providing vitally important insight into the historical and cultural contexts in which biblical texts were written and the events which they narrate. For example, knowledge of the political realities of first century Palestine under Roman rule enables us to understand the meaning of Jesus' admonition to "go the second mile" (Mt 5:41-42), just as historical information about the various movements within first century Palestinian Judaism shed light upon the narrated conflicts between Jesus and some of the Pharisees and Sadducees.

9. Emphasis on the realistic character of the synoptic Gospel narratives was not a retreat from the difficult issues raised by historical-critical scholarship. Frei distinguished between descriptive realism at the level of the narrative and the pre-critical notion that the Gospels are accurate reports of historical facts. Since it is Jesus' relation to God that identifies him, he argued, the interpretive category of factuality is inadequate for the

specification of this relationship. In agreement with Karl Barth, Frei maintained that the Gospels are not sources but testimonies. Frei was skeptical about the historian's, as opposed to the evangelist's, capacity to generate a character portrait of Jesus. Though he did not develop a systematic theology of revelation, Frei held that the biblical narratives are our sole epistemic access to God's revelation in Christ. They do not refer to a reality that is independently accessible to human reason or experience, but themselves render this reality to the reader by the Holy Spirit.

On the other hand, Frei believed that the biblical narratives have a loose and unsure connection with historical actuality. There are points in the Gospel narratives, such as the central events of Jesus' crucifixion and resurrection, where the logic of the story forces us to affirm that it matters greatly whether or not the event actually occurred. William Placher, one of Frei's students, contends that the integrity of the Christian faith is dependent upon the "essential correctness" of these narratives' depiction of Jesus' identity and character. Only the internal logic of the story itself provides the basis for determining which historical claims are essential to the truthfulness of these narratives' rendering of Jesus' identity. For example, one might conclude that skepticism about the historicity of the account in which Jesus told Peter that he could find a coin to pay the temple tax inside the mouth of the first fish he would catch (Matthew 17:24-27) does not undermine the integrity of the faith. But if Jesus had been dragged kicking and screaming to the cross, the Gospels' would indeed be an untruthful rendering of Jesus' personal identity. Hans W. Frei, *The Eclipse of Biblical Narrative: A Study in Eighteenth and Nineteenth Century Hermeneutics*, (New Haven, Conn.: Yale University Press, 1974), 12, 72-85, 119-20, 131-38, 150-51, 155-56, 307; idem., *Types of Christian Theology*, (New Haven, Conn.: Yale University Press, 1992): 80-91, 135-39; idem., "Response to 'Narrative Theology: An Evangelical Appraisal,'" in *Theology and Narrative*, 209-11; idem., "Theology and the Interpretation of Narrative," in *Theology and Narrative*, 102-103, 110-12; idem., "Conflicts in Interpretation: Resolution, Armistice, or Co-Existence?," in *Theology and Narrative*, 162-66; William C. Placher, *Narratives of a Vulnerable God: Christ, Theology, and Scripture*, (Louisville: Westminster John Knox Press, 1994), 95-96.

10. Edward Schillebeeckx, *Jesus: An Experiment in Christology*, (New York: Crossroad, 1987): 183-89.

11. Borg, *Jesus in Contemporary Scholarship*, 194-96.

12. Glen H. Stassen, *Just Peacemaking: Transforming Initiatives for Justice and Peace*, (Louisville: Westminster/John Knox Press, 1992): 39-

43, 190-91.

13. Frei identified the pattern discernible in the suffering and death of the innocent Jesus on behalf of the guilty, in order to bring about reconciliation with God, as "the pattern of union through the agonized exchange of opposites." Hans W. Frei, "H. Richard Niebuhr on History, Church, and Nation," in *Theology and Narrative*, 226, 230-33; idem., *The Identity of Jesus Christ*, 157-64.

14. Frei, *The Identity of Jesus Christ*, 157-64; Higton, "'A Carefully Circumscribed Progressive Politics,'" 71, 76-77, 79, n.2, 82, n.52 and n.53.

15. "Theological Declaration Concerning the Present Situation of the German Evangelical Church," in *The Declarations, Resolutions, and Motions Adopted by the Synod of Barmen, May 29-31, 1934*.

"Eternal God, Divine Mystery beyond Our Knowing"

Eternal God, divine mystery beyond our knowing, you call us to seek you with all our hearts. You have made us in your own image and placed within us a longing for fulness of life in communion with you. Although we have rebelled against you from the days of Adam and Eve, our first parents, until the present day, you have not abandoned us to our own ways. In the garden of your world, created and sustained by your Word of life and still expanding beyond the stars, you reign in gentle power as creation itself yearns for its healing and redemption.

We rejoice that your Word, eternally begotten from your own being, became flesh and was born of our sister, Mary, by the ministry of your Holy Spirit, and embraced our human condition. In this child of Bethlehem, who suffered, died and was raised for our sake, we celebrate your trustworthy and sovereign Word who alone leads us to your eternal embrace.

In a world continually tempted by the empty enchantments of self-centeredness and injustice, we ask you to make us the body of Christ, the church, a witness to your grace and peace. With the faithful in all times and places we praise you, unbegotten God, in the community of the Holy Trinity where, with Jesus Christ the Word and the Holy Spirit, you forever call us to choose life with you.

Thomas E. Dipko

Christ the Center

Kathryn Greene-McCreight

What does it mean for us to confess Christ as the Center? Does it mean that Christ is the focus of our worship? That Christ is the subject matter of our proclamation? That it is Christ who calls the church into being? That the love of Christ guides the inquiry we call theology? Certainly all of these are true and more. It is also true that Frederick Trost struggles to witness in his life and ministry to these truths of Christ as the center of the church's mission and witness. We also know how for Pastor Trost confessing Christ as the Center never meant a refusal to tend to the wounds of the world around him but by definition called him into works of love and reconciliation. I will seek then, in honor of Pastor Trost and of his ministry, to explicate what it might mean to confess Christ as the Center while keeping ever mindful of the connection between Christ and creation. I will do so with the help of Karl Barth, in particular his comments in his Church Dogmatics volume 3.1, in his material on the Doctrine of Creation. My hope is that through this section of Barth's Doctrine of Creation, in particular those subsections in 3.1 par. 41 which he entitles "Creation as the External Basis of the Covenant," and "Covenant as the Internal Basis of Creation," we might find the integral relation between Christ as the Center of our proclamation and the world as its inseparable yet distinct external basis.

Barth begins this section on creation and covenant with the statement that creation comes first in the works of the triune God and as such makes possible the history of God's covenant with humanity. For Barth creation is not simply the beginning of time, but it is the beginning of the covenant of grace itself. That covenant has its beginning, center, and goal in Jesus Christ. Creation, as the external basis of this covenant, is the "presupposition of the realization of the divine purpose of love in relation to the creature" (96). It is not a question of creation being the prototype of creaturely love but of divine love, which itself is the "inaccessible prototype and true basis of all creaturely love." Creation is itself the external basis of this covenant of divine love because it is a creation by God who chooses the creature as covenant partner. There is no external basis to this covenant except that wrought by God's activity in creation. Creation and redemption are therefore inseparably linked, even though they are not identical and indeed are non-negotiably distinct. This point is behind the debate between Barth and Brunner, to name only one example of Barth's refusal to allide creation and covenant of grace.

Creation is the external basis of the covenant of grace, or the bare datum of the existence of the creature with whom God in love has chosen to bring into covenant. This work of creation is God's and God's alone, and there is no external basis to this covenant other than that posited by God. The external basis of the covenant, God's activity in creation, means that the covenant partner is not the subject of another lord but God's property alone. This covenant cannot therefore be threatened in any serious way, for by its very creation the creature is destined for this covenant with God.

Creation is therefore the external basis of the covenant of grace. Barth is quick to point out that creation is not the internal basis of the covenant. Rather, the internal basis of the covenant is "simply the free love of God, or more precisely the eternal covenant which God has decreed in Himself as the covenant of the Father with his Son as the Lord and Bearer of human nature, and to that extent of the Representative of all creation" (97). As the external basis of the covenant, creation makes the covenant technically possible insofar as it establishes the sphere of creation and with it God's covenant partner in this sphere. This means that the "love of God could not be satisfied with the eternal covenant as such . . . [which] made necessary the existence and being of the creature and therefore of creation."

Barth shows how the first creation story, that is the first in canonical order, Gen 1:1-2:4a, develops this aspect of creation as the external basis of the covenant: "It describes creation as it were externally as the work of powerful but thoroughly planned and thought-out and perfectly supervised preparation, comparable to the building of a temple" (98). What will finally crown the narrative here is the creation of the partner for the man and ultimately the Sabbath rest of God, which signals the accomplishment of creation. "Rightly to understand this passage is to read it backwards" (99), insofar as everything leading up to this Sabbath joy points to this last event. As the climax of the passage is God's Sabbath rest and joy, Barth sees creation to be the "irruption and revelation of the divine compassion" (110). The creation itself holds the good news of the covenant of grace.

With this idea of the whole tending to the Sabbath, the seventh day, and reading the narrative backwards, Barth then reads the narrative "from the top" while holding in mind its goal, and turns to the first word of the Bible, *bereshith*, commonly translated as "in the beginning." Barth notes that this history has a beginning, unlike God, and as such, unlike God, also tends toward an end. The first word of the Bible promises an end, an end that transcends and yet is contained by and prefigured by God's Sabbath rest. Barth notes that there is an "indisputable literary connection" (100) between the beginning and the end of this creation account, Gen 1:1 and 2:4a, in part because both refer to "the heavens and the earth." It is the works of the divine *bara* which are the *toledoth*, the "generations of the heaven and of the earth." Both verses insist on creation as being the free and gracious act of God, not a birthing from godself as is usually the case in myth. Both are bookends to the first creation account, the first pointing toward the creation, the second drawing the account to a close.

The freedom of God displayed in the account is like, says Barth, that in Gen 6:5 in the Noah story in which God repents of making creation. The fact that God can repent of making humanity and the world points to God's distinction from the world and from the creature: "while it is not ungodly, [it] is not divine, so that to posit it at all is undoubtably a risk, since it is to posit a freedom which is distinct from the freedom of God" (109). This is the very risk that God took on in creating the world and the human creature in it. But as the author of creation rather than its mother, God's own freedom encloses the freedom of the creature such that freedom to do ill is not freedom at all but slavery. Commenting on Gen 1:3, "and God said," Barth says that the human creature may choose to deny this creative word, the very presupposition of his own existence, but doing so cannot "remove or abrogate it" (111). And any attempt at denying the word is to deny our own nature and existence.

The depiction of God's creating by speaking rules out any idea that the creature participates in creation or that the creation comes into being on its own or indeed, that creation emerges from the divinity itself as is assumed in myth. Creation itself is brought about by the command of God and as such hangs on that word. This emphasis on the divine utterance is unique among the creation accounts of the Ancient Near East and is the feature that is noted throughout the Bible, e.g. Ps 33:6ff: "By the word of the LORD the heavens were made." God's speech precedes all of creation, and as the Word is one with God. The Word is therefore not a creature but as speech is active in creation as one with God. And it is as speech, as Word made creature, that God communicates God's will for partnership with the creature.

And, says Barth, it is no accident that "the creative utterance at the creation of man in Gen 1:26 is described as a divine soliloquy: 'Let us make man'" (111). He notes that this divine soliloquy is a "consultation as though between several divine counselors, and a divine decision resting upon it" (182). He notices that the creative fiat is not directed toward any element of creation but rather inwards, "Let us," and as such is a "summons to intradivine unanimity of intention and decision." While traditionally this has been a locus for interpreters to read "into" the biblical text the Trinity in the "royal we," Barth is much more subtle. Without actually saying "This speaks of the Trinity," Barth says "What emerges characteristically at this point is the connexion between the *opus ad extra* and the *opus ad intra* which proceeds it; i.e., that God remains in Himself at the very time when in His utterance He proceeds out of Himself or vice versa, that the utterance of His Word signifies the execution of His inner decree" (112). God in his creative act is for his creation.

This inherent relatedness of God to the creature is not drawn simply from this one phrase. Barth continues to say that "'in our image' means to be created as a being which has its ground and possibility in the fact that in 'us,' i.e. in God's own sphere and being, there exists a divine and therefore self-grounded prototype to which this being can correspond" (183). That the creature should have this protype in God is a radical statement. Barth does not leave it there: "[T]he other phrase: 'In our likeness' means to be created as a being whose nature is decisively characterised by the fact that although it is created by God it is not a new nature to the extent that it has a pattern in the nature of God Himself" (184). And this is true only of humanity, not of the rest of creation, since it is humanity of whom it is said to be created in the image and likeness of God. The rest of creation, says Barth, participates secondarily in this image insofar as it finds its conclusion in this climax of all creation.

For Barth, the rest of creation stands as "something other than God" and "not of a counterpart." Indeed, Barth says that the human creature forms a "Thou" to God's "I" which no other creature can. This is, of course, where Barth speaks about the image of God, noting that the text says nothing to give us the impression that the image corresponds to any quality in humanity, either its moral or intellectual capacities. Rather, according to Barth, the image of God is in the relatedness of the human, male and female. Humanity is created in the image of God, male and female: humanity is "this being in differentiation and relationship, and therefore in natural fellowship with God" (185). This is not merely a statement about humanity as created here on the sixth day but itself forms a prototype of the yet-to-come: "The fact that he was created man and woman will be the great paradigm of everything that is to take place between him and God, and also of everything that is to take place between him and his fellows. The fact that he was created and exists as male and female will also prove to be not only a copy and imitation of his Creator as such but at the same time a type of history of the covenant and salvation which will take place between him and his Creator" (186). That a creature, namely humanity, could be allowed such an honor and play such a role is breathtaking. However, Barth is careful to say that there is "no question of anything more than an analogy" (196) and again "the *analogia relationis* as the meaning of the divine likeness cannot be equated with an *analogia entis*" (915). Here we see clearly how creation is the external basis of the covenant, insofar as creation holds the type of the covenant, and how creation and covenant are distinct, insofar as there can be no question of an *analogia entis*, a likeness in terms of being. There can only be an *analogia relationis*, a likeness in terms of relation.

After examining creation as the external basis of the covenant, Barth turns to consider the covenant as the internal basis of creation. His first point is that according to the text, the creature exists meaningfully; it has not come about as if by chance but as a purposed act of the Creator God. The act of creation is therefore "the revelation of the glory of God by which He gives to the creature meaning and necessity" (230). The creature was created in order to be the recipient of God's glory, in order to be a grateful being in thanks to God the Creator. Creation is thus the "formal presupposition of the covenant in which God fulfils the will of His free love" (230-231). This then is the external basis of creation, as we have seen. But creation's internal basis is that very covenant: "What God created when he created the world and man was not just any place, but that which was foreordained for the establishment and the history of the covenant" (231). The covenant in Christ is thus the goal of creation, not added on as an afterthought. The covenant of grace already characterises creation as such, as creation from God's own will to be in communion with the creature. Creation was therefore the formal presupposition of the covenant, and the covenant is the material presupposition of creation.

Barth says that no substantive difference exists between creation as the formal presupposition of the covenant and the covenant as material presupposition of creation. The one difference that does pertain is "in the respect of the direction and dimension in which it is considered" (232). In fact, Barth does not merely want to link creation and covenant in an external or material way alone; he sees creation as prefiguring the covenant and so turns to the second creation story, Gen 2:4*b*-25. This he calls a "history of creation from the inside" (232) with "an essential foreshortening of the teleology of the first" (233). While the first creation account was "prophetical" the second is "sacramental." The history of creation in Gen 2, by its sequel of the story of the disobedience in the garden, points to the history of the covenant, which begins when the human is disobedient and bears the consequences even while God remains faithful and controls the fallout of that disobedience. This creation account therefore is the "sign and witness of the event which will follow (234)." The very fact that the human is given freedom indicates the covenant, for the "freedom to obey is the sign of the fellowship already established by God and man at his creation" (264).

Again, the covenant is indicated in the very locus of the Garden of Eden. With its impossible geography at least one thing can be said, according to Barth, and that is that Eden is not the promised land. Rather, it is singled out as a "well-watered Garden," the dwelling for the first creatures, just as the land of Canaan, the land flowing with milk and honey, is singled out for the dwelling of Israel. The narrative tells us, according to Barth, that God's choice of the Holy Land for his people is not a coincidence but was "deeply embedded" in the world called forth in this narrative: "that this 'holy' land already had its prototype in God's creative act establishing all things; indeed, that the divine creative act had its meaning in the fact that it constituted this prefiguration" (268). God's creative act here for Barth prefigures the covenant.

This also happens in his reading of Gen 2 and Song of Songs in tandem, saying that the Song of Songs merely sharpens the question arising from Gen 2 (in particular v. 23, "Bone of my bones and flesh of my flesh"). What interests the authors of these texts, says Barth, was the "fact that in the relationship between man and woman—even prior to its character as the basis of the father-mother-child relationship—we have to do primarily with the question of an incomparable covenant, of an irresistably purposed and effected union" (313). The Song of Songs, notes Barth, is a continuous description of the utter joy, the "unquenchable yearning and the restless willingness and readiness with which both partners in this covenant hasten towards an encounter." Genesis 2 is similar and in its brevity even more pointed, for it tells us that only male and female together in their unity and relation equal humankind. Both are for each other, for covenant with each other, and cannot exist without each, for the man is not yet human insofar as it is "not good that the man should be alone" (Gen 2:18), and the woman cannot exist without the man for she is made from him. Genesis 2 sets out at the beginning what the Song of Songs holds as its goal, the two becoming one flesh (Gen 2:24). Barth says that this beginning and goal respectively is the covenant, the irrevocable covenant between male and female. It is of the substance of the covenant which God makes in creation.

The authors of Gen 2 and Song of Songs know that the broken covenant is still for God the unbroken covenant, the covenant intact and fulfilled from both sides (315). Barth says that this covenant is the inner basis of creation and as such it is also its goal. The covenant thus is viewed from this point in the narrative as the yet-unbroken covenant, indeed the covenant that cannot be broken. Barth says that the picture which Gen 2 and the Song of Songs offer is a clear reflection of the covenant of grace, most especially the covenant as kept not by Israel but by God. This is the case insofar as God found it "not good that the man should be alone" but made him a partner fit for him. In his divine freedom, God found "in no other people on earth what He needed; because as the One He is, YHWH Elohim, He willed to ignore the rest and to choose this people alone, without any merits of its own but solely on the basis of His own being, necessarily acknowledging it in the wisdom of His will, man as man could not recognize the completion of his creation in the fellowship of any of the beasts but only in that of woman" (318). At the creation stories, in particular Gen 2, we find the covenant of grace in the creation of humanity as male and female, which prefigures the call of Israel and the work of Jesus Christ.

Barth pushes this even farther and says that if left to its expression in the Old Testament in and of itself, the statement of the relationship of man and woman would give an ambiguous answer, that is, it would be an "insoluble riddle," an "unresolved contradiction" (320) to the question of the covenant of grace in the creation of humanity as man and woman. But Christians are not left alone with the Old Testament; we are given the expression indeed of the New Testament. Here we find Barth reading the Old Testament through the lens of the New Testament or at least in tandem with the New Testament. He states that the Christian church must read the Old Testament as forming a "single material context with the New." He argues that his interpretation of the Gen 2 creation story as bearing internally the covenant of grace demands that it not be read apart from Eph 5:32, "This mystery is a profound one, and I am saying that it refers to Christ and to the Church." Indeed Barth says that Eph 5 is a "commentary" on Gen 2:18 and therefore also on the Song of Songs and therefore also on the passages from the prophets which speak of YHWH as faithful lover and husband to an unfaithful Israel and therefore also on the creation narrative. Thus the Old Testament material cannot be read aright without this commentary from the New Testament.

Barth says that the Old Testament, when giving dignity to the relationship between the sexes, has in view its "prototype," the "divine likeness of man as male and female which in the plan and election of God is primarily the relationship between Jesus Christ and his Church, secondarily the relationship between YHWH and Israel, and only finally, although very directly in view of its origin, the relationship between the sexes" (322). Barth thus understands the primary relationship between Jesus Christ and his church to be the internal basis of creation, that is, of the story of the creation of humanity male and female in Genesis and here specifically in Gen 2. This primary relationship is also understood to be the internal basis of the election and calling of Israel by YHWH. Barth even goes so far as to say that it is because "Jesus Christ and his Church are the internal basis of creation, and because Jesus Christ is again the basis of the election and call of Israel, that the relationship between YHWH and Israel can and must be described as an erotic relationship." Israel in the prophets is portrayed as unfaithful, as a harlot, as an adulteress. That the prophets can speak of hope even within this breach of the covenant from the side of Israel, that they can speak of a renewed relationship between Israel and YHWH, that the Old Testament as a whole can proclaim the hope of restoration, its "true aim is the event in which, purified in baptism and sanctified by His Word (Eph 5:26ff.), the Church of Jesus will be presented to Him in glory without spot or blemish, holy and inviolable" (323). Interestingly, Barth can say of Ephesians that it gives a positive picture of the relationship between husband and wife. Many feminists would not agree by any means, but Barth cannot be so easily dismissed here. Barth argues that in Eph 5:28-30 "for the first time the relationship between man and woman is honoured as such, and not merely in the light of fatherhood or motherhood or posterity, which fade into the background in the New Testament." Here this relationship is again given its own glory as glowingly asserted in the Song of Songs.

Even this very limitation of the hope of the Old Testament to fulfilment in a future time, even in its prominence given to fatherhood and motherhood and the child yet to come, the ancestors yet to spangle the sky, even in doing so it points beyond itself, beyond all the generations of Israel to the end-time to the Son, the Bridegroom of his own people. "It can and must be said that with its normal observance of strict sobriety in this sphere the Old Testament pointed most powerfully beyond itself to the King given to Israel and rejected by it but exalted by God, the Son of God and the Son of Man, Jesus Christ." Here we see how Barth understands the Old Testament to stretch its grasp beyond itself, even according to its own plain sense. Indeed, Gen 2 and Song of Songs and such texts had Jesus Christ "objectively in mind," and as such they could not form only a "fringe and not the center of its witness" but that truly Gen 2 and its related texts form the "central witness to the Son, the expected One." But Barth does not leave us here, dazzled at his footwork through Scripture, but draws his whole argument throughout this section to a close with the simple statement: "But in view of this it may be seen that the centre could and had to have this fringe, and the creation saga this climax—the creation of humanity as the creation of male and female who were both naked and not ashamed" (324).

One always risks peril when one tries to summarize Barth's work, and this short sketch is not exempt, but we have at least seen how one can hold Christ as center, whether theologically, ethically, spiritually, and be at the same time fully "plunged" into the world around us. For Barth, the only reason that we are committed to works of justice and peace toward the mending of creation is precisely this fundamental relationship between creation and covenant. He manages to tie firmly Christ, and derivatively in him, Christians, to creation and therefore to its well-being and care. Barth does this, in fact, mentioning only rather briefly the witness of the prophets; it does not necessitate the prophetic word of judgment to understand the relationship of covenant and creation. There is no gap between theology and praxis, between the covenant and all creation. Of course this means that there is likewise no gap between theology and mission, for if the covenant is the internal basis of creation and creation the external basis of the covenant, all of creation exists by the very Word of God, without which all creation would return to the deep dark and formless void. Mission thus means not only outward acts of justice but also the preaching of the Word, which is Christ, the center of the covenant of grace.

The Church of the Living Christ

Henry A. Gustafson

From its beginning the people of the church have focused their attention on Jesus Christ and on what God has done in and through him. So centered were they on his role—past, present and future—that they soon began to be called "Christians," a term which they also used for themselves (Acts 11:26; 26:28; 1 Pet 4:16). The preeminent conviction which pervaded their lives and thought was that God had raised Jesus from the dead. This conviction has been central to Christianity. In the words of one New Testament scholar: "There could be no Gospel, not one account, no letter in the New Testament, no faith, no church, no worship, no prayer in Christendom today, without the message of the resurrection of Christ."[1]

The way the New Testament writers conveyed the news of his resurrection, however, differs greatly. None of them gives a description of the event itself, and the details as to when, where and to whom the risen Christ first appears vary considerably. And, since resurrection was not a common experience, they had to develop word-pictures in order to write about it. They said he "was raised," he "was lifted up," he "became a life-giving spirit," "he has taken his seat at the right hand of the throne of God," he "was exalted."

From this variety it becomes clear these early witnesses were not involved in some effort to arrive at harmony in their accounts or at uniformity in their language. What mattered to them was the conviction that God had raised Jesus. This conviction had two profound implications. It meant God affirmed the life which he had lived, and it meant he was alive, a living presence in their midst.

This first implication, God's affirmation of the life he had lived, was essential to the Christian movement. For so much of Jesus' story was difficult to accept. Respectable people often found his teachings and line of conduct offensive and unacceptable. Some who had begun to follow him turned away. And his ignominious death indicated to many that even God had forsaken him. The prevailing human judgment on his life had been one of condemnation.

But for those who experienced the reality of his presence that judgment was overruled. In raising him God affirmed his life. And from this perspective the Gospels tell his story. They tell of his being endowed with God's Spirit, of his intimate life of prayer, of his teachings about God's rule. And they tell about how he foresaw that his identity with, and ministry to, people in need—to the poor, to sinners, to the alienated and the ostracized—

would get him into trouble and how, nonetheless, he chose that life. For such a life conformed to his understanding of God's will, even though it led to his crucifixion. The Gospel writers concluded their narratives with the good news of Easter morning, the good news of God's "Yes" to that life he had lived.

Other New Testament writers also acknowledged God's affirmation of the life he lived. The author of Hebrews, using Psalm 8, says that Jesus "for a little while was made lower than the angels, (but) now (is) crowned with glory and honor" (2:9). His time of "lowliness" was one in which he, by sharing in the life of his brothers and sisters in faith, was enabled to sympathize with them in their weakness and help them in their times of trial. He became the pioneer and perfecter of their faith. Having endured this lowliness and suffering he was exalted, crowned with glory and honor, and seated "at the right hand of the Majesty on high" (2:14-18; 4:15; 12:2f.; 1:3).

Similarly, this juxtaposition of lowliness and exaltation appears in the letters of Paul. He commends to the Christians at Philippi the humility Jesus had demonstrated. "Let the same mind be in you that was in Christ Jesus, who . . . taking the form of a slave . . . humbled himself and became obedient to the point of death—even death on a cross. Therefore God also highly exalted him" (Phil 2:5-9). The exaltation is the affirmation of Jesus' life of service to, and costly identification with, people in need.

The primary event which Paul uses to refer to this costly identification is Jesus' crucifixion. It was at the heart of his message. "We proclaim Christ crucified," he wrote, "the power of God and the wisdom of God" (1 Cor 1:23-24). To be sure this crucified Christ was the risen Christ, but for Paul the victory does not overshadow the particular life which Jesus had lived and given for others. For in that life, with its passion and suffering, its "lowliness," he believed God had been at work. God's power and wisdom had been revealed.

For there love had been at work, both the love of Christ and of God. In Paul's words: "Christ . . . loved me and gave himself for me" (Gal 2:20), and "God proves his love for us in that while we still were sinners Christ died for us" (Rom 5:8). In the crucifixion, symbolic of Jesus' entire life and passion, Paul believed a divine action had been going on. Jesus' self-giving, his taking the form of a servant was an obedient response to God's love for sinners.

The second major implication drawn from their belief in Christ's resurrection is that Christ is alive, a living, spiritual reality to whom they can relate. God's act of raising Jesus meant that he was more than a hero, a person of great humility and compassion, a champion of the poor and marginalized, who had been given life after death. He had been exalted, had been given God's own name, and had come to share in God's power and authority.

This resurrection was not a restoration to the life Jesus knew before. It was not like that of a Lazarus, who presumably would have to die again. The character of this transition, says Paul, cannot even be imagined (1 Cor 2:9). He calls it a spiritual event. "It is sown a physical body, it is raised a spiritual body." There is a continuity between the Jesus of history and the risen Christ, but it is not substantive or structural. It is personal. The Christ Jesus who is alive is continuous with the Jesus of history. He is God's affirmation of the life Jesus gave for us. And to this living Christ we relate in the light of Jesus' life and ministry.

To convey the wonder of this event the early Christians told stories of his appearances. For many these were moving, life-changing, experiences: Mary Magdalene meeting the risen Jesus in the garden; the two disciples on the road to Emmaus; Saul's encounter, while he was still breathing out threats against Jesus' followers.

Also conveying their awe and wonder are the descriptions they used to speak of him. They said he was "the image of the invisible God" (Col 1:15), "the exact imprint of (his) very being," "the reflection of God's glory" (Heb 1:3). They said that "all things were created through him and for him" (1 Cor 8:6), "in him all things hold together" (Col 1:17), "he upholds the universe by the power of his word" (Heb 1:3), and "through him God was pleased to reconcile to himself all things" (Col 1:20).

These attributions were used for the Word of God and the Wisdom of God in their sacred writings. That Word/Wisdom was "in the beginning with God." He/She was the creator of all things, the source of life and light, the one who sustains the universe. (cf. Gen 1:1ff.; Ps 33:6; Prov 8:22, 30; Wis 7:22-27; 8:4; 9:9). She was one who guides, teaches, and saves her followers (Wis 9:18). Christians believe that Word/Wisdom, coeternal with God, was enfleshed in Jesus and continues to be known as the exalted living Lord, who is one with God, who bears God's own name, and is with us "always, to the end of the age" (Mt 28:20).

However exalted these and many other descriptions were they did not suggest to Christians the existence of a second deity. Their constant focus on Jesus Christ was consistent with their conviction that there is but one God. They subscribed to the Jewish confession: "Hear, O Israel: The Lord is our God, the Lord is One." Accordingly, Paul wrote: "For us there is one God, the Father, from whom are all things and for whom we exist."

And then added, "and one Lord, Jesus Christ, through whom are all things and through whom we exist" (1 Cor 8:5-6). In this text we observe a common characteristic in the texts making high claims about Jesus Christ. They are set within a monotheistic context. Their Christ is one who "has his being within the being of God." Their emphasis upon the centrality of Christ was possible within their basic belief that God was at work in him— creating, sustaining, and redeeming. And he is Lord, because God has given him God's own name.[2]

The appropriate response to this action of God in raising Jesus is faith. Jesus had humbled himself, God had exalted him, and people are invited to confess him as Lord. This confession involves believing that in the life he had given for sinners God's love was revealed. It involves trusting one's self to that love and imaginatively sharing in Jesus' life, death and resurrection. It involves obedience to the will of God as disclosed in Jesus' life. This belief, trust and obedience are the ingredients of the confession, "Jesus is Lord," and describe what is involved in being "saved" (Rom 10:9, 10).

The faith claim that God's love was revealed in the crucifixion of Christ had further far-reaching implications. If God could use the cross of Jesus—including the acts of betrayal, abandonment, and injustice—to a salvific end, then certainly God could use other human events and circumstances, such as Paul's "thorn in the flesh" and the diverse limitations to which the early Christians were subject (2 Cor 12:7-10; Acts 5:41). And consistent with this is the belief that "in all things God works for good" (Rom 8:28, 39). In every event and circumstance God is present and at work. This universal divine action, motivated by love, is experienced in a variety of ways—sometimes as liberation, sometimes as a loving purgative wrath, sometimes as reconciliation with God, or neighbor, or between groups and nations. Helping us to trace God's actions in all of these diverse occurrences of life is the story of God's self disclosure in the life lived out by Jesus Christ.[3]

Along with his role as revealer Paul sees Jesus Christ as our representative. In his death and resurrection we can participate. We can by imaginative faith re-present these elements of his story. Just as Jewish worshipers at the Passover festival re-present and share in the Exodus experience, so in baptism Christians re-present and share in the death and resurrection of Jesus Christ. In baptism we die with him and are raised to walk in newness of life (Rom 6:4; Col 2:12).

Here God's grace and demand are linked. We are raised to new life, but to experience it we must engage in the new ways of thinking and living that belong to that life (2 Cor 5:15-16). This includes a new way of regarding, looking at, evaluating, and judging others.[4] We are to do it from the perspective of the one whose life we share. He came to serve, and he taught that "Whoever wishes to be great among you must be your servant" (Mk 10:43-45). Therefore, to acknowledge his lordship, his authority to guide and direct our lives, is to be involved in an ethic, which is both personal and social. For the resurrection of our Lord is evident, as someone has said, not so much in a stone rolled away from the tomb, as in a church carried away by his lordship.

Notes

1. Günther Bornkamm, *Jesus of Nazareth* (New York, 1960), 181.

2. Edward Schillebeeckx, *Jesus* (New York: Crossroad Pub. Co., 1981), 491.

3. H. Richard Niebuhr, *The Meaning of Revelation* (New York: The Macmillan Co., 1946), 154.

4. Cf. J. L. Martyn, "Epistemology at The Turn of The Ages: 2 Corinthians 5:16," *Christian History and Interpretation,* ed. W. R. Farmer, C. F. Moule, and R. R. Niebuhr (Cambridge University Press, 1967), 274.

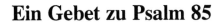

Ein Gebet zu Psalm 85

Von deiner Güte und Treue, Gott, leben wir.
Deine Güte und Treue sind verlässlicher Grund unseres Vertrauens.
Sie sind uns Wegweiser und Begleiter in die Zukunft deiner Welt.

Wir danken dir, Gott, für deine Güte und Treue von alters her:
Du befreist aus der Macht der Finsternis und schenkst Kraft und Hoffnung
zu einem neuen Anfang.
Du hälst deinem Volk die Treue und führst es aus Irrtum und Sünde zurück
auf deinen Weg.
Du lässt deinen Sohn Jesus Christus die Sünde der Welt auf sich nehmen,
damit wir Frieden haben.
Du schenkst uns die Gemeinschaft mit Menschen, die uns deine Güte und
Treue lebendig und gegenwärtig machen.

Wir bitten dich: mach auch uns zu Zeugen deiner Güte und Treue. Verbinde
die
Glieder deines Volkes zu einer Gemeinschaft, in der Güte und Treue gelebt
wird:
Hilf uns vergeben, wie du vergeben willst.
Hilf uns andere suchen wie du uns gesucht hast.
Hilf uns einladen zu dir, wie du uns eingeladen hast.
Gib uns Mut zu klaren Worten, wo Hass und Verachtung gesät werden.
Gib uns Kraft zu hilfreichen Taten, wo Gewalt und Unterdrückung
herrschen.
Lass den Geist deines Sohnes Jesus Christus in uns wohnen, dass wir nicht
nur den Opfern sondern auch den Tätern von Hass und Gewalt in Güte und
Treue begegnen konnen.

Gerhard Koslowsky

A Prayer While Listening to Psalm 85

Your steadfast love and faithfulness, God, are the source of our life.
Your steadfast love and faithfulness are the reliable foundation for our faith.
Your steadfast love and faithfulness are guide and companion to the future of your world.
We thank you, God, for your steadfast love and faithfulness from of old: you deliver from the power of darkness and grant energy and hope for a new beginning.
You remain loyal to your people and lead them back from error and sin.
You let your Son Jesus Christ take the sin of the world to make us whole.
You grant us communion with people making your love and faithfulness present and alive to us.

We pray that you will make us, too, witnesses of your steadfast love and faithfulness.
Join the members of your people to a communion of practiced love and faithfulness:
Help us to forgive as you are forgiving.
Help us to seek others as you sought us.
Help us to invite you as you invited us.
Give us courage for clear words where hatred and contempt are sown.
Give us strength for helpful deeds where violence and suppression rule.
Let the spirit of your Son Jesus Christ dwell in us to meet in steadfast love and faithfulness,
not only the victims but also the perpetrators of hatred and violence.

Gerhard Koslowsky

The Word of Life

Paul L. Hammer

It is a deep privilege for me to write on this theme in honor of Frederick Trost, for whom Christ has been the center of ministry. As friends and colleagues for more than thirty years, he and I have worked together on committees and boards of the United Church of Christ, shared occasions at St. Pauls Church in Chicago and in the Wisconsin Conference, collaborated in *No Other Foundation*, and rejoiced in his visits to his hometown of Rochester, New York, where his father was librarian at Colgate Rochester Divinity School for forty years and his mother in her 90s still resides.

How shall I approach my assigned theme? As a teacher of the New Testament for more than forty years, I decided simply to explore the ways some New Testament writers deal with Christ and the Word. This is a study of their use of the Greek *logos* to see how five New Testament writers relate Christ and the Word. The five are the Apostle Paul, Mark, Matthew, Luke, and John. This exploration reveals the diversity of New Testament writers in their common proclamation of God's Word in the Christ and gives canonical support for a continuing rich diversity among us in the life of the church today.

The Apostle Paul

Paul uses *logos* in a number of ways. Here I will limit myself to four texts where he links Christ and the word:1) the word of the cross, 2) the word of reconciliation, 3) the word of life, and 4) the word of faith. Each of these four terms is connected to *logos* linguistically by the Greek genitive case. We shall explore each in its respective context. In this essay I have translated *logos* as "word" consistently, though sometimes it is translated otherwise.

In his first letter to the Corinthians, Paul writes, "For the word of the cross is foolishness to those who are perishing, but to us who are being saved it is the power of God" (1 Cor 1:18). The cross points to the death of Jesus, and for Paul that death points to the love of God. "God proves his love for us in that while we were still sinners Christ died for us" (Rom 5:8). The word of the cross is the word of God's love for us in the death of Jesus, a love from which nothing in all creation will be able to separate us (Rom 8:39). The apparent foolishness and weakness of the word of the cross is finally the wisdom and power of God's love (1 Cor 1:24).

In what we know as his second letter to the Corinthians, Paul writes, "in Christ God was reconciling the world to himself, . . . and entrusting the word of reconciliation to us" (2 Cor 5:19). Why is Paul's theology of reconciliation so dominant in 2 Corinthians? I think Paul's own deep need for reconciliation with the Corinthians presses him to affirm a theology of God's reconciliation in Christ and of his own ministry and word of reconciliation. The language of Paul's theology is in part a grassroots product of the circumstances he had to face. The Corinthian situation called for God's word of reconciliation in Christ.

In his letter to the Philippians he writes, "It is by your holding fast to the word of life that I can boast on the day of Christ that I did not run in vain or labor in vain" (Phil 2:16). And what is that word of life? He writes earlier in Philippians, "For to me, living is Christ" (1:21); and he writes to the Galatians, "I have been crucified with Christ; and it is no longer I who live, but it is Christ who lives in me. And the life I now live in the flesh I live by faith in the Son of God, who loved me and gave himself for me" (Gal 2:19-20). The word of life is not primarily verbal. It is the life and death and risen new life of Christ in us.

In his letter to the Romans, Paul writes about "the word of faith that we proclaim" (Rom 10:8; though the Greek here is not *logos* but *rema*, rare in Paul but here it occurs in the Greek translation of Deut 30:14). The context makes it clear that, for Paul, in Christ "the word is near you, on your lips and in your heart." Christ himself is the word of faith that lives in us, in our external speaking and in our internal center.

The Gospel of Mark

When we turn to the Gospel of Mark, unlike Paul (whose letters say little about the words and deeds of Jesus and for whom the word and gospel focus on Jesus' death and resurrection), Mark brings us traditions of the words and deeds of Jesus. Paul, writing in the 50s of the first century and still expecting Jesus' final coming in the near future, focuses on the love of God in the cross and the power of God for new life in the resurrection. Mark, writing in the year 70, has begun to question the nearness of the end (even Jesus does not know the time, see Mk 13:32). For Mark, God's good news in Jesus stretches from his baptism to his resurrection and includes his ministry in word and deed. The continuing life of the church needed to know this too.

Mark proclaims Jesus himself as the gospel, but his use of *logos* is more limited than Paul's. In relation to Jesus, Mark limits his use to the spoken words of Jesus. "So many gathered around that there was no longer room for them, . . . and he was speaking the word to them" (2:2). "With many such parables he spoke the word to them" (4:33). "Those who are ashamed of me and of my words in this adulterous and sinful generation, of them the Son of Man will also be ashamed when he comes in the glory of his Father with the holy angels" (9:38). "Heaven and earth will pass away, but my words will not pass away" (13:31). We can see from these examples Mark's important understanding of "the word" as the words of Jesus.

But with his use of the verb form *legein* ("say") he brings a central message."Now after John was arrested, Jesus came to Galilee, proclaiming the good news of God, and saying, 'The time is fulfilled, and the kingdom of God has come near; repent and believe in the good news'" (1:14-15).

The Gospel of Matthew

Writing about the year 85 in the first century, Matthew probably knows and uses the Gospel of Mark, but he expands the story of Jesus to reach from his birth (with a genealogy going back to Abraham) to his resurrection appearances; and he weaves in five large blocks of Jesus' teaching (chapters 5—7, 10, 13, 18, 24-25), thereby intensifying Mark's view about Jesus' words.

For Matthew, Jesus becomes the supreme teacher in the tradition of Moses. Now his words are authoritative. Near the end of the Sermon on the Mount (5—7) Jesus says, "Everyone who hears these words of mine and acts on them will be like a wise man who built his house upon a rock" (7:24); and Matthew concludes, "Now when Jesus had finished these words, the crowds were astonished at his teaching, for he taught them as one having authority" (7:28-29).

Each of the other four blocks end with a concluding word about Jesus' teaching. "Now when Jesus had finished instructing his twelve disciples, he went on from there to teach and proclaim his message in their cities" (11:1). "When he had finished these parables, he left that place" (13:53). "When he had finished saying these words" (19:1; 26:1).

In chapter 13, Matthew highlights the center of Jesus' teaching as "the word of the kingdom" (13:19). It is a word for people to hear. "But as for what was sown on good soil, this is the one who hears the word and understands it, who indeed bears fruit" (13:23). As in Mark, Jesus says, "Heaven and earth will pass away, but my words will not pass away" (24:35).

During his earthly ministry, Jesus the teacher never tells his disciples to teach. But after his resurrection, Jesus says to them, "Go therefore and make disciples of all nations, . . . teaching them to obey everything that I have commanded you" (28:19). For Matthew, the authoritative teaching tradition of Moses and Jesus extends to the first disciples and now to us.

The Gospel of Luke

Writing about the year 90 in the first century, Luke, like Matthew, probably knew the Gospel of Mark, as well as the teaching material in Matthew (incorporating it in his own way). His narrative of Jesus, like that of Matthew, moves from his birth to his resurrection appearances, though with his own stories and a genealogy that goes back to Adam. Luke repeats some *logos* texts found in Mark or Matthew (see Lk 6:47; 9:26; 21:33).

In the prologue of his Gospel (1:1-4), Luke uses a phrase that is foundational for his Gospel and for the Acts of the Apostles, the second half of his two part work. The phrase is "ministers of the word" (1:2). For Luke, the Apostles were the first emissaries/proclaimers of the word about Jesus as God's Messiah to bring "good news of great joy for all the people" (2:10).

Luke uses *logos* language about Jesus' word some fourteen times in his Gospel, but the Acts throbs with the proclamation of the Word about thirty-six times in the post-resurrection and Pentecost-inspired witness of Jesus' first emissaries "to the ends of the earth" (Acts 1:8). If we can say that among the gospel writers Mark is the preacher and Matthew the teacher, Luke is the mission strategist who in the Acts wants to see the Word impact the whole Roman Empire. But here we shall limit ourselves to Luke's use of *logos* in his Gospel.

Like Mark and Matthew, Luke also speaks of the "words" of Jesus. After reading from Isaiah in his hometown synagogue to identify his mission, "all spoke well of him [Jesus] and were amazed at the gracious words that came from his mouth" (4:22). In a story of Jesus' healing, the people ask, "What kind of a word is this? For with authority and power he commands the unclean spirits, and out they come!" (4:36). When Luke speaks of Jesus' preaching ministry he writes, "Once while Jesus was standing beside the lake of Gennesaret, and the crowd was pressing in on him to hear the word of God" (5:1).

In Luke, Jesus defines his family with these words: "My mother and my brothers are those who hear the word of God and do it" (8:21). In the story of Mary and Martha, Jesus breaks with a tradition that forbade a woman to sit at the feet of a rabbi. "Martha had a sister named Mary, who sat at the Lord's feet and listened to his word' (10:39).

The two disciples on the road to Emmaus speak of Jesus as "a prophet mighty in word and deed before God and all the people" (24:19). And finally, the risen Jesus "said to them, 'These are my words that I spoke to you while I was still with you—that everything written about me in the law of Moses, the prophets, and the psalms must be fulfilled.' Then he opened their minds to understand the scriptures, and he said to them, 'Thus it is written, that the Messiah is to suffer and to rise from the dead on the third day, and that repentance and forgiveness of sins is to be proclaimed in his name to all nations, beginning from Jerusalem. You are witnesses of these things'" (24:44-48). This calls for "ministers of the word" both then and now.

The Gospel of John

When we come to the Gospel of John, we think immediately of the Word and *logos* language. "In the beginning was the Word, and the Word was with God, and the Word was God . . . . And the Word became flesh and lived among us" (Jn 1:1; 1:14). John links God's Word in creation with the Word in Jesus Christ and challenges any who would separate the God of creation from the God of salvation. The God of Israel is the God of Jesus Christ. When we speak of a theology of incarnation, of enfleshment, the Gospel of John is our primary source.

This Gospel states clearly the purpose of the signs written in it: "these are written that you may believe that Jesus is the Messiah, the Son of God, and that through believing you may have life in his name" (20:31). It challenges any who say that he is not the Messiah.

After the prologue, which proclaims the Word made flesh in Jesus, John's extensive use of *logos* languages points to believing in the word Jesus speaks, but in the context of this gospel, to believe in his word is to believe in him as the Word. Here are a few examples:

In the wedding in Cana story, his disciples "believed in him" (2:11). In the story of the Samaritans, "many more believed because of his word" (4:41). The official with the ill son "believed the word that Jesus spoke to him" (4:50). "Very truly, I tell you, anyone who hears my word and believes him who sent me has eternal life" (5:24). For this Gospel, eternal life is not only a quantity of life after death; it is a quality of life there and now.

John links the word with the truth. "Then Jesus said to the Jews who had believed in him, 'If you continue in my word, you are truly my disciples; and you will know the truth, and the truth will make you free'" (8:31-32). Jesus prays to God for his disciples, "Sanctify them in the truth; your word is truth" (17:17).

Jesus himself is the Word of truth. "I am the way, and the truth, and the life" (14:6); and he promises, "Those who love me will keep my word, and my Father will love them, and we will come to them and make our home with them" (14:23). The Word made flesh in the historic coming of Jesus comes to make his home now in our flesh as we keep his word. That word is the cleansing word of God's love. Jesus says, "You have already been cleansed by the word that I have spoken to you. Abide in me as I abide in you" (15:3-4a).

The ministry of Frederick Trost has been a ministry of Christ the Word. In his life and words he has kept the Word, and he abides in Christ and Christ in him. Thanks be to God!

Christ, the Only Foundation:
Thoughts on Home Improvement

Ute Molitor

For no one can lay any foundation other than the one that has been laid; that foundation is Jesus Christ (1 Corinthians 3:11).

This verse from Paul's first letter to the Corinthians is one of Frederick Trost's favorites, I've been told. Having known him for a few years now, I am by no means surprised. It is integral to the way he thinks and acts and breathes. It has been the nature and content of his work to unite the people of the Wisconsin Conference of the United Church of Christ and beyond in their faith in Christ, our true foundation. He has continuously asked all of us to consider what it means for our daily lives to draw our strength, hope, and calling from this foundation, to build on it and to invite the Spirit to dwell within us as individuals and as a church.

These are the very concerns Paul brings before the people of Corinth. When we look at the context of our verse, we find that Paul is trying to address divisions that have arisen within the church at Corinth. He has been informed that people are jealous of each other and quarrel. This does not seem to come as a great surprise to him because he has had to deal gently with their spiritual limitations from the beginning. "I fed you with milk, not solid food, for you were not ready for solid food. Even now you are still not ready, for you are still of the flesh." He is referring to the fact that the people argue with each other over affiliation. Some say that they belong to Apollos; some that they belong to Paul. In doing so they have missed the point of his teachings. Paul uses a diet of metaphors to clarify his beliefs, and I would like to focus on Paul's reference to building and, to put tongue in cheek, home improvement.

Paul says that he has laid a foundation among them; Apollos is building on it and must do so with care. However, the foundation is not Paul or his teachings: it is Christ himself. Christ is the cornerstone and the foundation. These are all images intended to say that any structure external or internal that does not put its weight, that does not rest its burden, on that cornerstone or foundation will crumble because it cannot stand up under its own weight. Paul also points out that we all will be asked to build on that foundation and that we have different building materials to choose from, such as gold, silver, precious stones, wood, hay and straw. He warns that we will have to be careful with our building because it will have to withstand the test of fire.

When I began to wonder about whether Paul was favoring one material over the other, I found myself going through my memories of working as a carpenter's helper in Philadelphia in 1991. When our motley crew of "Restoration Carpentry" built a two-story addition to a home, I had my first opportunity to see how the average house is put together in the United States. The foundation itself was solid, built by a crew of masons. We built a wood frame structure on top of that foundation. Once the frame was built we began the work of insulating. I had to cover the outside with blue insulation board, and the frame was filled with glass fiber insulation. We attached several diagonal metal braces on the outside to strengthen the structure and then added vinyl siding on the outside and dry wall on the inside. It occurred to me at some point in the process that I could break into the house through its outside wall using my Swiss army knife. It also left me with no doubt whatsoever that the first tornado could carry this house a few miles without much difficulty. A fire could consume it in no time. So much for wood and straw, I thought.

When I thought about gold, silver, and precious stone, I immediately pictured a palace and remembered a trip to Atlantic City with a number of visitors from the former East Germany. They wanted to see a casino and so we went to Donald Trump's Taj Mahal, a palace in its own right. It was properly bombastic and flamboyant, made to look as if it had been built of gold and silver, and precious stone. When we got there, all electricity was out in the underground parking garage, the elevators weren't working and employees had to lead visitors up through the system of underground staircases by the light of a flashlight. When we entered the sacred gambling halls we were overcome by the lights, the glitter of fake gold, and the sheer noise of the ring of slot machines and of coins dropping. It seemed to be a structure that had no lasting foundation, exterior or interior. It would crumble under its own superfluous weight even if the gold and the silver and the precious stones had been real.

Perhaps the question of what defines the outside of the structures we build is beside the point. Paul tells the Corinthians that they are God's temple in whom the Spirit dwells. This is a daring statement. He is asserting that God seeks to dwell in us through the Spirit. God comes to dwell in our interior spaces: the rooms where we store our memories, the drawing rooms of our imagination where we paint our dreams, the dark spaces where we go in despair. God lives there with us even when we feel as if our lives are falling apart or the structures we hold onto for comfort are crumbling.

Paul is saying that God dwells not only where a house is adorned with precious stone but also in the homes of the poor. God doesn't dwell only in the person who wears designer clothes and fine jewelry but also in the person who shops at St.Vincent's thrift shop or depends on the handouts of an agency. God doesn't dwell only in people who are adorned with titles and medals and other signs of accomplishment but also in the orphanage in Haiti, which some of our church members have visited, where the children have distended bellies and hungry eyes and a fierce desire to be held and loved.

It doesn't matter if our house or church is built of wood or gold or stone if there is room in it for God's Spirit to dwell. That Spirit is not separate from Christ and who Christ is. The Spirit that seeks to dwell in us is one with the incarnate one, Emmanuel, "God with us." This Spirit is one with the God who risked everything to be among us, the God who would rather be born among us a poor and homeless child than exert power from above, the God who enters what seems to be a God-forsaken world and is willing to suffer its hatred if that is what it takes to open our eyes to our own destructive ways. This is the God who is willing to be viewed as a fool in the eyes of the world in order to break down walls of division.

If we want to go about the business of spiritual home improvement, we can begin as individuals and as a church by prayerfully thanking God for dwelling in us and in others around us. We can invite the Spirit to open the blinders with which we have covered our eyes and to open our ears and hearts. These might be blinders of self-deprecation or pride, of selfishness or a need to save the whole world by ourselves. We can ask the Spirit to teach us true hospitality toward ourselves and others. This might mean that we will begin to learn to embrace our past or aspects of ourselves or our bodies that we struggle to accept. This might mean that we will be asked to reach out to people we don't like or don't know how to relate to. This might mean that we will truly have to learn what it means to share our wealth.

This Spirit might ask us as a church to tear down the walls and divisions we have built within and without the house of God. It is this extra weight as well as our acquiescence to a culture of opulence which has brought us to the point where we might crumble under our own weight. Furthermore, we too must be careful not to get lost in the battle over allegiances. "I belong to the Pope" or "I belong to Luther" or "I belong to Calvin, or Zwingli or Frederick or whoever is to succeed him." Paul reminds us that the Spirit will burn us with its fire when it is given room to do its work within and among us. It will burn away what is in the way of healing. The walls we have built will crumble. Whether we merely turn to ashes or rise up to share the warmth of God's love burning within us depends on whether we have given our hearts and homes to God in Christ who is our true foundation. Such surrender is foolish business. It is our business as the church of Jesus Christ, our one foundation.

The Promise behind the Purpose

Robert G. Hunsicker

Yogi Berra, the great catcher of the New York Yankees, who was known for his wit and wisdom as well as for his baseball skills, said one time, "If you don't know where you're going, you're likely to end up some place else."

To a certain extent that may be true of our understanding of the pastoral ministry. Two generations ago in his classic work *The Purpose of the Church and Its Ministry* H. Richard Niebuhr wrote about the indefiniteness, vagueness, and conflict which at that time characterized thinking about the ministry. Niebuhr noted that neither ministers nor the schools that nurture them are guided today by a clear-cut, generally accepted conception of the office of the ministry. [1]

The situation may not have changed significantly since Niebuhr wrote those words in 1956. The paragraphs that follow are a modest attempt to respond to the questions: *What is the vocation of the pastor?* and *What is the nature of the ministry to which the pastor has been called?*

The pastor is, first of all, one who has been *called*. The pastor is not someone who has been *hired* by a congregation to make certain the church operates smoothly and efficiently. (It seldom does.) The pastor is one who has been called by Christ to share in the work of Christ's ministry. Christ expressed his understanding of ministry with the words that Isaiah had written centuries earlier:

> The Spirit of the Lord is upon me,
> because he has anointed me
> to bring good news to the poor.
> He has sent me to proclaim release to the captives
> and recovery of sight to the blind,
> to let the oppressed go free,
> to proclaim the year of the Lord's favor (Lk 4:18-19).

The pastor's ministry is an extension of Christ's own ministry. The origin of the pastor's call is God's action in Christ. It is Christ who calls; it is Christ who empowers; it is the gospel of Christ the pastor proclaims.

The pastor's ministry is an extension of Christ's ministry; it is also part of the larger ministry of Christ's people. The writer of the Letter to the Ephesians reminds us:

The gifts [Christ] gave were that some would be apostles, some prophets, some evangelists, some pastors and teachers, to equip the saints for the work of ministry, for building up the body of Christ (Eph 4:11-12).

The task of the pastor and others in positions of leadership in the church is to equip the saints for the work of ministry. The fundamental call to ministry comes at the time of baptism. Baptism is ordination for ministry.

Robert V. Moss, Jr. who until his untimely death in 1976 served as president of the United Church of Christ, told his students at Lancaster Theological Seminary: "We have been called to be ministers to a ministering people." Moss added that the task of the ordained person is to work himself or herself out of a job.

Marva Dawn, in the volume she recently co-authored with Eugene Peterson entitled *The Unnecessary Pastor*, wrote that persons who are ordained need to remind those entrusted to their care that they are saints, the beloved baptized of God, gifted persons, created in God s image.[2]

In that same volume Dawn notes, "If we rediscover our pastoral call . . . we know that we are merely equippers, prodders, encouragers, and promoters of all the people so that each one fulfills his or her vocation in the church."[3]

What then is the nature of the ministry to which the pastor has been called? According to traditional Protestant understanding pastors are those who have been appointed to preach the Word, administer the sacraments, and care for God's people. The pastor has been called to love and nurture those whom God has entrusted to his or her care.

The pastor is not primarily an administrator, although certain administrative skills are important in the work of pastoral ministry. The pastor is not a therapist, although counseling is one of his or her basic tasks. The pastor is not essentially a prophet, although there are times when bold and courageous witness is required. The pastor is not a social worker, although faithfulness to the gospel frequently demands involvement with the larger issues of society. The pastor is not fundamentally a teacher, although teaching is an essential and vitally important element of pastoral ministry. The pastor is one who has been called to proclaim God's Word, administer the sacraments, and care for God's people.

Eugene Peterson, in the earlier mentioned work, wrote that we live in an age in which the work of much of the church's leadership is neither pastoral nor theological. Peterson added:

The pastoral dimensions of the church's leadership are badly eroded by technologizing and managerial influences. The theological dimensions of the church's leadership have been marginalized by therapeutic and marketing preoccupations. The gospel work of giving leadership to the community of the Christian faithful has been alienated from its source. . . . Rationalism and functionalism . . . have left pastoral theology thin and anemic.[4]

Those entrusted with the work of ministry in Christ's church have been called to care for Christ's people. The Romanian dramatist Eugene Ionesco said during an interview in 1969 at a time of great unrest throughout all of Europe: "One must first of all love the society one would change." That's true also for the pastor and his or her relationship with the church.

The pastor has been called to a ministry of care. At the same time the focus of the pastor's witness and work is Jesus Christ. It s to Jesus Christ that the pastor owes his or her ultimate loyalty. There is no other foundation (1 Cor 3:11). The framers of the Barmen Declaration, in rejecting the prevailing religious and political doctrines of their time, wrote:

Jesus Christ, as he is attested for us in Holy Scripture, is the one Word of God which we have to hear and which we have to trust and obey in life and in death.[5]

What Frederick Trost wrote in 1992 concerning the mission of the church is true also for the witness and work of the pastor:

It is the mission of the church to bear witness to the gospel of Jesus Christ. The church is called to point away from itself, as John the Baptist did (John 1:29), to the One in whom the Word became flesh and dwelt among us, full of grace and truth." (John 1:14). It looks to Christ who embraces the poor, brings release to the captives, gives sight to the blind, and offers the oppressed liberty and hope. It seeks to follow him.[6]

There is clearly in pastoral ministry that which is counter-cultural. In a society that tends to measure things in terms of success, the standard for pastoral ministry is faithfulness to the gospel. John Mulder, the President of Louisville Presbyterian Seminary, wrote several years ago:

The church needs to recover a biblical faith and a theological vision rooted in the cross and resurrection of Jesus Christ. . . . American Christianity is often only a pale imitation of the life of discipleship, sacrifice, and obedience portrayed in the New Testament. The gospel in America is colored by a pervasive hedonism at once materialistic and emotional. One longs to hear testimony of how Christ didn't make somebody feel "so good," or "more truly human," or how following

Christ didn t bring prosperity. American Christianity has a love affair with success, and it affects every sphere of the church's life.[7] This confession of faith can and should lead the Christian community to a passionate concern for social and political arrangements that are conducive to wholeness for all persons.

Pastors who are true to their calling will learn to love those entrusted to their care. They'll learn to accept them as they are with all their faults, frailties, and failures, knowing full well that at the very heart of the gospel is the truly good news that God has accepted all of us as we are. Those who are true to their calling will not be afraid to admit the brokenness of their own lives. They need to remind themselves constantly that their strength, like the strength of all God's people, comes from above. Martin Luther described the source of that strength as follows in his great Reformation hymn:

Did we in our own strength confide,
our striving would be losing;
were not the right man on our side,
the man of God's own choosing.
Dost ask who that may be?
Christ Jesus, it is he;
Lord Sabaoth his name,
from age to age the same,
and he must win the battle.

In the spring of this year the writer of this essay wrote a letter to Frederick Trost lamenting the fact that in so many ways the church in our time has allowed itself to become captive to the values of our culture. In Fred's reply dated May 13, 2000, he wrote:

Meanwhile, all one can do as a pastor is to seek to remain true to one's calling, equipping the saints, with all the flaws we bring to the task. But is there a more precious vocation than ours?

It is a precious vocation to which we, as those engaged in pastoral ministry, have been called. It is a vocation that involves bumps and bruises but also moments of great satisfaction and joy. It is a calling filled with both pitfalls and promises. At the heart of it all is the promise given by Christ himself to the apostles and indeed to all who have committed their lives to him, "Remember, I am with you always, to the end of the age" (Mt 28:20).

Notes

1. H. Richard Niebuhr, *The Purpose of the Church and Its Ministry* (New York: Harper and Brothers, 1956), 52, 50.

2. Marva J. Dawn and Eugene H. Peterson, *The Unnecessary Pastor, Rediscovering the Call* (Vancouver: Regent College Publishing, 2000), 244.

3. Ibid., 228.

4. Ibid., 60-61.

5. *The Book of Confessions* (New York: The General Assembly of the United Presbyterian Church, 1966), 8.11.

6. Frederick R. Trost, "A Theology of Mission," in *From Deep Night to Bright Dawn, Theological Reflections* (Cleveland: Make a Difference! The Campaign for the United Church of Christ, 1992), 2.

Discerning the Word: Scripture and the Ongoing Witness of the Spirit

Karl Allen Kuhn

"I know what the Bible says about homosexuality, and I don't need some theologian to tell me differently!" The man's concern was expressed with sincerity—no malice or even defensiveness but simply the earnest words of one who has come to believe that what scripture says is God's word. I appreciated his response, and in some respects agreed with him. Despite recent attempts by some interpreters to demonstrate otherwise, the New Testament texts that speak directly to the issue (1 Cor 6:9; 1 Tim 1:9-10; Rom 1:26-27) seem to be quite clear in their condemnation of homosexual activity.[1] In fact, my presentation to the church group of which this man was a part began by arguing this very point. Thus, his consternation with my eventual suggestion was certainly understandable. How was it that I could on the one hand agree with him on the Apostle Paul's rejection of same-gender sexual relations and yet be open to the possibility that homosexual unions may also give glory to God?

Underlying my seemingly paradoxical treatment of these New Testament passages that evening was a way of reading scripture that tries to hold together both the witness of scripture and the ongoing testimony of God's Spirit within the lives of individual believers and Christian communities. At its core is the conviction that God continues to deepen our understanding of God's will in new times and places, through scripture, prayer, and shared reflection upon our experiences as people of faith. Such continuing instruction is needed since—to use Paul's words—"we now see as in a mirror, dimly" and "know only in part" (1 Cor 13:12). The notion of God's continuing instruction through the ministry of the Holy Spirit is firmly rooted in the New Testament (e.g., Jn 14:15-17; 16:13-14; Rom 8:1-11; 1 Cor 2:12; 7:25-40; Gal 5:16-26), and holds a central place in Christian tradition. Commonly referred to as "illumination by the Spirit," it is seen as God's gift of helping believers to embrace within their own lives of faith the good news of God's love as revealed in scripture.[2] Yet herein lies the problem. What are we to do when particular insights that some believers perceive God is revealing to them are in direct contradiction to what the Bible itself teaches?

In Protestant tradition, scholars, clergy, and lay folk alike have often utilized three solutions to this problem. One approach is to suppress the alleged discoveries that some sense God is leading them to because it challenges our tightly held beliefs or because we hold to a strict form of the doctrine of *sola scriptura*: that scripture is the chief (or even sole) authority in matters of faith. Another common solution is to re-interpret the passage in such a way that it no longer says what most have thought it to mean (and what it may very well mean), thereby alleviating the contradiction. This appears to be with case with some of the recent interpretations (noted above) of 1 Cor 6:9, 1 Tim 1:9-10, and Rom 1:26-27. Or we might simply ignore the biblical passage that presents a problem. Undoubtedly, the underlying motivation for each of these methods is often to preserve the authority of scripture. To utilize any of these common solutions, however, is to weaken and limit the indispensable witness of scripture in our lives of faith. The Bible itself points to a better way. In the short essay that follows, I will briefly discuss scripture's own testimony to the progressive nature of God's instruction on how we are to live as God's people, and the implications that testimony poses for the way we are to meditate upon its teachings.

Scripture Itself Bears Witness to the Progressive and Continuing Instruction of God

On the whole, the Bible is dominated by narrative. Woven together into a canonical tapestry, most of scripture's many elements tell the story of YHWH seeking to redeem a fallen humanity. It is a story that extends from the genesis of our world to its climax in Jesus' life, death, and resurrection and beyond time, recounting the accomplishment of God's plan to reach out to God's human creatures and to call them back into right relationship with God, one another and creation. That this overarching narrative is to be seen as representing a progressive disclosure of God's will to redeem humanity is indicated by two of its features. First, and most obviously, the canonical casting of this revelation in the form of an unfolding narrative presupposes a progressive quality to it.[3] Second, the best information we have on how the scriptures were formed also suggest the progressive nature of the revelation it proclaims. This process was likely a dynamic one, involving intense reflection on sacred tradition and openness to God's revelation at moments of crises or in the wake of extraordinary events, in order to make sense of what God was doing in the present circumstances and what God expected of them.[4] Thus, the form of scripture as narrative matches and bears witness to how the Israelites and Christians perceived God to be at work in their midst: dramatically and progressively achieving and unveiling God's plan to call a stiff-necked people back to Godself.

Set within the context of this progressive narrative disclosing God's will for humanity and manner of accomplishing it are other genres of literature, such as the law codes, Psalms, and other wisdom traditions that instruct believers on what it means to be God's faithful people. In the laws of the Hebrew Scriptures, we encounter a dimension of revelation that is even more dynamic and in flux than the unfolding narrative in which they reside. From book to book and testament to testament, many of these laws are significantly recast or even superceded by new ones. The extensive changes these commands undergo, however, do not lessen their revelatory significance. Rather, in addition to providing helpful insights on what it means to be God's people, an equally important revelation they offer is that God's law changes over time. Terrence Fretheim offers the following assessment of the dynamic character of Israel's law.

> The integration of law and narrative throughout the Pentateuch (see chapter 5 on Leviticus) is a key consideration. God's gift of the law is not drawn into a code, but remains integrated with the story of God's gracious activity in the ever-changing history of God's people. Law is always intersecting with life as it is, filled with contingency and change, with complexity and ambiguity . . . This means that new laws will be needed and older laws will need to be recast or set aside.[5]

After illustrating this point by noting the recasting of specific legal codes given in Exodus by Deuteronomy, Fretheim adds,

> Internal tensions and inconsistencies between these laws, however, are not ironed out or considered a threat to the law's integrity. Rather, old and new remain side by side as a canonical witness to the process of unfolding law. Hence, *development of the law* is just as canonical as individual laws or the body of law as a whole.[6]

Examples of this "development of the law" abound throughout the Hebrew Scriptures. For Christians, however, perhaps the most revealing and decisive example of the law's development comes to us in the Sermon on the Mount (Mt 5:1—7:28). After announcing that he has not come to abolish "the law and the prophets" (likely a reference to the Hebrew Scriptures as a whole) but to fulfill them (5:17), Jesus goes on throughout the rest of Matthew 5 to offer his own recasting of several OT laws: "You have heard it was said . . . but I tell you. . . ." Some of Jesus' re-interpretations may simply be intended to get to the heart of the underlying spirit of the law (e.g., the laws on murder and adultery [5:21-30]). However, most offer quite radical departures from the original meaning and intent of the particular law in view, even to the degree that the previous laws given by God are essentially set aside: e.g., the laws on divorce (Mt 5:31-32 [see Deut 24:1-4]); taking oaths (Mt 5:33-37 [see Lev 19:12; Num 30:2; Deut 23:21) compensation/retaliation (5:38-42 [see Ex 21:24; Lev 24:20]); and loving one's neighbor (Mt 5:43-48 [see Lev 19:18]).

Jesus' recasting of God's commands in Matthew 5 marks a dramatic example of what Fretheim calls "a canonical witness to the process of unfolding law." Within scripture's narrative revealing the history of the relationship between God and God's people, climaxing in the life, death and resurrection of Jesus, how humanity is to live out its calling as God's people changes throughout. That such change has a *progressive* quality to it—that God's ongoing instruction is to help us to become more and more the people whom we are called to be—is indicated by two important elements. First, the placement of God's commands within the narrative of scripture presents the ongoing development of the law as part of God's unfolding plan to bring humanity back into right relationship with God, humanity and creation. In other words, one of the ways God accomplishes God's saving purpose is through such continuing and developing instruction. Second, the Gospel writers announce through their portrayals of Jesus as teacher that such instruction now reaches its culmination in Jesus, whose teachings far transcend those of his contemporaries (e.g., Mt 5:20; 7:28-29; Mk 1:21-28; Lk 2:46-47; Jn 7:14-52; 8:12-20) and even the stipulations of old (e.g., Mt 5:27-48; Lk 7:27-42; Jn 12:44-50; 15:1-17).

Implications: Redefining "Canonical"

Many, I think, in one way or another share this view of the progressive nature of God's instruction for how we are to live as God's people. The crux of the issue for the present discussion, however, lies in whether or not the progressive development of God's instruction manifested in scripture is to extend beyond the confines of the canon itself. This raises the question of what exactly is canonical about scripture. Is it simply its content? Or can the processes of development with respect to God's instruction on how we are to be God's people—a process that scripture itself reveals and implicitly approves of—also be received as authoritative? To what extent is the ongoing development of the law "canonical," as Fretheim suggests?

Paul Achtemeier, while emphasizing the developmental and dynamic nature of the biblical traditions, strongly argues that the canonization of the scriptural texts serves an important limiting function that effectively puts a hold on their further development.[7] Thus, the canon establishes a stable witness to God's work in history, culminating in Jesus, which faithfully proclaims the significance of those events. In Achtemeier's view, this limiting role of the canon also preserves as abidingly normative the New Testament writers' specific injunctions against certain behaviors, including homosexuality.

The attempt to legitimate homoerotic sexual contact as acceptable Christian "lifestyle" is another such attempt [to circumvent the limiting function of the canon], this time within the confessing Christian community. . . .In this instance, the limitations imposed by the canonical witness on certain ways of conducting a life in accord with the foundational Christian witness are themselves negated, and in that way actions can be declared acceptable which do in fact fall outside the hermeneutical limitation imposed by the canon.[8]

In my view, however, Achtemeier goes too far in extending the limiting function of the canon to specific injunctions issued by the biblical writers.[9] Instead, the confluence of two observations we have already discussed suggests another way of reading scripture that better appreciates its witness and canonical function within the life of the Christian community. First, there is scripture's own testimony to the ongoing revision of God's instruction concerning what it means to be God's faithful people. The dynamic and progressive nature of this instruction reveals that God does not simply want our adherence to a fixed set of laws. Instead, God desires our continual openness to God's ever-transforming instruction to which the biblical commands witness but can never completely contain.[10] Second, while the unfolding drama of salvation history reaches its culmination in Jesus, the New Testament texts themselves indicate that Jesus' instruction of believers will continue through the ongoing ministry of the Spirit (e.g., Jn 14:15-17; 16:13-14; Rom 8:1-11; 1 Cor 2:12; 7:25-40; Gal 5:16-26). Again, the reason this must be so is that we yet "see as in a mirror, dimly" and "know only in part" (1 Cor 13:12). The improving yet still deeply troubled human element of the yet-unfolding drama of God's salvation continues to necessitate a progressive path of illumination, a path that was also treaded—though magnificently so—by Paul and the other inspired writers of the New Testament. In light of this, the fact that scripture itself provides no indication that the dynamic nature of God's instruction is to suddenly cease is crucial. To insist, as Achtemeier does, that the specific injunctions of the New Testament concerning particular behaviors must stand for all time is to assign to biblical law a role that it has never before performed. According to his view, the canonization of the scriptures fundamentally—and problematically, I think—changes the function of the sacred tradition that it preserves.

In contrast, I believe these same two observations commend a way of embracing scripture both as God's witness to the sacred history of our faith and as an ongoing call to "meditate upon the instruction of the Lord day and night" (Ps 1:2). This approach to scripture understands "canon" to refer not only to the content of its witness but also to a way of reading sacred tradition that scripture itself embodies. The hermeneutic that scripture bears witness to is first of all one in which the sacred traditions of God's people are continually retold and celebrated as one, great, overarching history culminating in God's act of salvation in Jesus. Secondly, it bears witness to the need for those who embrace this great story as their own to continually reflect upon, together with other believers, what it means to live as those who are shaped by this story. For this ongoing discernment, God's instruction as presented in the Hebrew Scriptures and the New Testament, including its specific commands, is an indispensable resource for our lives of faith. The guidelines for behavior given in both testaments, when viewed within their narrative context and especially through the lens of Jesus' own instruction, are the starting point for discerning how we are to live as Christ's disciples. But in some cases, it may just be that through the Spirit, Jesus—the living Word—comes to us and says, "You have heard it was said, . . . but I tell you. . . ." and so calls us to discover even more deeply what it means to be God's people.

Many individual believers and faith communities are sensing Jesus' quiet but persistent voice. It is a voice revealing to them that those living in committed, same-sex relationships may also bear witness to the mutuality, care, respect, and love that is to characterize all of our relationships with one another. It is a voice disclosing that the best of these relationships, like the best of their heterosexual counterparts, proclaim and give glory to the ways of God. Many of our fellow believers disagree. But as others of us do the best we can to "discern the spirits," our strong sense is that it is the one Spirit at work in these relationships to reveal what it means to be the people of God.

Notes

1. Unfortunately, a detailed treatment of these passages and the debate they have produced is beyond the scope of this essay. By way of summary, challenges to the established interpretation of these passages as condemning homosexual activity usually rest on lexical or contextual grounds. With respect to 1 Cor 6:9 and 1 Tim 1:9-10, some have argued that the precise meaning *of arsenokoitai* (lit. "those lying with a male") is far from certain. For example, John Boswell, *Christianity, Social Tolerance and Homosexuality* [Chicago: University of Chicago Press, 1980] 107-14) and Darrell Lance ("The Bible and Homosexuality," *American Baptist Quarterly 8* [1989]: 140-151) both argue that the meaning of the term is difficult to discern and maintain that it more likely refers to male prostitutes. The recent translations of the NRSV and NIV, however,

disagree, and render the term "sodomites" (NRSV) or "homosexuals" (NIV). Favoring these translations is the fact that the components of the compound word *arsenokoites, arsen and koimasthai,* are found in the Septuagint's prohibitions against homosexuality (Lev 18:22- 20:13). These verbal correspondences suggest that among Jews *arsenokoites* became a standard designation for homosexuality or at least indicate that Paul would have likely had these Old Testament texts in mind when writing 1 Cor 6:9. Contextually, it is argued by some that Paul and the writer of 1 Tim were only referring to the specific practice of pederasty (adult males having sex with male minors playing the submissive role) given its common practice in Greco-Roman society. Robin Scroggs *(The New Testament and Homosexuality* [Philadelphia: Fortress, 1983]), for example, attempts to demonstrate that in the Greco-Roman world pederasty was "the one, basic model of male homosexuality" (126), and thus it was this specific, oppressive form of homosexuality that Paul and the writer of 1 Tim had in view when condemning homosexual activity. While Scroggs's proposal offers a valuable assessment of the cultural context of these passages and is still worthy of consideration, at least three serious objections can be raised against his argument: (1) While pederasty may have been the dominant model of *male* homosexuality in the Greco-Roman world, several of the hellenistic writers cited by Scroggs that argue against homosexuality also include references to female homosexuality (see *The New Testament and Homosexuality*, 59-60, 130-33) indicating that a more general view of homosexuality was at times also in consideration; (2) in Rom 1:26-27, the implied mutuality of the activity described, along with the parallelism of v. 27a ("men likewise gave up natural relations with women and were consumed with passion for one another") *and* the reference to female homosexuality (v. 26), all point to Paul's condemnation of homosexual activity in general; (3) even if we were to grant that the New Testament writers addressing the issue of homosexuality had only pederasty in mind (and this is very problematic in light of Rom 1:26-27), the argument that Paul and other Greco-Roman authors use to combat it—that it is "against nature *(physin)*"—would apply equally to any form of homosexuality. What is at issue when this argument is used is the *sexual activity* that takes place and *not* the specific form of the relationship itself (pederastic or mutual). While we may find pederasty a particularly dehumanizing form of relationship, Paul's whole-hearted embrace of the "against nature" argument in Rom 1:26-27 focuses on the sexual activity that is present in both pederasty and mutual homosexual relationships, including female homosexuality. The widely-criticized proposal put forth by Boswell *(Christianity, Social Tolerance and Homosexuality,* 107-14) that what Paul is condemning here in Romans is homosexual activity among those who are *by nature* heterosexual rests on an improper understanding of Paul's use of *physin* and the problematic assertion that Paul would have shared the modem understanding of sexual orientation. For helpful critiques on the specific issue of Boswell's treatment of the term *physin* in Rom 1, see Joseph Fitzmyer, *Romans* (AB 33; New York: Doubleday), 284-88 and Donald J. Wold, *Out of Order: Homosexuality in the Bible and the Ancient Near East* (Grand Rapids: Baker Books, 1998), 180-185.

2. For a recent discussion of this doctrine from a traditional perspective, see Gabriel Fackre, *The Doctrine of Revelation: A Narrative Interpretation* (Edinburgh Studies in Constructive Theology; Grand Rapids: Eerdmans, 1997), 1-25, 181-201. See also Hendrikus Berkhof, *Christian Faith: An Introduction to the Study of the Faith* (rev. ed.; Grand Rapids: Eerdmans, 1986), 63-68.

3. The progressive disclosure of God's unfolding plan to redeem humanity, much like the wilderness wanderings, does not follow a steady, straight path through the history it recounts. There are seemingly countless setbacks in the relationship between God and God's people and endless new beginnings. God's people seem nearly always incapable of embracing the blessing of new life YHWH repeatedly sets before them. Some of them even assent to the crucifixion of God's Son! But in their canonical (final) form, the scriptures proclaim that, despite all of these setbacks, God's plan to forgive God's people and to restore the blessings of creation is that towards which all of history has been moving and in the end will be accomplished.

4. See James A. Sanders, *From Sacred Story to Sacred Text* (Philadelphia: Fortress, 1987) for one of the more important discussions of canon formation and its progressive development. One key example of this canonical development was the reshaping, production, collection, and codification of major portions of the Hebrew Scriptures during the Babylonian Exile (587-538 B.C.E.), in part to help explain why such a disaster took place (because of Israel's unrelenting sin) and to announce God's eventual response (gracious restoration). Another occurs in the wake of Jesus' crucifixion and resurrection. In response to those revelatory events and Jesus' own teaching, Christians immersed themselves in the Hebrew Scriptures in order to make sense of God's long-awaited act of salvation occurring unexpectedly in a crucified and resurrected messiah, leading to the production of the New Testament texts. It was out of this merger of past tradition, present circumstance and God's inspiration that the biblical writers added to their sacred tradition believing that God was again at work revealing to them something crucial about their relationship

to God and God's activity in human history.

5. Terrence E. Fretheim, *The Pentateuch* (Nashville: Abingdon, 1996), 169.

6. Ibid.

7. Paul J. Achtemeier, *Inspiration and Authority: Nature and Function of Christian Scripture* (Peabody: Hendrickson, 1999), 152-156.

8. Ibid., 155.

9. Here Achtemeier and the many who share his view encounter a serious difficulty: Several commands issued by the New Testament writers are not seen by even many conservative Christians as binding. How many women continue to wear head-coverings in worship (1 Cor 2:2-16)? How many churches refuse to let women speak or teach in the community of believers (1 Tim 2:11)? To be sure, contextual and cultural factors are relevant to the understanding of these texts. However, the exact nature of the contextual issues underlying these texts is uncertain, and even if we could reliably discern them they would not alone account for the severity of the commands that are issued (especially 1 Tim 2). Moreover, the appeal to an underlying "principle" common to many evangelical interpretations of such problem texts often requires such an extensive degree of hermeneutical maneuvering that the final assessment of what the passage "means" is often quite different than the plain sense of the text. It is difficult to see how these methods are treating these texts as normative in the way that Achtemeier and others assert they must be. My position may be accused of placing us on a "slippery slope" with regard to biblical instruction: some may ask, "If some of the teachings of the New Testament are not binding for us, then what prevents any or all them from being put aside as well?" My contention is that nearly all Christians—liberal and conservative alike—have been essentially "putting aside" certain instructions for quite some time (and in many cases, appropriately so). In other words, all of us are already standing on this slippery slope, and the only means we really have to keep from tumbling down into the abyss of meaninglessness with regard to God's commands is the abidingly normative ministry of the Spirit.

10. Perhaps the lone exceptions are the two great commandments that Jesus announces: "You shall love the Lord your God with all your heart, and with all your soul, and with all your mind. This is the great and first commandment. And the second is like it, You shall love your neighbor as yourself. On these commandments depend all the law and the prophets" (Mt 22:37-40).

"Abounding in Steadfast Love and Faithfulness": The Old Testament as a Source for Christology

J. Clinton McCann, Jr.

When Augustine asked Ambrose for instruction on hearing the gospel of Jesus Christ, Ambrose directed him to the Book of Isaiah.[1] To contemporary pastors and scholars, it may seem strange to think of the Old Testament as a source for christology; but this should not be the case. The Christian Bible includes both testaments. So, when we Christians contemplate "The Centrality of Christ/the Word," it should be a reasonable expectation that both testaments offer testimony to Christ. In short, the Old Testament can and should be a source for christology.

By making this affirmation, I do not mean to advocate a return to pre-critical exegesis, nor do I want to suggest that we "Christianize" the Old Testament or see it as a "prediction of Jesus," thus ignoring its origin and transmission in the life of ancient Israel and Judah. I do want, however, to make the crucial apostolic affirmation that the God of Israel is the same God we profess to be revealed in Jesus of Nazareth. As Steve Motyer has recently put it:

> The God whom he [Jesus] teaches us to call "Father" is the God of Israel. And therefore . . . we regard ourselves as the people of that God, and those Scriptures as ours.[2]

So, as the title of Motyer's essay suggests, we Christians have "two testaments" but "one biblical theology." Because Frederick Trost has been a passionate practitioner and advocate of biblical theology, I am especially happy to offer the following exercise in biblical theology in his honor.

The Old Testament text upon which I shall focus is Ex 34:6-7, one of Israel's fundamental confessions of faith. I shall first explore the significance of this text within its context in the Book of Exodus. Then, I shall suggest how this text has a wider significance throughout the canon, including the New Testament, especially the first chapter of the Gospel of John and its portrayal of "the Word."

Exodus 34:6-7 in The Context of the Book of Exodus

God's revelation of the divine self to Moses comes at a critical moment in the unfolding story of the relationship between God and God's people. God has graciously delivered the Israelites from slavery in Egypt to freedom (Ex 1-15); God has offered the people instruction on how to stay free (Ex 19–23, including the Ten Commandments in 20:1-18 and the Book of the Covenant in chapters 21–23); and the covenant between God and Israel has been sealed (24:1-11). In particular, the people have promised twice to be obedient to God and God's commandments (24:3, 7).

It is crucial to notice that the very next time the people speak, they manifest their disobedience to God and the commandments (32:1). Their request for Aaron to "make gods for us" violates the first two of the Ten Commandments. God is inclined to wipe out the people and start over again with Moses (32:7-10); but remarkably, Moses talks God out of this plan (32:11-14): "And the LORD changed his mind about the disaster that he planned to bring on his people" (v. 14).[3]

Despite the announcement of God's change of plans in 32:14, the subsequent material in chapters 32–34 suggests that the future of God's disobedient people remains in doubt. From a historical point of view, the unevenness of the narrative reflects the development of the Pentateuch from several sources (JEDP, etc.). The literary effect of this unevenness is to highlight the crucial theological issue, namely, will God continue to be related to a disobedient people? God's address to Moses in 33:1-3 seems to contradict 32:14, and it puts the future of the people in doubt. Thus, Moses remains uncertain about God's abiding presence among the people (33:15-16), even after the divine self-revelation in 34:6-7 (see 34:8-9).

The uncertainty is resolved in 34:10, where the "covenant" God makes is, in essence, already a new covenant following the people's breaking of the covenant sealed in 24:1-11. In short, God will remain related to a disobedient people! Why? Because, as 34:6-7 puts it, God is "merciful and gracious, slow to anger, and abounding in steadfast love and faithfulness." The "awesome thing" (34:10) that God does is to forgive sinners!

This good news of God's amazing grace is reinforced by the placement of chapters 32–34 between chapters 25–31 and 35–40. Chapters 25–31 consist of God's instructions to Moses on how to build the tabernacle, and chapters 35–40 describe in detail how these instructions were carried out and the tabernacle was built. These chapters are very repetitive, and they are often viewed as rather boring; however, they have great theological significance. The people are told to build the tabernacle, "so that I [God] may dwell among them" (25:8). The instructions are given *before* Israel's disobedience in the golden calf episode (chapters 32–34), and the actual construction occurs *following* this episode. This sequence reinforces the good news that God will still "dwell among" God's disobedient people. As soon as "Moses finished the work" (40:33), "the glory of the LORD filled the tabernacle" (40:34); that is, God is present among the people. For people who have proven to be faithless and extremely frustrating to God (32:1-14), God's grace abounds.

But is the good news this simple? Well, yes and no. To be sure, 34:6 identifies God as "merciful and gracious, slow to anger, and abounding in steadfast love and faithfulness;" and 34:7 begins by proclaiming that God forgives "iniquity and transgression and sin." But what about the rest of v. 7? It continues as follows: "yet by no means clearing the guilty, but visiting the iniquity of the parents upon the children and the children's children, to the third and fourth generation." This tension between mercy and wrath, or grace and judgment, constitutes the basic interpretive issue for biblical theology. How is the issue to be approached?

As Phyllis Trible points out Ex 34:6-7 presents a "tension [between] God the lover and God the punisher."[4] Walter Brueggemann's language is a bit stronger. He suggests that the tension in Ex 34:7 is actually more of a disjunction, and he concludes that "God in the horizon and utterance of Israel is inescapably disputatious and disjunctive."[5] But does this tension or apparent disjunction suggest that God is capricious or unreliable? Or, does it serve some other purpose? As I see it, Ex 32–34 as a whole suggests that God is essentially a Lover rather than a Punisher. The function of the concluding lines of 34:7 is to suggest that "anything goes" is not acceptable with God and that there will always be destructive consequences of disobedience. These destructive consequences, however, are not God's will in the positive sense. Rather, they result from the people's choice to disobey and to go their own way. Exodus 34:8-10 actually suggests that the people are *not* punished. Indeed, logically speaking, grace is precisely the refusal to punish the guilty. To be sure, sinners will experience the negative consequences that their own actions set in motion, not because God wills punishment, but rather because God's will has *not* been observed.

Exodus 34:6-7 in the Old Testament Canon

The resonances of Ex 34:6-7 in the Old Testament canon create a trajectory that reinforces the conclusion that God is ultimately Lover rather than Punisher. As Rolf Rendtorff points out, Ex 32–34 and Gen 1–9 reveal a common pattern that forms a structuring concept for the books of Genesis and Exodus. The pattern is this: God creates or delivers; a relationship or covenant is established; humans disobey; and God graciously forgives and restores.[6] Moreover, Claus Westermann argues that the function of Ex 32–34 within the Pentateuch is to anticipate the entire prophetic canon. In other words, the pattern of Israel's disobedience followed by God's forgiveness, characterizes the subsequent story of Israel and Judah in the Former

Prophets (Joshua–2 Kings). As for the Latter Prophets (Isaiah, Jeremiah, Ezekiel, The Book of the Twelve), these books clearly warn Israel and Judah of the negative consequences of their idolatry and injustice; but they inevitably conclude with the promise of forgiveness and restoration.[7] While there are destructive consequences of the people's disobedience—that is, while the guilty are by no means cleared—the will of God in the positive sense is for the restoration of the people. In short, God is essentially "merciful and gracious, slow to anger, and abounding in steadfast love and faithfulness" (Ex 34:6), as in Ex 32-34 (see, for instance, Mic 7:18-20). Again, the canonical trajectory reveals God to be essentially a Lover rather than a Punisher.

Exodus 34:6-7 in John 1

The canonical trajectory involving Ex 34:6-7 is not limited to the Old Testament. The most obvious resonance of the Old Testament in John 1 is Genesis 1 (cf. Gen 1:1 and Jn 1:1, and note the importance of "light" in both chapters), but it seems that Rolf Rendtorff is not the first to have recognized a relationship between the opening chapters of Genesis and Ex 32–34 (and its context). So did the author of the Gospel of John, who cites both texts. The affirmation in Jn 1:14 that "the Word became flesh and lived among us" recalls Ex 25:8 ("make me a sanctuary, so that I may dwell among them"). Thus, the earthly Jesus is portrayed as the new locus of God's presence. This message is reinforced by the subsequent repetition of "glory" in 1:14, recalling Ex 40:34 and the notice that "the glory of the LORD filled the tabernacle" after Moses had "finished the work" (Ex 40:33).

But the work now being accomplished in Jesus is an even fuller revelation of the divine presence. Whereas Moses was not allowed to see God (Ex 33:20-23), the Word now made flesh makes God fully known (Jn 1:18; see 14:9). Given these resonances of Ex 25-40 in Jn 1, it is not surprising that Jn 1:14 also recalls the key Israelite confession of faith in Ex 34:6-7. In particular, "grace and truth" are the Greek equivalents of the Hebrew words translated "steadfast love and faithfulness" in Ex 34:6 (and elsewhere; see, for example, Pss 25:10; 40:10-11; 57:3; 85:10; 86:15; 103:8). This crucial word-pair is a sort of shorthand to describe the character of God, and it is John's conviction that Jesus fully embodies God's character.

From the resonances of Ex 25-40, especially 34:6-7, in Jn 1, it is obvious that the author of the Gospel was using the Old Testament as a source for christology. What may be less obvious is that John's use of Genesis and Exodus also serves as an invitation for us contemporary Christians to use the Old Testament as a source for christology. This is especially important, given the implication in Jn 1:17 that "grace and truth came through Jesus Christ," as if for the first time. Readers of the Old Testament sources on which Jn 1:14-18 depends, however, know better. God has *always* been steadfastly loving and faithful, as the stories of Israel and Judah make clear. Failing to realize this, we shall miss the crucial apostolic testimony that the God of Israel is also the God revealed in Jesus.

In the final analysis, of course the author of John's Gospel does not contradict this apostolic testimony. John 3:16 may be taken to imply that God only loved the world with the sending of the "only Son," but not so. The Gospel of John cannot imagine a time when the world was without "the Word" embodied by Jesus (Jn 1:1-18). In short, God has *always* loved the world. Creation itself begins the trajectory that takes us into the Book of Exodus, through the story of Israel and Judah, and into the Gospel of John; and it is a trajectory that consistently portrays God as essentially loving and faithful to the world, including a humankind that has been persistently unfaithful from nearly the beginning. In short, God is essentially Lover rather than Punisher.

The importance of reading the Old Testament as a source for christology is underscored too by the remainder of Jn 1, which proceeds to identify the Word made flesh as "the Messiah" (Jn 1:41), which is the Hebrew word meaning "anointed," a term that designated the ancient kings of Israel and Judah (see Jn 1:49). To be sure, one might infer the significance of the Messiah from the way Jesus is described in the Gospels, but the Gospel writers largely assume that readers will know what the Messiah represents. Of course, this is precisely why Ambrose told Augustine to read the Book of Isaiah. Failing to do what Ambrose counseled—that is, failing to use the Old Testament as a source for christology—we are apt to make the same mistake that many Christians have made throughout the centuries and still make. That is, we are apt to identify Jesus as our "personal savior" rather than the savior of the world (see Jn 1:29; see Isa 2:1-4; 9:2-7; 11:1-10; 42:1-9; 49:1-6; 52:7-10). In other words, failing to use the Old Testament as a source for christology, we risk the danger of failing to understand that God is and always has been steadfastly loving and faithful—indeed, nothing short of the unfailing Lover of the whole creation (see Jn 1:1-18; 3:16).

Notes

1. See Christopher Seitz, "Of Mortal Appearance: The Earthly Jesus and Isaiah as a Type of Christian Scripture," *Ex Auditu* 14 (1998):31.

2. Steve Motyer, "Two Testaments, One Biblical Theology" in *Between*

Two Horizons: Spanning New Testament Studies and Systematic Theology, ed. Joel B. Green and Max Turner (Grand Rapids, Mich. and Cambridge, UK: Eerdmans, 2000), 156. As Motyer recognizes, this affirmation raises the crucial issue of the relationship of Judaism and Christianity. He does not explore this issue in his essay, nor will space permit me to explore it in this essay.

3. See J. Clinton McCann, Jr., "Exodus 32:1-14," *Interpretation* 44 (July 1990): 277-281.

4. Phyllis Trible, *God and the Rhetoric of Sexuality* (Philadelphia: Fortress, 1978), 1.

5. Walter Brueggemann, *Theology of the Old Testament: Testament Dispute, Advocacy* (Minneapolis: Fortress, 1997), 705; see also 215-228, 269-272.

6. Rolf Rendtorff, "'Covenant' as a Structuring Concept in Genesis and Exodus," *JBL* 108 (1989): 385-393.

7. Claus Westermann, *Elements of Old Testament Theology,* trans. D. W. Stott (Atlanta: John Knox, 1978), 50. See also Raymond C. Van Leeuwen, "Scribal Wisdom and Theodicy in The Book of the Twelve," *In Search of Wisdom: Essays in Memory of John G. Gammie*, ed. Leo G.Purdue, Bernard Brandon Scott, William Johnston Wiseman (Louisville: Westminster/John Knox, 1993), 31-49. Van Leeuwen argues that Ex 34:6-7 played a major role in the formation of The Book of the Twelve, especially Hosea through Micah. I am also indebted to Van Leeuwen for originally calling to my attention the resonance of Ex 34:6-7 in John 1. In this regard, see also Motyer, "Two Testaments," 158.

Preaching the Word of the Cross

Gail R. O'Day

For Christ did not send me to baptize but to proclaim the gospel, and not with eloquent wisdom, so that the cross of Christ might not be emptied of its power (1 Cor. 1:17).

These words of Paul introduce his most focused discussion of what it means to preach the word of the cross, 1 Cor 1:18–2:5. Interestingly, it is in 1 Corinthians, not Romans and Galatians, that Paul reflects most on what it means for the life of the faith community to preach the crucified Christ. There probably is a correlation between this emphasis on preaching the cross and the myriad of community issues with which the Corinthian situation confronts Paul. The complexities of this particular community's life mean that Paul needs a living word to speak to a living community, and so Paul begins 1 Corinthians by focusing on the life-shaping and life-transforming power of preaching.

1 Corinthians is a New Testament book that should make contemporary Christians feel immediately at home. This letter from Paul to a nascent Christian community punches fatal holes in any myth about—or nostalgia for—the "golden days," the "good old days" of the church. What we see here is the first century version of our own communities: divisions among the members of the faith community, with different members attaching superiority to their theological blood lines (chs. 1–4); disagreements about sexual ethics, and what should or should not warrant church discipline (chs. 5, 7); community members suing one another in law courts (ch. 6); arguments about pluralism and multi-culturalism—how does one live as a Christian in the broader culture (chs. 8–10); rights of the clergy to support for their ministry (ch. 9); divisions over worship (chs. 11–14).

In the face of such a conflicted community, Paul does not simply focus on the variety of problems and try to give instructions on how to solve them. He does not begin his remarks to this community by telling them what behaviors they need to change, how they need to conduct their business, what management strategy or family systems theory they should employ to get their house in order. Paul would probably raise a quizzical and furrowed brow at the whole host of how-to ministry books that fill our bookstores. (That's if he were feeling polite—let's not forget that Paul was not exactly one to mince words when he disagreed with the way things were going— "You foolish Galatians! Who has bewitched you?")

Instead of following the path that has become so natural to contemporary Christian ministry, Paul takes a wholly different strategy. Paul assumes that the way to address practical problems in a community is with theology, not advice. Paul does not separate the practical and the pastoral from the theological. For Paul, theology is not to be isolated from ministry as an intellectual pursuit; christology is not abstract words about who Jesus is. Theology and christology are integrally linked to who the community is and will be. Paul thought that topics that the contemporary church tends to dismiss as too "heavy" were at their heart not only preachable but were indeed the very essence and purpose of preaching and of pastoral ministry.

For the Corinthian church to get its community life back in order, the Corinthians had to be reminded of who they are—and how and why they are a community of faith. Instructions on how to live as a church have to be preceded by what it means for this group of people even to take shape as a church. Throughout 1 Corinthians, Paul does not address himself primarily to the problems that beset the community—although they are his constant point of reference—but to the community's identity as a people of Christ, as a people to whom, for whom, and with whom the word of the cross has been proclaimed.

Paul's affirmation of his vocation as a preacher of the gospel, not a baptizer (1 Cor 1:17), is spoken in response to sectarian quarrels among the members of the Corinthian church:

> There are quarrels among you, my brothers and sisters. What I mean is that each of you says, 'I belong to Paul,' or 'I belong to Apollos,' or 'I belong to Cephas,' or 'I belong to Christ'(1 Cor 1:11-12).

The reason for the quarrels may be difficult to grasp at first glance, because at one level, there is nothing wrong with claiming "I belong to Christ." If those words are an affirmation shared by all, it is a statement of Christian unity. But clearly some in Corinth are saying, "I belong to Christ" as if Christ is their possession and no one else's. They claim that direct membership to Paul, or Apollos, or Cephas (Peter), makes one somehow better, a superior Christian.

Paul responds to the Corinthians' claims ironically and not altogether kindly: "Has Christ been divided? Was Paul crucified for you?" (1 Cor 1:13) These two ironic, almost sarcastic questions set up Paul's reference to his vocation as preacher of the gospel and his words about the message of the cross that follows at 1:18. The Corinthians seem to think that their sectarian squabbling (which might feel uncomfortably close to denominational divisions in our own context) is acceptable because it is only about them and their relationship to one another. Quarrels and divisions in the church are acceptable behavior because they are an inevitable symptom of human nature.

Paul counters quite pointedly that the Corinthians are wrong about the ramifications of their behavior. Quarrels among themselves are not simply about them—they are about God and Christ. They threaten to betray the very framework of the gospel Paul is called to preach. Paul's questions work both sides of the problem. The first question, "Has Christ been divided?" asks the Corinthians to look at what their words and arguments say about Jesus. Is Christ divisible into many little parts, available to any for the taking: some parts here; other parts there? Paul's most eloquent answer to this question will come in the metaphor of the body of Christ in 1 Cor 12. The second set of questions, "Was Paul crucified for you? Or were you baptized in Paul's name?" moves even more pointedly to the sectarian claims that seem to shape this community. One's identity as a Christian does not come from the individual communion into which one is baptized—hence Paul's distancing of his own role as one who baptizes—but one's Christian identity comes from the crucifixion of the one indivisible Christ.

The indivisibility of the crucified Christ is what Paul is called to preach and is what is at risk in the Corinthians' preoccupation with the diverse forms of their own Christian lives. Paul does not disparage baptism but reminds the Corinthians that baptism is not the starting place for their own individual and disparate lives as Christians. Instead, baptism gives them their place in a story that began before them and that they are welcomed into by virtue of the word of the cross. Preaching Christ is so important and central to Paul because everything disintegrates without this word.

In response to these quarrels and divisions, Paul reintroduces the Corinthians to the theological world that is the source of their identity. In 1 Cor 1:18–2:5, Paul speaks eloquently of wisdom and foolishness, power and weakness, and of the centrality of the cross in defining all the terms of the conversation. The quarreling Corinthians, in their insistence on claiming privilege for one group of believers, are like those who demand signs and wisdom (1:22). Conventional categories of power and wisdom have been inverted by the cross, but the Corinthians come perilously close to accepting the world's norms rather than the new norms introduced by the cross: "we proclaim Christ crucified, a stumbling block to Jews and foolishness to Gentiles, but to those who are called, both Jews and Greeks, Christ the power of God and the wisdom of God" (1:23-24).

The logic of the structure of 1 Cor 1:10–2:5 also points to the decisive role of the cross in the preaching and ministry of the church for Paul.

As has been noted, he begins with the community's present experience of divisions (1:10-16) and then offers a description of the theological world that they put at risk with their quarrels (1:17-25). In the remainder of this unit, Paul combines theological and experiential language in order to show the Corinthians the ways in which their experience and God's identity are inseparable from one another. In 1:26-31, Paul uses the language of power and wisdom to talk about the Corinthians' own experience of Christian community. In 2:1-5, Paul views his own ministry through the theological lens of power, wisdom, and the cross. Paul shows the Corinthians that he chooses the foolishness and weakness of the cross (2:1, 3, 4), and that he has worked intentionally in his preaching to communicate to the Corinthians that this cross-shaped foolishness and weakness is also the ground out of which they live and move and have their being (2:2, 5). The Corinthians' notions of power and wisdom lead only to quarrels and divisions; the power and wisdom of God, as known in the cross, lead to salvation.

Paul's words, "For I decided to know nothing among you but Jesus Christ and him crucified" (1 Cor. 2:2), are at the heart of all his preaching to the Corinthians. Throughout the letter, Paul does indeed know nothing among this community except Jesus Christ and him crucified. Paragraph after paragraph, community problem after community problem, Paul confronts the Corinthians with the transformative and decisive reality of the death of Jesus: "For our paschal lamb, Christ, has been sacrificed" (5:7); "For you were bought with a price" (6:20); "The cup of blessing that we bless, is it not a sharing in the blood of Christ? The bread that we break, is it not a sharing in the body of Christ?" (10:16); "For as often as you eat this bread and drink the cup, you proclaim the Lord's death until he comes" (11:26). Finally—and only finally—Paul turns from the death of Jesus to the resurrection in 1 Cor 15. But even then, Paul grounds the resurrection in the death of Jesus and in the proclamation of that death (15:1-11).

Paul's words to the Corinthians about the centrality of the proclamation of the crucified Christ raises important questions about the authority of the preacher and of the word the preacher brings to his or her community. The word one preaches has its source in the cross and must be shaped by the cross to be authentic.

1) Is there a fit between the message and the form of the proclamation? Is the emphasis in proclamation on "lofty words and wisdom," glib speech and easy answers, or on a message that unflinchingly embraces "Jesus Christ and him crucified"?

2) Is there a fit between the message and the one who proclaims it? Does the preacher, like Paul, come to the ministry of preaching "in

weakness and in fear and in much trembling" (2:3)? As Paul also wrote to the Corinthians, "For we do not proclaim ourselves; we proclaim Jesus Christ as Lord and ourselves as your slaves for Jesus' sake" (2 Cor 4:5).

Paul's words call the church to search for evidence of the crucifixion and its shaping influence in its preaching. All members of the Christian community are, to a degree, "broken" by the word of the cross. We know Jesus' suffering; we know the cross; we know human suffering. Any message that we preach needs to attend to those realities for all who receive the word, "so that the cross of Christ might not be emptied of its power (1 Cor 1:17). Paul invites first and twenty-first century Christians to live out of and into the word of the cross.

"Almighty and Eternal God, in Every Age and Land"

Almighty and eternal God, in every age and land you have called men and women to speak your word and to do your will. For your wondrous gift of Jesus Christ and for the light he has brought to the world we are grateful. For the way you have led us to learn of Christ and awakened in us the desire to be his disciples we are thankful. To you, O God, we give our special thanks for your providence that calls some to be apostles, pastors, and teachers in our day.

Guide, O God, those persons you have called to be preachers so that they may speak your word boldly because they know you and yet speak humbly because they know you only in part. May pastors be those who speak your truth and may they also share your love without limit.

O Good Shepherd, lead those who shepherd the people of your congregations so that many will praise you, love you and your church, and faithfully serve you. May we who bear the name Christian, walk not far from Christ, in whose name we pray.

Walter J. Olsen

Jesus Christ and the Christian Vocation to *Politeia*

Stephen J. Patterson

These people who have turned the world upside down have now come here. . . . And they are going against the decrees of Caesar, saying that there is another emperor, Jesus (Acts 17:6b, 7b).

Frederick Trost, in a lifetime of service to the church has never shied from the radical call to discipleship that implores one to "turn the world upside down." To understand the claim of Christ on one's life is to receive it as a claim on one's whole life, not just the private sphere of personal piety. To hear in one's own life a word of grace as *God's* Word is to receive this Word as a hope for the whole world, not simply one's private world of satisfied devotion. In his life and his ministry, none has embodied this more than Fred. So it is that I would offer these reflections on the Christian vocation as inadequate payment on a debt we all owe to him for his devotion to prophetic public witness.

Let us begin with the Christian vocation itself. What does God call each and every person to do? This is a question we might pose to Jesus himself. When asked by a scribe to name the most important commandment of all, Jesus responded not with one command, but two: "'You shall love the Lord your God with all your heart, and with all your soul, and with all your mind, and with all your strength.' And the second is this, 'You shall love your neighbor as yourself'" (Mk 12:29-31). This is the two-fold vocation we all share: the love of God and the love of neighbor.

But why in this story does Jesus name two commandments, not just one, as the scribe asks? Matthew, in re-presenting Mark's version of this story, adds words that bring out the significance of this two-fold claim. The second commandment, he says, "is like unto the first" (Mt 22:39). To love God *is* to love one's neighbor; to love one's neighbor *is* to love God. This great truth, repeated again and again in the Christian tradition, is grounded in the claim that God's very nature is love. To love God is to be devoted to love itself. As the writer of 1 John so aptly put it a generation after Matthew, "Let us love one another, for love is of God, and anyone who shows love is born of God and knows God. Anyone who does not show love does not know God; for God is love" (1 Jn 4:7-8). The vocation of each and every person is to show love: to create for others an experience of the love of God we ourselves can see and know in the life and work of Jesus Christ.

But what does this mean, really? Many North American Christians hear these words of Jesus gladly but receive them within a cultural context that suggests their meaning is personal and private, not political or public. The love of God and neighbor is the basis of our private ethics but not at all the principle around which we imagine the way the world ought to work, even at the highest levels of economic and political life. There other norms prevail: competition, self-sufficiency, survival of the fittest. Consequently, many North American Christians lead two lives: a private life of compassion and care for others and a public life that is "dog-eat-dog."

The roots of this curious schizophrenia are manifold. One is a European theological tradition that is wary of attempts to associate Christianity too closely with any particular social or political program. The Nazification of the German church in the 1930s and '40s serves as a stern warning against all that can go wrong with such attempts. Perhaps more relevant for most North American Christians is our constitutional tradition of keeping the state out of matters pertaining to religious faith. This separation of church and state, a unique development in western culture, has proven to be crucial for ensuring our religious liberty and the flourishing of diverse forms of religious expression across the American cultural landscape. But it has also been an excuse for many Christians to view their political choices as somehow free of the principles that govern their private lives. The same person who responds enthusiastically to the request to take a casserole to an ailing parishioner, might in the next moment be heard to favor cuts in government programs that provide nutritional support for children, on the grounds that taxes are too high.

As difficult as it is for North American Christians to integrate their religious and political lives, do it we must. When the scribe who asked Jesus about the greatest commandment responded in agreement with Jesus' answer, Jesus said to him, "You are not far from the realm of God" (Mk 12:34). Here Jesus uses an expression that was typical of his way of speaking about his ministry: "the realm of God." This word, "realm," often rendered "kingdom" in traditional Christian parlance, is in fact a very political term. The Greek word it translates is *basileia*. Its chief use in Jesus' day was in reference to that great political entity that dominated the life of Jesus and every other peasant living in the Mediterranean basin in the first century of our era: Rome. *Basileia* means "empire." There was but one empire in the world that Jesus knew, the Roman Empire. To speak of another *basileia*, another empire "as God would have it," was an act of high treason. Rome considered *itself* to be God's empire, and its emperor God's son.

But Jesus spoke constantly of the Empire of God, a practice that distinguished him from all but the most brazen street philosophers of his day. And the empire he spoke of was not at all like that which swept across his world in one violent coup after another. In God's Empire the poor reign, the hungry are fed, the outcast are drawn in. What the "dog-eat-dog" world of imperial Rome spit out as refuse, Jesus and his followers gathered up into a new empire grounded in an experience of love-ultimate, unmitigated love, gracious love, God's love. Jesus did not think of this new empire as something private, apolitical, other-worldly, or strictly future. He said, "The Empire of God is not coming with signs to be observed; nor will they say, 'Lo, here it is!' or 'There!' Just look! The Empire of God is in the midst of you" (Lk 17:20-21).

The way in which Jesus confronted the Empire is illustrated by a story in the Gospel of Mark, in which Jesus is asked whether or not Jews ought to resist paying the Roman tribute. Here was the heart of the matter for Jews living under imperial rule. Jesus was not foolhardy. He approached this question with great cleverness, but his meaning should not be misconstrued. His answer is well-known:

> "Bring me a denarius and let me see it." And they brought one. Then he said to them, "Whose head is this, and whose title?" They answered, "The emperor's." Jesus said to them, "Give to the emperor the things that are the emperor's, and to God the things that are God's" (Mk 12:15-17).

In modern American culture this reply has often been misunderstood as a blueprint for the separation of church and state, for dividing sacred from secular concerns. But this misses the point entirely. In Jesus' world there was no separation of church and state, sacred from secular. For Jesus, a Jew, there was *nothing* that did not belong to God. "The earth is the Lord's, and the fullness thereof" (Ps 24:1). This was equally true of Romans, who saw their rule as an all-encompassing God-given peace, the *Pax Romana*. So what did Jesus mean by this reply? In it he employs the skill of a clever street philosopher, constantly in danger of entrapment by his opponents. They mean to trap him between the authorities on the one hand and his tax-oppressed audience on the other. He eludes them with a reply that itself begs a question: "What *does* belong to God, and what to Caesar?" Now his opponents must reveal *their* assumptions. They are caught in their own trap. If they admit Caesar's claim, they will be stoned by the Jewish crowd; if they do not, they will be arrested. But no one in the crowd that day would have missed the clear sub-text so elusively laid out by the unanswered question in Jesus' reply: God and Caesar are not the same, and one must choose between them.

In the end Jesus was not satisfied with the power of the clever rejoinder to settle disputes on the street. Eventually he was to take his Empire of God into the very seat of imperial power in his own land, Jerusalem. There he confronted the political figures who set the economic and social agenda in Rome's province of Palestine. These leaders, too, knew that Jesus was not interested in a merely private faith. And so they executed him on a cross, the Roman method for dealing with peasant protesters who criticized imperial values and priorities. In this fate, Jesus' life was joined to those of the great Hebrew prophets of old—Amos, Hosea, Jeremiah—who spoke a word of God in the political sphere in spite of the consequences they knew might result. In proclaiming his resurrection, Jesus' followers staked their claim that his word was indeed God's Word, that his Empire truly was "of God." This claim of faith remains ours today.

Politics—*politeia*—in its most general sense is the negotiation of how we will structure human life together. If the church is to be the church of Jesus Christ, it cannot forswear its legitimate interest in *politeia*. For the gospel of Jesus Christ speaks exactly to this: how shall we structure human life together such that everyone may experience the ultimate reality we now know to be true, that God is love? How shall we embody love in every sphere of human life, not just our private affairs? How shall we create an empire that is "of God?"

The preaching of Jesus about the Empire of God comes to us as a claim upon our lives in their entirety, a call to participate fully in what Christ has wrought. It is not a partial claim, nor one that engages us merely privately, but wholly. To respond faithfully to this claim, the church must always be engaged politically. It must watch after our common life, doing all it can to promote in the political sphere the kind of love and care that are Christ's, even though their unlikely vehicle may even be a government about which we have become so cynical. For the church there is no secular realm. As Paul the Apostle asserts, all legitimate power and authority comes from God (Rom 13:1-7). When it is exercised in the cause of love, care, and compassion, it deserves our respect and support, not cynical indifference. When it is not, it is the church's calling to hold accountable those who would use power and authority to selfish ends, to oppress, to do violence, to divide human communities.

In such times the church will not be a welcome voice in the halls of power. This, too, was an experience early Christians knew well. In Acts, when Paul and his companions come into Thessalonica preaching the gospel of Jesus, they do not receive a warm welcome. To the local authorities their patriotic opponents complain, "These people who have turned the world upside down have now come here. . . . And they are going against the decrees of Caesar, saying that there is another emperor, Jesus" (Acts 17:6-7). Sometimes this is indeed our calling: to turn the world upside down. For in all we do, our ultimate loyalty is never to any government, however just or corrupt. We know another emperor, Jesus, and another Empire that is "of God."

What Is Meant by "Telling the Truth"? The Case of Dietrich Bonhoeffer

Carl J. Rasmussen

The conclusion to Bonhoeffer's *Ethics* (the sixth edition) is a short fragment called "What is Meant by 'Telling the Truth'?"[1] Although the text does not disclose it, Bonhoeffer wrote this short fragment in Tegel prison in Berlin, under interrogation by a military judge, Judge Manfred Roeder. We know from notes that Bonhoeffer left, notes that constitute follow-up responses to his interrogator, that he was lying to protect his co-conspirators, a fact he made no attempt to conceal from history.[2]

The question Bonhoeffer addresses here is a large one, one central to Bonhoeffer's theological career: "What is truth itself and how does our speech relate to it?" As Bonhoeffer puts it, "The real is to be expressed in words. That is what constitutes truthful speech. And this inevitably raises the question of the 'how' of these words" (363). In short, the question addressed is the fundamental theological question: "If one is to say how a thing really is, *i.e.*, if one is to speak truthfully, one's gaze and one's thought must be directed towards the way in which the real exists in God and through God and for God" (365).

Bonhoeffer begins the chapter, neither with ethical abstractions, nor with his personal dilemma. He begins with the dynamics of a particular institution: the family. He considers what is required of parents and children when they speak to each other. He observes that the truthfulness of a child towards parents is different from that of the parents toward the child. As he puts it, the life of the small child lies open before the parents, and what this child says should reveal to them everything that is hidden and secret. But the parents cannot be open to the child. From this observation, Bonhoeffer concludes that telling the truth depends upon the particular situation in which one stands (363).

We must here confront Bonhoeffer the myth. Bonhoeffer's ethics of the concrete situation is neither an example of relativism nor the ethics of individual conscience. To the contrary, Bonhoeffer's ethics derive from authority and obedience, which is to say, from discipleship. For Bonhoeffer, only in the concrete situation do authority and obedience disclose themselves. Moreover, they disclose themselves only within a divinely ordained institutional framework. Four institutions in particular, four "mandates," carry the special ontological status of God's command. As such, their status is beyond question. These mandates are government, church, family and vocation. Through such institutions, individuals are gathered into community. Through such institutions, individuals find it possible to live for others in deputyship. Such institutions are in a sense constitutive of our individuality. Understanding any situation ethically involves acknowledgment of these mandates. It also involves acknowledgment that truth is not a simple matter. As I have suggested, Bonhoeffer wrote this fragment while lying to a military judge about his involvement in an attempt to overthrow his own government by force.

Bonhoeffer's location of truthfulness in specific situations, which occur within the structures of divinely mandated authority, shapes his ethics. Bonhoeffer expressly rejects any Kantian abstract, formalist ethics. Kant advanced a formal rule to generate universal ethical rules: Kant's categorical imperative. Kant more than any other figure is Bonhoeffer's opponent in the *Ethics*. Bonhoeffer's ethics derives from mandates, not rules. Hence, ethics is not a matter of individual conscience. It is a matter of obedience to institutions which are constitutive of individuals and in which individuals are free to live. Moreover, because it involves specific instances of obedience, ethics is not a matter for systematic study. Indeed, Bonhoeffer suggests that within the mandates ethical questions arise only as peripheral, or extraordinary, events. To suggest that ethical questions are reducible to some method is to deny their seriousness. Precisely because the mandates require of us obedience, only in extraordinary times of disunion among the mandates do ethical questions arise at all.

By contrast, the theoretical ethicist (by whom Bonhoeffer means Kant, perhaps Reinhold Niebuhr as well,[3] and really any systematic ethical thinker) requires of individuals ethical determinations concerning each individual action. For Bonhoeffer, such *ethics* falsifies experience. Such ethics is a form of narcissistic individualism which seeks its own justification and which leads to destruction of the self and community. Such an ethics is in Bonhoeffer's terms irresponsible. Bonhoeffer uses a particular Kantian example in his chapter. It is an example that he cites twice in the *Ethics*: Kant said that he would tell the truth to a criminal looking for a friend of his who had concealed himself in his house. The irony of Kant's example for Bonhoeffer's situation requires no comment. It should not surprise us that Bonhoeffer draws a conclusion different from Kant's example. Bonhoeffer would "lie" for his friend.

Bonhoeffer's ethics of obedience undermines any doctrine of correspondence. Speaking the truth does not involve some kind of correspondence between thought and speech. He points out, for example, that one may speak flatteringly, presumptuously, or hypocritically without uttering a material untruth, yet the words may nevertheless be untrue because the speaker disrupts and destroys the reality of the relationship between husband and wife, for example (365). An individual utterance is always part of the total reality which seeks expression in this utterance. Therefore, it must take into account the person addressed and the context. As he says, "If my utterance is to be truthful, it must in each case be different according to whom I am addressing, who is questioning me, and what I am speaking about" (365). The truthful word is not in itself constant; it is as much alive as life itself (365). Moreover, the location of truthfulness in the particular means that telling the truth is something that must be learned. It is a matter of experience within the framework of the mandates. It is a question of knowing the right word on each occasion. Finding this word is a matter of long, earnest, and ever more advanced effort on the basis of experience and knowledge of the real (365), including the interrelationship of the structures of authority in which we live. For Bonhoeffer, only people of maturity and experience can understand how to speak truthfully.

For Bonhoeffer, the view that truth is the correspondence between thought and speech can serve only the cynic. Bonhoeffer notes that it is only the cynic who claims to speak the truth at all times and all places to all people in the same way and thus displays a lifeless image of the truth. The cynic makes no allowance for human weakness but rather destroys the living truth between people. The cynic wounds shame, desecrates mystery, breaks confidence, betrays the community in which he lives, and laughs arrogantly at the devastation he has wrought and at the human weakness which cannot bear the truth (366). Bonhoeffer says that there is a truth which is of Satan.

> Its essence is that under the semblance of truth it denies everything that is real. It lives upon hatred of the real and of the world which is created and loved by God. It pretends to be executing the judgment of God upon the fall of the real. God's truth judges created things out of love, Satan's truth judges them out of envy and hatred. God's truth has become flesh in the world and is alive in the real, Satan's truth is the death of all reality (366).

What then is a lie? Given Bonhoeffer's view, it is very difficult to say what constitutes a lie. Having dispensed with a correspondence theory of truth, Bonhoeffer rejects the usual definition of a lie as a conscious discrepancy between thought and speech. Bonhoeffer's rejection carries dramatic implications. Lying is not a deliberate deception of another to his or her detriment. For Bonhoeffer, deception of the enemy in war, for example, is not lying (368-369). But what is a lie?

The lie is primarily the denial of God as He has evidenced Himself to the world. "Who is a liar but he that denieth that Jesus is the Christ?" (1 Jn 2:22). The lie is a contradiction of the word of God, which God has spoken in Christ, and upon which creation is founded. Consequently the lie is the denial, the negation, and the conscious and deliberate destruction of the reality which is created by God and which consists in God, no matter whether this purpose is achieved by speech or by silence (369).

Christ is the center: He alone is the truth, and any theory of what it means to tell the truth must originate in this center. Bonhoeffer acknowledges a danger in his position. It creates the suspicion that the truth can and may be adapted to each particular situation in a way that destroys the idea of truth and makes truth and falsehood indistinguishable (366). Moreover, Bonhoeffer suggests that his position may be misunderstood to mean that one may adopt a calculating or superior attitude towards another; that one has discretion to decide what one is prepared to tell. Yet, these dangers must be encountered:

> The word in the family is different from the word in the business or in public. The word which has come to life in the warmth of the personal relationship is frozen to death in the cold air of public existence. The word of command, which has its habitat in public service, would sever the bonds of mutual confidence if it were spoken in the family. Each word must have its own place and keep to it (367).

An important means of mitigating these dangers is a necessary reticence concerning language. As a writer, Bonhoeffer is extraordinarily spare. He was careful with words. Bonhoeffer's reticence about words made him skeptical of the mass media in words that should give us pause:

> It is a consequence of the wide defusion of the public word through the newspapers and the wireless that the essential character and the limits of the various different words are no longer clearly felt and that, for example, the special quality of the personal word is almost entirely destroyed. Genuine words are replaced by idle chatter. Words no longer possess any weight. There is too much talk. And when the limits of the various words are obliterated, when words become rootless and homeless, then the word loses truth, and then indeed there must almost inevitably be lying. When the various orders of life no longer respect one another, words become untrue (367).

To illustrate how words can become untrue, he sets forth the central example of his chapter, (which along with his personal dilemma and the Kantian example represents a third case study for his text). He considers a teacher who asks a child in front of the class whether it is true that the child's father often comes home drunk. The allegation is true, but the child denies it. Bonhoeffer observes perceptively that the lies of children and of inexperienced people are often to be ascribed to the fact that these people are faced with situations that they do not fully understand (368). The child's answer can indeed be called a lie, but according to Bonhoeffer it contains more truth, it is more in accordance with reality, than if the child had betrayed his father's weakness (368).

Here, as this fragmented essay disintegrates, in the shadow of his personal cross, we have a powerful if final glimpse of Dietrich Bonhoeffer, pastor and theologian:

> In our endeavors to express the real, we do not encounter this as a consistent whole, but in a condition of disruption and inner contradiction which has need of reconciliation and healing. We find ourselves simultaneously embedded in various different orders of the real, and our words, which strive towards the reconciliation and healing of the real, are nevertheless repeatedly drawn into the prevalent disunion and conflict. They can indeed fulfill their assigned purpose of expressing the real, as it is in God, only by taking up into themselves both the inner contradiction and the inner inconsistency of the real. If the words of men are to be true, they must deny neither the fall nor God's word of creation and reconciliation, the word in which all disunion is overcome (370).

Notes

1. All quotations in the text are from Dietrich Bonhoeffer, *Ethics*, ed. Eberhard Bethge, trans. Neville Horton Smith, based on the 6th German Edition (New York, N.Y.: MacMillan Publishing Co. 1965).

2. See Eberhardt Bethge, *Dietrich Bonhoeffer: A Biography, Revised Edition* (Minneapolis, Minn.: Fortress Press, 2000), 813, 829, 841. Dietrich Bonhoeffer, *Letters and Papers from Prison,*, ed. Eberhard Bethge, trans. Reginald Fuller, Frank Clark and John Bowden (New York, N.Y., MacMillan Publishing Co., 1972).

3. See the sole reference to Reinhold Niebuhr in the *Ethics,* 191.

"Dear God, Creator of the Universe"

Dear God, Creator of the universe and every living thing, come near to our hearts as we strive to live in cadence with your Word. Remove the scales of indifference and pettiness from our vision so that we are enabled to comprehend the breadth and depth of your creative love in all things and amidst all peoples. Toward that end focus our being on the embodiment of full and gracious life in Christ Jesus, our Teacher, our Savior, and our Light. Then, in your infinite mercy, O God, grant us the strength and will to accomplish in word and deed that which we proclaim in faith and prayer.

Max J. Rigert

"Peace Be with You"

John 20:19-29

Joachim Rogge†

No discussion! After Easter, after resurrection, Jesus came. No discussion about the circumstances. He is present. No explanation, but he speaks. To whom? To the disciples, who were afraid. There was no triumphalism in their hearts. For them the catastrophe was complete.

It seems to me that we are not privy to the interior situation of the disciples, but several things are obvious. They were sad, they were resigned, they had no more hope. There was no clear vision about the future. The doors were shut, understandably. This situation is similar to circumstances in which Christians and non-Christians find themselves today. Disappointment, closed doors and hearts, isolation, little joy about the life given by God. Very often we live after Easter, not knowing Easter took place. We live between an "unknown" Easter and the coming of the risen Lord to the anxious disciples.

We are not aware that Jesus comes and stands among us. He stands in his light amidst our darkness which, in fact, is no more darkness. The church father, Augustine, said that the one who refuses to believe that Christ is present is like a person who covers the sun in order to walk further with a lantern. But what to do and what to hope, when one has lost hope?

Hope. This is the saving and helping word that comes not from inside. It comes from outside. Jesus comes with his word after Easter. Not with a discussion regarding heaven and earth. And his message is so simple that he does not give the occasion or the challenge for long-lasting debates among us. Everybody can take this word, this message into his or her heart. Our response is the decision between life and death. Jesus wants life, our life, our passion, our joy, which is transferable to other people.

The risen Lord, says simply, "Peace be with you." He says this three times, without explanation. And the disciples answered nothing. They were strongly surprised. Perhaps they were full of doubt. They probably thought all possibilities, all hopes were gone. Without any comment, Jesus showed them the signs of the terrible event: his hands and his wounded side. Almost two thousand years ago the disciples saw this. But we, his followers today, have only the word, "Peace be with you." This word of life is very often disturbed or destroyed among us because the words of desperation, hopelessness and darkness are stronger. Yet peace is not only possible, peace is reality among Christians and non-Christians, if we believe and live this word. We have clear advice for living in the peaceless world. The only problem is that we do not believe Jesus Christ himself is our peace who has "broken down the dividing wall of hostility" (Eph 2:14).

I come from the country in which (some time ago) the dividing wall of hostility was broken down. New freedom, new liberty has been given as a gift of God to us. And now Christians are called to fill in the dangerous vacuum of conquered hostility. What shall be the new content of freedom and liberty? The content is Jesus Christ, our personified peace.

The disciples were glad. Are we also glad? We are the ambassadors of Christ among all men and women in the world. Jesus is sent by the Father and now we are sent by our Lord Jesus Christ. What is the message? What is the content of our life? Too often we ourselves bring trouble, disappointment, resignation, and depression to people in our environment. Our salvation is connected with our message from God that everybody who has contact with us shall go away more happy than in the moment he or she has met us. Our sense of life is that we meet all people with the joy that is in God and from God. The main question in our life is (and will forever be) which spirit is in our heart? Jesus did not discuss spirits and spiritualism. But he brings us the new reality, the foundation, and root of everlasting joy. He says, "Receive the Holy Spirit!"

What is the content of the newly-given spirit and spirituality? It is a very concrete reality. It is forgiveness! We have seen in our social environment in the former German Democratic Republic (GDR) an exciting example of life-bringing forgiveness. Following reunification, a Protestant pastor, who had suffered for a long time with his ten children under the regime of Erich Honecker, nevertheless took this man and his wife into his home when they had no place else to go. The break-through of forgiveness aids the world and builds bridges between military, political, and economic confrontation. The social engagement of Christians on behalf of Christians and non-Christians on God's behalf, helping to heal the thousands of wounds of bleeding humankind, is now crucial.

From the Holocaust of the Jews to the massacres in El Salvador, we see obviously that the Holy Spirit of our Savior is given but not received. The darkness of terrible ghosts seems to rule humankind. But the Spirit of the risen Christ is really given! The reality of non-believers is as old as the life-giving message. Shortly after the meeting of Jesus with the disciples, Thomas, who was absent at that exciting moment, said he could not believe. He seeks another demonstration. He wants to see the prints of the nails in Jesus' hands, and he requests a chance to place his hand in Jesus' side. This was the presupposition for his faith.

Do we have similar presuppositions? We ask, "Where is God in his mercy in this tormented world?" Let us ask the question differently, "In whose name are we involved and participating in the future of the world?" Let us not dismiss too quickly this question from our hearts.

And now another scene. Jesus comes anew eight days later. Once more there is no discussion, no rebuke to the non-believer Thomas. Jesus was once more among his disciples. He knew the doubts of Thomas, he knows also our doubts. He will fulfill Thomas's requests. "Put your finger here," he says. Thomas notably avoids further debate. He accepts the Lord as the Lord. "My Lord and my God," he says. Only with the heart are we able to see well. Blessings are given to those who have not seen and yet believe. Our physical eyes may get darker, but the trusting faith can get stronger. Not our often irritated eyes conquer the world, but God's promises. "This is the victory that overcomes the world, our faith" (1 Jn 5:4). We come from the victory of our risen Lord and now we go to the victory of the Lord who wins for us our future and the future of the world.

Confessing Christ and the Unity of the Church

Nikolaus Schneider

Christianity is divided into many churches and denominations. Unity always was a great task and at the same time a source of anger and conflict. There are good reasons for John's Gospel quoting Jesus: "I ask not only on behalf of these, but also on behalf of those, who will believe in me through their word, that they may all be one . . . so that the world may believe that you have sent me" (Jn 17: 20).

From its very beginning Christianity has had to struggle with the problem of divisions. This problem is not simply a matter of discussions about different opinions. This is a severe and serious stumbling block. There is a relationship between the credibility of Christ and the experience of Christianity in the world. A divided Christianity diminishes the witness of Christians and churches, and it even diminishes Christ himself.

Missionary societies suffered because western Christianity exported its patchwork situation into the missionary fields. This experience was one of the reasons for the world missionary conference of Edinburgh in the beginning of the twentieth century that eventually led to one of the roots of the World Council of Churches (WCC).

The competition among the missionary societies and the western churches, including the Roman Catholic Church, indicated a lack of spiritual power. The societies and the churches confused their efforts to proclaim Jesus Christ as the only hope and savior for the whole creation with the struggle for their own dignity, power, and influence. The danger was and is that the churches are serving themselves and not Christ or God.

The ecumenical movement is the one great effort to overcome this destructive and Christ-diminishing competition. Growing understanding of theological issues and traditions and of the organization of the churches as an expression of their faith and common actions to proclaim the gospel and help the needy were and are the methods and tools. The ecumenical movement was strong after World War I and World War II, but now we have to face the reality of a growing weakness: lack of interest from the side of the mainline churches, the self-centered interest of the Lutherans in their special talks with the Vatican, the opposition of the fundamentalist churches and others against the WCC by slandering it as purely political, the self-serving actions of the Orthodox Churches and, above all, the lack of a convincing vision. The Protestant churches especially have lost their strong ecumenical engagement, allowing the confessional world alliances, including the Vatican and the Lambeth Conference, to act on their own. At present Christianity is not growing together but falling apart. This is not promising for Christian unity. We seem to be looking backward to times that should be left behind.

From the very beginning, Christianity was not organized as one big church. It was a variety of movements with developing formal structures. According to Ernst Käsemann, the multitude of confessions and denominations is a consequence of the variability of the New Testament kerygma. There is a rightness to a diversified Christianity, but how do we avoid hostile controversies and movements in churches that separate us from each other?

The idea of *episkope* by presbyters, bishops, synods, and councils was developed to maintain unity by deciding and communicating the confession of one truth and declaring different opinions as heretical. These instruments worked for a while, but they could not prevent Christianity from being split into two bodies, the Orthodox and Roman Catholic churches (1054). The Reformation was the second major separation, and we now have three large church families. Speaking more precisely, we have to mention the pre-Reformation movements of the Waldensians, the Hussites, and the Anabaptists, who unfortunately have been misjudged because of the Münster events (1525).

These separations happened for many different reasons. One reason was the connection between the Bishop of Rome and spiritual, juridical, or even political and military power and coersion. The Pope was and is welcome as a servant of the unity of the church but not as a governor or a dictator. Christianity outside the Roman Catholic Church therefore must regret the decision of Vatican Council I: In questions of doctrine and when speaking *ex cathedra*, the Bishop of Rome was declared to be free of error. This is unacceptable for Orthodox or Protestant Christians.

This decision was made in the second part of the nineteenth century, in a time of deep revolutionary change. It can be understood as an attempt to be safe in unsafe times, to establish truth against scientific developments, to assure a feudalistic society against democratic subversive activities, and to prevent open discussions in times of questioning everything.

Following the self-understanding of the council fathers, this type of unity under the rule of the Bishop of Rome could be understood as an effort to maintain Christian unity, and as a consequence the Roman Catholic Church sees itself as the safe harbor for the truth of the gospel.

Most recently the Vatican reaffirmed its specific understanding of the Roman Catholic Church in its *Declaration Dominus Jesus.* This document explains the Roman Catholic understanding of Jesus Christ, with which we agree; the Roman understanding of religions, which we can understand; and the self-understanding of the Roman Catholic Church in relation to other churches, with which we must disagree.

The Vatican seems to be saying that the Roman Catholic Church is synonymous with the Church of Jesus Christ: there is a *subsistentia* of the true church of Christ in the Roman Catholic Church (No. 4). The declaration underlines that it is dangerous to read and explain the holy scripture without reference to the tradition and the doctrinal authority of the church (No. 4). And it speaks of the Roman Church as "our holy mother," so that other churches can only be named as "daughter churches" and not as "sister churches" (No. 8). The declaration claims that Jesus Christ himself founded the church and therefore established the uniqueness of *this* church (No. 16).

The document insists upon a historic continuity between this Christ-founded church and the Roman Catholic Church of our times by apostolic succession. The Lord's church, a society in this world, becomes a reality in the Roman Catholic Church, conducted by the successor of Peter in communion with the bishops. Despite all the divisions in Christianity, according to the document, the church of Christ continues to exist in the full sense only in the Roman Catholic Church. The effectiveness of different churches (e.g., the Orthodox) and ecclesiastical societies (the Protestant) depends on the fullness of grace and truth given to the Roman Catholic Church (No. 16).

According to this view, by God's will the bishop of Rome owns the primacy over the whole church in an "objective sense." But there are "part-churches" in close connection with the Roman Catholic Church that have preserved the apostolic succession and the real Eucharist. Ecclesiastical societies, which did not preserve these two elements are not churches in the real sense of this word. Yet baptism into these societies incorporates into Christ, creating a certain community with the Roman Catholic Church (No. 17).

This document understands the church of Christ as being on the way to the kingdom of God, centered as "church for others." This concept has some positive aspects but carries the danger of underestimating the church (No. 19). The document ends with the assurance that Pope John Paul II confirmed and rectified this declaration with assured knowledge and by the power of his apostolic authority.

Protestant churches must be disappointed by this declaration. It is true that this paper conveys a recognized position of the Roman Catholic Church. But after a long period of ecumenical work, in particular after the declaration about justification in October 1999 in Augsburg, there was the expectation of an ongoing development of understanding between the churches.

We must join others in the ecumenical community, including many concerned Roman Catholics, and object to the document's tenor. It is not acceptable to identify the church of Jesus Christ with the Roman Catholic Church. Even the choice of words hurts: "Church" means the Roman Catholic Church alone. The document never uses the term "Roman Catholic" but only "Catholic." Protestants have to maintain that this is an incorrect use of the term. Catholic means the whole world." In this sense, Protestant churches are also catholic, evangelical-catholic churches. We cannot accept the terminology that implies exclusivity in this document, and likewise we have to be careful about our own use of words.

Protestants have to point out that all ecclesiastical doctrine not based on holy scripture is heretical. How can anyone be expected to accept the autocratic spirit of this document? By contrast Protestant churches stress that the unity of the church cannot be achieved by possessing Christ but only by confessing Christ.

Confessing Christ first of all expresses a certain understanding of the relation of Christ to his church. This relationship depends on his freedom and love at the same time. No church is allowed to proclaim ownership of the presence of Christ in its midst. It is and remains and will ever be his sovereign decision whether he will be with any Christian and any church. Christian churches can only hope and believe that he bound and binds himself through his love, as a free act of love.

No theory about possessing Christ is acceptable. Christians and churches only can confess their own belonging to Christ as an expression of faith. It is in our act of confessing this that we realize the communion between Christ, his brothers and sisters, and his churches. We believe that confessing Christ is not a work of our own free will, knowledge, or insight: "And I am sure, that he who began a good work in you will bring it to completion at the day of Jesus Christ" (Phil 1:6). Paul is equally clear about the impossibility of anyone owning Christ: "Not that I have already obtained this or am already perfect; but I press on to make it my own because Jesus Christ has made me his own" (Phil 3:12).

Any doctrine about "objective conditions" is making God an "object" of our thinking; "objective" theories about God are the product of human thinking and wishing, idols of our fantasy.

Very often Protestant theology has to explain its understanding of subjective and objective. The act of confessing Christ is not an expression of subjective and wishful thinking or speaking: it is the Lord's work. This side of the relationship between God's action and human action provokes the question, how can a human being be sure that confessions really confess Christ as Lord and are not the product of dreams, special ideas, or individual whims? Confessing Christ or confessing subjective, personal insights: how is it possible to avoid confusion?

There is no final security, but there are hints, and I would like to mention only three of them:

- Confessing Christ means to confess the biblical Christ.
- Confessing Christ means to confess Christ the Jew.
- Confessing Christ means to confess the living Lord.

In studying the Bible we will find that the biblical reports about Jesus Christ and the confessions about his life and work are really different expressions of the faith of the biblical authors. Although these reflections about Jesus Christ are inspired, they are not dictated. Confessing Christ cannot mean to erect an abstract theory of everlasting truth: truth must be found in certain situations and in certain conditions of life. Christ himself inspired his friends to express their confessions in biblical terms and their acts of confession responded to certain challenges and followed historical demands of people. This opens up the space for our own confessing: It can be appropriate to our time, our challenges, our demands. At the same time, it must be the reflection of the same spirit that created the confessions of the biblical authors. So it has to be examined: Do we confess the loving and healing Christ? Is it the Christ who suffered the cross of violence and injustice? Is it the Christ that will create a new heaven and a new earth and has begun the renewal of creation through his presence among us? Is it the Christ who guides our feet into the way of peace? Is the confession appropriate to his own proclamation of his mission: "The spirit of the Lord is upon me, because he has anointed me to preach good news to the poor. He has sent me to proclaim release to the captives and recovery of sight to the blind, to let the oppressed go free, to proclaim the year of the Lord's favor." (Lk 4:18)?

Confessing Christ therefore has to inspire us to stay by the side of the poor, to fight for justice and peace, and to break the chains of slavery. Confessing Christ has to be biblical in this sense or it is reduced to confessing anyone imaginable.

Confessing Christ means to confess Christ the Jew. For centuries Christian scholars taught that Christianity superseded Israel. Following this doctrine, Christ was the knife to cut off the Jews from the covenant between God and God's people. We must counter this image, for the Christian churches entered into the covenant between God and God's people. God didn't cancel the covenant: God's trustworthiness is everlasting. Confessing Christ cannot be expressed as a condemnation of the Jews. Christians and Jews have to confess their faith in communication with each other and direct it as their common witness to the world. Christians have to learn about the Jewish understanding of the holy scriptures. They have to learn about faithfulness that depends completely on God a whole life long and how to use God's name with respect. They have to learn how to fear God's holiness.

Christianity has to discover its Jewish roots to keep in touch with the lifestream of God, the creator and father of Jesus Christ. Confessing Christ means to confess the living Lord. The act of confessing has to be the expression of a living relationship: we must confess Christ in the presence of our immediate life situation.

Those who confess must be convinced that the confession is heard not only by human counterparts but also by God. It has to be honest and true. Believing in the living Christ is the expression of a faith that is related to the crucified and resurrected Christ. The life witness of Jesus of Nazareth, Christ living on earth, is the model for the Christ-following church. The present Christ is the presence of his inviting way to proclaim the gospel, his care for the sick and marginalized, his deep belief in his Father, his teaching about the kingdom of God coming as peace and justice. The presence of Christ forms the healing and reconciling profile of the church.

Confessing the biblical, Jewish, living Jesus Christ is proclaiming and creating the unity of the church. The unity of the church is the union of all Christ-experiences and teachings. It is not an exclusive union but open to Israel and Christian brothers and sisters. Unity seeks for spiritual, theological, and organizational union under the guidance of Jesus Christ. But unity starts by confessing Christ, in whom and through whom unity already exists. The next step is to overcome confessional and denominational limitations and to be reconciled to the diversity in which we live, knowing that we already are One in Christ.

"Yes," "No," and "Prayer"

Bryan C. Sirchio

I should begin this essay by confessing a certain degree of discomfort with the whole business of attempting to reflect on the "Centrality of Christ/The Word." It's not that I don't like the topic, or that I do not consider Christ to be, in a sense, the "Center" of all that is. Christ is, as we are reminded in the so-called hymn to the Cosmic Christ in Col 1:15ff, "the image of the invisible God, . . . for in [Christ] all things in heaven and on earth were created, things visible and invisible; . . . all things have been created through [Christ] and for [Christ]." The problem for me is that the Christ is simply too vast to transcend and somehow try to reflect back upon conceptually. Christ is the Center, but Christ is also dynamically present at every imaginable personal and social margin. Christ is not just "The Center," Christ, as part of the Trinity, is the One in whom "we live and move and have our being" (Acts 17:28). "Center" somehow seems too small, although I do understand what we are trying to get at here. Furthermore, there is the important and provocative discussion of the difference and relationship between the Cosmic Christ and the revelation of God in and through Jesus of Nazareth, the Word made Flesh. Fortunately (I think), this can of worms is beyond the scope of this essay. But let me just nail my colors to the mast and confess that my christology, even after all these years in mainline Protestant circles, is high. I cannot neatly separate the Cosmic Christ from the humanity of Jesus the carpenter (or vice versa), and I both surrender to and embrace the mystery of the Incarnation.

I am often amazed by the unique freedom which we human beings have been given. As far as I can tell, we seem to be the only ones in all of God's creation who have been granted the freedom to choose to actually displace Christ—for a while anyway—from the center of our personal lives and our communities. According to scripture, there will indeed come a time when all human beings will confess the centrality and sovereignty of Christ ("every knee shall bow and every tongue confess" Phil 2:9-11). But the simple truth is that for our brief time on earth, we are not forced to acknowledge and celebrate Christ as the driving energy and focus of our lives. And of course, many of us do not.

As I meditate on the notion of the centrality of Christ, the image of a target keeps coming to mind, with Christ being the target's bull's eye. I cannot help but think of the rather well known definition of sin as "missing the mark." I am also reminded of Kathleen Norris's reflection on the meaning of righteousness in her popular book, *Amazing Grace.* Norris notes that the Hebrew word, *hesed*, which we often translate as righteousness, means "for one's aim to be true." This definition speaks deeply to me, because it seems to honor the *intention* to hit the mark, even if one does not always strike the bull's eye. I appreciate this approach to righteousness because it leaves room for grace, and God knows I need grace. Despite my most earnest attempts to aim the arrow of my life at the bull's eye—to live out my faith in Jesus Christ as the Center of my life and as the Center of Life itself—I must also quickly confess that many of my "shots" have missed the target altogether, let alone the bull's eye.

I do not want to beat this target metaphor into the ground, but given the fact that so much of our theological work is extremely conceptual and intellectually oriented, maybe it's a good idea to keep playing around with this more poetic image. The truth is that while Christ may be the target at which individual Christians are aimed, God is the Archer who aims us. That is grace. God (the Abba of Jesus) is the Archer. Christ is the target's bull's eye. I guess that makes us the arrows. We are arrows, created by the Archer, fashioned and formed to travel straight and true, and to reach the mark at which the Archer has aimed us. And yet we are unusually "free" arrows. Somehow we have been invited by the Archer to help determine and therefore even alter the very nature and course of our brief flight through time and space.

I am not much of an archer, though I do own a bow and some arrows. Each arrow has three feathers on it, and as far as I can tell, the primary thing I can do to keep the arrows "true" is to make sure the feathers are in good shape. Once the feathers are missing or bent out of shape, the arrow no longer flies as it was intended to. So I do my best to keep the feathers smooth and in place. Well, forgive me if I'm forcing the issue, but I'd like to use the three feathers of the arrow to represent three essential dimensions of being "living arrows" in the Archer's hands. The three feathers are called "Yes," "No," and "Prayer."

The "Yes" feather represents all that we are called to embrace or "say yes to" as we journey toward and into the heart of Christ. "Yes" to the fullness of God poured into human form in Jesus. "Yes" to the life and teachings of the Nazarene. "Yes" to the mysteries of stable, cross, table, basin and towel, and empty tomb. "Yes" to the witness of Jesus Christ as the One to whom we return again and again for clues as to what it means to be a human being fully alive. "Yes" to love, to justice, to mercy, compassion, forgiveness, and community. "Yes" to the very "person" of Christ being formed within us through the indwelling presence of the Holy Spirit. "Yes" to all the fruits of the Spirit (Gal 5) which grow naturally out of our lives when our connection to the "Vine" (John 15) is nurtured. "Yes" to humble, sacrificial service and costly grace. "Yes" to God's dream of Shalom and Jubilee and loving neighbor as self. "Yes" to one's own gift and call, that smaller piece of God's dream for the world which each of us is meant to help carry for a while. "Yes" to participation in the circle of believers. "Yes" to being "church," "called out," the living body of Jesus Christ in the world today. "Yes" to standing with the victims and the oppressed and the lonely and the marginalized and the powerless and the voiceless. "Yes" to the dignity of the image of God in all persons, including ourselves, and "yes" to the beauty and integrity of the created world. "Yes" to love in all its expressions and forms.

The "No" feather represents all that we are called to reject or "say no to" as arrows released by the Archer and aimed at the bull's eye of Christ-centered living. "No" to envy, selfish ambition, jealously, and egocentrism. "No" to extreme juxtapositions of wealth and poverty, and "no" to the overindulgent lifestyles and stockpiled assets of a wealthy few in a world in which tens of thousands of children die of starvation each day. "No" to all forms of idolatry and infidelity. "No" to what Walter Wink has so aptly coined, "the domination system." "No" to institutions and structures of greed and exploitation. "No" to "lording power over" individual persons and entire nations and races of persons. "No" to manipulation and dehumanization. "No" to prejudice and put-downs. "No" to hatred and bitterness and vengeance and retaliation. "No" to "might makes right." "No" to anxiety, stress, alienation, and emptiness. "No" to what Gandhi referred to as the "seven deadly sins":

1. Politics without principle

2. Wealth without work

3. Commerce without morality

4. Pleasure without conscience

5. Education without character

6. Science without humanity

7. Worship without sacrifice

God knows that to be living arrows aimed at the mark called Christ, there are many clear "nos" to say; "no" to anything and everything that violates the law of love.

The third and final feather is the feather of "Prayer." It is in and through prayer that we move from being mere proponents of a moral or ethical code to being in intimate and living relationship with the God of

Jesus. It is through prayer that our Christian yeses and nos become deeply personal and heart-felt responses to the *voice* of God rather than a list of obligations or duties or even worse, propaganda for an ideological agenda. It is in and through prayer that we discern which controversial yeses and nos must be spoken and acted upon, and which issues are not "our crosses to bear." It is through prayer that we find clarity and strength to stand firm and perhaps pay a price when our nos and yeses are offensive to the dominant culture, or to other brothers and sisters in Christ who see things differently. It is through prayer we discern God's timing for our yeses and nos and God's ways of saying "yes" and "no" through us.

Prayer is the difference between knowing when our "hour is not at hand," and when it is time to "set our faces toward Jerusalem." It is in and through prayer we are given the grace to "see the logs in our own eyes before we attempt to remove the specks in the eyes of others," and to love even (if not especially) those whom we are most tempted to demonize and disregard. It is through prayer, and perhaps most specifically through the form of prayer known as Divine Silence, that we "hear" those things to which we must say "yes" and "no" in Christ, and it is prayer that enables us to wait upon God when clear yeses and nos are not forthcoming.

"Yes," "No," and "Prayer." If we would live in such a way that our individual and corporate lives bear witness to the centrality of Christ, we will find ourselves doing whatever is ours to do to keep these three "feathers" in good condition. And there are certain things that are indeed ours to do; we can choose to recognize and honor our own need for spiritual disciplines. Our "feathers" are regularly groomed and maintained through study of scripture, accountability to others in intimate fellowship, confession, solitude, journaling, spiritual direction, and countless other inner and outer disciplines. But grace will find us again and again trusting ultimately in the Archer, the One who aims and follows every shot—those which hit the bull's eye—and those which miss the mark because the arrows themselves somehow got "off true." Grace means that the Archer will always find us, and perfectly restore our "feathers" if we will allow ourselves to be touched and returned us to the quiver until it is time for us to be aimed once again and released toward the mark of Christ-centered living.

When invited to write this essay and thus participate in the *Festschrift* related to the retirement of Frederick Trost, I inquired as to whether or not I was supposed to make specific references to Pastor Trost's ministry in the essay itself. I was told it was fine for me to do so, but it was neither required nor expected. In light of my essay's primary image, I would like to end this essay by simply offering Fred a rather unusual compliment. For close to two decades, the God of Jesus Christ has worked through Frederick R. Trost to faithfully and courageously help countless individuals, hundreds of congregations, the Wisconsin Conference, the United Church of Christ in general, and the church at large, to try to "keep our feathers straight." In so doing, he has helped us to move through time and space in a more true fashion, and he has helped us to remain focused on the "mark of the upward call of God in Christ Jesus" (Phil 3:14). Thank you and God bless you, Fred.

"Majestic God, How Easily We Imagine Your Glory"

Majestic God, how easily we imagine your glory! "Immortal, invisible" we have called you. "Wise," we have made your name. We have hid you in light, held you distant and inaccessible. This we have sung. This we have believed. And it has seemed better for us this way. Because, when we banish you to the farthest corner of your magnificent heaven—when we ask you to watch us from a distance—we can have our way with you: believing what we will, owning you when we want, absenting you too often from our peculiar days.

Yet, with a majesty strange beside the one we imagine, you refuse to let us make you obsolete! As we live peculiar lives, so you became peculiar in Jesus from Nazareth. Hands calloused by carpenter's tools, fingers splintered by the wood's stubborn grain, an overflowing of wine for a wedding feast already too spirit-filled, multitudes fed with one meager lunch, filthy wounds made clean with spit and mud, adulterers forgiven, tax collectors and sinners claimed as honored banquet guests, thieves invited into Paradise, flesh split and broken with too-familiar nails and wood, and a tomb left coldly useless: can this One really be your Son? Can this One really be God?

If he is not—if he cannot—if your universal irrelevance and ethereal almightiness did not become peculiar in Bethlehem's birth and on Calvary's cross—then how can you be our God? Yet he is your Son! Yet he is very God! So *his* peculiarity is forever woven into our own. And we dare to ask. We *must* ask: "What would Jesus do?" We ask because he *did* do. And because he is still *doing*, through his Spirit that deigns to dwell in us.

Majestic God, perfect your majesty in peculiarity, both in his and in ours, that we might know your truth in him, that we might practice your peace through him, that we might taste your joy because he has named us, and claimed us, and made us his own. Lord Jesus, be near to us, peculiar with us. For you are our Christ, our God!

Charles E. Mize

Jesus Christ, the Word of God

Joanne Thomson

I am the vine, you are the branches (John 15:5a).

To be honest, I have always been suspicious of things that grow outdoors: things like vegetables, flowers, and grass. It may be my upbringing, which was urban and quite concrete-friendly. It was not uncommon for people where we lived to pave the small remaining islands of dirt on their property and then paint them green. Gardening has only been thrust upon me later in life, after moving to the Midwest and the suburbs where there is grass to tend and hosta to befriend. I have not, by any means, become a born-again gardener. I have not gone quietly into the world of nature but have raged, raged. The most wonderful aspect of gardening I've discovered so far is that everyone else in my family hates it too. So when I head outdoors with a shovel or rake, I do so with a smile on my face, since. I can count on their avoiding me like the plague, which translates into time unbothered and alone. Weeding and digging are the price of solitary peace.

Therefore it is with some chagrin that I share the story of the pumpkin in the compost bin. In early summer, I noticed that a weed of truly epic proportions had sprouted from the compost bin. I sighed, frustrated yet again. Here was one more sign of the utter perversity of the natural world. The greens in the compost were supposed to die and turn into dirt. They were not supposed to become weeds the size of New Jersey. How could anyone actually take nature seriously—much less find meaning there— when it so stubbornly refused to follow its own rules? I mentally filed the chore away for some future date: "Kill monster weed in compost."

But then we went away on vacation. And I procrastinated on garden duty. And when next I rounded the corner to where the compost bin stood, I gasped: something out of a 40-year-old Japanese horror movie was growing in my back yard. The monster weed was now a Godzilla weed, winding across a path and invading the hosta across the way. Worse yet, it obviously planned to reproduce itself, like Sigourney Weaver's alien. Huge yellowish-orange blooms had appeared, which clearly meant this weed had decided to go forth and multiply. In a panic, I dragged my husband outside. "Will you look at this thing! What are we going to do? How did it get in there? What is it?" Calmly, he answered: "It's a pumpkin. You put the Halloween pumpkins in there last year. They've grown, that's all, just like they're supposed to. Congratulations."

"I am the vine, you are the branches."

To be honest, I have also always been suspicious of the Gospel of John. John has seemed to me vague and mushy. "As you are in me and I am in you, may they also be in us." But what does it all mean? "Then lay the hay down where the goats can get it," as Garrison Keillor would say. Give me the plain talk of the synoptics: Pick up your cross; Turn the other cheek; Play through the pain; Eat your peas. The synoptics have a beginning, a middle, and an end. They don't meander around in a circle like John. In the synoptics, we're going to Jerusalem; we have suitcases to pack. In John, on the other hand, Jesus maddeningly spends four chapters just saying goodbye.

But lately, by the grace of God, it has been through the Gospel of John that I have most richly received the Word of Life. And that is so, I believe, precisely because John gives us a Jesus who truly finds a home in our world. John's Jesus literally puts on our skin, in a way that a synoptic Jesus does not. From the Prologue itself, in the midst of the lofty theological language, comes the statement, "the Word became flesh and lived among us." Lived among us. I get the feeling John's Jesus actually likes us.

You know what your mother used to say in response to naughty behavior: "I always love you, but I don't always like you." Mark's Jesus surely feels that way. But you get the impression that John's Jesus really likes us too. The Word truly came to dwell within the world; the Divine chose to enflesh itself—just as the fish lives within the ocean, can't live without it but is never of it; is engulfed and surrounded but does not, cannot, drown—so Jesus, the Word, lives among us and actually enjoys the swimming. John's Jesus is not afraid to get too close to humanity. He does not hold himself back from us in order to avoid the logical impossibility of the Word alive within the world. John's Jesus seems not to be afraid of anything and certainly not logic.

To some extent, this is just simply Incarnation 101: the Word became flesh. But the fully human Jesus opens the door to a "big question": Where exactly is the line between Word and world? How exactly do we avoid making God human, or making human beings god? This has been a big question for Christians since, oh, the lifetime of Jesus of Nazareth, and it is a hot debate for Christians like us right now. How do we discern the distinctiveness and transcendence of the Word over against the world and its language and culture? For some, the possibility that Word and world are not, in fact, identical is itself to be debated. Others seem to find, perhaps as a corrective, that the Word must always stand over against the world, as though Word and world are eternal adversaries.

Lately it has seemed to me that we debaters should take an extended vacation in the Gospel of John. "I am the vine, you are the branches." From the compost, which surely is a metaphor of creatureliness and death if ever there was one, grows life. Unplanned by human agency, unanticipated, unrecognized, and unappreciated, comes life. Jesus the Word grows, not in spite of the world or apart from the world, but from the nourishing soil of the world and for the sake of the world. And even though the Word lives as close to the world as skin to a skeleton, the Word nevertheless lives according to its own nature and purpose, not according to the devices and desires of the world. Jesus identifies with us so closely that he even dies, but he does not become death. The Word is in the world but in order to save it, not to serve its purposes. Truly an impossibility, and a glorious one.

"God so loved the world."

It is helpful to remember why the Word has immersed itself in the world, namely for our salvation. The Word has come into the world to save it from itself. The Word has come to change the very nature of the world. We call this a "new creation." The Word will reorder all that is and will do this by means of love alone. The Word will create the world anew, so that our destiny will no longer be death but life.

Let us not underestimate the cosmic enormity of the job God has taken on. God's purpose is not to solve the problems of the world but to save the world, to impose the true *Logos* on a disordered reality. Let us not underestimate how disordered this reality truly is. One of my fellow students in divinity school chose a vocation (journalism) that has enabled me over the years to watch him at work from afar. Maybe it's because I knew him back when he was a regular person that his byline catches my eye. Chris Hedges has made a specialty of writing about ugly wars. Sadly, he has been very busy. His resume reads like a synopsis of global tragedy: Palestine, Kuwait, El Salvador, and on and on, and most recently Kosovo.

Not long ago I read a reflection he had written. He told a personal story from Sarajevo in 1995:

There was no running water or electricity, and little to eat; most people were subsisting on a bowl of soup a day. Families lived huddled in basements, and mothers, who had to dash to the common water taps set up by the United Nations, faced an excruciating choice---whether to run through the streets with their children or leave them in a building that could be rubble when they returned. The hurling bits of iron fragmentation left bodies mangled, dismembered, decapitated. We slipped and slid in the gore, heard the groans of anguish, and were, for our pains, in the sights of Serb snipers, often just a couple of hundred yards away.

But the horror is even worse than it appears, if that's possible, because there is absolutely no reason for it. Or, rather, the horror is created only to justify more horror. Chris reflects on his later experience in Bosnia:

There was no reason for the war in Bosnia. The warring sides invented the national myths and histories designed to mask the fact that Croats, Muslims, and Serbs are ethnically and linguistically indistinguishable.

Invent a war to invent some hatred, to invent more war to invent more hatred. A sane person must ask, "What kind of a world is this? What are human beings made of, to commit such acts for the sake of—what? To commit murder in order to create a reason to murder? Why do we do it? Simply to have the experience of the power to destroy? What kind of creatures are we?"

It is probably true that for most ages other than our own and in most places other than the affluent West, it is more easily obvious that death is the force that ultimately defines human life. To be in "being," to be part of the created order, means, above all, to be subject to death and, along the way, to death's dear allies: violence, poverty, hatred, all forms of destruction. People like us generally operate as though life is innocent until proven otherwise. Most of the world most of the time has no choice but to do the opposite.

Jesus came into this world to change it. Jesus, the Word, is the *Logos*, no less than the *order* of all that is. He came not to heal the sick but to heal sickness; not to release the prisoners but to end captivity. He came not to raise the dead to life but to lay resurrection at the foundation of existence. When measured against the monstrous sum of human suffering, most of the time, a vine growing from a compost bin is not much of an answer. Yet that is precisely the assurance we need beyond all others: God is doing something unnatural with our natural world. God has broken the back of death. God has replaced the rules that govern the present order. Jesus Christ has joined us now in the beauty and the muck of this life; so that, instead of endless repetitions of variations on the only themes we can imagine, a vine will grow, and we will be its branches.

"Word of Prayer, Word of God, You Give Us Words to Pray."

Word of Prayer, Word of God, you give us words to pray.
World Lover, you give us the world to love, the bread to live, this day.
Whirlwind, you give us the breath for what we say.
Work us, we pray, from formless clay to works of art today.

When we rise from beds of rest or pain
Wake our bodies and souls to defy gravity again,
Shake from these eyes the deposits of sleepiness and sin,
Take us up and out, inspired and aspiring, as we take you in.

When we step out to work or play, make our day, we pray,
A carnival of incarnate revival over carnal decay,
A festival of faith over festering dismay,
A triumphal march with the Maker of the way.

Then, when we lie down to rest or retire,
Regenerate us with your generous spirit, gently come,
Revive us with your resurrecting fire,
Receive us at last in our everlasting home.

Thomas O. Bentz

"In the Beginning Was the Word"

Eugene S. Wehrli†

In the beginning was the Word.
The Word was with God
and the Word was God.
He was in the beginning with God. (John 1:1-2)

The full identity and inter-relationship between God and the Word is made clear. God, in God's very being, has always been a God seeking to reveal self, eager to share self and to make self known. Hence God is a God of Word, of communication. In this sense God is not desirous of being hidden from God's creatures. Stated in human terms, God has always sought to express self. Never has God sought aloofness. Expression belongs to the very being of God. "In the beginning" is reminiscent of the Word in Genesis and suggests that God is engaged in a new creative act. The culmination suggests that it is a new community that is born of the will of God.

All things came into being through him,
And without him not one thing came into being.
What has come into being in him was life,
And the life was the light of all people.

This self-expressive God reached out to establish a larger community in creation which was to be life-giving and enlightening for all humanity. To use Genesis words, "It was good." Here we see the coming of Jesus set within God's universal purpose from the beginning. From creation God has been acting to express that which is now fully made known in the "only begotten Son."

The light shines in the darkness,
and the darkness did not overcome it.

God has always let the light shine and there is no darkness that can either overcome it or comprehend it. The light is God's power at work exposing all darkness. It is at this point . . . that John inserts the historical reference to John the Baptist—he is the one whose role it is to bear witness to the light. In that function he is a type of the true disciple of Christ whose role is to witness to the Light of the Word (cf. John, chapter 9). The prose "interruption" (in the lyric) enables John to portray the meaning of our discipleship in relation to the light coming into the world.

He was in the world,
and the world was made through him,
yet the world did not know him.
He came to what was his own,
and his own people did not accept him.

The experience of God's self-revelation in human history does not lead to inevitable success. In fact the light coming into the world has experienced a multiple history of rejection—even from "God's own."

Nevertheless, . . . there is also a community created by God's entering into history which is responsive to the light, walks by the light and is willing to live by the light. Those persons who "receive him," "believe in his name" are empowered by that new relationship to become what they were not by birth, namely, "children of God." In their new birth they are generated by the will of God and live by that will. For this relation a natural birth is not sufficient, nor is the birth a self-achieved creation, rather they are the persons receptive to God and so they are new persons. The result of the revelation is a creation of a new people who go by the name, "the children of God." So the poem continues:

But to all who received him,
who believed in his name,
he gave power to become children of God
who were born (not of blood,
nor of the will of the flesh,
nor of human will)
but of God.

The Incarnation, the Word become flesh, is now affirmed. The language of the poem is not precise; it is poetically free. The language is even confusing if one tries to get technical. If the "Word become flesh" is not announced until verse 14, who or what is referred to in verse 9 ("the true light")? There it is announced that the light "was coming into the world." Likewise in verses 10-12, who or what was not received? We might say that it was the Word with which the whole began, God's self-expression of the Word.

Here we see working the christology of the early church. It was not Jesus who was with God from before creation, but it was God's active Word. Yet that Word became fully empowering and generative only when it became flesh and entered fully into human experience. And because that reality is so powerful for the Christian community, when they talked of

God's self-revelation from the beginning, they could only grasp it as it had been incarnated in Jesus the Christ. When John refers to "the Son" throughout he is affirming the reality of the self-expressive being of God that the Word embodies in the Prologue.

Yet because the Word has become flesh in human history, when Christians talk of the Word they have to think of the Word in fully personal and relational terms which the expression "Word" does not communicate. If the reference were just to the abstract concept of "Word," then "it" would have seemed to be most appropriate. But in this poem from the beginning the Word is talked about in fully personal and relational terms. This becomes even more true in the Gospel where John stresses the relationships of Jesus to God and of Jesus to his followers.

In the pivotal verse 14 there is an amazing change of pronouns. Up to now the hymn has spoken in the third person, but suddenly it shifts to the first person pronoun. The Word dwelt among *us*, and "We have beheld his glory, glory as the only Son of the Father." It has moved from a cosmic view into the language of communal experience and the recital of lived faith. This is our experience as we are included in this hymn. We are the ones who see the glory of God in Christ Jesus. This is not a rational test of faith for an objective witness; rather this is a personally involving claim that has overwhelmed us in the midst of life in the world. It is the community of faith, corporately, that shares the rich experience of the Word become flesh. It is this community that is the new creation of God—a people of God's own gracious act. Consequently, the gifts are all ours personally.

And from his fullness we have received,
grace upon grace.

The benefits of the Word become flesh are ours. No longer can one think of the impact of the Incarnation (solely) in the scheme of the cosmos. We know it in our personal lives. We have received such abounding grace that what was once felt to be grace hardly even deserves the name anymore in the light of God's super-generosity which "we" know.

The communal reality is enlarged when one remembers that in the statement "The Word became flesh and dwelt among us," the term "dwelt" really means "tented" and brings to memory the rich tradition of God's sheltering presence with the Hebrews as they wandered in the wilderness. The Incarnation is God's continuing and powerful presence with us in our wildernesses. Even more as the Hebrews saw the glory of God revealed in God's dwelling with them in the wilderness, so now in Jesus Christ the full glory of God shines, transforming everything.

In its broadest scope, Christmas is that transforming presence of God in history that means we can all know and see God, and we have available that shining glory which illuminates and transforms every dark corner.

Music in Relation to the Centrality of Christ, the Word

Paul Westermeyer

In the beginning was the Word, and the Word was with God, and the Word was God. . . . And the Word became flesh and dwelt among us, full of grace and truth; we have beheld his glory, glory as of the only Son from the Father (John 1:1, 14).

For Emil Brunner the Prologue to John's Gospel meant that "the 'word of God' is first of all 'what God says to us,' the content of [God's] communication. But," said Brunner, "God wills to do more than 'say something' to us, or even to 'communicate' something to us; the content" of God's communication, he continued, "is the very self of God. . . . The word is not sufficient." Where the very self of God is imparted "there is more than speech: 'The Word became flesh.'" Verbal communication through speech is insufficient. It's too weak. "Only what we call the Incarnation, the coming of God to us in person is sufficient for this communication." The one who speaks is "not merely speech but life, the life of a person."[1] Robert Jenson recently began a lecture with his point of departure this same passage from John's Gospel.[2] Jenson indicated he regarded John's Prologue as a gloss on Genesis 1, then said that, contrary to a well-known hymn, there never was any "silence of eternity."[3] "In the beginning," he said, "was the Word." The Trinity was speaking, was in conversation from the beginning. If I understood him correctly, he thought Luther and Tertullian were among the few theologians who had understood this.

Evidently we have two fundamental realities to contend with here. Starting with Jenson (or Luther and Tertullian), the *first* is that the Word, not silence, was from the beginning, with God. Indeed, the Word was God, from the beginning. The *second*, this one related to Brunner's point, is that the Word became flesh and dwelt among us in Christ, in person. Our topic asks about music in relation to the centrality of Christ/the Word. It means we have to consider music in the context of these two realities. As soon as the topic is articulated in this fashion, one is immediately struck by two further realities, less complementary ones than the first two. They may be stated as questions, or groups of questions.

Does the Word from the beginning give sound a unique significance? If that question is answered affirmatively in any way at all, it gives rise to a cluster of other questions. Does music itself, which presumes sound as its raw material, also then have a unique significance? Since words are incipiently musical, especially when they are dialogical as Jenson suggests they were from their beginning in the triune being of God, is music even more fundamentally set in play from the beginning? If so, is it related to the very being of God? If that is so, how is the sound of the universe related to God? At this point the question becomes "incarnational," if you will, because we're not dealing with sound in the abstract but with God's creation where sounding form always happens within the confines of the harmonic series. All cultures in the world as we know it have to confront God's created order of sound when they make any music. This is true no matter what the specific musical syntax may be, whether Eastern, Western, pentatonic, tonal, modal, pandiatonic, twelve-tone, or whatever, because no sound can avoid the givenness of a stack of pitches above it ordered in mathematical ratios and relationships. Albert Blackwell has persuasively discussed this.[4]

Even more significant, perhaps, in this first cluster of questions is Luther's realization. It never ceased to amaze him that words were used to communicate the Word of God and that, wonder of wonders, words could be sung. Words and music both come from the "sphere of the miraculous audible things," to use Oskar Soehngen's phrase that describes Luther's thought. Both words and music therefore communicate the gospel.[5] In this light does music take on even greater significance than it does in its relation to the created order? Is it a bearer of the Word?

Realizing music's importance, even if only some of these questions are answered affirmatively, cannot stop a second cluster of questions that point in a different direction. The central question here is how music can bear a Word that after all is an Incarnate one? If the Word of God for Christians, as Brunner indicates, is the Word made flesh in Christ, in what sense can music bear that Word, the Word that is a person? One can sing words, to be sure, but how does one sing a person? How does one sing Christ in the flesh? Is music not a bearer of the Word?

It would seem that we are now confronted with two further realities, this time the quite complementary ones to which the church has referred with the shorthand "word and sacrament." The *first* of these expresses the importance of spoken and sung words that point to the Incarnate Word and do in fact bear it among us. The preacher, with, as Karl Barth suggested, the Bible in one hand and the newspaper in the other, speaks words in the hope that they will be heard as the Word of God. That is, the preacher and congregation trust that the good news—the gospel—and grace of the Incarnate Word will be borne among us by poor human words. Words point to and indeed in some sense then can be understood to "bear" the Incarnate Word.

Music does the same thing but in a different way. The musician cannot relate to the daily newspaper's moment the way the preacher can but must instead compose and rehearse music, sometimes with a group of singers and instrumentalists, well before—and with little hope of modification at—the time of its use. Like J. S. Bach, the musician composes music with the Bible and hymns, not so much the newspaper, in hand. The composer is especially attentive to the readings in the lectionary and the hymn of the day for the specific occasion. She or he then writes music in the hope that the words it breaks open will be heard as the Word of God. That is, the composer writes music as the preacher writes a sermon, praying that the good news—the gospel—and grace of the Incarnate Word will be borne among us. Music bears the words about the Incarnate Word and in some sense then also "bears" the Incarnate Word but in this case with the contextual breadth of polyphonic possibilities that are not open to the preacher. One of the best examples of music's polyphonic capacity to communicate breadth is the last movement of Bach's *Christmas Oratorio* where the baby Jesus is proleptically viewed through the paschal mystery of cross and resurrection: at the manger the tune associated with "O Sacred Head" is set with trumpets and timpani to a Christus Victor text about the death of sin and death. No preaching can provide this kind of breadth and context, while no music can provide the preacher's laser-like beam.

Choosing to emphasize the spoken and sung word has not left the church unable to enact something more. While it is true that in some sense spoken and sung word bear the Incarnate Word, the question about how the Incarnate Word as person can be sung is not a mind game. It helps explain why the church has affirmed a *second* reality, in this case a sacramental one. Brunner says that "God wills to do more than 'say something' to us, or even to 'communicate' something to us, [that] the content" of God's communication is the very self of God. If that is true, then nature in the sense of the physical stuff of space, not only the musical stuff of time, is called into play in the communication of the Incarnate Word to us. That is, God comes to us in the person of Christ and inhabits our space not only at one particular place in history but in all our places in all our histories—in our assemblies at worship, as Vatican II reminded us,[6] and, to use Luther's formulation, "in true flesh and blood under the bread and wine."[7] The gospel and grace of the Incarnate Word are borne among us not only in the sound we sing and hear but are also sacramentally enacted among us in the space we inhabit and touch. Music is related to both: we sing words about the Incarnate Word, and we sing around the table where the Incarnate Word is host.

Keeping the paschal feast each Lord's Day at word and table as the church's practice and ideal should come then as no surprise. Various groups, to be sure, have emphasized one of these realities at the expense sometimes of the other, but for most of the church most of the time the two have been held together in some fashion or other. Our current ecumenical consensus about the importance of word and supper weekly reflects the church's best practice and suggests that health requires both in vital integrity. Time and its sound are important but so are space and its touch because the Incarnate Word reigns over all time and space and dwells with us in all time and space. Music is related to both the word in time and the table in space, more intrinsically to the word as part of the "sphere of the miraculous audible things,"[8] more as articulation of time around the space of the table.

Reflection on these matters can be complicated. It is fashionable to attack such reflection. The truth is that important topics garner complex thought. We should not be surprised at that, nor should we think things could be otherwise. Another simpler, more earthy form of discourse, however, is also sometimes appropriate to such topics. That is the case here.

The church sings its song around font, ambo, and table, most visibly perhaps as a motley crew of hard-headed, thick-skulled, self-centered egotists, each of whom wants this or that at the expense of the other. Though the song we as church have to sing is one song by one body of Christ before one Triune God, we seem nonetheless to have as little capacity for singing it together as we do to exercise compassion for one another or to overcome our silly divisions or to care about the world we are called to serve. Yet God sustains us in our weakness and sends us singing and doing in spite of ourselves. Sunday after Sunday the church gathers to celebrate and sing the Paschal mystery, day by day it sings its prayer, and bit by bit it manages to care for the neighbor and to concern itself with justice. All this is broken, to be sure, sometimes massively broken or even hidden, but it goes on nonetheless from age to age.

Reflection on this mystery is not complicated at all. It is crystal clear that God sustains the church, not we, for we seem able to do little more than make a botch of our song and everything else we do. That anything positive gets sung or accomplished is a mystery and the biggest surprise of all. But in spite of ourselves, by God's grace, we can look back and see that more has been sung and accomplished than we thought. We have indeed "sinned against [God] in thought, word, and deed," as the Prayerbook says, but by God's grace we are also forgiven and "strengthened in all goodness,"[9] with more health and favor than we could imagine in our wildest dreams. For that mystery a song of thanksgiving is the inevitably reflexive response of the church.

On top of this, or maybe in it, or under it, or somewhere in its midst, God raises up faithful servants for us. Their feet are made of the same clay as all the rest of us, and they make botches as well as anybody else. But they nonetheless are those who, with their gifts and maybe in spite of themselves, in season and out of season do many good things. Some of them preach the word and preside at font and table. Some of them lead us in our song. Some of them teach. Some of them communicate the gospel in our world, if necessary, as St. Francis said, with words. Some attend to our needs, some bind up our wounds, and some help us to seek justice. Some exercise oversight so that others may lead with their gifts, may sing, and may be Christ's body in the world.

Such servants, like the one we honor here, make it possible for the church to be what it is and to do what it is called to do. For example, those who exercise oversight, though they themselves are not the leaders of the song, make it possible for others to lead the rest of the body in song. This is no small thing at a time when some "leaders" of the church have chosen to misplace their energies in attacks on the music of the church that sings of Christ the Incarnate Word and in attacks on the musicians whose very vocation is to carry out this task. It is well to remember that a bishop named Ambrose is called the father of church song. Partly that is because of his ability to write durable hymn texts, no doubt, which not all bishops could do or should try to do, but partly it is because of his organizational skills in supporting the church at song. That sort of support for the song *is* the responsibility of all bishops. Of the servant we honor here it can be said that he preached, presided, and exercised oversight faithfully, so that the body of Christ could be built up in its manifold richness, a richness that includes the church's music.

There is yet one more thing to be said. Those who exercise oversight also are responsible for stimulating and sustaining both the highest quality of complicated theological reflection as well as the simpler, earthier discourse about important topics that require such attention. Those with oversight support these efforts for the sake of the work and witness of the church in the world, and, let us be certain to add, for the sake of the church's music as part of that work and witness. The servant we honor here has made this responsibility a priority. That he has done this in the face of a contrary spirit both in the culture and in the church itself is to be celebrated with gratitude. Thanks be to God.

Notes

1. Emil Brunner, *Revelation and Reason,* trans. Olive Wyon (Philadelphia: The Westminster Press, 1946), 109.

2. Robert W. Jenson, "God and the Language of Worship," lecture at The Crisis of Christian Worship, St. John's University, Collegeville, Minn., June 6, 2000.

3."Dear Lord and Father of Mankind," *Lutheran Book of Worship* (Minneapolis: Augsburg Publishing House, 1978), # 506.

4. Albert L. Blackwell, *The Sacred in Music* (Louisville: Westminster/John Knox Press, 1999), chap. 11, specifically p. 71. Blackwell's discussion is not so convincing at the sacramental and some of the theological points, but it is hard to refute his logic that the overtone series is inescapable.

5. Oskar Soehngen, "Fundamental Considerations for a Theology of Music," *The Musical Heritage of the Church,* ed. Theodore Hoelty-Nickel (St. Louis: Concordia Publishing House, 1963), VI, 15-16.

6. See, for example, *The Documents of Vatican II,* ed. Walter M. Abbott (New York: Guild Press, 1966), the Church, I, 4 (p. 17), and the Liturgy, I, 7 (p. 141).

7. Martin Luther, "A Treatise on the New Testament, That Is, the Holy Mass," *Luther's Works,* vol. 35, ed. E. Theodore Bachman (Philadelphia: Muhlenberg Press, 1960), 86.

8. Soehngen, VI, 15-16.

9. *The Book of Common Prayer* (New York: The Church Hymnal Corporation, 1979), 360.

"God of Life and Breath"

God of life and breath, we praise you and give you thanks. In the fullness of time, you chose to be with us, God in-the-flesh. You came to us, not just as idea or thought or ethereal being, but as Jesus Christ, Word Incarnate. You lived with us, laughed with us, cried and walked and prayed with us. Through Jesus' life, death, and resurrection, you live among us still.

Ah, Holy Jesus, how blessed we are that you are our God! We ask your forgiveness for those times we would rather keep you distant and removed. How much easier it is to think of you as an intangible concept, holy and antiseptic. Or we limit you to our own image of good teacher and friend and peace-maker. How loved we are that you are our God, come to us in-the-flesh!

Thank you, Jesus, for loving us enough to get your hands dirty. Thank you for touching us with words we can feel, for hearing our pain, our anger, our sorrow, and our joy with compassion and understanding. Thank you for speaking the wisdom of the ages in stories and actions. Thank you for calling us to be your body, claimed, forgiven and set free to speak and to live your word of hope and joy in the world.

Be with us now, Holy Spirit. Fill our lungs and our lives with your breath. Give us courage to listen for your voice calling to us when we are too busy or afraid, speaking words to us that inspire justice and challenge the powers of this world. Come to us, abide with us, Word Incarnate. We pray all these things in the name of the One who was, who is, and who is to come.

Susan R. Schneider-Adams

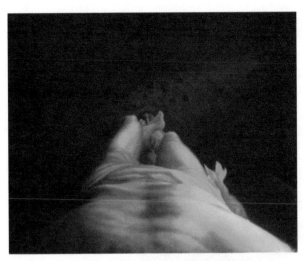

"And You Are in Me"

oil on canvas
Thomas A. Duff

"Flight into Egypt"

oil on canvas
Thomas A. Duff

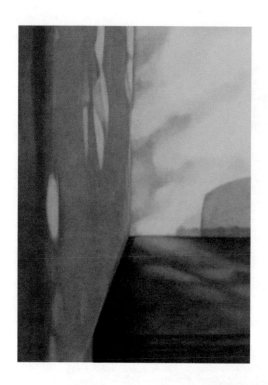

"Reflection"
Colored Pencil
Jane Suddendorf

"Sanctuary"
Colored Pencil
Jane Suddendorf

"Christ at Emmaus"

(oil on wood)
Paul Gerhardt Trost

"Blessed Are the Merciful"

(oil on wood)
Paul Gerhardt Trost

"Christ on the Sea of Galilee"
(oil on wood)
Paul Gerhardt Trost

"The Lord's Supper"
(acrylic on wood)
Paul Gerhardt Trost

SECTION III

THE VOCATION
OF THE PASTOR

Everything to Everyone:
The Vocation of Christian Ministry

Raymond P. Adams

Few readers of Calvin's *Institutes of the Christian Religion* would be surprised to find him approving Paul's injunction to the Corinthian Church that "all things should be done decently and in order" (1 Cor 14:40). Turning his attention to the ordained ministry (Book 4, chap. III), he writes:

> If any one would be deemed a true minister of the Church he must first be duly called; and secondly, he must answer to his calling; that is, undertake and execute the office assigned to him. This may often be observed in Paul, who, when he would approve his apostleship, almost always alleges a call, together with his fidelity in discharging the office.[1]

Calvin, helpfully, further distinguishes between the external, formal call of the church, and the secret call of God, "The good testimony of our heart [is] that we undertake the office neither from ambition nor avarice, nor any selfish feeling, but a sincere fear of God and a desire to edify the Church."[2]

The interplay between the "external" call of the church, and the "internal" call of God to the individual is a fascinating one. In the context of a local church, the interplay between the church's call and the internal motivation and calling of its pastor can be extremely creative: the faith of the church community is nurtured through preaching of the word and the administration of sacraments; and the congregation recognizes the local and global community in which it is set as the realm of God, and responds to its needs with love and commitment. The interplay can become destructive where minister and people have different agendas, where vision is lost to pragmatism, and fear of failure impedes faithful risk taking.

Yet today, for a new generation of ministers, it can no longer be assumed that the call of God is co-terminus with the institution of the church, as opportunities arise for ministry outside the structures. At times, the call of the church is but a launching pad for the increasing number of ministries through para-church organizations or (in the case of non-stipendiary ministries in the United Reformed Church in the United Kingdom) ministries in secular employment. Though this remains a small proportion of the total number of those ordained to word and sacrament, there is a desire to be at the cutting-edge of engagement with society, economic structures, and the powers which affect people's lives. It shows (very often in the churches' ambivalent response to these ministries) the potential detachment of ministry from the church in the traditional sense, and from any meaningful ownership by the church. It is salutary to put this alongside the assertion from the *Baptism, Eucharist and Ministry* document:

> The ordained ministry has no existence apart from the community [the church]. Ordained ministers can fulfil their calling only in and for the community. They cannot dispense with the recognition, the support and the encouragement of the community.[3]

And Bonhoeffer's belief:

> The Church is her true self only when she exists for humanity. As a fresh start she should give away all her endowments to the poor and needy. . . . She must take her part in the social life of the world, not lording it over men, but helping and serving them. She must tell men whatever their calling, what it means to live in Christ, to exist for others.[4]

Ministry breaking out of traditional moulds is nothing new but can be seen as part of the prophetic tradition of the Bible and the church: a proper response to the circumstances we live in where, in order to reach the majority of the population (certainly in the UK) who are untouched by the gospel, there needs to be a diversity of missionary initiative to reach those parts that conventionally-expressed Christianity fails to touch.

Walter Brueggemann maintains:

> The task of prophetic ministry is to nurture, nourish and evoke a consciousness and perception alternative to the consciousness and perception of the dominant culture around us. . . . Prophetic ministry has to do not primarily with addressing specific public crises but with addressing, in season and out of season, the dominant crisis that is enduring and resilient: of having our alternative vocation co-opted and domesticated. [5]

The enduring domestication of vision has to be tackled from both inside and outside church structures. Yet the nature of society and increasing demands made on ministers puts certain constraints on the practice of ministry. It leads to what is viewed by some as healthy diversity but to others is a dangerous slide towards fragmentation. From an entirely British context, there are several influences on the shape of ministry today:

1. The long process from the Enlightenment through postmodernity has championed the individual for good reasons, but the icon of self-fulfilment often sits uncomfortably alongside a Pauline concept of

service (2 Cor 4:5-12), and struggles even with the idea of self-fulfilment-in-community. This is true for those coming into ministry as well as congregations. "Ownership" in the Congregational tradition has led too often to a state where the local church has seen its minister as its employee, and treated him/her as such. Yet there is a proper sense in which the church "owns" its ministry (as noted above in the quotation from *Baptism Eucharist and Ministry*), and the nature of that, in terms of affirmation, joint commitment and support needs to be redefined in this new century, lest ministries are seen as go-it-alone products of the spirit of the age, which leaves the minister unsupported and even criticized for engaging in ministry beyond the walls of the church.

2. Paradoxically the decline in church attendance in Britain (and in many parts of Europe) resulting in fewer ministers serving wider areas, and more churches, means that it is impossible for a minister to embrace all the functions of the ministry of the church. The roles of pastor, prophet, teacher, evangelist, and servant have to be shared, so that ministers need, more than ever, to be gifted for collaborative working and skilled at team-building. For those coming in later years into ministry it can be quite a shock to realise that the skills required to work with volunteers are quite different from managing a company or being the head teacher in a school.

3. The increasing acceptance that ministry and mission of the church is the calling and responsibility of the whole people of God, is evident in the statement of the Lambeth Conference in 1988 which affirmed "Five Marks of Mission." The United Reformed Church has challenged its member churches to use these marks of mission as benchmarks for their corporate life, church programs, and ministry. They should set as priorities their call

- to proclaim the good news of the kingdom;
- to teach, baptize, and nurture new believers;
- to respond to human need by loving service;
- to seek to transform unjust structures of society;
- to strive to safeguard the integrity of creation, to sustain and renew the life of the earth.

While training programs exist to help leaders and members take on the tasks necessary to meet some of these commitments, there needs to be good co-ordination and the willingness of church members to take up new responsibilities.

4. Government policies in the UK now encourage greater partnership in society between local government and the voluntary sector

including the churches. There is an increasing recognition of the spiritual dimension of life but continued caution about formal religion. This brings with it a growing number of requests from healthcare trusts, the police, fire, and ambulance services, universities, colleges, factories, industry, town-centre stores, prisons, and private schools that the churches provide chaplains. New European Regional Development structures are being set up across the United Kingdom, to bid for European Community funding to regenerate communities with employment opportunities in areas of deprivation. In an increasingly ecumenical way, churches are becoming involved in these developments and on a regional scale are being asked from among thier church leaders to nominate someone (deemed to be independent of the political process and business interests) to chair these commissions.

Given all these developments, an increasing number of church reports try to define for local churches what ministers are for. It is not because of a loss in confidence in the role of minister within the life of the church but because it is in the nature of contemporary society that one of the constants is change. The URC General Assembly 2000 *Book of Reports* recently offered the following definition for the guidance of its local churches:

- Ministers should be able to organize and administrate, but they are not called to be managers.
- Ministers should be able to lead worship winsomely, but they are not entertainers.
- Ministers should be able pastors, but they are not therapists or counsellors.
- Ministers should share people's lives, but they are not casual visitors.
- Ministers should help break "the strange silence of the Bible in the church" but should be able also to speak of the God who is beyond scripture.
- Ministers should be students of scripture but need not be academic scholars.
- Ministers should know what is going on, but are not called to be sociologists or political scientists.
- Ministers should have a prophetic detachment, surrendering neither to the cynicism of the world, nor to the nostalgia of the church.
- Ministers should be men and women of God yet know their way round the world, acting as interpreters between the community and the church.

- Ministers should have soft hearts and hard heads; they should not have soft heads and hard hearts.

- Ministers should be good team players: with their colleagues, their elders, and their members.

- Ministers are not the private property of their congregations. They are called to care not only for those congregations but also to be ministers in District, Synod, and Assembly and should encourage their churches to see these relationships as means of mutual support rather than distant bureaucracies.

- Ministers in the United Reformed Church are, by definition, ecumenists.[6]

Whatever definitions we come up with, they exist against the background of a changing and challenging world. A minister of word and sacrament is so to the Christian community, yet the Word became flesh and the sacramental takes us beyond the table where bread is broken and wine outpoured to a world that is itself fragmented and increasingly "unoverseeable," i.e., impossible to grasp in its totality.

There are two models of ministry (among the many) whose validity remains strong in a changing social landscape:

1. The minister as the one in the church who, regardless of individual skills and local requirements, is called to dream and proclaim an alternative reality to the fixed and sometimes cynical view of the world as an unchangeable order.

The lead-in to the miracle of feeding the 5000 in Mark 6:35-37 shows Jesus challenging his disciples to use their imaginations, but they cannot. They are bound by the framework of the marketplace: "What are we supposed to do? Go and buy huge quantities of bread and feed everyone?" The same incredulity is exactly that of people today confronted by world poverty, or asylum seekers. Ched Myers has suggested that the only miracle in this gospel story is "the triumph of the economics of sharing within a community of consumption, over against the economics of autonomous consumption in the anonymous marketplace."[7] And further, in John's version of the miracle (Jn 6:3-15), the pivotal point of opportunity for Jesus to transform the reality of hunger is a child's willingness to give up his five loaves and two fish.

Ministers need to be dreamers who believe in the power of God to transform the world, who see the routine liturgical actions of breaking bread and pouring wine as potent images of God s creation given to be shared equally amongst all God s people; and who commit themselves to explore and express these things further and more deeply in the life they share with their people.

The example of the Colombian priest Camillo Torres, who refused to celebrate the Eucharist until justice had been achieved for his people, shows starkly the power of the "alternative reality," to be proclaimed in hope, and by declining to accept injustice and oppression (in whatever form it takes) as normal . All these things are to be discerned and declared while ministering through word and sacrament.

2. The minister is called to be the person representing all, and the person-for-all: the focus of the ministry of the whole church, who is "publicly and continually responsible for pointing to its (the church's) fundamental dependence on Jesus Christ, and thereby provide, within a multiplicity of gifts, a focus of its unity." [8] The minister is also, in the oft-quoted and misquoted phrase, "all things to all people" (1 Cor 9:22, *tois pasin gegona panta,* lit: "I became everything to everyone"). New Testament scholar Morna D. Hooker explains this as a "ministry of interchange."[9]

Paul is not trying to be like a weather cock changing in the wind but, discussing the rights and privileges of an apostle, summarises his ministry by using the same formula five times: "For though I am free, . . . I have made myself a slave to all so that [in order that, *hina*] I might win more of them" (1 Cor 9:19ff). To the Jews he became as a Jew (putting himself under the law); to the Gentiles (outside the law) he put himself outside the law. He identified himself with those he sought to win for the gospel. Paul therefore willingly gives up the freedom of his identity in order that men and women might share, not in what *he* became—that is, a slave like them so that he is thus identified with them—but in what *he essentially was and is:* one who is called and redeemed by Christ. This is clearly a parallel with the redemptive self-emptying *(kenosis)* of Christ himself, through which action they and we have a share in what he was willing to abandon. Christ was rich, and we too become rich; he knew no sin, and we become the righteousness of God in him. Prof. Hooker summarizes:

> It is not that Christ changes place with men and women. Though he identifies with them, he remains what he is—without sin, Son of God, in the form of God. And when they become what he is it is because they are now identified with him—they are in Christ. [10]

This redemptive act of exchange becomes a model for the church's ministry (not, of course, that we can or need to set ourselves up as redeemers. What Christ has done is once and for all). Yet it is through the ministry of incarnation that we can identify with others and lead them to Christ.

We see it again in Philippians 2:4-7, where Paul urges his readers: "Let the same mind be in you that was in Christ Jesus, who, though he was in the form of God, did not regard equality with God as a something to be exploited, but emptied himself, taking the form of a slave, being born in human likeness." That ministry of identification with others is also universal in its scope.

A recent conversation the writer had with the chairman of the governing body of a college of education elicited his view that the newly appointed chaplain should be there as a "listening ear" for the school principal but should avoid the excesses of his predecessor, who had stood up to the governing body on a particular issue and was perceived to behave like a trades union representative for the staff. This puts in a nutshell the privilege and essential role of ministry—not to be impartial but freely becoming "Jew," "Gentile," "slave" in order to bring the love and righteousness of God to bear in the workplace as well as the sanctuary; to be prophetic when the situation requires it but to acknowledge its fundamental dependence on the inward call of God to sustain, direct and renew each one involved in the task, as we accept, in Isaac Watts' words: "new works of duty done for thee."[11]

Notes

1. John Calvin, *Institutes of the Christian Religion,* Bk. IV, chap. III, trans. Henry Beveridge; (London: James Clark & Co, 1957), 322.

2. Ibid., 323.

3. *Baptism, Eucharist and Ministry,* Faith and Order Paper, no.111 (Geneva: World Council of Churches, 1982), 22.

4. Dietrich Bonhoeffer, *Letters and Papers from Prison,* trans. Eberhard Bethge (Fontana Books, 1959), 166.

5. Walter Brueggemann, *The Prophetic Imagination* (Philadelphia: Fortress Press, 1978), 13.

6. Reports to the General Assembly of the United Reformed Church (July 2000):19-20, quoting from *Great Expectations: a study pack to help churches discover themselves and their future,* (URC Wales Synod 1998), 59-60.

7. Ched Myers, *Binding the Strong Man* (New York: Orbis, 1988), 205f; quoted in Timothy Gorringe, *The Sign of Love: Reflections on the Eucharist* (London: SPCK, 1997) 33ff.

8. *Baptism, Eucharist and Ministry,* 21.

9. Morna D. Hooker, "A Partner in the Gospel: Paul's Understanding of Ministry," in *Epworth Review*, 25.1 (1998): 13.

10. Ibid., 73.

11. Isaac Watts (1674-1748), "My God, my king, thy various praise," based on Psalm 145:110, stanza 2.

On Becoming a Parson/Person

Browne Barr

Recently a very able woman invited me to participate in her ordination. In the invitation she frankly explained to me that she wanted me to offer the Charge unless her home pastor could make the long trip from his home to take part in the ceremony. In that event she would ask me to read the lesson. However, that was complicated because she had long promised her college professor of religion a part in the service; but the professor had been so ill there was little likelihood she could be there. There was still a slim chance she would come, and in that case would I be willing to offer the call to worship?

A few days before the scheduled ordination, the ailing professor suddenly recovered and announced her delight that she could be present, as did the home pastor. The woman seeking ordination, in great embarrassment, asked me if I would be willing to give the benediction, the call to worship having been assigned to someone else that morning in a moment of liturgical generosity.

"No," I gently told her, "I can't do that. The benediction is yours–your first official act."

"Oh, well," she replied. "That's okay. "I've given lots of benedictions already."

Further conversation revealed that this good, well-educated, devout woman regarded ordination, and especially the title "The Reverend," the prerogatives provided by the church to anyone who had finished the work required in a divinity school or seminary for a Master of Divinity degree. Her examination by the Ordaining Council had been a cordial affair where she had been given an opportunity to bear witness to her faith but there had been no serious theological conversation or probing inquiry about the work of a pastor. She had earlier made clear that she sought ordination only as a teacher of religion.

You would think that anyone who aspired to the life of a teacher would be especially keen not to fail so great an examination as the one for ordination, but it did not seem to be large in her consideration, not nearly so important as to cut a place, however small, for her major friends in the service itself. To be sure, the sense that no one ever failed the examination was further ingrained, at least in this case, by the practical arrangements: the examination was held in the afternoon and the long scheduled and advertised ordination was held that same evening. All on the same day! It reminded me of the difficulty some members of an Ordaining Council had when they *tried* to postpone approval of an ordination. The argument not to postpone was strong and won out for they already had been twice interrupted by the arrival of some dignitary hunting the restroom and also by the smell of the pot roast cooking in the church kitchen.

This report of the trivializing of ordination is not exaggerated, but it would be no great concern if it were except insofar as it achieves and participates in a trivialization of the vocation of the pastor. By turning the service into a production, we trivialize the Christian religious experience which is an encounter with the Almighty and Living God. It is the experience by which the church lives and is called the public worship of God and is the chief responsibility for which men and women are ordained.

The vocation of the pastor is "to preach the gospel, to administer the sacraments, and to bear rule in Christ's church!" For this we ordain women and men; for this we give them authority over us; for this we provide for them and their dependents; for this and for nothing else! To provide ordination for many related tasks, education, counseling, calling, etc., is to dilute the purpose of ordination and to demean the priesthood of all believers.

Preaching the gospel is not some self-righteous person banging us over the heads with the Bible, and his or her authority is not the authority of civil state or personal eccentricity. Preaching is not outlining the commandments, it is not laying down the law of Moses to us, it is not threatening us with eternal damnation nor is it helping us through the day with sweet platitudes. Preaching is a conversation which leads us into the presence of God. It draws us into a place of incomparable beauty where our sins become intolerable and are bathed in the light of Christ's face. It holds us where our lives are renewed, our great good resolves are refreshed. The imperative mood is out of place; the indicative reigns. We hear what draws us to goodness and light as great art plunges us into silence and music may running.

We are all prodigals, and we need to be open to hear and respond to the Divine Parent's voice, week upon week, so persistent is our separation from God and so profound our need. That this is so seldom our experience and our lives are so lacking in the moral energy and direction such worship provides, is sober judgment on every ordained person in our ranks.

But there is more than that, more than just us and our private destinies. As P. T. Forsyth reminds us, "Any conception of God which exalts his Fatherhood at the cost of his holiness . . . unsettles the moral throne of the universe." Perhaps this is the word we need the sacraments to hear, where the word reaches beyond and beneath our words in the crucified Christ. Without it we have "no due sense of the human tragedy, the moral tragedy of the race. . . . It robs faith of its energy, its virility, its command, its compass, and its solemnity. . . .We have churches of the nicest, kindest people, who have nothing apostolic or missionary, who never knew the soul's despair or its breathless gratitude."[1] All humankind is at stake and congregations turned inward never know that. To declare this mystery, to proclaim this history, to preach from this divine energy is to renew and reenact the saving work of Christ. It is to give it new life within our being and refreshed power between communities of persons until every living thing shall rise up in that transcendent mystery glorifying God and enjoying God forever.

We are entering a century where science itself is trying to unlock us from its prison as it compels us to confess the mystery of creation and of our creation, to confess the vastness of eternity and much which we acknowledge but cannot understand, to release us from an age which defines us by our vocation to enter one which honors our not-knowing, forgets our doing and celebrates our being.

It is an age, as I have written elsewhere, where we "may well be prompted to take a more sober view of coincidence, a more reverent view of Providence, a readier and gentler openness to the heavenly leaf falling into the flowing stream, God in Jesus Christ entering human history. It will summon congregations, leaning forward in their pews or moving toward the holy table, to plead with the preacher, 'Don't tell us what you know! Tell us what you don't know, so together we may worship God.'"[2]

Such a pity that women and men ordained to such a wonderful task are known as "Reverend." To begin with such a title is mostly used ungrammatically. "Reverend Kolops," we say. But reverend is an adjective, like honorable. We do not say of the governor, "Honorable Jones." So it should be, if we insist on using it, The Reverend Mr. Jones or the Reverend John Jones. But that is straining, dotting every "i." But we don't consider the strain when the ordained person is called "Reverend" and she knows that she is not good and she cringes inside. Please don't call me "good," she wants to plead. The gospel is not broken if I, who proclaim it, am a struggling sinner nor is it elevated perceptively if I am a saint. It rests in fragile vessels but it is not dependent upon them. Only in this knowledge could anyone bear to be ordained or dare to undertake that central task in the church of Jesus Christ.

In an earlier time the minister was known as the "Parson." That sounds strange and old-fashioned to us but some words need to be recycled. Maybe this is one. For "Parson" comes from "Person" and the clergyperson was regarded as the Person in the town, The Representative Human Being, not in the sense of being perfect but of being whole. I know a few people like that. They just seem to have their hands on life in a magnificent, collected, discerning, nonjudgmental way. They know they are not perfect and need to pray a lot, but they are not forever apologizing. They make mistakes but are not undone by them. Somehow they seem to understand that they are not God. They simply are becoming full human beings, laughing and crying and loving and being loved and pressing on for the high calling of God in Jesus Christ. Somehow that feels appropriate for Christian character aspiration, for lay people and clergy alike.

Notes

1. P. T. Forsyth, *Positive Preaching and Modern Mind* (Beecher Lecture, 1907), 355.

2. Browne Barr, "To Be a Pastor to People Who Can't Even Predict the Weather," *Theology Today* (January 1997): 503.

About You, among Others

Martha Ann Baumer

Recently, I sat in the Abbey on the island of Iona, part of an assorted congregation gathered for an informal celebration of the Eucharist. Presiding and preaching was the current Warden of the Abbey, Brian Woodcock. He spoke directly to those who had been there for the week's conferences. At the Abbey the focus had been Celtic Christianity and at the nearby MacLeod Center, peace in Northern Ireland. He told us that the week had not been about Northern Ireland or about Celtic Christianity but "about you." He described how in the study and conversation surrounding these two topics, what was really happening was some sort of involving and changing of the participants themselves. To learn information, to think together about implications, to be in relationships with others, whether new friends or old, compatible or not, to care about faith and peace and justice is to discover one's self in new ways, it is to be affected and changed in the process. It is "about you." I was not among either of the groups, but I heard a clear message. When I try to distance myself in the learning process, when I think the sermon is interesting but not aimed at me, when I think I'm just an impartial observer, I'm really kidding myself. It is about me.

Pastoring, I am sure, is like that. It is about you and about me. It is about pastors and about lay folk and about all whom their lives touch. In honoring Frederick Trost, we think particularly about pastors, for they and their work are dear to his heart and his ministry. The pastor is called to be a servant of Christ, to represent the church to itself and to the world. And Frederick Trost has done that so well. There are various images, roles, tasks, titles, and responsibilities for the pastor. The descriptions and prescriptions are helpful, but, finally, as we see in Pastor Trost, it is about the person, "about you."

For a year now, I have been at work developing ways in which my seminary can support its recent graduates as they begin their ministries. The program comes from observations of the needs of the church and its clergy. Many new pastors have had little experience of the church and those with significant experience often find themselves in very different circumstances from what they had known. Many came to seminary without prior academic training in disciplines easily related to theology, its content, and methods. Most are in a role that they may have observed or otherwise understood but which they are discovering in new ways as they live it. Whatever their preparation and prior experience, the first pastorate or chaplaincy is the crucible in which the various pieces become blended and molded and the pastor emerges in the form that is likely to provide the basic shape of that person's ministry from then on. Those first years seem crucial and the resources available to the new pastor vary greatly from one situation to the next.

It is not only new pastors who are being formed. Though the process may be less noticeable, all are continually changing, hopefully growing, as they experience their lives and work. Pastoring is a continuing, personal process. The person of the pastor cannot be masked, put aside, ignored. The pastor does not adopt her pastoral persona for certain functions as a suit of armor in which to do battle; granted, she will move from task to task and the particulars will change accordingly. Pastoring is "about you," and each of us is constantly being affected and molded as we go through life. We're never finished learning and growing and we need to take responsibility for our continued development as we seek to be faithful to the Christ, to the church, and to those who are particularly affected by our lives. It is easy to ignore that, or even to try to reject it as being true, and we often do so. I believe a far healthier and more faithful way is to embrace personal change and growth as an essential element of being a pastor.

Perhaps the first step is to recognize and welcome the fact that pastoring is personal and is a continuing process. Theological education, particularly in church-related seminaries, attempts to engage persons in the process of developing foundations and criteria for ministry. Such requires participants to look hard at their personal faith, their relationships in every direction, their understandings of basic foundations of life, such as who is God and who or what authors our life and work. It quickly becomes "about me," even as we strive to maintain some sort of objectivity and to gain even larger and more varied perspectives about life and faith.

Virginia Samuel Cetuk of The Theological School of Drew University notes, "theological education is not about learning, it is about change." She goes on to add, "it is precisely about changing students' worldviews and receptivity to others; it is about changing their self-understandings in relation to God and others; it is perhaps even about changing their dreams."* Though I would argue that learning itself is about change, I strongly agree with her point.

Change is the nature of life and certainly of ministry. It never stops. As the pastor enters ordained ministry, faces new situations, moves to a new community, engages different persons, change happens. Every time she reads a book, prays seriously, listens to a complaint, becomes a parent or grandparent, loses a spouse, change happens. The pastor approaches every new day with his particular set of experiences and his particular identity.

That contributes to the shape of what he sees and hears and the ways in which he understands. The experiences of the day in turn shape the pastor, and she will approach tomorrow a different person. Sometimes the change is minuscule; often the individual resists any change and may even try to deny it. But I suggest that we both acknowledge the personal nature of pastoring and also seek to grow positively as persons of faith and as pastors as we welcome and engage life and ministry.

Surely this is a way of life for every faithful Christian, not to be taken lightly. God claims to be making all things new and is not only doing so but is inviting us to join in the process. What a privilege! The Ephesians and we are admonished that "speaking the truth in love, we must grow up in every way into him who is the head, into Christ, from whom the whole body, joined and knit together by every ligament with which it is equipped, as each part is working properly, promotes the body's growth in building itself up in love" (4:15-16). Not only are we invited to grow, we are reminded we do not do so alone.

The pastor is called by Christ and the church to represent the church to itself and to the world. The pastor does not function, ever, in isolation anymore than the baptized live in isolation. We are always part of the body of Christ. For the pastor, the claims may be more intense because pastoring itself belongs not to the individual but to the church of Jesus Christ. Representing the church, as the pastor does, requires carrying the church's faith and heritage within oneself and being aware of how and when to share that appropriately. The pastor has agreed to be a teacher and a leader of the community of faith. The interaction is virtually continuous with the players always changing. Sometimes the pastor is intersecting with the world on behalf of the church; sometimes she is functioning primarily within the faith community; sometimes both. Basic to it all, of course, is our relationship to Christ. Pastoring is relating and relating is always personal. It is about you, about me, about us.

There are risks in all of this, some of them obvious. To welcome and engage personal change is to risk one's life. We do so with confidence because of the constancy, the will, and the compassion of the triune God. In pastoring, it means learning with and from one's people and the communities of which the pastor is a member. It means intentional biblical and theological study to examine and develop anew in each context the basic understandings and criteria that shape preaching, judgments, counseling, understanding of and participation in the whole church of Jesus Christ, reaching out to proclaim the gospel in mission. It means welcoming insights from other disciplines, knowing and caring about discoveries and inventions and new understandings that shift the realities of life. It means tending to relationships with care, taking the time and giving the attention to listen carefully to the other. It means reaching out to others for companionship and support. Most new understandings and insights require shaping and practice before they are honed to appropriate use. Such happens in continual conversation as ideas and understandings are tried, remolded, tried again, given rest, applied in other contexts, seen from different vantage points.

Engaging the pastoral office as a growing, developing way of life requires letting go of that which no longer fits or serves faithfully. One key to such is being able to accept the forgiveness of God and to forgive oneself. Some things need to be let go; forgiveness says we are given new life in Christ. Churches often fail to give the pastor the time and space for healing and renewal; pastors are often unable or unwilling to claim the need for this time or do so inappropriately. Yet, without receiving forgiveness and letting go, growth and therefore life are endangered. It is not possible to grow without change. Change often includes pain. And pain requires healing.

Along the way, the pastor must also acknowledge and give attention to what we've come to call "boundaries." If pastoring is about the person, then the person needs to know where he starts and stops, what is appropriate in various relationships with various persons, when to say "yes" and when to say "no." To accept responsibility for the life God has given to me, I must live it and not someone else's. To accept the love God has given to me and to all, I must care for others with respect for each and for all. Those boundaries are always in danger of being hidden or being eroded. Like all fences, they require tending. This, too, is part of the reality of pastor as person.

While pastoring is "about you," it is not *all* about you! As members of the community of faith, the body of Christ, we do none of this alone. The pastor's living and growing is done among those who can and generally do offer the support, love, correction, guidance, counsel, and care required. Most of us could more intentionally and carefully seek such support and welcome it when it's available than we now do. We are not left to our own devices though we may think or act as though we are. We claim the company of the triune God who has promised to be with us, who keeps promises, and who often comes to us in human forms.

While pastoring means personal growth and change, it is not an individual self-improvement program. It is not for the sake of the pastor, except as the pastor is a beloved child of God and a member of the body of Christ. Pastoring is for the sake of the body and its members; it is for the

Christ. It is growing and maturing as a child of God among and with all the children of God, as a member of the body whose particular vocation is that of pastor. It is living and growing with and for the church of Jesus Christ.

That sermon I heard at Iona didn't end with comments about the week's study. The Warden continued, talking of the eucharistic meal we were about to share. He recalled for us that as we receive the body and blood of Christ so we become the body of Christ in the world, called to live accordingly. The Supper, he told us, is not only about God, it is "about you." Thus we are fed, called, made new, empowered. Thus we belong to the Christ and in him to one another. Thus we know who we are and what we do. Pastoring is personal; the pastor/person belongs to Christ. Whatever the risks, whatever the losses, whatever the outcome, we are in the hands of the One who is love and life. That, and only that, makes it all possible.

Note

* Virginia Samuel Cetuk, *What to Expect in Seminary* (Nashville: Abingdon Press, 1998), 45.

"I Hear Your Voice Calling"

I hear your voice calling—

    beckoning me from the shadows of my soul,

    encouraging me to live in your light and share in your joy,

    nurturing a renewal of spirit,

    awakening a love that is the motivator of my heart.

Holy God, grant that I have the grace to answer as I shout

    thanks and praise to you, O my Creator.

I hear your voice calling—

    challenging me from complacency,

    prompting me from my comfort zone to stand beside the needy and the broken,

    pushing me to be a voice for the voiceless and power for the powerless,

    persuading me to walk with others the road to wholeness.

Holy God, grant that I have the courage to answer as I cry

    thanks and praise to you, O my Redeemer.

I hear your voice calling—

    surrounding my spirit through the daily-ness of life,

    allowing me to acknowledge a deep and steadfast faith,

    ever-abiding throughout my life's journey,

    reassuring that your presence is constant and true.

Holy God, grant that I have the will to answer as I mindfully lift

    thanks and praise to you, O my Sustainer.

Beth A. Faeth

The Hospitality of Christ and the Church's Resurrection: A "Performed" Christology as Social Reformation

Mark S. Burrows

Lord Jesus Christ, you did not come to the world to be served and thus not to be admired either, or in that sense worshiped. You yourself were the way and the life—and you have asked only for imitators. If we have dozed off into this infatuation, wake us up, rescue us from this error of wanting to admire or adoringly admire you instead of wanting to follow you and be like you.[1]

Jesus' direct question of his disciples, "Who do you say that I am?"[2] has been central as a guiding norm in the church's emergence and growth within diverse cultures. Indeed, it establishes what Paul Tillich called the principle of "correlation," a method of engagement used for apologetic and didactic purposes alike by which Christians through the ages have sought to engage cultures with the gospel message on their *own* terms.[3] Such an interrogative approach has led to losses and gains in the "original" memory of Jesus, though one might say with some confidence that Christians until the period of the western Enlightenment were little concerned with recovering the "original" Jesus, the Jesus of "history"[4]—at least as *we* now understand history. Theirs were other interests, above all, the task of articulating the gospel of grace in cultures increasingly distanced from the Galilean, Jewish context out of which Jesus arose. And this meant that their attempts to answer this simple but demanding question shaped the formation of their faith and life. As one New Testament scholar, John Dominic Crossan, has suggested in the opening lines of his study of the so-called "historical" Jesus, "In the beginning was the performance; not the word alone, not the deed alone, but both, each indelibly marked with the other forever."[5]

This "performed" christology, to take Crossan's point a step further, was a confrontation in the first instance not with a concept or an intellectual question, but with a person: one might well say that Jesus not only poses this question of his contemporaries (and, through the Gospel texts, ours as well) but actually *becomes* the question that confronted Jews and pagans of all varieties and throughout the ages of the church's formation. Indeed, the emergence of the primitive church and its growth into a position of cultural ascendancy is to a large extent a story of struggle with precisely this person. And it is quite clear that this query remains at the heart of the church's witness—not only its endeavors to speak "to the nations" (*ad nationes*) from age to age, but its efforts to remain critical of itself and of its propensity toward accommodation with other "Gospels" or complacence toward its own. For it is the person of Christ who sets the measure for our life in community. Who *we* say Christ is shapes the character of our life and mission, in and to "the world."

Yet it is always the case, as Albert Schweitzer reminded us in *The Quest of the Historical Jesus,*[6] that our attempts to answer this question—to *live* in answer to this question—often stumble into idolatries of our own making. We all too readily make Jesus into *our* image, honoring what seems "tasteful" to us and ignoring or dismissing what puzzles, offends, or embarrasses. To paraphrase Schweitzer, the question we have tended to pose in this quest is: "Who do you *want* me to be?" Kierkegaard saw this clearly for an earlier generation when he condemned our tendencies to admire rather than live in imitation of Jesus the Christ. As he put it in characteristically acerbic tones, here describing what he called "the calamity of Christendom":

There is in Christendom an everlasting Sunday babbling about Christianity's glorious and priceless truths, its gentle consolation, but of course one bears in mind that it is eighteen hundred years since Christ lived. The sign of offense and the object of faith has become the most fabulous of all fabulous characters, a divine Mr. Goodman. One does not know what it is to be offended, even less what it is to worship.

And he concludes from this strident criticism that "Christendom has abolished Christianity without really knowing it itself," and thus he argues that our task is to "attempt again to introduce Christianity to Christendom."[7]

To hear such a driving criticism—and to have "ears to hear" that this might have something to say about *us*—is to come to the heart of the matter before us. Jesus' question evoked historical and prophetic echoes for his first hearers—who had not yet seen what his life would lead to. The "crowds," as the text reminds us, wondered whether he might not be Elijah, John the Baptist, or one of the prophets (Mt 16:13ff; Mk 8:27ff.; Lk 9:18ff). But they—together with the disciples—had no premonition of the cruel fate awaiting this teacher and healer; the scene that follows this periscope in the accounts of Matthew and Mark, Peter's "rebuke" of Jesus, suggests how difficult it was and is to "hear" a gospel that announces life only in the midst of death. And it is precisely this dimension of the interrogation that we must hold before us: this is a story that must offend *us*, that must continue to measure *us*, if we would hear it faithfully. Or, to put this another way: if Jesus' question results only in historical curiosity or in coffee hour pleasantries, we have not yet heard it with the full force of its scandal nor can we hope to know what it means to be church.

Let us stay with this approach for a moment longer, since there is surely something to be said for the crowd's logic and for Peter's evasion, something that continues to tempt us as we respond to Jesus' direct question. For it is a much more attractive invitation to honor or admire a great teacher, or even a true prophet, than it is to follow one destined for an ignominious death at the hands of his compatriots. And thus we, with the crowds, are sorely tempted to accept Jesus in terms of our own more manageable hopes, messianic or prophetic, for political salvation and to define the character of Christian life in other terms—e.g., as a "moral" way of life, based perhaps on the Beatitudes; or, variously, as a "social" witness to the injustices evident in our world grounded in his identification with "the poor." Or, with Peter, we seek to ameliorate the force of Jesus' own announcement of his fate, particularly when we also know that he tells us to follow *him* by taking up *our* cross. Should we blame ourselves (or others) for such evasions? After all, Jesus' rebuke of Peter—"You are an obstacle in my path, because you are thinking not as God thinks but as human beings do"—sounds not entirely unreasonable as the response of "weak vessels" like us. We remind ourselves that we live within a *Christian* culture, and are not therefore confronted with the same stark options that faced the early apostles. We are not altogether sure that we want to—or, indeed, that we *need* to—follow Jesus all the way to the cross, particularly if there are less difficult options to pursue. And thus we seek to find ways, often quiet and subtle, to evade the force of this question altogether, since we know that it is a question about *us*, about *our* faith and courage.

If this is a general challenge facing Christians through the ages, it is true with peculiar (if not often perverse) force for witnesses to the gospel in churches (such as ours) whose survival is rooted in the voluntarist tradition. What we most want to avoid, it often seems, is scandalous preaching—to "introduce Christianity into Christendom," as Kierkegaard put it with ironic force. Too often our efforts as preachers—either intentionally or implicitly—have softened the force of this question, preferring to find ways to "get a hearing" by speaking the gospel in a melody that is harmonious with culture or one that offers inner healing, a cheap sort of grace, or "church growth" rather than gospel confrontation. And so we preach "peace where there is no peace," and avoid the "hard saying" of Jesus that he came to bring a sword.

What I would like to suggest is that this question is one of conversion, of *our* conversion, an invitation to become followers rather than admirers, at one extreme, or critics, at the other, of Jesus' witness to the embodiment of divine righteousness. As such, it brings into conversation christology and ecclesiology, yoked as these were for earliest Christians under the rubric "body of Christ" (*soma Christou*). What we say about Jesus, in other words, determines how we will come together as "church" (*ekklesia*). On the basis of this convergence (i.e., of christology and ecclesiology), I would like to get at the query "Who do you say that I am?" through three questions: first, "Who belongs at table?" as this is reconstructed from the Gospel narratives; second, "Who belongs in the body?" as we understand this in Paul's witness; and, finally, "How should we invite *out*siders—*in?*" on the basis of our identity "in Christ." For it is in asking about the nature of our communion that we find a central way of "hearing" and responding to Jesus' question.

"Who Belongs at Table?"

To ask this question is to stumble upon one of the central responsibilities we face when we gather to "give thanks" (*eucharistia*) in Christ's name, above all when we come together for the holy meal of Communion. For we all—the "words of institution" establish one of the fundamental principles of ecumenical convergence—recite Jesus' instruction to his disciples: viz., to eat bread and drink wine "in remembrance" of him, as words constitutive of our identity.

What will it mean to "remember" Jesus? *Whom* are we remembering? This memory requires, in the first instance, that we recognize that we *all* are stewards of a "new covenant" of forgiveness, ministers of the divine acceptance of sinners. The early disciples, imitating Jesus in this act, would have re-membered in quite concrete terms the kind of table fellowship he kept—which was unsavory, to say the least, since Jesus insisted upon eating with "outsiders," with people who just did not belong in "good" company. When we affirm in the communion liturgy that the covenant in his blood has been "poured out for many for the forgiveness of sins" (Mt 26:28), we mean to say that the preparation for this table is something God has already achieved *in Christ!* Jesus apparently welcomed *many* to his table simply because they sought such fellowship with him, often to the annoyance not only of his critics but of his disciples as well. And, in the culture of this period, acceptance at table was at one and the same time a most public *and* intimate declaration of communion. As a consequence, one normally ate with those of similar or better rank, if possible, in order to maintain or elevate one's social status. In this case, of course, it is clear that some things never change. Jesus exemplified an apparently self-defeating social strategy: he did precisely the opposite, risking his reputation by eating with those who sought him out, often those on the margin of Jewish society whose very presence at table was a clear public offense.

When we remember Jesus in this meal, we with the disciples should remember the kind of host Jesus was—because his "table manners" declared who people perceived him to be, perhaps prompting the references to Elijah (who was expected at every Passover) and John the Baptist (who apparently welcomed, without condemnation, the crowds at the Jordan who sought forgiveness).

Paul offers a penetrating insight into this question from another angle when he identifies the divisions within the Corinthian church as the source of their "sacramental" improprieties: "For when you come together, it is not really to eat the Lord's supper. For when the time comes to eat, each one of you goes ahead with your own supper first, and one goes hungry while another becomes drunk. . . . Do you show contempt for the church of God and humiliate those who have nothing?" (1 Cor 11:20-2). The inequalities—social, economic, political—within the community disrupted proper table fellowship! Or, to put this another way: the Corinthian factions could not "re-member" who Jesus was as long as they constructed barriers within the body, divisions of status that were foreign to Jesus' own hospitality at table. Again, the character of Jesus' table fellowship established the norm for that of the early Christian community, according to Paul: proper memory—or, more accurately, right social practice on the basis of right memory—became the very condition of authentic experience of the supper.

For the apostle, the question of social reconciliation had to be faced *before* one came to the table, such that one's "table manners" determined in advance whether one "ate worthily" and thus entered into Christ's covenant in the meal. Recalling Jesus' practice, Paul reminds us that table fellowship stood as the place to demonstrate who it was the community gathered to remember. Bonhoeffer relied on this apostolic insight to explain Jesus' "transcendence" not in metaphysical but in physical terms—viz., as the expression of one who gave his life "even unto death" *for others*.[8] Indeed, he also makes the connection between christology and ecclesiology, arguing on the basis of this vision of Christ's "transcendence" that "the church is the church *only* when it exists for others."[9]

To ask "Who belongs at the table?" and to act upon this memory is in a very real sense an answer to the question, "Who do people say I am?"

and to the more direct rejoinder, "But who do *you* say I am?" Will we stand with those who wanted to see only a prophet, a great teacher, a healer? Will we rebuke Jesus, with Peter, because we do not want to follow the call "unto death"? Will we only "keep company" with Jesus when to do so seems to offer us advantages "in the world"? Or will we risk hearing the good news of the One who pursued "the way of the cross" (Luther) and whose life announced "peace" to those far off (Eph 2:17)—to us, first of all, and to those still living at the margins of society? Will we come to this table remembering the character of Jesus' hospitality—and, if necessary, violate on the basis of that memory the contemporary codes of social status, *in order to embody Christ at table* by breaking bread with "the least" of these (Mt 25)? We cannot answer Jesus' question in abstractions; we *will* answer it in the patterns of our affiliations, within and outside the church. The question is not *whether* but *how* we will do so.

"Who Belongs in the Body?"

To pose this second question is to pursue the same dynamic raised in the first: we demonstrate who we think Jesus was on the basis of our fellowship in the "body." Here one might recall Paul's familiar description of the church's unity and the equality of membership, based on our having been "clothed . . . in Christ" through baptism (see, for example, Gal 3:8), as an illustrative answer to this question. But this reminder has not been forceful enough, historically speaking, to disrupt patterns of inequality, discrimination, and even segregation that have fractured and continue to divide the one body of Christ. Let us rather respond to this question by first recalling Jesus' strange and disturbing parable about the wedding feast (Lk 14:15-24; Mt 22:2-10), which in Luke's Gospel stands as a direct correction of bad table manners (see Lk 14:1; his instructions to "the guests" at v. 7, to the "host" at v. 12, and to "one of those at table" at v. 15).

In Luke's account, the host of the banquet, after his servants returned without the invited guests, fell into a rage and sent them out again to invite "the poor, the crippled, the blind, and the lame"—in a word, the "outsiders" who deserved no place at the table. And after that, seeing that there was still room at table, he sent the servants out with orders to bring people in "by force," if necessary, so that the house would be full. This is, to be sure, a peculiar and troubling account of how to host a party—and, by analogy, a self-defeating strategy according to popular approaches to what is called "church growth."

The complex parable reminds us of one simple truth: viz., that the host of the divine kingdom wants a full house, and relies on strange practices to achieve this end. What this story might teach us about membership in the body of Christ seems clear, if also disturbing: the parable reminds those of us who are often more anxious to ascertain who is *worthy* of attendance at table that many not included in the original guest list—i.e., those "far off," to recall Paul's phrase—will be included, one way or another. The burden falls upon us, who claim to be "servants" of this host, to realize this mission. And this will mean for us, as Jesus meant it for his Jewish audience, that we must seek to liberate the *church* of parochial attitudes and segregationist policies or tendencies if we would know what it means to be "in Christ," to live as the "body" of Christ. We might here put the question the other way around, asking outsiders to our communities to construct *our* doctrine of God on the basis of the commitments they observe among us—not only in our patterns of acceptance *within* the community but in the character of our hospitality to those outside. The patterns of our fellowship, in other words, "incarnate" who we think Jesus is.

"How Should We Invite *Out*siders—*In*?"

This seems a strange question in relation to our point of departure, but the logic should now be clear: we will bear witness to the One who invites *us* into fellowship insofar as we invite *others* into that fellowship—with God, through Christ, and with *each* other, again through Christ. Ecclesiology is the place where the integrity of christological affirmations must finally be tested! This means that we must reduce theological or christological abstractions to very concrete terms, and measure the faithfulness of our vocation as "ambassadors" for Christ—persons through whom God appeals for a community more "catholic" in its faith *and* life (see 2 Cor 5:20)—in "real" and quite ordinary terms. It will mean that communities in which reconciliation is a genuine goal (if not also an occasionally experienced "end") will begin to understand Jesus by "incorporating" the kind of hospitality he exemplifies, and this in a broken world, hardened by tribal fears and parochial hostilities. But this is to say that the doctrine and practice of church—the patterns of our "congregating," as it were—become the most fundamental means by which we answer the question, "Who do you say I am?"

It also suggests that we have become far too complacent in our churches with the disfiguring status quo that exists in our neighborhoods and in our world. What might it mean if we were to begin to see our identity "in Christ" as creating new and more catholic communities, something that civil law can envision—usually by attempting to prevent its opposite—and occasionally even enforce, but a goal grounded in a mystery that it cannot itself generate? How might we view the "other," defined in terms of a broader "household" of faith than we are often able to see because of denominational, racial, or ethnic differences, if we grounded our faith in a *common* inheritance, and if *we* saw *ourselves*—and particularly those of us who pride ourselves as being "the first"—as those "far off" from God? How might our churches bear witness to an alternative vision of community in a world that seems to be increasingly connected (and thus dependent) in market terms and yet disjointed (and thus independent) in terms of our mutual obligations to one another, moral, political, or economic? What would it mean to put in practice Jesus' instructions to those who come to a party—and, particularly for those of us who represent the "first" within the "first world," to take the place of *least* honor and greatest service among those gathered at the global banquet with limited resources? Perhaps ours is not only the burden of "forcing" guests to come to the feast but of ourselves taking "the lowest place" at table so that others might also have a place to share in the meal, though this must be the subject of another discussion.

All this suggests that the question before us is not one that we are allowed to pose in abstract terms, nor is it one that we should direct first of all to outsiders. Rather, it is the question we must raise with critical force toward *ourselves* within our communities of faith, hoping that this question might expose the idolatries which separate us from one another and impose burdens of hospitality that we have not yet dared to imagine—leading, in short, to the liberation of the church from the bonds of fear and greed, of sin and death. Directing this question back to ourselves, as an expression of the church's identity as the body of Christ, calls us to account for our faith in the visible form of our life, to "incarnate" our faith in the One who died for us "while we were [God's] enemies" (Rom 5:10). This means, of course, that the faith we profess is only as deep, as broad, and ultimately only as *real,* as the "catholic" character of the communities in which we gather to worship the Christ of God. Amid the horizon of strife in which we find ourselves, the creation which is "groaning in travail" for its liberation (Rom 8:22), and a "land of death" strangled by injustices on every side, there is no time for "an everlasting Sunday babbling" about the truth or rightness of our cause. In opposition and resistance to such prattle, we must begin to invest our energies in local—and, insofar as this is feasible, "global," strategies of reconciliation (the gospel announces nothing less than this!), thereby envisioning the church as a community uniquely entrusted by God for this mission and thus "embodying" Christ as it were *in* and *for* the world. To do this, we must dare to be scandalized by Jesus, to recall Kierkegaard's driving point, to be properly "offended" by his table manners—but then to learn from his witness and follow him in embodying something of his vision of the divine reign.

This will call us to resist the fracturing and ultimately dehumanizing structures of our society and even to engage the powers of death itself, not through pious or even prophetic rhetoric alone but through communities that incarnate Jesus' vision of a more "catholic" hospitality. Our answer to the question of Jesus' identity must lead us toward an "embodied" or performed christology, one that becomes the guiding norm for more radical forms of congregational life. Only in this way—this *via crucis*—are we able to resist the "corinthianizing" tendencies that have so disfigured both church and society through the ages and in our own context.

Jesus warns us that this "way" will be a difficult one; it will require us to trust in a costly grace, since it will call us to become more deeply and concretely converted to a truly "catholic" vision of Christian life than we have often dared. But there is no other way, no shortened detour, to discern who this Jesus is. In his memory we must re-think, and re-form, what it means to be congregations *in and if necessary against the church*, remembering that we are people of a covenant not of our own choosing— viz., as a people chosen by God to bear witness to "a new creation" (2 Cor 5:17), in a world yearning both for genuine creativity and for a life in community that is authentically "new."[10] And if John Donne was correct in his prophetic vision of modernity that "'Tis all in peeces, all cohaerence gone,"[11] and W. B. Yeats accurate in his suggestion that "Things fall apart, the centre cannot hold; mere anarchy is loosed upon the world," then we must begin to see that the church as a community of "reconciled diversity" (Congar) stands in a unique position of responsibility, and opportunity in the current context.

This means, finally, that we must allow the question about Jesus' identity to measure our life as the "body" of Christ in and for the world, living one's faith out in the church, as a response to Jesus' witness of hospitality, his life *for others* (Bonhoeffer). Only in this way will we move toward a properly "performed" christology, measuring our faith by the integrity of our mission and seeing in this commitment *in Christ*—which is an embodiment *of* Christ—an insight into the very "catholicity" of God. In this way, and in no other, will we learn what it means to "take up our cross" as servants of the Servant, to follow Christ not in admiration of "a most fabulous of all fabulous characters, a divine Mr. Goodman" (Kierkegaard) but in imitation of the crucified and risen Lord. In this following and *only in this following* is death ultimately transfigured, a penultimate embodiment of social "re-formation" that marks our hope in a final consummation of the divine reign in space and time. As we endeavor to perform christology in this manner and journey in this way of the Cross, we are able to pray that the *church*—and through her the society in which she lives—might also be "resurrected" with Christ (Rom 6:4) unto newness of life.

The theme of this essay, the hospitality of Christ, has shaped the life and witness of Frederick Trost. I offer this piece as an expression of friendship and gratitude, for the courage of his faith and the deep beauty of his life. The great truth Fred has taught so many of us is that servanthood is God's gracing gift for us, and that following Jesus "on this way" is not only a calling but a life, one shaped by God's invitation that we come to the feast with gratitude and joy.

Notes

1. Soren Kierkegaard, *Practice in Christianity*, trans. Howard and Edna Hong (Princeton, 1991), 233.

2. See Mt 16:13-20; Mk 8:27-30; Lk 9:18-21.

3. See, for example, Jaroslav Pelikan, *Jesus Through the Centuries: His Place in the History of Culture* (New Haven, 1985).

4. On this point, Morton Smith has rightly noted the difficulty of the endeavor: "Trying to find the actual Jesus is like trying, in atomic physics, to locate a submicroscopic particle and determine its charge. The particle cannot be seen directly, but on a photographic plate we see the lines left by the trajectories of larger particles it put in motion. But tracing these trajectories back to their common origin, and by calculating the force necessary to make the particles move as they did, we can locate and describe the invisible cause. *Admittedly, history is more complex than physics*; the lines connecting the original figure to the developed legends cannot be trace with mathematical accuracy; the intervention of unknown factors has to be allowed for. Consequently, results can never claim more than probability; but 'probability,' as Bishop Butler said, 'is the very guide of life.'" See *Jesus the Magician* (New York, 1978), 6; emphasis added.

5. John Dominic Crossan, *The Historical Jesus. The Life of a Mediterranean Jewish Peasant* (San Francisco, 1991), xi.

6. *The Quest of the Historical Jesus: A Critical Study of Its Progress from Reimarus to Wrede*, trans. W. Montgomery (New York, 1910). For a recent discussion of this "quest," see also James M. Robinson, *A New Quest of the Historical Jesus, and Other Essays* (Philadelphia, 1983), and, for a radically altered methodology, Crossan, *op. cit.*

7. See *Practice in Christianity*, 35-36.

8. See his *Letters and Papers from Prison*, ed. Eberhard Bethge (New York,

1967), 209-210: "The experience of a transformation of all human life is given in the fact that 'Jesus is there only for others.' His 'being there for others' is the experience of transcendence. It is only this 'being there for others,' maintained till death, that is the ground of his omnipotence, omniscience, and omnipresence. Faith is a participation in this being of Jesus....The transcendental is not infinite and unattainable tasks, but the neighbor who is within reach in any given situation."

9. Ibid., 211. His conclusion is startling in its radicality, though this must be understood within the context of the state-supported German church: "To make a start, it should give away all its property to those in need. The clergy must live solely on the free-will offerings of their congregations, or possibly engage in some secular calling. The church must share in the secular problems of ordinary human life, not dominating, but helping and serving. It must tell [people] of every calling what it means to live in Christ, to exist for others."

10. On this point, see the analysis of the "culture of separation" and the call to "reconstitute the social world" in which we live, as depicted by Robert N. Bellah, et al., *Habits of the Heart. Individualism and Commitment in American Life* (Berkeley, Los Angeles, London, 1985), 277-96.

11. J. Donne, "An Anatomie of the World: The First Anniversary," reprinted in *The Poems of John Donne*, ed. Herbert Griersoon (Oxford: 1912), 231. Donne, of course, is here commenting on the dissolution of the last vestiges of medieval society, though his words sound ominously "modern" in tracing the consequences of this unraveling in an industrial and even post-industrial age. W.B. Yeats, "The Second Coming," from *Michael Robartes and the Dancer* (New York, 1921), 91.

Called to Ministry

Jake Close

Anyone who writes about the "vocation of the pastor" risks stepping into a quagmire. If the ideal pastor actually existed, writing about pastoral vocation would be an easy task. There is, however, no such entity. There are pastors to be sure. That is a reality we can observe. But within this array of existing pastors, there are many notions about what constitutes a call to the pastorate. The churches who authorize the ministry of these pastors must also accept responsibility for defining "call" and holding all pastors to accountability in that office. Accordingly, the United Church of Christ has a code of standards by which the ordained minister must live. It begins as follows:

I believe that God calls the whole church and every member to participate in and extend the ministry of Jesus Christ; that the privilege of witnessing to the gospel in the church and society belongs to every baptized Christian; that God empowers the ministry of the church and its members by the Holy Spirit; that the church nurtures faith, evokes gifts, and equips its members for service; and that God calls certain of the church's members to various forms of ministry in and on behalf of the church.[1]

This initial paragraph celebrates the vocation (call) of the whole church and all members to the service of Jesus Christ through our baptism. Thus all who are baptized are under the yoke of God and therefore submit to the discipline of engaging regularly in prayer, reading and studying scripture, and rendering loving service in the name of Jesus Christ. The code goes on then to say, on behalf of the ordained ministry, "God calls certain of the church's members to various forms of ministry in and on behalf of the local church." The one called to ordained ministry then affirms:

I have been called by God to be a minister of the Lord Jesus Christ and ordained by the United Church of Christ to preach and teach the gospel, to administer the sacraments and rites of the church, and to exercise pastoral care and leadership. I will seek to witness to the ministry of Jesus Christ. I will preach and teach the gospel without fear or favor. I will speak the truth in love. I will administer the sacraments and rites of the church with integrity. I will diligently perform the work of ministry which I have agreed to perform.[2]

This then, is the church's stance on the standards by which one is called to do ordained ministry.

I will seek to witness to the ministry of Jesus Christ.

Matthew 28:19-20: "Go therefore and make disciples of all nations, baptizing them in the name of the Father and of the Son and of the Holy Spirit, and teaching them to obey everything that I have commanded you. And remember, I am with you always, to the end of the age."

1 Timothy 4:12: "Let no one despise your youth, but set the believers an example in speech and conduct, in love, in faith, in purity."

Each one of us goes about this witness in a way that makes use of our individual gifts and reflects our creativity. In my own experience I have tried to embody the pastoral call with deep engagement in the community. I have honored this commitment by working to lead both the church and the community to an understanding of what it means to witness to Jesus Christ by involvement in places of great need.

I have sought to bring attention to the compassionate love of Jesus to those needing adequate housing through being instrumental in founding a chapter of Habitat for Humanity. I have sought through service on the board of directors of a local chapter of the United Way to show that the love and compassion of Jesus exists in the many forms of ministry embraced by the various agencies represented in that organization. These are examples of the ways in which I have sought to give witness in the larger community to the love of Jesus Christ for a world so desperately in need of divine and human love.

I have sought, albeit imperfectly, to witness to the love of Jesus in my home with my wife and children day in and day out. In addition to the familial ties that bind us, there is the deep sense of love expressed on many levels in the gratitude I feel for God s grace and the need to respond to that love and by loving those nearest and dearest to me. By God's grace the love of family expands to embrace the faith community, and the love that we share at the Lord's table is itself our witness. In loving and being loved, we tell others that we belong to the God of love: "By this everyone will know that you are my disciples, if you have love for one another"(Jn 13:35).

I will preach and teach the gospel without fear or favor. I will speak the truth in love.

2 Timothy 1:7: "For God did not give us a spirit of cowardice, but rather a spirit of power and of love and of self-discipline."

In the call to the vocation of the pastor there are two challenges that can threaten the integrity of the pastor. The first involves the ability of the pastor to proclaim the gospel free of personal bias. No one is immune to the temptation to ride the hobbyhorses of our own strong opinions. The challenge is to make sure that what we preach and teach is tested against scripture, tradition, experience, and reason. There is a constant need to examine one's own thinking in light of these restraints in order to guard against fear and/or favor. In the passage cited above, we are assured that we are not given "a spirit of cowardice but rather a spirit of power and of love and self-discipline." Self-discipline is key in exercising those restraints against the excesses of ego.

A second and perhaps more serious threat is that experienced by a pastor who is prevented by personal needs or problems from speaking the "truth in love." Entering the pulpit with a chip on the shoulder because of a personal slight or out of sorts over some institutional rift is not compatible with speaking the truth in love. These are troubled times in the lives of many churches, and often the effects of inadequate pastoral leadership can result in barriers to civility. It is Jesus Christ whom we represent, not ourselves. The call to the pastor is to re-present Jesus to those to whom we minister. Admittedly it is hard to disengage ourselves from cultural conflict and personal sensitivities, but it is always wise to carry with us the image of Jesus, to "let the same mind be in you that was in Christ Jesus" (Phil 2:5).

I will administer the sacraments
and rites of the church with integrity.

Luke 24:30-31a: "When he was at table with them, he took bread, blessed and broke it, and gave it to them. Then their eyes were opened and they recognized him."

When the sacraments and rites of the church are administered, the presence of Christ should be recognized. That is to say, the celebrations should be joyous and reverent so the participants know that these are actions of the church that recognize Christ as the head of the church. Baptism, for example, should be a joyful act of the church at worship, celebrating the welcoming of a new member into the church whether the new member is a child or an adult. The celebrant then understands that the efficacy of the rite is in the relationship of Christ to the church and those persons receiving the blessing of Christ through the church.

Weddings are perhaps the most trouble-filled rites administered by clergy today. In my experience weddings are too often looked upon as a prelude to a party. It is incumbent on the officiant to prepare the couple in advance to understand the deep spiritual significance of this occasion. The pastor's responsibility extends to helping all who are participants in the wedding to appreciate their part in a service of worship that celebrates the steadfast love of God, whose power for covenanting brings two people together in marriage, surrounded by a community of love. And finally the pastor is called to help the couple realize that God's presence in this event is a presence that reaches beyond the wedding into the marriage.

Likewise, confirmands need to be prepared to understand that the rite of confirmation is more than a rite of passage in the same category as passing the exam for a driver's license. We need to understand that preparation for confirmation is not so much about gaining knowledge as about establishing a relationship with the church and the Lord of the church. Since confirmation is a long process of creating awareness of the significance of full church membership in those approaching adulthood, care should be given in interpreting this purpose to those presenting themselves for confirmation. Many adults, years after going through confirmation, are heard to remark regretfully: "I wish I had paid more attention in confirmation class." Their words should be an incentive to us all to fulfill our obligation of conveying to confirmands the urgency and scope of the confirmation process and also to insure that the learning experience and the sense of community don't end with Confirmation Sunday.

The administration of the sacraments can only be done with integrity if those involved have an understanding of Christ's presence in the sacraments and in all of life. If that is so, Christ is honored and so are the recipients of the blessings that come from the acts of the church.

I will diligently perform the work of ministry
which I have agreed to perform.

1 Timothy 6:11-12: "But as for you, man [woman] of God . . . pursue righteousness, godliness, faith, love, endurance, gentleness. Fight the good fight of the faith; take hold of eternal the life, to which you were called and for which you made the good confession in the presence of many witnesses."

The affirmation for the ordinand stresses in two places that persons are called to be pastors and teachers; both are indispensable to the work of the church. We can say that there is this difference in the two tasks: The pastoral office involves responsibility for discipline, administration of the sacraments, admonition and exhortation. Teaching, on the other hand, involves presiding over the interpretation of scripture in order that pure and sound doctrine may be maintained among believers.[3]

It could be assumed that someone who had received a call to pastoral ministry, undertaken extensive training, gone through the call process to a local setting, and the procedures of ordination would be eager to embrace an opportunity for pastoral service in the church with energy and integrity. It seems that would be the case, but there are persons who enter this ministry and find themselves in the office on the first day of a new call without a clue as to what needs to be done except to prepare for the worship service the following Sunday. The demands of pastoral ministry are so varied, ranging from weekly worship to pastoral calling in hospitals and homes, to the administrative tasks of meeting with boards and committees, to teaching confirmation and Bible studies, to pastoral counseling, to working with families in grief situations, to community involvement, and a host of other tasks too numerous to mention. The variety can be a great blessing, but it can also be overwhelming to the new pastor.

The church needs to make a continuing effort to work with seminaries and mentors to aid in the preparation and support of new pastors and their ministries. Local churches need help through the search process to learn ways they can aid in fostering growth so that people of energy and talent do not languish.

It is a marvel that the work of ministry gets done with all that is asked of clergy. The grace of God and the power of the Holy Spirit working through the churches are responsible for providing an effective pastoral ministry.

The vocation of the pastor is one to be embraced by those called to it. Paul Scherer had it right when he said:

We should . . . clear out of the road all the nonsense we have picked up . . . in the matter of the call to the Christian ministry. There is such a call; and when it comes, it comes straight from God. I believe with all my heart that a man [woman] must hear it and feel its imperious constraint before he [she] can ever give himself [herself] with any wholehearted devotion and abiding wonder to this stewardship of the gospel.[4]

Finally, the vocation of the pastor requires perspective and a sense of humor. Perspective will help us to see that the whole of ministry does not rest on our personal resources. The God who has called us into the service of Jesus Christ provides for us in this awesome responsibility. It is not about our egos. A healthy sense of humor will help us to maintain the balance needed for this call that involves the people of God so intimately. The notion that a gracious God seeks a wayward humanity in love and care is enough to sustain both perspective and a sense of humor.

Notes

1. *Manual On Ministry*, United Church of Christ (New York: United Church Press, 1986) 20.

2. Ibid.

3. John Calvin, *Institutes of the Christian Religion*, vol. II (Grand Rapids, Mich.: Wm. B. Eerdmans, 1957), 319.

4. Paul Scherer, *For We Have This Treasure* (New York, Evanston and London: Harper & Row, 1944), 4.

"O Lord, Give Us Pastors"

O Lord, you call women and men to be pastors in your church,
to lead worship, proclaim the gospel, celebrate the sacraments, and teach
the faith.
Refresh them constantly with the wind and fire of your Spirit
that they may show forth the fruits of your kingdom:
love, joy, peace, patience, kindness, goodness, fidelity, gentleness, and
self-control.

O Lord, give us pastors who are like the first apostles,
leading your church in mission,
witnessing, working, sharing, constraining, winning—
in the world but not of it—
to spread the light and love of Christ.

O Lord, give us pastors who are true shepherds
and people who are strong and undivided,
hungry for the riches of the kingdom,
and thirsty for springs of living water,
so that all may be your Body in the world.

O Lord, give us pastors who can speak the prophetic word
to make known your living truth.
Give them a clear vision to speak your word
that all your people may be recalled
to simpler living and holier discipleship.

O Lord give us pastors who are servants—
servants of the servants of God—
so that all may be built up in faith,
your kingdom may be extended,
and your peace made known throughout the world;
through Jesus Christ our Lord.

Michael F. Hubbard

By God's Mercy

Jon S. Enslin

The office of pastoral ministry is best described within scripture. No biblical description of ministry is clearer or more radical than Paul's in his second letter to the church at Corinth, the fourth chapter.

Paul begins with an amazing statement: "Therefore, since it is by God's mercy that we are engaged in this ministry." The ministry of the church, and specifically the pastoral ministry, is a result of God's *Eleos*, God's mercy, God's compassion.

This is a startling statement coming from someone like Paul. Reflecting upon his experience in ministry, one would hardly characterize his life after conversion as enjoying the fruits of God's compassion. His ministry resulted in imprisonments and beatings, shipwrecks and an untimely death. What kind of strange God do we worship, whose mercy is expressed in such things?

Paul has two things in mind. There would be no church, no ministry, were it not for God's mercy in Jesus Christ. We are founded on grace, and it is grace that we proclaim. It is God's compassion that enables any ministry to occur. Had God not sent Jesus, we would still be in our sins, destined for destruction.

But I believe that Paul means more than the redemptive act of Jesus in the declaration that our ministry springs from God's mercy. God could simply have saved us as God created us: by proclamation. Many ways could have been used to make clear to humanity the fullness of God's grace, but God chooses to include human beings in the process of redemption. God not only assures us of eternity, but God prepares us for eternity by involving us in the eternal destiny of others. Eternal community begins now, as we care for one another, pointing one another toward the Holy One. We are privileged by God with mission.

Rarely does the church grasp the enormity of this. Often the church does mission begrudgingly. We would rather become caught up in matters of housekeeping or structure, in the erection of buildings or the study of texts. Mission makes us uncomfortable. Talking to another human being about our gracious God somehow offends our privacy of spirit. It is a task done haltingly, often unwillingly. We are not sure what words to use. There are times we are not even sure of the reality of our own redemption.

The fact is we have the privilege of impacting another human being by God's grace in a manner that will affect that person permanently, ultimately. There is no higher responsibility and no greater privilege than making an eternal dent in the life of another human being. All other work pales next to that which will last through the refiner's fire. Nations will cease. Buildings will crumble. Financial markets will be irrelevant. Theories will be seen as woefully inadequate. People will live forever. You and I are blessed with the opportunity to impact others eternally.

Paul also makes clear that for this to happen, we must speak the truth. Deceitful, shabby, manipulative methods cannot lead people to God. We are only able to prepare people to live through the refiner's fire by means that themselves will live through that fire. We must tell the truth about the One who is Truth.

Paul continues: "for we do not proclaim ourselves; we proclaim Jesus Christ as Lord and ourselves as your slaves for Jesus' sake." Our ministry is not about us! The good news is not, "Come and meet my pastor." We invite people to meet the Holy One. It is Jesus who is proclaimed. Whenever the pastor becomes the focus of the congregation's life, the gospel is at risk. Whenever the congregation, its ethnic heritage, its customs and liturgical styles, becomes the focus of its life at the expense of truth-telling, the gospel is at risk.

I must express some frustration with the apparent unwillingness of many clergy to exercise truth-telling. Careful theological work is replaced with pop culture. God's will gives way to personal opinion. Clever gimmicks supplant clear and bold witness. We are more interested in being loved than announcing God's love. Having a following is more important than enabling people to follow Jesus. This can be seen in the apparent ease that people have in "belonging" to a church without any agony about their lives, their congregations, or the world.

The end result is that the church, especially the congregation, is often seen as being owned by the members. One active lay person in our synod had the courage to say it clearly. At a congregational meeting called to adopt the model constitution, he objected to the first sentences in the constitution dealing with the nature of the church: "All power in the church belongs to our Lord Jesus Christ, its head. All actions of this congregation are to be carried out under His rule and authority." When someone asked why he objected, he responded, "What if we want to do something that Jesus doesn't want us to do, or we don't want to do something Jesus wants us to do? Who owns this church?"

It is not *our* church. We cannot own it, any more than we can own the One who calls us together. This ministry is not about the pastors. This ministry is not about the church. We proclaim Jesus Christ as Lord. Everything else, everyone else is subservient.

Of course, we cannot speak the truth without knowing it. Martin Luther asserts that the prime task of the pastor is to get theology right and then to preach in clear, easy to understand language so that the youngest neophyte in the congregation understands God's love and its implication for his or her life. Without being centered on the Word, without sound theological work, the church is adrift. How can we take on the powers and principalities that seek to sway the world from the Holy One without that clarity of faith and thought? Scriptural study and prayer are essential tools for ministry.

Does this mean that only brilliant thinkers and eloquent preachers can serve as pastors of the church? Of course not. In comparison with what we proclaim we ourselves fall very short. Paul suggests this is by God's design. The "treasure" of the gospel has been entrusted to "clay jars," common household utensils, domestic gear. It's not the special china that it used at the banquet table but the everyday earthenware that is indeed disposable. There is divine design in this: "so that it may be made clear that this extraordinary power belongs to God and does not come from us." While we have gifts and talents, it is not our excellence that invites God to call us into mission. It is our humanness. None of us are indispensable. We are honored by the service, not served by our honor.

I recently met with a retired pastor unwilling to let go of his ministry in his former congregation. After a lengthy discussion he finally announced he would give up all but ministering to three shut-ins in the parish. "We have a special relationship. Nobody else could serve them as well as I," he declared. I reminded him that when he brought the scriptures and sacraments, he was bringing Jesus to them, not himself. He was not their savior. "The new pastor can bring Jesus to them as well." This ministry that starts out as privilege as a result of God's mercy often is seen as entitlement. When people respond in faith to our ministrations, we fail to remember that God working through us has caused the faithful response, not our own excellence. We are merely common, clay pots.

It is singularly interesting that Jesus impacted the world in a way no other spiritual leader has by calling as disciples those whom the society saw as less than competent. They were not the brilliant theologians or scholars of Judaism. They carried little credibility among the religious leadership. They were the objects of scorn and even ridicule. But they did one thing well. They entrusted themselves to the power of God, and their fragility became their witness. It is that very fragility that is at the center of the witness. It is no accident that the Greek word for witness, *martus*, has become our word for one who dies as a result of faith. The world does not respond well to the lordship of Jesus Christ. The world seeks to run its own way, to do its own thing. All the world is in rebellion, and that rebellion finds its expression in various ways.

One major expression of rebellion is our denial of death. We hang on to life as though by seizing it we would never lose it. We cover up our signs of age with cosmetics. Balding men have hair transplants. When people die, we paint them and exhibit them before we entrust them to the ground in hermetically sealed caskets to guarantee the absence of decay. We do this theoretically to permanently implant in our mind a beautiful memory of the deceased. In fact, we do it to deny our bondage to decay. It works no more for us than it did for the pharaohs. A friend of mine once asked, "When is the last time you've seen a hearse pulling a U-haul?" People try. Occasionally someone will be buried in their Cadillac or take all their jewelry with them. That merely results in rusted cars and useless baubles in the earth. To a culture consumed with the here and now, an accountability in eternity is not necessarily good news.

Thus the intriguing paradox. Those who proclaim *Life* are often "afflicted in every way," even killed. This is especially true under dictatorships, where the lordship of Jesus directly conflicts with the presumed lordship of the dictator. It is often also true in more subtle ways in our own culture. Faithful pastors are often the object of attack and inappropriate gossip. Their very frailty is used against them. Their absence of perfection is seen as faithlessness. But those threatened by the lordship of Jesus are the fools. Those who know the *Truth* are not intimidated by death. They know we have to die to live.

It should surprise no contemporary pastor that this ministry is not easy. I invite all pastors to reread the words of Paul. "We are afflicted in every way but not crushed; perplexed, but not driven to despair; persecuted, but not forsaken; struck down, but not destroyed; always carrying in the body the death of Jesus, so that the life of Jesus may also be made visible in our bodies. For while we live, we are always being given up to death for Jesus' sake, so that the life of Jesus may be made visible in our mortal flesh. So death is at work in us, but life in you" (2 Cor 4:8-12).

As a seminary student I was told the responsibility of the pastor was "to preach as a dying man to dying men." (We were all male in those days.) The ultimate task of the pastor is to lay bare the incredible vulnerability of humanity, to be honest about the reality of death, even joyous in its promise. If the lordship of Jesus Christ means anything at all, it means that clay pots, even if shattered and returned to the earth, will one day be shining and pure at the table of the Holy One. Even if this is contrary to almost everything in our culture, it is nonetheless the "good news." In the face of doubt and ridicule, suffering and even death, God's mercy invites us to proclaim this news with boldness and clarity.

Prophet, Priest, and Pastor

James R. Gorman

Frederick Trost is and will remain always a pastor of the church who has a high view of its sacramental life and a bold sense of its prophetic calling. So many of his delightful stories about parish life were from the days of his urban pastorate on the near north side of Chicago. I was privileged to be his assistant at St. Pauls Church in the mid seventies. His most compelling stories about that unusual parish come from a period of time eight years before I arrived. One story always touches me deeply. It takes place in August of 1968. The Democratic Convention was in town and Richard Daley was "dah Mair." Pastor Trost, along with one hundred colleagues, made his way to Lincoln Park where the "hippie" demonstrators had been cornered by the police.

The Chicago police, which "hizzoner" once said were there "not to create disorder but to preserve disorder," moved on the demonstrators with tear gas and night sticks. Chaos ensued and Trost, along with several hundred hippies, found his way back to the gymnasium of St. Pauls Church about seven blocks west of the park. St. Pauls Church was one of the grand old churches of the Evangelical and Reformed tradition, having once been the spiritual home of the Oscar Mayer and Wieboldt families. Finding hippies in the ecclesial domain of the princes of wieners and department stores was an incongruity beyond comprehension. But there they were.

The young folks were in a state of derivative chaos from the park. The noise against the cement block walls and hardwood floors of the gym was deafening. Worries about the presence of drugs and alcohol were on the minds of the young pastors who had risked their careers by inviting this protesting, unwashed cadre into this house of prayer.

Three elderly women from the congregation had volunteered to help get the young folks settled in and had been preparing something for them to eat. These women, Edna Mae Haddock, Emily Wahlenmayer and Erna Knaphurst were part of God's little diaconal army, ever ready to sustain the homeless and give comfort even to the misguided, no questions asked. One of the women, who thought that it might be time to settle down and get some rest, walked right into center court. Her sensible shoes and formless dress made her a stunning presence among the tie-dyed and Jesus-sandaled. The place quieted down immediately. In the silence she welcomed the young people and said that they were guests in the house of God and she was pleased they were there. Then, filling entirely the expectant silence, she recited the 23rd Psalm from memory and suggested they all get some rest. And they did.

In part I love this quintessentially Trostian story because of its gospel romance. But mostly I love this story because in the telling of it, Pastor Trost tells us something deeply significant about his view of the divine offices of ministry. For there at center court is the confluence of the prophetic, priestly, and pastoral offices[1] of the work of Christ which we inherit in both the lay and professional ministries of the church. The story represents the view of the office of ministry that is so much the gift of Frederick Trost's sense of the church.

In Old Testament studies while I was in seminary in the early seventies, no subject was more popular than the prophets. This was so because we were pretty sure that prophecy was to be our main vocation in the new church "we would be building" or deconstructing, depending on who you talked to in those days. As students in those prophetic years streamed to Walter Brueggemann's prophets classes, he quickly discovered that we came with some fundamental misunderstandings about the prophetic office. Moreover, these misunderstandings were pervasive not only among his student body but also in the larger church itself. To correct these misunderstandings he did the only thing Brueggemann knew to do. He wrote his first book and made it required reading for his classes.

This book, *Tradition for Crisis*,[2] written in the year of the Tet Offensive, the deaths of Martin Luther King Jr. and Bobby Kennedy and the Democratic Convention, was a study of the prophet Hosea, and it evokes a theme that would occupy much of Brueggemann's scholarship throughout his career. His theme was, "How can we Christians be eager listeners to, and fresh appropriators of the catholic tradition and apostolic faith, shepherds of the continuing community, while at the same time prophetic in our confrontation of decidedly modern problems?" In fact, says Brueggemann, there is no inherent contradiction if you rightly understand the meaning of the prophetic office. The real problem lies in a misunderstanding of Old Testament prophecy alive today in church and culture, one which lifts up the prophetic task to the neglect of the priestly and pastoral.

The misunderstanding about the prophetic office was the result of several generations of scholarship which, as Brueggemann put it, "assumed that there is a sharp discontinuity between the religion of the Torah and the faith of the prophets."[3] The sixties polarization in the church between social-action liberals and reactionary conservatives will, he said "prophetically" in 1968, "no doubt get worse before it gets better." In fact, the polarization between the priestly, pastoral, and prophetic offices in the church has indeed gotten worse and more pronounced in the mainline Protestant church.

There, however, at center court in the gymnasium that Oscar Mayer built was the extraordinary confluence of the prophetic, priestly, and pastoral offices of ministry. There was solidarity of the church with the protestors. There was the ancient psalm filling sacramentally an expectant silence. And there was the shepherd astounded by and deeply proud of what his flock was able to do.

A few years ago I was visiting with one of the saints of my current parish who was in the last days of her ninety plus years. She handed me her copy of the Heidelberg Catechism all marked up with an adolescent scrawl, German on the left and English on the right. I turned to the first question—the one to which Pastor Trost had always directed us—and to my amazement there was his family name! "Was ist dein einziger Trost im Leben und im Sterben?" "What is thine only comfort in life and in death?" In the question there was a kind of genealogical drivenness toward the pastoral task. How could Trost be anything else but a comfort? But in the daring answer there is the foundation of the prophetic calling. "My only comfort in life and in death is that I am not my own but belong body and soul, in life and in death, to my faithful savior Jesus Christ."

If our Christian identity is first of all *Sola Christi* then all other allegiances are measured, circumscribed and penultimate. Our calling as ministers in the church of Christ is in the three-fold office of Christ, prophetic, priestly and pastoral. The balance of these is crucial for the continuing witness of the church and the spiritual, not to say psychological, health of its leadership. For how can we be prophetic without an abiding sense of the bodily presence of the Lord who is our Shepherd?

Notes

1. The traditional construct of Prophet, Priest, and King belongs to John Calvin in the *Institutes of the Christian Religion* (II, xv) but can be traced back to Chrysostom's notion of that which is received in baptism. The use of "Pastor" in the place of "King" is a well-honored move in the discussion about the offices of ministry derived from the offices of Christ, but there is not room here to defend it.

2. Walter Brueggemann, *Tradition for Crisis* (New York: Harper & Row, 1968).

3. Ibid., 11.

"Our Gracious and Eternal God"

Our gracious and eternal God, we give thanks for our lives which you create and our living which you guide. We trust in your promise to be with us in and through each dawning day.

We are grateful for your call to ministry, a call that sends us as servants and not masters, a call that requires a heart bigger than our ego, a call that needs us to recognize and reduce the hurt we see in others and ask for forgiveness when that hurt is caused by our brashness or our indifference.

In our ministry, O God, help us know the need you have for us to understand before we are understood, the need you have for us not to amputate the gospel, not to take away its arms and legs, its holy presence in each dawning day, a holy presence that may be experienced by others when we are with them. In a word help us to walk the talk and talk the walk, for one without the other shortens our reach and deadens our step.

May we experience ministry in relationship and not in isolation, in partnership and not in dictatorship. Help us realize the great power in ministry, a power entrusted to us when people bring their pain and share their inner journeys. May we listen with a heart that understands and a response that strengthens.

In our ministry, dear and gracious God, in our effort to bring justice and mercy, understanding and compassion, grace and presence, may we always know that you discern our needs and regard us with compassion. Help us to know that our need for your blessings is no less than those with whom we share ministry.

In marvelous and unspoken ways, in soft and quiet manner, in the elation of a good sermon, and in the reality of a forgotten meeting, we ask for your Presence, your Word and your Love, so that we can be instruments of your healing and your comfort and your strength.

We pray in the name of Christ in whom and for whom we live and move and have our being.

Mark H. Miller

Social Witness Today:
The Promise of Generous Orthodoxy

George Hunsinger

Christians are called to bear social witness to Christ in two ways: first, through the ordering of their common life and second, through direct action in the surrounding world. Ecclesial ordering and secular intervention comprise a unity in distinction. They are not alternatives and may well at times blend together. Nonetheless they are ranked in a particular way. Priority belongs (in principle) to the ordering of the church's common life. The church does not have a social ethic so much as it is a social ethic. A church whose common life merely reflects the social disorders of the surrounding world is scarcely in a strong position for social witness through direct action. In such cases—and where is this not the case?—the gospel must progress in spite of the church and against its failures. Here too there is more grace in God than sin in us. Note that social witness, whose direct action cannot always wait for the proper ordering of the church's common life, must proceed on several fronts at once. Nevertheless, social witness in discipleship to Christ requires the church to be a counter-cultural community with its own distinctive profile. It must stand over against the larger culture when that culture's values are incompatible with the gospel.

No doubt a church that emphasizes distinctiveness at the expense of solidarity falsifies itself by becoming sectarian. A church that loses its distinctiveness, however, through conformity and capitulation, evades its essential vocation of discipleship, especially when it means bearing the cross for being socially dissident. A Christian is an unreliable partisan who knows that peace with God means conflict with the world (even as peace with the world means conflict with God). "You are the salt of the earth; but if the salt has lost its taste, how shall its saltiness be restored?" (Mt 5:13). "You are the light of the world" (Mt 5:14). Disciples are not above their teacher (Mt 10:24).

The very idea of "social witness" implies an orientation toward the centrality of God. It means that Christian social action, whether within the community of faith or the larger world, is more than an end in itself. This action does not simply aim to alleviate social misery in the form of hunger, nakedness, homelessness, terror, illness, humiliation, loneliness, and abuse. Efforts to name and oppose social injustice, no matter how important and necessary, are only one aspect of "social witness." As Aristotle has pointed out, any given action or policy can be an end in itself while also serving as the means to a greater end. As important as bread is to us, we do not live by bread alone. Human flourishing, as we know from the gospel, depends on more than the alleviation of social misery and the satisfaction of earthly needs. The main purpose for which we were created is to glorify and enjoy God forever.

This purpose is acknowledged by social witness in at least two ways. First, Christian social witness is parabolic in intent. It aims, in all its forms, to enact parables of God's compassion for the world. Although not all needs are alike, with some lesser or greater than others, God cares for us as whole persons in all our needs. The highest purpose for which we were created is not always remembered in this context. Being created to live by and for God, we know a need that only God can fulfill. Being creatures fallen into sin, moreover, we also endure a terrible plight, fatal and self inflicted, from which we are helpless to free ourselves but can be rescued only by God, without which rescue we would be cut off from God and one another forever. According to the gospel, God has not abandoned us without hope to this plight, for God does not will to be God without us. On the contrary, God has spared no cost to rescue us. The point is this: No human action, not even by the church, can do for us what God has done, or be for us what God indeed is, at the deepest level of human need. Human action can nonetheless, by grace, serve as a witness. It can point away from itself to God. It can enact parables of compassion that proclaim the gospel. In addressing itself wholeheartedly to lesser needs, Christian social witness points at the same time to God as the only remedy for our greatest need. Christian social witness, in its efforts to alleviate social misery, is thus at once an end in itself while also serving as the means to a greater end.

Secondly, social witness cannot be parabolic in intent without also being analogical in form. It must correspond to the content it would attest. It cannot point to God without corresponding to God. Correspondence to God is the basic criterion of social witness, and it is this criterion that makes faithfulness more important than effectiveness. The validity of Christian social witness cannot be judged by immediate consequences alone. It must rather be judged, primarily, by the quality of its correspondence to God's compassion as revealed and embodied in Jesus Christ. No social witness can be valid which contradicts faithful correspondence, even when that means leaving the consequences to God. Consequences are in any case greatly overrated with respect to their predictability and controllability, just as they are also commonly misjudged when uncompromising faithfulness results in real or apparent failures.

It is no accident that the words witness and martyr are semantically related. The promise of the gospel is that faithful witness, whether successful in worldly terms or not, will always be validated by God. To believe that supposed effectiveness in violation of faithfulness is promised similar validation can only be illusory. No comprehensive policy of social action, regardless of what it is, will ever be without elements of helplessness, tragedy, and trade-off in the face of human misery. It is always a mistake for faithfulness to overpromise what it can deliver in resisting evil or effecting social change, though it may sometimes be surprisingly effective, or even compatible with maximal effectiveness, depending on the case. Social witness *qua* witness, in any case, cannot allow itself to be determined primarily by the question of effectiveness but rather by faithful correspondence to the cruciform compassion of God.

A recurring phenomenon in the history of Christian theology has been the displacement of central truths by lesser truths. Usually these displacements are more or less temporary. Nevertheless, they can cause great confusion while they last. Polarizations and animosities typically form between two groups—those in their wisdom who passionately reject one truth that they might recover the centrality of another, and those who do much the same thing only in reverse. In such cases the solution arises when central truths are allowed to be central and lesser truths are allowed to be lesser. The truth of neither is denied, and room can even be found for allowing the lesser truths, perhaps previously unnoticed or neglected, to assume the urgency of situational precedence.

During the last 25 years or so, the church has increasingly witnessed the emergence of victim-oriented soteriologies. The plight of victims, variously specified and defined, has been urged by prominent theologians as the central soteriological problem. It can scarcely be denied that the history of the twentieth century has pushed the plight of victims to the fore. Nor can it be denied that the church has too often seemed ill-equipped to bring the plight of victims, especially victims of oppression and social injustice, clearly into focus for itself so that reasonable and faithful remedies might be sought. Victim-oriented soteriologies have undoubtedly made an important contribution to a better understanding of the church's social responsibility.

Polarizations and animosities have developed, however, to the extent that the plight of victims has displaced the soteriological plight of sinners or even eclipsed it. Victim-oriented soteriologies have unfortunately tended to define the meaning of sin entirely in terms of victimization. Sin ceases to be a universal category. It attaches to perpetrators and to them alone. Since by definition victims *qua* victims are innocent of being perpetrators, they are to that extent innocent of sin. If sin attaches only to perpetrators, however, victims can be sinners only by somehow becoming perpetrators themselves (a move not unknown in victim-oriented soteriologies). Victim-oriented soteriologies, with their bipolar opposition between victims and perpetrators, display a logic with sectarian tendencies.

How the cross of Christ is understood by these soteriologies is also worth noting. The cross becomes meaningful because it shows the divine solidarity with victims, generally ceasing to find any other relevance, at least positively. (In extreme cases the theology of the cross is trashed as a cause of victimization. But such denunciations, when meant *de iure*, exceed the bounds even of heterodoxy and so cease to be of constructive interest to the church.) The cross, in any case, is no longer the supreme divine intervention for the forgiveness of sins. It is not surprising that more traditional, sin-oriented soteriologies should react with unfortunate polarization. When that happens, sin as a universal category obscures the plight of oppression's victims, rendering that plight just as invisible or irrelevant as it was before. Atonement without solidarity seems to exhaust the significance of the cross, and forgiveness supposedly occurs without judgment on oppression.

The task of generous orthodoxy in this situation is to dispel polarization by letting central truths be central and lesser truths be lesser but in each case, letting truth be truth. No reason exists why the cross as atonement for sin should be viewed as logically incompatible with the cross as divine solidarity with the oppressed. Good reasons can be found for connecting them. The great historical ecumenical consensus remains, however, that the central significance of the cross, as attested by Holy Scripture, is the forgiveness of sins. This established consensus pervades every aspect of the church's life, not least including baptism and the Lord's Supper. It has by this time withstood all the onslaughts of unbelieving modernity (so that the only question today is not whether the ecumenical consensus will survive but whether those churches devitalized by modern skepticism will). No ecclesial catechesis can be valid that fails to affirm the forgiveness of sins as the central truth of the cross.

Lesser truths, however, ought not to be pitted against central truths. Lesser truths, moreover, gain rather than diminish in significance when decentered, for they no longer have a role foisted upon them that they cannot possibly fulfill. Generous orthodoxy attempts to do justice to both central and lesser truths in themselves as well as to their proper ordering.

The oppressed have always understood that the cross brings them consolation and hope by placing God into solidarity with their misery. The African-American spiritual is exactly right when it laments, "Nobody knows the trouble I've seen. Nobody knows but Jesus." The gospel does not obscure that our Lord was "mocked and insulted and spat upon" (Lk 18:32), that he was "despised and rejected" by others (Isa 53:3). Admittedly, the church has not always kept pace with Scripture in recognizing that "The Lord is a stronghold for the oppressed, a stronghold in times of trouble" (Ps 9:9). It has not always prayed fervently enough with the psalmist: "May he defend the cause of the poor of the people, give deliverance to the needy, and crush the oppressor" (Ps 72:4), nor has it always acted conscientiously enough on the basis of such prayers. Social witness has a perpetual obligation to solidarity with the oppressed. This obligation, however, is entirely consonant with the truth (which can be displaced only at our peril) on which the entire gospel depends: "For our sake he made him to be sin who knew no sin, so that in him we might become the righteousness of God" (2 Cor 5:21).

When the universality of sin is recognized as the central soteriological problem, the results can be liberating. All illusions are dispelled, for example, that though others may be needy, I am not, and that I am therefore somehow above others if I am in a position to help them in their need.

Acknowledging my need, conversely, brings no implication that I am beneath others who may help me. When recognition is accorded to the universality of divine grace, moreover, I am freed from moralistic forms of obligation. For when grounded in the reception of grace, social obligation is not an externally imposed duty, but a response to the needs of others in gratitude to the God who has already responded so graciously to me. My response to others is based on a solidarity in sin and grace. It occurs as an act of witness to the gospel and through participation in the grace of God. "Walk in love, as Christ has loved us and gave himself up for us" (Eph 5:2).

Our lesser needs are related to our central need by a unity in distinction. Concern for the poor and needy stands in inseparable unity with the forgiveness of sins, without displacing it or becoming a substitute for it. Concern for the poor and the needy has a solid basis in traditional faith, as when linked with the petition for daily bread in the Lord's Prayer. Through the recovery of sound catechesis, concern for the poor, among other things, could become more deeply embedded in the life of the church. A person who fears and blesses the Lord "opens her hand to the poor, and reaches out her hands to the needy" (Prov 31:20). It will be a great day when congregations not only give money to help the poor but also create situations in which the poor feel welcome to participate in the life and work of the congregations themselves.

This essay has been excerpted from George Hunsinger, "Social Witness in Generous Orthodoxy: The New Presbyterian Study Catechism," Princeton Seminary Bulletin 21 (2000): 38-62.

"O God, Whose Gracious Will"

O God, whose gracious will and Word sustain my life, to you be all praise, honor, and glory. I come to you in need of help. Hear, O Lord, my prayer. Once again I face the daunting task of proclaiming your gospel. Without your help I know I will never find the words that speak to the needs of your people. As I begin to prepare another week's sermon, give me eyes to see and ears to hear the truth of your Word. Give me clarity where there is confusion, courage where there is fear, faith where there is doubt, and hope where there is despair.

Forgive me for thinking that I can preach your Word in my own wisdom and keep me from giving in to frustration when I cannot. Forgive me for acting as though preaching were a burdensome task rather than a challenging opportunity to share your love and truth. Forgive my reluctance to wait upon you in silence, for my laziness in prayer, for expecting you to inspire my careless preparation.

Gracious God, help me never to forget that when I preach to others, I also preach to myself. Help me to proclaim the truth of your gospel in a spirit of love; save me from arrogant speaking, compromising silence, and personal prejudice. Help me to interpret your truth with words and images that will be clearly understood by those who listen. May your Spirit use my words to awaken the careless, strengthen the faithful, comfort the afflicted, and edify your church. Speak to each person the word they need to hear; teach them how to meet the comforts, conflicts and challenges of life with faith in all their aspirations and in all their fears, in all their joys and in all their sorrows, in life and in death, lead them to an ever closer relationship with Jesus Christ.

Paul A. Quackenbush

Easter before Easter:
A Sermon for the Doing of Ministry

F. Russell Mitman

Now a certain man was ill, Lazarus of Bethany, the village of Mary and her sister Martha. Mary was the one who anointed the Lord with perfume and wiped his feet with her hair; her brother Lazarus was ill. So the sisters sent a message to Jesus, "Lord, he whom you love is ill." But when Jesus heard it, he said, "This illness does not lead to death; rather it is for God's glory, so that the Son of God may be glorified through it." Accordingly, though Jesus loved Martha and her sister and Lazarus, after having heard that Lazarus was ill, he stayed two days longer in the place where he was. Then after this he said to the disciples, "Let us go to Judea again." The disciples said to him, "Rabbi, the Jews were just now trying to stone you, and are you going there again?" Jesus answered, "Are there not twelve hours of daylight? Those who walk during the day do not stumble, because they see the light of this world. But those who walk at night stumble, because the light is not in them." After saying this he told them, "Our friend Lazarus has fallen asleep, but I am going there to awaken him." The disciples said to him, "Lord, if he has fallen asleep, he will be all right." Jesus, however, had been speaking about his death, but they thought that he was referring merely to sleep. Then Jesus told them plainly, "Lazarus is dead. For your sake I am glad I was not there, so that you may believe. But let us go to him." Thomas, who was called the Twin, said to his fellow disciples, "Let us also go, that we may die with him." (John 11:1-16)

"My brother, your friend, Lazarus is sick," Mary sent word to Jesus. This is the same Mary who had fallen to Jesus' feet and had anointed them with a costly ointment while the disciples grumbled over such a devotional extravagance. This is the same Mary who with her sister Martha had invited Jesus to a dinner party. This is the same Mary who had been mesmerized by Jesus' teaching while her Type-A sister fussed with the crockery in the kitchen and complained that Mary couldn't lift a finger to help her. "Lazarus is sick. Lazarus would like the pastor to visit him." Mary sent the word.

For some reason John has Jesus committing the unconscionable error of tarrying two days before making the pastoral visit. Maybe there was a good reason for the delay. Maybe he had received death threats. But suddenly he says to the disciples, "Let's go to Bethany. . . . Our friend

Lazarus has fallen asleep." Remember, Jesus is speaking through John, who liked to preach in words with double meanings. "Our friend Lazarus has fallen asleep, but I am going there to awaken him." Thomas and the others are the literalists. To them there is only one meaning for a word, only one interpretation: "Lord, if he's sleeping everything's okay. Just sleeping off the fever. He'll be all right. A couple of aspirins, and he'll be okay, after he sleeps it off. Just sleeping." Jesus replies, "Lazarus is dead, my brothers. Lazarus is dead."

When Jesus arrives, he finds that Lazarus has already been in the tomb four days. Now Bethany is near Jerusalem, some two miles away, and many of the Jews had come to Martha and Mary to console them about their brother. When Martha hears that Jesus is coming, she goes to meet him, while Mary stays at home.

Martha says to Jesus, "Lord, if you had been here, my brother would not have died. But even now I know that God will give you whatever you ask of him."

Jesus answers her, "Your brother will rise again."

And Martha replies, "I know that he will rise again in the resurrection on the last day."

Jesus says to her, "I am the resurrection and the life. Those who believe in me, even though they die, will live, and everyone who lives and believes in me will never die. Do you believe this?"

She answers, "Yes, Lord, I believe that you are the Messiah, the Son of God, the one coming into the world" (Jn 11:17-27).

Lazarus died four days ago. The casket is closed, the grave is covered, the funeral is over, the mourners have gone home, the flowers are fading. And those left to grieve still grasp for reasons. It's Friday, not yet Sunday.

"Oh, Lord, if you had been here, my brother would not have died."

"If only"—how often have we who would be healers heard these words uttered in grief's seemingly endless litany? Perhaps we have chanted and prayed "if only" ourselves. "If only," a mother kept repeating, "If only I had spent more time with my daughter when she needed me, then maybe this wouldn't have happened." "If only I had been there when Gilly was brought to the hospital," a physician-father kept groaning after he received the telephone call saying his daughter had been killed instantly in an automobile accident." "If only I had been there when my father died," I castigated myself for months. "If only, if only," the grievers grieve—Friday's grief that yearns for Sunday's relief.

"Your brother will rise again," Jesus says to the grieving.

"Oh, I know he will rise again in the resurrection on the last day," at the end of time. Textbook theology. Theology comes quickly to trained tongues: easy answers to tough questions. And death is the toughest.

"I am the resurrection and the life. Those who believe in me, even though they die, will live, and everyone who lives and believes in me will never die. Do you believe this?" Jesus asks.

"I am the resurrection and the life *now*. Mary, Martha, sisters, brothers, I am the resurrection and the life *now*. This is Easter before Easter *now*. Do you believe this *now*? Do *you* believe this now?

I remember well. It was my first funeral fresh out of seminary. Archie Heller was the name of the deceased. I didn't know Archie; he didn't know me. I was a "rent-a-preacher," as one of my colleagues identifies those whom funeral directors call upon to offer eulogies for the ecclesiastically unconnected. I didn't know Archie's family—rather, families, because Archie had been married twice, and both families were there glaring across the aisle from each other in Finnegan's Funeral Home.

Mr. Finnegan asked me before I went down that aisle, Do you want to use a lectern?

"No, I'll just stand there next to the coffin. And, so I did, with my fresh copy of the Evangelical and Reformed *Book of Worship* in my hands. "I am the resurrection and the life, sayeth the Lord," the service begins. Some of you are old enough to remember? I remember well. "I am the resurrection and the life," I tried to intone in my 25-year-old stained-glass voice. And with each word, my breath got shorter. I was having an anxiety attack right there next to Archie's coffin. I had never been to a funeral before in my life, yet I was supposed to be saying something to proclaim the meaning of resurrection to those who had come to mourn Archie's passing. I didn't know whether I believed it myself. You see, I had been to seminary! By the Twenty-third Psalm I was hyperventilating. Was I going to die, too? I subconsciously asked my 25-year-old self. Maybe I was dying, and they'd lay me out there next to Archie. "I am the resurrection and the life. Those who believe in me, even though they die, will live, and everyone who lives and believes in me will never die. Do you believe this?" Do *you* believe this? Do *I*? Do you and I believe that the now is an Easter before Easter?

After Martha makes her perfunctory statement about the resurrection, she returns and calls her sister Mary and tells her privately, "The teacher is here and is calling for you." And when Mary hears this, she gets up quickly and goes to him. Now Jesus has not yet come to the village but is still at the place where Martha had met him. The Jews who are with her in the house, consoling her, see Mary get up quickly and go out. They follow her because they think that she is going to the tomb to weep there. When Mary finds Jesus, she kneels at his feet and says to him, "Lord, if you had been here, my brother would not have died."

When Jesus sees her weeping and the Jews who came with her also weeping, he is greatly disturbed in spirit and deeply moved. He asks, "Where have you laid him?"

They answer him, "Lord, come and see." Jesus begins to weep. So the Jews remark, "See how he loved him!" But some of them say, "Could not he who opened the eyes of the blind man have kept this man from dying?" (Jn 11:28-37)

Lazarus died, Jesus wept—two people trapped in life's tragedies. One died, one grieved. A friend died, a friend grieved. When people are trapped in tragedies, life is lived in clipped sentences, two-word sentences—one is the subject, the other the predicate; one the noun, one the verb—that's all. Life hurts too much to speak in more than two-word sentences. Lazarus died. Jesus wept. To say the words hurts too much. There can be no embellishing adjectives that might dilute the pain or adverbs that try to rationalize the tragedies. Lazarus died. Jesus wept. In between and around the edges there is only an empty silence. There doesn't seem enough breath left to get anymore out.

Yet those who stand outside grief's perimeter need to fill in the empty silence with sympathy-card commentaries. "See how he loved him!" the onlookers cry. "Isn't it wonderful, see how he loved him!" Of course he loved him. We say the dumbest things when a silent presence, a quiet embrace, a caring touch is all that is necessary, and anything more is a noisy gong or a clanging cymbal. TV nightly news is there with its action camera to video the grief of a slain teenager's friends. While lying cozily between the sheets and watching the 11:00 news we can say, "See how she loved her!" We want to keep our distance when people get trapped in tragedies, and whisper behind a hand the dumbest things, "See how he loved him!" "Ain't it a shame, ain't it a shame?" Life seems to get stuck on Friday, always on Friday, and never gets to Easter, never gets to Sunday. "Ain't it a shame?" Eleven o'clock tomorrow night the chronicle of tomorrow's tragedies will be unwrapped on the TV tube once again: "Ain't it a shame? Ain't it a shame? See how he loved him!"

Then Jesus, again greatly disturbed, comes to the tomb. It is a cave, and a stone is lying against the entrance. Jesus says, "Take away the stone."

Martha, the sister of the dead man, says to him, "Lord, already there is a stench because he has been dead four days."

Jesus replies, "Did I not tell you that if you believed, you would see the glory of God?" So they took away the stone. And Jesus, looking upward, prays, "Father, I thank you for having heard me. I know that you always hear me, but I have said this for the sake of the crowd standing here, so that they may believe that you sent me." When he had said this, he cries with a loud voice, "Lazarus, come out!"

The dead man comes out, his hands and feet bound with strips of cloth, and his face wrapped in a cloth. Jesus says to them, "Unbind him, and let him go." (Jn 11:38-44).

It was a cave. Lazarus's tomb was a cave, and there was a stone there. "Take away the stone!" Jesus commanded. A cave? A tomb? A stone? Sounds like Easter, doesn't it? Sounds like an Easter before Easter, doesn't it? It sounds like the one who was himself in Easter's tomb is commanding before Easter, "Take away the stone! Take away the stone!"

"Lord, already there is a stench in there," Martha warned. "It stinks in there." The Greek text is more graphic than the English, and the King James Version gets it right: "He stinketh." Lazarus has been dead for four days. He stinks. The American way of death shields us from stinking corpses, and the American way of life protects us from stinking situations.

"Wouldn't you rather be in Florida?" the billboard asks me while thirteen inches of slush freezes into ice. Of course, I'd rather be in Florida when it seems that even hell is freezing over, but I've got all these stinking things to do here. I want to be in the Easter parade, but I'm schlepping along on Friday's procession here. And it stinks! It stinks to high heaven! Innocent men and women are sentenced to carry Friday crosses, and it stinks. Bad things happen to good people, and it stinks. A mother of three is sent off to a hospital in a screaming ambulance and fights for her life in the emergency room while the driver of the car that hit her staggers away anesthetized by the six-pack under his belt. And it stinks. Ministry somehow always is engaged where it stinks, where people are trapped in Friday's messes.

"Take away the stone!" Jesus commanded. So they took away the stone. They took away the stone that separated Friday from Sunday. They took away the stone, and now it was Sunday, now it is Easter before Easter. And Easter's resurrected Christ calls from *outside* the tomb, "Lazarus, come out! Lazarus, come out!" "Come out!" Jesus is on the *outside* calling us to come out of the stinking messes where ministry and mission always have their beginnings but sometimes get stuck.

Come out, Jesus calls us. Come out of the tombs that have held the church bandaged in bondage to the secular "isms" waging their age-old wars. Come out of the tombs that have kept you closeted in your fears and entombed you in your rationales. Come out, come out of the shadows that keep life partial and imprison the truth in lies and deceptions. Come out, come out of the negativity that enshrouds your churches in "But we can't do that," or "But we never did it that way before." Come out, come out of the stinking mess that wants to reduce life to a garbage heap of Golgotha and a valley of dry bones. Come out, come out of Friday's death wish and death watch. Come out of Friday's death and, even before it's Sunday, step into Sunday, step into Easter's life. Lazarus, come out! Come out!

A Life That Belongs to God

Teruo Kawata

Frederick Trost is one of the consummate pastors—and pastor to pastors and churches—in the United Church of Christ. He is a theologian and scholar, an articulate preacher, a compassionate pastor, and a person who translates his convictions into his living with great faithfulness, sometimes at risk to himself. I am honored to have been asked to contribute an essay to this book honoring him as he comes to the time of retirement from his service as Conference Minister of the Wisconsin Conference of the United Church of Christ. He has been a respected colleague and friend to many of us.

God's Summons

I begin my reflections on the vocation of a pastor by recalling that the word "vocation" is rooted in the Latin, *vocare,* to call. In our common language we have come to use the word to speak of any occupation or profession. Indeed, many have entered their particular field of endeavor out of a sense of "calling." But for many of us, the ministry was not one profession among many from which we chose. It was a response to a "call." H. Richard Niebuhr, with John Calvin, speaks of the "secret call." He describes the "secret call" as that inner persuasion that God is summoning or inviting one to take up the work of ministry, which then was affirmed by the church in the act of ordination (the ecclesiastical call).[1] In our experience the call came not because of our merits but out of God's initiative, for reasons beyond our understanding often, and sometimes, in spite of our denials and resistance.

We would remember Moses' call and his deep reluctance (Exod 3:1-14). He made every excuse that we have heard and made ourselves, but God would not let him go. There are some among us who know something of Moses' reluctance.

Then we would remember Isaiah's call (Isa 6: 1-8). Overwhelmed by the *mysterium tremendum*, to use Rudolph Otto's words, Isaiah gave himself saying, "Here am I, Lord. Send me." Some among us know that experience too.

Then there was Paul who was yanked out of what he believed was his vocation and turned around (Acts 9:19) to be the primary theologian of the church. The Bible is full of stories of persons who have been "called" to use their lives as instruments of God's purposes and in responding have had their lives radically turned around.

The beginning of the vocation, then, was a personal encounter with God, in which we were confronted by a reality, a mystery beyond our comprehension, yet which persuaded us and brought us to an at-one-ness with the ultimate and with ourselves. And living in response to that awesome grace that freed and enabled and empowered our lives we came to that sense that we were being called to use our lives as instruments of that grace.

Some pastors are able to point to a moment when the call and their response came dramatically and clearly. For others of us it has been an ambiguous journey, sometimes with a great deal of inner struggle. We have begun with Moses' "Who? Me?" (Exod 3–4). There have been the struggles about one's adequacy, struggles about what one must give up of one's own dreams and plans. There has been that inner nagging about one's own motivations. But we moved, whether by circumstance or a continuing searching, toward that goal which led us to ordained ministry, and our lives have been powerfully changed and blessed, beyond our deserving or expecting. One cannot help but recall Henri Nouwen's poignant description of those of us in ministry as *The Wounded Healer*.[2]

A Ministry Among Ministries

I would have us remember that in the United Church of Christ and in its antecedent communions, there has been the strong theological affirmation rooted in the Reformation that ministry belongs to the whole people of God. But with the Reformers, we have also affirmed a special call to the vocation of minister of the church.

Accordingly, the Constitution of the United Church of Christ states, "God calls the whole church and every member to participate in and extend the ministry of Jesus Christ by witnessing to the gospel in church and society" (paragraph 17).[3] And in paragraph 19, "Ordination is the rite whereby the United Church of Christ . . . recognizes and authorizes that member whom God has called to ordained ministry."[4]

I put this in front of us to keep two principles in focus: one, that ours is a ministry among ministries, not higher or lower but alongside, and two, and more importantly, that the ministry is to be an instrument of God. In that context then I reflect on the "vocation of a pastor."

An Instrument of God's Word and God's Grace

To stimulate my own thinking in preparation for writing this essay I spoke to several colleagues whose ministry and perceptions I hold in high respect and from whom I have learned. In response to the question, "What is the vocation of a pastor?" in every instance they said, in essence, "To preach and teach the Word of God and to be an instrument of God's grace." That's where I am. In the near 50 years of ordained ministry I would like to think—and I hope—I have kept that central to all that I have done.

There are several Biblical images that have served to guide our thinking, I believe. There is the prophet, the priest, the teacher, the shepherd, the healer. We have used such words as: to confront the world with God's vision for its children, to be a change agent, to care about people. We have used the best we could learn of the tools and skills for bringing about social change. We have used the best we could learn of the conceptualizations and tools of modern psychology and the human potential movement to help individuals come to a fuller sense of themselves and of their life's potential. We have used the learnings from the field of organizational development to help the church move toward health and vitality. And while one or the other emphasis may have dominated at certain periods in our lives and according to the perceived needs of the world in which we were set at the time, the center has been the call to be an instrument of the love of God given to us in Jesus Christ, in word and in deed.

To be a "pastor" locates one's ministry in a particular context, namely, that of being the pastor or "shepherd" of a community of faith. The word "pastor" is derived from the Latin and means, "shepherd." The shepherd images in the Bible are rich and varied. There is the shepherd with whom there is "no want . . . who leads beside still waters and restores the soul" (Ps 23). There is the shepherd who "feeds his flock" (Isa 40:11). The shepherd "seeks out and rescues" (Ezek 34:12). The shepherd "leaves the ninety-nine and goes after the one that is lost" (Lk 15:4). In talking about the vocation of a pastor, one of the colleagues placed first and foremost the responsibility for caring about people. Under that, she subsumed everything else: the preaching of the word, to being with people when they were ill or grieving, to give one's heart and energies to social justice. That's what loving people in Jesus' name is all about, she said. And she did and does. That's why I honor her ministry.

Nourishing the Church

Another dimension of being a pastor is that one is charged with the care of the church. as institution. That is to say, besides a caring ministry and a preaching and teaching ministry, there is the ministry of helping the church be a healthy and vital community. One minister once talked of administration in the church as *administrivia.* Indeed, it was that to him, and the life of the congregation he served reflected it. I have often said one of the responsibilities of the pastor is to be "the chief executive officer" of a local church. Some are uncomfortable with importing such language into the church. They say, moreover, it reflects a top-down mentality that does not serve the church well. It does not have to. The role of a chief executive officer, or a pastor if you will, is that of helping the church be focused on its purpose, helping the church discover and develop the ways in which it will fulfill its purpose. Whatever it is called it does not matter. The important thing is that the pastor see her or himself as the enabler of the community, the church, to be a healthy and effective instrument of the Word of God.

Renewed by God's Love and Mercy

I want to conclude this essay with words from President Hugo Sonnenschein when he retired from the presidency of the University of Chicago. When asked in a closing interview about the future of the university, he said among other things, "They don't serve when they swerve from their most serious purpose."[5] He could well have been speaking about the pastor.

One colleague whom I had consulted spoke of the vocation of a pastor as that of sacrificing for the sake of the gospel. In an earlier time, it was commonplace to speak of ministry or giving one's self to the mission, as making a sacrifice for the Lord. For the most part, persons going into the ministry today do not use the language of "sacrifice" very often. But what this pastor was identifying is that in responding to "the call,"one's life no longer is entirely one's own. It belongs to God and God's purposes. And so we find ourselves living in the tension between what the "vocation" is calling us to and what we want and often feel we need or ought to do. Sometimes that tension is lived out with a great deal of pain, and sometimes with a great deal of guilt.

I am aware there are some ministers who do not share this perspective. Over the fourteen years that I served as Conference Minister I have been with many pastors and churches as they have struggled with their continuing relationships. Apart from the gross violations of the standards of conduct that are acceptable as the pastor of a congregation, the kinds of things the people have most often spoken of are: he or she is lazy, he or she is too concerned about her or himself and not enough about the congregation, he or she rambles in the pulpit as if he or she had not really prepared. These are distressing comments about a pastor. Acknowledging that a pastor/congregation relationship depends on what both give to it, the pastor carries the larger responsibility. We have said "yes" to God and we have presented ourselves to the church as having been trained and are now prepared to give ourselves to this calling. We stand before God to account for what we have done to fulfill this "calling."

With all of its burdens and with the burden of our own inadequacy for the calling, we have found a richness and blessing which have brought deep satisfaction and joy. God's people are an amazing people who live with such courage and grace, that we have found ourselves blessed more than we can fully say. The grace of God is far more than we can ever think or deserve and in God's never failing mercy and love is our freedom, our renewal, and our fulfillment.

Notes

1. H. Richard Niebuhr, *The Purpose of the Church and Its Ministry* (New York: Harper & Row,. 1956). 64-65.

2. Henri Nouwen, *The Wounded Healer* (New York: Imago Books, 1979).

3. Constitution and ByLaws of the United Church of Christ, 1984, para. 17.

4. Ibid., para. 19.

5. Hugo Sonnenschein, "What It Was Like To Be President: An Interview," *University of Chicago Magazine* 92, no. 5 (June 2000): 25.

Proper Pastoral Posture:
The Role of Knees in the Vocation of the Pastor

David J. Michael

Pastors are in charge of keeping the distinction between the world's lies and the Gospel's truth clear. Not only pastors, of course—every baptized Christian is part of this—but pastors are placed in a strategic, countercultural position. Our place in society is, in some ways, unique: no one else occupies this exact niche that looks so inoffensive but is in fact so dangerous to the status quo. We are committed to keeping the proclamation alive and to looking after souls in a soul-denying, soul-trivializing age.

So writes Eugene Peterson in the introduction to the book he and Marva Dawn have recently co-authored, intriguingly titled *The Unnecessary Pastor.* In a time and place that conspire to make us unnecessary, as the world measures necessity, it is no easy matter for pastors to keep in mind that we belong to Christ alone as we work at keeping clear the distinction between the world's lies and the gospel's truth. The pastoral vocation puts us in charge of attending to the church's identity, its understanding that it is the very body of Christ in a world badly in need of his redeeming work. In such a world, we need a posture which can strengthen us to hold firm against the myriad temptations to become chaplain to the culture or a religious functionary always attentive to the needs of the people —needs that too often run counter to the demands of the gospel. We need a posture which can assist us to "equip the saints for the work of ministry, for building up the body of Christ (Eph 4:12).

The apostle Paul has identified this proper pastoral posture for us in his letter to the Philippians, where he offers us a magnificent hymn of praise to Christ our Lord. Paul writes, in part: "Have within yourselves the same disposition of mind as was in Christ Jesus. . . . He emptied himself, and took the very form of a servant, and became one of us. He became obedient, even to the extent of accepting death on a cross. And for that reason, God has highly exalted him, and granted to him the name which is above every name, that at the name of Jesus, every knee should bow and every tongue confess that Jesus Christ is Lord, to the glory of God the Father" (Phil 2:5-11).

What Paul has given us here is a compelling picture of what our faith is all about and, correspondingly, what pastoral ministry and the ministry of the whole church is to be about. It has to do with bowed knees and confessing tongues, with persons acknowledging who is Lord and who is the only source of authentic life. Here is Paul, once the arrogant, aristocratic opponent of Christ and his church calling every one of us to drop to our knees when we hear Jesus' name, that name we use (or ought to be using) more often than any other in the daily exercise of the pastoral vocation.

On our knees, says Paul: that's the proper posture for those who seek to serve the gospel of Jesus Christ. On our knees in humility, in penitence, in obedience, giving honor to the one whose "name is above every name." Talk about unnecessary! What posture could possibly seem more unnecessary, in fact more useless for our time and place than a posture of humility and obedience, honoring One who demands sacrifice, discipline and unswerving loyalty? How can you live for self and bend the world to your will when you're on your knees? The answer, of course, is that you simply cannot: which only illustrates that the world's lies and the gospel's truth are irreconcilable.

The vocation of the pastor requires postures other than kneeling, of course. Both physically and in terms of attitudes of the heart, a variety of postures are needed. Pastors need to *stand and stretch out* hands in love, with arms open to *embrace* others with the affection of Christ. We need to stand with our *feet planted firmly and arms akimbo* in the face of evil and opposition to the gospel. We *walk arm in arm* with friends in the faith, we *sit patiently* with those enduring hard times, we *run urgently* with the good news, we *raise our arms* in a victory salute when truth prevails, and we *stand on tiptoe* as we wait in hope and eager longing for the reign of Christ to arrive in its fullness. And yes, honesty demands acknowledging that the pastoral vocation will find us *holding our heads* in defeat, *turning back* in fear, *raising clenched fists* in anger and frustration, *wallowing* in uncertainty and self-pity, and *falling flat on our face* (time and again)!

Many postures for many circumstances—but essential to them all, behind them all, is the singular posture with which every ordained servant of Christ must begin and end each day: on our knees, honoring Jesus Christ, humbly seeking his forgiveness and mercy for self and others, offering ourselves again and again in obedience to his will. Yet we assume this posture with hope, because we know that the Lord of the church will lift us to our feet again, and set us once more on the path he would have us travel.

The pastoral vocation requires some expressions of ministry which are either awkward or impossible in any posture other than that of kneeling. Imitating the mind of Christ, as Paul calls us to do in the Philippian letter, demands that *servanthood* be the focus and style of ministry. On the night of his betrayal, Jesus took a basin and towel and knelt to wash the feet of his disciples, calling us to do the same; and it can't be done in any position other than on our knees. The Samaritan on the Jericho Road had to bind some wounds and lift a fallen man; such a ministry requires kneeling. Coins, sheep, and people get lost, and need to be searched for; they can't be found without kneeling. Jesus tells us that it's necessary to become like children in order to have a share in the realm of God; stiff knees keep us from seeing the world as does a child. Paul says that he planted the seed of the word, another watered it, and God gave the growth; planting seeds can't happen with unbent knees. Jesus could not get though his Gethsemane experience except on his knees—we cannot expect to get through our Gethsemane experiences in any other posture. It is the only proper posture for pastors.

Before we knew the difference between our knees and our nose, most of us were brought before a gathered community of faith, held in the arms of our parents, to receive the grace of baptism. A few years later, we again came before the gathered saints to claim the church's faith as our own and to kneel as we confirmed our faith in Jesus Christ. When we came again before the gathered people of God to be set apart for the office of ordained ministry, we knelt once more and hands were laid upon us as a mark of grace. That posture and the attitude it represents is the sign of both our personhood and our ministry. It is in kneeling that we find the strength we need to fulfill our calling; it is in kneeling that our obedience to Christ finds direction, and it is in kneeling that we give honor and allegiance to the One who has called us to ordained ministry. It is not the *power* of Christ which drives us to our knees before him. It is instead that amazing love of God for us which leads us, in gratitude, to the most appropriate posture for the pastoral vocation.

We ought to be sobered by the fact that pastors are someone's itemized deduction. From the moment of ordination, if not before, the source of our income and livelihood becomes what the Internal Revenue Service calls "charitable deductions." We need to take that fact with considerable seriousness. If we are to validate our vocation, something had better be happening in the lives of those who claim us as a charitable contribution. St. Paul, in another of his letters, says to the Corinthians, "Are you not my workmanship in the Lord? You are the seal of my apostleship" (1 Cor 9:1-2). That is his way of saying that those Corinthian Christians, and what is happening in their lives, are evidence that what he is doing has validity and is blessed by God.

This is not an easy criterion with which to live, but it makes great sense as a validation of our vocation. Who we are and what we do ought to result in people who are increasingly finding their way to *their* knees at the name of Jesus. It is the vocation of the pastor to nurture a climate in which people find, in the life of the congregation, those resources of our faith that can move them toward health, wholeness, and maturity (as measured by the mind of Christ). Is a more firm and steady sense of self-worth being built on the foundation of a growing trust that we are valued and loved by God in Christ? Is there a growing sense of freedom, a larger capacity to find joy, a greater sensitivity to and compassionate action on behalf of the oppressed, the rejected, the "unproductive," both close at hand and far away? The issue is not " Have we arrived?" The issue is whether there is movement in some of the people entrusted to us—movement toward wholeness and maturity as defined by Jesus Christ, measured by how far each has come from his or her own personal starting point.

Proper pastoral posture reminds us that we are not the ones who change or move lives, but it is the One to whom we bear witness who causes lives—and congregations—to move and change. And while we are called first to be faithful, not successful, it is still true that we are called to be *both* faithful and effective. If our faithfulness seems to bear little observable fruit, it may well be that we have neglected or forgotten that primary pastoral posture.

"Let this mind be in you which was also in Christ Jesus. . . . He took the form of a servant" (Phil 2:5,7). This is the warrant for the style of ministry of every baptized Christian, and it is crucial for those called to the vocation of pastor. We are called and ordained to be good stewards of the church's fundamental dependence on Jesus Christ, custodians of the church's memory of who it is and to Whom it belongs. As we preach and teach, administer the sacraments, exercise pastoral care and leadership, being servant leaders can be lonely work, easily misunderstood. It can appear unnecessary to minds that do not conform to the mind of Christ. It is, however, the only style which has God's stamp of approval, and therefore its ultimate validation is sure and certain.

Meanwhile, we need all the others who join us in this bent-knee servant ministry. One of the realities of the vocation of the pastor is the simple recognition that in almost any congregation we serve, there are saints whose faith is firmer than our own, whose grasp of the biblical perspective is deeper than our own, and whose sensitivity to God's will for the church is surer than our own. Because Jesus took the form of a servant and became obedient even to death, "God has highly exalted him and given him the name above all others, that at the name of Jesus every knee should bow and every tongue confess that Jesus Christ is Lord, to the glory of God the Father." That day has not yet fully arrived, but as surely as God keeps promises, it *will* arrive. Until then, we need one another within the body of Christ. Until then, let us see to it that we are on our knees together with all with whom we serve, adopting the only posture which can prepare us to confess the sovereignty of Christ in word and deed, and faithfully proclaim the gospel of reconciliation in the face of the world's lies.

For all but my first few years of pastoral ministry, Frederick Trost has been both a tangible and intangible presence in my life, a person whose powerful Christian faith and passionate thirst for authentic ordained ministry have served as inspiration, goad, and challenge for me in the discharge of my pastoral vocation. I am glad to submit these thoughts in honor of him, in celebration of our companionship on the way, and in gratitude for his refusal to be domesticated by anything other than the gospel.

"Strangers and Foreigners on the Earth"

For people who speak in this way make it clear that they are seeking a homeland. If they had been thinking of the land that they had left behind, they would have had an opportunity to return (Hebrews 11:14-15).

Holy God, as a minister in Christ's church, these words have always been important to me.

They have helped me to understand my own calling.

How many times I've wanted to turn back, to go a different way.

And, at times, I've had the opportunity.

But I confess that I am indeed a stranger and a foreigner in this place

—forever seeking a homeland.

How could I turn back? How could I ignore my longing for justice, peace, and love?

I rejoice and give thanks that you encourage me and others to *speak in this way.*

May your love and grace continue to inspire our work, and lead us toward home.

In the spirit of Christ I pray.

Jeffrey Suddendorf

The Mission of the Pastor

Robert F. Morneau

When I was asked to write this essay on the mission of a pastor, my mind turned immediately to several pastors who enriched my own ministry in a variety of ways. They have witnessed to and spoken of what shepherding the flock really means. A cumulative "job description" of a pastor emerges from their gospel-centered lives.

At the top of the list is the seventeenth century Anglican priest George Herbert (1593-1633). Not only does his poetry speak eloquently of a faith-filled parson but his reflections on the pastor's life articulate his vocation of being an instrument of God's love and mercy. Here is the way Herbert summarizes the mission of the pastor: "A Pastor is the Deputy of Christ for the reducing of Man to the Obedience of God."[1] In paraphrase, the pastor is the representative of Christ to bring us back from error to live in obedience to God.

Pastoring is about listening and responding to the voice of God. That voice can be heard in sacred scripture, in the rich tradition of church history, in the joys and sorrows of the community, in the subtle (and not so subtle) stirrings of our heart and conscience. The pastor helps people hear God's call and challenges an appropriate response. Reducing people to the obedience of God is a noble, risky undertaking.

Pastor George Herbert realized, of course, that he himself must live in obedience to the Lord. He writes about the ministry of preaching, a primary task of the pastor: "For in preaching to others, he forgets not himself, but is first a Sermon to himself, and then to others; growing with the growth of his Parish."[2] Herein lies authenticity: the preacher listens and responds to what God has in mind. This is also what causes considerable embarrassment in the preacher's life since he/she knows full well that we ourselves do not measure up to the fullness of the gospel's demands of loving, showing compassion, forgiving seven times seventy times.

In his poem "Trinity Sunday," George Herbert gives us an implicit mission statement of the pastor. The task of Christ's deputy is to make known a trinitarian God, to face and acknowledge personal sin, to beg God for those theological virtues that govern the Christian life. Here, in nine lines, is a rule of life for all pastors as well as a song of great faith:

Trinity Sunday

Lord, who hast form'd me out of mud,
And hast redeem'd me through thy blood,
And sanctifi'd me to do good;

Purge all my sins done heretofore:
For I confess my heavy score,
And I will strive to sin no more.

Enrich my heart, mouth, hands in me,
With faith, with hope, with charity;
That I may run, rise, rest with thee.[3]

A second pastor, coming out of the world of fiction (but for that no less real than George Herbert) is George Eliot's Dinah Morris, a female Methodist minister in the novel Adam Bede. Listen to Dinah's discernment process as she explains to Seth Bede why she cannot marry him:

God has called me to minister to others, not to have any joys or sorrows of my own, but to rejoice with them that do rejoice, and to weep with those that weep. He has called me to speak his word, and he has greatly owned my work. It could only be on a very clear showing that I could leave the brethren and sisters at Snowfield, who are favoured with very little of this world's good; where the trees are few, so that a child might count them, and there's very hard living for the poor in the winter. It has been given me to help, to comfort, and strengthen the little flock there, and to call in many wanderers; and my soul is filled with these things from my rising up till my lying down. My life is too short, and God's work is too great for me to think of making a home for myself in this world. I've not turned a deaf ear to your words, Seth, for when I saw as your love was given to me, I thought it might be a leading of Providence for me to change my way of life, and that we should be fellow-helpers; and I spread the matter before the Lord. But whenever I tried to fix my mind on marriage, and our living together, other thoughts always came in—the times when I've prayed by the sick and dying, and the happy hours I've had preaching, when my heart was filled with love, and the Word was given to me abundantly. And when I've opened the Bible for direction, I've always lighted on some clear word to tell me where my work lay. I believe what you say, Seth, that you would try to be a help and not a hindrance to my work; but I see that our marriage is not God's will—He draws my heart another way. I desire to live and die without a husband or children. I seem to have no room in my soul for wants and fears of my own, it has pleased God to fill my heart so full with the wants and sufferings of his poor people.[4]

A major part of a pastor's vocation, whether married or not, is pastoral care. Just as Jesus came to serve so too the designated, public disciple of the Lord is to do the same. That means that one's attention is on the needy: the suffering and dying, the poor and marginal, the lonely and forgotten. Dinah Morris had a heart rich in empathy, a compassion so strong that her own needs found only secondary place in the scheme of things.

This passage from Adam Bede also highlights the importance of God's word in discerning which direction divine providence is drawing us. Pastor Morris took seriously human love as a viable way in which she might be led to specify her unique calling. In her prayer and discernment process, however, God's word indicated that something else was being asked of her. What freedom she demonstrates in following the divine call regardless of the sacrifice!

Three words capture Dinah Morris's life as a disciple: "I'm called there."[5] Like George Herbert's understanding of his vocation, Dinah also knew that obedience was the heart of the matter. She said "yes" to whatever the Lord would ask of her, be it marriage or not, working in Snowfield or elsewhere, heading for missionary land or staying near home. The double grace of freedom and compassion led her into a servant leadership role that has much to say to our times in which individualism and narcissism dominate so much of our culture. Someone recently commented that many people today live an "uncalled life," having no goals or ambitions outside their own self-fulfillment.

A third paradigm, this one back in "real" history, is Pope John XXIII, the pastor who called Vatican Council II, a council that has revolutionized the Roman Catholic Church and the ecumenical movement as well. Although Pope for only a short time, October 28, 1958, to June 3, 1963, he demonstrated to the world the humanity behind the office of a pastor as well as the source for his spirituality and faith.

First of all, Pope John XXIII's humanity. Shortly after becoming Archbishop of Venice, Angelo Giuseppe Roncalli (Pope John XXIII's baptismal name) went home to bury his sister Ancilla. On the train ride back to Venice after the funeral, Roncalli's assistant heard the future pope "murmur: '*Guai a no se fosse tutta un illusione.*' With the rhythm of the train and the rain beating down on the windows, the mysterious remark, 'Woe to us if it's all an illusion,' was imprinted on Capovilla's memory because 'it revealed a disconcerting aspect of the genuine humanity in my patriarch, who was normally always so strong and self-controlled.'"[6]

Pope John XXIII was no stranger to doubt. He had to wrestle with the human condition as do all pastors of souls. Faith is often tested by the death of those who are close to us. As the poet Emily Dickinson reminds us, we cannot "still the tooth that nibbles at the soul." It was precisely this and other human qualities—wit and compassion and sensitivity—that endeared this Pope to millions of people both inside and outside his own church. No pedestal here but a fellow pilgrim who, on riding a train from his sister's funeral, wonders if anything makes sense.

What is the secret of ministry? What is the glue that holds together the life of Christian pastor? Again, we have in Angelo Roncalli a mentor and a model. On his deathbed, after having been anointed by Bishop Canisius Van Lierde O.S.A., the pope said:

> The secret of my ministry is that crucifix you see opposite my bed. It's there so that I can see it in my first waking moment and before going to sleep. It's there also, so that I can talk to it during the long evening hours. Look at it; see it as I see it. Those open arms have been the programme of my pontificate: they say that Christ died for all, for all. No one is excluded from his love, from his forgiveness.[7]

There are other metaphors to govern the life and ministry of a pastor. Some find the image of John's Gospel—the vine and the branches (Jn 15)—to be the central symbol to depict their callings. Others might turn to the Emmaus story (Lk 24) or Psalm 23 (shepherd image). For Pope John XXIII it was the crucified Christ who inspired and empowered him to serve with such compassion and inclusivity. No one was excluded from the Lord's mercy, no one was denied the love made visible through the Incarnation. Every day and every evening Roncalli saw this vocation hanging before him. No surprise that he had the strength to call a Council that would change the world.

Conclusion

The vocation of a pastor embraces many diverse elements: governance, teaching/preaching, celebrating sacramental life, caring for the needy, doing the work of justice. One pastor put it this way: "We have the opportunity to be present to people during crucial moments of their lives as they celebrate new life, seek forgiveness, reach maturity, enter marriage, deal with suffering, and face death. We have the truly challenging task of helping people apply their faith to their daily lives and, in turn, receive the gift of serious conversation with good people about matters of ultimate concern."[8]

Ultimately the mission and vocation of the pastor is to be a good steward, one who receives God's gifts gratefully, nurtures them responsibly, shares them charitably, and returns them to the Lord in great abundance. St. Paul reminds us that we are stewards and ambassadors of the mysteries of God. What a noble and awesome task.

A Wisconsin poet, the Carmelite Jessica Powers, speaks about living a spiritual life, a life of the Holy Spirit. When all is said and done, only two things are required of the pastor and the people: to be good listeners and good lovers. This is our vocation.

To Live with the Spirit

To live with the Spirit of God is to be a listener.
It is to keep the vigil of mystery,
earthless and still.
One leans to catch the stirring of the Spirit,
strange as the wind's will.

The soul that walks where the wind of the Spirit blows
turns like a wandering weather vane toward love.
It may lament like Job or Jeremiah,
echo the wounded hart, the mateless dove.
It may rejoice in spaciousness of meadow
that emulates the freedom of the sky.
Always it walks in waylessness, unknowing;
it has cast down forever from its hand
the compass of the whither and the why.

To live with the Spirit of God is to be a lover.
It is becoming love, and like to Him
toward Whom we strain with metaphors of creatures:
fire-sweep and water-rush and the wind's whim.
The soul is all activity, all silence;
and though it surges Godward to its goal,
it holds, as moving earth holds sleeping noonday,
the peace that is the listening of the soul.[9]

Notes

1. *George Herbert: The Country Parson, The Temple*, Classics of Western Spirituality, ed. John N. Wall, Jr. (New York: Paulist Press, 1983), 55.
2. Ibid., 83.

3. Ibid., 184.

4. George Eliot, *Adam Bede* (New York: New American Library, 1981), 45.

5. Ibid., 43.

6. Peter Hebblethwaite, *Pope John XXIII: Shepherd of the Modern World* (New York: Doubleday & Company, 1985), 241.

7. Ibid., 501.

8. James Bacik, "The Practice of Priesthood: Working Through Today's Tensions,"*Priesthood in the Modern World*, ed. Karen Sue Smith (Franklin, Wisc.: Sheed and Ward, 1999), 64.

9. *The Selected Poetry of Jessica Powers* (Washington, D.C.: ICS Publications, 1999), 38.

Shepherds of the Particular

David S. Moyer

Lord, to whom can we go? You have the words of eternal life (John 6:68).

Where do people go for words of eternal life? The minister of a large urban church told of surveying the neighborhood around his church, a neighborhood that was changing and contained a large number of younger professional people. One question in the survey asked whether these persons were seeking any kind of spiritual renewal for their lives. Ninety percent answered that they were. Of the group who gave a positive answer, eighty percent indicated that it would not occur to them to seek this spiritual renewal in a church.

How is it that many persons in a culture which leaves them wishing for a greater sense of clarity in their spiritual lives would not seek out the church? There are many trends, both cultural and theological, that lead people to seek something that transcends self in places other than the church. The mix of value systems in today's world offers plenty of "theologies" and therapies, but the church and its ministry also share responsibility for a lack of clarity in communicating the gospel in a way that makes clear its transcendent power.

The church once made a self-conscious claim to be the keeper of words of eternal life. Those words were the gospel, the particularity of the revelation of God in Jesus Christ. In recent years such a claim has come to sound exclusive to modern ears, so accustomed to the sound of self-definition and the authority of individual experience and reason. Embarrassed by the "scandal of particularity," and wishing to avoid its sounding like a scandal of exclusivity, the church has run the risk of offering a theology in which God is in danger of becoming domesticated to our cultural value systems, and the gospel is robbed of its power.

The theme of this section is the "vocation of the pastor," so I would like to focus on tracing a trajectory of pastoral identity that has contributed to this situation and then to offer some signs of hope that I observe in current pastoral practice. It is the question of the "particularity" of God's revelation in Christ that I believe is at the heart of pastoral identity in Christian ministry. It isn't easy to find ways to bring an ancient and sometimes odd word into the current marketplace of competing ideas and value systems. Jesus' disciples found it difficult as well. In the text above, Jesus teaches about the particularity of his own body as the "bread which came down from heaven," but his disciples say, "This is a hard saying. Who can listen to it?"(Jn 6:60)

Communicating the uniqueness of the revelation of God in Christ is at the center of the role of Christian pastor. In the past generation or two, as liberal culture questioned traditional grounds of authority, many mainline pastors grew increasingly uncomfortable representing a tradition that so clearly found authority outside the self. In the 1960s there was a strong impetus for the minister to be a professional among many professionals who were ascending into a growing professional class in United States society. Some of us began to have "itchy ears" for the call of voices that promised the comfort of cultural accommodation.

We pastors saw ourselves as counselors, adopting much of the language of psychology and seeking to find a synthesis out of psychological terms and understandings that would help people, when we lost confidence in the power of the gospel to heal. Some of us understood the problems of the world as going beyond the individual and saw social workers helping people and confronting injustices in society. We saw people in various helping professions gaining the status of a master's degree with 40 credit hours, while we clergy spent 120 hours getting another bachelor's degree. This explains our move to convert the degree to the Master of Divinity and the modicum of additional status we thought it might provide.

Some clergy were captured by the seductive political scene of the 1960s and 70s, a time of turmoil and change that seemed to be pointing to a more humane society, to greater equality, economic justice, and diversity. When we clergy spoke on these issues, we spoke in a language that provided a thin veneer of theology covering what we thought were the "real" issues of social and political engineering. The wave was rolling, and we were anxious to catch a ride.

As the economy heated up and organizational theory took off, we clergy followed, going through a time of seeking to be the manager of the little engine that could change the world, the church. The role of pastor was seen as the manager of a voluntary organization. The "minister as manager," planning programs, doing good, organizing for mission was a common theme of writing about pastoral identity in the final quarter of the twentieth century.

We also spent a lot of time in the past generation of ordained ministry in defining ourselves by what we were not. One reason we were so afraid of using biblical or traditional language was that the growing fundamentalist church and prominent conservative preachers were using it in ways we could not abide, and we wanted the world to know we weren't them.

These personal vocational ambiguities were not the result of some evil intent on the part of pastors, some inordinate pride or arrogance. Often the opposite was true. Pastors were discouraged. We were not feeling the same kind of support or affirmation that had existed for much of the time since Colonial America, namely that clergy were often the most educated and respected persons in a community and the primary source of help. Now cultural trends were leading in another direction, and pastors were feeling left behind.

In its institutional life, the mainline church was also moving away from the particularity of pastoral identity and toward a more "functional" view of ordination. There was less emphasis on spiritual gifts and more on the leadership needs of the community of faith. For example, the *Manual on Ministry* of the United Church of Christ lists seven "Faith Affirmations" in its section on "The Church's Expectations of Its Candidates for Ordination":

Is compelled by the gospel of Jesus Christ.

Has a sense of having been called by God and the church to ordained ministry.

Has a sense of vocational direction.

Is committed to the mission of the church.

Can clearly articulate a personal theological position.

Can clearly articulate a theological understanding of ordination.

Can relate his or her understanding of ordained ministry to the ministry to which he or she has received a call.

With the exception of the first item on the list, and to a lesser extent the second, these can hardly be called faith affirmations at all. They are, in fact, completely functional in their intent, and yet they are called "faith affirmations." The manual goes on to a much more extensive list of self-consciously functional things that are expected. The institutional shaping of the ordained is clear in our expectations. We are to be "compelled by Christ," to be sure, but we are primarily to be attentive to the functional needs of the church as organization.

None of what is suggested here is meant to demean other professions or to deny possibilities of human progress or the ability of modern therapies to help persons. I do not mean to diminish the skills needed for pastoral work or organizational skills required to lead a church.

Knowledge of other disciplines is needed in order to refer and to support persons who are receiving help from a variety of sources. Knowledge of other fields of knowledge allows us to offer a prophetic perspective that both critiques and receives critique in the debates around the enormous ethical issues of our day.

The point is that the gospel will only be served and the world will be better served, if we offer the particular and peculiar story that has been entrusted to us, the story which Paul said was "Christ, and him crucified." Certainly, this story will at times be a stumbling block in our dialogue with the world, but it is the unique thing that we can bring to the table.

Having briefly described what I think are trends and issues that have influenced the vocation of Christian ministry in the mainline church, it is now time to turn to some small beginnings that may offer an alternative vision of ministry and be a foundation for renewing vocational identity. The first sign I want to point to is the return to scripture. There is a growing renewal of interest in scripture and in seeking both its instructive and its spiritual power. There is a recovery of the sense of "holy writ," God's word standing beyond our experience.

There is an increase in the use of scripture as a powerful component of pastoral care for persons who are troubled. There is an increase in pastoral practice in what one pastor describes as not only using scripture "in" pastoral care but using scripture "as" pastoral care. This understanding reminds me of being called to a hospital to try to help a parishioner who was extremely anxious about a serious surgery. She was panicked, and no matter what her family or the nurses tried, including various medications, she could not be calmed down. The needed surgery was at risk. When I spoke to her, it had no effect. Then I did something which, for me, in those days, was unusual. I read from the Psalms. The transformation was amazing. The power of the Holy Spirit in the word had a power that all our human endeavors could not muster.

To trust the word is essential for ministry. To believe that it has its own power, beyond our own words, and that the Holy Spirit speaks to the heart and exerts a presence and a power that is transcendent and efficacious is at the center of our work. It has been neglected for too long, and it is good to see it returning to a place at the center of pastoral vocation.

For the past five or six years the various committees and gatherings of our Association have begun with a very simple reading of the gospel text from the lectionary for the following Sunday. This has become such a lively and important part of our being together, that sometimes the discussion continues long into the other agenda items. This is undoubtedly frustrating to some, but for others, like the lay woman who signed up for another term, saying, "I wouldn't want to miss the Bible study," it is at the center of the work we do.

A Lutheran pastor tells of how she insists that being a member of the church board is not just a position of administrative or programmatic leadership but involves spiritual leadership. Therefore, if you accept a term on the board, you are committing yourself to one-third work on church business and programs, one-third study of the scriptures and Christian tradition, and one-third service to others. If there is a two-hour meeting, it is evenly divided into Bible study, business, and reporting on pastoral care and service opportunities in which the leaders have participated in the past month. The pastor's evaluation is that they have gotten much more efficient at their administrative tasks and that a sense of priority has been given to the total work of the body of Christ.

Another pastor told of reading a book for a seminary class on church meetings, and how he has begun to make the council meetings a service of worship, with candles and symbols of the faith in the middle of the table, and a time of scripture and singing and prayer as part of every monthly meeting. This approach has transformed meetings, as the work of the council is placed in the context of God's word. The guidance of the Holy Spirit is overtly sought, and there is a sense of meaning beyond the moment that goes into decision-making.

There is also a renewed interest in a broader and deeper understanding of ordination. Committees on the Ministry are looking for a stronger background in traditional theological studies, to see that the student is a person of faith who is informed by a hermeneutic of trust and love for the tradition along with an appropriate hermeneutic of suspicion which is essential for a church in continual need of reform. There is less tendency to accept personal spiritual narratives in the place of an ability to articulate a tradition and an attempt to move questions of ordination to a ground beyond humanistic issues such as self-enhancement, growth, and free-floating spiritual insight. Committees are seeking dialogue with seminaries on course offerings, as well as mentoring and faith formation; on the shaping of a pastoral identity along with academic progress.

These anecdotes certainly do not constitute a trend, but they are hopeful signs that the vocation of pastor is turning a corner in the mainline church. If so, it is something to build on as we seek to strengthen pastoral identity in the particularity of the Christian story. The recovery of the particular, and at times peculiar, story of the life, teaching, death, resurrection, and current presence of Jesus Christ as the heart of pastoral identity will be a welcome development for the church.

It is a story which has sustained a community for over 2000 years, and it may give those who have not heard it pause to consider whether their spiritual needs might be met in the church. To reclaim the sense of the particularity of God's revelation in Christ may at times make us appear odd in the midst of the modern world and its worship of progress and its trust in the marketplace of personal choices. Yet the history of the story we claim is full of examples when Christ's people were seen as odd and out of step. Remarkably, it has often been those moments when the church's ministry was most transformative. A growing trust and joyful participation in this particular, gracious work of Christ is the foundation of hope in the vocation of pastor.

The Pastoral Office

Robert D. Mutton

*For neither the light and heat of the sun, nor any food and drink, are
so necessary to nourish and sustain the present life as the pastoral
office is to the preservation of the church in the world.* (John Calvin,
The Institutes of Christian Religion)

*How are they to believe in him whom they have never heard? And how
are they to hear without a preacher?* (Romans 10:14)

During my last sabbatical, I took on the task of trying to discover
what help could be offered to clergy just beginning in parish ministry. My
contention was that the first five years of ministry set the stage for what
will follow. If pastors get off on the right foot, then they can continue to
develop a solid pastoral identity and learn from the inevitable mistakes
and failures. On the other hand, if their pastoral identity is undefined, it is
more likely that they would repeat the mistakes of the past.

I interviewed thirty-five people about their first five years in
pastoral ministry. Some of them had been in the ministry for ten years or
more, some less. Each interview took about two hours. It was a wonderful
and emotional time. I was honored to be permitted into this tender and
vulnerable place. Most people had never talked about the first few years,
often painful times. Many were lonely, some frightened, and some more
confident than was healthy. One scene was repeated over and over: "It's
the first day of work, and I'm sitting in the office at the pastor's desk: now
what is it that I do?" Some were in tears; some were terrified; all were
hoping for the phone to ring to give them some direction on what to do
next. This incident characterizes the crisis in our understanding of
pastoral identity.

Just what is the pastoral office? The answer matters to people, to
their spiritual growth, to the community of faith. There is a story told of a
woman pastor, the first woman pastor in a particular parish in the Chicago
area. She was presiding at her first funeral, and an older woman, one of the
matriarchs of the parish, asked if she could ride with her to the interment.
Following the service at the graveside, the older woman got back into the
car and said, "Well, there now. I can go back and tell the others not to be
afraid; she can do a funeral."

From the *BEM* document (*Baptism, Eucharist and Ministry*,
World Council of Churches, 1982) we have an ecumenical consensus:

In order to fulfill its mission, the Church needs persons who are publicly and continually responsible for pointing to its fundamental dependence on Jesus Christ and thereby provide, within a multiplicity of gifts, a focus of its unity. The ministry of such persons, who since the very early times have been ordained, is constitutive for the life and witness of the Church. . . . As Christ chose and sent apostles, Christ continues through the Holy Spirit to choose and call persons into ordained ministry. As heralds and ambassadors, ordained ministers are representatives of Jesus Christ to the community, and proclaim his message of reconciliation. As leaders and teachers they call the community to submit to the authority of Jesus Christ, the teacher and prophet, in whom law and prophets were fulfilled. As pastors, under Jesus Christ the chief shepherd, they assemble and guide the dispersed people of God, in anticipation of the coming Kingdom.

Even with help from the *BEM* document, we still find in our free church tradition a difficult time answering the question "Just what is it that pastors do?" Calvin in his *Institutes* has no confusion; his understanding of the pastoral office, the ordained ministry, is clear and strong. The pastoral office bears responsibility for preserving the church. *BEM* states that the ministry of pastors is constitutive for the life of the church; pastors call the community to obedience. These are high understandings of the pastoral office in comparison to our confusion. Therefore, let us look at our tradition's understanding of ordination and the ordinand's vows to discern what they have to say about the pastoral office.

The classical Protestant answer is five-fold:

1. Ordination is the public testimony by which God's call is openly declared to be approved by the church.

2. Through ordination the ministry of word and sacrament is committed formally to the ordained.

3. Through the vows the one who has been called becomes obligated to the church in the sight of God to render the faithfulness in the ministry that the Lord requires.

4. The church is reminded that this pastor has authority to teach.

5. In ordination the whole church earnestly prays to "commit to God" the ministry of the one who is called, expecting that God will accompany this ministry.

Next, looking at the United Church of Christ *Book of Worship*, we find these ordination vows:

Do you, with the Church throughout the world hear the word of God in the scriptures of the Old and New Testaments, and do you accept the Word of God as the rule of Christian faith and practice?

Do you promise to be diligent in your private prayers and in the reading of the scriptures, as well as the public duties of your office?

Will you be zealous in maintaining both the truth of the gospel and the peace of the church, speaking the truth in love?

Will you be faithful in preaching and teaching the gospel and administering the sacraments and rites of the church, and exercising pastoral care and leadership?

In summary, these things stand out as central to the pastoral office:

1. A call from God confirmed by the church.

2. The authority to study the scriptures and the tradition and to teach, preach, and administer the sacraments.

3. The responsibility to provide spiritual leadership and be a spiritual resource.

In our quest to understand the pastoral office, these are our beginning points. But what do they mean? The first one, the call—and the gifts from God that go with the call, for we understand that whatever is needed will be provided—needs to be distinguished from the last two. The first is a condition; the last two are tasks, yet the last two are totally dependent on the first.

The Call and the Gift (the Charism)

I remember my pastor's advice when I told him that I thought I was called to ordained ministry: "If you are able to do anything else, do it." At the time, as a young and enthusiastic person, I did not take that to be a word of encouragement. Yet later in life his meaning became clear to me. If one is so compelled that it is impossible to do anything else, there is a good possibility that one has a call.

In my conversations with the thirty-five folk I interviewed, all could identify a clear call. The calls varied in content and intensity. One woman was happily teaching at a university and uninterested in the church. She had no relationship with any congregation, but while she was walking across campus one day, she was called into ordained ministry. She left everything and followed. Another, a young man who grew up in a congregation had no dramatic conversion but was converted weekly as he lived in the midst of Christian people whom he admired, who loved him into the ordained ministry. In all the interviews people felt a calling, one beyond their baptism. Without this sense of call, no one can enter the pastoral office.

The sacrament of baptism shares with the rite of ordination a call to ministry. Both confirm what has already happened. God has acted in this individual, and the church confirms God's call and prays for the continuation of God's grace. The pastoral office is inhabited by one in whom God has acted. It is God who has called and it is God who provides the gifts for this office. This is fundamental. Without a call, the pastoral office is nothing more than a job, a profession, a career, and when it is such, there is nothing to sustain the person in times of deepest despair.

Studying, Preaching, Teaching, and Administering

If the call is fundamental, then these responsibilities are at the heart of pastoral ministry. When persons are ordained, they are called "pastor and teacher." The term *teacher* is a confusing term to many. Are they to teach in the church school; are they to teach a Bible study? What exactly are they to do as teacher? First, their education has given them authority to teach; they study from a wide range of disciplines and are knowledgeable in various fields related to the Bible and the traditions. They have assimilated a body of knowledge and are able to teach it with authority, and thus they provide a way to open up the tradition. They are therefore to make available to their congregation the teachings of the church. They are not the answer-givers, nor does their knowledge preclude the teaching role that is given to other members of the congregation. Their task is to interpret in light of the tradition. The key here is that the pastor is the teacher of the church and its tradition, and one's personal viewpoint is not the focus.

William Willimon of Duke University Divinity School tells this story (*Christian Century*, February 7-14, 1996:136-7.):

In a church history course in my last year at YDS [Yale Divinity School], the professor invited an Orthodox priest to lecture. He gave a rather dry talk on the development of the creed. At the end of the lecture an earnest student asked, "Father Theodore, what can one do when one finds it impossible to affirm certain tenets of the creed?"

The priest looked confused, "You just say it. It's not that hard to master. With a little effort, most can quickly learn it by heart."

"No, you don't understand," continued the student. "What am I to do when I have difficulty affirming parts of the creed, like the Virgin Birth?"

The priest continued to look confused. "You just say it. Particularly when you have difficulty believing it, you just keep saying it. It will come to you eventually."

Exasperated, the student, a product of the same church that produced me, and a representative of the '60s pleaded, "How can I with integrity affirm a creed in which I do not believe?"

"It's not your creed, young man!" said the priest. "It's our creed. Keep saying it, for heaven sake! Eventually it may come to you. For some, it takes longer than for others. How old are you? Twenty-three? Don't be so hard on yourself. There are lots of things that one doesn't know at twenty-three. Eventually it may come to you. Even if it doesn't, don't worry. It's not your creed, it's *our* creed."

Teaching and preaching are not just a matter of disseminating the personal opinion of the one who has studied. Teaching and preaching are making available the tradition of the church in the equipping of the saints for the mission of the church.

One of the ways that the ordained minister equips the congregation of the saints is by making the tradition accessible to individuals dealing with personal and corporate issues in the life of the community. If the congregation is in conflict, the role of the ordained goes beyond making a social system response. Many lay people among us, in fact, know systems better and have better conflict resolution skills than ordained folk. Therefore when conflict arises, the ordained person has the special task of looking to the tradition and asking, "Did the Corinthians have similar problems?" In other words, the teacher, preacher, pastor relies on a specific body of knowledge, not *all* knowledge, but a *body* of knowledge, that enables her/him to make available the tradition. This knowledge then is for *one* purpose, and that is to equip the congregation for its ministry. It is my contention that what will equip the congregation is the Bible and the tradition interpreted by one who has been called by God and given the charism (the gift). This pastoral minister, whose experience, focused through the scriptures and the tradition, will serve to equip us all for the call to servanthood.

Spiritual Leadership

If the call is fundamental to the pastoral office, and study, teaching, and preaching are at the heart, then the root of the pastoral minister's responsibility is spiritual leadership. The primary role is that of inviter. The continuing spiritual task is that of offering an invitation to a relationship. It is to remind us just where our dependency can be rooted and where we can be sustained. The relationship with God in Jesus Christ is the root, and the ordained one is called to remind us and direct us, and most importantly, invite us. The first question in the mind of the cleric when a person comes into the study for counsel on a family problem is "How is your relationship with God?" The next is "How is my relationship with God? Can I with conviction invite this parishioner into this relationship because I know it, trust it?" Listen to Roberta Bondi from her book *In Ordinary Time* (Abingdon Press, 1996) talk of this relationship:

> Before anything else, above anything else, beyond anything else, God loves us. God loves us extravagantly, ridiculously, without limit or condition. God is in love with us; God yearns for us. God does not love us in spite of who we are or for who God knows we can become. According to the wonderful fourth and fifth-century teachers I have learned from, God loves us hopelessly as mothers love their babies, and as tiny babies love everyone who smiles at them. God loves us, the very people we are; and not only that, even against what we ourselves sometimes find implausible, God likes us.

This is the content of the continuing invitation offered by the ordained. This is the relationship that is to be trusted. For if the saints are to truly to be equipped, this relationship must continually be proclaimed and encouraged.

One last image of the pastoral office that draws together the call that is fundamental with the heart and the root of our vocation appears in Frederick Buechner's book *Telling the Truth* (Harper & Row, 1985). He writes:

> So the sermon hymn comes to a close with a somewhat unsteady Amen, and the organist gestures the choir to sit down. In the front pews the old ladies turn up their hearing aids, and a young lady slips her six-year-old a Lifesaver and a Magic Marker. A college sophomore home from vacation, who is there because he was dragged there, slumps forward with his chin in his hand, the vice-president of a bank who twice that week has seriously contemplated suicide places his hymnal in the rack. The pregnant girl feels the life stir inside her. A high-school math teacher, who for twenty years has managed to keep his homosexuality a secret for the most part even from himself, creases his order of worship down the center with his thumbnail and tucks it under his knee. The preacher pulls the little cord that turns on the lectern light and deals out his note cards like a river boat gambler. The stakes have never been higher. Two minutes from now he may have lost his

listeners completely to their own thoughts, but at this minute he has them in the palm of his hand. The silence in the shabby church is deafening because everybody is listening to it. Everybody is listening including even himself. Everyone knows the kinds of things he has told them before and not told them, but who knows what this time out of the silence, he will tell them? Let him tell them the Truth.

The ordained one, the one who inhabits the pastoral office is responsible for pointing us to our fundamental dependence on Jesus Christ, that is, the Truth.

"Most Gracious God"

Most Gracious God, you have called and I have answered, "I will go. Send me to minister in the name of Jesus." I have committed my life to serving you. I have learned that the road is not predictable and not without risk, but you have sent Jesus to lead the way. You have provided the Holy Spirit to empower and sustain me. Through those who love me, you have given me your word to carry for a lifetime and to give to all I meet in every circumstance and condition. Thank you, O God, for the influence and example of my brothers and sisters in ministry, those who have gone before me and those who work alongside me. They have left the imprint of their sacrifice and dedication on my heart. They have lifted me up and brought me closer to you. Thank you, loving God, for the sacred gift of ministry.

I have rejoiced with the children in their love for you, their enthusiasm for life and learning, and their invitation to "stand on tiptoe" to see what is yet to come. I have been honored to hear the passion in the concerns of youth: their hopes, dreams, and fears, and the fervor of their prayers. The poor, needy, sick, and dying have taught me what faith is and from whom it comes. They have taught me how to live in faith hour by hour and moment by moment. When their legs can no longer support them, their faith carries them on the road to Bethlehem with a smile, a tear, a memory, the familiar words of a hymn, a prayer. And they carry me with them. Let me remember always to listen and look beneath the noise and appearances to discover the sacredness within your Holy People. In their faces, I have seen the face of Christ.

When the ways of the world threaten to distract me, let me hold fast to the servanthood of Jesus the foot-washer, the servant of all. Sustain in me a clear vision and a steadfast heart as I strive to bring good news to the afflicted and release to those in bondage. With your help, let me lift up the downtrodden. Strengthen me in Christ so that I may do that which is good and honorable and just in every situation. Let me recognize when it is time to rest. Let me accept the refreshment of your Holy Spirit and the laughter and hospitality of those I meet along the way. And let me remember always to lay aside the burdens I carry in the guise of responsibility and to carry nothing with me for the journey except my love for your holy people and Jesus Christ, my Redeemer and Sustainer.

Dorothy A. Palmer

The Glory of Ministry:
A Sermon on the Text of 2 Corinthians 3:3

Charles L. Copenhaver †

Recently "The Glory of Ministry" by Charles A. Copenhaver, Pulpit Digest, (May/June 1981), caught my attention. The sermon was preached at his son's ordination on June 20, 1980. Today the son, Martin B. Copenhaver, is senior pastor of the Wellesley Congregational United Church of Christ in Massachusetts. Asked for permission to use the sermon for publication, Martin wrote: "I would be particularly delighted to see this sermon included in the volume dedicated to Frederick Trost, someone I have known and admired for years." I couldn't agree more, "The Glory of Ministry" speaks about "our" vocation in a most sensitive, profound, and challenging way. It is about our "common life" with both ecstacy and agony, which according to Bonhoeffer in Life Together *gives "a pastor no right to accuse his congregation before God. Rather, let him make intercession and give thanks for his congregation. Thankfulness is the key to greater spiritual resources."*—Erwin Pegel

Wherein lies that glory? Surely it is not to be found in financial gain. Ministers on the average are paid much less than any other professional group in our society and considerably less than most laboring groups. The glory is not in the money. Seldom is the glory found in power. There is little room for a minister in the power structures of our secular society. Nor is the glory realized in recognition and fame. With the few exceptions of the nationally known evangelists on radio and television, how many ministers can you call by name? These are the standards for success by which glory is measured in our society—money, power, and fame. No one of them is adequate to describe the glory of ministry. The glory of ministry is something very special. In many important ways it is unique.

How can it be described? St. Paul wrote to the Christians in Corinth: "Show that you are a letter from Christ written not with ink but with the spirit of the living God . . . not on tablets of stone but on tablets of human hearts." You are to be a person relating to other persons, your life a letter, as it were, from Christ. Not cold ink on dry paper nor a chisel carving on hard tablets of stone. Rather, a life communicating the good news, the gospel, the very riches of Christ to others. O, the glory of that!

The glory of ministry then is to declare the good news—the best news in the whole world, the best news for all time and for all time. How awesome this is. Surely we know that "We have this treasure in earthen vessels," as St. Paul said. We know our weaknesses and our unworthiness, for we are not better than others. We are tempted, even as they are. We would be strong, but we are ashamed of our weaknesses. We would be courageous, but fear is no stranger to us. We intend to love all, yet there are times when the unlovely are difficult to love. We mean to forgive but some things strike us as unforgivable. So it is that Christ stands before us and we say, as did Simon Peter when he confronted Christ, "Depart from me for I am a sinful man, O Lord."

His patient response to our confession is, "Go forth as a letter from Christ—writing the good news on human hearts." Imagine that! Isn't it astonishing? You spend a lifetime doing what most certainly is the most important thing in the world, declaring the good news of God to the lonely and loveless, the proud and stubborn, the weak and fearful, the lost and wounded, the successful and self-righteous. Consider. Your words and your actions, your life and the way you live it, your response to failure and your reaction to success, your strength in the shadowed valleys of sorrow and your spirit in sun-drenched times for joy, how you heal when you hurt and what happens when you feel grievously misunderstood, your ability to love the unlovable and forgive what would seem to be unforgivable, your strength in weathering a storm of unjustified criticism and your patience in dealing with conflict, your resources for standing tall and strong for what you verily believe—all of these a letter from Christ being read day by day by others and all being written hour by hour on tablets of human hearts. Astounding? To be sure. Terrifying? Of course it is, Are we worthy for this? Certainly not. And yet, by the grace and mercy of God, this is the glory of ministry: that God can use us even such as we are.

This means that we are to be committed for life to proclaim the gospel and to place lives under its power. To give your life to this end is an awesome and in a sense a stunning thing to do. There are times when every fiber of your being cries out, as did David when he stood before the Lord: "Who am I, O Lord God . . . that thou hast brought me this far?" It is well that this should be so. If it ever not be so, then we are lost to both the true and spiritual nature of our calling and the glory of ministry.

It is the glory of ministry that our lives are to be inescapably woven into the lives of others. In this we carry constantly on our hearts the concerns of countless in our congregation, and there are times when the weight of that burden may seem unbearable. The hurt and wounded in spirit make their way to us, and they come in the hope that the minister will, at least more than others, hear and understand. The apprehensive and fearful seek us out, trusting that we can help them find antidotes for their anxieties. Those who are in grief following a heartbreaking loss turn to us that they may pick up the scattered pieces of their lives and begin again. The guilt-ridden spill out their shame before us, seeking the solace that can come only from the assurance of God's forgiveness. The losers in life look to us for fresh encouragement and new hope. The sick in body wonder whether our Lord, the great physician, can help them. So they come in steady stream, often smiling in countenance yet with hearts that weep.

A man said after reading a very pessimistic book that the author left the reader feeling there was nothing left for him but the point of a revolver or the power of the cross. Life can do that to people. A minister witnesses this in the lives of others. It is the minister who can turn them from the point of the revolver to the power of the cross. No wonder then that there are times when he is emotionally drained and weary in spirit for he shall have given much of himself to them. Yet here is the source of our greatest personal fulfillment and here is the glory of ministry. Ernest Poole in his novel, *One of Us*, says of John Valliant, a minister, "He gave men strength by rousing the God asleep inside of them." That's what we are about.

Then there is the glory of ministry in the shared joy. Here are two young people standing before us, hearts beating a bit faster in their happiness and eyes shining with excitement. It is their wedding day, the day of days in their lives. How great is a minister's privilege to speak to them of God's love and to call down God's blessings upon them. They are there, you are there, and God is there. Surely it is a blessed and glorious moment. And what greater moment in life can there be than that moment when you take a warm and tender infant in your arms and baptize a new life in the name of Christ and his church? Here in your arms is the very miracle of life, God's power of creation and the mystery of existence itself. Look deep into the eyes of the parents, hold close the wee one, and surely you will know God is present at that moment. The glory of it!

Then there comes a time when the ultimate mystery confronts us, and we gather to remember a life past and confidently commend that life to God's everlasting love and care in the name of the resurrected Lord. To speak with assurance the great promises of our faith, to bring about in the grief-stricken the healing silence which marks an acceptance of the inevitable, and to gently guide those who are left back into the mainstreams of life is a glory of ministry.

There are those—and some within the church—who would hold that a minister is unacquainted with real life. Not so at all. A minister sees life and he sees it whole, at its best and at its worst. He may see more real life in a week that the average person might encounter in a year, It is the glory of the ministry that we are called to be with and to serve all kinds and conditions of people in the name of Christ. Though we are Christians, we are to confess our common humanity with people of all faiths. Though we may be white, we are to declare a God who is color-blind. Though we may be relatively poor, we are to minister to rich and poor alike. Though some may think of us as liberal or conservative, such distinctions mean nothing to us and are not known in the kingdom of God. Though we may be well educated, we know that no one enters the kingdom of God by degrees. Though we may be young, we love both young and old alike. Even St. Paul saw it, so we see: "Here cannot be Greek or Jew, circumcised or uncircumcised, barbarian, Scythian, slave, free man, but Christ is all, and in all." There is the glory of laboring for the Lord within the fellowship of believers in Jesus Christ, bound together by a common loyalty and common love, the church.

Let us not be dishonest nor deceived. There is no such thing on earth as a perfect church, for there are no perfect people. Neither is there a really good church, for we are the church and most of us are not that good. It is as simple as that. A church can break both the heart and the spirit of a minister. He is a public figure, open and vulnerable to the critical opinions and unfair judgments of any in the congregation and out. He can be blamed for much that is not his fault, and often he has no other resource except to take such blame in silence. A church can make a minister a lonely and bruised person. Yet a church can be patient, long-suffering, thoughtful, supportive, kind, and compassionate.

There is the glory of ministry within the church. Samuel H. Miller spoke of the church in such a way that it cries out for repetition:

Here we may be cast down, but we praise God! We may not know the answer to all our fears and tragedies that overwhelm us, but we praise God! We stand in the midst of troubled times and do not know what the morrow will bring forth, for we are not prophets or the sons of prophets, but we praise God! We found in our own lives mysteries we cannot understand, problems we have not solved, but we praise God! This is the house where [we] with all [our] doubts and sins and darkness may come and shut the door on all the running tides of this world's fashion and listen for the still small voice that has spoken to [us] from the creation of the world. This is the house of God, when in our souls we stand on the solid ground where we live, and in the circumstances where we grapple with mystery, and in those places where we need something more than the world can give.

Never lose sight of the glory of ministry. Even in the darker days—and they are a part of every life—remember that a minister is to be "a letter from Christ . . . written not with ink but with the spirit of the living God, not on tablets of stone but on tablets of human hearts."

Editor's note: This sermon was first preached in 1980, and the use of masculine pronouns is both a reflection of common usage and a reference to a specific ordinand.

Reflections on the Pastoral Ministry and Service of Dietrich Bonhoeffer

F. Burton Nelson

The life and legacy of Dietrich Bonhoeffer (1906-1945) will be remembered in numerous ways as we look back on the tumultuous twentieth century. He will always be remembered as a noble and courageous martyr for his Christian faith. His faithfulness to the death has been celebrated by his inclusion among ten twentieth-century martyrs sculpted over the entrance to Westminster Abbey in London.[1]

He will also be remembered for his active opposition to the unbridled tyranny of Nazism, issuing in his direct involvement in the resistance movement. For four dangerous years (1939-1943) he served as a civilian member on the staff of the *Abwehr,* the counterintelligence agency of the armed forces in Nazi Germany.[2]

Further, his contributions to theology and to the life of the Christian church throughout the world will be perpetuated long into the twenty-first century and perhaps beyond. Most notable among these contributions are the sixteen volumes of his writings, published initially in Bonhoeffer's native German and now being translated into English.[3] The massive biography by Eberhard Bethge, his closest friend, will serve for all time as the standard record of this abbreviated life, cut short by murder at the age of thirty-nine.[4]

Indelibly important is the pastoral character of Bonhoeffer's life, initially as a parish pastor, subsequently as "a pastor to pastors," a continuing model of pastoral ministry "without portfolio."

Parish Ministry and Service

The Bonhoeffer family, living in the capital city of Berlin in the 1920s and 1930s, was not enthusiastic about young Dietrich's decision to prepare for ministry in the churches of the time. His own brothers sought to convince him that the church was a poor, feeble, boring, petty bourgeois institution. His scientifically-trained physician father, Dr. Karl Bonhoeffer, was to write at a later time, "When you decided to devote yourself to theology, I sometimes thought to myself that a quiet, uneventful minister's life, as I knew it, . . . would really almost be a pity for you." [5]

In spite of these sentiments, Dietrich prepared for the ministry, which would occupy his few adult years. His first appointment brought him to a German-speaking Lutheran congregation in Barcelona in 1928 at the young age of twenty-two.[6] During that time there were about six thousand Germans in Barcelona; the congregation numbered about 300, with about 40 in attendance at the services. His days were brim full of pastoral ministry—preaching, visitation, pastoral care of the unemployed and the sorrowing. He was to stay in Barcelona for just a year, although he was wholeheartedly invited to continue. It was a time for honing pastoral skills, such as preaching, counseling, visitation, teaching, organizing, leading. Beyond all that, however, was the evolving of profound vocational attributes: caring, encouraging, relating, theologizing, sympathizing, loving.

These attributes and these skills were to be further refined during Bonhoeffer's year at Union Theological Seminary in New York, 1930-31. Deepening and maturing continued in classroom studies and in relationships with such stalwart minds as Reinhold Niebuhr, Harry Ward, Eugene Lyman, John Baillie, J. W. Bewer, and Harry Emerson Fosdick. He was likewise forever enriched by his friendships with Union students Jean Lasserre of France, Erwin Sutz of Switzerland, Paul and Marion Lehmann, and Frank Fisher of the United States. Especially formative was his experience at the Abyssinian Baptist Church of Harlem. He was frequently there at services on Sunday, as well as teaching catechism in a Sunday school class, all the while absorbing the passion for justice, equality, and fairness that he found in the African-American community. His attachment to the singing of such spirituals as "Go Down, Moses," "Swing Low, Sweet Chariot," and "Nobody Knows the Trouble I've Seen" never flagged. In fact, later he taught them all to his students at the Finkenwalde Seminary.[7]

Bonhoeffer's ordination as a pastor took place at St. Matthias Church in Berlin November 15, 1931. Shortly thereafter he began teaching a confirmation class at Zion Church in the Berlin district of Wedding. Fifty children learned the rudiments of the faith under his tutelage, compelling him to further hone his skills in communication and caring. His biographer paints a vivid picture of this significant period of his life:

> The Wedding experience had a deep impact on Bonhoeffer. When it was decided that he should continue with the class until they were confirmed, he reduced his other commitments to the minimum. A student remarked, "Not only could we eight confirmation pupils visit him in his apartment on Oderbergerstrasse, but even in his parents' home on Wangenheimstrasse." Thus he lived in the same district as his

working-class pupils. . . . He devoted his free evenings to his confirmation candidates. They were allowed to come and see him uninvited, to play chess or take English lessons. Each received a present at Christmas. On weekends he took them on trips to youth hostels. Such exercises in community living were still unknown in ordinary German parishes.[8]

The aforesaid pastoral ministries were instrumental in the shaping of Dietrich Bonhoeffer's own vocation. Though brief in time, each experience served to cultivate both his skills and his attributes. It was his London residency, however, which constituted a marked leap further. Just as his native Germany was being introduced to the Nazi, Hitler-dominated era which would forever change the course of history, Bonhoeffer was called to London for the longest of his parish experiences. During his eighteen months in Britain's largest metropolis, he served two small German-speaking congregations, one in Sydenham, Forest Hill, the other in London's East End, St. Paul's. Both of these congregations were small in number, but they were otherwise quite different. About thirty to forty parishioners worshiped in the Sydenham congregation, a parish of the United Church. Many of the congregants were prosperous merchants, and a few were German diplomats. St. Paul's was connected with the Reformed Church, having a background of over two centuries. About fifty worshipped there each Sunday, comprised primarily of tradespeople. Bonhoeffer proved to be an energetic and faithful pastor, introducing children's services, youth clubs, Nativity and Passion plays, financial assistance for German refugees, and a revival hymnal.

The months in London sharpened Bonhoeffer's perspective on the developing church struggle in his homeland. Far from abandoning his involvement with the churches there, he stayed in touch with Pastor Martin Niemöller and other trusted leaders, as well as mobilizing the German pastors of the London area toward an anti-Nazi stand. He saw the church struggle as a watershed for all the congregations in Germany, ultimately asserting that Christianity and Nazism were forever incompatible. He saw, too, the importance of the fledgling ecumenical movement, anchored in a close relationship with Bishop George Bell of Chichester. He constantly urged a solid theological warning that compromise and appeasement of Nazi ideology would destroy Christ's kingdom and his people.[9]

The London pastorates came to a conclusion in 1935 when Bonhoeffer received a call back to Germany to serve the Confessing Church, which had come into being the previous year at the famous

Barmen Conference. He then became the director of one of the five Confessing Church seminaries, situated first in Zingst, near the Baltic Sea, and then in Finkenwalde, the first station on the main railway line from Stettin to the east. He became the pastoral shepherd to about twenty-five candidates for ministry in the Confessing Church. In his own vision of what this preparation school might become, he saw beyond the disciplines of theology, church history, Biblical studies, homiletics, and pastoral care to a place of brotherly help and fellowship. He yearned for a well-ordered, well-regulated common life, a common obedience to the commandments, deepest inward concentration for service outward, and prayer, meditation, study of Scripture, brotherly discussion, and open confession.

One of his students, Wolf-Dieter Zimmermann, was to write about this experience years later:

> Each Saturday evening Bonhoeffer addressed us, as a pastor, guiding us to live in brotherhood, and working out what had been experienced during the last week, and what had gone wrong. Thus we gradually grasped that this experiment in life together was a serious matter. And gradually we became ready to fall in with him and to do with zest what were asked to do.[10]

It was during these Finkenwalde days that Bonhoeffer articulated many of his keenest and sharpest insights for the church s ministry: the importance of discipleship in the life of the Christian and in the life of the church; the affirmation of Jesus Christ as the living center of the Christian faith;

1. the importance of preaching;
2. the utter necessity of a disciplined daily life of prayer;
3. meditation, intercession, and exposure to scripture;
4. the emphasis on care for the sick, the elderly, the troubled, the outcast, the dying, and the grieving;
5. the faithful celebration of worship and the sacraments;
6. the sincere practice of confession;
7. the active quest for justice and peace.

All of these pastoral concerns were an integral part of shaping a vocation for life. Bonhoeffer himself served as a flesh-and-blood model for his students, as well as for the pastors already active in parish ministry.[11]

When the Gestapo finally closed the doors to the Finkenwalde school in 1937, a new phase of pastoral training evolved, the collective pastorates, primarily in eastern Pomerania. Bonhoeffer's ordinands were now cast in the role of apprentice vicar, continuing to study and matriculate under the most trying of circumstances. In March of 1940, all the ordinands were conscripted into the army, thereby bringing to an abrupt conclusion this creative and resourceful experience in theological education.[12]

Bonhoeffer's own ministry continued, however, especially through the circular letters that he wrote regularly to his students. Most of them were now living in harsh conditions in the military, many in the midst of combat, suffering, and death. He reminded them of their ongoing vocation no matter where they were: "certainly none of us is ever released from the responsibility of being a Christian and no one may deny that he [or she] is a pastor." [13]

Parish Ministry and Service Today: Echoes of Bonhoeffer

The life and legacy of Dietrich Bonhoeffer, his writings and his martyrdom do not constitute the only pattern and model for contemporary church ministry. There are many other voices of the twentieth century that deserve to be heard as we continue to shape the vocation of the ministry for this new century. His voice is one to be heeded, however, because of the challenges and insights that permeated his own perceptions and conceptions of ministry. Frederick R. Trost, early in his own ministry, recognized in the writings of both Karl Barth and Dietrich Bonhoeffer, and in the struggles of the church living during the Nazi years, guideposts for authentic Christian living and faithful church ministry.

It was in his congregation of St. Pauls on Fullerton Avenue in Chicago in the early 1970s that a Bonhoeffer Festival was celebrated. The keynoter that day was Professor Paul Lehmann of Union Theological Seminary in New York, who had been one of Bonhoeffer's most intimate and trusted American friends. My own friendship with Lehmann began that day and continued until his recent death. One unforgettable moment for me was his accompanying me to the docks in New York harbor and pointing out the spot where he bade Bonhoeffer farewell in 1939, never to see him again in this life.

For many of the nineteen years of Frederick Trost's Conference ministry I have been privileged to receive the Confessing Christ newsletter which carries the byline, "Encouraging Serious and Joyful Theological Reflection in the Church Today." It is instructive to note how frequently quotations from Barth and Bonhoeffer, as well as the Barmen

Declaration, appear. It is noteworthy as well that the title of this group's occasional papers has been *Life Together,* reflective of one of Bonhoeffer's most inspirational writings.

On February 4, 2000, Pastor Trost wrote me an invitational letter on Bonhoeffer's birthday, which I shall always retain in my files, along with the newsletter and the occasional papers:

> I have been thinking of you today for several reasons, including the birthday of Dietrich Bonhoeffer. For your devotion to teaching and interpreting his theology over many years, I remain very, very grateful. In my pastoral ministry of nearly forty years, Karl Barth and Dietrich Bonhoeffer (among the contemporary theologians) have helped me the most in coming to understand the nature of the church and its witness and in the attempt to craft sermons. To return to them again and again is like dipping into a deep well of fresh water![14]

It is both a pleasure and a privilege to salute Frederick R. Trost. In both parish and Conference ministry he has worthily exemplified the vocation of the pastor. His pastoral skills and pastoral attributes are indeed echoes of those portrayed by such twentieth century notables as Dietrich Bonhoeffer. He has indisputably rendered yeoman's service in the ongoing cause of Christ.

Notes

1. In July, 1998 Queen Elizabeth II of England unveiled the sculptures of ten twentieth-century martyrs, representing the thousands of Christians whose personal lives were sacrificed in witness to their faith. In addition to Dietrich Bonhoeffer, those included are: Grand Duchess Elizabeth of Russia, Esther John of Pakistan, Martin Luther King Jr., of the United States, Maximilian Kolbe of Poland, Manche Masemoia of South Africa, Janani Luwum of Uganda, Oscar Romero of El Salvador, Lucian Tapieda of New Guinea, and Wang Zhiming of China.

2. For a succinct description of this involvement in the resistance, see Geffrey B. Kelly and F. Burton Nelson, *A Testament to Freedom: The Essential Writings of Dietrich Bonhoeffer* (San Francisco: Harper, 1995) 35-38, under the heading "A Double Agent."

3. See *A Testament of Freedom,* Appendix 2, The Dietrich Bonhoeffer Works Translation Project, 527-529. The project is scheduled to be completed by 2005.

4. Eberhard Bethge, *Dietrich Bonhoeffer: A Biography,* rev. and ed. Victoria J. Barnett (Minneapolis: Fortress Press, 2000). This monumental

version of the classic biography appeared just a few weeks prior to Bethge's death in March 2000.

5. Ibid., "The Decision to Become a Theologian," 34-44.

6. For further accounts of Bonhoeffer's Barcelona ministry, see Eberhard Bethge, *Dietrich Bonhoeffer,* 97-120 and *A Testament to Freedom,* 7-8, 47-48.

7. See Bethge, *Dietrich Bonhoeffer,* 147-166, and *Testament to Freedom,* 9-12, 33-35, 382.

8. Bethge, *Dietrich Bonhoeffer,* 226-227.

9. Bethge's *Dietrich Bonhoeffer* offers a comprehensive description of Bonhoeffer's major pastoral experience in London, 325-417. See also *A Testament to Freedom,* 19-20, 217-252.

10. From Wolf-Dieter Zimmermann and Ronald Gregor Smith, eds., *I Knew Dietrich Bonhoeffer: Reminiscences by His Friends* (New York: Harper and Row, 1966). Pastor Zimmermann is still alive and well, residing in Berlin. On December 6, 1984, he was a guest of the Wisconsin Conference of the UCC in Madison, where he spoke on "Barmen."

11. The first volume to be published in the English edition of the Dietrich Bonhoeffer Works, *Life Together* and *Prayerbook of the Bible,* reflects this significant collection of concerns. It is edited by Geffrey B. Kelly, translated from the German edition by Daniel W. Bloesch and James H. Burtness.

12. Eberhard Bethge's *Dietrich Bonhoeffer* describes the workings of these collective pastorates in detail, 587-596. See also Jane Pejsa, *Mission to Pomerania: Where Bonhoeffer Met the Holocaust: A History and Traveler's Journal* (Minneapolis: Kenwood Publishing, 2000).

13. *Testament to Freedom,* 434-459.

14. I did accept the kind invitation and presented a five-hour seminar on 5 May 2000 at the Wisconsin Conference UCC Center, using the theme "The Legacy of Dietrich Bonhoeffer for Parish Ministry in the Twenty-First Century."

"You Have Called Us, O Lord"

You have called us, O Lord
    and we have responded with gratitude and joy
        for the opportunity to serve in the vocation of
            Pastor-Teacher-Servant Leader.

We give you thanks
    for the challenges and opportunities,
        privileges and struggles,
            brokenness and healing,
                that come with our sacred calling.

We give you thanks, too,
    for the gifts bestowed
        through the inspiration of your Holy Spirit
            that make our ministry in your name possible.

For relationships that grow into genuine friendships,
    authenticity that risks honest expression
        and vulnerability that enhances genuine community,
            we give you thanks.

For faith that develops into a deeper sense of your presence and mystery,
    for hope that undergirds our convictions,
        and love which compels us to welcome strangers and pray for enemies,
            we give you thanks.

Grant all who serve as ambassadors of your gospel
    a deep appreciation of your grace;
        a joyful, playful, transforming grace
            that motivates as it empowers,
                judges as it forgives,
                    convicts as it comforts and heals.

Grant us a faith that will be up to the challenges of discipleship in these often
perplexing and radically changing days.
    A faith rooted in wonder not rigidity,
        trust not control, boldness not timidity.
        A faith willing to take risks for the sake of the gospel.

Deliver those entrusted with the audacity of proclaiming the gospel
    from the complacency that would masquerade in
        timid sermons, pretty liturgies
        and cozy fellowship.

Forgive too the spiritual arrogance
    that basks in the delusion that it is ultimately up to us to
        fix this person,
            this world,
                or even ourselves.

Freed from such self-delusion and complacency,
            we pray for the courage of our convictions to serve You
                in this particular time and place
                in which we have been called.

When the journey gets too difficult,
    when our energies become depleted,
        when despair begins to crowd out hope,
            remind and restore us by your love that will not let us go.

You have called us, O Holy One,
    and so we ask that You consecrate and utilize our gifts,
        be they naturally endowed or spirit-induced,
            for the extension of your reign of love, justice,
                compassion, and truth.

Douglas M. Pierce

A Reformed View of the Servant Leader

William H. Rader

"What we need is leadership!" A white-haired member of the pulpit committee of an inner-city church looked pleadingly at the pastoral candidate. The committee had confessed that neither they nor anyone they knew had the answers that would enable the church to turn from its steep decline. They hoped for a pastor with vision who would lead them out of the wilderness of declining membership, financial deficit, and burnt-out lay leadership into the promised land of church growth, financial stability, and fruitfulness.

Not only inner-city churches call for leadership; the call is widespread throughout the church, and in society at large. One influential response is that made by Robert Greenleaf, an official of a large corporation. In the 1970s, Greenleaf developed the concept of servant leadership, for which he finds support in the New Testament. Greenleaf's thinking has gained considerable attention from pastors and pastoral theologians.[1] In my own attempts to understand my vocation as pastor, the image of servant leader has played an important role. My question has been "How can I grow as a servant leader?"

While on this quest, I came upon some unexpected warning signs. Donald Messer points to dangers inherent in the paradox of servant leader: Congregations want both gentle care and aggressive direction.[2] The strongest warning is raised by Edward Zaragoza who recounts critiques of the concept of servanthood by women theologians who claim that the use of the term "servant" perpetuates the oppression of women. Servant is the role women have been expected, even forced to take. To use this term for the pastor's vocation is to ignore certain justice issues and support an obstacle to the struggle for liberation.[3]

The term "servant leader" is really no better than "servant" alone, as Zaragoza sees it. Carefully analyzing the material which Greenleaf takes from the New Testament in developing his servant-leader paradigm, Zaragoza finds a theology considerably at odds with Christian teaching. This theology is individualistic, and results in an "operative ecclesiology that has ministry reside chiefly in the pastor, rather than in the church as a whole." Also, the strong goal orientation of the servant-leader idea emphasizes works, such as completing tasks and having the right answers. The trouble is that in the servant-leadership mold, good works take precedence over faith, results over relationship, function over love.[4]

Although I find the work of Zaragoza, as well as his forerunners Susan Dunfee, Jacquelyn Grant, and Ada Isasi-Diaz provocative contributions to the servant-leader controversy,[5] I want to offer a response by shifting the focus of the servant image. My alternative, a product of the Reformation, is still used as a title for pastors in Switzerland: The vocation of the pastor is to be a servant of the divine word, *verbi divini* minister.

One advantage of the term "servant of the divine word" is fairly obvious. The servanthood it speaks of is not on the level of interpersonal or intergroup relations, where the concerns of Zaragoza and those for whom he speaks are lodged.[6] Objections come immediately to mind, however. Isn't the term "servant of the divine word" too impersonal, too removed from the pastor's work with human beings? *Verbi divini* minister may evoke images of a scholarly recluse, who slaves over the scriptures, wrestling with biblical commentaries, but avoiding the contemporary world.

Despite the dangers, I find the term *verbi divini* minister promising. Far from being narrow, it opens up wide vistas. The divine word is not bound to the pages of the Bible. But neither is it independent from the Bible. The Word has become flesh, but it has not stopped being the word. In one way my study of scripture is like the polishing of the lens through which I look at life: my own, that of members of my parish, of the congregation as a whole, and of the wider community. In another way, scripture is the prime means by which nourishment comes to me as a servant of the word. For as Zwingli says, "The shepherd dare not lead his sheep to any pasture that he himself has not been nourished in. . . . He must listen to the word of the Good Shepherd, trust and follow him . . . be led to grazing and nourishing by him, the Word which he would proclaim to others."[7] What happens when I as a pastor listen for the divine word?

Part of my service of the divine word is to listen for the word in people's lives. A member who has been active in our inner-city congregation all her life is now in her mature years wondering how much her activity has really done for sharing God's word. Margy has a genuine yearning to talk with others about faith. Near the close of a Sunday School lesson on Matthew 28:16-20—"Go therefore and make disciples"—Margy said, "I don't feel I'm really doing that." Others in the class agreed they weren't either. I suggested that we pray each day during the week asking God to give us an opportunity to follow the Great Commission. We were to take notes in our journals and share about it next Sunday. In the sharing time, Margy told about an airplane trip she had taken. She said to the woman in the next seat. "Isn't it wonderful that God has given us the knowledge and abilities to build a wonderful machine like this!"

In contrast to Margy's approach, mine had been quite negative. In a waiting room with the television blaring, I had assumed that being a witness would mean speaking to people who don't care at all or who are even antagonistic. But listening to Margy reminded me that the divine word is already at work in the lives of the persons I meet. I'm sure the divine word is at work in Margy, and the word came through to me afresh as I listened to her struggles to be a witness for Christ.

My reflections on praxis seem to be corroborated by literature on pastoral care. More and more, pastoral theology is exploring the conviction that the study of the documents of scripture and the study of the living human document have many parallels and connections. One pastoral theologian venturing in this direction, Donald Capps, states:

> Technically, hermeneutics is concerned with interpretation of texts. Yet, in recent years, the principles of hermeneutics have been applied to phenomena other than texts, and there have been proposals for applying hermeneutics to the sphere of human action. . . . There is every reason to believe that this idea will be equally useful for interpreting pastoral actions such as those that fall under the general heading of pastoral care.[8]

Principles of hermeneutics can be applied not only to individuals, but to the congregation as a whole. In a recent work on preaching, Leonore Tubbs Tisdale entitles a chapter in her book "Exegeting the Congregation."[9]

Discerning the divine word in the congregation is an essential part of leading the congregation, as John McClure brings out in *The Round-Table Pulpit: Where Leadership and Preaching Meet.*[10] While the term "servant of the divine word" says nothing explicitly about leadership, it includes leadership, for the Word leads. The servant of the divine word takes very seriously the conviction that the Word made flesh is our leader. Jesus Christ is the head of the church, and the one whom we follow. Furthermore, a key strategy for leadership is to ask good questions. The servant of the divine word will aim to be so steeped in the biblical word and so attentive to the word in the life of the congregation that she will be able to ask questions that will lead the congregation to greater self-awareness and faithfulness. Participants in Bible study will be encouraged to ask: "What do we hear in this passage about what God wants for our church and our neighborhood?"

The neighborhood around the church is also an arena where the pastor serves the divine word. I will never forget the neighborhood around the first church I served out of seminary; it was First Reformed Church, in the inner-city of Cincinnati. For the first six months I kept asking, "How can there be a place like this, with its racial tension, hostility, and violence? How can people live in such poor, crowded, dirty conditions? How can God let this go on? Where is God?" The questions were driving me to despair, and I wondered if I could stay. Then one afternoon, in the shadowy narrow passage between two tenement buildings, I saw a figure. I was sure it was the figure of Jesus. Perhaps I was superimposing on that passageway a memory of a painting I had once seen, but the experience was very real for me. The eyes of my heart were enlightened (Eph 1:18). My questions were answered: God was not far off, but suffering the ongoing squalor and poverty; God was here, in the midst of it all. The Word became flesh and dwelt among us, full of grace and truth, even in the ghetto. In Jesus Christ, God has come and shares in the suffering. The divine word is here, present and active even in the worst conditions. In this conviction I stayed and served.

As well as being attentive to the divine word in the congregation and in the world around the church, the pastor will listen for the word within the pastor's own soul. The need to do this was powerfully brought home to me in a crisis near the end of my official ministry there. Despite prayer, study of scripture, and use of all the help we could find, our inner-city church had not seen a turn from its decline. There were some good signs, but mostly they seemed too little and too late. My questions were "How can things go on like this? Why does God not answer our prayers? Where is God?" These questions came to apply not just to the church and its neighborhood, but to myself. I became hopeless and believed there was no way left. From my youth I had felt God calling me to work for racial justice and understanding in the inner city. Now here I had been given an opportunity to do some significant work, and I had failed. I felt that my whole ministry was a failure. I was filled with guilt and regret. The ghetto was now in my heart.

I received help from many servants of the word: a spiritual counselor, a psychiatrist, friends, and a loving wife. In retreats, both individual and group, in peer groups, in silence and in reflective Bible reading, I was gradually given healing for my own soul. As a pastor in need of a great deal of pastoral care, the eyes of my heart were enlightened. At last I saw that God was here too—here in the ghetto of my heart. In Jesus Christ, God was sharing the pain and guilt and burden of sin. The word is at work in my heart. The word is also at work in the hearts of others whom my life has touched. Whatever the fate of this particular church, what is done for Christ will last. Coming to know this more deeply than ever before, I have been made whole again in Christ.

By putting the emphasis on faithfulness rather than on success, the concept of servant of the divine word has been very helpful to me. The literature often gives the impression that if a pastor is truly a servant leader, the people will follow. But often I did not have followers. That is, in crucial areas where I was convinced of directions in which I should lead the church, I was not followed. I agonized about this, continually asking, "In what ways have I not been a good enough servant leader?"

It certainly is important to examine oneself, and it often is the case that a pastor, certainly this pastor, has fallen short in many ways. But to accuse oneself continually leads to despair. The shortcomings may not always be the pastor's. In fact, James Dittes claims that ministry is grief work because instead of being followed by the members of one's congregation, the minister is often forsaken by them.

To be a minister . . . is to be forsaken regularly and utterly by those on whose partnership one most relies for identity, meaning, and selfhood, as these are lodged in the vocational commitment. In their forsaking ways the minister's call is rebuffed and repudiated and grieved for over and over and over again.[11]

Dittes aims to help the pastor deal with the grief that is a necessary part of the pastor's calling. He urges the pastor not to deny the limits and death in the partnership with the congregation, nor to deny that there was ever any real life there, but to work through the grief. This can be done in light of trust that what is ultimately important is not the achievement of visible results, but faithful service to the divine word.

Sometimes the gift is granted a pastor to see something of the fruit of service to the divine word. Not many months after I had been helped to work through my long-accumulated grief, I got a surprise phone call. It was from Bill, who had been a teenager when I was pastor in Cincinnati. Bill was one of the crowd of youth who had no families to speak of, had very limited horizons, and were often at risk of falling into alcoholism and crime. Like a number of other young people in the neighborhood, Bill had found a home in First Reformed Church. Now, after more than 40 years, and after First Reformed Church had closed its doors, Bill, who was traveling near our present home, wanted to spend some time with us. Until late into the night, Bill told about his wife, children, and grandchildren, about their life in the church they now belong to, and about other First Reformed youth, many of whom are still in the Cincinnati area and active in their churches. None of them is in jail. Above all, Bill spoke his thankfulness, and the thankfulness of the whole group, for what the church had done for them, for how they had been taught the love of Jesus in both word and deed. Bill remembered those who over the years had given themselves to be servants of this love as members of the church staff. What delighted my wife and me perhaps most of all in this wonderful cornucopia of blessing was that Bill is now a business partner at the same elementary school in the inner city that he attended as a child. He's serving it in all kinds of ways, meeting needs of this underprivileged school with generosity, creativity, and verve.

Sometimes the pastor is given to see that some of the seed she has sown has brought forth grain thirty, sixty, and a hundredfold. Then the pastor's soul sings the *Nunc Dimittis*. For the servant of the divine word has seen a sign of the fulfillment of God's promise:

So shall my word be that goes out from my mouth;
it shall not return to me empty,
but it shall accomplish that which I purpose,
and succeed in the thing for which I sent it (Isa 55: 11).

Notes

1. Robert K. Greenleaf, *Servant Leadership: A Journey into the Nature of Legitimate Power and Greatness* (New York: Paulist Press, 1977).

2. Donald E. Messer, *Contemporary Images of Christian Ministry* (Nashville: Abingdon Press, 1989), 103-106.

3. "Servant leadership enjoys center stage as the predominant paradigm for ordained ministry today." Edward C. Zaragoza, *No Longer Servants, but Friends: a Theology of Ordained Ministry* (Nashville, Abingdon, 1999), 12.

4. Zaragoza, *No Longer Servants,* 82.

5. Susan Nelson Dunfee, *Beyond Servanthood: Christianity and the Liberation of Women* (Lanham, Md.: University Press of America, 1989). Jacquelyn Grant, "The Sin of Servanthood and the Deliverance of Discipleship," *A Troubling in My Soul: Womanist Perspective on Evil and Suffering,* ed. Emilie M Townes (Maryknoll, N.Y.: Orbis Books, 1993), 199-218. Ada Maria Isasi-Diaz, "Un poquito de justicia—A Little Bit of Justice: a Mujerista Account of Justice," *Hispanic/Latino Theology:*

Challenge and Promise, ed. Ada Maria Isasi-Diaz and Fernando F. Segovia (Minneapolis: Fortress Press, 1996), 325-339.

6. Zaragoza's own theology of ordained ministry, which takes its cue from John 15:15, "I do not call you servants any longer . . . but I have called you friends," proposes a paradigm shift from servant leadership to friendship.

7. Zwingli, "Der Hirt," *Hauptschriften*, ed. F. Blanke, O. Farner, R. Pfister (Zurich: Theologischer Verlag, 1940), II , 260.

8. Donald Capps, *Pastoral Care and Hermeneutics* (Philadelphia: Fortress Press, 1984), 12. Another work in the same vein is Charles E. Winquist, *Practical Hermeneutics: a Revised Agenda for the Ministry* (Chico, Ca:. Scholars Press, 1980).

9. Leonore Tubbs Tisdale, *Preaching as Local Theology and Folk Art* (Minneapolis: Fortress Press, 1997), 56-90. Similar work has been done by Lucy Atkinson Rose, *Sharing the Word: Preaching in the Roundtable Church* (Louisville: Westminster/John Knox Press, 1997).

10. John S. McClure, *The Roundtable Pulpit: Where Leadership and Preaching Meet* (Nashville: Abingdon Press, 1995).

11. James E. Dittes, *Re-Calling Ministry* (St. Louis: Chalice Press, 1999), 15.

Pastors in the Chain of Trust

Rembert G. Weakland

Being called to be a pastor can be intimidating. Few vocations exist today where the one called is expected, by reason of the calling itself, to be so totally God-like. In its biblical context the vocation to be a pastor means to bring to one's ministry those qualities that God manifested toward the people in the Old Covenant and the qualities Jesus claimed for himself toward all humanity in the New Covenant. A pastor, by etymology and content, is called to be a shepherd, in the same way that God in the Old Covenant and Jesus in the New show us how to be shepherds. To have God and Jesus as such direct biblical models for a calling places significant demands on the one responding to the call. No wonder such a calling causes one to be anxious and fearful. How can anyone ever measure up? The only optic that permits one to say yes to being a pastor is total reliance on God. One must accept the role with deep humility, conscious of being a broken vessel, a fallible instrument, an inadequate substitute. One must realize that God, as the loving Father, and God's Son Jesus Christ remain the good shepherds; all other human persons are but imperfect, broken instruments through which God alone shepherds. The great miracle is that Jesus Christ chose to carry on his pastoring mission in the church through human persons with all their foibles and imperfections.

The Pastor in Scripture

In the Old Covenant we hear the psalmist pray: "The Lord is my shepherd, I shall not want" (Ps 23). With God as shepherd, there is no need to fear. The same shepherd has special concern for the weakest among his people: "He will feed his flock like a shepherd; he will gather the lambs in his arms, and carry them in his bosom, and gently lead the mother sheep" (Isa 40:11). After the prophet Ezekiel pointed out the existence of false shepherds among God's people, he reminded the chosen people that God would claim his sheep and save them. No need to fear. God will look after the sheep, guard them, rescue them, lead them, pasture them, and bring them to rest: "I will seek the lost, and I will bring back the strayed, and I will bind up the injured, and I will strengthen the weak, but the fat and the strong I will destroy. I will feed them with justice" (Ezek 34:16). But God will also separate the bad from the good. God is very aware of the bad shepherds who seek only personal gain. Finally, God promised to appoint one shepherd: "I will set up over them one shepherd, my servant David, and he shall feed them: he shall feed them and be their shepherd" (34:23).

Thus, God promised to appoint shepherds with this same love and concern that he has shown his people and spoke of the "righteous branch of David" as the fulfillment of the promise that there would be God-like shepherds among the chosen people. Jeremiah repeats this same prophecy (23:4-5).

Jesus was aware that he was the long awaited Good Shepherd. He talked of seeking out the lost sheep, setting that lost one on his shoulders, and, with joy, bringing it back to the flock (Mt 18:10-14; Lk 15:4-7). But the lengthy exposition of this image and the way Jesus claimed it for himself is found in the Gospel of John 10:1-16. Here Jesus is the gate through which the sheep pass. He it is who calls each by name; he walks ahead and they follow. But he goes further when he talks about the contrast between himself and the evil shepherds by saying he would lay down his life for his sheep. He also seeks to have but one flock and one shepherd. No other passages are so effective in pointing out the nature of Jesus' ministry as those where he describes himself as the Good Shepherd.

When we Christians call someone a pastor, this history of the concept of the Good Shepherd in its totality comes to mind. The lineage has two mirrors against which one must measure himself or herself: God's providence and care for the chosen people of old and Jesus' qualities of love and concern that permitted him to even lay down his life for his sheep. How moving and surprising it is then when Jesus in John 21:15-17 tells Peter to feed his lambs and his sheep. This God-like task is passed on to frail, human persons. What trust Jesus had in the human person whom he had created, knowing as he did all their sinfulness and weakness! Peter, in turn, realizing the awesome mission he has received from the Lord, passes it on to the presbyters of his day: "Now as an elder myself (*sympresbyteros*) and a witness of the sufferings of Christ, as well as one who shares in the glory to be revealed, I exhort the elders (*presbyterous*) among you to tend the flock of God that is in your charge, exercising the oversight, not under compulsion but willingly, as God would have you do it—not for sordid gain but eagerly. Do not lord it over those in your charge, but be examples to the flock. And when the chief shepherd appears, you will win the crown of glory that never fades away" (1 Pet 5:1-4). Knowing his own weakness and the weakness of all the ministers in the church, Peter still realized it was the Lord's wish that Jesus' pastoring role continue on through history through fallible, broken human beings.

The Good Shepherd in Today's Context

Thus, a pastor today is not a glorified business manager of a large corporation but a Christ-like figure for others. Those who share Christ's ministry must fear falling into the attitudes or role-models our contemporary society offers us. Instead, the gospel attitudes for the pastor today, to be authentic and related to the ministry of Jesus Christ, must be of a different sort, related more to the spiritual well-being of those entrusted to one's pastoring care. Since each person in the "flock" is unique and has specific needs, the approach to each one must be different. Moreover, each brings special gifts and graces to build up the community. The pastor walks with each one, helping to discern how each can bring his or her gift to serve the community of faith and the world. But the image of the false shepherds should also not be forgotten. They still abound and the pastor must be on guard lest charlatans invade the flock with easy, cheap promises of salvation that are nothing but distortions of the gospel message, of the cross, and of the final judgment.

Many today, however, do not resonate with the image of the Good Shepherd. Our people, because of our urban culture, think the image of the Good Shepherd is a quaint one and of no significance to today's faithful. Few people have ever come directly in contact with shepherds and the details of their lives. Commentators can tell us much about the life of shepherds in Palestine before and at the time of Christ, but the image of the Good Shepherd remains either very vague and romantic or totally foreign to our experience. (For contemporary teens I have often used instead the image of the lifeguard as more familiar to them, but every image substituted for a biblical image limps.)

Moreover, most people today do not appreciate being called sheep. Sheep are known to be weak, defenseless, vulnerable, dependent, and helpless creatures. No one wants to see the disciples of Christ characterized by this image. Its deficiency lies in the fact that there is no growth principle within it. There is no moment when sheep cease to be sheep and acquire the qualities associated with fully mature Christian personalities. Yet the image of the shepherd and the sheep is excellent for pointing out our inability on our own to work out our salvation and our utter dependency on God.

Perhaps an image more appropriate for our day that would complement the one of the shepherd and the sheep is that of the teacher. Our logic must follow these steps. Every baptized person, by reason of accepting to be a follower of Christ, must become more and more like Christ. If Christ is the Good Shepherd, then all Christians are called to participate in this pastoring aspect of Christ's role and mission. Every Christian is called to be a Good Shepherd, like Christ, and fight against the "Cain syndrome" within us. We are not isolated atoms but are responsible one for another. We are all "pastors" and must be open to being pastored by others simultaneously.

If this is true, and I believe it is, then the designated pastor's role is to train other pastors, to look upon all those entrusted to his or her care as other pastors whose full pastoring potential is yet to be realized. In this respect he or she is like a teacher who rejoices as students become independent of the teacher and move out to learn by experience what was taught to them and then, in turn, to teach others. The success of a teacher is to create independent students who can contribute to the world on their own initiative. A good pastor, thus, sees his or her task as developing the pastoring talents of others, bringing out what is best within them, and rejoicing in their independence and co-pastoring roles. Perhaps one could say it is like the lifeguard who sees his or her role, not just as saving people or preventing harm from coming to them, but as one who teaches others to swim and to look after each other.

If the image of the shepherd and sheep is a bit distasteful to us, it is because we fail to see that pastors are called upon to help all the baptized realize their vocation as shepherds, sharing in the pastoring ministry of Jesus Christ.

Pastoring and Confirming Faith

There is a tendency in American culture to see the role of pastor as the one to initiate programs, as the one responsible for finding answers and solutions to every problem and challenge the community or individual must face. Our American Pelagian culture feels there is no problem for which we cannot devise an adequate program. Pastors attend many workshops to find new programs in the hope of stimulating the interest of the flock in what discipleship is all about. At least in the tradition I come from, the pastor is also expected to have the correct answer to every theological question that arises.

The role of the pastor is not to have all the answers, whether on the level of existential reality or on the level of programmatic change. It is not even his or her task to have all the theological insights and knowledge that will explain away or diminish the difficulties encountered in today's contemporary world. But it is the task of the pastor to confirm the people in their faith and in their baptismal faith commitment. Sometimes this is best done, not by giving solutions, but simply by praying together, by placing the difficult situation in God's hands, by having more trust in God. Jesus told Peter that he would pray for him that his faith not fail and that, once truly converted, he could then strengthen in faith the others: "Simon,

Simon, listen! Satan has demanded to sift all of you like wheat. But I have prayed for you that your own faith may not fail, and you, when once you have turned back, strengthen your brothers" (Lk 22:31-32). Jesus did not provide a program for his disciples to prepare them for his suffering and death. He prayed for them. The pastoring role that has been passed on to leaders in the Christian community is, above everything else, one of strengthening people in their faith.

Many pastors today fall into the temptation of thinking they must be therapists trained in all the clinical arts and skills of psychology. Although such skills may help, the task of the pastor is exercised on a different level—that of faith. Giving easy answers and ready solutions on a psychological, material, social, or even theological level is not what the task of the pastor is all about. In many ways the pastor's role begins and even becomes most significant when easy solutions fail or are found wanting and unacceptable. It is then that one must fall back on faith and trust in a loving God. How God in love deals with us is such a mysterious and marvelous reality that the pastor will never exhaust probing its depths. Faith-solutions cannot be substituted for psychological or material ones as therapeutic cures, but they go beyond the physical healing to another kind of level of inner peace that comes only with trust in God's providence and an unshakeable faith in God's goodness. The pastor, as much by example and prayer as by word, lays the ground for such faith; God's unceasing love does the rest.

The vocation or calling to be a pastor works itself out, then, primarily on the level of faith. As the pastor confirms others in the faith, they, too, are made capable of confirming others in the faith, and so the chain of trust grows and expands. The pastor's role is like the stone thrown into the sea, where the rippling effect cannot be and should not be measured. Over and over again, the pastor is reminded that, in the end, it is God who does it all and is pastoring through us, and, at times, in spite of us.

In Earthen Vessels

Donald G. Nelson

We have this treasure in earthen vessels, to show that the transcendent power belongs to God and not to us. We are afflicted in every Way but not crushed: perplexed. but not driven to despair; persecuted, but not forsaken; struck down, but not destroyed (2 Corinthians 4:7-9).

My first church was a small American Baptist church on Madison's east side. My calling to pastoral ministry occurred in my teen years at Morgan Park Baptist Church in Chicago. I went to college and then to seminary, graduating from the University of Chicago Divinity School in 1962. I was called/appointed to Glendale Community Baptist Church in Madison, Wisconsin, that same year. We moved into the parsonage with high expectations. I was twenty-six years old.

I began my ministry by starting a Bible study group, which seemed like a sensible thing to do. Seven came to the first meeting in our home, including John, who carried a large King James Bible with index tabs, it showed signs of vigorous use. John was not happy with my appointment as pastor. He knew the University of Chicago was a liberal institution. The study group soon became an inquisition. John peppered me with questions to test my orthodoxy. Caught off guard. my answers were feeble and tentative. I tried to regain control, but I had scant training in group dynamics. I had planned to study scripture. Instead I was studied. Despite the serving of sweet cookies, the evening ended on a sour note. I began to understand in lily gut Paul's "earthen vessels" analogy.

A pleasant younger woman did not come back for our second and third meetings. I assumed that she had been alienated by the rancor of the first session. I finally found the courage to talk to her face to face. To my great surprise. she told me that she had come to see how we had furnished tile house and having observed the decor, her need was satisfied. I commended her for her honesty.

These experiences brought my soaring expectations to a forced landing. It became clear to me that pastoral ministry would involve a healthy dose of crisis, wounding, and struggle. I began to understand Paul's relationship with that flock of dysfunctional Christians at Corinth. Ministry must involve acceptance of people as they are while holding tight to a vision of what they might become in God's love and grace. What was more difficult was accepting myself without losing hope for what I might become in the providence of God. Acceptance and change became the two poles of my calling, both for myself and the people I served.

Many words may be used to describe the varied work of the pastor: shepherd, leader, counselor, friend, administrator, teacher, learner, healer, role model, preacher, fund raiser, prophet, priest, conflict manager, disturber of the peace. The vocation is impossible on its face, yet God has used the clay pots of pastors' lives to bring some good into the world.

In the same person, the pastor is both human and created in the image of God. Because a pastor is human, he or she knows struggle, anxiety, and weakness. In her or his relation to God, peace and purposefulness are experienced. As St. Paul said, we are clay pots containing a great treasure, pointing beyond ourselves to the glory and power of God. Our prayer is that we might be a door or a window, and not a brick wall. Sometimes, by the grace of God, that prayer is answered.

Our humanness can disturb some people. When a pastor's shortcomings are revealed, shock, disappointment, and anger can result. But weakness dealt with honestly can also endear and connect the pastor with others. It is terribly hard to live with perfection. When a pastor fails, some will feel compassion, particularly those who also have stumbled. It is a freeing experience for a pastor to say: "I was wrong. I apologize. With God's help, I will do better."

A high-school student in my confirmation class once affirmed me in an interesting way. "Pastor, don't take this the wrong way, but I am almost glad that you are divorced. It makes you more human and real." Her words came to me during a crisis of self-worth. What to me was a disaster, to her was an opportunity.

Of course, pastors are called to a high standard. They must be careful not to abuse their position or take lightly the claims of Christ. They must strive to love God and others on a daily basis. But, God help us if we secretly think that sin is largely confined to folks in the pew, since "all have sinned and fall short of the glory of God" (Rom 3:23). What unites pastor and people is a common human experience as sinners and a common human experience as recipients of God's amazing grace.

In an age of specialists, the pastor remains a generalist. In a time when people are subdivided into narrow classifications, the pastor embraces all of human experience—the good, the bad, and the indifferent. She or he may feel inferior to the brain surgeon, the carpenter, or the electrical engineer. The pastor may envy those who are super competent in a given field. Yet in an increasingly fragmented world, the pastor performs a vital function. He or she reminds people that human need and human struggle change little over the span of recorded history.

A love letter written on papyrus in 1000 B.C.E. in Egypt expressed the same longing and emotion as a letter written in the 21st century. Years ago in the sixties, I read some words of the Greek philosopher Socrates to my congregation, without identifying the source. Socrates was bitterly complaining about the youth of his day and their disrespect for parents and contempt for virtue. I then asked my congregation to identify the writer. Several hands shot up. Everyone knew who said those critical words about young people: Spiro Agnew, the Vice-president of the United States in the Nixon administration! A vital pastoral role is that of making connections and affirming the fundamental unity of all people in every age and in every culture. Yes, change is everywhere. But the human heart still beats with eternal rhythms.

Most pastors are perfectionists. In my second church in Beaver Dam, Wisconsin, a trusted member once said to me: "Don, you are such a perfectionist!" I was shocked. I denied it. But later that day in honest self-reflection, I pled guilty to the charge. Most pastors are perfectionists. It is only with great difficulty that we can affirm the beneficial role of failure in human experience. We find it hard to be clay pots. Yet, it is in failure and perplexity that we fully appreciate the love and grace of God.

My home church in Chicago was graced by a large oil mural of Jesus as the Good Shepherd. The mural towered over the central choir loft and the central pulpit. It portrayed Jesus with staff in one hand and a distressed sheep in his arm. Behind him followed a flock of sheep. The painting was pure perfection, except for the left foot of Jesus. It was almost a club foot, misshapen and swollen. Many in the congregation noticed this artistic failure. After a number of years, the deacons decided to hire a skilled artist to give Jesus a proper left foot. With great expectation the congregation awaited a properly fixed Jesus. When the great day arrived, the foot was barely changed and did not match the right foot. We adjusted and finally came to love our Shepherd Jesus with the bad left foot.

The church of Jesus the Christ often has a bad left foot. We are called to serve and love this church, remembering always that "We have this treasure in earthen vessels, to show that the transcendent power belongs to God and not to us" (2 Cor 4:7).

The calling of the pastor is a very high calling, for it consists in preparing the soil of life so that God might take root in the daily experiences of the pastor and the parishioners. The energy and life force for the growth of gospel seed is in God's hands. But we as pastors are invited to spade the garden, prepare the soil, and water the tender shoots of faith as they emerge. There is mystery in church life. Sometimes, we do everything right and our expectations for great success soar, only to discover that the perfect plan left out the work of the Holy Spirit. At other times, our bumbling efforts result in change and growth. I prepare a great sermon. I have no doubt that it will make a significant impact on Sunday morning. The auspicious Sunday arrives and the sermon goes into cardiac arrest. God surprises me. On another Sunday, I enter the sanctuary with acute anxiety. The sermon seems to me like dust. My mouth is dry with worry. Amazingly, this message serves God and touches hearts. The surprising God is always working with us, humbling us in our arrogance and lifting us out of our discouragement. God is not finished with you or with me. We are works in progress.

The demands of pastoral life can wear the pastor down. It is important for survival to renew energies, to take at least one day a week truly off with cell phone left on the kitchen table. Jesus alternated between time alone and honest engagement with people. It is a good model for all who would follow the Christ.

Insights I've needed have usually come to me through others. About twelve years ago, I attended one of the Development Groups for clergy in our Southwest Association. These valuable groups permit clergy to discuss the challenges of ministry in a confidential setting with colleagues. I was quite agitated that day over a crisis in my congregation. I was moaning and groaning about the incident. One of my fellow pastors turned to me with a steady gaze and said: "Congratulations on your crisis." I was stunned into silence. I was being congratulated for having a mess on my hands? I asked for an explanation. "Well, Don, a crisis can lead to change, so now you have an opportunity on your hands, for no significant change ever takes place without a crisis." Lightning struck. I had a vision. I went back to my church that afternoon seeing possibility. My gloom lifted. I thanked God for the wisdom and concern of my clergy friend. My attitude turned around that day and I was able to deal with the crisis in a more productive way. As pastors we need to stay healthy in heart, mind, and body. Sharing burdens with others is indispensable. We are designed for community.

Despite his bad press in our era, I love the apostle Paul. He possessed a passion to take the good news of Jesus to the Roman provinces. He faced incredible obstacles. His physical health was fragile.

He faced opposition from the Jewish community and from some in the Christian community who were skeptical about the reality of his conversion. He was chased out of town, jailed, beaten, and shipwrecked. In his Corinthian correspondence, Paul bares his soul, defends his ministry, and is open about his hurt and disappointment. The church problems in Corinth would push most of us to despair. But Paul's love for that church would not permit him to abandon them. Despite the problems, despite the neglect of Christian teaching, despite the quarreling factions, despite all he still regarded them as saints in Christ's church, redeemed and redeemable. As the "chief of sinners" Paul could relate to a fall from grace. Paul as pastor and teacher saw more than problems. He saw the people of God. Christ's love for them and his love for them would not permit him to turn away.

As pastors, we are called to love and serve a family of women and men, boys and girls, young and old. We are not called to be perfect but to do our best with the help of God. God invites us to speak the truth in love, to speak truth with words and actions. In failure, we ask for God's help. In success, we give God credit. All that happens to us and through us is grist for the mill of God. We are clay pots that hold the treasure of the gospel. God will use us for his glory. God will use our frailties and our failures. Not one of our experiences needs to be hidden or thrown away. God will use us as we are and help us to become what we need to be. May the God of all love and grace sustain us and renew us and make use of us.

The Minister as Servant of the Word

Mark E. Yurs

Pastoral ministry is in something of an identity crisis today. The surrounding culture is changing in ways that are well documented.[1] The culture of the church is changing too, pulling long-established certainties out from under the pastor and not yet offering anything to replace them.[2] Meanwhile, steady advances of secularism upon and within the church press the pastor to fulfill a role that members of the business community can readily understand if not manipulate and control. Further, increased entitlement thinking on the part of parishioners encroaches on what was once known as the authority of the pastoral office. Entitlement thinking would fashion the pastor according to a consumer agenda that is based on a demanding market and would expect the church s leader to produce, in timely fashion, a quality spiritual "product," convenient to enjoy and in accord with a host of subjective specifications.[3]

The seriousness of the new challenges ministers face today notwithstanding, it is my judgment that it is modern arrogance and heresy to believe our times are so radically different from other days that they demand unparalleled responses. My thinking is closer to that of Andrew W. Blackwood when he decided, "'the acids of modernity' are almost never new except in name."[4] Such a perspective helps us see that the more we attempt to fit the times, the more likely complications are to develop. It helps us notice we are better served if we keep to the demarcations of ministry as defined by the wisdom of the past. I am persuaded we will find our way through today's identity crisis by keeping to a truth that has honorably withstood a host of yesterdays. I refer to the thought that the minister is a servant of the Word.

The Minister Is a Servant of the Word.

To speak of the minister in this way is to delineate the pastor's primary allegiance and line of accountability. It is rather common, particularly in times of conflict between pastor and parish, to view the pastor as an employee of the church whose performance is under the direct supervision of the congregation or certain members of it. While it is true that the minister works in and through the church, it is not true that the minister acts at the whim of the church. As Charles E. Jefferson contended long ago, the pastor is a servant, to be sure, but not the drudge of every little despot that may come along, whether in the parish or the wider community.[5] First and foremost, the minister is a servant of the Word.

The Word whom the minister serves is Jesus. We recognize that Jesus is the living Lord and not a dead hero. This means the minister's primary task as a servant of the Word is not to safeguard a body of doctrine already spoken or oversee a cultus already developed and unchanging. To be sure, there are aspects of this in our work, but the primary task of our vocation is to witness to the living Christ who is still speaking and acting.

This living and active Word is at the heart of ministry. The Word is our authority and our effectiveness. We have nothing else to offer, nothing else upon which to stand. We are earthen vessels of this great treasure (2 Cor 4:7) and, if there be any effectiveness in us at all, it is as a result of this treasure working and speaking through us (2 Cor 3:4). To be a pastor is to be at the disposal of the Word of God so the purposes of God can be established insofar as God intends for them to be established in and through the life and ministry of the local church.

The Minister Is a Servant of the Word through Prayer.

Prayer stands at the forefront of the work of a minister because it is at the heart of every Christian life. Prayer is our primary means of relating to God. By grace, God initiates relationship with us and invites us to enjoy the blessings of being in relationship with God. The shape of this relationship is one of conversation, and the conversation is prayer.

While all Christians are called to pray, the pastor has a vocation to pray because the pastor ever stands at the meeting place between heaven and earth. Barbara Brown Taylor contends ministry began on and around Mt. Sinai. There God called Moses by name, engaging him in conversation on sacred ground. Later, the people, fearful of God, ask Moses to do their speaking and listening for them. They ask their leader to stand in their stead before the Lord (Ex 20:19).[6] Without pausing to trace ministry's roots to this text or to some other, it is plain to see how Moses models the pastoral vocation. The minister is one who, at times, often as preacher and as pastoral visitor, represents God to the people. By the same token, the minister is one who, just as often, represents the people to God. This happens when the pastor prays for the people, whether during the course of public worship, private conference, or personal devotion. In either case, prayer is the means of service. By way of prayer, we hear the word God would speak, and by way of prayer we speak the word our people would like God to hear.

It is true to say all ministry grows out of prayer and feeds back into prayer. Prayer is our chief means of loving the people of God, for by it we can lift them, one by one, to the throne of grace, where we can be confident they will receive everything they need from the only one who has both the will and the power to give what is best. Not only that, but prayer is our central contact with God whereby we surrender to the Lordship of Jesus Christ, listen for and learn the will of God for today, and begin to find both the courage to attempt and the power to accomplish what God would have us do. Just as the disciples learned of a kind of demon who could not be cast out except with prayer, so we who pastor soon discover there is much we cannot do unless we pray. Likewise, prayer keeps us going when we fail, for it is when our heads are bowed and our hearts are broken that the Lord speaks the word of forgiveness that alone is life for today and hope for tomorrow. So it is that the minister is a servant of the Word through prayer.

The Minister Is a Servant of the Word through Study.

Study is second only to prayer in pastoral life and work. Every Christian is called to love God with his or her mind. The pastor has a peculiar vocation to study. John Calvin's well known dictum is "none will ever be a good minister of the Word of God, unless he is first of all a scholar." [7] As far as this policy is concerned, there is little cause to amend the Genevan Reformer, save to allow for gender-inclusive language. Unless the pastor studies with depth, how can there be anything but shallowness in the pulpit?

The program of study the local pastor pursues is in place not simply for the purpose of gaining intellectual prowess or academic stature. Its function is to probe the frontier along which the church exists and where lives are lived. This edge between today and tomorrow is where God is active as the living Christ in the power of the Holy Spirit. By way of our study, all of which is to take place in a spirit of prayer, we can discern much about the activity of God today. This makes concentrated study fundamental to our witness as pastors.

Chief in our studies is the study of scripture. We pour over the Bible, not to find a sermon, but to see our Master. Blackwood, like Calvin, wrote in days before the church was sensitive to the need for gender-inclusive language. If we forgive him for being a product of his time, there is much we can learn from his remarks about the pastor's approach to scripture:

The main idea is to discover something about the Triune God, who reveals Himself in countless ways, always with reference to the needs of His children here on earth. Above all does He wish to make Himself known to a minister during hours of devotion, so that he in turn can lead others to find God through devotional reading of the Book. [8]

While the Bible is thus the primary object of our study, doctrinal theology is a close second. Theology, Barth reminds us, is the church's self-test of its language about God.[9] If we are to serve the Word faithfully and with effectiveness, we need to submit our thoughts and our words to this test on a regular basis. Depending upon the bent of a person's mind, there is much to be gained from the further study of a wide assortment of books, whether in the realm of fiction, biography, history, science, or some other such field of interest. God is truth, and we must be prepared to find the truth anywhere and everywhere. As long as we are rooted in scripture and sound doctrine, there are few books that will be an utter waste of time and there are many that will yield some fruit for preaching, teaching or pastoring. The whole idea is that we pastors are, by vocation, seekers after wisdom (Prov 15:14).

The Minister Is a Servant of the Word through Preaching.

Thus far we have been thinking of the minister's inner life or of the pastor as a person. We turn now to ministerial functions and come first to the work of preaching. To be sure, preaching is not simply a function of ministry; in very real terms it is part and parcel of the minister's identity. "Preaching," says Sr. Joan Delaplane, O.P., the first woman president of the Academy of Homiletics, "is not something I do; it is something I am."[10]

Preaching has been called everything from thirty minutes to raise the dead to work the angels envy. I define it as proclaiming the good news of God s activity in Jesus Christ so persons can respond, as the Spirit leads, with knowledge, faith, love, and obedience. However it is defined, preaching is indispensable to Christianity. The Word has prominence throughout scripture, and Jesus intended for his disciples to preach. In the days of his flesh, and during the period between his resurrection and his ascension, he sent them forth as witnesses. Preaching is essential not simply because of this commission, but also because of Paul's affirmation that faith comes through hearing (Rom 10:17).

Preaching has both a theological priority and a functional one. The functional priority stems from Acts 6, where it is recounted how the apostles appointed others to serve in certain capacities so they could devote themselves to the ministry of prayer and proclamation. The theological priority is expressed in Bullinger's conviction that the preaching of the word of God is the word of God,[11] and in Bonhoeffer's affirmation that the human word of preaching is not a phantom body for the Word of God but actually a fresh incarnation of the Word of God.[12]

The Minister Is a Servant of the Word through Teaching.

Jesus lived as a teacher as well as a preacher. So do pastors. We who are ordained and installed are done so as pastors and teachers. Thus, it is expected, by the denomination if not by the congregation we serve, that we will devote a significant amount of time to teaching in the local parish.

Some teaching will occur through sermons. Ideally, even more will occur through classes and other formal occasions. Along the way, we dare not neglect to notice that some will happen indirectly by virtue of our bearing. In other words, our example will speak as loudly as our words, if not more so.

Charles E. Jefferson looked upon teaching in the church as a more exacting and difficult work than preaching. Evangelism, he thought, was rather easy. The more cumbersome task is training the new converts in the ways and beliefs of Christians.[13] Perhaps if we gave more time to this more demanding task, today's mainline denominations would not be complaining of malaise. Without claiming to be able to turn a church around, and without claiming that teaching alone can lead to congregational renewal and strength, I do report my experience that parishioners want and appreciate teaching. They want to know what their pastor thinks and what their denomination believes about certain issues that appear in the popular press and perplex human society in general. They want to know more about the Bible and the Christian faith. They do not want to be told what to think, but they appreciate being tutored in how a Christian thinks. The minister who helps people at this growing edge of life and faith is living out his or her vocation as a servant of the Word.

The Minister Is a Servant of the Word through Public Worship.

Worship is the arena in which the church most closely approximates its ideal. It is in worship that the congregation is most deliberately directed toward God, glorifying and enjoying God, openly and gladly praising God and testifying before others. It is in worship that the congregation is most open to God and ready to receive what it is God would offer. It is in worship that the people of the congregation are their most humble before God, ready to be honest about themselves and contrite of heart. Similarly, it is in worship that the members of the congregation are their most unified with one another under God, fully at one as a fellowship of peace and love.

The minister is certainly not solely responsible for the quality of a congregation's worship, but the minister surely has some responsibility. Part of our pastoral vocation is to direct people in their approach to God. We have, as it were, a priestly function, and are charged with handling sacred things for the sake of order in the church. The true mediator is Jesus in the power of the Spirit, but the church has put the minister in a middle position as far as worship is concerned for the sake of the traditions of the church and the souls within the church. As with prayer, we who pastor and thereby serve as worship leaders at times represent God before the people and at times represent the people before God. It is our task in worship to be vessels of the Word and of human words, all for the sake of God, the upbuilding of the church, and the individuals who are part of it.

The Minister Is a Servant of the Word through Pastoral Care.

It is part of the ministerial vocation to relate to the individuals of a congregation on behalf of God. This task is not wholly fulfilled in public or before groups but requires private conference with individuals. This is the call to love, to intercede, to bear one another's burdens, to weep with those who weep and to rejoice with those who rejoice. Indeed, this is a call that is spoken over every Christian, but it comes especially to the pastor. Here the distinction between the lay person and the pastor as a provider of care is one of oversight. All are called to care, but the ordained leader is called to a position of oversight in the hope of assuring a balance of care throughout the congregation.

The shape of this ministry is varied. Just as the Lord Jesus walked the earth as one with compassion, so do the Lord's servants make their way with compassion individually expressed. At times the pastor serves the Word by offering a ministry of comfort whereby the pastor helps a parishioner sense the present help of God; elsewhere it is a ministry of guidance whereby the ordained friend helps a lay person discern the will of God or hear the promise of God. It is my judgment that, for the most part, parish administration is a function of pastoral care, for through it we who pastor labor to spot gifts, equip the saints, encourage cooperation, enhance community, and oversee the church's ministry, complete with its interpersonal relationships and individual disciples in need of nurture and care.

All the above makes it plain that the task of ministry is large. Any one task is large enough, but the pastor of a local congregation is called to accept them all with a degree of grace and the promise of growth. Even so, it remains true that there is no greater honor that can come to a person than the invitation, "Come, be our pastor."

Notes

1. On contemporary cultural changes, particularly in terms of how they impact church and ministry, see Robert Wuthnow, *Christianity in the 21st Century: Reflections on the Challenges Ahead* (New York: Oxford University Press, 1993).

2. On contemporary changes within the church, see John Killinger, *Preaching to a Church in Crisis: A Homiletic for the Last Days of the Mainline Church* (Lima, OH: CSS Publishing Company, 1995).

3. On the issue of entitlement thinking, see G. Lloyd Rediger, *Clergy Killers: Guidance for Pastors and Congregations Under Attack* (Louisville: Westminster/John Knox Press, 1997), 20f.

4. Andrew W. Blackwood, *The Fine Art of Preaching* (1937, rpt.; Grand Rapids: Baker Book House, 1976), 16.

5. Charles E. Jefferson, *The Building of the Church* (New York: Macmillan, 1910), 243-244.

6. Barbara Brown Taylor, *Mixed Blessings* (Cambridge: Cowley, 1998), 59.

7. As quoted in Donald G. Bloesch, *Essentials of Evangelical Theology,* II (San Francisco: Harper & Row, 1979), 93. The reference is to Calvin's Sermon on Deut 5:23-27.

8. Andrew W. Blackwood, *The Growing Minister* (Nashville: Abingdon Press, 1960), 41.

9. Karl Barth, *Church Dogmatics* I.1, trans. G. T. Thomson (Edinburgh: T. & T. Clark, 1936), 11.

10. Joan Delaplane, The Berger Lectures, University of Dubuque Theological Seminary, Dubuque, Iowa, April 26, 2000.

11. See James S. Stewart, *A Faith to Proclaim* (New York: Charles Scribner's Sons, 1953), 42.

12. Dietrich Bonhoeffer, *Christ the Center,* trans. by John Bowden (New York: Harper & Row, 1966), 53.

13. Jefferson, *Building of the Church,* 69, 75.

"I Come to this Time and Place"

Father in Heaven,

I come to this time and place not out of routine but out of need. I need and even hunger for your presence in my life and within me. Please hear my cry. Help me to remember it is your call to serve that I have responded to, not my own vanities. Help me to trust that you will give me the gifts I need to serve. I do not have to do this on my own. I see such need and there is so little of me to go around. I seem to trust myself more than I trust you. I ask that your Spirit be poured out upon me, that I will be filled and renewed, that I will be able to walk closer to you, that I will speak your words and extend your hands to others.

Gracious God, I do not ask in this time only for myself. I lift up to you those who are ill, those who face death, those who grieve, those who are lost, those who are bitter, those who are wounded, those who are hungry, those who know joy, those who are at peace. Thank you for the work of this congregation. They labor diligently in teaching others, in sharing the good news, in caring for the sick and hungry. Bless their ministries. Pour your Spirit upon them that they may be renewed and draw closer to you. I lift up the special project we are doing. I lift up our need for someone to serve in this special way. Loving God, I am bold to also lift up this community in which we serve you. May our ministries be a blessing to it. May you bless the entire community.

Eternal One, thank you for your promise to always be with me. I am grateful that you are faithful even when I am unfaithful. I thank you for your grace. Thank you for carrying my burdens. Thank you for your call to be among these people. I see your Son in each one. Thank you for hearing my prayers, even those prayers which have no words. I ask all of these things in the name of your Son, Jesus Christ.

Denise Cole

SECTION IV

THE MISSION
OF THE COMMUNITY

"Most Gracious and Merciful God"

Most gracious and merciful God,

We offer you thanks and praise for the abundance of life given to us;
   for your breath that sustains our bodies,
   your word that feeds our souls,
   your Son whose life, death, and resurrection keep hope in our hearts,
   and your church that draws us together in faith.
For all these, we sing Alleluia!

Through the waters of baptism,
you call us to witness to your will and word for a broken world.
You set before us a table of plenty, that through the feast of discipleship,
we might be filled with the blessings of your holy name.
You ask us to go forth from your table to
feed the hungry, shelter the homeless,
comfort the sick, and visit the prisoner,
that those held captive by the trials of life
might know the grace and joy of your abiding presence.
You extend to us the gift of forgiveness and redemption,
that we might become true sons and daughters of your kingdom
   here on earth.
You offer these gifts, yet we squander them and worship other gods.

In your great mercy, O God, receive us in our brokenness.
Fill us with your grace, capture our wills,
strengthen our hearts, use our lives, lift our voices.
That all we are might reflect your love and hope for all creation.

We boldly ask these things in the name of our Savior, Jesus Christ.

Gail A. O'Neal

Dietrich Bonhoeffer and the Confessing Church

Victoria J. Barnett

Interest in the life and theology of Dietrich Bonhoeffer continues to grow, particularly among lay Christians in this country. Increased attention in recent years to the Holocaust has led many Christians to study the history of their church more critically. Because of his involvement in the Confessing Church and the German resistance, and his eventual martyrdom, Bonhoeffer is a central figure in this history. His theological writings trace the deepening reflection and critique of a Christian thinker who was intimately connected to the political developments of his times.

This renewed interest in him is especially striking when we recall that in 1945, immediately after the defeat of Nazism, Bonhoeffer and his closest followers within the Confessing Church were little known outside Germany and fairly controversial inside it. The old guard within the German Evangelical Church re-established itself fairly quickly. It is true that many representatives of that old guard (such as Berlin Superintendent Otto Dibelius, who became Bishop of Berlin after the war), had been members of the Confessing Church, but their difficulties with Bonhoeffer only showed how much of an outsider he had always been in the Confessing movement. In a sense, Bonhoeffer took the Confessing Church more seriously than its leaders. When he told his students that whoever broke with the Confessing Church had broken away from salvation, he was going where few could follow.

Bonhoeffer lived and worked on the edges of his church. In 1933 he was a very young man, just beginning his career. During a crucial period of the German church struggle, from October 1933 until April 1935, he was not even in Germany but was serving as pastor to a German congregation in London. When he returned from England, his work for the Confessing Church in Germany consisted of teaching seminarians at an underground seminary in the hinterlands of Pomerania. When he appeared at Confessing synods, it was usually to cause trouble: putting up signs attacking Reich Bishop Müller and the Aryan paragraph around the town of Wittenberg during the infamous "Brown Synod" in 1933 or leading the very vocal protests of his Finkenwalde seminarians at the Steglitz Synod in 1935.

What postwar Germans had the most trouble accepting, however, was his involvement in the German resistance and in the 1944 plot to assassinate Adolf Hitler. For years, many Germans viewed the conspirators as traitors to their country and found the involvement of a member of the clergy especially troublesome. Invited to attend a 1945 memorial service for Bonhoeffer, Bavaria's Bishop Hans Meiser refused because he viewed Bonhoeffer as a "political" martyr, not a religious one.

Like many of his colleagues, Meiser didn't quite know how to categorize Dietrich Bonhoeffer; and, indeed, Bonhoeffer transcends many of the usual categories. He was a dedicated pastor and preacher, and a brilliant scholar who could have had a prominent academic career. The accounts of his youth work reveal someone with an obvious gift for working with young people. His complex role in the German resistance was truly unique—as a German respected by his ecumenical colleagues, a friend who truly ministered to his co-conspirators, and, above all, as a theologian who reflected on the ethical dilemmas of resistance and the role of the church under a dictatorship with a depth shown by few others, before or since.

Because of all this, many people today share Meiser's dilemma, albeit in a somewhat different form. Perhaps all of us tend to seek out the Bonhoeffer we are most comfortable with: Bonhoeffer the resister, or Bonhoeffer the author of *The Cost of Discipleship*, or Bonhoeffer the Confessing Church pastor, or Bonhoeffer the teacher. Christians from very different points of the religious and political spectrum—from liberation theologians to anti-abortion activists—can find something to like in Bonhoeffer.

Yet, as Eberhard Bethge showed in his wonderful biography of Bonhoeffer, all these different aspects are related. There are deep connections between the thoughts of the young theology student who studied with Adolph von Harnack, the vicar in Barcelona, the critical friend of Karl Barth, the ecumenist, the author of *Sanctorum Communio*, *Ethics*, and *Letters and Papers from Prison*, and the resistance figure. His earliest writings contain the seeds of the most radical thoughts that come later. While it is certainly not the case that one phase of Bonhoeffer's life led naturally and seamlessly to the next—how would this have been possible in the chaotic situation in which he found himself!—it is possible to see how one thing prepared him for the next. For Bonhoeffer, the deep spirituality and prayer that he taught to his students at the Finkenwalde seminary was present as he traveled on behalf of the resistance, and it emerges with poignancy and power in his prison writings.

Our task today, then, is not to pick out the Bonhoeffer we like but to reflect on his journey as a whole. How did he get from *Sanctorum Communio* to *Ethics*? What is the common thread between the different phases of his life and work? I suspect Bonhoeffer might have answered this question the same way he did in "After Ten Years," his 1941 essay to his fellow conspirators. "Who stands firm?" he asked. "Only the man whose final standard is not his reason, his principles, his conscience, his freedom, or his virtue, but who is ready to sacrifice all these when he is called to obedient and responsible action in faith and in exclusive allegiance to God—the responsible man, who tries to make his whole life an answer to the question and call of God."

This notion of answering God's call with one's whole life is central, I think, not only to understanding Bonhoeffer but to interpreting his legacy in its entirety. It goes to the heart of the idea of a public witness of the church that combines word and deed. Particularly in these times and in our own society, it has become very difficult for many of us to understand what God's call to us is, and how that should be expressed in the world in which we live. If faith has meaning, it has to be not only on Sunday mornings or in the privacy of our prayers but in our daily lives, our work, our relationships, our very identities as friends, spouses, parents and citizens. This meaning is neither easy to discern nor to practice. We can return home from church with great insights and the best of intentions, and, hours later, find that they have been lost in the mundane events of our lives.

Bonhoeffer struggled with this. In many ways, of course, his struggle was far more dramatic than ours, for it occurred against the historical backdrop of great evil; he confronted great and unusual decisions. Yet, many of his writings seem timeless because he is wrestling with these questions in words that sound so familiar that they could have been written for us. In the 1944 baptismal sermon for Bethge's son, Bonhoeffer wrote of the old world that had passed and no longer made sense, and added: "We have learned, rather too late, that action comes, not from thought but from a readiness for responsibility. For you thought and action will enter in a new relationship; your thinking will be confined to your responsibilities in action."

In such times, "confessing Christ"—one of the hallmarks of Frederick Trost's ministry—entails more than we think. Naturally, it includes a firm foundation of tradition, and an understanding of theology and the confessions. But it must also include this "readiness for responsibility," which took Bonhoeffer to such unexpected places. Bonhoeffer did not take the easy way out by simply discarding those aspects of his tradition and theology that were proving problematic. In the spirit of true responsibility, he stretched his tradition, rethought his theology, and brought both into dialogue with new ideas and political realities. He did not see religion or faith as a fixed set of rules that simply had to be followed, nor did he view action as sufficient when it had no foundation in belief.

Perhaps that is the key to understanding Bonhoeffer. We have to place the resistance figure next to the author of *The Cost of Discipleship*. Bonhoeffer's perspective on many things changed as time passed; he himself acknowledged that he had abandoned or revised some of his thinking. Throughout, however, he remained consistent in his readiness for responsibility, and in the openness within his heart and mind for the call of God.

This was not just the outcome of a solid doctrinal foundation, or a matter of remaining true to Christ's teachings. There were many in the Confessing Church who did those things. In and of itself, faithfulness to doctrine does a pretty good job of taking care of the heretics—in Bonhoeffer's time, the German Christians—but it's not what is ultimately required to withstand evil. It was responsibility to God's call, not doctrine, that led him to widen his heart and to stand in deep sympathy with the victims. This is what he writes in "After Ten Years":

> We are not Christ, but if we want to be Christians, we must have some share in Christ's large-heartedness by acting with responsibility and in freedom when the hour of danger comes, and by showing a real sympathy that springs, not from fear, but from the liberating and redeeming love of Christ for all who suffer.

To many of the good Lutherans in Barmen, the central message of the Barmen confession—*Solus Christus*—meant a strong doctrinal position with which to draw a line against heresy. For Bonhoeffer, *Solus Christus* went beyond that; it was yet another step on the way to a form of responsibility that, in its very large-heartedness, opened him to new forms of witness.

This is why Bonhoeffer wrestled so deeply and freely with the theological questions of his age, and why he experimented in Finkenwalde with forms of spiritual life that weren't parts of the German Lutheran tradition. It's why many leaders of his church considered him a gifted but problematic upstart, and why they couldn't take him seriously as a theologian after 1945.

They blamed his politics, but it wasn't really his politics. If Bonhoeffer is taken purely as a hero of the resistance—a political foe of Nazism—his essential core is left out. Even interpreting him as a political foe whose religious convictions led him to resistance doesn't convey entirely what happened to him. Taken as whole cloth, Bonhoeffer's life reminds us that the way in which we think through our faith, live it, and witness it will always be an imperfect and patchwork process. Surprising things are demanded of us, at odd times and in unexpected places. Faith entails the unexpected, the turn in the road for which we think we are unprepared but which we realize, in retrospect, served a purpose much greater than we expected or that we alone could have planned.

Bonhoeffer's historical importance, and his integrity and faith as a disciple, have become more evident with the passing of time. This is why he continues to be read today, and it's also what makes (and made) him truly ecumenical. We read his writing the way we read any great spiritual writings, not because we're biographically interested, but to search for clues that make the spark of the divine more transparent to us in our times.

Bonhoeffer was acutely aware that God had put him in this world to do certain things, and he did them. There are not many people in history of whom that can be said, and it shines through his work. In some of his writings—such as "After Ten Years"—the spark shines through like a floodlight, and we have not only proof of Bonhoeffer's greatness but a sense of what God is about on this earth. At such moments Bonhoeffer, like the other great spiritual figures in human history, gives us a glimpse of how we can live and act in the world as people of faith. That, in turn, enables us to see new possibilities for our church and its mission, even in the darkest times.

Some Reflections on Conversion

Dale L. Bishop

Before I began my tenure as Middle East Area Executive for the United Church Board for World Ministries and the Division of Overseas Ministries of the Christian Church (Disciples of Christ), I enjoyed an earlier incarnation as a scholar of Iranian languages and religions. I became somewhat of an expert on Zoroastrianism, the religion of pre-Islamic Iran, and a religion believed to have influenced Judaism during the Babylonian captivity, and consequently Christianity and Islam. The prophet of Zoroastrianism, Zarathustra (*Zoroaster,* to the Greeks), who probably lived in eastern Iran sometime during the second millennium B.C.E., depicted the world as a battleground between the forces of good and evil, the "truth" and the "lie," order and chaos. Human beings were created to be warriors in the struggle for the redemption of creation, and they were to be judged on the basis of the choices they made. For those who chose righteousness, there was the reward of "paradise" (itself an Iranian word); for those who followed the way of the lie, there was to be an afterlife of unremitting torment until the final days, when the cosmos would be cleansed by an all-consuming fire.

My studies of Zoroastrianism took me to India, home of most of the world's remaining Zoroastrians. In India, through the largesse of the Fulbright Fellowship program, I lived among and studied the Parsis, as Zoroastrians are known there. Theirs is a dwindling community, perhaps on the road to extinction, not because the religion has lost its appeal or its majesty but because Zoroastrian forebears from Iran, in flight from the Islamic conquest of Iran in the 11th century, had agreed upon arrival in the region of Gujarat never to engage in proselytism. This political arrangement over the years came to be translated into an ironclad religious doctrine whereby conversions to the faith are forbidden. Any increase in numbers of Zoroastrians will be achieved by procreation alone, and the birthrate of this prosperous community is very low. To make matters even more dire, intermarriage is forbidden, and the children of such unions are not considered to be Zoroastrians.

This experience with the Parsis in India compelled me, perhaps for the first time, to deal with the existential dimensions of the issue of conversion. As a scholar, and as a Christian, I tried to maintain an appropriate distance from the community I was studying. But I came to love the Parsi community, to feel almost a part of it, to share its anxieties about the future even as my admiration for the elegant simplicity of the

Zoroastrian world view grew. (Zoroastrians, for example, are spared the always vexing "problem of evil" in their positing the omniscience, but not the omnipotence, of God. The good will ultimately triumph but only because human beings, endowed with wisdom, will make it so.) This affection for the community and its tradition was made all the more poignant by my awareness that Christian missionaries of the English Methodist variety had sown confusion among the Parsis by their proselytizing efforts in the mid-nineteenth century.

On the Sunday before I departed India, at the small Church of North India congregation I was attending, a twelve year-old Parsi boy was baptized into the Christian faith. The joy that Christians feel with the enlargement of the Christian family was for me, I will confess, tempered by my awareness of the sense of loss that I was sure was being experienced by the Parsi community. The witness of the Zoroastrian faith that had nourished world culture was, I feared, being gradually extinguished. In my subsequent years as Middle East Area Executive for the UCC and Disciples, I was to witness a similar sense of loss among Middle Eastern Christians when family members, under social pressure or because of intermarriage, or out of genuine conviction, converted to Islam. Members of religious minorities, particularly small religious minorities, feel such losses especially keenly. For Christians in the Middle East, conversion, except in the rarest of cases, is a one-way process. Depending upon the particular society, apostasy from Islam can literally be lethal, while conversion to Islam is socially, and often economically, beneficial.

It is, perhaps, in the nature of religious faith, particularly the Abrahamic ones, that faithful people gravitate toward the polarities of certainty. Even the formulation of questions about "conversion," or "evangelism" or "evangelization"—terms that have distinct meanings but are frequently used interchangeably—reflect this polarity, this desire to hear "the right answer." Our missionaries and staff are, for example, frequently asked whether we are engaged in evangelism among "unreached peoples." The expected, or hoped for, answer often is an unqualified "yes." An attempt to explore the complexities of the issue may be met with the accusation of "universalism." One is either a faithful Christian, or a relativist universalist.

Others are equally certain in their uncertainty. The same question about conversion, slightly modified to, say, "you're not trying to convert people, are you?" may reflect a horror at the thought that our church could be involved in any enterprise that smacks of the "imperialism" of mission. Since in our society gospel has become inextricably entwined with culture, the argument goes, we have nothing to say to, and in, the world. How dare we foist our beliefs on others, when, as we all know, there are many roads to God? To modify the title of this book of essays in honor of Frederick Trost, "in essentials, respectful (and sometimes not so respectful) disagreement."

This polarity of certainty, which I will confess, I have depicted in its most rigid form, cannot reflect the complexity and the variety of the mission experience and may have the unintended result of actually restricting our understanding of the activity of the Holy Spirit. In our effort to be faithful to what we understand to be God's will, we may, in fact, be trying to comprehend that will, to enclose it in our own human limitations. The actual experience of mission, on the other hand, has been an experience of mutual witness, of the transformation of what may have originally been conceived to be a one-way process to a process of mutual conversion in which both parties are somehow transformed, often, or usually, within the context of their own respective religious traditions.

The career of Frank Laubach, a revered missionary of the American Board, who served among Muslims in the Philippines, reflects this process of breaking open the limited expectations of mission, the very human effort to restrict God's options. Laubach originally went to the Philippines with the expectation that he would convert Filipino Muslims to Christianity. Like many missionaries who have witnessed within the Islamic context, Laubach discovered that it was very difficult, well nigh impossible, to convince Muslims to change their self-identification from "Muslim" to "Christian." In what he himself could only describe as a mystical experience, a moment of religious revelation, Laubach realized that he needed to expand his understanding of what would be a true a experience of conversion. He encountered a group of Muslims praying, and he joined them. "He is Islam," the Imam said of Laubach. "No," replied Laubach, "a friend of Islam." Laubach's subsequent career represents one of the glowing moments of Christian mission, the inauguration of a literacy movement much copied around the world, called "each one, teach one," and the beginning of a relationship between Christians and Muslims in the Philippines that reflected their mutual quest for faithfulness to God.

What really happened in this encounter between Christian mission and Islamic society? I would argue that true conversion took place. Laubach had a profound impact on those among whom he taught. Even though they did not change their self-identification as Muslims, they were introduced to an understanding of Jesus that was reflected neither in their historical experience of Christianity, which had come to the Philippines as a conquering European religion, nor in their current experience of the faith as a small minority in a predominantly Christian society. Jesus, as they experienced him through the humble love of his servant Frank Laubach, became their friend, and no longer an icon of political dominance. At the same time, Laubach himself had a conversion experience, not "becoming Islam," as the Imam had suggested, but becoming a friend of Islam, a religious tradition that encourages community and mutual responsibility. Neither party to the process changed their self-identification, but both emerged profoundly changed, closer to God, perhaps, than they would have been had there been no mission.

Which brings me back to that polarity of certainties we encounter within our own faith community. It is, indeed, tempting to attempt to quantify the results of mission. Ours is a society that wants to know the "bottom line." Early missionaries of the American Board even plotted out a mathematical model for the conversion of the world, based upon an "each one, teach one" assumption rather like Laubach's later pedagogical model. But God works within the human heart, and the Spirit, from the very first Pentecost, has been notoriously unpredictable, inspiring people with the reality of the gospel even when it is communicated in different tongues and to different cultures, perhaps even within different religious traditions. Human beings may be the vehicle for conversion, the enfleshment of the Word, but actual conversion depends upon God alone.

By the same token, however, the church will only live if it lives by mission. Zoroastrianism, with its high ethical standards and compelling cosmology, is approaching extinction in large part because of the fateful decisions of generations of leaders who agreed, first out of political necessity and later under the weight of tradition, that the Zoroastrian faith was only for those who were already Zoroastrian. A faith that once challenged the political status quo and inspired a coherent moral vision became the special preserve of those who, out of conviction or burdened by expediency, determined that it was not a faith to be shared, but one whose esoteric secrets were to be preserved among a diminishing group of those who had been born into the tradition.

It would be my hope that one of those "essentials of unity" in our beloved United Church of Christ would be a fervent commitment to mission and witness, that we would continue to insist the Word becomes flesh among us, whether in the sharing of people in our churches with partners around the world, or in the receiving of evangelists from partner churches whose faith has been tested and deepened by hardship, poverty, and the encounter with other people of faith, that we would also open ourselves to those other people of faith in our own society. The journey of mission is an uncertain one, for it challenges the neat communal structure that humanity has imposed upon God's world, and opens the possibility of wholeness, or *shalom*. In embarking on this journey, we should anticipate conversion: of those whom we encounter, of ourselves, and indeed of the world.

"Our Lord, Jesus Christ"

Our Lord, Jesus Christ, we thank you for your good news
and for those who witness to you in this world.

We also thank you for the challenges we encounter.
Thank you that you love women and men, youths and children all over
the world.

Help us to bring your word to people by telling them your stories,
and teach us to spread your promises. We are waiting for God's reign.

Strengthen your Christian family all over the world
so that together we work for your justice and peace.

Thank you that you send out people,
that they leave their familiar surroundings to serve you.

Help us to learn from one another all over your wonderful world.
Encourage us to face the problems of poverty and violence.

Fill our hearts and minds with your Holy Spirit
so that we can act creatively and lovingly in the place where we live—
in our families and circle of friends, in our congregations and
neighborhoods.

Bless those relationships and friendships.
Without you we can do nothing.

Deliver us from pride and selfishness so that we serve you with words
and deeds.

Bless those for whom we are caring in hospitals, through projects like
Habitat for Humanity, in poor countries, in institutions for elderly
people and for young children.
May we be conscious that the goods and talents we have to share are
your gifts.

We praise you today and for the rest of our lives
for yours is the power and the glory forever.

Iris Susen-Pilger

Conspiring with Amos:
Prophetic Critique and Public Witness in a Time of National Triumphalism

Theodore A. Braun

These are dangerous days for the church in the United States. Located in the belly of the richest, most powerful, most self-indulgent nation on earth, the church is vulnerable to a seduction and captivity that tames theological hermeneutics, co-opts prophetic critique, and domesticates its life and mission.

We see this in the ways the church has so often adopted the values, assumptions, and ideological lenses of the nation, proclaiming a gospel of personal fulfillment but not one that confronts the powers, principalities, and domination systems that impact us and compete for our loyalty. Walter Wink refers to these as unjust economic relations, oppressive political relations, biased race relations, patriarchal gender relations, hierarchical power relations, and he points to the use of violence to maintain them all.

We live in a time of national self-congratulation. We have won the Cold War; we have a booming economy and the world's most powerful military machine; we have the ability to force our wishes upon almost every other nation on earth; and we can fight wars without losing any of our own combatants.

In the midst of all of this triumphalism, however, there are two important theological questions that confront and challenge us: the God-question and the neighbor-question. "Who is our God?" or, more directly in this day of multiple idolatries, "In which God do we place our trust?" And secondly, "Who is our neighbor?" "To whom does God call us to be neighborly?"

Our nation has a basic credo, "In God We Trust." It is imprinted upon every piece of United States currency, and reaffirmed every time we give or receive it. It became our credo in 1864 after the secretary of the treasury, Salmon P. Chase, received a letter from a Pennsylvania clergyman asking that "the Almighty God" be recognized in some way on US coins. Chase took the request to Congress which passed legislation approving the idea, and it was signed by President Abraham Lincoln. On July 30, 1956, Congress passed legislation confirming these four words as "the national motto."

It is apparent, however, given the contextual location of this statement of faith and the network of financial temples that expedite its circulation among our population, that this God so trusted in is a "market economy" God, a god of financial success undergirding consumerist and materialist values, whose bottom line is profit and whose blessings are affluence and power. Jesus called this god "Mammon."

In our nation, we are in an unprecedented time of wealth production. We now have more millionaires than the rest of the world combined, with each day bringing into existence an estimated sixty new millionaires. Large expensive new homes are being built across our nation; stores and catalogs offer an expanding surfeit of consumer and luxury items. We are in the process of privatizing more and more segments of our social resources and public domain, turning them into profit-oriented enterprises for the benefit of wealthy individuals and corporations, despite the fact that with this approach we see a growing gap between rich and poor, and increasing numbers of people falling into the cracks.

Even those who are not participating greatly in this pandemic of "affluenza" but are molded by its ethic still spend significant amounts of their own money to buy clothing and equipment that prominently display corporate symbols, company logos, and trade mottos, liturgical vestments and accessories that celebrate this market economy God.

From all over the world wealth is flowing into our nation through debt servicing, distorted export trade and manufacturing relationships, privatization, and financial speculation. When nations such as Cuba and Yugoslavia have resisted entering our market economy system, we have sought to destroy their resistance.

In this triumphal *Zeitgeist*, the church needs to give solid theological attention to the alternative value system in God's upside-down kingdom/dominion, its different bottom line, and the ongoing need for idol-breaking, re-formation, and being born "from above," i.e., what it means to live in a vocation of holy subversion within this domination system and in a stance of solidarity with those who are its victims and non-beneficiaries. Jesus had a name for one of these victims: "Lazarus."

The second question has to do with our neighborliness. A crucial justice test for us in the United States is our relationship to one of our nearest southern neighbors: Cuba. For 450 long years it was a political and economic colony of Spain and the United States, but in 1959 it finally won its independence. Refusing to recognize the virtue, dominion, and beneficence of our market economy God, it opted for a different organizing ethic.

Cuba began to construct an alternative model of society: social, economic, political, and cultural relationships built on justice, equity, and solidarity, guaranteeing everyone, and especially the most vulnerable, access to basic social services. It gave priority to public health, education, employment, social welfare, the ending of racial and gender discrimination, and the development of a democratic electoral process that was accessible to all citizens and not dependent on the corrupting power of money. It also sought to develop a personal ethic not dependent on, or measurable in, material goods, and a bottom line based on service rather than profit.

To help fund this undertaking, Cuba nationalized foreign property and assets (offering the United States a twenty-year reimbursement plan which it refused), and began the systematic development and redistribution of its economic resources on behalf of greater equity and justice. Amaziahs and other establishment functionaries in the United States were greatly upset by these developments and complained to our nation that "Cuba has conspired against you in the very center of your hemisphere." The United States then began a forty-year effort to destabilize and overturn Cuba's revolutionary enterprise, an effort that included sabotage, invasions, bacteriological warfare, and a blockade.

At first Cuba was able to survive with the assistance of the Eastern bloc, but when that support folded, Cuba went through some difficult years of hardship and suffering, especially since food and medicine were also blockaded. Any other nation would have collapsed, but Cuba survived for several important reasons:

1) The vast majority of the people, especially those whose circumstances had been helped most by the revolution, continued to support its direction and values, and to trust the government and its leadership.

2) Cuba's campaign against an individualistic ethic, its development of neighborhood *koinonia* and support groups, and its emphasis on empathy and compassion for others, especially for those in need, gave its society a strong cement to hold it together.

3) Cuba's democratic electoral system, "People's Power," which was accessible and accountable to all the Cuban people, was not vulnerable to penetration by US money and client candidates (as happened with the Sandinista government just before it collapsed).

This is not to portray a trouble-free picture of Cuban society and developments. There have been serious problems along the way: Soviet influence brought hierarchical arrangements and a verticalism that were not Cuban, but this was superseded by a new commitment to the teachings and ethics of Cuba's primary mentor, José Martí. Official governmental atheism (especially during the period of Soviet aid) was a foreign emphasis that was finally ended in 1992 when Cuba became a lay, secular state. The oppressive forty-year war encouraged a defensive mentality that worked to protect the revolution against revisionist viewpoints and dissidents (many of whom were indeed funded and undergirded by the United States), a mentality that tended to become overly rigid. But there have been a number of steps taken to make Cuba's democracy more participatory.

A complicating factor for people in the United States has been the fact that our corporate media have made broad use of the interpretive lenses supplied by the most extreme and embittered elements in Miami's exile community, lenses that purported to reveal an environment of persecution, human rights violations, a lack of freedom and democracy, and a ruined economy. Left unspoken in this exile hermeneutics was this element's dislike for Cuba's thoroughgoing mixing of races and its restrictions on wealth accumulation and capitalist enterprise.

All through these years Cubans kept insisting that life in Cuba was neither heaven nor hell, but somewhere in between. The 1959 triumph of the revolutionary struggle brought many changes to the life and mission of the church. Catholic and Protestant schools were nationalized; in the early 1960s many church members who had developed a North American mentality and consciousness emigrated to the United States, and some conservative church members even took part in counter-revolutionary activity.

But over the years, as the benefits of the revolutionary development began to be experienced in the society, church members discovered it to be a kind of "shalom" laboratory and began taking leadership roles in their neighborhood, union, and professional organizations. The Cuban Council of Churches has taken the lead in fostering ecumenical relationships and providing opportunities for lay theological education. It helped bring more than a million Bibles into Cuba, and has been working on projects of green medicine, green agriculture, and ecologically sustainable development. During recent years, there has been a religious revival going on in Cuba, with churches full of new members.

One of the most remarkable aspects of the Cuban ethic of compassionate solidarity and service has been its international medical program. For many years Cuban doctors have served in poor areas of African and Latin American countries. Then in 1999 Cuba cut its national defense budget to convert a former Naval Academy into a Latin American School of Medical Sciences where 4,500 students from eighteen Caribbean and Latin American countries, mostly from poor backgrounds, are now enrolled in a six-year program.

The students receive a medical education, housing, tuition, books, and a stipend completely free of charge. The first two years are spent at the school, and the last four years studying and working in Cuban hospitals and clinics, focusing especially on community-based approaches and preventive medicine. The students are committed to serving for at least five years in the public health program of their home country when they return. Cuba has also offered to include poor African Americans from our inner cities in this program.

The seven-month captivity of Elián González in Miami and in the Washington area did much to reduce the power of the far right group in the Miami exile community and has brought a new political alignment in Congress that bodes well for changes in the laws undergirding the boycott. The church has also played an important role in this opening. The Cuban Council of Churches and our National Council of Churches (NCC) took an active role in facilitating the visit of Elián's grandmothers to Washington, and the NCC and Social Justice office of the United Methodist Church helped raise financial support for an attorney to represent Elián's father in his effort to reclaim Elián.

Increasing numbers of US citizens have been traveling to Cuba, and cultural and trade delegations have been multiplying. Some dozen US cities have established sister city relationships with cities in Cuba, and a growing number of US and Cuban congregations have established sister church relationships. Pastors for Peace has moved large quantities of humanitarian supplies and equipment (buses, computers, medical supplies) to Cuba, and Church World Services has also taken down humanitarian supplies. There is a growing cloud of eyewitnesses in the United States who can tell what they have seen and heard in Cuba. Jesus acknowledged the importance of such eyewitness accounts in his instructions to John's disciples (Lk 7:18-23).

In this situation of longtime alienation and enmity, the church needs to continue and intensify its prophetic task of calling for an end to our nation's inhumane and cruel boycott of the Cuban people. It is a *kairos* moment calling for repentance and reparation for the pain and suffering we have caused our brothers and sisters in Cuba, a time for reformation, reconciliation, and celebrating at a common table.

When one confesses Christ in a triumphal time, there is always the danger of turning him into an icon. The Jesus who welcomed women, Samaritans, the poor, and "impure" of his day into full membership in God's family and to full seating rights at God's table does not fit easily into iconolatry. We are continually challenged to deal with Bonhoeffer's central question, "Who is Christ for us today?"

Confession, trust, and reconciliation will mean plumbing the biblical claim that the breaking down of walls of hostility and the reconciling have already taken place through the Prophet of Nazareth, the Announcer of Jubilee, the Healer of Brokenness, the Breaker of Purity Codes, the Overturner of Commodity Tables, the Criminal of Golgotha, and the One who walks with us along our Emmaus roads.

Public Witness: Word and Deed

W. Sterling Cary

The church is called to be a reminder to the world of God revealed in Jesus the Christ. The life of the church must be consistent with its proclamation of the lordship of Jesus the Christ. Frequently the life of the church reflects its cultural setting rather than the redemptive presence of its transcendent Lord.

The Protestant church tends to be a neighborhood church and as such is often shaped by neighborhood traditions and values. I had the opportunity to observe the impact of culture on the life of the church in the early 1950s when I was a student at Union Theological Seminary in New York. During one of my summer vacations at Union, I worked as a minister to migrant farm workers in upstate New York. These migrants were appreciated as workers on the farms where they harvested crops, but they were unwelcome guests in the nearby village. On weekends when they went to the local movie theater, they were forced to sit in a designated seating section. Learning of this injustice I went to the theater with them, urging that they follow me and sit in the general seating area. Fear of losing employment, however, kept them from following me to the non-designated area.

Disturbed by this discrimination I approached a local Presbyterian pastor, asking him to join me in visiting the theater management to demand an end to this racist policy. The pastor explained that the arrangement was an acceptable practice in this part of the state, and though he opposed it, he could not be expected to "get up on the cross" with me. Clearly, this pastor was obeying the dictates of his cultural setting rather than the teachings of his Christian faith.

In America, being shaped by neighborhood means having parishoners of the same class, race, and political affiliation. Thus, instead of being a community that reflects the diversity of the global village, church membership tends to be homogeneous. Attend any local church for the weekly worship service and you will inevitably experience racial and ethnic separation rather than global community.

The mission of the faith community must be that of bearing witness "to a more excellent way" (1 Cor 12:31). The church is called to transcend the exclusionary boundaries of neighborhood, race, ethnicity, and class if the church is be an authentic reminder of the God revealed in Jesus the Christ. Time and again Paul writes not to the church of a neighborhood but to the church at Rome, Corinth, or Galatia. The New Testament understood a church to be the residents of a city rather than the inhabitants within the more limiting boundaries of neighborhood. Neighborhoods tend to be homogeneous enclaves, but our mission as the faith community is that of celebrating the diversity of God's human family.

The mission of the church is that of being a community where there is the nurturing of loving, caring relationships. Paul calls the church "the body of Christ" (1 Cor 12:27). Being the church means being the incarnation of divine love. As Jesus responded with love and compassion to the needs of the ostracized and rejected ones—even of a Zacchaeus (Lk. 19:5)—so also is the church called to restore to individuals their sense of worth which comes in knowing that one is loved and valued. Many are the times when persons seeking refuge from the strain and stress of existence turn to the church for the healing power of Christian fellowship. They come in desperate need of "the balm in Gilead" only to return to the outside world empty and disillusioned. In our contemporary mass culture, an individual tends to become a nameless face in the midst of the multitudes that crowd the streets of urban America. Deep is the hunger within for affirmation, recognition, and relationship. In our impersonal world a person can weekly attend worship services in large urban congregations without ever being called by name or experiencing relationship with a kindred worshiper. Strangers often sit in the very same pew without greeting or extending the peace of God to each other. The church must be a community that facilitates healing, reconciliation, and caring if it is to be God's instrument in enabling worshipers to experience the lifegiving power of divine love.

Within the faith community Christians are to minister to one another; there is to be a mutual bearing of burdens in times of struggle or grief and a sharing of celebrative times of joy. At the same time that we are called to minister to one another, we are also called to minister to the world, to engage in ministries of public witness:

"For I was hungry and you gave me food, I was thirsty and you gave me something to drink, I was a stranger and you welcomed me, I was naked and you gave me clothing, I was sick and you took care of me, I was in prison and you came to see me."

When, Lord, did we do these things?

"Just as you did it to one of the least of these who are members of my family, you did it to me" (Matt 25:35-37).

The church's ministry of outreach is in obedience to our Lord's Word: "Other sheep I have which are not of this fold" (Jn 10:16). The church is to provide that cup of water for those who thirst for fellowship and support in their times of aloneness and despair. The unwed mother, the young adult being destroyed by drug addiction, the senior citizen failing in health and forsaken by children. Wherever the church is located we are surrounded by anguished cries for help, cries that demand the response of the faith community. We must be involved in the lives of those who are as sheep without shepherd.

In reading the New Testament we are reminded that the church exists not exclusively for the cultivation of individual piety; the church is also called to respond to the needs of neighbor. Recognizing the claim of neighbor is in keeping with our Lord's word, "But a Samaritan while traveling, came near him; and when he saw him, he was moved with pity" (Lk 10:33). The church must be involved in the struggle to create a society where those who hunger are fed, where the homeless are housed, where the sick have access to health care, where all have access to meaningful employment. The voice of the church must be raised in the struggle to build a world order based on justice and freedom. We must reach out in support of the victims of war, famine, disease, racism, sexism, oppression, and exploitation. As the body of Christ we are called to be God's redemptive presence in the life of the world.

The church's public witness must be rooted and grounded in the word. Our witness must be an expression of God's purpose for humanity: "that is, in Christ God was reconciling the world to Godself, not counting their trespasses against them, and entrusting the message of reconciliation to us" (2 Cor 5:19). There is no blueprint for effecting this ministry of reconciliation. How do we as church communicate the love of God to those whose life situations have silenced their singing? How do we communicate the love of God to those who are in prison for crimes they did not commit? How do we communicate the love of God to children in "Third World" countries who live in communities of unpaved streets, no public sanitation systems, limited supplies of sanitary drinking water, and in regions of the world where there is constant hunger for food? How do we communicate the love of God to the millions in distant lands where primitive health care condemns them to death from AIDS? There must never be debate on whether the church should be engaged in ministries of healing and reconciliation, but there is cause for debate on how best to engage in those ministries in our contemporary situation.

In its mission as a faith community the church must be concerned about sin, but sin must not be thought of simply in terms of the actions of individuals. The church must speak the word of God to a society that is characterized by an ever widening gap between the haves and the have-nots. A society where the privileged few have both winter and summer homes while there is an alarming increase in the number of citizens who are homeless. Many of the homeless work full-time jobs receiving minimum wages with no benefits. If we believe that "God so loved the world" (Jn 3:16), then as church we must join with those who are seeking to alleviate the sufferings of our brothers and sisters whose cry for justice and mercy goes unanswered. Walking with God means walking with the wretched of the earth. We must be lifegivers, to those who inhabit a valley of death.

The church that prays "thy kingdom come" must actively participate in efforts aimed at preparing the way for the coming of that kingdom. Empowered by our Lord, the church must battle the forces of death and destruction. The church must speak God's word of "No" to all the negative forces that threaten to dehumanize the lives of God's people. The church must be mindful that our intercessory prayers for the people should be manifestations of a commitment to working at redeeming the world in which they live and move and have their being. In urban, suburban and rural communities the church must be present in word and deed, communicating God's "No" to all of the demonic powers and principalities that are at work seeking to frustrate the human quest for fullness of life. The church must be that place of sanctuary for all the seekers of abundant life.

We must confess that as church we have frequently absented ourselves from the struggle to redeem the times. "Were you there when they crucified my Lord? Were you there when they nailed him to the tree?" As church we must confess that we were there when humanity rebelled against the purposes of God for human history. The church must ask the question "Were we there?" when the curse of slavery tormented the lives of African Americans. Were we there when our nation inflicted massive destruction and death upon those identified as the "enemy"? The church is to tell the story of God's love for a fallen creation and to bear witness to that redemptive love in our life and ministry.

The earthly church reflects the "humanness" of an imperfect humanity, but by the grace of God, in spite of that "humanness," the church has been a redemptive presence in the life of the world. Through the life and witness of the church, sinners have been inspired to accept Jesus the Christ as Lord and Savior. The preaching of the gospel has strengthened and empowered those bruised by the adversities of day by day living. The church has been used by God in the reconciliation of individuals, races, and nations. The global church has been and continues to be engaged in ministries of education, health care, development, and faith proclamation.

The church has not always been faithful to our Lord. The church confesses its unfaithfulness, accepts God's forgiveness, and is sustained in its witness by the knowledge that the living Lord has conquered the powers of sin and of death!

"As God Has Called You, Live Up to Your Calling"

Ephesians 4:11-16

David C. Chevrier

Those are thunderous words. They almost give me chills when I think about the implications of what they mean. Somehow, it seems we like to think, or at least I like to think, that no one has a claim upon my life but me. Who I am and what I do is my decision, and I only have to answer for myself. That's why these simple straight-forward words of Ephesians are so powerful and devastating:

As God Has Called You, Live Up to Your Calling.

We are a *called people*. We have been called to from across the chasm. God has chosen to be in touch with us. For God every calling is always a calling forth. We are called to come forth; to follow is to be on our way acting in Christ's name.

Live up to your calling: These are the beginning words of ministry. God has called us and addressed us. How are we now to respond? It is in this call and this response that lies the heart of ministry. It might be important to add at this point that this letter to the Ephesians was not written to the leading person at Ephesus (not to the Rev. Dr. Ignatius or Theresa). These words about calling and ministry were written "To the saints who are in Ephesus and are faithful in Christ Jesus"—to the *whole* body of Christ.

And where are *we* being called today? Where is the ministry of the church to be found and what form is it to take? I would like to suggest that the place of the church's ministry today is at *the edge*. And where is the edge today? It's the same places where it was for Jesus. The edge is always where few dare to go: the leper colonies, the homes of tax collectors, all the "unclean." It is standing before Pontius Pilate or Herod or wherever the springs of decision are being made. It can be in the midst of the crowd, in the marketplace teaching and healing, or meeting with one person, face to face, at the well, encountering that other in his or her full humanity.

The edge is a place, but more than that it is a *direction*, a movement. The church stands on the edge when it allows its building to be used by groups who have no place to lay their heads, who have been turned away, excluded, cast out, rejected elsewhere. Giving a place to those who have no place fulfills in a very deep way the biblical meaning of sanctuary: a safe place, a holy place, a place of welcome, a place of peace and blessing.

What form does life take at the edge? The passage from Ephesians speaks to us and helps us see what God calls us to:

But each of us was given grace according to the measure of Christ's gift .... The gifts he gave were that some would be apostles, some prophets, some evangelists, some pastors and teachers, to equip the saints for the work of ministry, for building up the body of Christ (Eph 4:7, 11–12).

Because of God's initiative, God's action on our behalf, our ministry must be seen as a response to that grace and those gifts.

The gifts are as varied and as diverse as the variety and diversity of the people of God, yet it is the *same* Spirit that gives them. No one has all the gifts, yet all the gifts are to work together for the service of God in the world. Let's look at three of these gifts more closely for in them lies the form of our ministry. The gifts of being prophets, pastors, and apostles were not just given to the church at Ephesus; these are the same gifts given to us today for God's love is eternal and the gifts are constant. These are our gifts which must be used to equip God's people in the service of God. So in order to be able to recognize these gifts in ourselves and others, let us take a closer look at them.

Some to be Prophets: Prophecy is not so much foretelling the future as it is living in the future. As Paul puts it in Romans 8: "We know that the whole creation has been groaning in labor pains until now." It is living as though this new birth is about to happen, that we are the midwives to this divine revolution. It is being so caught up in the vision of the new creation that because of the way we live the vision is made visible, partially fulfilled right now. "The commonwealth of God is in the midst of you . . . is at hand . . . is near," says Jesus. Yet prophecy, if it is to be Christ-like, if we are to be the body of Christ, must be lived very deeply in the world as it is. It means agonizing with the pain of the world and identifying with the poor and oppressed and struggling with them in their desire for justice and peace. And because of that agony and that identification and that struggle, prophecy means calling all God's people to help bridge the gap between what is and what should be and what can be because with God *all things are possible.* Prophecy is living at the edge, challenging the world to live up to and live out the vision.

Some to be Pastors: To be a pastor means to have the courage to be vulnerable to others and to dare to be vulnerable to the world's opinion and hostility. To be vulnerable means to be open to being wounded, to be a wounded healer. The pastoral function/office/role/responsibility is fulfilled when members of the body of Christ are able to stand up in our midst and share their deepest joys and sorrows, hopes and fears, not just for themselves but for others so we become members one of another, brothers and sisters in Christ. Like the Good Samaritan, we are willing to risk being robbed of everything in order to help someone in need, to risk losing one's life in order to find one's real self, to be detoured from our personal plans and schedules and desires for the sake of someone abandoned and alone. Compared to the ways of the world, Christ's way in the world always looks foolish and stupid, like a Suffering Servant, like a sheep being led to a slaughter, like one despised and rejected. To be a pastor is like leaning over the edge.

Some to be Apostles: The apostles are the ambassadors, the delegated representatives, the messengers. They are the ones who are first sent to the edge, ambassadors on our behalf, which does not mean they are the most diplomatic but rather the most honest. Messengers must be straightforward and direct. Apostles are aliens in a strange land willing to enter occupied territory to travel to the front in order to proclaim release to the captives and recovery of sight to the blind. Yet even at home the apostle is still an alien, no longer able to adapt to the patterns and style of life of this world. The apostle stands as a living contradiction to the usual, the conventional, the accepted ways of the world. The apostle continually denies the standards of this world in allegiance to a higher standard of truth and goodness and beauty. So apostles live at the edge of the world while being immersed in the world and struggling to move that edge until it covers the whole world.

These are God's gifts to us as prophets, pastors, and apostles. Yet how do these work together to be used in the service of God, as the body of Christ? Perhaps a story from the Jewish tradition can help us:

Once a long time ago, somewhere in Lithuania, a certain Eleazer Lipman, known for his wealth and generosity, met a beggar on his way to the village. He stopped his carriage and invited the beggar to get in. The beggar politely refused saying, "I still haven't earned anything all day."

"How much do you possibly earn in a day?" asked Eleazer Lipman.

"A lot. Twenty-five ducats maybe."

"I'll give them to you. Come along."

"No," said the stubborn beggar, "I can't do that."

"Why not? You won't lose anything."

"True, but money isn't everything. I must think of the people who regularly, once a week, open their doors and hearts to me. If they don't see me today they will worry."

"Don't let that bother you. I'll go from door to door to reassure them on your behalf. But do come along. I can't bear to see you walk so far."

Dropping his mask, the beggar, actually a messenger of God in disguise, congratulated Eleazer on passing the test.

This is life at the edge. It is living a life that is outrageous and reckless, risky and unconventional, willing to do the unexpected and contradictory. Perhaps it is time for the church not to be so fearful and so important and so preoccupied with its own concerns and agenda and survival that it can't stop to pick up passers-by on the road. Perhaps it is time for the church to get down from its carriage and make the rounds of the neighborhood on behalf of the beggars and homeless, to so agonize with the victims that we cannot bear to see them walk so far. And that may mean being vulnerable; it may mean standing in conflict with the world; it may mean identifying with the outcasts. In short, it may mean living up to our calling as prophets and pastors and apostles.

Speaking the Truth in Love

If the church is to take sides in these very desperate times in which we live, let it be on the side of recklessness and not safety, risk and not solvency. Let it be on the side of honesty and not diplomacy, on the side of conflict and not convention, for that is what it means to live at the edge, to be the body of Christ. If the church is not free to be outrageous, then it is not free.

So in that spirit let us rejoice and live up to all of our gifts:

For those who have the gift of music and song, let them make music, for God's revolution needs joy and gratitude and inspiration.

For those who have been given the gifts to build, let them put their hands and arms together, for everything is to be restored and made new.

For those who have been given the gift to listen, let them open the ears of their hearts so that someone can hear the cries of pain and we can respond quickly.

For those who have been given the gift of speech, translate the cries of pain into words that can grasp and grab our hearts, giving us visions we can see.

For those who have been given the gift of tenderness, be gentle with those far off and those nearby, and teach the rest of us. Please, please teach the rest of us how to be sensitive so we can express our care.

For those who have been given the gift of patience, wait for us who are slow to get it, wait for us who speak without listening, wait for those of us who act without being touched so that we might come along also.

Whatever your gifts, remember there is no task too small, no job to menial, no work too unimportant, no act too insignificant, no prayer too silent. For when life is lived at the edge, the small becomes great, the servant becomes the leader, and the slave the master of us all.

"O Chamada para Missão"

Eu escuto sua voz, o Deus, me chamando para o servi o de missão.
Eu escuto sua voz me chamando para a união com todos os povos,
De todos as nações,
De todas as culturas,
De todas as cores e raças,
De todas as crenças,
Para se juntarem para um universo de paz enquanto nós celebramos nóssos
Diferentes caminhos, para trazer seu Reino aqui e agora. Pois isto é a
missão da Igreja.

Mas sei que sem a igualdade para toda a sua creação,
Sem justi a social,
Sem justi a económica,
Sem justi a política,
Sem igualdade sexual, cultural e religiosa,
Seu Reino nunca virá.

Eu escuto sua voz no vento, chamando sua igreja para esta missão.
Eu escuto sua voz nos gritos dos famintos,
Os pobres,
As crian as abandonadas,
Os sem terra,
Os desencantados,
Os que procuram a fé,
Chamando a igreja para esta missão.

Mas estou sozinho, Deus,
Eu escuto sua voz em toda parte mas sozinho o que posso fazer?
A missão da Igreja me chama pois com a Igreja,
Não estou sozinho.

Sua missão me chama e aqui estou, Deus.
Ajude-nos a estarmos prontos para servir sua missão, a missão da Igreja,
Pois a Igreja é o corpo de Cristo,
Suas mãos no mundo.

A missão da Igreja me chama.
Eu escuto o chamada,
Ajude nos, Deus, a fazer
Seu Reino de paz hoje e agora!

Barbara de Souza

"I Hear Your Voice, O Lord"

I hear your voice, O Lord, calling me to your service of mission.
I hear your voice calling me to union with all your peoples,
of all nations,
of all cultures,
of all colors and races,
of all faiths,
to join together for a universe of peace
as we celebrate our different paths
to bring to fruition your reign in the here and the now.
This is the mission of the church.

But I know that without equality for all your creation,
without social justice,
without economic justice,
without political justice,
without sexual, cultural, and religious equality,
your reign can never come to fruition.

I hear your voice in the wind,
calling the church to this mission of peace.
I hear your voice in the cries of the hungry,
the disenfranchised,
the abandoned children,
the landless,
the disenchanted,
the faith searchers.
But I am alone, Lord,
I hear your voice all around me, but alone what can I do?
The mission of the church calls me, for with the church,
I am not alone.

Your mission calls me, and here I am, Lord,
Help us be ready to serve your mission, the church's mission,
for the church is the body of Christ, your hands in the world,
a witness to the world.

This mission of the church calls me,
I hear the call; help us, Lord, to bring
your reign of peace in the here and the now.

Barbara de Souza

The Church in a Capitalist Society

Uwe Dittmer

The following observations move from an outsider's view to an insider's insight into the church in a capitalist society. The perspective is that of a Christian who lives in the former German Democratic Republic (GDR), now the Federal Republic of Germany (FRG).

The Capitalist Society from Beyond the Border

Citizens of the GDR before 1990 knew about the Federal Republic of Germany exclusively by means of television. Only elderly people had some experiences from earlier times and from visits to the West that were allowed to people over 65. The FRG seemed to most of us to be the "Golden West," though the propaganda of the GDR presented the West as a capitalist society filled with contradictions.

After the sixties, a generation grew up that received only vague impressions of the West, and these were from stories, television, and highly welcomed parcels sent by friends or relatives. The dreams were filled with blue jeans, coffee, bananas, and the beautiful cars of western relatives, when those relatives were allowed to visit. East German people did not really get to know about the everyday problems of the West, such as increasing prices, high rents, unemployment, and homelessness. The image East Germans had of the West remained excellent.

The Church from Beyond the Border
History: from Stuttgart to Darmstadt

After World War II, the church formulated the *Stuttgarter Schuldbekenntnis*. This confession of guilt opened the door to the ecumenical movement. Some were deeply disappointed, however, to see the conservative church leaders of the *EKD* (Evangelical Church in Germany) turning back toward the twenties. These persons met in 1947 in Darmstadt as *Bruderrat der Evangelischen Kirche in Deutschland* and decided on a *Wort des Bruderrates der Evangelischen Kirche in Deutschland zum politischen Weg unseres Volkes*. They used very clear language and confessed guilt in terms of the developments that led the church on the wrong way. "Not Christendom and occidental culture, but repentance and turning towards the neighbors . . . that's what our people and we Christians ourselves urgently need." But the bishops of the *Evangelische Kirche* went the way of Christendom and occidental culture. The *EKD* remained *Volkskirche*. New ideas survived only in brotherhoods, groups of the Student Christian Movement, some more progressive groups, and aspects of the *Kirchentag*.

The Church as *Volkskirche*

When they thought about *Volkskirche* many Christians in the East had no positive feelings. They remembered the contract with the state in the West when the church took over responsibility for the *Militaerseelsorge* (military chaplaincy). They felt that the church had been ensnared by the administration of the state and had almost lost the chance of critical distance. Leading members of political parties participated in church councils (*Kirchenleitungen*), but the question of their first loyalty was seldom raised. Many of them supported the Lutheran "doctrine of the two kingdoms" that allows double loyalty and supports the conviction that the church must keep out of political issues.

The Church as Employer

There were more critical aspects. We in the East got the impression that the church in the West generally, as the second largest employer in the FRG, cast its lot with the rich. The trade unions automatically took their stand on the other side. From abroad that seemed entirely absurd. It looked like a prolongation of the 19th-century tradition in which the church as part of the monarchy took its stand against the labor movement.

The Church and the "Third World"

The church seems to be unable to confess its own part in the guilt related to poverty in the "Third World." Too few people understand that the poor are not poor by themselves but that they have been made poor by northern companies, institutions, and states. Insights from a new reading of the Bible that took place as a part of liberation theology were seldom accepted. The modern official church that came out of the Reformation in 1517 didn't want any kind of current reformation. They had forgotten that the church is supposed to be an *ecclesia semper reformanda*.

The Church We Have Experienced since 1990

In 1990 Christians and churches voluntarily joined the present church in a united Germany. We were given no chance to share our experiences of the GDR time. We had *new* experiences: some of us became millionaires; others were homeless; the majority fell in between. Some of the STASI-coworkers became coworkers of the Secret Service of the FRG; others were made lepers. Some became winners, others losers. The majority got a better life than they ever had before. The church we now experienced was similar to what we observed previously from beyond. The fellowship of sisters and brothers in Christ, that had been working very well over decades, was soon suffocated by the *Loccumer Erklaerung* which made us part of the EKD in spring 1990.

The Church in the Covenant with God, Entirely Committed to God's New World

What the Church Is Not:

- The church is not a political party. But that does not mean it is never partisan and has no political options.
- The church is not a social organization. But that doesn't mean it isn't similarly organized.
- The church is not an association to cultivate traditions. But that doesn't mean it neglects its own traditions.
- The church is not an association to promote fine arts. But that doesn't mean the arts are not at home there.
- The church is not a trade union. But that doesn't mean that the laborer's rights are not a major concern.
- The church is not an employers' association. But that doesn't mean there are no church employees.
- The church is not a welfare organization. But that doesn't mean it doesn't help many people.

But what then is the church, called by YHWH as part of God's people and listening to Jesus Christ?

Orientation by Jesus

It has been said, "Jesus proclaimed the kingdom of God, but the church came into being." This remark implies a question about whether the church is close to what Jesus proclaimed. Jesus proclaimed the kingdom of God. More exactly, he proclaimed: "The kingdom of God is at hand," it is "in the midst of you." All that Jesus said is part of this proclamation. He proclaims the world as it is strongly wanted by God, and therefore it is possible to repent and to change. Jesus teaches his friends to pray: "Your kingdom come," and "Your will be done on earth."

Everything in Christianity has to be focused on this goal or it has nothing to do with Jesus. In parables and deeds Jesus has taught and shown what it means to live toward God's world. And he challenged his disciples to follow, to imitate him, as seen in the following examples:

Matthew 14:13-21: Thousands are listening to Jesus. At supper time Jesus' friends give reasonable advice: "Send the crowd away to make sure they all get something to eat." But what would happen if they all would run or walk toward the next small village? Youngsters strong and quick enough would get the opportunity to buy. The next group, probably adults strong and healthy, would also find food. But the elderly, the sick, the disabled, and mothers with small children would get no food. Nothing would be left anymore to be bought. Bad luck, but that's the way it goes.

Therefore Jesus says to those who were supposed to understand the rules of God's world: "You give them something to eat."

"That's impossible. We haven't got enough for all, just for ourselves. Send them away. You know, everyone has to take care of him-or herself. That's how it works in our world."

Jesus doesn't agree. He takes bread and fish, gives thanks to God, and shares it with the hungry. And by sharing, Jesus' friends get an exciting experience and learn about God's world: All things are possible if we follow seriously the rules of God's new world.

Matthew 20:1-16: Jesus tells a parable of an employer giving all workers the same amount of money at the end of the day, though the workers started on the job at various hours, some early, some late. The vineyard owner doesn't pay on the basis of the output of their work but on the basis of what they really need for their daily life. The all-day-long workers don't need more than the part-time workers. Jesus gives an example of overcoming the deep gap between the rich and the poor, the employed and the unemployed.

John 8:3-11: "Punishment must follow sinful acts"; this is the watchword of the legalists in this story. Jesus doesn't justify adultery, but he shows how to handle human lapse and guilt. The world that lives according to God's will has new rules that even the church doesn't always put into practice.

Jesus proclaims the nearness of this *new world* of God. Nearness means achievability, possibility. Why not live that way since God makes it possible?

Opposing Arguments

Do you really believe that we ever will be able to achieve God's world?

- If I say yes, you will accuse me of a loss of reality. If I say no, you will accuse me of a lack of faith. You yourself are only interested in keeping the status quo alive. Therefore you shift the world of God into another world.

- There is no alternative between yes and no. The promise of the near *new world* of God is to be understood as a promise running along with us, running in front of us, drawing us in the correct direction according to the will of God that is God's help to anthropogenesis.

- Proclaiming Jesus as the savior of the world, inviting people to follow Jesus—this is unbearable as long as we practice the opposite of what we proclaim. To follow Jesus is mostly a matter of discipline, not of possibility and practicability.

The church is suffering a crisis of credibility. The church itself declares by its own structures and decisions: "We don't believe what we proclaim." This way the church no longer has anything important to say. And what it is doing, others are able to do just as well. Perhaps even better.

The Church within Capitalism

The church within capitalism has the same task as the church within socialism. There are simply different accents and emphases. The "yes" and "no" that the church gives to society must focus on the humanity of political, financial, economic, scientific, and environmental developments and must serve all people and society in its entirety by "mutual commitment (covenant) for justice, peace, and the integrity of creation."

What the Church Can Do:

- The church can give an example for a more just distribution of wages than now exists.

- The church can look for allies in its struggle in favor of the creation.

- The church can give an example for a sisterly and brotherly way to deal with its own coworkers, in particular with people traditionally disadvantaged and discriminated against because of race, color, gender, disability, and sexual orientation.

- The church can give an example for a value-oriented and spiritual way of life which is the opposite of a modern hedonistic and nihilistic lifestyle.

- The church can give examples for an existence that favors all kinds of helpless persons.

- The church can give examples for peace-keeping and peace-making.

- The church can clearly oppose practices in politics, economy, and society based on recklessness and greed. Memoranda that hurt nobody are of no use.

- The church can take a stand openly in the name of YHWH without looking for weak compromises, and not losing the call of God to be and to live as the people of God among many others who are nevertheless God's beloved children.

The Structure of the Church
(which is also its preaching, according to Barmen III)

A church can exist in base communities rather than parishes. Such groups will be joined by families and singles, elderly and young. Some—children, for example—may have their own groups, open for new members. Most groups will be organized as serving groups, choosing their special tasks and projects: peace initiatives, the environment, "Third-World" concerns, human-rights, women's issues, the rights of gays, and diaconical ministry. These groups will pray and celebrate worship services, enjoy Bible studies and festivities, and will keep on learning and teaching. A church existing in such groups will surely do a great deal of networking and cooperating. Synods will no more be assemblies mainly for legislation but for networking and open discussion.

Does the church of Jesus Christ really need to have its own extensive administration? Isn't it enough to have space for the bishop (or conference minister) and some coworkers? The church in Germany needs to experience a new reformation and, I'm sure, this will happen during the present century. I hope it won't be too long until Christians from the grass roots start reforming. And I'm pretty sure that they will partially learn from the United Church of Christ. But I'm also quite sure that nothing will happen if we ourselves won't pray and start and go forward and listen carefully to the Spirit of YHWH. Vamos caminando!

All Hail the Power of Jesus' Name: Reflections on the Public Witness of the Church

Jerry L. Folk

And Jesus came and said to them, "All authority in heaven and earth has been given to me. Go therefore and make disciples of all nations, baptizing them in the name of the Father and of the Son and of the Holy Spirit, and teaching them to obey everything that I have commanded you. And remember I am with you always, to the end of the age" (Matthew 28:18-20).

"Growing the church" seems to be emerging as a major or even the major concern of many mainline Protestant churches today. When explaining this emphasis, church growth advocates often appeal to the passion for mission so central throughout the New Testament. The risen Jesus' commission to his disciples in Matthew 28 is one of their favorite texts. They understand their church growth programs to be an appropriate response to this commission. I believe, however, these programs often misunderstand the vision of Christian mission that lies at the heart of the Great Commission. They leave out or, at best, seriously underplay the public witness of the church, perhaps because it is the most controversial, counter-cultural, dangerous and difficult to market dimension of Christian mission.

A Declaration

Jesus does not begin his commission to the disciples by telling them what they are to do. He begins with a word about authority. Jesus declares to his disciples, "All authority in heaven and earth has been given to me." At the heart of disciple-making is the proclamation of Jesus' authority over heaven and earth. If we are to proclaim that authority with power and credibility, we ourselves have to believe and trust in Jesus' authority. More than that! Inspired by the Holy Spirit, we ourselves must seek to accept and live under Jesus' authority. Then, and only then, will we be free from subservience to the powers and principalities of this world, free both to be and to make disciples.

"All authority has been given to me," Jesus declares. The public witness of the church rests on this declaration. It is, at its heart, a witness to the power and authority of God over heaven and earth. The public witness of the church is a continuation of the witness, which according to the synoptic Gospels, was at the center of Jesus' own ministry. "Repent, for the reign of God has come near!"

The Nature of Jesus' Authority

There is in the New Testament a mystery deeper and far more surprising than Jesus' assertion that all authority has been given to him. Jesus reveals to us the nature of God's authority and shows us that God exercises authority in a profoundly revolutionary way. God rules the world through a love that embraces even the enemies of God, a love that sacrifices and suffers as all true love does. God rules the world through a Messiah who was crucified for the sake of love and who, while dying on the cross, loved the very ones who nailed him there. God rules the world through a risen Savior who is servant of all. The wounds on the risen Jesus' body bear witness to the depth and power of God's love and to the truth that nothing is stronger than this love, not even death itself. Public witness to this truth and to its significance for public life is an essential dimension of the church's mission. When we neglect this witness or push it to the margin of our missionary activity, we betray Jesus Christ. But when we pursue this witness boldly, we threaten the powers and principalities of this world and put the church and ourselves in danger.

Engaging the Powers

The powers of this world believe they are in charge, that the world belongs to them, that they can buy it and sell it, exploit it or abuse it and all who live in it for their own profit, pleasure or entertainment. In modern western society, characterized by extreme materialism, individualism, affluence and narcissism, it's often not only leaders who believe this but ordinary citizens as well. Being in this world, we ourselves, both individually and as churches, are inevitably infected with this belief.

Whenever we bear public witness to true authority, i.e. to the authority of Jesus, an authority exercised through suffering love, we expose and challenge the false authority of worldly power, even when it is found in the church. This provokes conflict, embroils us in struggle, and puts us in danger. If our church growth programs never lead us into conflict with worldly power, if all people always speak well of us, if our way is too smooth, if no one is ever offended by our message, perhaps our disciple-making is defective. Perhaps we are neglecting or marginalizing our call to witness boldly and publicly to Jesus' authority.

Church Growth and Discipleship

Failing to see the importance for the church's mission of Jesus' declaration about his authority is one way, but not the only way in which some church growth programs misinterpret and misapply Matthew 28:18-

20. Church growth programs also often emphasize Jesus' command to baptize while overlooking his equally important command to make disciples or they separate the two from each other. But the central commandment in Jesus' commission to his disciples is to "go and make disciples of all nations." The rest of the commission explains what this means. It means "baptizing them in the name of the Father and of the Son and of the Holy Spirit, teaching them to obey everything that I have commanded you."

The command to baptize, to incorporate people into the body of Christ, comes between Jesus' charge to make disciples of all nations and his charge to teach them to obey all he commanded. This positioning makes it clear that we cannot separate baptism and church membership from discipleship. If we do, we are marketing cheap grace. "Cheap grace," Bonhoeffer said, "is the deadly enemy of our Church . . . . Cheap grace means grace sold on the market like cheapjack's wares. The sacraments, the forgiveness of sins, and the consolations of religion are thrown away at cut prices . . . . Cheap grace is grace without discipleship, grace without the cross, grace without Jesus Christ, living and incarnate."[1]

In his "Letter from Birmingham City Jail" (1963), Martin Luther King, Jr. speaks eloquently about the tragic results of separating church membership from Christian discipleship. He writes,

I see the church as the Body of Christ. But, oh! How we have blemished and scarred that body through fear of being nonconformists . . . . The early Christians rejoiced at being deemed worthy to suffer for what they believed. In those days, the church was not merely a thermometer that recorded the ideas and principles of popular opinion. It was a thermostat that transformed the mores of society. Whenever the early Christians entered a town, the people in power became disturbed and immediately sought to convict the Christians of being "disturbers of the peace." . . . Things are different now. Far from being disturbed by the presence of the church, the power structure of the average community is consoled by the church's silent—and often even vocal—sanction of things as they are.

King continues with a warning. "If today's church does not recapture the sacrificial spirit of the early church, it will . . . be dismissed as an irrelevant social club with no meaning for the 20th century. Every day I meet young people whose disappointment with the church has turned into outright disgust."[2]

The Great Commission is not about membership recruitment. In giving us this commission, Jesus calls us to be disciples and to make disciples, to acknowledge, proclaim, and accept his authority by obeying and teaching others to obey everything that he commands. What is this "everything?" Does Jesus impose a new legalism on the world? This is certainly not his intention in Matthew 28 or any other place in the Gospel of Matthew. Jesus does radicalize the law. But he also simplifies it by reducing it to a single commandment: the law of love. "You shall love the Lord your God with all your heart, and with all your soul, and with all your mind. This is the greatest and first commandment. And a second is like it. You shall love your neighbor as yourself. On these two commandments hang all the law and the prophets" (Mt 22:37-40).

God Is Love

Peter F. Ellis, in his commentary on Matthew, writes that for Jesus, "Everything in the Law and the Prophets is not only summed up in the love command but is subordinate to and subject to the love command for its interpretation . . . . Where love of neighbor is in conflict with any other law, even the law of the Sabbath . . . the law of love takes precedent.[3]

In the Sermon on the Mount, Jesus illumines the radical nature of love as he understands it with these words. "But I say to you, love your enemies and pray for those who persecute you, so that you may be children of your Father in heaven; for he makes his sun rise on the evil and on the good, and sends rain on the righteous and the unrighteous" (Mt 5:44-45). In these words, Jesus also gives us a glimpse into the very heart of God as he knows and experiences God. God reigns over the world through love, the same radical love Jesus practiced when, from the cross, he prayed for those who nailed him there (Lk 23:34). These words point forward to the First Letter of John, which tells us that the God who made and rules the world, the God who sent Jesus into the world, is love (1 Jn 4:8). Jürgen Moltmann underscores the radical nature of this declaration in his book, *The Trinity and the Kingdom*. He points out that Christian tradition has always understood these words to be not only an assertion about the way God relates to the world but also a revelation about the innermost nature of God's divine being and life. In other words, "God not only loves, but is love."[4]

The public witness of the church is a radical witness. It is a witness to the authority of Jesus, the authority of God over the world, an authority exercised through the power of suffering love. This witness is an integral part of Christian mission to the world. The church must make this witness not just in its proclamation but also in its life. Whenever it fails to do so or does so in a muffled or equivocating manner, the church is unfaithful to its whole mission.

Mission and the Market

Market studies may reveal that there is no great demand for this witness, that it is not a saleable product. And in a world that divinizes the market, it is hard to dismiss such studies. But no matter how popular the worship of Mammon-Market may be, the disciples of Jesus know that Mammon-Market is not God. The market did not make the world, and it does not own the world. The promises of his prophets notwithstanding, Mammon-Market cannot save us. And we cannot be disciples of two masters: both God and Mammon. We have to choose whom we will serve. If we choose God, the going will not be easy, especially in this 21st century world of the globalized and divinized market.

If we decide to take up our cross and follow Jesus along this dangerous way, we would do well to carry with us in our hearts the words with which Jesus ends his Great Commission. Jesus did not begin his Great Commission with a commandment, and he does not end it with one either. He began with an assertion. "All authority in heaven and earth has been given to me!" He ends with a promise. "Remember, I am with you always, to the end of the age." Jesus' command to make disciples of all nations is framed by a declaration and a promise. This assertion and this promise sustain us in the difficult work of Christian mission. Faith in this assertion and this promise gives us the courage and hope we need to remain faithful and steadfast to our call. This faith is the victory that conquers the world (1 Jn 5:4b).

Notes

1. Dietrich Bonhoeffer, *The Cost of Discipleship* (New York: Macmillan, 1949), 35-36.

2. Martin Luther King, Jr., *Why We Can't Wait* (New York: Mentor, 1963), 91-92.

3. Peter F. Ellis, *Matthew* (Collegeville, Minn.: The Liturgical Press, 1974), 152-153.

4. Jürgen Moltmann, *The Trinity and the Kingdom* (New York: Harper & Row, 1981), 57.

The Healing of the Nations

Reinhard Groscurth

"I love to tell the story" of *Kirchengemeinschaft,* this very special relationship between the United Church of Christ (UCC) and one of its mother churches, the Evangelical Church of the Union in Germany (EKU), formally expressed by the respective synods on both sides of the Atlantic in the years 1980 and 1981 but informally prepared since the foundation of the German Evangelical Synod of the West in 1872. And it would be easy to explain again how the term *Kirchengemeinschaft,* introduced by Dietrich Bonhoeffer in 1936[1] and used again in the year 1973 by the so-called Leuenberg Concord between Lutheran, Reformed and United churches in Europe and Latin America (now altogether 101 churches), has been rightly applied to the communion existing between the UCC and the EKU. That story, however, has been told more than once[2] and to carry coals to Newcastle is not appropriate.

Nevertheless, when we consider the nature and purpose of the church we should not forget that there is a history in each local, regional and national expression of the *one, holy, catholic, and apostolic church.* We should also keep in mind that the relationships between these "expressions," the different branches of Christianity, are in themselves part of the mission. How churches relate to each other, how they share their common history and how they try to realize the "fully committed fellowship" (New Delhi 1961) is in itself a sermon; if the process of sharing fails, the credibility of the church is at stake. Protestant churches in many parts of the world—more than their Anglican, Orthodox, or Roman-Catholic counterparts—have been inclined far too long to live in isolation and to become somewhat narrow minded and perhaps even nationalistic. The ecumenical movement of the 20th century has helped to stop this trend; it has encouraged those churches to discover their common roots and—to quote a title by the famous ecumenical pioneer and first General Secretary of the World Council of Churches, Dr. Willem A. Visser't Hooft—"The Pressure of our Common Calling".

It must be stressed, however, that the emphasis on history and on links from the past is not sufficient to describe the nature of the church nor to discuss the tasks for today's public witness. Even if we add the need for a critical evaluation of the present situation ("roots" plus today's problems) we will not succeed. There are so many predicaments in our world that we quickly become inclined to jump from one activity to the next and get breathless very soon. I am convinced that one has to look beyond the horizon of our "normal" life. If we look further, we may be able to get a glimpse of God's future. Theologically speaking: Eschatology is needed to find ecclesiological answers.

There is one particular biblical vision that may help us to overcome the border between today and the future of God. It is found in the last two chapters of the New Testament. Their summary: A new heaven and a new earth will come and all things will be new. Interestingly enough there are not only visionary descriptions of the glory of God and of the changes of the entire *kosmos,* but also the rulers of this present world ("the kings of the earth," Rev 21:24) and the nations are mentioned: They also will be changed, they will be healed (Rev 21:24-26; 22:2). There will be, to quote the Greek word for healing, a *therapy* for all the nations.

In reviewing the synoptic Gospels we discover that the Greek word *therapeuein* is used again and again for the healing miracles that Jesus performs. Health and healing are essential aspects of his ministry. But this is not limited to him: He passes on his authority, *exousia,* to the disciples, the original twelve (Mt 10:1ff.) and the seventy (Lk 10:1 ff.). To be sure: Healing is not the only task given to the followers of our Lord, but it is also part of their commission. Obviously both for Jesus Christ and for his disciples healing is not limited to the "believers"; most of those miracles are described as a public witness by which even the rather strict borders between Jewish and pagan persons are overcome.

If we relate this commission to heal, given by Jesus to his followers in the Gospel, to the vision of the "healing of the nations" in the Book of Revelation, it becomes possible to discover our own place in this *Heilsgeschichte*: We may be able to contribute to the healing process in our present time. And though we will definitely not be able to produce God's kingdom on earth, we may be in a position to witness to this kingdom which will certainly come and in which there will be no more violence, suffering and tears.

Can *Kirchengemeinschaft* between two churches become a *therapy* at least for the two nations in which they exist? And could this lead to a public witness in our present world? One should be modest in every evaluation and refrain from the so-called success-stories. Fairly often they represent the doctrine of "justification by works." But with this in mind and without going into too many historical details, I may be permitted to present briefly a few examples.

On February 11, 1936, President Dr. S. D. Press of Eden Theological Seminary wrote to General Superintendent Otto Dibelius, Pastor Gerhard Jacobi, and Pastor Martin Niemöller and told them that Eden Seminary had decided to confer on them a D.D.,[3] an honorary doctorate of divinity. To Niemöller he wrote: "It has fallen on you under peculiarly trying conditions to preserve the liberty of the Christian gospel. . . . You still stand firmly for the complete freedom of the gospel at the present critical moment." Of the three persons so honored probably Niemöller was the most endangered. In 1937 he became Adolf Hitler's "personal prisoner" and spent seven years in a concentration camp. After the war he declared that with some probability this title, indicating international recognition, saved his life.

After the war both the Evangelical and Reformed Church and the General Council of the Congregational Christian Churches, together with many other churches in the USA, paved the way to reconciliation with their former enemies, the Germans. The hands of friendship were extended in a remarkable way. One of my own recollections of that time: Big freighters unloaded in the seaport of my hometown Bremen, CARE parcels on the hooks, many of them bearing the inscription "In the name of Christ." Among those who worked for the reconstruction of Europe from the very beginning were Dr. Carl E. Schneider and Dr. Howard Schomer, to name only two from the two traditions which in 1957 joined to become the United Church of Christ.

Healing of the nations: It was in the years 1960–1962 when in our country many children were born with severe limitations, often with very short arms and with restricted movement—a sad consequence of their mothers' taking thalidomide during their pregnancies. Soon afterwards the government of the Federal Republic of Germany invited Dr. Harold Wilke for five months as an adviser for parents, teachers, nurses, and medical doctors. As a person without arms he proved to be a living witness to the special abilities God can provide. H. Wilke's regular visits to both parts of Germany (besides all his visits to so many other countries in all continents) and his appeals to provide access for people with wheelchairs became influential far beyond the borders of the church. "The Healing Community" (so one of his books) is a vision which nobody should forget.

In 1961 the infamous "Wall" was erected throughout Germany. The East German government tried to cut all existing links between East and West and exerted its power particularly on the churches. The EKU tried to avoid a total separation—after all their union existed since 1817! Thus in 1972 two independent but connected regions (*Bereiche*) were formed. Throughout the following seventeen years the UCC did everything possible to stress the unity of the partner church. The experiences of the great number of visitors from the UCC to the Eastern part (behind the "Iron Curtain") and of those often isolated Christians in remote villages provided at the same time spiritual and political insights which should not be forgotten. Fraternal workers, moving more or less freely between East and West, were helpful go-betweens.

Questions of peace and war—"a just peace church"—how to deal with minorities and migrant workers, the dichotomy existing between God's justice and our rather fragile attempts to create greater justice between the nations, the dilemma of the death penalty (totally abolished by the Germans after the murder of those millions of people before and during the war)—all these and many other themes have been in the discussion between the UCC and the EKU. More than once it was stressed that in *Kirchengemeinschaft* interference is more important than the exchange of diplomatic niceties. Obviously this is demanding.

Last but not least, one should mention the common theological roots and the enormous task of passing on the torch of faith to the next generation. How do we deal with the change of values and find a new style of living? What can we do for mutual "faith enrichment" (theme of General Synod XIII in 1981)? Thanks be to God that there have been bridge-builders aware of these basic questions, among them Dr. Frederick Trost, who has always kept in mind the roots of our common faith, who has been conscious of the predicaments and promises of our present time and who together with so great a cloud of witnesses is expecting God's future in which even the nations shall be healed.

Notes

1. D. Bonhoeffer, "Zur Frage nach der Kirchengemeinschaft," *Ev. Theologie,* Jahrgang 3, (1936): 214-233.

2. Louis H. Gunnemann, *United and Uniting. The Meaning of an Ecclesial Journey*, (New York: United Church Press, 1987). Reinhard Groscurth, "The Challenge of Mutual Recognition among United Churches," in: Michael Kinnamon and Thomas F. Best, *Called to be One in Christ.* (Geneva: World Council of Churches, 1985). In German many sources are available in the volume *Kirchengemeinschaft im Schmelztiegel: Anfang einer neuen Ökumene? Anfragen und Dokumente aus der United Church of Christ*, ed. Frederick Herzog and Reinhard Groscurth. (Neukirchen, 1989).

3. James Bentley, *Martin Niemöller, 1892–1984,* (New York, 1984), 92.

"Oh Dios y Padre Nuestro"

Oh Dios y Padre nuestro,
que por la obra redentora de tu Hijo,
llamas con la fuerza de tu Espíritu a la unidad,
a todos los humanos de toda raza, lengua y nación;
permanece en los empobrecidos de la tierra y haz
que apresuren la llegada de tu Reino
con la oración de sus múltiples sufrimientos.

Por el mismo Cristo tu Hijo,
que vive y reina contigo en la unidad del Espíritu Santo,
por los siglos de los siglos.

Samuel Ruiz Garcia

Our God and our Father,
through the redemptive work of your Son and the power of your Spirit,
you open the door to unity for all humans of all races, languages, and
nations.
Remain with the poor of the earth.
May their prayers and their great suffering hasten the arrival of your reign.

Through Christ your Son,
who lives and reigns with you in unity with the
Holy Spirit, for ever and ever.

(translation from the Spanish, Marcia Fry and Thomas S. Neilsen)

The Child as Redeemer and Victim: Theology and Global Reality

Kristin Herzog

"Let the little children come to me, do not stop them, for it is to such as these that the kingdom of God belongs"(Mk 10:14). For centuries this has been a popular baptism text and a topic for sentimental pictures, but in its original setting it probably had nothing to do with baptism or familiar sentiments.[1] Jesus' words have a revolutionary character. "Unless you turn and become like children you will never enter the kingdom of heaven" (Mt 18:3); "Whoever does not receive the kingdom of God as a little child will never enter it" (Mk 10:15; Lk 18:17). "Whoever welcomes one such child in my name welcomes me, and whoever welcomes me welcomes not me but the one who sent me" (Mk. 9:37). Such words must have touched a raw nerve in Jesus' disciples who had just quarreled about getting first place in heaven when he put a child in their midst and insisted that it was a model for being "the greatest" in the kingdom of God (Mt 18:4). He was "indignant" (Mk 10:14) when they wanted to keep children away from him.

Jesus does not make dogmatic statements, but his words are visions that like lightning illuminate the skyline of God's kingdom. Children to him are the concrete representatives of all those persons of no account who are under God's special protection. They are not unfinished human beings, raw material to be shaped by knowledgeable adults, as the Greco-Roman world assumed.[2] Jesus turns things upside down: the adult disciples are the ones to be taught, and "the child becomes the lesson."[3] Not only ages and social positions are revalued, but even genders: he "took [the children] up in his arms" (Mk 10:16; 9:36), a very feminine gesture.[4] He does not ask women to be better mothers, but he asks his male disciples to do what mothers usually do.[5] He asks them, so to speak, to bend down to the child's level, to be spiritually daring and socially caring. Where this "bending" or reaching out is missing, there is no divine life, no partaking of God's reign (Mt 18:6), no *talitha cumi,* helping the child to rise and grow (Mk 5:41).

The context of the disciples' quarrel about their status is as revealing as other stories surrounding the texts about children: the pleading widow and the Pharisee and the tax collector (Lk 18) and discussions on marriage and divorce, poverty and riches (Mk 10). The overall message appears to be that where God rules, things are different from human standards: the humble are exalted, the poor are rich, women get their rights, and the last shall be first. "Whoever becomes humble like this child is the greatest in the kingdom of heaven" (Mt 18:4). Humility in the Hebrew Bible as well as the New Testament is not a state of mind but "an objective state of . . . dependency."[6] Jesus is not describing the innocence of children but the character of God who is always on the side of the most needy, vulnerable, or marginal beings. His observation of children playing in the market place (Mt 11:16-19; Lk 7:31-35) shows that he did not romanticize children but knew they could be as stubborn and discontented as adults.

The point of Jesus' sayings concerning children is neither a call to individualistic spirituality nor to social activism. Heart and mind cannot be separated from concrete action and from life in community. The mystery of sharing in the kingdom of God lies in the unity of a childlike dependence on God and a concrete "receiving" of children. Jesus is not an anti-intellectual promoting naiveté. After all, he asks his disciples to be "wise as serpents" (Mt 10:16). What the child models for him is the ability to live and grow by receiving, to be free and active without being "in control." The message of the Reformation finds a confirmation in Jesus' sayings about children because they imply that only by grace we are able to discover and use our own creativity.

One New Testament exegete has stated that "Jesus' conscious concern for children has no analogies in the history of religions."[7] Much research still has to be done to confirm such a statement. The Jews of antiquity appreciated children so much that they never abandoned sickly or deformed newborns the way Greeks or Romans did. "Children have a fundamentally positive significance and role in Old Testament-Jewish tradition. They are seen as a divine gift and sign of God's blessing."[8] They are bearers of the tradition and therefore will continuously be drawn into dialogue with their parents about the exodus history (Ex 13:14; Deut 6:20-25). Even more: the messianic age will be initiated by a child who will bring peace and justice to all living beings: "For a child has been born for us, a son given to us; . . . authority rests upon his shoulders" (Isa 9:6); "the wolf shall live with the lamb, the leopard shall lie down with the kid, . . . and a little child shall lead them" (Isa 11:6). We are used to reading these verses as pointing to Christ, but they were originally prophesying a concrete prince on the throne of David, so they had political as well as spiritual implications.

The idea of a redeemer child appears even in antique mythology and philosophy as the image of future peace, harmony with animals, and the return of the Golden Age.[9] One aspect of this child's divinity is often its birth by a virgin. For example, according to legend, the Buddha was born around 563 C.E. in today's Nepal as son of a royal couple. In the form of a white elephant with six horns he entered the side of his mother, Queen Maya. Nine months later, when she walked through the gardens, she reached up to a branch, and the child appeared from her side. Gods made music and threw flowers to celebrate the child. The blind began to see, the mutes were able to speak, prisoners were set free, and peace entered the world.[10]

One of the five greatest gods of Hinduism, Ganesa, the God with the head of an elephant, was born in even more miraculous circumstances. This symbol of vitality, humor, and kindness did not even need a virgin's womb but was created by Siva for his wife, the goddess Parvati, from a piece of her sari.[11]

Surprisingly, Islam accepts the virgin birth of Jesus.[12] There are also various stories about the prophet Muhammad's love of children, and, according to the Koran, Jesus' ministry began as soon as he was born; even as an infant he proclaimed the life he will live and the wonders he will perform.[13]

Also in our day there are redeemer children thought to have divine powers, and frequently they are politically influential. There is, for example, the fourteen-year-old 17th Karmapa of Tibetan Buddhism, who during the past year fled to India because the Chinese government did not permit him to receive the proper Buddhist instruction. Karmapas are chosen as children and are supposed to liberate their followers from an endless cycle of birth, death, and rebirth.

Much closer to home we find a redeemer child even in ancient American history. The half-god and mythical hero Dekanawida was born from a virgin of the Huron tribe. Together with his disciple Hayonwatha he founded the famous Iroquois League of Peace that is thought to have influenced Benjamin Franklin and the U.S. Constitution.[14]

What can we learn, then, from these multiple, persistent images of the child as redeemer in totally different geographic, cultural, and religious settings? The child is the irrepressible symbol of hope, peace, and justice, not only among human beings but for all of creation. Why, then, are millions of the world's children victims of neglect?

One in five children in the U.S. is living in poverty. Every two hours a child or youth under 20 is killed by a firearm. Every four hours a child or youth under 20 commits suicide. More than a third of the homeless families who sought shelter in 1997 were families with children, and the number has increased. What does it say about our concern for children when a childcare worker earns a little over $12,000 a year without any benefits while the average professional football player receives 182 times that much?[15] Six to seven million U.S. children are now taking mood-altering drugs like Ritalin.[16] School children have murdered their classmates, and violence among teenagers is epidemic in the cities. Child abuse is much more frequent within families and among acquaintances than between strangers and is aggravated by the media and the general public which commercialize and sexualize children. There is also a "legislative child abuse" that demands "family values" while cutting programs that benefit children.[17]

If we look abroad, the picture is even more disturbing: 32,000 children under age five die daily on this globe from preventable or curable diseases. An estimated 300,000 child soldiers have been recruited in Africa, Asia, and Latin America. About 250 million children work for starvation wages to enable their families' survival. An estimated one million children are this year being forced into sexual trafficking.[18] There are some 11 million AIDS orphans worldwide. While 2% of children under five in the U.S. suffer from developmental problems related to hunger or poor nutrition, in Peru they represent 26%, in Sierra Leone 35%, and in Vietnam 44%.[19] Two hundred fifty children die each day in Iraq on account of the U.S. embargo.[20] The Kosovo war has once more proved children's massive victimization by war, and Tschernobyl will forever remind us that children are most vulnerable from environmental pollution. By last year, 191 nations had signed the United Nations Convention on the Rights of the Child, but it has not been ratified by the United States and Somalia.

What, then, is the churches' task? The Methodist bishops are to be commended for raising the consciousness of their members concerning the plight of children, but much more has to happen in theology and the churches in order to witness to the radicalism of Jesus concerning the child as model.[21] He did not preach a dogmatic principle but practiced a vision. The child as bearer of transcendence is a paradox to be verified in a way of life, in conscience. We have to be sensitized, for example, to the relationship between the massive suffering of children on this globe and the growing gap between rich and poor: the top 1% of households of the U.S. hold almost 40% of the nation's wealth.[22] We also can be more imaginative in including children in our worship. David Cunningham has tried to relate his understanding of the Trinity to a necessary "polyphony"of voices in our worship services that intentionally includes children. He sees Black and Hispanic church services as models in this regard.[23] Early Christian worship developed out of ritual play.[24] The serious playfulness of children could make our worship services less abstract.

God redeems humankind by appearing in the form of a vulnerable refugee baby, challenging us to answer any baby's cry to the world, to learn from the child's natural receptivity, and to nurture its growing life. In eliciting our love and care, children become agents of our own transformation. They teach us to blurt out the truth, to forget grief and quarrels quickly, to make daily new beginnings and discoveries, to trust instead of craving control. Our global reality of victimized children and idealized redeemer children is not God's reality. Godself as victim and redeemer child is struggling to be recognized in the 32,000 children in our world who should not die today. This divine presence in "the little ones" is the very "glory above the heavens" that is chanted by "the mouths of babes and infants" (Ps 8:3, cf. Mt 21:16).

This essay is lovingly dedicated to Frederick Trost, a true friend to Frederick and Kristin Herzog, and a friend of children.

Notes

1. See Joseph A. Fitzmyer, *The Gospel According to Luke,* X–XXIV (Garden City, N.Y.: Doubleday, 1985), 1993; and Ingetraut Ludolphy, "Zur Geschichte der Auslegung des Evangelium Infantium," in Gerhard Krause, ed., *Die Kinder im Evangelium* (Stuttgart: Ehrenfried Klotz Verlag, 1973), 35f.

2. Robin Maas, "Christ as the Logos of Childhood: Reflections on the Meaning and Mission of the Child," *Theology Today* 56, no. 4 (Jan. 2000): 457. "The child's value lay almost entirely in the future—in the promise of maturity (as heir, producer of wealth, defender of the nation, or bearer of more children) rather than in the concrete reality of the present."

3. See Hans-Ruedi Weber, *Jesus and the Children: Biblical Resources for Study and Preaching* (Geneva: World Council of Churches, 1979), 46.

4. See Judith Gundry-Volf, "Mark 9:33-37: Discipleship of Equals at the Cradle and the Cross," *Interpretation* 5, no. 1 (January 1999): 58.

5. The earliest artistic representations of Christ do not show him as a domineering ruler but as a youth with feminine traits. See Thomas F. Matthews, *The Clash of the Gods: A Reinterpretation of Early Christian Art* (Princeton: Princeton Univ. Press, rev. ed., 1993), 124f, 29.

6. Weber, *Jesus and the Children,* 32.

7. Ulrich Luz, *Das Evangelium nach Matthäus, EKK* 1,3 (Zürich/ Neukirchen-Vluyn: Neukirchener Verlag, 1997), 115 (translation mine). Surprisingly, Milan Machovec (in former years a Marxist) supports this

thesis and points to Karl Marx's praise for Jesus' love of children. See his *Jesus für Atheisten* (Stuttgart: Kreuzverlag, 1973), 7, 117ff.

8. Judith Gundry-Volf, "To Such As These Belongs the Reign of God: Jesus and Children," *Theology Today* 56, no. 4 (January 2000): 470; and Thomas Wiedemann, *Adults and Children in the Roman Empire* (New Haven: Yale Univ, Press, 1989), 36f.

9. Heraclitus, *Fragments: A Text and Translation with a Commentary*, by T. M. Robinson (Toronto: Univ. of Toronto Press, 1987), 37, 166, 119f; and William Berg, *Early Virgil* (Univ. of London: Athlone Press, 1974).

10. See Patricia Eichenbaum Karetzky, *The Life of the Buddha: Ancient Scriptural and Pictorial Traditions* (Lanham, N.M.: Univ. Press of America, 1992), Introduction; and Huston Smith, *TheWorld's Religions: Our Great Wisdom Traditions* (New York: Harper Collins, 1991), 82f.

11. Paul Martin-Dubost, *Ganesa: The Enchanter of the Three Worlds* (Mumbai: Project for Indian Cultural Studies, 1997), 42, 94.

12. Koran 3:78, 19:93. See also Smith, *The World's Religions,* 236.

13. William E. Phipps, *Muhammad and Jesus: A Comparison of the Prophets and Their Teachings* (New York: Paragon/Continuum, 1996), 120, 146f , 91.

14. See William N. Fenton, ed., "The Constitution of the Five Nations," Book III of his volume *Parker on the Iroquois* (Syracuse, N.Y. Syracuse Univ. Press, 1968); and Elizabeth Tooker, "The League of the Iroquois: Its History, Politics, and Ritual," in *Handbook of North American Indians,* ed. Bruce G. Trigger (Washington, D.C.: Smithsonian Institution, 1978).

15. This is a question asked by Marian Wright Edelman. See Children's Defense Fund, *The State of America's Children, Yearbook 1999* (Washington: Children's Defense Fund, 1999), xi, xii, and *Yearbook 1998,* xviii, 6f, 11.

16. ABC News Program of January 2, 2000.

17. Henry A. Giroux, "Stealing Innocence: The Politics of Child Beauty Pageants," in Henry Jenkins, ed., *The Children's Culture Reader* (New York: New York Univ. Press, 1998), 266-271.

18. *The Christian Century* (April 19-26): 449. See also Rita Nakashima Brock and Susan Thistlethwaite, *Casting Stones: Prostitution and Liberation in Asia and the United States* (Minneapolis: Augsburg Fortress, 1996).

19. *State of the World's Children 2000* (New York: UNICEF, 2000), 90-91.

20. See James Wall in *The Christian Century* (April 19-26, 2000): 443.

21. Rainer Lachman stated in the *Theologische Realenzyklopädie:* "For systematic theology the child continues to be neither subject nor topic of scholarly reflection." TRE, vol. 18, art. "Kind" (Berlin/New York: De Gruyter, 1989); translation mine. Only recently theology in general has taken the topic seriously. *Concilium* dedicated a whole journal issue to "The Child in the Center" in 1996, and *Theology Today* concentrated on the topic in January 20. Wm. Eerdmans will published a volume on the child in theology in the fall of 2000.

22. Geneva Overholser in the Durham *Herald-Sun ,* Oct. 21, 1999.

23. David S. Cunningham, *These Three Are One: The Practice of a Trinitarian Theology* (Oxford, U.K.: Blackwell, 1-99) 275-297.

24. Bernard Lang, *Sacred Games: A History of Christian Worship* (New Haven: Yale Univ. Press, 1997.

Building the City of God:
The Mission of the Christian Community

John Huebscher

Saint Augustine once defined a community as a place where the people love certain things in common. So it is fitting that Christians take seriously the mission of building a community for doing so involves giving witness to values that bind people together and foster the justice and peace that are vital to the common good.

Some may question whether such a concern with the secular community is appropriate for a community grounded in religious faith. Public witness, however, is inseparable from faith. Indeed, the very foundations of Christian faith call us to such witness. Moreover, they call us to a particular kind of witness, that which places the needs of the poor and vulnerable at the center of our concern. At the same time, our Christianity calls us to give witness consistently, humbly and with charity so that the method of our witness models the very values to which we call the rest of the community.

Let us first consider some basic truths that serve as a wellspring for so much of our advocacy. The Christian tradition has flourished over two millennia in part because believers have drawn from its teachings and symbols, which communicate truth beyond words, to nurture their faith and help them transmit this faith to their children.

Central among these is the mystery of the Trinity. The Trinity communicates two foundational truths that define our lives and give them direction.

The first of these truths is that human life is sacred. When we "sign" ourselves in the name of Father, Son, and Spirit we affirm, in word and symbol, that each of us, in who we are and what we do, reflects the image and likeness of God. We recall also that he who died on the cross and ascended to the Father, though divine, is also human. And Christ's connection to the transcendent is mirrored in every human life.

So, life is indeed sacred. Every one of us matters. No person is defined by someone else's choices. None of us exists as a means to some one else's happiness.

The second truth grounded in our belief in the Trinity is that human life is social. As creatures made in the *image of a Triune God*, that is of a God of three *persons* who interact with each other for all eternity in loving relationship, we cannot truly reflect that image unless, we too, love other people and unless our faith has a social dimension.

Thus does our Triune God call us to leave the upper room of our personal lives and take the gifts of the Spirit into the village square, to all nations, even to the ends of the earth.

And if these teachings and symbols help us grasp why we must speak to the concerns of the community, the Scriptures tell us what our message must be. Ours must be a voice for justice—justice for all—but especially for those left outside the door. Just as we take the gospel to the ends of the earth, so are we called to bring the cause of those at the margins of society to the attention of those at its center.

As the prophets tell us, it is to our treatment of those at the margins of society, the widow, the orphan, and the stranger that God looks to judge the society. And in the gospel passage of the sheep and the goats Christ sharpens the challenge. For in that passage he makes clear that those in prison, those who are ill, those who are hungry, those who lack clothing, indeed all those who suffer are important. They are not important because that is where God looks to judge us. They are important because it is in the needs, the lives, and the very faces of such people that the Son of God is to be found.

That is why we take up the cause of the unborn child and the family on welfare. That is why we welcome the immigrant and the refugee. That is why we plead for the life of the person on death row. That is why we advocate for those without health care. That is why we speak truth to power on behalf of those who have no power. That is why our faith remains so relevant to the needs of our times.

Thus do Christians enter the public square as people who are sacred and social, guided by a faith that calls us to solidarity with all people. And if this is who we are and where we come from, what do we do with this identity? Where, now, must we go? Having come together in our faith, how do we live and model that faith to others?

Reading the signs of the times, I suggest that we offer, through the quiet dignity of our own example, a model of consistency, humility, and civility to the debates in our community. For these traits are too often lacking in the village square today.

Let me begin with consistency and focus on the importance of the consistent life ethic to our collective ministries. The Wisconsin Catholic Conference statement "The Consistent Life Ethic, A Demand of Discipleship," defines an ethic as a habit or a value that guides a person in his or her decision-making. Simply stated, a consistent life ethic directs one to evaluate his or her choices, be they public or private, in light of their impact on human life and dignity.

"The Consistent Life Ethic" challenges the trends of individualism and social isolation by reaffirming that we are all responsible for each other. It affirms that life is sacred by holding up the value of life whenever it is threatened. It affirms that life is social by asserting that acts against the dignity of life for some endanger the right to life for all.

Consider the story of Cain and Abel: Recalling Cain's question, "Am I my brother's keeper?" we are told the answer is a resounding "yes." But this responsibility for our brother extends far beyond the lineal family, culminating in the mandate of the Great Commandment to love our neighbor as our self.

It is this love to which Christians are called to give witness. As the Good Samaritan did in loving his enemy, as Pope John Paul II did in forgiving his assassin, as Cardinal Bernardin did when he forgave the young man who accused him of abuse, as Sister Helen Prejean does in *Dead Man Walking*, as we are called to do every day.

But if we are to be consistent so must we be humble. Our certainty of purpose and our commitment to the truth must never blind us to our own frailty. For our right to life is not grounded in the fact that we are worthy. Recall once more, the example of Cain. Neither Cain, nor any of us has earned our dignity. We must recall this whenever the issue of worthiness surfaces in debates over welfare, capital punishment, or euthanasia. When debates over whether those at the margins of society are worth our protection, we must ask our society the hard questions: Who are we to judge whose life is worth living? Was Christ born to redeem humankind because we deserved to be redeemed? Does God's mercy to any of us depend upon our behavior? Where would we be if God had answered that question "are we worthy?" as we so often answer it today?

It is reasonable to ask whether this lack of humility may be one reason for the coarseness in public discourse today. Too often, we are so convinced of our own virtue we refuse to see virtue in others. Too often we are willing to question or doubt the purity of an opponent's motives or even the authenticity of his or her faith.

It is often said that Christianity is a "hard" religion in the sense that the demands of the gospel are not easy to live up to and this is certainly true. It is not easy to live in a religion that says life is sacred from womb to tomb, that insists on fidelity for life in marriage or that demands obedience to doctrines one may not fully understand or support. It is easier to pick and choose those tenets to which we will adhere.

But neither is it easy to accept a smaller profit so one's workers can enjoy a just wage, to be generous to those who may not work as long or as hard as we do, to consume less of what we want so others may have more of what they need, to open our neighborhoods, our borders and our hearts to those of different races or backgrounds, to show mercy to someone who has murdered or maimed someone we love. Here, too, it is easier to turn a deaf ear to what our tradition asks of us.

Our humility should remind us that it is a rare person who can do all of those things consistently and cheerfully, and that few, if any, of us have embraced the whole of the message from day one. Each of us has struggled—and most of us continue to struggle—to be faithful to all that our faith asks of us. As such, each of us has, at one time or another, been a "cafeteria Christian" who has fallen short of the ideal.

Remaining mindful of our own failures can serve to make us more tolerant of other's frailties and limitations. Recalling the detours in our own journey of faith may make us less inclined to speak ill of someone who may be in a different place on the road. And from our humility will flow civility and charity to our opponents.

In the movie, *Mass Appeal*, Jack Lemmon plays an experienced pastor mentoring a seminarian. Lemmon asks the young seminarian, who thinks he has all the answers, if he loves his parishioners. "I love what they could be," he responds. "But," Lemmon then asks, "can you love them for who they are?"

Charity calls us to love others as they are. By doing so, even when their vision and choices differ from ours, we bear witness to the consistent life ethic. Charity and civility are the nutrients that draw fruit from the soil of "common ground." Cardinal Bernardin saw this. As he put it near the end of his life:

> We should presume that those with whom we differ are acting in good faith. They deserve civility, charity, and a good faith effort to understand their concerns. . . . We should put the best possible construction on differing positions, addressing their strongest points rather than seizing upon the most vulnerable aspects to discredit them. We should detect valid concerns and legitimate worries that may underlie even questionable arguments.

Charity to opponents is a necessary foundation to compassionate policies. Moreover, it is vital to securing an enduring commitment to such policies. Thus, we are called to speak in ways that bring people together instead of driving them apart, in ways that challenge, not chastise, discern not demonize, and enlighten not enrage. For an opponent in debate is still a neighbor. A person of a different political party or philosophy is still a sister or a brother. A person with a different vision of church is still a daughter or son of God.

The challenge to speak with consistency for the vulnerable and with humility and civility to those with whom we differ is an imposing one, as one would expect from a faith that challenges. We must be prepared for failure and setbacks. So it is appropriate to invoke another foundation for our Christian Faith, the symbolism of the cross.

The cross is both a reminder and a promise. It is a reminder that no victory comes without pain or suffering. But the cross also promises that no defeat, no matter how ignominious, is final. Easter does follow Good Friday, though always in God's good time, not ours. With that reminder and that promise ever before us, we Christians enter the third millennium of building the City of God by working as one for justice with consistency, civility, and charity to all.

"God, Ever-loving and Ever-just"

God, ever-loving and ever-just, you are our anchor and our wings. You hold us fast in the knowledge that we are yours; you set us free to discover the ways of discipleship and faith. We praise you for your constant presence in this ever-changing world, a world you have created and nurtured, a world for which unity is your dream and peace your hope.

O God, we confess that sometimes we get lost in the world that swirls around us. We get caught in the undertow, and it seems to take all our strength just to keep ourselves afloat. We become selfish about our time and about our needs, and we block out the pain of others, while you call us to be selfless and self-giving.

O God of such amazing grace, empower us to reflect the love and service that Jesus so embodied. Set our feet in places where there is hurt, that we might be instruments of healing and solace. Grant to us the vision and voice of prophets, that we might be advocates for justice and makers of peace. Stretch our compassion and expand our love, that our witness may be plain and our faith find action.

These things we pray for the sake of your realm among us, for the sake of all your children everywhere. In the name of him who is Servant and Savior.

Shari K. Prestemon

Baptism and Its "Shapeless" Protestants: Some Aspects

Christoph Keienburg

In the east of Westphalia, near the city of Büren, where Europe now runs its largest high security prison for deportable refugees from all over the (third) world, the majestic castle of Wewelsburg surmounts a huge valley. Heinrich Himmler, *Reichsführer SS*, once chose this site to be the center for the Third (World) Reich. From the north tower, which was to be the naval of the renewed Germanic kingdom, the empire would be ruled. For the remodeling of the medieval castle's tower into a *Thingstätte* for the *SS-Führer* of the whole Reich, free labor was made available by the nearby concentration camp of Niedernhagen. There were communists, Jews, gypsies, "anti-social elements," but most of the inmates here belonged to the group of the so called "earnest Bible students."

To an outsider the behavior of this group of prisoners would appear to be peculiar: In contrast to all the other prisoners who were condemned to be here because of race, sexual orientation, political opinion or subversive action, who never would be released and whose destiny was to be "destroyed by hard labor," these people seemed to remain here by their own decision. It was said that if they once agreed to lift their right arms to salute the *Führer*, if they once gave up their unintelligible resistance against the military draft (which so many Protestants and Catholics, with enthusiasm or with a mixture of contrition and obedience, had responded to), from one moment to the next they could liberate themselves from this nightmare of slave labor, hunger, and death. But though from other concentration camps single cases were reported, in Niedernhagen not one conversion took place. These strange inmates obviously answered to a power that succeeded in controlling them completely (and that even prevented them from raising a single arm).

Somehow, they were different. As in other concentration camps, part of the structure of violence in Niedernhagen was the unequal distribution of food which provoked a daily struggle for the available bread. But among this group (and those whom they were in touch with) no one died of starvation. Once in a while the SS-guards were amused at the cheerfulness of these emaciated bodies, chasing each other around the courtyard. At the end of the game, when his companions had caught him, one of them was dipped into the rain water cistern. Too far from where the action took place, the SS could not hear the transforming words spoken over the basin. They never would have imagined that what they were witnessing was a baptism, a procession from a world of grief into a kingdom that obviously had more to offer than the empire which erected its ridiculous tower up the hill. A kingdom whose citizens would be among those who finally were to be rescued. And whose King expected an unconditional loyalty.

In Niedernhagen and other places the "severe Bible seekers" earned the name under which they are known, deprecated, and smiled at still today: "Jehovah's Witnesses." After the dissolution of the camp, after the death of hundreds of inmates, after the tumbling down of Himmler's mythical tower, some of the SS guards applied for membership in this other kingdom.

II

What do our churches of today, UCC and EKU, have to offer children and adults when they respond to the Word and are commited to the risen Lord? Into what reality do we—in obedience to God's will—draft people? In both contexts the sacrament is stuck in a kind of schizophrenic situation: On the one hand there is a huge hermeneutical apparatus, mounted over a more than slippery exegetical landscape, screwed together with a bunch of psycho-sociological insights. Whatever the sacrament is considered to be—a performative act, a *rite de passage*, a *billet d'entrance* into a particular social group, an exterior sign of an interior assent, an incentive to a family feast, a condition or a result of faith, the start of a pilgrimage or the destination of a tour, a symbol of death and rebirth, co-crucifixion or anointment to kingship, priesthood, prophetical office— every church boasts of an elaborate, flawless baptismology.

On the other hand the churches often appear to baptize whomever they can grasp, at the same time deploring the loss of depth and seriousness in the acceptance of this practice. Their hermeneutical efforts to reconquer sense and wholeness, gratuity and grace seem to be surpassed by the allegedly more impressive narrations that surround them. Their liturgical performances suffer from a lack of self-evidence: Lukewarm water goes with tulips and swimming candles. For the child's soul's sake, hell and devil have been eliminated from the prayers, and the hymns from the first tunes on make clear that in this ceremony—besides an unforeseen flickering of the candle—nothing dangerous can happen. High theology above flat waters.

III

In the same region where fifty years ago two kingdoms were disputing over the hearts and bodies of the inmates of the Niedernhagen concentration camp, a young couple of today, born into a once secret

Lutheran congregation in Russia or Kazakhstan and now longing for a decent life in West German society, knock at the parish door and want their child to be baptized.

"Are you baptized yourself?"

"Well, I don't know. My aunt did something to me in our living room."

"Did she use water?"

"Yes."

"Well, that's something! Why do you want your daughter to be baptized?"

"She has all the documents, she has been vaccinated; why should we not do what all the others do as well?"

Any interpretation of the irrefutable ontological quality, the soteriological significance, and the ecclesiological consequence of baptism for this child of God will fail in front of the current situation where the petitioners know: The relevant question is how to enter at lowest cost into a ritual, which obviously is as necessary for the conquest of normality as it is completely irrelevant for life itself.

For the Baptist in the Mexican High Sierra (who never would submerge an *infant* into the baptistery) it is a matter of fact and lies beyond the necessity of interpretation: His/her dedication to Christ sealed in this Holy Moment is one decisive step on a long voyage that liberates him/her and *the whole community* from *all* the evils of this world. Therefore at least some secular evils such as alcohol, drugs, nicotine, dance, promiscuity are to be banned *right now*, together with all the other invisible companions of the devil.

For the catechumenate, the way with many steps, the *katecoumenoi,* (catechumens) are asked to take one step after another on their pilgrimage out of the darkness into the brightness of Easter morning. Accompanied by daily exercises of purification and filling of soul and body, this way is a process of mutual incorporation. While the believer, by fasting, breathing, praying, gradually begins to prepare for the break with evil and for the inhalation of the divine atmosphere (and so develops techniques that would help her/him in the lifelong battle through which he/she will have to stand), this divine atmosphere—in the dogmatic tradition considered to be the body of Christ or the community of saints—takes possession of her/him. Baptism on this voyage is not a singular act, not just one *cairotic* moment; it is a necessary, irreversible step on the itinerary.

IV

The current practice in both the UCC and the EKU suffers from the fact that the gratuity of grace granted, promised, performed, gifted in the act of baptism, apparently has dispensed the aspirants (and the celebrants and congregation too) from any kind of preparation or after-treatment, (aside, perhaps, from the hint of the presiding pastor to turn to the page of the hymnal where they can find the Apostles' Creed during the service). Instead, all stress is laid on the moment. From the organized church's perspective there is an enormous accumulation of things that *should be believed* during the ceremony (often the parents of the baptized infant or the confirmand escape from this intellectual and emotional exaction by beginning the mental preparation for what comes after the service). But there is little that *may be done* as a matter of course, unquestioned, and beyond subjectivist personal options or psychological patterns, few that really would nourish the baptized on his/her way as king, prophet, priest, member of the community of saints, steward in God's household or whatever profile the sanctification of the individual shall gain in the long run of his/her life.

The *factus brutus* of being baptized is not embedded into any structure. Plenty are the powers that claim respect in life: the golden hammer of the *simul justus et simul peccator* bangs over the heads of all those who, once in a while, startled by the gospel, could realize that they *are* already citizens of the only real kingdom, that they *have* left the gray zones between life and death, and that the struggles and sufferings they are witnessing in their lives are nothing else than Christ's own struggle on his way to bring light, bread, water, life in fullness to his world.

A church that exempts so easily the aspirants (or their parents and godparents) from a process of cleansing and clearance on the way to the baptistery and that leaves them—in the true sense of the word—"un-in-formed" after having crept out of it: Is this "yes at no cost," presented as a "service to the customer" when it is really an act of *serving* a child of God who is called to make his/her steps on a risky road, into a new, undiscovered landscape? The hasty attendance to the "wants" of the "member," regarding his/her "desires" and "preferences": will it really help the other to grow up in faith, to learn to live up to his/her incomparable, unknown, and unforeseeable commitment in face of the dangerous, tremendous, and attentive reality, which in baptism claims possession over this child? Or will it simply perpetuate a structure of infantilism in which at best the future "member" "attends" a "church" in order to get fed by those who anyway know better?

Our churches talk a lot about the gift of baptism; they practice it as if it were theirs. But it just isn't. Baptism distinguishes them from all other religious traditions, and it distinguishes every single believer from any other human being in the world. So evil has to be banned. A whole life long. The Holy words and the Holy meal have to be digested. A whole life long. The way to peace and justice has to be discovered. A whole life long. And day by day death has to be confronted. There is a new *shape* that makes a distinction, a smell, a sound, a breath, a way to walk, a way to love, a way to struggle, a way to die and to resurrect.

V

The young Russian-German couple, really interested, really affected, really open, as if to ask: "What type of vaccination will our child receive now, when they pour water over her head? Against what will she be immunized by the name pronounced with so much solemnity? What measures do we have to take in order to prevent her from any reversion?"

The parents do not carry the dogmatic ballast on their shoulders; they do not have to be liberated from the boring truism that has inflicted and darkened the calling of so many baptized human beings. They want the best for their child. Should they not come to know that "to get into" means "to leave from," and "to be filled with" implies "to get rid of"? Should they not have a right to discover what "no" corresponds to the unconditioned "yes" that is about to grasp their child to turn her upside down and downside up?

Does the church really have the right to withold its guidance because it fears that demand and exactation could cause frustration or anger, that the strangemess of the word and the archaism of her religious labor could evoke laughter or shaking heads or—worst case for so many servants of the word—"misunderstanding"? Never even running the risk of denying a baptism or banning a camera from the choir or a chrysanthemum from the font—how can the church in full power hand over the *exorcistic* forces of the mystery to those who deserve them to master their lives? Never having forced anyone to look at, to name, and to confront the powers that limit and bind, suffocate and strangulate the textures of life, how can the church assist the Spirit to develop the *exodal* dynamics, breaking rules and values, life scripts and family structures, prison cells and chains of injustice and consequently to discover the *other country*?

VI

In the concentration camp of Niedernhagen some young men were so impressed by the solidarity and atmosphere of love that the community of the "earnest Bible students" emitted, that they requested to be part of the community and to be baptized. For them it was a clear decision: To belong to this community would involve facing a long way of suffering and certain death. From the ideological point of view of a religious, sectarian organization it was a favorite situation (new members!), and so it might have been from the religious point of view of the (secret) leading committee (souls saved for Jehovah's kingdom!). But the council, whose members over a long time had seen the death of so many believers on the way of succession, informed the young candidates of its decision: It asked the aspirants to withdraw their petition. For the elders it had become clear that Jehovah did not want more young lives to be sacrificed. "We are convinced that He has accepted you as citizens of His kingdom and wants you to get out of here. We will keep on praying for you." The young men reacted sadly, but finally they accepted. Whereas the leaders of a sect, in the midst of hell, in a struggle for illumination that had been urged on them by their own baptism, had fathomed the depths of the godhead.

"O Most Compassionate and Enriching God"

O most compassionate and enriching God, restorer of all life,
we gather as your family and people
to be fulfilled in the presence of your Holy Spirit.
You call us out of obscurity, confusion, and denial
to stand fast in the struggle for the integrity and decency of the human spirit.
Help us to have the courage and strength to do what is right and holy.

Lord God, teach us the grace to see beyond our selfishness
that we may serve you by serving others,
especially those whom our society deems "last, least, and lost."
Help us to feed the hungry, clothe the naked, give shelter to the homeless
and refugees,
lift up those oppressed by great tyranny and violence,
and give voice to those who have no voice.
Help us to witness together as Jesus in our time and world.

Eternal Hope, help us always to offer our lives as vessels through which
your presence shines,
even in the darkest corners of existence.
Take us—body, mind, and soul—as a holy offering of service to the world,
even if that service leads us to our own cross.

In the name of Jesus the Christ, Holy and Eternal, we offer our prayer.

Thomas S. Neilsen

The Church's Choice: Prophecy or Extinction

Daniel C. Maguire

Christian theology and preaching is full of talk about salvation, about being saved and redeemed. That talk presents a question that every age must answer for itself. What is it that we are being saved from and what kind of redemption do we need?

Add to this question a significant factor: the weakening of the main stream. Christian churches, at the dawning of the twenty-first century, are in decline. Their relevancy is questioned. A principal reason for this, I submit, is the lack of focus in the churches on the actual "salvation" and "redemption" needs of planet earth along with its peoples and all of its exuberant life forms. The reign of God is a capstone principle of biblical religion. What it means is that the destructive, cold-hearted, earth-wrecking penchant of humanity—captured in theology under the rubric of "original sin"—needs to be challenged. The biblical poets dared to dream that God would step into history and, with a blessed embrace, turn it around, moving us from war to peace, from devastation to flourishing, and from solitariness to solidarity. That is the divine protocol implied by the phrase "reign" or "kingdom of God." That biblical dream is mocked by the current state of the world and of human society. Whatever Jesus and the prophets did, they didn't save the world.

Pause for a moment and take a look at the real state of the planet. It's hard to do that. It's so painful that it is almost like looking at the sun. We self-protectively turn our gaze away from the facts of modern life. Of course, it's easy to do that when you live where we live. The United Nations, an institution that is more into prophecy than most "people of faith," illustrates our sin with a champaign glass model of the world's wealth. Most of us live in the cup where the champaign bubbles. That is, the top 20 percent of the human race income-wise. We receive 92 percent of all world income, leaving 18 percent to the remaining 90 percent of suffering humanity. And there is more bad news. Let's dare to look at it.

All life depends on crop land and on the earth's generous waters. Topsoil, that precious and thin layer of life support, is washing like blood into the seas and rivers, blowing away in the wind, and being paved over. In thirty years, China, where one of every five humans lives, lost in crop land the equivalent of all the farms in France, Germany, Denmark, and the Netherlands. Forty-three percent of the earth's vegetated surface is to some degree degraded, and it takes from 3,000 to 12,000 years to develop sufficient topsoil to form productive land. On a typical day on planet earth seventy-one million tons of topsoil are lost. If we were losing huge quantities of gold, it would be a lesser tragedy.

Oysters, of all creatures, are another witness to earth's woes. The oysters do for sea water what our kidneys do for us. They purify and filter the water as they feed themselves. The fabled Chesapeake Bay once enjoyed a thorough filtration by the massive oyster population every three days. Thus cleansed, the Bay flourished. It was fish heaven. Now the oysters are so depleted that the filtration occurs only a few times a year with portentous results. Similarly, mussels, as they busily take in vast quantities of water to glean out microscopic plankton, perform the filtering process for inland waters in the United States. Seventy-seven percent of them are either extinct or endangered.

The major rivers of the heavily populated nations are all polluted. Remember that less than one percent of the earth's water is drinkable by humans. Life grew on earth because we are "the water planet." And yet we are busily poisoning this most precious of resources. Potable water is not evenly distributed on planet earth. Most of Africa, the Near East, northern Asia, and Australia are on the short end of the water supply; and they suffer from chronic water shortages. It has been said that if one glass of pure water were the cure for AIDS, most people on the planet would have no access to it. Water wars are already in the offing. Notice that negotiations between nations in the Middle East are beginning to talk more of water than of oil.

The seas were the original source of life and they have been since the beginning of the earth a generous mother. Yet the richness of the seas is spoiling like the land. Of the seventeen major world fisheries, nine are in decline and all the others are threatened by unsustainable fishing practices. As far as the analysts' eyes can see into the future, we are faced with declining supplies of fish per person. Indeed, per capita supplies of water, fish, meat, and grain are declining. The world grain harvest is now regularly below consumption, drawing down grain stocks to the lowest level on record.

Until recently we thought the world was infinite. We wanted all poor nations to "develop" so they could live like we do. Now we know that the earth could sustain only about 3 billion people if they ate a typically American diet, and there are over six billion of us on earth. We know too that if China were to eat fish at the same rate as Japan does, it would require the entire fish product of the earth. In a word, there are limits to what the earth can produce. For the so called "developing" nations to consume like we do would take ten planets. This one is too small. For Holland to consume the way they do requires the equivalent of 1.4 Hollands. They import the rest. The rest of the world is our plantation, and many of its peoples are our slaves.

Not surprisingly, people, in solidarity with the decedent earth, are dying too. When it comes to impoverishment, the rule seems to be women and children first! Four million babies die yearly from diarrhea in the euphemistically entitled "developing world." Next come the women. Dr. Noeleen Heyzer of the United Nations says: "Poverty has a female face." Women constitute 70 percent of the world's 13 billion "absolute poor," and "absolute poverty" means you do not have the basic necessities of life. Every year, up to 60 million people die from hunger related causes and over a billion people lack the calories for an active working life.

Microbes and viruses that found a life for themselves in the forests, have accepted deforesting humans as their new hosts. As Joel Cohen says: "The wild beasts of this century and the next are microbial, not carnivorous." More than thirty new diseases have been identified since 1973, many of them relating to our new and ecologically dangerous lifestyles.

Meanwhile, there are more of us. It took 10,000 generations to reach the first 2 ½ billion; it took one generation to double it. Till the middle of the next century, the momentum is unstoppable. Overall fertility rates have been declining over the past 40 years, but mortality rates are dropping even faster, and so our numbers inexorably grow.

World population is like a triangle, with the reproductive young at the wide base and the old at the narrow top. Until the model comes closer to a rectangle, with a more balanced distribution of young and old, the growth will not stop, nor does anyone expect it to. *And over ninety percent of the growth is in the poorest parts of the world.*

The results of all this earth-wrecking do not stay overseas. Try as they might, affluent nations cannot become gated communities hidden safely away from the pollution of poverty. The results of ravished ecologies overseas come home to us. Those poisons arrive in air, water, and strawberries. Acid rains fall on the affluent and the non-affluent alike. Professor David Orr of Oberlin College gives us some of the scary data: male sperm counts worldwide have fallen by 50 percent since 1939. Human breast milk often contains more toxins than are permissible in milk sold by dairies. At death some human bodies contain enough toxins and heavy metals to be classified as hazardous waste. Almost eighty percent of European forests have been damaged by acid rain. Fifteen years ago I was driving through the Black Forest in Germany and a sign hung by the road: *Der Wald stirbt!* ("The forest is dying!") And so it is. Scientists say the two greatest tragedies to hit this planet were the blasting by comets and asteroids 65 million years ago that ended the reign of the dinosaurs. The second greatest disaster, they suggest, was the arrival of the human race.

Back to the Bible

Now how about this talk of salvation and the witness of the church? What do people nourished by the Jewish and Christian moral revolutions have to say about all of the above? Are they in the forefront of efforts to rescue the poor of the earth and the generous and battered earth itself? No, they are not. Religions who would be the moral heirs of the prophets should be building prophetic lobbies (churches) fueled by scriptural study and a fiery prophetic indignation at the ongoing rape of the earth and its poor. The Bible's mandate is clear. We have just not had the generosity or the nerve to see it. What the Bible offers (among many other stunning challenges) is a radical theory of justice and some profound thoughts on social conversion.

Biblical justice, called *Sedaqah* in the Hebrew scriptures, is downright un-American. It is biased, prejudiced, and partial in two ways. It is biased toward the poor and against the economically secure. Unlike the Roman Tacitus who said the gods are with the mighty, the Bible says our God is a "God of the humble . . . the poor . . . the weak . . . the desperate . . . and the hopeless" (Judg 9:11). When Job defended his virtue, he went right to the tradition of *Sedaqah* to do it. He said he had been "eyes to the blind, feet to the lame, . . . a father to the needy" and he took up the cause of people he didn't even know. (Job 29:12-20) Churches to be authentic must be effective lobbies for the poor, including the poor earth. Otherwise they are a pathetic irrelevancy.

Shock Therapy

Salvation for us on this earth may not be feasible. If current trends continue, we will not survive the next millennium. What is needed is major cultural change—culture being what people love and hate collectively. The salvation needed is to change the heart of so-called homo sapiens, not just individually, but collectively. We have to get into the affections of people. Technology won't save us. We need a societal rebirthing of awe and reverence. The prophets of Israel knew this and they bequeathed us elements of social conversion. In the brevity of this essay, we can follow the prophets through four doorways into the heart: *delight, anger, tears*, and *mind-blowing shock*.

Delight is a form of pleasure shock, and we don't delight enough in the gifts given to us on this planet. When writing about delight, Aquinas mistakenly used the incorrect Latin word *dilatatio*, which means, instead, stretching or broadening. It was a happy mistake. Delight stretches us so we can receive a new and congruent good. This can be verified because when delight stretches us to new awareness, the stretching is sometimes so great it produces tears. Orgasm and pain produce the same grimace. There are practical conclusions to this. Without the stretching caused by delight there is no learning. Theology, preaching, or liturgy that does not delight leaves us as it found us, or worse. No delight, no growth was Thomas's point. The literary power that pulses from Micah to the Psalms to the Sermon on the Mount gives us lessons on delight-filled, passionate teaching. *Cor ad cor loquitur;* only the heart speaks to the heart. All learning is a passionate *eureka!* Neurophysicists tell us that emotion is the key to lasting memory. It is also the key to moral growth. Boring, pedantic theology, dry sermons, rote religious education, let *them be anathema!*

Anger bristles through the prophets, and why not? The biblically astute Thomas said that anger looks to the good of justice, so that those who are not angry in the face of injustice, love justice too little. Thomas cited John Chrysostom's dictum: "Whoever is not angry when there is cause for anger, sins!" Therapeutic culture sees anger as a malady to be cured. Prophecy sees it as the awakening of the soul and the passionate key to conversion.

Tears. We have everything to fear from the tearless. The old Roman Catholic liturgy had a prayer begging the gift of tears. This prayer used to befuddle me as a young victim of our jejune Anglo-Saxon culture. The prayer begged divine power to break through the *duritiem*, the impenetrable hardness of our hearts and bring forth a saving flood of tears. Unless our eyes "run down with tears and our eyelids flow with water," we will come to a fearful ruin (Jer 9:18-19).

Finally, *shock.* Shock specialists is what the prophets were. Simple, sensible approaches won't do it and so the prophets turned bizarre and eccentric. Isaiah wandered around "naked and barefoot" for three years (20:2-4). Micah was also drawn to the streaker tactic: "Therefore I must lament and wail; I will go barefoot and naked" (1:8). The nudity caught on. When Saul stripped himself naked, the people asked: "Is Saul also among the prophets?" (1 Sam 19:24) Jeremiah harnessed himself to a yoke and was seen, understandably enough, as a "madman" (27:2-3; 29:26). Ezekiel cut off his hair with a sword and scattered it to the winds (5:1-2). Jesus was so intemperate he was seen as "a prophet like one of the old prophets" (Mk 6:15). He was a scandal because, as Walter Brueggemann says, he violated "propriety, reason, and good public order." And so did they all.

To what end? And how could it apply to our as yet unborn psychology of societal conversion? The prophets intuited that only outrage speaks to outrage. Outrageous insensitivity is thick-shelled. Only shock gets through. The Berrigans spoke and no one listened; they burned government records and were heard. Martin Luther King preached and enjoyed anonymity; he led a boycott and was killed by the overwhelming impact. Notice that it is not "either/or" but "both/and." The Berrigans continued to speak, and King continued to preach with even more effect until he met a prophet's death. Prophecy is essentially eccentric—coming from Greek—"outside the center." The center is where the addicts of comfort and safety dwell. Prophecy leaves them and pushes to the edges where new horizons can be seen. Resistance to the dominant consciousness anchored as it is in ill-gotten privilege is the essence of prophetic eccentricity.

These four hints on how to move the tectonic plates of our cognitive affectivity present huge challenges to our inbred stoicist epistemology. They threaten our confidence in logic and technique. They call attention to our almost total neglect of the constitutive role of affect in all moral and religious understanding and hence in all religious and moral education. They reveal our poverty in the realm of ritual and liturgy. We are queasy when we hear that Hindu ecologists use dance, song, art, and drama more than lectures to raise ecological literacy. We have a lot to learn about social conversion, but the prophets gave us a whopper of a start.

Gandhi said, "As human beings our greatness lies not so much in being able to remake the world—that is the myth of the Atomic Age—as in being able to remake ourselves." It is to that prophetic mission that the Christian churches are called.

Are We Asking the Right Questions about Peace?

Charles McCollough

A major part of Frederick Trost's ministry has always been public witness in word and deed. I remember seeing him sitting in a corner of the courtroom where we were to go on trial for witnessing against the Contra War in Central America. Fred was already writing his next public statement, explaining how the gospel calls us to civil disobedience in our time just as Bonhoeffer was called in his time to act against politically sanctioned evil. The call for our action on behalf of peace needs updating in each age. In our time of "humanitarian intervention," we find it necessary to work hard at understanding the gospel's call. Fred is always doing that work of theology in word and deed. This paper is written in the spirit of Frederick Trost's ministry of public witness.

The Problem

Recent military missions by the United States, the United Nations, and the North Atlantic Treaty Organization have challenged standard Christian responses to military actions. How does the church reply when asked what Christian ethics says about participation in "peacekeeping," "humanitarian intervention," or "humanitarian rescue" missions such as those in Kosovo, Bosnia, and East Timor? When a conscientious Christian considers whether or not to participate in or support a US, UN, NATO, or other military force deployed to enforce international law or a peace agreement, where does that Christian go for guidance?

The Past

Based on our experience of past wars, three or four approaches to military action have evolved for Christians to consider. The early Christians struggled with whether or not to fight in wars of any kind. Some were pacifists who refused to serve in the Roman armies. When Christianity replaced the Roman state in the fourth century and Rome was sacked in the fifth, Augustine wrote a long history of Christian thought on war. He, and later Thomas Aquinas, condensed just-war theory into five principles for going to war and two more principles to observe while participating in war. These principles were not meant to justify war but to limit it: (1.) War must be declared by a legitimate authority. (2.) War must be waged with good intent. (3.) It must lead to a good outcome, to conditions that are better than they were before the war. (4.) War must be the last resort after all other means are exhausted. (5.) War must be defensive and not offensive.(6.) The means used to wage war must be proportional to the ends. (7.) Non-combatants must be immune from attack.

These requirements, if met, allowed a Christian to participate in war or a military/coercive action in order to restrain evil and limit the harm done. A third approach emerged in the Middle Ages that sought to justify Christian war-making as a crusade against infidels. In our era of the Viet Nam War, a fourth approach was posed that attempted to distinguish between absolute pacifism and participation in a just war. The names for this approach were fluid: "selective pacifism," "selective conscientious objection," or "just peace." This approach sought to allow for police action and some forms of clear self defense but not participation in a war such as the one in Viet Nam, which, it was argued, just-war theory itself ruled out. Indeed, most modern wars are unethical based on just-war principles; to cite one reason: modern weaponry no longer allows for the protection of non-combatants. Some argue, therefore, that there is no need for the fourth approach, and the debate continues about the adequacy of just-war principles for modern warfare, especially military actions intended for "humanitarian" purposes.

Post-Cold-War Wars

Where should a Christian stand on what is called "humanitarian rescue" or more generally, "peacekeeping"? The question goes beyond Christian ethics as such. The US military itself is confused about whether its armies are soldiers or policemen. For example, in Kosovo NATO troops (known as KFOR) are there to do peacekeeping. General Klaus Reinhardt is commander of KFOR, which is trying to keep Serb and Albanian Kosovars from attacking each other. One such effort is securing the Northern border of Kosovo proper to prevent the flow of Serbian arms and agents. Reinhardt says, "Normally the military does not do such work" (*New York Times,* 22 February 2000). Short on police to patrol the area, Reinhardt has had to send in KFOR troops, who are also frequently involved in mediation and relief assistance.

Confusion

This confusion of roles was examined in "Soldiers of Great Fortune: Is America's Military Training Warriors or Humanitarians?" by Bob Shacochis in *Harper's Magazine* (December 1999) He points out some religious dimensions of the new confusion of military roles:

> After a decade of America's secular jihad against ruthless disorder, it is the sacred and profane pairing of the humane warrior . . . that much of the nation and much of the world finds curious, puzzling, suspect in its claim to virtue. Repeatedly throughout the bloodshed in Kosovo, the punditry referred to the "new military humanism," the defense of human rights, as a righteous, or self-righteous, form of armed conflict. (p. 45)

Where does just and unjust peacekeeping or war-making begin and end? Given the chronic distortion of language about military action, how can Christians trust words like "peacekeeping"? Were not the Roman armies "keeping" the "Roman peace" in Jesus' time?

What is meant by terms such as "humanitarian intervention," "new military humanism,"or "humanitarian rescue"? Is it not a positive good for US military helicopters to fly rescue missions in Mozambique or to insure the Israel-Egypt peace agreement or to keep Turks and Greeks apart in Cyprus? Yet, how can we be sure our military actions are not merely keeping the peace for American hegemony? Dominant empires throughout history rarely saw themselves as occupying armies but as rescuers and protectors of weaker nations, that is, as "peacekeepers".

Perhaps we are asking the wrong question. Maybe we cannot get a clear answer to the question of a Christian position on war as it is posed. The question of fighting or not fighting a war usually surfaces so late in our consciousness in a war-making situation that we cannot get a clear ethical answer; the lateness of the question inevitably limits our options. Rather than asking whether or not Christians can ethically fight in a war and then arguing over the various theories of just war or just peace, we can ask another question. Rather than the either/or question of to fight or not to fight, as if those were the only options, what if we ask another question: What ways can a Christian make and keep the peace? This third option, beyond fighting or not fighting, turns out to have numerous ethical actions that are frequently unknown or ignored. A look at the stages of international conflict helps us see these options better and put the relatively small part of conflict that is war-making in its place. Asked this way rather than at the last minute before war erupts, we are given more options and answers. The key is early, preventive action before a war breaks out.

A Clarification

Two steps are needed to advance toward some clarity for a Christian ethic of peace work: one is a clarification of terms; two is an analysis of the stages of international conflict. For a careful analysis of the stages of international conflict I will rely on a book by the United States Institute for Peace (USIP) and written by Michael S. Lund, entitled *Preventing Violent Conflicts: A Strategy for Preventive Diplomacy*, Washington, DC: 1996. The author was a senior scholar at the USIP and has a Ph.D. in political science and a B.D. from Yale Divinity School. Despite his divinity degree, Lund's book is aimed clearly at secular, international policy makers in the State Department and elsewhere. His goal is to convince Washington that the post-Cold-War world offers a window of opportunity to head off wars before they begin. He says, "[T]he United States could take the initiative by proposing the creation of a conflict preventive regime along the lines spelled out here" (196).

He is not promoting Christian ethics but rather national interest which, of course, is the bottom line for national policy. Yet his analysis of stages of conflict is helpful for our purpose of determining a Christian ethic of peacekeeping.

Terms

Lund unfortunately continues the Orwellian use of terms that adds to the confusion. In his war-making stage, he uses the terms "peacemaking" and "peace enforcement." I will simply call this stage of hot war what it is, "war-making." In addition, we now have terms used to describe limited "military intervention with humanitarian intent," "humanitarian intervention," and "virtuous intervention." The Presbyterian Church has made an extensive study of post-Cold-War micro interventions and named them "warfare for humanitarian rescue." We will come back to this term later. The term "peacekeeping" is used by Lund in a slightly different way, usually referring to the task of keeping warring sides apart or guaranteeing a negotiated cease fire. We will use the term "peacemaking" to refer to the peace and justice work *before* a hot war has begun. Peacemaking will be used to include "preventive diplomacy," the governmental work of diplomacy. Peacemaking also includes, however, non-governmental efforts before wars start. We will use "peacekeeping" to refer to the enforcement of an agreement in a period *after* a hot war has ended.

Figure 2.1. Life History of a Conflict

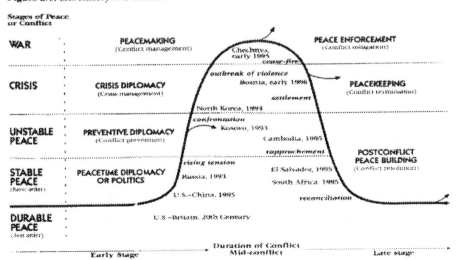

Stages of International Conflict

Lund's delineation of the stages of conflict is helpful in that it shows the stage of war-making is only a small part of the progression of international conflict. The chart is helpful in visualizing the larger areas of peacemaking and peacekeeping. Those stages are laid out on a chart (see above) with the intensity of conflict on a vertical axis beginning with (1.) a durable peace, then moving up to (2.) a stable peace, (3.) an unstable peace, (4.) crisis, and (5.) war. The chart's horizontal axis is time or duration of a conflict, moving left to right from early to mid to late stages of a conflict.

Lund has a complex elaboration of this chart that is beyond the scope of this paper, but the schema is helpful in visualizing his main point, preventive diplomacy. By focusing on preventive, as opposed to reactive diplomacy, such a "regime," as he calls it, would move away from reliance on a massive military involvement world wide and on diplomacy that reacts only after crises have moved to warfare. Rather this new regime would have the State Department working with the UN, and regional bodies, such as the Organization for Security and Cooperation in Europe (OSCE), would be organized to prevent wars before they reach the crisis and war stages. More on OSCE later.

The schema also helps the church visualize the huge area of peace work available *before* a hot war happens and the huge area of peace work *after* it begins. On both the vertical and horizontal axes, we can see that hot war is temporary in intensity (violence) and in duration. There are vast levels of time and relative peace when preventive diplomacy must happen. By looking at the whole picture of conflict, we can get a better grasp of a Christian approach to peacemaking and peacekeeping rather than being locked into a reaction to war-making.

New Kinds of Peace Work

Clearly the early stages of conflict allow for more effective conflict resolution. Before the crisis or war stage the parties to the conflict are not yet polarized with mobilized armies, and they have yet to demonize their enemies. Each stage, in fact, requires various strategies of diplomacy. According to Lund, however, the current framing of the debate in foreign policy does not allow for these differentiated strategies. Rather, the debate usually posits military intervention on the one hand and isolation on the other.

Lund's third option of preventive diplomacy involves not only a new foreign policy but a regime that puts many trained personnel in the field—persons trained in mediation, civil society building, and conflict prevention to monitor emerging conflicts and empowered to act to prevent the unstable peace from deteriorating into a crisis that may eventually become a war. This preventive diplomacy is suggestive of a Christian approach also, for the life of grace and good works is a precondition of peacemaking and peacekeeping.

A Model for Preventive Diplomacy

Lund gives a number of examples of successful preventive diplomacy such as the efforts in Macedonia, Hungary, and Estonia. Macedonia, with its ethnic tensions, Serbian threats, and in addition, a crisis-level conflict with Greece, could have gone the way of Bosnia or Kosovo when it voted to break away from Yugoslavia in 1991.But preventive steps were taken, beginning with OSCE observers who gave the early warnings, and eventually troops under UN's authority were sent. This UN mission was the only one of the sixteen UN operations around the world with a preventive mission, and the measures worked. Macedonia as a fledgling multi-ethnic democracy has survived with continued assistance from OSCE in its development of democratic institutions including a multi-ethnic police force.

How the Organization for Security and Cooperation in Europe Works

The OSCE model, though it is only beginning its efforts and is virtually unknown in the US, not only illustrates preventive diplomacy, peacemaking, and peacekeeping but is, I believe, worthy of aggressive support by the church. We need, besides good theory, examples that promise to continue working successfully to prevent war. OSCE "is a regional arrangement under Chapter VIII of the Charter of the United Nations" and "a primary organization for the peaceful settlement of disputes within its region and a key instrument for early warning, conflict prevention, crisis management and post-conflict rehabilitation" ("Charter for European Security," OSCE, Istanbul Summit, December 1999).

OSCE consists of 55 states between the Atlantic and the Urals, all of which have equal status in the organization. There are currently 1,400 staff members throughout Europe and increasingly in Central Asia, who are developing emerging relationships with the Mediterranean nations of Algeria, Egypt, Israel, Jordan, Morocco, and Tunisia. Japan and the Republic of Korea also have begun joint work with OSCE. Decisions are made by consensus through a permanent council with a rotating chairman-in-office. OSCE has a vast number of peacemaking and peacekeeping tasks from conflict prevention to refugee resettlement, civil society building, support for human rights, police training and deployment, and all the functions of non-violent peacekeeping, including assistance in economic, environmental, and political development toward democracy, assuring free elections, free press, protection of minorities, and the rule of law. OSCE has put in the field Rapid Expert Assistance and Co-operation Teams (REACT) which were to be fully operational in June 2000.

Other Successes

The efforts of OSCE were not successful in stopping the wars in Bosnia and Herzegovina or Kosovo, but the organization is fully functioning in these countries and others to keep the peace by resettling refugees, building democracies with free elections, and nurturing prosperous, peaceful, multi-ethnic societies. In addition to Macedonia, Hungary, and Estonia mentioned above, its successes include police work in Croatia, removal and destruction of Russian military equipment in Moldova, building democratic institutions in Belarus, preparing for free elections, maintaining security, and confidence-building in the Ukraine, Crimea, Armenia, and other eastern nations of the former Soviet Union.

These brief references to the work of OSCE serve to illustrate a kind of peacemaking, including preventive diplomacy and peacekeeping for the future, that holds promise even though it is widely ignored in the US media and most congressional offices. There are many other peace organizations at work, but OSCE has the support of the UN and governments in Europe and a mandate to carry out many tasks needed to make and keep peace.

Peacemaking and Preventive Diplomacy and the Church

Where does the church come into this effort? First, we are called to confess our inertia. We seem content, as in a failing marriage, with a cold or unstable peace. We have settled into merely keeping the lid on violence or hot wars, resulting in a kind of silent anguish but also a deep yearning for meaningful community and peace. We do not dare dream of real, stable peace—a New Jerusalem, which is a necessary vision of the Christian faith, and literally, a city of shalom or peace. A real peace where tools of growth replace weapons of war is the biblical dream we must seek and the essence of our heavenly banquet celebrated by a common humanity where all are welcome— our Eucharist. And we commit ourselves to that dream "on earth as it is in heaven" routinely in our Lord's Prayer as well as ultimately in our baptism.

The Presbyterians' Peace-making Agenda

We can learn from the Presbyterians, who have struggled hard with the peace issue both in their attempts to respond to post-Cold-War conflicts and through their active peacemaking programs. The Presbyterian General Assembly passed a resolution on "Just Peacemaking and the Call for International Intervention for Humanitarian Rescue."

Don Shriver, former President of Union Theological Seminary, wrote a thoughtful commentary on violence in general and on this resolution applying it to the war in Kosovo. ("Taming of Mars: Can Humans Contain Their Propensity for Violence in the Coming Century?" a pre-published manuscript from a series on *God and Globalization: Theological Ethics and the Spheres of Life in a Global Era* [Valley Forge, Penn.: Trinity Press International, vol. 2, forthcoming])

He concludes an "open ended," highly qualified, interim endorsement of the military action in Kosovo which is called "humanitarian rescue." It is interim because he, like the Presbyterian resolution, declares that "just peace making . . . agrees with the pacifist that war is contrary to God's will for humanity and cannot ever find war to be morally justified." Yet the next sentence states an apparent contradiction: "However, it simply realizes that there are times when the powers and structures of human life are so threatened by the policies or actions of an international outlaw that there is no other course of action to take but, in great agony and without a sense of righteousness, to restrain an evil threat by military means." (Minutes of the 200th General Assembly, 1998, part 1, p. 450, quoted by Shriver, 34).

We are left to wonder whether to call this statement a contradiction, a paradox, or what. Shriver does point out that the Presbyterian resolution "strengthens the lastness of the last resort" principle. The fine line here between "just-war" theory and "pacifism" requires extremely careful analysis and prayer.

The agony over "carrying guns with a heavy heart" (Reinhold Niebuhr), on the one hand, and standing by as innocent victims cry out for humanitarian rescue, on the other hand, hang in almost perfect balance on our moral scales. One senses in reading Shriver that a slight breeze could tilt the scales either way to a straight pacifism or to a firm endorsement of the use of military force. Jesus did teach non-violent resistance to evil. Yet images of our failure to stop the trains to Auschwitz haunt our Western consciences. Was not Kosovo morally the same? Shriver points out that ultimately the answers are religious answers, agonizing as they may be. But we are always too late to catch up when wars break out. For all these reasons, the church simply has no excuse to avoid praying, thinking, learning, preaching, and acting on peace before, during, and after a hot war chokes our options to an either/or of fighting or not fighting.

But as it stands, the church, "so consistently mandates the muffling and bypassing of conflict in its own ranks that it lacks resources of experience for contributing to the resolving of conflict in the secular arena"

(Ibid., p. 29). In other words, the church has to get its own house in order and get serious about peacemaking and peacekeeping in a culture of peace in the church and in society.

If We Get Serious about Peace

First, we must begin with peace education in the churches and in our communities. We know so little of the peace efforts in churches other than our own or in OSCE and other agencies that it is a major task to *inform*. We can learn to employ preventive diplomacy in local areas. Otherwise, when it comes to advising young people about military service, deciding on support for a military action, or preaching for or against a war effort, the church has to start *de novo* on each occasion.

Second, in addition to serious education about peace, we must establish highly disciplined skill training in conflict mediation in Conferences, Associations, and local churches. A few UCC Conferences recently have formed conflict resource teams who go to mediate local church conflicts and educate them about conflict resolution. But these are poorly funded and maintained by self-sacrificing volunteers. The teams rarely move beyond dealing with internal church battles to deal with community issues. We need greater numbers of trained mediators supported by adequately funded programs merely to help our frequently conflicted churches, not to mention conflict mediation in our communities and wider mission work.

Third, we need informed citizens' political action. Not only have new forms of military action and military weapons emerged in recent times, but new and promising alternatives to war have as well. What is needed most is the recognition that there are many stages between peace and war, between an unstable peace and a hot or cold war. When people become aware of these stages, then the possibilities for war prevention, preventive diplomacy, peacemaking, and peacekeeping can be developed. Unfortunately, most international peace programs such as arms control, bans on nuclear testing and land mines, foreign aid, and adequate support for UN efforts are stymied. Even the little progress we have made in nuclear arms control is now threatened by the call for a new national missile defense system. The defense budget climbs to over $300 billion a year even without real military threats. So an informed and active citizenry is essential to elect and watchdog officials who seek the real security of international cooperation and common security.

Fourth, Christian theology has always warned against human self-delusion and self-righteousness, so checks and balances must always be built into governmental structures. Our "national interest" is thus not an adequate justification for military intervention. Every tyrant of any nation can claim "national interest" as reason for war making. A minimum standard in deciding for military action is that such action always have international approval and cooperation.

The United Nations was founded for this purpose but has, since the end of the Cold War, been starved for adequate funds even as it is increasingly called on for peacekeeping missions, especially in the neglected crises in Africa. This fourth criterion calls for renewed insistence on the United States to pay its dues.

In conclusion, the answer to the question: Can a Christian support military action variously named, "peacekeeping," "humanitarian intervention," or "humanitarian rescue"? is "Yes, *if.*" The *if* is a large one that takes into account our small world with its big weapons. Such support would have to meet all these criteria: (1.) Be authorized by the UN to protect against self-delusive or self-righteous national actions. In our world, nation states can no longer be ordained as the last legitimate authority. (2.) The purpose must be humanitarian rescue, protection of a population, or the prevention of human catastrophes, not national, economic or other limited interests. (3.) The military action must not risk causing a worse situation, such as nuclear fallout. (4.) All other means of preventive diplomacy must be exhausted. This criteria is rarely followed in current military action but must be adhered to for Christian support. (5.) The military action must be to defend, rescue, or protect persons and nature, and not for the goals of inflicting punishment, seeking revenge, or attaining economic benefit. (6.) While in the pursuit of such objectives, military action must employ the minimum force needed to accomplish the goals. (7.) If non-military civilians are at risk of harm, the action must not begin.

These big "ifs" are, of course, updated just-war principles which in our time are virtually impossible to honor. If they are not used to justify war but rather to limit it, and if all seven are strictly adhered to without exceptions or equivocations, we would likely be restricted to vast regimes of preventive diplomacy and universal and life-long training in peacemaking, teaching, learning, and practice. Very few nations could meet all of these criteria. However, the Organization for Cooperation and Security in Europe is making an impressive effort in this direction, which suggests that such peacemaking and peacekeeping are not impossible and can be done—must be done. Such vast efforts are not beyond the scope of Christian calling; indeed this seems to be what being peacemakers is about.

Sanctuary: Radical Truths of Faith

Michael McConnell

The principal of the local Chicago elementary school seemed to stare at me for an eternity. I was sitting in her office one hot August day in 1982 attempting to register for classes two children of the refugee family from El Salvador that had just arrived into public sanctuary at Wellington Avenue United Church of Christ.

Wellington had just become the first congregation outside of a border state to declare sanctuary for Guatemalan and Salvadoran refugees fleeing the violence of their lands. Sanctuary, as the church had proclaimed on the July 25th welcoming ceremony, was the reviving of an ancient religious tradition that allowed those being persecuted to seek refuge or sanctuary within the church, until true justice could be done.

As Wellington's pastor, David Chevrier, said that day, "We live in a time of encroachment by the state, a violation of the holiness of even the most basic human rights. A demonic domination has been unleashed that is profaning the human through torture and terror. It is time to provide a safe place and cry our *'Basta!* Enough! The blood stops here!'"

The congregation at Wellington believed that persecution existed and that justice would not be done. The Immigration and Naturalization Service's own statistics told the story. In spite of over twenty-five thousand people being killed in El Salvador and thousands of murders and disappearances in Guatemala, over thirteen hundred refugees in 1982 applied for political asylum in Tucson and none were granted it. Nationwide over twenty-two thousand applied and only seventy-four were granted asylum. That three percent rate was to continue for several years, while people coming from communist Poland or Russia were gaining asylum at a 60 percent rate.

The principal had just asked me for official papers proving the ages of the two children that I wanted to register. I hesitated to answer. While I knew that it was perfectly legal for undocumented children to attend classes, I was worried that the truth could jeopardize their ability to continue their education or worse, lead to their capture by INS agents.

In 1982 no one knew what northern immigration agents might do. With a large office in Chicago and some recent highly publicized raids on factories fresh in our memories, we had been preparing for INS raids on the church itself. Around the clock monitors had been set up with an outpouring of volunteer help stepping forward, even when it meant spending the night sleeping in the church.

As I sat there, contemplating the various stories that I could make up, I came upon the principle that would guide the rest of my efforts in the sancturary movement. Even though the movement was just a few months old, the declaration of sanctuary was a statement of faith based on telling the truth. It told the truth about the realities of violence in El Salvador and Guatemala. The sanctuary movement also told the truth about the complicity of the United States in arming dictators, who were themselves in power due to the historic interventions of the US military.

I decided that it this movement were going to succeed, it would have to be based on the truth. So I told the principal that this family did not have any papers because they had to flee their country very rapidly and that carrying papers with them could have endangered their lives.

"Is this that family that was taken into sanctuary at Wellington Avenue Church?" she asked in what seemed to me an excessively stern voice. That's when she stared at me for what seemed like an eternity. The eternity part related to my wavering on the truth principle. Neither her voice nor demeanor indicated that this was going to end well for the family. But either out of stubborn adherence to this recently formulated principle or sheer lack of creativity for conceiving lies, I answered, "Yes."

Another eternity of stares followed. "Well you just go back and tell David Chevrier (the pastor) and the congregation that I am so proud of what they have done. And as far as the documentation is concerned, just have the church issue a baptismal certificate indicating their ages and that will be sufficient."

I had an almost identical experience when registering a third child Caytano for high school. Again as I explained that he had no papers prvoing his age, the African-American social worker asked if this was the family that she had seen on television, who were fleeing the violence in El Salvador. With the success of the elementary school behind me, without hesitation I answered, "Yes."

She not only immediately registered him but added that whatever additional assistance he needed, she would be glad to provide. In fact, she was grateful to have the opportunity to help. Again and again I found people of goodwill who responded either out of humanitarian need or prophetic anger, willing to go the extra mile to help.

Wellington itself had responded to a plea from the Tucson Refugee Support Group. In a letter dated May 31, 1982, a little over two months after Southside Presbyterian Church in Tucson had publicly declared sanctuary and taken in refugees from El Salvador, the group wrote: "This letter urgently requests a life-affirming response from you. Will you join in making your church a sanctuary for Central American refugees?"

They also made clear the risk involved. "Sanctuary is a serious responsibility for all persons involved. Should the government take action, the possible legal consequences may include being charged with harboring an illegal 'alien' (section 274 of the Immigration and Naturalization Act of 1952). Conviction may result in participants being fined up to $2,000, and/or being imprisoned up to five years (for each 'alien')."

They concluded with the core of the contradiction facing people of faith both in Central America and the United States. The biblical witness was unequivocal on how to treat the stranger. The Old Testament law in Leviticus stated, "When a stranger sojourns with you in your land, you shall not do him wrong. The stranger who sojourns with you shall be to you as the native among you, and you shall love him as yourself" (19:33, 34).

The life of Jesus also made abundantly clear that those who follow Christ welcome the stranger and the outcast into their midst. In the case of the Good Samaritan (himself an outcast), he shared in the risk of the road by helping those lying in need. Since it was common for robbers to feign injury and then attack the passersby who offered assistance, the Samaritan was willing to risk his own safety in order to respond to a stranger in need.

The Tucson group wrote: "When the state imposes limits on communion and fellowship, the prophetic faith is, in affect, outlawed. Under these circumstances, passive protest merely trains us to live with atrocity. Our government declares that sheltering a fellow human being from torture and murder is a felony. Civil disobedience is now our only nonviolent defense of this inalienable right of conscience."

First, the government of the United States armed the military and paramilitary squads who were killing and torturing people causing them to flee their own countries. Then the US government refused those victims refuge and considered those who aided them criminals.

But the government could do no other. To admit that what was happening in El Salvador and Guatemala were international human rights violations would have been to admit the failure of a foreign policy that supported the perpetrators of those atrocities. The refugees arriving in our midst were the living witnesses to the 50,000 disappearances in Guatemala and the 10,000 people killed each year in El Salvador. Their testimony had to be silenced. The government thought by arresting sanctuary workers, they could squelch the truth of the refugees. They were wrong.

In 1984, just after Stacey Merkt, a church member transporting refugees to a safe haven was arrested, the Chicago Religious Task Force decided to openly transport a refugee family to Weston Priory, Vermont. We intended this as an open defiance of the Immigration and Refugee law and as an act of solidarity with both the sanctuary workers and refugees who lived in constant fear of detection.

If the government thought that a high profile arrest would stop the sanctuary movement, we wanted to assure them that it would not. A highly visible caravan that numbered from three to thirty cars at various points of the eight-day trip from Chicago to Weston Priory, Vermont, stopped at several sanctuary churches and Quaker meetings along the route.

At each stop, caravan organizers told supporters that the simple act of feeding and harboring these refugees for a night was enough to break the letter of the law that the Immigration and Naturalization Service (INS) was using to try Stacey Merkt as a felon. Upon arriving at Weston Priory, the Benedictine monks and 500 supporters greeted the Excot family, Felipe and Elena and their five children. Elena, upon entering the monastery said that she was very happy, and yet it was the saddest day of her life. She was expressing her grief at having to leave her country and live in exile.

Felipe was a catechist who was the only one of 24 catechists from his area of Guatemala to survive a military massacre. He lived in corn fields for months, trying to visit his family and provide for them. Finally the threat of military patrols made him decide to flee to Mexico. There he met a priest who was part of the clandestine Mexican church aiding refugees from Guatemala and El Salvador, who sent him to Tucson and then on to Chicago.

Felipe was one of the hundreds of devastating truths that walked across the US border and penetrated the hearts of the faithful within congregations either declaring or contemplating declarations of sanctuary. Something profound and mysterious happened to members of US congregations as they encountered the stories of refugees. People of faith began to see the reality of Central America from the perspective of the poor. We saw dirt streets with houses patched together with cardboard and metal signs. We read the Gospels from the perspective of an empty stomach, or through the eyes of those who didn't expect to be alive the next day.

We began to view history from "underneath" and hear the biblical parables through the ears of those in situations very similar to first century Christians—persecuted, outcast, clandestine, poor. Sanctuary, through the testimonies of refugees, told the truth: the truth about Central America, the truth about US complicity in violence, the truth about the Christian faith. And for many, that truth set them free.

"O God, Whose Glory Shines"

O God, whose glory shines from the face of Jesus Christ and from whose outstretched hand flow all good gifts—life and breath and every good thing—give us again and again the gifts we so rarely think to request: the companionship of your Holy Spirit on the way of our pilgrimage; your living Word correcting, admonishing, healing, and strengthening as our need may be. Enhance the faith that can still find you present to us in the quiet hours of the night when we are troubled by conscience or fear or worry. Be with us in our relationships and all our dealings, our conversation and our work, so that we be found honest, trustworthy, gentle, and kind.

By the presence of your Spirit, open and encourage our own spirits so that we are ready to receive the human gifts others are so ready to bestow: comfort in our times of trial, laughter in our times of joy, seriousness of intent in our mutual work, and constancy in our friendships. Open our ears to hear subtle inflections, to see sadness or anguish in other's eyes, the empathy that joins life to life. May we hear anew, freshly spoken, your word, O God, you who comforts and strengthens us for the tasks to which we have been assigned. We pray for the church here and in every land, and for all institutions by whose compassion and labors the burden of pain is lightened, by which the light of hope is restored and life is sustained.

O God, by whose gift of love we are moved to care for others, strip from us the insulation that hides their need and dampens our compassion for them. Reunite us by your grace, sustain us by your power, open our hearts, and temper our minds for new tasks.

We pray in the name of the Son you gave to the world for the sake of our reconciliation with you, even Jesus Christ our Lord.

This prayer was written for Sunday worship at First Congregational UCC, Madison, Wisconsin, where Frederick Trost was a member.

Wells B. Grogan

With Confession and Assurance, Humility and Audacity

Mary Ann Neevel

It was Dietrich von Hildebrand who wrote, "Humility implies a heavenward aspiration that carries with it a breath of greatness and holy audacity." The connection of humility with holy audacity is a testimony to the profound complexity of the public witness of the church. We tend to think that such a witness requires boldness, even brazenness. Indeed, we might look upon church-related activists as being anything but humble. Yet, I would argue that it is a deep and faithful humility before God which most surely prompts and supports the church's public witness.

When I first learned that Frederick Trost was a tax resister in regard to the use of money for military weaponry, I felt a sense of awe. However much time I have spent in my life opposing one or more aspects of our military policies, I knew that I wasn t ready to take that brave step. Yet, I've never heard Fred talk about it very much. It was simply something that, for him, had to be done. What he does speak of—often, and at length—is the necessity of theological reflection. Out of the tradition of Dietrich Bonhoeffer and the Confessing Church in Germany, he has drawn the lessons of faithful theological work and faithful witness in the midst of the world's demands and turmoil.

It is crucial for our life together, and for our witness in the world, that when the church gathers to worship God, we offer in humility our confession and hear again the words of assurance of God's forgiveness in Christ and God's grace-filled love. All faithful witness is grounded in worship. It is grounded in the words of the prophets and in the teaching of Jesus. It is grounded in a community of faith where we are known and accepted as members of Christ's body in the world.

Confession provides for us a way of humility. In confession, we recognize our own creatureliness before God, we are led to seeing and owning our sin—both personal and corporate—and to identifying the lack of justice in the world around us. At the heart of *The Rule of St. Benedict*[1] is the seventh chapter, On Humility. For Benedict, humility was the ladder by which we ascend to that perfect love of God which casts out fear. Humility, far from making us grovel in our own sin, helps us ascend to the confidence of loving God and losing fear. But another monastic, Bernard of Clairvaux, found that rather than ascending the ladder of humility with the great Benedict, he was better prepared by his own life's experience to slide down it, following the degrees of pride: All I can say is that I can teach only what I know myself. I could not very well describe the way up because I am more used to falling down than to climbing. St. Benedict describes the steps of humility to you because he had them in his heart; I can only tell you what I know myself. Then he adds: However, if you study this carefully you will find the way up. [2]

In this age of human genome projects and computers, we need to study carefully the ways of humility taught by Jesus in his preaching and parables. We need to listen again to the wisdom of Benedict and learn that it is God, not we, who judges the world. In her commentary on the *Rule of Benedict,* Joan Chittister offers insights for the edification of us all: Benedict is telling us that true humility is simply a measure of the self that is taken without exaggerated approval or exaggerated guilt. Humility is the ability to know ourselves as God knows us and to know that it is the little we are that is precisely our claim on God. Humility is, then, the foundation for our relationship with God, our connectedness to others, our acceptance of ourselves, our way of using the goods of the earth and even our way of walking through the world, without arrogance, without domination, without scorn, without put-downs, without disdain, without self-centeredness. The more we know ourselves, the gentler we will be with others. [3]

That aspect of our formation as Christians comes not only from the confession, not only of our own true identity as humans, but especially of God's identity as God. Each time the church gathers for worship and praise of God, we reorient ourselves in regard to whose world this really is, and whose justice we really seek. To be confronted with the profound goodness of God and a perspective on justice which lifts up those who are poor, weak, and oppressed in a magnificat of praise is to be formed as the body of Christ which will view the world with the eyes of faith.

Benedict's wisdom offers a path toward deeper trust and faith. Each part of the church is on that journey: individuals, congregations, denominations and communions, councils and the wider ecumenical community. There are times when those who speak publicly on issues seem far from us, and we would do well to remember the prophets and to be reminded that those speakers, too, have been formed by congregations of the gathered faithful. There are times when deeds of compassion, companionship and hospitality speak louder than words.

I think of the community of Billings, Montana, and its witness against bigotry when people from many backgrounds came together to each hold a menorah as they walked in the city streets. I think of those churches who have declared for themselves that they are "open and affirming," "reconciled in Christ," "more light" congregations who welcome all persons as those whom God has redeemed and loved. There are times when discernment is difficult and it takes a lonely voice crying in the wilderness to point the way to truth. I have met more than one person in the upper midwest who remembers when Marian Anderson brought her beautiful voice to our cities, only to be denied a place to stay in the local hotels. It was the voice of my fifth-grade teacher expressing her deep dismay about the situation that drew me into a growing awareness of all racial prejudice.

One of the central concerns of the ecumenical movement over the past few years has been the inter-relation between ecclesiology and ethics. The World Council of Churches held three consultations, reported in *Ecclesiology and Ethics: Ethical Engagement, Moral Formation and the Nature of the Church.*[4] Part of this initiative was an attempt to heal a long-standing division between two streams of the ecumenical movement—Faith and Order, and Life and Work. There were two important and overarching convictions guiding the study, which are worth repeating here: 1) that ethical reflection and action . . . are intrinsic to the nature and life of the church , and 2) that ecclesiology and Christian ethics must stay in close dialogue, each honoring and learning from the distinct language and thought forms of the other.

In other words, it is crucial that wholeness be sought and sustained in our understanding of the church's public witness. That wholeness brings together what we learn from scripture, the experience of the church over the centuries, the integration of theology and ethics, and our understanding of Christian discipleship, spirituality and holiness in the context of the everyday world. However much we might be attracted to one or another of those things as the rationale for witness, we must listen to all of them with openness to new comprehension of where God is leading us.

Conversations in the Faith and Order Commission of the Wisconsin Council of Churches have reflected that desire for wholeness. In a recent meeting, one of the representatives proposed that since most of our denominations were involved in difficult discussions regarding human sexuality, and especially homosexuality, and since those discussions reach into ecumenical relationships, the commission should engage in them as part of our Faith and Order agenda for the coming year. While our conversations in the past have been more focused on ecclesiology, it is apparent that we will bring ethical concerns into that dialogue, and the level of trust is such that we look forward to it. This small gathering of the church always begins its work with worship—with confession of our faith, confession of our sin, and with an assurance that God's forgiveness, power and love prevail. Each person present is grounded in a local congregation, and each has been stretched toward a shared ecumenical vision which is both informing and joyful.

Stanley Hauerwas once said, "the church does not have a social ethic; the church is a social ethic."[5] The church provides not just an ethical theory, perspective, or set of pronouncements. The church in its own life and being lives an ethic, which derives from its corporate character as "the people of God," *koinonia*, "the body of Christ," "covenant people," "the household of faith." The WCC report adopts this perspective: "Thus in speaking of the *ethos* of the household of faith we mean the way of life, the distinctive patterns of thinking, feeling, and acting, which characterize those who live within that household." In other words, the public witness of the church cannot be set apart from our life together as Christians. The church lives its faith publicly, and while we may distinguish our actions—as does the General Synod of the United Church of Christ—between resolutions of witness to the world and prudential (internal) resolutions, all are visible to others as opinions and deeds of the church.

Arne Rasmussen, in an article in *The Ecumenical Review* of the World Council of Churches, enlarges upon the Hauerwas statement by saying,

> Ethics is then nothing else than discipleship, sanctification, spiritual life, or however one wants to describe the Christian life. It has to do with the whole of life and not with specific universal duties, and no sphere of life is outside of it. In this sense Christian ethics is inevitably a theological ethics (in contrast to autonomous ethics); it is embedded in the whole network of Christian convictions, practices, rituals and dispositions. . . .The life of the church is constituted by a set of social practices such as worship, witness, works of mercy, discipling and communal discernment. . . .Communal discernment is of course another name for ecclesial ethical reflection. In the Christian understanding these practices receive their meaning from the place of the church in God's purpose for creation. The internal goods of these practices are then the glorification of God and the fulfillment of God's creational and saving purposes.[6]

While we may not articulate such understandings on a regular basis in the life of a local congregation, perhaps we ought to. There has been great change during the last century in regard to the church's role in society. From being a cornerpost on Main Street acting in concert with a prevailing societal and political ethos to offer the religious perspective, most of our urban and suburban congregations now find themselves competing with youth (and adult) soccer games, weekends away, and times of solitude with a cup of coffee and the thick Sunday paper. Spirituality has come to mean a lonely pursuit—like bowling alone—instead of a relationship to God and self which is shaped and formed by historic faith community tradition.

Dietrich Bonhoeffer, in his little volume *Life Together*, lifts up the understanding that the body is the proper metaphor for the Christian community. We *are* members of a body, not only when we choose to be, but in our whole existence. Every member serves the whole body, either to its health or to its destruction. This is no mere theory; it is a spiritual reality. [7] It *is* a reality for many of us, but there is also the fact that a plurality of perspectives shape our lives. We live in a pluralistic complexity of identities in the world, so that different groups in different places may regard the same person in a variety of ways. Identity in the place of work might feel different from identity as a parent or as a vacationing traveler. Bonhoeffer's haunting question, "Who am I?" could well be our own. Hopefully his response will also be ours: "Whoever I am, you know me, O God. You know I am yours."[8]

The formation of our identity as Christians is also complex. We do not live and act on our own. The clues for our ideas and behaviors come from parents, siblings, friends, and neighbors. Our understanding of what is good and what is right is not just the end of the process of personal reasoning but something we receive from others, absorb from our environment, appropriate from thoughts that we criticize and modify. We do not choose for ourselves accounts of virtue, but draw on the resources of the community and its stewardship of tradition that nurtures new generations. It is the story of our faith, told and retold, which shapes our moral vision, so that we come to discern a distinctive way of seeing and acting. The thought I would offer is that this is one aspect of confessing our faith and saying publicly that we are neither our own or alone. We are shaped and formed by God and community.

The biblical prophets offer an example of being shaped by community and tradition. I think especially of Jeremiah, who was a descendent of one of the two chief priests of King David, Abiathar. Abiathar was a Levitical priest, meaning that he derived his theology from the older traditions of the Hebrews: the exodus from Egypt, the wilderness wandering, the gift of the land of Canaan, and the Covenant of Sinai. Abiathar had served King David well, but was banished by David's successor Solomon, for supporting Solomon's rival. Jeremiah honored this heritage. His strong criticism of the house of David and the Jerusalem temple comes in part from his conviction that the older traditions were more faithful to God. Indeed, Jeremiah was presented as the prophet like Moses.

He preached repentance and a return to the ancestral faith—that was his heritage. But he also advocated acquiescence to the Babylonians as the sole means of avoiding national destruction. You can imagine that Jeremiah gained powerful enemies within Judah. His laments reflect his experience of persecution, yet his vision of the future remained clear. If Judah continued to resist Babylon, it could only lead to destruction. Jeremiah preached in the places of power, even the temple itself, assaulting the theological undergirding of royal religion and arguing that obedience to the commandments and covenant of Moses (and not temple worship) was Judah's only hope for survival. This has always seemed to me to be the heart of his message:

> Thus says the LORD:
> Do not let the wise boast in their wisdom,
> do not let the mighty boast in their might,
> do not let the wealthy boast in their wealth;
> but let those who boast boast in this,
> that they understand and know me,
> that I am the LORD;
> I act with steadfast love, justice, and righteousness in the earth,
> for in these things I delight, says the LORD (Jer 9:23-24).

It points to one aspect of confession: an honest perception of things of which we might boast, and a call to boast only in the understanding and knowledge of God.

Public witness in matters of justice and peace is not an easy path to follow without the support of a community of faith. Holy audacity is grounded in humility, which in a biblical kind of reversal gives authority and power to the one who speaks for justice. Indeed, it is only with humility that we can see the holy in our midst. Then we no longer put ourselves in God's way but allow God to work in and through us. Justice is God's work, and if we see it only as ours and only in our terms, we will lose the way.

So with confession and assurance, with as much wholeness as we can embrace, with humility and audacity and with great hope, the church continues to combine ecclesiology and ethics into its task of being the body of Christ in the world. For we have this assurance: that through Jesus Christ "we have obtained access to this grace in which we stand; and we rejoice in the hope of sharing the glory of God."[9]

Notes

1. *The Rule of St. Benedict*, ed. Timothy Fry (Collegeville, Minn.: Liturgical Press, 1981), 201.

2. Quoted by M. Basil Pennington, OSCO, in *Weavings* 15, no.3, (May/June 2000): 19, from Bernard of Clairvaux, *The Steps of Humility and Pride*, XVI 44.

3. Joan Chittister, *The Rule of Benedict: Insights for the Ages* (New York: Crossroad, 1996), 773-774.

4. *Ecclesiology and Ethics: Ethical Engagement, Moral Formation and the Nature of the Church*, ed. Thomas F. Best and Martin Robra (Geneva: WCC Publications, 1997).

5. Stanley Hauerwas, *The Peaceable Kingdom*, (London: SCM Press, 1984), 99.

6. *The Ecumenical Review* 52, no. 2 (April 2000): 184.

7. Dietrich Bonhoeffer, *Life Together* (New York: Harper & Row, 1954), 89.

8. Translation of *Wer bin Ich?* from *Widerstand und Ergebung*, in *A Testament to Freedom: The Essential Writings of Dietrich Bonhoeffer*, ed. Geffrey B. Kelly and F. Burton Nelson (San Francisco: Harper, 1990, 1995), 381-382.

9. Romans 5:2, NRSV.

Word and Deed. Word In Deed. Word *Indeed!*

David L. Ostendorf

It was that turbulent Chicago summer of 1968 that Frederick Trost's reputation spread. Word got around that with his leadership St. Pauls United Church of Christ had opened its doors and floors to shelter protesters gathered for the now-fabled Democratic convention. Even before that auspicious act, wayward college students had made their own way to the church to hear this booming preacher at Sunday worship, to be enthralled by the music and worship, and to be inspired to hope anew. These many years later it is our honor to honor him as one who has throughout his ministry sought to keep before us the power of God's word.

Word and Deed

My own journey of faith had only recently taken new turns at that turbulent time. Its foundation had been firmly set at home, but its growth began as I finished high school and entered college to be exposed to new realms of thought and analysis. Born a boomer into a working class family, I was always deeply nurtured in faith and action. Even as a child I could tell an unknowing adult where they should not shop because the store was not unionized. There was in my home no separation between faith and a life of justice. My father was a deeply believing trade unionist, and after thirty years on the shop floor he was elected as an International Representative to serve his membership and organize new locals. My mother has always been active in church and taught by deed that one's faith is lived out serving others. The expansiveness of her faith still shocks her contemporaries and others much younger in years: she gives no quarter when it comes to matters of inclusiveness and justice.

The link between God's word and human deed was implicit in my home and was never really discussed. Church was on Sunday; the rest of the week was work. Old German quietude on matters religious ran deep in both family and congregation; faith was not worn on one's shirt sleeve. I can recall few times when discussion centered on the relationship between word and deed, yet the link was always there by example. Somehow the power of God's word had inoculated an undemonstrative people to live out their faith in quiet service. Still, at home, the separation between pew and picket line was virtually indistinguishable.

Word in *Deed.*

Thus inoculated and activated, my early call to ministry was thereafter shaped and formed by the startling dichotomy, indeed the disconnect, I felt between what faith proclaimed and what it did—or did not do—to shape a world of justice and righteousness. I began to take ever more seriously the faith mandates for justice and, finally, after seminary, ordination, and more graduate education, realized that the academic teaching vocation I thought I was called to was a diversion from the course God was laying out for me.

In 1974 I returned with my own family and a colleague to Southern Illinois to begin work in the coal fields. On the heels of the energy crisis, the state sought to capitalize once again on its vast coal reserves, promising a new boom to communities that had barely survived the previous bust, and inviting coal companies to help themselves to the land and the wealth that lay beneath it. Putting word and gifts into deed, the Illinois South Conference of the United Church of Christ provided seed money for us to begin our organizing efforts to stem the exploitation of both land and people. For five years Roz and I and other colleagues carried our commitments throughout the state, rooting deeply with people, churches, and communities struggling to balance the need for jobs and justice with the care of the land, towns, and cities where they lived. The commitments begun in that period carried on long past our departure, in partnership with the church, and still live on today.

What we tried to do in these early years of ministry was to move beyond word *and* deed, and to make manifest word *in* deed. This is more than a game of theological semantics. It was and is the *conscious and intentional* commitment to live out God's word in acts of justice and hope with and among a people under assault. It is to take seriously God's desire for a just creation by working with both believers and non-believers to secure—to taste and see and experience—the fullness of life promised by a loving and just God. It is to make *explicit and vocal* the yearnings of the people for justice and wholeness, and to work with the people *to make those yearnings real* in their own place, in their own lifetime. It is to move beyond the quiet acceptance of word and deed lived out implicitly to an innate understanding that every act of life might reflect the radical call of God to put word into deed.

Word *in* Deed.

Organizing to get better land reclamation policies after strip mining; to curtail mine blasting so homes would not be damaged; to stop the nation's largest coal company from mining almost on top of a town or through a river; to secure fair rates from an electric utility that for years had run roughshod over its customers with relentless price increases; to gather low-income truck farmers into a market where they could sell their produce for a fair price.

In 1981 God called us from a stint in the nation's capital back to the heartland prairies, to begin a grueling decade of ministry with farm and rural people throughout the nation. Arriving in Des Moines that summer, we had no idea what was ahead. By the following fall and winter we had begun working with farmers being pushed off the land by a deadly combination of staggering interest rates, low commodity prices, and falling land values. By mid-decade we were organizing with rural people across the region, and building ties with farm and rural groups throughout the nation. Our commitment to mass peaceful protest alerted the world to the plight of those who work the land and those who live from it, including small business owners and factory workers. New public policies were developed and won to keep family farmers on the land. Numerous new leaders stepped forward and grew into prominence. Farms and jobs were saved—and lost. And partnering with many churches and church leaders, we did in deed practice what God's word called us to.

It was in the middle of that decade that we were also thrown into action to counter the growing presence of organized hate groups that attempted to ply their racism and anti-Semitism among rural folk stricken by the economic crisis. Using the Bible and religion to promote their hateful cause, these groups began to pop up across the Midwest urging listeners to take up the gun, to strike back, to train for armed conflict. They stirred people up to target the "true enemy," particularly Jews who were allegedly the real force behind the crisis. Realizing that there had to be a concerted and organized commitment to counter this development, we began working with the larger church to stand fast and strong against the hatred, again trying daily to put word into deed. In countless seminars across the country and in Canada we educated, trained, and organized church and rural people to counter the scripture-based, organized racist and anti-Semitic movement, a work we continue to this day in light of that movement's staying power and its deep, cultural influence in this nation.

Word Indeed!

A new decade brought new growth in my ministry, as I realized that there was even more God had to teach me about word and deed, and word in deed. By 1992 I felt a restlessness that would not go away. I prayed deeply for God's guidance and direction, not knowing what it was that I was being called to. A new seed had been planted in my spirit, yearning to grow.

As I look back a decade later, I know that God was beckoning, pushing me to a deeper immersion in the word than I had ever imagined. It became clear that if both church and community were to be revitalized and renewed, and if acts of justice were to be more truly grounded in and grown out of faith, the word of God itself had to be fully engaged in new ways with and among the people of God. In an increasingly secularized society, where the church itself had become so deeply acculturated with the social, economic, and political powers, and where there was still a deep yearning for spiritual meaning among the people, God's word indeed had to be wrestled with in new ways.

So began a new part of my own faith journey. Taking lessons and learnings from the biblical reflection process utilized by base Christian communities, we began the long, challenging process of developing a genuine faith-based organizing process that would provide congregations and the communities they serve a new sense of purpose and mission. This organizing process is deeply grounded in participatory, contextual Bible study—engagement with and by the word of God in order to better understand what that word means for us in our own places in this day, regardless of whether we live in neighborhoods or communities under assault, or in places that are relatively prosperous.

It is the word indeed that now fires new life in congregations and parishes grounding their life together in the biblical and theological reflection process that is at the heart of this faith-based organizing methodology. From their engagement with and by God's word at every meeting, and in regular gatherings of believers across many denominational lines and traditions, the people of God are being inspired to new acts of mission and justice involving their own members and other citizens in the community—building new and powerful relationships with one another and with those whose voices are seldom heard. And from that new grounding in faith, the people are putting word *into* deed in ways they had not previously imagined.

So it is that mainstream Protestants, Evangelicals, Pentecostals, and Catholics are gathering in one community at a common table around God's word, breaking down old racial and economic barriers, and exploring the development of a community credit union to serve poor neighborhoods. So it is that one small, fired-up, open country church has become the stimulus for a county-wide project that is likely to address affordable housing issues and other social and economic impacts from metropolitan sprawl. So it is that a group of churches in another state has joined forces to address immigrant worker issues. So it is that in another place, churches grew a Unity Coalition out of their commitment to counter organized racist activity. And so it is that God's word, indeed, is birthing powerful new deeds of mission and justice from churches seeking new life and hope in the new century.

Word and deed. Word in deed. Word indeed! God's word must be the everlasting source of our life as a people in mission. Engaged in and by that word, we are called to create a radically different community—a just, beloved community—where all have a seat and a place setting at a common table laden with the bread of life, and where no one goes away hungry or in need. Thus fed, we serve one another, and together join the arduous and liberating journey for justice.

"Holy, Holy, Holy Lord"

Holy, Holy, Holy Lord, God of power and might, heaven and earth are full of your glory, O God most high. Blessed are we that you have come to us in Christ and have entrusted to us the joyful responsibility of continuing Christ's ministry in this world. Open our eyes to see your face in the face of our neighbor, our ears to hear your voice in the music of their voice, open our hands to extend your hospitality to those in need, open our hearts so that we might embrace the world with your love. Empower us, we pray, with your Spirit so that the love we bear might bring a greater measure of justice to the oppressed, the hospitality we extend truly refresh the weary sojourner; the song we sing bring joy to those in despair; the care we offer acknowledge our common creation in your image. In the name of the risen Christ, we pray.

Mark X. Pirazzini

A Theology of Engagement and a Covenant of Community

Carmen Porco

So we, who are many, are one body in Christ and individually we are members of one another (Romans 12:5).

Humankind has developed too many masks that prevent us from knowing one another. We measure worth and identity in economic, educational, and professional constructs. The absence of acceptable criteria in these areas diminishes us into various forms of poverty. Today, the well-to-do stand in poverty just as the have-nots do. I believe we are all struggling to right the injustices by various acts of charity and searching. Our attempt to create community lies in how we define our worth and relationships both as individuals and as institutions. If we fail to recognize our interconnectedness, we undermine our very efforts to connect with one another, and we are further impoverished, regardless of our material success.

In the Christian context, the idea that we are all related to one another and interdependent upon one another is inescapable. Our success and failures are tied to the fate of the brother/sister who is known or unknown. I, as a Christian working in the ghettos of America, have come to realize the truth of theological constructs which enhance the community of humankind and stand against the societal constructs of oppression. Our capitalistic system extols the advantages of free-market competition; those who aren't aggressive are to blame for their own failure. We, as a people, have come to define materialistic values as Christian values and to equate financial success with God's blessing.

Such a paradigm causes us to further divide our ability to relate to one another with respect and to build the covenant of community that we must uphold as Christians. God's covenant, unearned by even the most brilliant and successful, provides the challenge and opportunity to equalize humanity in community and be redeemed in unconditional love.

Engaging in a theology born of mutual respect, interdependent relationships and the search for the essence of Christ as the core values for success will point to peace, unity, equality and redemption amongst the poor and rich. This "Theology of Engagement" will revolutionize our perceptions about the estrangement of the poor and the nature of poverty as well as the worth of materialism and "Americanism" as blessed by God, and hence deemed success. I must affirm my brother/sister, regardless of race, ethnicity, educational level, wealth or social status, as a child of God, not as the accumulation of social, economic or educational achievements. The continuum of humanity must not be broken and divided by the human constructs of value and success. Nowhere is this of greater significance than in working with communities of poverty.

The church is called to minister unto the least of these, my brothers and sisters. Churches are just beginning to regard the domestic poor as they have the poor in foreign missions for some time, where the people and their culture are viewed positively and blame is laid on the government as either oppressive or lacking in resources to provide for its citizens. The United States, the richest and supposedly the most successful nation, struggles with the question of the poor and ends up blaming the poor for their own lot in life. Witness the rhetoric of welfare reform; both sides of the aisle espouse the idea of personal responsibility as a way of sidestepping their own responsibility. Examine how various departments of government have developed the "Office of Faith-based Relations." I conclude that the church must not fall victim to being the apostle of "the System," but must instead guard the values and resources of a nation and seek to equalize the delivery of services and resources to individuals. The covenant of God is grounded in grace, justice, and love, not the free market system: *grace* freely offered, without distinction, to all; *justice* to organize the delivery system to enhance and nurture all people; and *love* to motivate appropriate angles of vision.

Caring and extending grace is the first step in the continuum of community. The call to unconditional love separates Christianity from all the other disciplines. Charity without discipline allows us to contribute without mutual accountability, but grace requires reciprocity. Helping the poor by giving them resources for short-term needs such as money to pay the rent, or food to see them through the end of the month or volunteering for short periods of time by mentoring a child makes us feel successful. We do this generally out of the need for making a positive contribution to people and our community. Unfortunately, this approach plays into the victimization of all parties.

I offer the opportunity to examine the idea of disciplined compassion: a compassion that doesn't try to overcome the pain, suffering and oppression of a materialistic system by replacing it with immediate rewards and short-term relationships to momentarily connect the haves and the have-nots, but rather offers a long-term systematic approach to enabling people to meet their own holistic needs.

If the church is to succeed in the war on poverty, it must engage in a war on opulence. Until we see how we have fallen victim to the measurements of worth and success of a materialistic society, we will only succeed in briefly placating ourselves and those who are already victimized. Love is the first step; unconditional love sustains and unites individuals and institutions in the creation of a better society because it removes the artificial mask of meaningfulness, and allows authentic relationships.

Unconditional love enables me to be blind to the measurements of success in our materialistic world and permits me to see my fellow human as another child of God, my equal in the sight of God. Who am I to determine the degree of God's claim on each of us? As a Christian, I must not become confused by the need of the system to mainstream all into the normative economic order. It is my ministry to treat my brother/sister as myself and seek to build bridges to the resources necessary for my brother/sister to design his or her own destiny.

Hence, I offer a more proactive theology that can enhance the fulfillment of the covenant of God in all humanity. In the light of this theology of engagement, we see a continuum of service requiring us to ask the question, "How do the poor provide a service to humankind?" This question is no harsher than God asking what service *you* are rendering to humanity. None is deserving and all suffer, yet each is asked in his or her own way to render unto Caesar that which is Caesar's and unto God that which is God's. We must all learn to distinguish the values of the social system and its demands from those of God: to seek justice, to love kindness, and to walk humbly with one's God. Rich and poor, educated and uneducated, those of status and those lacking status come together in the covenant of grace, which gives hope to humanity. Until the church adopts a theology that sees the poor as contributors to and healers of society, we as Christians will be violating the essence of Christ. Until we discover the service that the poor can perform as part of the community, we rob ourselves of the same grace that was extended to us as undeserving and impoverished. Until I extend this grace with unconditional love, I cannot claim to be a Christian.

The theology of engagement which I am offering has four components: first, trust in the capability of our fellow humans, regardless of economics; second, their involvement in identifying the resources needed, methods for obtaining those resources and ways to utilize those resources for self-determination; third, focusing on the internal community and building the capacity for leadership and servanthood; and finally, building bridges to the mainstream community for both social and spiritual relationships. The people in a community of poverty need to create the system that serves them so that their various needs are met, rather than pieced together by multiple outside agencies with conflicting purposes.

Working in low-income housing has provided me with the opportunity to practice this theology of engagement. Six housing developments in Wisconsin serve as the platform for radical change. At the outset, they were the setting for financial ruin, community disintegration, deteriorated housing stock, high turnover, high crime, drugs and violence, elevated school dropout rates, and high unemployment rates. The church had been involved over a five-year period implementing a theology which diminished the poor people whom they were attempting to serve. At the end of this time, the common theme of the clergy and laity involved was, "I just can't understand why we did not succeed. We did everything for them that we could. We had Bible classes, we tutored, we even advocated for them on issues of importance." After some weeks of evaluation, I met with those involved and asked them questions. How did you involve the people in defining the problem? How did the people plan the programs to meet their specific needs? How were the people responsible for the resources allocated to the community? How were the people asked to be accountable? How were the people involved in evaluating the outcomes?

In summary, the clergy and laity did not believe that the people could handle this level of responsibility and accountability; after all, they were on welfare, uneducated, undisciplined and unskilled. One offered a more honest answer: "I did not think we could trust them with this responsibility." These are not statements from Christians; these are statements from Christians who have victimized and impoverished themselves with the core value of "Americanization." The essence of Christ helps me realize that all are capable. Some are more processed and have more credentials than others. Some are so conditioned by the core values of the system that they can't see the command implied in being a Christian: stand apart from the divisiveness of a system that blinds you from seeing the dignity and worth in the "least" of these among you.

We needed to implement a theology which had the courage to see that in the eyes of God we are no different from the poor: sinners not deserving, not competent, not contributing members of the community, and subject to victimizing ourselves. In so doing, we are able to trust the people to join in a covenant of hope by extending to them both opportunity and responsibility along with the resources to design their own destiny. The people extend the same grace in return as that extended to them, by not victimizing those in a different socioeconomic position or seeing them as "the enemy."

Not only are individuals in communities of poverty disconnected from the mainstream, but communities of poverty often lack institutions with the resources they need for quality of life. Where they do exist, they too are disconnected from the mainstream. A theology which affirms the belief that poor people are capable and can contribute to refining mainstream society needs to focus on building these resources, the internal capacity for leadership, and the institutions within the communities of poverty, drawing from the people in the communities themselves. Our planning process with the people identified a need for a learning center with a holistic program. In the process of engagement, we remembered the value of teaching people to fish, as opposed to taking them out fishing. The people were asked to define their problems and needs. They were asked how they could provide the services to meet their needs. How would they operate the learning centers once built? Their worth and capability to provide services as well as receive them was implicit in this theology of engagement, which further required them to be inclusive of other needs outside their own housing community.

The idea of poor people serving the broader community also included their role in advocating for justice against systemic injustice. Funding these learning centers provided great obstacles, which led us to examine the property tax codes. Country clubs, sororities and fraternities were property-tax exempt, yet not one multifamily low-income housing development was exempted by code. With the residents, we succeeded in gaining exemption by effecting changes in the legislative language of the statute. Working with the Department of Housing and Urban Development then allowed us to use funds previously paid in taxes for social program development on an annual basis. We built four large Community Learning Centers equipped with high-end computer labs, day-care centers, Head Start classes, an employment center, conference rooms and offices. Two centers opened in Madison, Wisconsin in 1995 and two more in Milwaukee in 1998 with an emphasis on education and employment, as the residents had planned.

During this period, twenty-four residents have been hired and continue to be trained on all aspects of running a community-based organization. This required regulatory changes at HUD. Managers, lab technicians, Head Start teachers, property managers and maintenance persons have been hired to operate the housing and learning centers. For the first time, the community has the resources and the institutional tools to serve humanity and the opportunity to provide leadership.

What does it mean to teachers in a school system who come to the low-income community learning center and receive instruction on new software from the youth in our community? What does it mean to a community of low-income residents when the mayor of the city chooses their centers as the place to kick off the community leaders' reading and mentoring program instead of the city's own centers? What does it mean when the state university asks low income people to host a delegation from the Ukraine to explain how the people can build community? What does it mean to the community when the government (HUD) chooses to make this program a national initiative?

Hope abounds, people are transformed and the community begins to accomplish educational excellence and employment placement. Pat, the program coordinator of the Northport center in Madison, a resident of the community for eleven years, and Jackie, the Packer center's program coordinator, a resident of twelve years, demonstrate the success of the educational programs. Before the centers were in operation, the grade-point average of the 402 kids at these two sites was 1.4 on a 4.0 system. Within two years, the grade-point average rose to 3.2. The dropout rate was reduced from the high teens to below 3 percent. The behavior of the students as affirmed by the school principal and teachers changed dramatically. The referral rate due to violence and acting out, near 40 percent, was reduced to under 1 percent. One of the middle school principals said "I can tell the students from Northport and Packers from the rest now. They no longer stick together in their own group; they are mingling with students from other socioeconomic backgrounds. They are also involving themselves in extracurricular activities and not just staying with sports, and finally they are providing leadership in our technology centers. In addition, over 150 people were trained and placed in employment of choice, all in livable wage jobs. It raises the question of who is empowering whom?

Low-income housing developments are communities filled with wealthy souls that lack only the resources to demonstrate their intention to uphold community values which *allow* the village to bring up the child. This theology and the creation of these centers allowed residents to have a symbol of significance just as those living in a gated community have. Just as the children succeeding in these housing communities now have the confidence to reach beyond their comfort zones, we are finding that the larger mainstream community is now reaching to our communities for services. Our community is now seen as an education community and not a low-income housing development. With the proper theology of acceptance and the internal development of community leadership, our residents have been seen as productive contributors to the mainstream society. With that acceptance comes mutual acculturation in the human community with no pretenses about success or failure. Instead, we've gained wisdom about the processes needed on all sides to maintain and nurture the sense of community and people.

The program base is composed of diverse institutional partners that would never come to serve and be served in this community unless they had seen the richness of both the human and technical competency of our community. For too long, the church has been in the business of charity, and low-income people have been in the business of begging or being placated. Neither is good for the other. We must realize the unity of the body of Christ and our own relationship, as members, to the body. For through God's grace, both those who have affirmed Christ as Lord and Savior and those who may not have affirmed this are invited to the Lord's table. As host, we must make sure the table can seat all.

This article is written in celebration and in honor of the witness and ministry of Dr. Frederick Trost, whose engagement of word and deed builds upon the covenant of God in the world and who has graciously extended to me the invitation to the rich communion of his friendship.

"Let Your Light Shine"

Barbara Rudolph

You are the light of the world. A city built on a hill cannot be hid. No one after lighting a lamp puts it under a bushel basket, but on a lamp stand, and it gives light to all in the house, In the same way, let your light shine before others, so that they may see your good works and give glory to your Father in heaven (Matthew 5:14-16).

My god-children are of elementary age. They love to tell jokes and ask funny questions. "Where does the sun never shine at all?" they have asked me. They provided the answer when I failed to have one: "In the shade!"

"Where there is much light, there will be much shade," says a German proverb. Most of the time such popular wisdom sayings are correct, but with Jesus this saying is not true, and that is good. In the Sermon on the Mount he says "You are the light of the world."

Let's have a closer look: To whom is Jesus saying this? To those who live in the shadows of life, those who are not in the sunlight of public recognition, those who are overshadowed by the dark clouds of suffering and powerlessness. In the passage prior to the Sermon on the Mount we find a description of these people: sick, afflicted with various kinds of diseases and pains, demoniacs, epileptics, and paralytics; a great crowd of all sorts of people from Galilee, the Decapolis, Jerusalem, Judea, and from beyond the Jordan (Mt 4:24-25).

In the Greek text these people are called *ochlos*, which has a negative tone to it like "vagabonds." To these *ochlos*, to this mob, Jesus says: "You are the light of the world." The names of those who heard this have not been recorded for posterity, but Jesus lifted them out of the darkness of history, out of the shadows of life into the bright sun light. The shadow play becomes a play of light, the mob, the vagabonds, become bearers of light. Thus Jesus spoke to the people on the mountain and thus does he speak with us: "You are the Light of the world."

After all, the sun shines even in the shade; the light breaks through the darkness. I step out of the shadows into the bright light of God's love, which shines on me because Jesus' word is addressed to me. I joyously accept this for I need it more than anything else. What lifts me to the sun, to the light, is not what I do and achieve, not what I think and feel, rather the light *reaches* to me and shines on me. Just as on a summer morning when I step out of the shadow of the house into the morning sun and the light warms me and shines through me, so it is with the love of God, which intends only the good for me.

"You are the light." At the beginning of creation, God created first the light. Thus, I am valued and honored.

I am the light of the world, says Jesus in John's Gospel. Thus I am valued and honored.

The *ochlos,* the vagabonds, the mob, without exception are placed on God's side, into the light of his love, without "ifs" or "buts," unreservedly. Who from the *ochlos* in our congregation needs this light, and what shadow in my life needs this light? We pause to allow this light to shine upon us. And we sense how great God's love is—the hidden and secret darknesses of my life, the twilight of guilt and failure, the shadow of illness and death—yes, the light of heaven, descending into the realm of death, will not separate me from God.

We welcome this assurance, in the safety of our sanctuary, during a protected time of worship. We need this time out for ourselves, to hear it, to receive it, to repeat it, to make it our own: "You are the light of the world."

We need this for the world in which we live, for the world into which we return from this service, for tomorrow, and the day after tomorrow. Jesus looks at us and says: "You are the light of the world." Do we desire Jesus' eyes embracing us as we leave the sanctuary? Will we trust the light to shine even when we enter into unprotected places? It can encourage us, too, that Jesus speaks to the *ochlos,* the vagabonds, the mob, in such an astounding way. The bright light of this promise breaks in on the many facets of everyday life.

Dennis is five years old and has a disability. His parents are often overtaxed and edgy. They have two other children. Time and nerves are often stretched to the breaking point. The teacher in the special kindergarten smiles at the parents when they come for consultation. "Dennis is such a joy and he is so much fun. He is our sunshine," she tells them. The parents feel good as they hear this and Dennis is radiant.

Daniela is thirteen years old. Her parents laid down the rules: straighten up your room, do your homework, be home at the set time. She complains: "My parents are always picking on me and are never satisfied." Her grandmother is not interested in reminding her of her shortcomings. When Daniela visits Grandma, she prepares her favorite dish and inquires about her newest boy friend. "You are always my sunshine," she says. And Daniela beams with joy.

Maria, forty-four years old, is stressed out: family, housework, and a part–time job. Sometimes she is not sure how long she can make it. But then she comes into the office one morning and her co-workers greet her. The sun is shining! Maria shines too.

Hans is seventy-eight years old with a body that has been worn out by years of hard work. His wife died two years ago. He continues to accept the invitation of the bowling team to play with them. His friends say to him, "Hans, without you bowling is not much fun. We need you." And Hans beams with happiness.

Who talks to us in this way? Where does the light of God's love, broken into human words, shine into our lives in this world? Do I learn to become aware of it in the safety of the sanctuary, during the protected time of worship, and do I take the time to allow it to illumine me to become more attentive to God's light in the world in the multi-colored facets of life? It goes with us on life's way, and we need it more than we might want to admit.

We know about people whose lives have been penetrated by God's light even in their darkest hour of sorrow and guilt: Dietrich Bonhoeffer, facing certain death, experienced this in the darkness of his loneliness and fear; in the Gestapo prison (1944) he wrote these lines: "By gracious powers so wonderfully sheltered, and confidently waiting, come what may." And in the fifth verse of this famous poem he asks God: "Let warm and bright the candles burn, which you have brought to shine in our darkness."

Heinrich Albertz, theologian and politician, was Berlin's minister of the interior when, during the time of student unrest, Benno Ohnesorg, a student, was killed in a police action. So different from other politicians at that time, he took responsibility for this death. Such courageous action is still doing us a lot of good. He often said that faith and confidence in the love of Christ encouraged him to take this step which reaches into the darkness of our guilt.

"You are the light of the world." The light wants to shine in the world, just like the sun is shining in the shadow. We know about people living in the shadow, who depend on this and who wait for the light of Christ to reach them too.

In our neighboring church some refugees found sanctuary. They had been scheduled for deportation to the former Yugoslavia. The congregation fought with the city council for a resident permit to allow the family to stay. In many papers interviews with the pastors were printed. Christian people brought light into the darkness of the deportation praxis often at their own risk.

In Moers we have a safe house operated by the Catholic church. Here women who have been abused by their spouses can find refuge with their children. The violence in families is very high, but Catholic women bring light into the structures of power and violence. Doing this they are personally at risk.

It has become apparent that Western Christian civilization has its dark side; it is a world in which people are urgently in need of being guided by the light of love which Jesus preached on the mountain: "Let your light so shine before the people, that they may see your good works." Jesus knows what the world really needs: engagement and advocacy for people living in the shadows of life. It can be inconvenient and bring trouble, but Jesus knows about that, too. He put himself at risk and ruined his reputation as he turned toward the people on the darker side of life, as he found himself in the shadows.

Therefore, permit me to say something critical at the end, even if it is my personal impression. Sometimes parents and grandparents tell a child or grandchild: "You are my sunshine." Jesus said: "You are my light." The second part of the sentence, however, we have ignored. At birthdays and at Christmas, children are often the center of attention, like stars in the flood light on the stage, like little princesses and princes showered with presents and every wish fulfilled. And the children cannot save themselves from being raised into little egotists and materialists. It is good for children and young people to be sunshine illuminating the darkness. It also encourages children in their faith if the light of love not only shines upon them but also upon people on the dark side of this world.

In our congregation, parents give their children a money box for the World Children's Fund on their first birthday. Every Sunday some money is deposited into the money box. Parents tell their child: "You have a sister in South America whom you do not know, but she lives with you in this your world and she will be happy to receive your help." What a wonderful experience for the child to learn about the great light of God's love which has been withheld for too long from others!

Therefore, "Let your light so shine before the people that they may see your good works and praise your Father in heaven."

Translated from the German by Erwin Pegel

Remarks On Globalization

Max L. Stackhouse

The following is excerpted from an address delivered to the Student Christian Movement in Bangalore, India, in 2000. It contains themes that were developed both in research at the Center of Theological Inquiry, and out of church and academic conferences on this topic in Australia, Fiji, China, Japan, Europe, and South Africa, as well as India.

The issue of globalization has taken on weight for me in recent years due to the ways in which the United Church Board of World Ministries has invited me to be involved in a number of ecumenical and international opportunities. Yet, I am not convinced that the current stand of our church is very profound and I am trying to press the inquiry deeper. As I listen to the voices of friends and colleagues on this matter, I find there are many points on which we agree. We must fight oppression. We must defend the defenseless. We must bring about greater equity within our nations and between them in the emerging global economy; but I am also convinced that the ideology of neo-Liberalism on one side and of the Liberationism that emerged in the decolonial period is fundamentally inadequate to grasp what is happening. I will try to tell you with what I disagree, and why.

It is at the point of understanding of the "social" part of Christian Social Ethics that the disagreement flares up. As I mentioned, we are largely in agreement on the ethical matters that demand a critique of injustice and on the deeper Biblical and theological reasons for that concern. But we disagree about the social dynamic of globalization.

The main point of my disagreement can be stated simply. Many (clearly not all) Indian Christians (and other thoughtful and morally concerned people) appear to have a very definite "standard view" of globalization. They see it as a dynamic economic juggernaut, late-capitalist in form, without social boundaries or moral purpose, possibly a new version of the old colonialism that India has struggled to overcome. Further, the word "capitalist" is understood through Marxist ideological glasses—not that everyone is a Communist but that certain analytical categories expressed in the philosophy of Marx govern the modes of analysis. The wider social context is read through that lens, and some parts of the context are taken as compelling evidence that this definition is fully correct. The evils of Indian society—the poverty, the marginalization of the Dalits, the oppression of women, and the destruction of the environment are all seen as the product of globalization understood in this way.

If the standard view is correct, we must all fight globalization. We would have no disagreement. Justice would demand it, and no serious theological stance could approve or tolerate it. But what if this standard view is lopsided, ideological, and obsolete? What if this view is not what globalization is at its basic levels? What if reading the world through these lenses falsifies the social data? And what if these are not the decisive effects of globalization?

For instance, when was there not poverty in Indian society? When was there not the marginalization of Dalits? When was there not the oppression of women? When did the great Gangic plain become desertified? Many of these things were well entrenched before anyone ever imagined the word, let alone the reality of globalization, or even the reality of colonialism. The evidence that these are caused by or even made greatly worse by globalization is hard to find. To blame these problems on globalization could mislead us as to their real causes and thus prevent an effective response.

Of course, we cannot say that these were the only features of classic Indian culture; but neither can we say that these are the chief effects of globalization. More likely, it was the globalization of certain ideas of human rights and social justice, of democracy and economic opportunity that has made us all more conscious of these problems. All who have a sense of globalization have also a sense that all persons must be treated with dignity as full members of society, that women should be seen as the equal partners with men in the common life, that we should limit ecologically-damaging practices, such as free-range cattle grazing.

Nor does it help to appeal to the size of the slums in the many great cities of India as proof that globalization is making things worse for people, as some have done in our discussion. The growth of mega-cities all over the world has been a major story for more than a century, as new means of agricultural production have pressed many off the land, and new methods of industrial production have drawn the energetic and eager into the towns. Of course, the human situation is often harsh, raw, and bitter in the cities; but only some want to go back to their former status, and fewer do go. They know that the social conditions, opportunities, and social stigmas there are worse.

I think India can expect more and more migration to the cities, as the cities become the ganglia of globalization. Putting priorities on basic infrastructure for city-dwellers would be the most important single strategy to help the masses of India find their way in a globalizing era, and if this is done with a spirit of self-help, and not only by new forms of government dependency, the long range involvement of people in their own destinies is likely itself to improve life. Those church activists, advocacy, and social service groups who work with these populations are in fact building the future. Discouraging as the work may be now and again, it is vitally important.

Perhaps because I come to this land every few years, as a kind of visiting uncle, I can see what I believe is also present in the technical economic data: growth and dynamic development that those of you who live here all the time may not notice—just as you may not notice the growth of a young man or woman whom you see every day. My impressions fit with the best evidence that the most respected scholars offer. They show that the indicators of well-being are in fact improving. The life-expectancy is longer, the death rate for children is down, the number of people in abject poverty is reduced from more than 50 percent at Independence (and an estimated 75 percent in the early 20th century) to less than 40 percent and some say less than 30 percent. To reduce the poverty rate that much, even if the population continues to grow so that many people are affected, is rather amazing.

Moreover, the mass famine that characterized some periods of India's history is behind it. Fluctuations will come and go in this or that decade or half-decade: the monsoon may not be good, the relationships to supportive countries abroad may change, the policies in one economic area or another may fail, or international competition (such as with fisheries) may wipe out a significant industry for thousands (and damage the ecological situation as well). Further, these fluctuations are most difficult for those parts of the population—and they are vast—who have no safety net. Those with the standard view will seize on these facts and make them central to what the standard view expects: the inevitable polarization of the classes.

But these facts may not be the big story of Indian life over the last century or so. What is more remarkable, in fact the great untold story, is the growth of the middle classes. Life may not yet be very secure for many in this category, and the pressure of struggle to keep from falling back may be great; but the level of life-style and discretionary income (that not immediately necessary for survival) is exploding at tremendous rates. It does seem to be the case that the very rich are getting more rich faster, that the upper-middle classes are getting more rich, but not quite so fast, and the lower middle class is getting richer more slowly, and the very poor are dividing into two groups: those who are progressing up the ladder of material well-being very slowly and those who are making no discernable gains at all. The struggle to work for this last group does not demand a resistance to globalization; in fact, it could be that globalization will, over time, do more to aid them than to functionally demand that they stay in traditional social roles.

Most peoples around the world have decided that capitalization, the accumulation of concentrated wealth to make the massive investments that are necessary for the plunge into the future with its demand for new institutions, should not be only in the hands of politicians or their appointees (who turn out often to be relatives and contributors to their campaign funds). Thus, other potentially capitalizing centers—families, cooperatives, companies, corporations, and banks (and their managers, their "stewards")—have begun to play that role, and people who know how to operate in this environment are paid tremendous salaries (which they cannot possibly use, and which they therefore invest).

In many societies, the legal arrangements are not in place to make these centers of finance as accountable as they perhaps should be; and certainly the problems of transparency and corruption become significant. These not only prove that a totally *lassez faire* economy is not viable, they damage the overall well-being of the society and drive away those who might invest (from inside or outside) but find the demanded, illegal "transaction costs" (bribes and "black money") distasteful morally and dysfunctional economically. Thus, important reforms are very necessary to keep such practices in check. But I know of no major government and no viable political party anywhere in the world that wants to return to centralized control of the economy—or to the traditional economy. Globalization of just laws and moral practices facilitates the globalization of economic inclusion.

This non-governmental control of capital does mean, for a while at least, that the distance between the top and bottom will not decrease rapidly. The bigger point, however, is the fact that larger and larger percentages of the people are gaining from the new possibilities and want to keep them than any other known possibility, although some at the very bottom do not gain from them.

A more accurate view of globalization will take these realities into account. It will also recognize that even these significant shifts in economic life are but one aspect of a massive social change now underway. We cannot ignore the social, political, cultural, technological, moral and religious factors that have set the deeper conditions which have generated this phenomenon.

There are several things that globalization, understood in these more complex terms, is not, or at least not quite, although people often confuse them with globalization. It is not quite "modernization," even if some aspects of modernization lead to globalization. Modernization was essentially a "developmentalist and statist" model, whether the revolutionary Marxist one or the evolutionary "Liberal" one. These developmentalist models had the vision that each nation would have to go through the stages that the West went through, and that the state, either by borrowing the "sweat equity" of the people or fed by the largess of bank loans, would lead the world to modernity.

It proved a false model. Modernization everywhere brought us vast semi-rationalized bureaucracies, with all their myriads of permits, passes, and permissions to do just about anything—a great occasion for corruption. It also turns out that the states are poor economic producers. They may be good re-distributers of wealth in certain ways, but they are not good at generating wealth. Besides, modernization was often advanced as a purely secular vision of human well-being, and it proved to have no stable moral core.

Besides, some nations leapfrogged over the predicted stages, precisely by forming their own kinds of corporations—the Samurai companies of Japan, the *chaebol* of Korea, the "General's corporations" of Taiwan, etc. Meanwhile, the governments that borrowed the most to do this from the top down developed the fewest corporations and are the countries now with the greatest debts.

It looks to me as if the new "socialist market economy" of China's militantly anti-religious government, the "technocratic capitalism" of Indonesia's secular military rulers (which the people are trying to contain with new democratic arrangements), and the "mixed economy" of India, are among the world's leading contenders for the way of the future—not only because of their vast populations, but because they are major experiments in the world options. I am at present betting on India, in spite of all the corruption and problems, in large measure because it is the most open to globalizing influences, has a mostly functioning democracy, and is (so far) open to deep influences from religious ethics.

Nor can we say that globalization is quite the same as "internationalism." That was the sentiment that built the League of Nations and then the United Nations Organization; but it is hardly able to manage the geopolitics of the world, let alone the new geoeconomics. No, the powers of globalization have surpassed the capacity of even coalitions of nations to halt the processes of globalization. Indeed, few nations really want to. Every democratically elected nation in the world now has a government that is adjusting itself to, and for, globalization, in spite of resistance from some quarters of the population. The strongest resistance comes from the elders of the old sub-cultures who recognize that much of what they worked for will be altered. Besides, every country that energetically opposes globalization is in very bad shape: Afghanistan, Somalia, Burma, Libya, Rwanda, Iraq, Cuba, Zaire, Iran, North Korea, for example.

These considerations are the ones by which the specifically economic factors have to be interpreted, and then in comparative and historical perspective. What are the economic effects?

I agree with Simon Kuznets, the older Nobel Prize Economist who argued with the "developmentalists," with Amartya Sen, the current Nobel Prize Winner (rather than C. T. Kurian who recently critiqued his new book), my friend Henry Jacoby, a leading environmental economist from M.I.T, and David Landis, of Harvard, author of the new, massive survey of *The Wealth and Poverty of Nations*. Of course, they are economists, who are as bad as theologians on agreeing on things; but they seem to be in accord with the fact that open systems, with transparency, accountability, and transnational agreements under a just law, are the most likely ways to allow the people and the environment to flourish, and to control the worst negative effects.

Thus, I tend to come to these conclusions:

1. Globalization is unavoidable. Only to oppose it, not to learn how to shape it, is to plan one's own defeat, and to have the next generation distrust you for false prophecy.

2. It will bring what Schumpeter called "creative destruction": some people will be winners and some losers. Those with a moral passion will work eagerly to reduce the number of losers.

3. Governments can do some things to ease the pain of transition by wise public policy; but many of their efforts must be to ready the next generations for the impact of globalization.

4. The mixed results of globalization will be more positive than negative if religiously and morally committed people engage the questions and bring their visions of justice wisely to them.

5. There are openings in the processes of globalization at personal, corporate, political, technological, NGO, and legal levels to moral and spiritual influences that could alter the course of globalization, to make the corporations more responsible, accountable, and transparent, to undertake programs that protect the most vulnerable people and ecological regions, and to draw as many as possible into

the process of global development so that they are not left out entirely.

In other words, if globalization is like a bull-dozer in a village, we had best learn to drive it and not just flee from it, or shout at it from a (usually safe) distance, while it completely alters the landscape, which, frankly, is what some "third world theologians" seem to have been doing for a decade, with little effect. It does not help people learn to drive in traffic, if we only portray them as pedestrian victims. Besides, some who shouted against it the most loudly have worked to get their children in on it.

But, as I mentioned at the outset, we are already agreed, I think, on the basic moral principles and purposes. Our debate was about social analysis. We did not go very far into specific strategies, for that requires a detailed knowledge of the operational possibilities on the ground, which I do not have, although I indicated that I thought the moral and spiritual influences of our common faith can and should be making a more vital contribution than they are at present. Still, if some continue to be absolutely opposed to globalization and persist in holding to the standard view of it without revision, the burden of proof will be on them. Fewer and fewer will heed them, and the cost in the lives of people will be greater than if we help people cope with, and learn to shape globalization. I did not hear a viable strategy outlined to make the standard view effective throughout the evening.

My message to you, as a visiting uncle and as a fellow Christian, is a message of hope and love. What is coming is not all bad, and it can help things. It will have negative sides too. What does not? But learn how to let it help.

The message is also an invitation or a challenge. If you have only a negative image of globalization, consider revising your understanding, re-grinding your glasses. See this phenomenon through some new lenses. If you do not agree with me, develop your own revised vision. I am not telling you what model you must have; but I am telling you that I do not believe that the old standard view will help, and that there is strong evidence to suggest that it is likely to hurt. I may be wrong, but if you think that in any respect you may be wrong too, then we must develop something better than the standard view. I, myself, have learned from this night and hope to continue learning. Perhaps we can all go deeper in the future.

A Feast That Moves:
Real and Missionary Presence in
Lutheran-Reformed Full Communion

John H. Thomas

Augustus Lutheran Church in Trappe, Pennsylvania, a significant place in the history of North American Lutheranism, is an early colonial congregation founded by the patriarch of the German Ministerium, Henry Melchior Muhlenberg. Muhlenberg is buried in the church yard outside the original sanctuary and is pictured in a stained glass window in the vestibule of the current church. Augustus Church was the location for a gathering of delegates to the national church meetings of the Evangelical Lutheran Church in America and the United Church of Christ in the spring of 1997 as both churches were preparing to vote on *A Formula of Agreement* establishing full communion between the ELCA, the UCC, and two other Reformed churches: the Presbyterian Church (USA) and the Reformed Church in America.[1] Much of the theological dialogue leading to the historic votes on full communion centered on the question of real presence, an issue that has divided Lutherans and Reformed since the famous Colloquy at Marburg in 1529 where Luther and Zwingli found themselves unable to agree on the mode of Christ's presence in the sacramental meal. So it was appropriate that much of the discussion at the Trappe gathering focused on how these twentieth century descendants of Luther, Zwingli, and Calvin view the question of presence. "Where, and how, is Christ's presence 'located,' and in what sense is that presence 'real'?"

The dialogues leading up to the vote on *A Formula of Agreement* answered the question in the following way: "The Reformation heritage of our churches in the matter of the Lord's Supper draws from the same roots and envisages the same goal: to call the people of God to the table at which Christ himself is present to give himself for us under the same word of forgiveness, empowerment, and promise."[2] As was the case in most of the North American and international Lutheran and Reformed dialogues, exploring the meaning of this assertion, and gaining confidence that it accurately reflected the reality of each of the participating churches was a major challenge. Much of the conversation that day in Trappe dealt with what "real" really means for Lutheran and Reformed Christians in North America today.

At the conclusion of the session the leader proposed that the ecumenical challenge was not simply to resolve historical questions but also to discern together how to respond to contemporary mission challenges, or to borrow from the titles of two of the dialogues, how do we move from *Marburg Revisited* to *Our Common Calling*? With that question as a kind of benediction, participants departed through the vestibule past the gaze of Muhlenberg. On another wall of that vestibule, however, was a painting that echoed the leader's question. The Victorian portrait depicted a large cathedral, nearly empty save for a group of priests huddled around the high altar in the distance. Shadows enveloped most of the scene except for two figures in the foreground of the painting bathed in light near the door to the nave of the cathedral. One was Christ, embracing in compassion an old woman who was a beggar. The message was clear. The real presence encountered at the altar is also and always a missionary presence encountered in the midst of need. The feast that defines the church is a feast that moves, a movement that has a clear trajectory from the center toward the margins of life after the way of Jesus whose pilgrimage led him to a cross outside the walls of the city. Kosuke Koyama, in a compelling address at the Eighth Assembly of the World Council of Churches, spoke of a "Centre God who runs out to the periphery. . . . The light shines from the periphery, not from the centre. . . . The church is the body of Christ who runs to welcome the broken world."[3] What would it mean for Lutheran and Reformed Christians to celebrate together a "feast that moves?"

The relationship of the "real" and "missionary" presence, while not a formulation of the dialogues themselves, was on the agenda of most stages of Lutheran-Reformed dialogue. Yet it has often been an agenda item left largely incomplete. In part this is due to the preoccupation with the Reformation debates over the nature of the sacramental presence. This, after all, is where Lutherans and Reformed parted company, and thus it made sense for efforts at rapprochement to begin with a "revisit" of Marburg. It was also due to the fact that restoration of [full] communion was based on satisfying the requirements of unity outlined in the Augsburg Confession: "For the true unity of the church it is enough [*satis est consentire*] concerning the teaching of the Gospel and the administration of the sacraments."[4] As a result, reflection about doctrine has taken precedence over reflection about praxis in the dialogues, and the theme of witness and service in the world has tended to be named as a future agenda to be addressed by churches that have *already* achieved full communion. Witness and service are named, for example, in the Leuenberg Agreement as one of four elements of the "declaration and realization" of church fellowship.[5] *Toward Church Fellowship,* the 1989 report of the international Lutheran and Reformed Dialogue, recommends the development of "common witness and service in the world," reminding us:

We are called to proclaim and live the love of God to humanity in its need, to remove the causes of human suffering, to defend justice and peace in the community and in the whole of creation. Failure to take up this duty, tolerance of injustice and all forms of suppression, become counterwitesses which contradict our faith.[6]

Finally, *A Common Calling,* the report of the Theological Conversations on which Lutheran-Reformed full communion in North America as articulated in *A Formula of Agreement* was based, names "declaring God's justice and mercy" as a task in an "agenda for the future together."[7] In spite of these good intentions, however, it must be confessed that the churches which have achieved full communion either on the basis of *The Leuenberg Agreement* or *A Formula of Agreement* have yet to take up this agenda in a compelling way. As one participant in the Leuenberg process has put it, "The Achilles' heel of the Leuenberg Fellowship is without doubt the difficulty we experience in arriving at a common witness and service. This problem has been with us for 25 years."[8]

One of the problems leading to this "disappointment" of a central hope and expectation of full communion may be the way in which issues of justice, peace, and the integrity of creation are related to the questions of "real presence" that have dominated dialogue and reflection to this point. It is not the case that these critical questions have been absent. But they have been separated from the sacramental questions in somewhat parallel reflections on the relationship between the Lutheran emphasis on "two kingdoms" and the Reformed emphasis on the "sovereignty or kingship of God." This theological reflection has been rich. By making ethics, mission, and justice separate topics alongside that of the nature of sacramental presence, however, Lutherans and Reformed have tended to relegate the former to the status of "addenda" or "next steps" in their common work.[9] Might it be possible for Lutherans and Reformed to give new energy to themes of common witness and service by moving them from "next steps" into the midst of the sacramental reflection that has always been center stage in the dialogues, acknowledging that it is just as important to speak of the "missionary presence of Christ" in the sacrament as it is to establish the real presence of Christ in the sacrament?

In 1994, representatives of the Leuenberg Fellowship met to continue their theological dialogue as a part of the on-going Leuenberg process. Echoing themes found in international Faith and Order documents like *Baptism, Eucharist, and Ministry*, the report of the meeting identified both eschatalogical and ecclesiological aspects of the Lord's Supper in ways that creatively relate "real" and "missionary" presence:

In the Lord's Supper we celebrate the dawn of the kingdom of God in the hope of a final renewal of creation. The Lord's Supper is thus an event of new covenant and a prophetic sign of the universal salvific will of God and of the future Lordship, in which God will be all in all. In this way the Lord's Supper is a feast of joy in the midst of sorrow, a feast of forgiveness in the midst of all guilt, a feast of fellowship in the midst of all division. . . .

In the Lord's Supper the church becomes visible as communion. At the same time each eucharistic celebration is the sign, remembrance and challenge of the fact that the received gift stands in the communion of all believers and in the solidarity with the world to which God's redemptive will is addressed.[10]

The relationship of real to missionary presence is reiterated in a recent statement on "the nature and purpose of the church" by the World Council of Churches:

Through the Lord's Supper the all-renewing grace of God penetrates and restores human personality and dignity. The eucharist involves the believer in the central event of the world's history. As participants in the eucharist, therefore, we prove inconsistent if we are not actively participating in the ongoing restoration of the world's situation and the human condition.[11]

This apprehension of the relationship between real and missionary presence places Lutheran and Reformed theological reflection squarely within the broader ecumenical dialogue, and in an important way moves both of these Western traditions into closer contact with Orthodox understandings which speak of "the liturgy after the liturgy," of a liturgy that "is not terminated in the prayerful intimacy of the worship but continues with diakonia, apostolic mission, visible and public Christian witness." In the words of Romanian theologian Ion Bria, "[The liturgy] must be seen as the starting event of the Christian movement for mission, the point of departure given to the church for pursuing its vocation in the wider society."[12]

For too long Lutheran and Reformed Christians have detected— and debated!—the movement of God in a feast that from a human standpoint has been largely static or sedentary. A preoccupation with this static feast has made it difficult, even when sacramental divisions have been overcome, to engage together in missionary witness and service. By noting, however, that the real presence is always and everywhere a missionary presence, that eucharist and mission are inextricably linked together, Reformed and Lutheran Christians are caught up in a feast that moves, a feast in which solidarity with the oppressed and the marginalized, and with the creation itself, is no longer an addenda or a next step but is in fact part of the feast itself.

Past the Muhlenberg window and the Victorian portrait in the vestibule of Augustus Church, there is a memorial stone walkway honoring the 18th century Ministerium that Muhlenberg established as the first expression of an organized Lutheran presence in North America. The walkway is made up of replicas of the corner stones of the churches that belonged to that early body. Many of those churches in their formative years, and some still to this day, are Union Churches, housing both Lutheran and Reformed (United Church of Christ) congregations. Pilgrims to this shrine of colonial Lutheranism find themselves literally tracing the steps of early Lutheran and Reformed dialogue in this country, a journey marked by pain and promise, by cooperation and competition, by warm affection and bitter caricature. As both traditions now move past the milestone of the establishment of full communion in 1998, and as we honor the faith and witness of Frederick R. Trost whose own life is so richly blessed by the tradition of the Evangelical Synod with its blending of Lutheran and Reformed resources, may we gather around a Presence that is both real and missionary, celebrating together a feast that moves!

Notes

1. Lutheran Reformed dialogue in North America is summarized in the reports of several rounds of theological conversation: James E. Andrews and Joseph A. Burgess, eds., *An Invitation to Action: The Lutheran-Reformed Dialogue Series III* (Philadelphia: Fortress Press, 1984) contains the reports of the third round (1981-1983) and the first round, *Marburg Revisited* (1962-1966). Also included is the text of the Leuenberg Agreement which was adopted by Lutheran and Reformed churches in Europe in 1973. Keith F. Nickle and Timothy F. Lull, eds., *A Common Calling: The Witness of Our Reformation Churches in North America Today* (Minneapolis: Augsburg Fortress, 1993), contains the report of the Lutheran-Reformed Committee for Theological Conversations held from 1988 to 1992. *A Formula of Agreement*, summarizing the results of the previous dialogues, was acted upon by four churches at Assemblies and Synods in 1997.

2. Nickle and Lull, *A Common Calling,* 49.

3. Kosuke Koyama, "Rejoice in Hope," in Kessler, Diane, ed., *Together on the Way: Official Report of the Eighth Assembly of the World Council of Churches* (Geneva: World Council of Churches, 1999), 40.

4. Augsburg Confession, Article 7.

5. Leuenberg Agreement, IV.1.a. paragraph 36, in *An Invitation to Action*, 71.

6. *Toward Church Fellowship: Report of the Joint Commission of the Lutheran World Federation and the World Alliance of Reformed Churches* (Geneva, 1989), 25, 29.

7. *A Common Calling*, 59-61.

8. André Birmelé, "The Implications of the Leuenberg Agreement for the Communion of Churches," in *Rowing in One Boat: A Common Reflection on Lutheran-Reformed Relations Worldwide* (Geneva, 1999), 42.

9.See, for example, *Marburg Revisited*, which presents its conclusions in three separate sections, one dealing with "The Lord's Supper," one dealing with "Creation and Redemption, Law and Gospel, Justification and Sanctification," and one dealing with "Ethos and Ethics—Christian Service in the Modern World." See also *An Invitation to Action* in which a joint statement on "The Sacrament of the Lord's Supper" is divided from joint statements on "Justification" and "Ministry."

10. "On the Doctrine and Practice of the Lord's Supper," in *Leuenberger Texte* (Frankfurt am Main, 1995), 73.

11. *The Nature and Purpose of the Church: A Stage on the Way to a Common Statement*, Faith and Order Paper 181 (Geneva, 1998), 39.

12. Ion Bria, *The Liturgy after the Liturgy: Mission and Witness from an Orthodox Perspective* (Geneva, 1996), 28.

"Lord Jesus, I Look at My Hands"

Lord Jesus,

I look at my hands and wonder about yours:

The calluses developed through long labors in wood,
The stain of mud and spit from reaching down into the earth
        to heal the creatures of the earth,
The soiled wetness from washing the feet of your friends.

Sometimes late at night finds me staring at my hands, Lord.
The day is done but so much has been left undone.
And some has been done that I wish could be taken back.
So I stare at my hands and pray to you.

Some say there are secret signs in hands, a future to be unfolded,
Awaiting only the proper reader.
But there are no secrets here, in my hands.

There's a scar from my first penknife clumsily closed.
It makes me remember the sting of iodine and the patience of my mother.
There's a finger made crooked by a poorly-caught ball.
Arthritis will find a ready-made home here.
A ring of promise hangs tightly there,
Binding a finger swollen with minor temptations guiltily savored.
With your faithful grace, the promise still remains
And the ring, though dulled, still holds.

Of course, these hands are not nearly so ruined as yours,
Stained as they are with mud and spit and tears and blood.
Lord, why were your wounds never healed?
Why weren't your wounds even closed?
Could it be that there was more work for them to do?

Could it be that your hands, scarred as they were,
Are not so unlike mine?
Could it be that my work
Is not so unlike yours?

Now my hands fold in fear and humility, and I offer you my prayer:
Your hands in mine, dear Jesus, your hands in mine.

Stephen P. Savides

An Invitation to the World

Bennie Whiten, Jr.

In the late 1960s I participated in a television program under the auspices of the New York City Council of Churches, then called the Protestant Council, with Dr. Norman Vincent Peale, then the Senior Minister of the Marble Collegiate Church, and Dr. Charles Spivey, who at the time was directing the Social Justice Division of the National Council of the Churches of Christ in the United States. It was not billed as a debate but it turned into one as the topic of discussion was the role of the churches and clergy in the Civil Rights struggle that was unfolding in those years. Not surprisingly Dr. Spivey and I were advocating an activist role in the struggle for faith communities to which Dr. Peale responded, "I'm just an evangelical preacher who is concerned to convert the hearts of men."

Having grown up in the Black church tradition with its strong emphasis on conversion, I was not hearing something I had not heard before. Yet, I have remembered those words for more than three decades as they encapsulated the tension that exists among believers regarding the mission of the community in terms of public witness. For me there was also a bit of irony in the fact that two Black clergy, both of whom had grown up in conversion-oriented, evangelical traditions, were saying to this distinguished leader "There's more to be said. What is the work of the converted heart?"

For me the answer to that question is exquisitely expressed in a section of the United Church of Christ Statement of Faith as adapted by Robert V. Moss:

> God calls us into the church to accept the cost and joy of discipleship, to be servants in the service of the whole human family, to proclaim the gospel to all the world and resist the powers of evil, to share in Christ's baptism and eat at this table, to join him in his passion and victory.

To me, this portion of the Statement of Faith states clearly whose we are and what we are to be about as God's people.

At the same time I am not unmindful that as sincere followers of Christ we may tend to emphasize one aspect more than another in being responsive to God's call and that was the nub of the difference in our conversation. For many the beginning point is found in the Great Commission of the risen Christ in Matthew 28:19 while others find their marching orders in Luke 4:18-19. This has led to a word or deed dichotomy and weakens the witness of the community in and to the world. I find it helpful to remember Paul's words in 2 Timothy: "All scripture is inspired by God and is useful for teaching, for reproof, for correction, and for training in righteousness, so that everyone who belongs to God may be proficient, equipped for every good work" (2 Tim 3:16-17).

What often seems to be missing from such discussions is an irenic spirit and an irenic theological consciousness. Thus we fail to see what elements we might affirm in the position taken by the other and effectively deny the possibility of finding a creative dialectic. One person who has embodied that spirit and consciousness for me has been Frederick Trost with his continuing call for "joyful theological reflection" by pastoral theologians for which he is an exemplar. I believe this is because he is a serious student of both the Lutheran and Calvinist traditions of which the United Church of Christ is heir. In simplistic terms, the former placed emphasis on the reign of God beyond history while the latter accented God's redeeming work in history. It may be that much contemporary discussion of the mission of the community in the world, which often seems to come to an either/or reduction, is a distortion of the two traditions. What is to be eschewed is an unreflective activism as well as the "paralysis of analysis."

We need to be chary of those who come with all the answers and need to make our own offerings with a spirit of humility. We are indeed "stewards of the mysteries of God" and must acknowledge that our understandings are limited and finite but must not let that become an excuse or reason for passivity in terms of public witness. Our calling is to proclaim the gospel in word and deed. Jürgen Moltmann says,

> The gospel is the liberating word of the God who is to come. Just as the coming kingdom is universal. So the gospel brings the liberation of men (*sic*) to universal expression. It seeks to liberate the soul and the body, individuals and social conditions, human systems and the systems of nature from the closedness of reserve, from self-righteousness, and from godless and inhuman pressures. It takes place in the world, in language, for the purpose of hearing and believing; but the freedom to which it calls reaches further and seeks to place the whole of life in the sphere of the hope of the kingdom. . . . Consequently the divine pardon stands at the centre of every proclamation of the gospel, the pardon that liberates men and women from the compulsion of evil, from the control of the powers, from fear of forsakenness, and from the apathy of the empty life, and that gives them courage for a new life for the kingdom in fellowship with Christ.*

Such an understanding of the gospel frees the community for its mission in the world without the arrogance of claiming to possess all the answers for every human situation. It frees us to work with persons of faith and persons of no faith in joining in God's redemptive work of justice and liberation. Knowing ourselves to be a community of forgiven, pardoned sinners, and knowing this comes only by God's gracious act, we are able to engage in acts of kindness, works of mercy, and deeds of love.

To deepen our understanding of the mission of the community in our time is not a dilettantish endeavor. There is a resurgence of a kind of fundamentalism in all the major religions of the world which would shackle us into narrow strictures and structures and which would deny the freedom to which we have been called as persons made "in the image and likeness of God." Unless communities of faith are clearer about their mission those forces will prevail. Pastoral theologians, to use Frederick Trost's term, must themselves be deeply rooted in the Word as they reflect on the everydayness of life and provide leadership to the flocks entrusted to their care. The mission of the community is the mission of the whole people of God but that people must be "equipped for the work of ministry."

The mission of the community is not to provide the blueprint for a new kind of social order nor a utopian vision of what our human communities may become but rather it is to proclaim and bear witness to a radical grace which is available to all. Roozen and Hadaway in their book, *Rerouting the Protestant Mainstream*, set before us a vision of the church "spiritually alive, justice oriented, and radically inclusive." Such a community is clear about its public witness because it is rooted and grounded in the Holy Spirit, knows its head Jesus Christ stands in the tradition of the prophets with the unequivocal call to justice, and welcomes all because it knows it exists, not by virtue of its worthiness or goodness, but by the grace of God.

This community does not speak to the world in triumphalist terms. It does not seek to impose its agenda on the world around it. Rather it offers to the world the invitation it has heard and accepted, "Come unto me, *all* ye that labor and are heavy laden."

Note

* Jürgen Moltmann, *The Church In The Power of The Spirit*, (New York: Harper and Row, 1977), 223.

"You Have Been Good to Us"

You have been good to us, gracious God! For sunshine and rain, for the new growth of spring and the autumn harvest, for the beauty and bounty of your creation that sustains us, for loved ones with whom we share not only our tables but our lives, we pour out our gratitude. You have been good to us, gracious God!

[We name our joys.]

You have been good to us, gracious God! We have more than we need. Dwell with us now that we may be not only inspired to share but prompted to work for a more just world in which all your children have enough to eat and reasons for joy.

We remember that all people will not gather with loved ones on this day. Not all your children will have enough to eat. Not all people will wake in the morning to a day full of promise. We ask you to be with those who are lonely or hungry, suffering from illness or sorrow.

We especially remember *[Names]*.

You have been good to us, gracious God! We are grateful for the communities that gather to bear witness to your goodness and hope for the world. Strengthen our faith and deepen our commitment to proclaim the good news. By the witness of our worship and work together may others come to know your presence and power in their lives. May we live each day reflecting the gift of life and love you have given us in Christ in whose name we pray.

Bonnie B. Van Overbeke

Living and Dying in the Community of the Church

Charles A. Wolfe

We do not live to ourselves, and we do not die to ourselves. If we live, we live to the Lord, and if we die, we die to the Lord; so then, whether we live or whether we die, we are the Lord's. For to this end Christ died and lived again, so that he might be Lord of both the dead and the living (Romans 14:7-9).

When, at the age of forty-three, Tom Petersen joined our church in 1994, it was not as a dying man wanting to make sure there was a place where his funeral could be held, although, as it turned out, he was a dying man. In February of 2000, Tom died of the brain tumor which had been partially removed in 1991. It should have surprised none of us, except for the fact that nine years is a fairly long time to live after surgery on an astrocytoma. No, Tom Petersen had come to Plymouth Church as a man amazed and gratified to be alive. Fear, Tom once told me, is the greatest cause of human sin. Tom, probably drawing from his own experience, was convinced that fear is behind almost every form of sin: greed, hatred, envy, pride—every form of selfishness—is motivated by fear. That, Tom might have said, is why in almost every biblical story of angels, the first word out of the angelic mouth is "fear not." Before anything else, "fear not."

Tom's final illness began on the first weekend of September 1999. His wife, Lou Ann, noticed it in the sudden forgetfulness he exhibited at times on Friday, a forgetfulness that became painfully apparent to her on Saturday and had her calling for help on Sunday morning. His teenage son, Andrew, an only child from his first marriage, had been with Tom on Friday evening. Andrew had planned to go out that evening with a high school friend but changed his mind for some reason, and on the last absolutely lucid, clear-headed night of his life, Tom and Andrew spent an evening in deep conversation as father and son. Sunday morning Lou Ann telephoned in tears to say that Tom was not remembering anything and could not possibly handle the preparation of Communion elements as he was scheduled to do. It was the beginning of the end.

Pastoral ministry to the dying is rarely an easy task. It is particularly difficult when the dying one has not achieved great age, has hundreds of gifts to share with the world, and is a parishioner with whom one has much history. Such was the case with Tom and Lou Ann.

When the partner of Lou Ann's brother died, I presided at the burial; his service was the first one I had done for someone who had died of AIDS. I had come to know Lou Ann's brother and his partner through Lou Ann when I agreed to talk with them about the partner's intention to commit suicide during a visit to Madison. It had been a surreal several days, beginning when the two men checked into a hotel and invited me to have dinner with them. As though it were a perfectly everyday conversation, the partner explained that he'd been suffering with AIDS for a decade, knew the disease well, having watched a number of friends die of it, and intended to get out while he could still make that decision. We talked at length. I suggested there might be other avenues available to him; he disagreed. The following day the two of them visited cemeteries, picked out and purchased a grave site, and made pre-arrangements with a local funeral home. As a sort of joke, they also purchased a tie as a gift for me because the partner, who had worked as a fashion model, had been unimpressed with my choice of tie the previous evening.

Lou Ann and I had talked together about the suicide plan; we had, in fact, together talked with a counselor from Hospice Care who assured us that pain control was possible, and that no one should feel they had no option but to commit suicide.

The next morning four people met in the hotel room for prayer: Lou Ann's brother, his partner, his partner's father (a lawyer from one of the Dakotas) and me. Three of us left the AIDS sufferer in the room as requested to make his own choices, and spent an anxious morning together. At noon we returned to the hotel room, expecting to find a body, and found, instead, the partner in bed sleeping, breathing very slowly. By afternoon he had awakened, feeling hung-over from an overdose of medications which, he insisted, should have been absolutely lethal.

The two men, after another couple of days, returned to their own home in New York. There, after suffering a series of strokes which left him blind, the man with AIDS died about two months later. His body was cremated and buried on the plot he had selected with his partner in Madison, Wisconsin. Tom and Lou Ann joined Lou Ann's brother, her parents, and the partner's father at the graveside service.

When a pastor has been through such events with a family, there develops a depth of trust and easy intimacy. Tom was a lover and master of word play in which we both delighted. Sometimes, during Sunday morning coffee hours, for example, he and I would engage in a kind of surface banter which any bystander would likely have thought pure foolishness, as it often was. But, in the midst of it, we would sometimes make sudden drops to deep places of self-revelation, theological insight, or awe-filled wonder. Tom was owner and artistic director of Brave Hearts Theater, an experimental venue for performing arts which had been his own creation. Tom understood his work as a calling, a vocation from God. Therefore, he was convinced that if it was meant to be, as something God was calling forth into the world, it would happen; and, conversely, if it did not happen, then it must be because God had other plans. The loss of the lease for Brave Hearts had Tom scrambling for another place during the summer of 1999. When Tom's memory loss emerged in September it was within a week of his having lost the space for Brave Hearts and the entire theater mailing list, due to a computer crash. The irony was apparent to Lou Ann, who perceived it as a kind of awful omen that the computer and Tom should, almost simultaneously, suffer memory loss.

The response of our congregation when the tumor became active again in September of 1999 was gratifying but not surprising to me. Tom's many friends from the theater community in Madison organized a benefit which raised several thousand dollars. The congregation of Plymouth Church, about 250 members, contributed more than $2300. With a neighborhood friend and Plymouth's parish nurse coordinating them, friends and church members were organized so that at least one meal a day was brought to the Petersen's home from about mid-September until his death in February. Some members would stop by and offer to stay with Tom so that Lou Ann could take a walk or run errands. Others came in and would simply slip into the kitchen to wash dirty dishes or sweep the floor.

It was an astonishing urban event for them to open their home on the east side of Madison so people could come and go, often without knocking, sometimes without even announcing themselves, if Tom and Lou Ann were upstairs resting or out of the house.

It is testimony to the depth of Lou Ann's faith that it enabled her to receive help and see that opportunity for service as a gift to the givers.

Tom showed remarkable improvement between September and Thanksgiving with a regimen of tumor shrinking drugs, daily prayers at St. Benedict's Center, acupuncture, and herbal remedies, and an astonishing appetite. Tom had always been thin—appearing even anemic at times—but with short-term memory loss he had no idea how long it had been since he last ate, and Tom became a nearly constant eater!

There were other, more painful dislocations that accompanied Tom's memory loss. During this period Tom and Lou Ann were in church most Sundays. It was sometimes uncomfortable to be with Tom when, for example, he was convinced that he was in Wisconsin Rapids where he had grown up; or became anxiously insistent that something needed to be done about a situation which, obviously, he found disturbing but was unable to tell us about with long-term memory unavailable. It was clear in such moments that Tom's intensity, an integral part of his "normal" self, was undiminished by the tumor. Members of the congregation were wonderfully able, for the most part, to "roll with the punches," to provide appropriate responses.

This was possible because in all things, in moments of lucidity and in moments of being completely lost, Tom, as well as Lou Ann, and, increasingly, all of us discovered ourselves to be surrounded by compassion. To be with passion, literally, but to be, more accurately, with caring. Christians, Jews, agnostics and others came and went from the house, and in the midst support was given from caregiver to caregiver, conversations found depth of meaning, in even the most casual exchange there was a sense of caressing one another in passing with a smile, a look, a word, of compassion.

Always there were prayers. On December 30, the eve of New Year's Eve, and at the peak of Tom's physical wellness in all of this, a Service of Healing and Renewal was held at Plymouth Church. Many gathered, not just Christians, and fewer than fifty percent were from within the congregation. With Petra Streiff, our parish nurse, and me leading the worship, people came together to pray, to sing, to name those in need of the compassion of the community of faith and the healing of God and to pray again.

With every visit to his home, Tom would ask me to pray with him. And so I would pray: for strength, for healing, for guidance and patience, for wisdom, for love, for peace, for grace. At the end of my spoken prayer, as we sat holding hands, Tom would often add his own few words: "Help me, God, to do whatever it is that you want of me," or "I love you, God, and want only to do what you want me to do, and to be the person you need me to be." Always Tom's spoken prayers were prayers for obedience.

On Thursday evening, February 24, I received a phone call from a friend of Tom and Lou Ann's with the message, "We think Tom has just died." I hurried to the house to find Lou Ann, the woman who had called, and a neighbor couple who were close friends gathered there. Tom's body lay still on the mattress on the floor of the upstairs bedroom. Tom had not moved in several days, except for his eyes which seemed to follow movement in the room. He'd had a CAT scan ten days before when his mobility had become greatly impaired; the tumor had increased five or ten times during the months in which Tom had showed improvement. His family had come for visits and gone during that last week, knowing that Tom was slipping away. His last words had been to Lou Ann when, after two days of saying nothing, and seeming detached and unable to do more than sip a little liquid, Tom had turned to her, and said, "Pray with me." A few weeks before, as they were driving between their home and St. Benedict's Center, Tom had hesitantly described to Lou Ann an experience he had had. He was hesitant because he feared it might disturb her, but he thought it of great importance: It was like a dream—but it was not a dream—it was far more real than a dream, Tom had said, and then gone on to describe being in a place where he became aware, in a bright and shining moment that he was with Jesus. Tom added, "I think God was there too."

On the evening of his death, Tom's son, Andrew, had come to play the cello for his father. The mellow tenor music filled the house. Later Lou Ann and her friend sat with Tom singing hymns. His breathing had been slow and slowing for most of the day. Periods of apnea came. For ten seconds, or fifteen, Tom would not breathe. Then there would be a great inhalation and a return to the measured, slow in and out. At the end of a hymn they looked over at Tom and saw he was not breathing. They paused in silence, waited a little, five seconds, ten seconds, fifteen, and Tom did not breathe again.

There is in this story of living and dying in the church something to be said of pastoral ministry: of the pastor's role. The living of Tom Petersen's death was, for me, a time of profound enrichment and humility. The number of members who expressed their appreciation to me for my role was a continual surprise because, it seemed to me, my role was far from central. Almost never did I do any actual work. Early on, I had accompanied Tom and Lou Ann through a series of radiation treatments for Tom when the tumor of 1991 began to grow again. Twice I had physically traveled with them to the treatment center. I assisted, on two occasions, in physically carrying Tom from one place to another in the last weeks; I puttered to reglue a broken rocker which refused to be mended. I visited, I offered prayers, I encouraged and commended others. But I did not organize; I made no food. I was not the catalyst to make things happen.

One tends to think of the pastoral role, as the word's origin suggests, as one of shepherding, of wielding the shepherd's staff, protecting the flock from enemies, leading to places of pasture and still waters. None of that seemed urgently necessary in this event, although all of it happened: pasture and water were found in abundance, whatever enemies may have been were driven off by the fact of the flock's staying together. And these things happened without the offices of the pastor as shepherd.

I am reminded of Jesus' words recorded in John's Gospel, " I am the good shepherd. . . . I know my own and my own know me, as the Father knows me and I know the Father; and I lay down my life for the sheep . . . so there will be one flock, one shepherd" (Jn 10:11*a*, 14, 15*b*, 16*b*). When we consider the One who is the Good Shepherd, we quickly recognize that the pastor may have another, very different role. Perhaps it is, as I have begun to think of it for myself, as only another one of the sheep, one entrenched in the midst of the flock. If there is a role of leadership to be modeled, perhaps it is this one: that of the sheep who wears the bell about his neck, the one the other sheep follow when the way is not clear, whom they follow because they hear the clanging of the bell up ahead. It is the job of this sheep not to worry overmuch about whether or not the flock will come along—for they will. The only concern this member of the flock need have is to follow the shepherd, to follow the Good Shepherd, so that the rest of the flock be not led by some other bell in some other way.

The story that I have shared is fully true in so far as my memory and sensitivities have been able to record it. Whatever errors of fact or misapprehension may be contained are my errors. I am grateful to Lou Ann Erickson Petersen, and to her brother Rick Erickson, for permission to publicly share their stories, and through their stories, also their faith. I am even more grateful for the faith to which they have borne testimony in the course of the months of this narrative.

Kirchengemeinschaft:
A Covenant in Mission and Faith

Kenneth R. Ziebell

Among the causes to which Frederick Trost has devoted himself with great energy and effectiveness in his commitment to the Mission of the Community/Public Witness/Word and Deed has been the special relationship between the United Church of Christ and the Evangelical Church of the Union (EKU), the united church in Germany. Known as *Kirchengemeinschaft*—"full church communion"—this relationship is an expression of the Mission of the Community in a global context, as these churches on different continents in different sociopolitical systems have committed themselves to share in mission partnership.

Kirchengemeinschaft received formal affirmation in a resolution adopted by the UCC's 1981 General Synod in Rochester, New York, which called for "the development of a UCC/EKU covenant for joint action in faith enrichment and mission outreach." That action laid the groundwork for a relationship which in the following two decades and no doubt far beyond would deeply enrich the faith and the mission of both churches and of countless of their members.

The UCC action in 1981 responded to corresponding resolutions adopted by the EKU the previous year. At that time, however, Germany was a divided nation, with a communist government in the (East) German Democratic Republic and a capitalist/democratic society in the (West) Federal Republic of Germany. The two were on opposite sides of a menacing confrontation line between two hostile military blocs. As a consequence of that political division, German churches had also been compelled to divide organizationally into separate structures in East and West. Thus it was necessary for the EKU-West and the EKU-East separately to adopt resolutions affirming *Kirchengemeinschaft* with the UCC.

It may have been remarkable enough that a beleaguered church facing threatening government restrictions in East Germany, a strong established church in West Germany, and a historically and culturally diverse UCC living in the "superpower" of the West could find common language to affirm their unity in faith and commitment. Yet even more challenging were the questions: What could these churches in three different situations say to one another which would be relevant and substantive, in the words of the UCC Synod resolution, for "performing the tasks which God requires of us now"? And what could they say jointly that would contribute to "strategies for witness in common tasks of justice and peace for the whole world"?

The posing of these questions highlights a key characteristic of that Synod resolution and of the *Kirchengemeinschaft* relationship that it affirms. Far from merely supporting friendly contact between the two churches, the resolution lays out a specific agenda which is to be the substantive content of the relationship. In the words of the resolution's title, it is to be "a covenant in mission and faith." The agenda begins, as just noted, with "witness in common tasks of justice and peace for the whole world." Its second item is "strategies for exploring and recasting the catholic, evangelical, reformed, and covenantal aspects of our theology for issues of faith today." The third task, to assure that the relationship never become ingrown or exclusive, directs that these mission and faith strategies be explored "for their possible significance in the relationships of our two churches with the other churches with whom we are jointly called to discipleship."

The Synod resolution also makes reference to other factors which might have provided the motivating force for *Kirchengemeinschaft*. There were significant historical connections which had importance for many in the churches. There was the fact that both churches are members of the international grouping identified as "united and uniting churches." Discussions at the consultation of united and uniting churches in 1975 in Toronto, in fact, provided particular impetus for the UCC-EKU explorations which resulted in the Synod decisions in 1980 and 1981. While acknowledging these factors, however, the resolution makes clear that at its heart *Kirchengemeinschaft* is not a celebration of history or an exercise in structure but is a commitment to joint action. Through its history it has brought blessings of many kinds to many people, but always at its best it has been a forum for Christians of similar backgrounds but in different societies to work, witness, and serve together on critical issues of mission and faith.

In the initial years of *Kirchengemeinschaft* this international community in mission was for many UCC members the source of a profound enrichment of their understanding of Christian faith and mission, as they became personally acquainted with EKU members in East Germany. They met fellow Christians who were maintaining a faithful witness despite suffering the consequent personal restrictions and disadvantages imposed by an atheistic communist government. The relationship offered a uniquely privileged opportunity for first-hand encounter with this twentieth century demonstration of Christian faithfulness at severe personal cost.

In addition, these contacts with East Germany offered UCC participants—and to some extent their EKU-East counterparts as well—a radically different perspective on the prevailing "Cold War" mentality, in which citizens on each side were commonly led to view the opposing side as a threatening and irreconcilable adversary. After they had visited fellow Christians "on the other side" of the political dividing line, the supposed enemy could no longer be viewed as the faceless demon of popular rhetoric. Instead, after the visitors had met personally a variety of people like themselves going about normal lives with joys and sorrows, aspirations and goals similar to their own, they felt compelled to work for mutual understanding and conciliation across the "Cold War" dividing line rather than accepting blind condemnation and hostility.

The collapse of the communist system throughout eastern Europe in 1989 and the subsequent unification of East and West Germany brought a new dimension to the life of the EKU and consequently to the UCC-EKU relationship. The EKU-West and EKU-East, formally divided for four decades now became structurally reunited, but it quickly became clear that those years of partially separate history had left Eastern and Western churches with substantially different situations and perspectives. Despite the enormous political changes which had occurred, the *Kirchengemeinschaft* relationship was in fact still joining churches in three different situations: the Eastern part of the EKU, severely weakened by its recent history in terms of resources and power; the Western segment of the EKU, a strong and influential element in a society which had become a dominant political and economic force in Europe; and the UCC, struggling with new challenges in an increasingly secular US society which was now the sole "superpower" on the world scene.

Thus *Kirchengemeinschaft* has continued to pursue its task of "joint action in faith enrichment and mission outreach" through sharing among Christians who have a common commitment but who live in a variety of social situations. In their ongoing pursuit of that joint commitment and in their participation in one another's experiences, members of the UCC and EKU continue to find inspiration and renewal and to understand themselves as part of a mission which has worldwide scope.

During the two decades since its formal affirmation *Kirchengemeinschaft* has come to assume an increasingly "grassroots" character through the multiplication of direct relationships between UCC Conferences and EKU Regional Churches (*Landeskirchen*), partnerships between individual congregations of the UCC and the EKU, and cooperative contacts involving educational and diaconal institutions of the two churches. The result has been a massive web of interactive involvement whose participants have learned from personal experience the global dimension of Christian faith and mission. In fact, now and for the future, the scope of the activities of *Kirchengemeinschaft* organized in local and Conference/*Landeskirche* settings far exceeds plans initiated nationally.

These shared encounters between UCC and EKU congregations and members have yielded important mutual benefits in that each church can find its own life and mission strengthened through its experience of the other. In an effort to identify some specific ways in which this happens, the EKU in 1998 issued a small booklet entitled "What we, the churches of the EKU, can learn from the United Church of Christ." The booklet lists such topics as Stewardship of Gifts, Stewardship of Money, Worship, Religious Education, Church Leadership, Inclusiveness, and Church and Society as areas in which its members have observed in the UCC qualities that might enrich its own life. A corresponding testimony from the UCC perspective is in process of being drafted.

Of course, participation by Christians in any contacts with churches in countries other than their own offers a powerful personal awareness of being part of a global community of faith. But unlike partnerships the UCC maintains with churches in less developed parts of the world, the UCC and the EKU live in, to some extent, similar socioeconomic circumstances. As the EKU booklet puts it: "There is a social comparability between the two nations. Both societies are highly industrialized and increasingly secular with similar social endemics." Since US and German congregations find themselves facing similar situations and problems, there is a particular relevance in the exchange of experiences and perspectives between UCC and EKU members. Again, in the words of the EKU booklet, these discussions on "topics concerning witness and service within the congregations . . . can lead to reciprocal stimulation."

Both Germany and the United States are dominant economic powers on the world scene as well as influential political powers—in Germany's case, as a leading member of the European Union. The people of both countries enjoy abundant benefits as a result of their position in the world. At the same time, responsible citizens of both countries are deeply troubled by persistent failures to resolve issues of peace and justice and rightly recognize their special responsibility to work for the discovery of solutions. Within these countries the gulf between rich and poor continues to grow, as the affluent are becoming richer, while a growing proportion sinks deeper into poverty. The same trend prevails on a global scale, as rich countries such as the US and Germany accumulate greater wealth, while the less developed nations fall further behind.

As the EKU booklet recognizes, both the EKU and the UCC "are committed to building a society based upon justice." *Kirchengemeinschaft* offers a channel for congregations and members to explore together the particular responsibility these churches face to provide guidance and take action in support of a just social order.

Among the specific common dilemmas confronting both societies are, for example, issues of immigration and refugees. Migration into the US from Latin America and to a lesser extent Asia is changing the country's demographic composition. Likewise immigrants and refugees from many sources have been attracted to Germany in search of economic opportunity. Conflicts result in both countries both among political leaders and in local communities as to whether these changes are a source of strength to be welcomed or a threat to be resisted. In too many cases hostility has led to violence. As the churches in both countries seek to formulate actions and policies to address these issues, members of the UCC and EKU have the opportunity to exchange experiences, problems, and successes from their respective situations to help one another become more faithful witnesses for the just society to which they are committed.

Thus, as the 21st century begins, *Kirchengemeinschaft* continues to provide a demonstration of The Mission of the Community in action globally. Circumstances have changed radically since the EKU and UCC affirmed their special relationship in 1980 and 1981. Throughout that time they have found opportunities in sharing experiences and insights to enable their members to be mutually strengthened in their faith enrichment and mission outreach.

The 1981 UCC General Synod resolution refers to *Kirchengemeinschaft* as "a gift . . . which can have a very significant impact upon our life as a church." That gift continues two decades later to offer valuable opportunities for joint action in mission and faith.

"Eternal God, You Spoke"

Eternal God, you spoke and the heavens and earth, all life,
      was created through your word.

You spoke and Sarah and Abraham left for the promised land.

You spoke and prophets—men and women together—proclaimed
      your justice.

You spoke and your Word was made flesh in the unique face of
      Jesus Christ.

Send us your Spirit, that we may not only listen to your word of peace
but also make peace with our neighbor.

Send us your Spirit, that we may listen to your word of justice
and that it may become reality in our love for those who long for justice.

Send us your Spirit, that we may not only listen to your word of creation
but that we may care for earth and its creatures.

Eternal God, thank you for the presence of your word among us,
for your eternal love, and for the privilege of your call to serve your
people everywhere.

Hans Wilhelm Fricke-Hein

SECTION V

REMEMBRANCES

Waiting and Wonder

Christine M. Trost

When my brother Paul and my sisters Marianne, Margaret, Sarah and I recently reflected on our memories of life in the parsonage, two words were frequently mentioned—*waiting* and *wonder*. For nearly all of us, our experiences of waiting were the first to come to mind, but the experiences we lingered over as we reminisced were those of wonder that we had as children witnessing the ministry of our father.

Christmas, for our family, includes many cherished traditions and lots of waiting. In fact, we have made waiting into one of our traditions. As children, we would rise early on Christmas morning. Before we were allowed to descend the stairway and search for our stockings, we waited at the top of the stairs, sometimes for what seemed like an eternity, until the candles were lit, the incense was burning, and the 1954 recording of "Lessons and Carols" from King's College at Cambridge University was playing on the stereo. Our early morning celebration was usually cut short due to the 9:00 a.m. German service, which was followed by the 11:00 a.m. English service. (St. Pauls always had Christmas Day services, regardless of what day of the week it was.) After the service, we would wait, as we did every Sunday, while our father greeted everyone who came to celebrate the birth of the Christ child. He would also meet visitors and people with special needs and requests, privately, in his study. Sometimes, my mother would take us home before he was done and we would wait just a little while longer for our dad to arrive. There were a few years when we were certain, on his way home, he was delivering the last of the dozens of (now fragrant) fruit baskets that had filled the back of our station wagon to sick and elderly parishioners who could not attend the Christmas celebration.

Finally, he would return and we would enjoy our Christmas dinner followed by what we, as children, most looked forward to—present opening! In our family, present opening also involves waiting, but this is the kind of waiting that we most enjoy: Each present is opened individually but not before guesses are offered by all with regard to its contents. After the present is opened it is passed around for all to view and comment on. Only once the opened gift has made its way around the circle do we start in on the next gift. The effect of this (combined with our late start) was to extend our Christmas celebration over several days. It is a testament to our love of this tradition that we continue it today when we celebrate Christmas together.

We have many other memories of waiting. Paul remembers waiting at the printers on Saturday afternoons, while our dad carefully proofread the

Sunday bulletin one last time. (This was especially hard to do those times when it was the last stop before leaving on our family vacation.) I remember waiting in the car outside of Grant Hospital while my father visited, prayed with, and offered communion to elderly and ailing members of the congregation. I also remember playing at the cemetery while my dad conducted internments. Margaret remembers how we would wait to be picked up from school, sometimes the last to leave the playground, because of funerals, hospital visits, or emergency phone calls.

Sarah reminded me that even though there was a lot of waiting, it usually entailed fun or reward. Waiting for our father to finish greeting people after church gave us time to play outside on the church's front lawn, in the gym, or, when he was not meeting people in his study, underneath his desk. Pastoral calls and hospital visits were followed by ice cream cones or milk shakes; and every time our dad picked us up from school, late or not, the car would veer "out of control" and pull to the side of the road when Schmeissing's German bakery on Lincoln Avenue came into sight.

My father devoted nearly every weekday afternoon to making pastoral calls. Many afternoons he would offer to give my mother a break and bring us with him. This is when our wonder began. We experienced wonder as elderly German ladies invited us into their homes, offering us fruitcake and homemade marzipan. To us, these women were both strange and wonderful. They overcame our shyness, caused by the strange smells and the sound of German being spoken, with their kindness and generosity. We also experienced wonder as we watched our father minister to women like Carmen. Carmen was an elderly German-speaking woman who lived alone in public housing but was barely able to care for herself. Her small apartment was cluttered and dirty; it also smelled bad. In spite of our discomfort at the sights and smells, when our father visited her he greeted her with the same warmth and generous spirit that he extends to everyone he meets. He laughed at her jokes and listened to her complaints with compassion and understanding. Occasionally, when she came to church, she would correct my father's German (sometimes in mid-sentence) from her pew. He would graciously accept her instruction, even though she was not always correct.

Marianne, especially, remembers the controversies that our father took on, like the time he invited young Vietnam War protesters, who were being beaten and gassed by Chicago police during the 1968 Democratic convention, to find shelter in our church. Not all of the church's members supported the idea of "hippies" sleeping in the gymnasium at St. Pauls. Nor did they agree with his opposition to the war, which he passionately explained in a Sunday sermon broadcast live on Chicago television. (As a result of this sermon, the station executives determined that in the future they would telecast religious services from the studio in advance so they could be edited if needed.) The fact that most of the members of St. Pauls, including a large number of refugees who had fled communist regimes in Eastern Europe and the Soviet Union, did not leave the church on account of his outspoken opposition to the war in Vietnam attests to his ability to lead his congregation to the foot of the cross by reconciling different points of view with compassion, sensitivity, and conviction.

Marianne also remembers Don and Jack, two severe alcoholics who were homeless and visited our parsonage regularly for a bite to eat and a few dollars; and Earl, a young man who was never quite the same after taking LSD, but who had a gift for playing the piano. Over the protests of some on the church staff, our father invited Earl into the sanctuary to play his beautiful music. We all remember the time that Becky, a homeless woman in her 30s, was found sleeping under the flowering crab tree on the front lawn of St. Pauls on Easter morning. Some of the members wanted to remove her from the church grounds, but Dad let her sleep.

The compassionate care and acceptance that our father extended to those who are left out and live on the margins of society filled us with wonder as children. As adults we better understand how consistent these actions were with his vision of church and community and the living Word. Through his opposition to the Vietnam War and later the Reagan Administration's war on the peasants of El Salvador and Nicaragua; his acts of nonviolent civil disobedience and the arrests that sometimes followed; his refusal to pay taxes that would be used to produce nuclear weapons; and his welcoming of homeless, alcoholic, and disturbed people into our church and home, he showed us and his congregation how to live out our faith in and through our daily lives. Following the example of his theological mentors, Dietrich Bonhoeffer, Karl Barth, and Abraham Joshua Heschel, among others, he brought us closer to understanding God's mysterious, wondrous, and essential call to us—that we be fully present in this world as disciples of peace, compassion, love, and justice.

We have many other memories, too many to list, but a few that deserve special mention. Sarah remembers how, on Saturdays, our dad would open up the gym and we would play full-court basketball all afternoon. (This is possible to do with a family of seven!) Margaret remembers the sound of Dad typing late into the night on Saturday evenings. (I now realize that Saturday basketball would always mean a late night of sermon writing for our father.) Marianne remembers late-night phone calls from people in distress followed by the sound of Dad putting on his shoes and walking out the front door. And Paul remembers our father's sermons, including the conviction in his voice, the humor he would use, and the vivid stories he would tell to illustrate his message. We all remember waking up to the beautiful music of Bach on Sunday mornings; the sound of Dad singing hymns by heart in his deep, booming, joyful, powerful voice during worship at St. Pauls; and hours spent greeting friends old and new at coffee hour, followed by our special Sunday dinner at home.

We remember the fun we had in Sunday school and confirmation class; our trips to St. Pauls family camp at the UCC retreat center (Tower Hill) in Sawyer, Michigan; and the hundreds of church events that we attended, including square dances in the gym, *Frauenverein* luncheons, Advent workshops, and making felt banners for the sanctuary. We also remember being called upon at the last minute to serve as acolytes, read the Scripture (which I so loved!), and play our instruments for the German service. One of our favorite memories was helping to prepare and serve the annual "Silent Supper" that took place in the darkened, candlelit nave of the church on Maundy Thursday. I remember savoring the taste of pita bread, cheese, and grapes as I listened to people around the table read the Scripture followed by periods of silence. Together, these memories created for us as children a lasting impression—church was a fun, beautiful and awe-inspiring place. It was a place of community, where we felt loved and welcomed. God was present.

The lessons each of us has taken away from our experiences of waiting and wonder are different. As adults we have chosen to interpret and apply them differently to our individual lives and to the development of our faith. However, after reflecting together, there is one lesson we share in common. It is rooted in the daily actions and demonstrations of faith that we witnessed as we watched and waited for and wondered at the ministry of our father. Through his example of integrating faith into daily life, we have learned to recognize and respond to God's presence in our own lives.

If you ask my father what accomplishment he is most proud of, he will answer that it has been raising us, his children, with my mother. Given his many other accomplishments, I used to think this was a strange response until I had a child of my own. Now, as an adult and a parent, I can better appreciate and understand the challenge of providing for a family of seven on a pastor's salary; and the difficult, demanding, and sometimes conflicting tasks associated with being both a father of five and a pastor to a congregation of over 1000 members.

What fills me and my brother and sisters with wonder today is how well he succeeded at both vocations. We also know that his ability to be both a father and a pastor, an inspirational teacher and a passionate leader, and a model of tolerance, compassion, and conviction to us all would not have been possible were it not for our mother. Her equally patient, strong, wise, generous, and gentle spirit has been an essential source of support and nourishment in our lives and throughout our father's ministry. The lessons of faithfulness, compassion, and stewardship that we have learned from our mother, in her role as the wife of a pastor and all of the numerous, unpaid and often unacknowledged demands and responsibilities that this entailed, as a teacher of special ed children; as a food pantry director; and as a mother of five, are equally memorable.

There is a story my mother tells about the time my father came home late from a meeting at the food pantry he had helped get started. Earlier in the day, he had bought a new overcoat to replace his old coat, which had become tattered and thin. My mother remembers it was a bitter cold night, but when he walked through the front door he was not wearing his new coat. On his walk home, he had given his coat to a man he'd met on the street, a man who was shivering and without a coat. At first, my mother was, in her words, "flabbergasted": Given the small size of our family budget, which she arduously stretched in many creative ways every month, how could he give away his new coat? After the dust had settled, she tells us, it provoked in her a new understanding of faith in action. I should add that her ability to understand this truth and to be understanding, in the face of meals that went cold while waiting, late nights spent alone with us while my father was working, vacations interrupted with emergency phone calls, and "new coats" that were given away, is an equally significant part of this story. If our parents have raised us well, it is because they have both provided us with models of faith and action.

Among my father's spiritual teachers, as noted above, was the great Jewish biblical scholar, Abraham Joshua Heschel. Books by Rabbi Heschel occupy a prominent place in my father's study and are well-worn. From the writings of Heschel he learned many things, including the vital fact that "the deepest wisdom a human being can attain is to know that his or her destiny is to aid, to serve." Our parents believe this truth deeply. Recalling our childhood in the St. Pauls parsonage, we remember the waiting but also the wonder of this beautiful theme in our parents' lives.

I gratefully acknowledge the generous contributions of my brother and sisters in the writing of this essay.

Biographical Note:

Christine resides with her husband, Douglas, and their six-year-old son Reed in Berkeley, California. In 1999, Christine's sister Margaret and her eight-year-old son Luke also moved to Berkeley following the death of Margaret's husband, Rich Tanaka. They share a duplex and are enjoying raising their sons together. Margaret owns a business devoted to health and the preservation of the environment, which allows her to teach and train others. She is also involved in developing a food program for impoverished children in Haiti. Paul lives in nearby Sonoma, California. He is an artist who specializes in oil paintings on wood and canvas. The themes of Paul's art reflect the faith in which we were raised. Sarah and her husband John reside in Tucson, where Sarah is a clinical psychology doctoral student at the University of Arizona. Marianne, her husband, Adam, and their two-year-old daughter Grace also live in Arizona. Marianne cares for their daughter Grace at home while she pursues her interest in grant writing.

Frederick Trost: The St. Pauls Years

Thomas R. Henry

The year Frederick Trost became the associate pastor of St. Pauls United Church of Christ in Chicago was the year America's "Camelot" came to a violent end with the assassination of President John F. Kennedy. The "Fabulous Fifties" were being left behind and the "Dawning of the Age of Aquarius" was just ahead. It was a new era for church and society marked by civil rights speeches, anti-war sermons, youth and social activism, and slogans like: "America: love it or leave it," "We shall overcome," "I am somebody," and "Give peace a chance." Indeed, the times were changing, and the changes were coming rapidly for the nation, for the cities, and for St. Pauls Church.

Right out of Yale Divinity School and newly ordained, Frederick Richard Trost came to St. Pauls Church in Chicago in 1962, as an assistant pastor. The following year, he was honored with the title of associate pastor, and in September, 1964, he became the senior pastor of St. Pauls, an historic church in Chicago, founded by immigrants from Prussia in 1843, as the *Erste Deutsche Evangelische Lutherische Saint Paulus Gemeinde.* At the time of Fred's arrival, the church had undergone almost 120 years of changes, evolving from an ethnic congregation to an inclusive urban congregation, yet maintaining its historical ties with weekly worship services in the German language and a German women's organization, the *Frauenverein.* Over those years the German Evangelical Lutheran St. Pauls Congregation had become St. Pauls Evangelical and Reformed Church, and then in 1957, it had become part of the United Church of Christ. When Fred came to St. Pauls, the United Church of Christ was only five years old, and the St. Pauls church building, rebuilt after a 1955 Christmas night fire, was no older than the denomination. So, with a young denomination and a new building and a 28-year old senior pastor, it seemed God was making all things new at old St. Pauls.

But when God makes all things new, there is pain as well as pleasure; excitement and energy, but suffering, too. The old ways struggle to survive, and the new ways have yet to stand the test of time. God was making all things new, not only at St. Pauls, but also in the city of Chicago and in the United States of America. It was during such a time that Frederick R. Trost served at St. Pauls United Church of Christ. The years were 1962 to 1981.

President John F. Kennedy was assassinated in the year Frederick was chosen associate pastor, and the Rev. Dr. Martin Luther King, Jr. gave his "I Have a Dream" speech in that same year. The Civil Rights Act of 1964, the most sweeping civil rights legislation in the history of the country, was passed the year he was installed as senior pastor. But in 1964, the United States Congress also gave the President greater authority to launch military attacks against North Vietnam, and for the first time the phrase "urban crisis" began to be used to describe what was happening in the nation's cities.

The neglect of city neighborhoods and schools, the promise of the growing suburbs, and the brand-new, multi-lane expressways prompted people to leave cities like Chicago in record numbers. While many church members would continue to "come home" to St. Pauls from their new places of residence beyond the city, others would not. The pastoral task at all city churches became much more difficult. During the years Frederick Trost was at St. Pauls, several neighborhood churches closed. A Methodist church was converted to other uses, a Baptist church and a Presbyterian church were torn down, and a Lutheran church became a condominium. Led by Frederick Trost and a committed group of layleaders, St. Pauls UCC held on and survived and even thrived.

Through the years of Frederick's pastorate, seven associate pastors served with him. By the time that I came to St. Pauls as an associate pastor in 1974, Fred Trost had been senior pastor for ten years. Herbert Davis, Mark Miller, James Serdy, and George Knight had been associate pastors before me, and Gordon Smith and James Gorman were associate pastors with me. Of all the things I remember about the years of service with Fred, what I remember most is his love of ministry and his support and encouragement of his associate pastors.

Even with the decline in the number of members in the church and the increase in the annual operating budget deficit to several thousands of dollars, he never spoke of retrenchment or defeat. Frederick Trost believed in the ministry of St. Pauls Church, and therefore argued constantly with those who were succumbing to the pessimism that was permeating urban churches. He maintained a full staff and encouraged us to try new programs and to do things in new ways. Fred even supported us in doing some things that made him personally uncomfortable. And he somehow found the funds to cover the costs. When church members complained about what one of the associates was doing, Fred always publicly defended us, and then found a way to privately nudge us toward finding a different (less inflammatory) means to achieving the same end.

One of the private and personal ways Fred Trost communicated with associate pastors, and also with members of the congregation, was through note writing. During those St. Pauls years he was a prolific note writer. Some notes were typed on his electric typewriter, and you could often hear it humming in his study. These were his reflections on some occurrence or aspect of the ministry, and they were sometimes several pages long. Others were handwritten and quite personal. When we received one of these handwritten "Trost Notes," we knew he cared about whatever it was that was happening to us and had taken the time to let us know. The most special notes came at Christmas time, handwritten in both red and green ink, telling us how much we meant to him and to St. Pauls during the year that was almost past.

Fred was a pastor. Although he took his prophetic function very seriously, preaching against the atrocities in Vietnam and for the necessities of civil rights, Frederick Trost was first and foremost a pastor. The story is still told today in the congregation about what he did in 1968, when he and his associate pastors gave sanctuary in the church to several hundred young anti-war protestors who had come to Chicago to demonstrate outside the Democratic National Convention. On order of the mayor of Chicago, who wished to rid the city of these nuisances, these high school and college age young people were being tear-gassed in the park nearby the church. Fred believed this to be an emergency situation that required immediate attention from the Christian community. He conferred with the church council and then offered refuge in the church building.

These kids filled the gymnasium and youth center, sleeping on the floors and being fed by some of the women of the church whose own children and grandchildren were of the same age. They were highly agitated by the action of the mayor, the police and the National Guard, and some of them were scared, but one of the older women was able to calm them by standing in the middle of the gym and reciting the Twenty-third Psalm. That is a moment yet-remembered as a deeply spiritual moment. However, some members of the congregation were not to be calmed. They considered the act of providing sanctuary to the anti-war protestors to be unpatriotic, and they stirred up emotions among others in the church. Fred and his associate pastors spent the days following the crisis personally calling or visiting every member of the congregation, interpreting the action as the necessary Christian response, but also listening to the concerns of those who disagreed with the action. Frederick Trost was pastor to the protestors, and he was pastor to those who were against the protestors.

Recalling these and other difficult times, Fred preached a sermon in 1972, in which he said: "We are a family. We are related through our Lord to each other. And it should be possible therefore to face the most difficult questions, and to disagree, without being cut off from each other." Because he deeply believed these words he spoke, and acted faithfully on his belief, he was respected and loved even by those who fervently disagreed with him.

Lest it seem like the Trost years at St. Pauls, from 1962 to 1981, were consumed by crisis, it is important for me to say that there was a lot of laughter amid the tears. In fact, Fred's laughter could be heard from blocks away. When he was happy, everyone around him was happy. His laughter and his good spirit were infectious. He had a powerful way of drawing people into his happiness, into his enthusiasm, and into his faith, and he often did this with a hug.

I remember Frederick Trost as a worship leader, and there are two experiences which, for me, capture his spirit. The first occurred on a communion Sunday at St. Pauls. He and I were standing at the table. I had my head bowed and was leading the congregation in the prayer of confession. When the prayer was finished and I raised my head, Fred was gone. I knew not where nor why. It seems he'd noticed the chalice and communion bread were not on the table. While everyone's heads were bowed, Fred disappeared. Then, as we all lifted our heads and began to sing the hymn that followed the assurance of pardon, Fred reappeared, lifting high the bread and cup, processing in from the sacristy, with piety and ceremony, as if we had planned it that way. Frederick Trost very much liked things to go as planned, especially in worship, but he also had a way of improvising that looked like planning.

His improvising also served him well at an Easter Sunday communion. At the early service, the communion bread was still frozen and would not easily be broken. Again, with great ceremony, Fred turned away from the congregation and toward the altar, and speaking some scriptural-sounding words he made up on the spot, he used all of his strength to literally break the bread. Following that service, the associate pastor's wife, who shall remain nameless here, suggested we put the loaf for the second service in the oven to thaw it. (Those were the days before microwaves.) And so it was done. And so it was forgotten. And so at the festival service that Easter Sunday, the toast was broken. And later that day, much later that day, Fred laughed.

On many communion Sundays as I stand at the table, I can still hear his laughter. His spirit will always be present at old St. Pauls, a congregation which through his faithfulness to Christ and his love of the church began to grow younger every day.

A Tribute to the Ministry of Frederick Trost

James Fellowes

My parents spared no expense in educating their children. At fourteen I left home to attend a fine boarding school for privileged kids. Then, it was on to a great university, later to one of the leading graduate schools for an MBA. Nor did they spare any energy teaching us the rights and wrongs of life: ample doses of discipline followed every wrong decision. Because of their great love they were even quicker to identify my strengths and encourage me to reach my full potential. Educating their children about life was their greatest single priority; they were good at it.

But, was it enough? Was I really prepared for my twenties—for life's big decisions and for the world out there with all its attractions and well-concealed trapdoors?

It was a winter Sunday morning in 1976 and I was closing in on my thirtieth birthday. I scooped up our newly-born daughter and my wife Deby and walked a short distance to St. Pauls Church in Chicago's Lincoln Park neighborhood. It was the first Sunday morning worship experience in our six-year marriage.

I had suggested to Deby that attending church would be the right thing to do now that we had the responsibility of parenting. Both of us had come from church-going families. Moreover, the church down Fullerton Avenue just looked great. The chance to carve out an hour of quiet reflection in such a place was no small attraction given the abrupt changes in our life style in recent weeks.

But the invitation to church carried deeper significance. Buried deep within I carried a burden and I carried it alone. The pain was rooted in moral failure: a widening gulf between who I was and who I knew I was to be. In short, I had found one of those trapdoors in life.

Curiously, there was something else equally profound stirring alongside the burden. The experience of witnessing our first child's birth had awakened wonder and amazement as only that moment can. The thrill left a trail of questions on the ultimate issues of life. These two strong feelings, one so troublesome and the other so joyfully awesome, churned away as we made our way to church in search of answers that cold Sunday morning.

A rather large man rose from the first pew. He turned to us and welcomed us in the name of Christ. He registered his hope that we "might sense the presence of Christ among us." His arms were open and he smiled when he spoke but not like someone trying to sell us something. He was genuine. We were instantly drawn to Frederick Trost.

We attended regularly, then joined the church. About a year later I was asked to serve as an elder. At this stage of spiritual development I was still checking the page profile of other members' Bibles to get my bearings as to where I might find one passage or another ("Looks like about 80 percent of the pages are turned to Romans. Yes. Here it is!") I had but one qualification to serve as elder: a humbled heart with eagerness to learn.

Frederick Trost became my teacher and I his eager student. Like anything else, I discovered there were levels of understanding in what I was learning. It was fairly easy for me to grasp and accept the concepts that had been introduced to me as a child: God loved me; God had a good plan and purpose for my life; we honor God by being obedient or a good neighbor and so forth.

To get to the next level was not so easy. My teacher introduced me to scripture that was not so familiar and to the writings and works of Augustine, Luther, Bonhoeffer, Barth, and others. These were men I recognized but about whom I knew very little. Their writings were often difficult to grasp, but I at least sensed validity in their thoughts. They challenged the flimsy world I knew so heavily influenced by '70s American pop culture.

I was especially interested in what the Bible had to say about sin and was surprised by its pervasive theme in scripture. My teacher had marvelous stories and illustrations, which brought depth to themes of repentance, forgiveness, and grace. Connections were made to my own life's burdens. Like a difficult jigsaw puzzle the pieces were joined in clumps before there was a glimpse of the whole. In time, though, the pieces met at the cross where I could process who I was, how to leave my burdens behind, and how I needed to go forth.

It was just four years that I sat in the pew at St. Pauls Church quietly, but intently, soaking up what I could. Fred was then called to the Wisconsin Conference in Madison and we moved along to a Chicago suburb. Our paths diverged. More than twenty years have since passed.

Nevertheless, I now view Frederick's ministry as a personal gift from God with life-changing effects. This work was by no means completed in these short years, but it was begun. I now held a compass in hand and took my bearings from absolutes I had earlier dismissed.

In spite of divergent paths, this relationship has strengthened over the years. The more I have come to know him as a friend, the more I have appreciated this unique person. I would identify four qualities that meet in

Frederick Trost with powerful effect: immense personal integrity, an impressive blend of passion and compassion, an exquisite command of language, and an intense interest in others.

With respect to personal integrity I am reminded of a quotation that Fred himself has used to describe the principle of personal integrity. It is one of those simple reminders I have tucked away which helps me stay on track. Long ago St. Jerome described a person of faith as one in whom "the heart and the tongue and the hand all agree." This would best fit Frederick Trost: a man whose life is anchored to God's word and who could only speak and act in concert with his calling as a minister of God.

Secondly, Fred is a man of great passion and compassion. Anyone who knows him at all understands that his emotions are a powerful (perhaps legendary) force in driving him effectively toward his goals. He may well be an intellectual, but by no means does he "intellectualize" a thing. He is a man of action with eyes that reveal intensity to his good purpose and compassion for those in need.

Thirdly, Fred's command of language is exquisite. His mastery of the German language allowed our small German-speaking congregation at St. Pauls to hear God's word clearly preached in their native tongue each Sunday morning. With respect to English, I have first hand knowledge, however. He has the remarkable gift of bringing clear expression to the concrete and the abstract alike. I have come to appreciate this increasingly as Fred has written to me periodically over the years on a wide range of topics. From beautifully crafted Christmas letters (always with a pen and ink "noel" candle), to a touching memorial tribute to his son-in-law, to sharp criticism of the "School of the Americas," to "proud father" updates on his children, his thoughts are expressed with great beauty and precision. Many of these letters have been tucked carefully into my business case and taken with me for months on end for reading and re-reading in airports, train stations, and hotel rooms. There is always more to learn.

Finally, he is intensely interested in others. He engages with others to understand, to encourage, and to assist is some way. He sees the best in his friends and his colleagues. Conversation seems to turn in the direction of his doing most of the questioning and listening. The word that begins with "self" that best fits his character is "selfless."

There would only be a handful of people who have touched my life as Frederick Trost. Because I have learned so much, I have chosen to describe our relationship in the context of teacher and student. To leave it there, however, would be to shortchange it of its full richness.

We have become great friends in the wider context of our wives and families. Deby and Louise add a most welcome element of warmth and charm to our gatherings, to say nothing of their sense of what is really going on within our families. We have marveled at the pursuits and accomplishments of Marianne, Margaret, Christine, Paul, and Sarah. We thrill in every victory! A painting which hangs in our den entitled "Blessed are the Merciful" painted by Paul Trost reminds us of our calling as Christians.

I am grateful to God for his provision in my life in the person of Frederick Trost from whom I have learned so much. I have concluded that my parents were masters in teaching me what they could about life, but we need others to come alongside us in life to continue the good work. Learning is a life long process. We learn most from those we admire.

Thank you, Fred and Louise, for your good ministry and for your warm friendship which we dearly cherish.

Confessing Christ Today

Gabriel Fackre

"Who is Jesus Christ for us today?" asked Dietrich Bonhoeffer. What is *our* today, the context now in which the church is called to confess Christ? Some say it is the spiritual hungers of our time, not the secular setting Bonhoeffer faced. Others, the struggles for real bread, the plight of the poor and oppressed. Yet others, the new paradigm of science and technology. Still others, the postmodern mood that questions our very ability to know either the issue or the response, a postulate itself, one more diagnosis of today.

Whatever *context* we choose to address—and why not more than one from this and an even larger list?—we do so with a *text* in hand. Jesus Christ, as he is attested for us in Holy Scripture, is the one Word of God which we have to hear and which we have to trust and obey in life and in death.[1] Our Barmen forebears taught us well. So did Bonhoeffer who pointed us to Christ the Center. Amidst the flurry of proposals, challenges and ideologies of the hour, never forget the Archimedean point, the one Word!

Some of Barmen's progeny sought to pass on that learning by making it front and center in the charter of the United Church of Christ. Thus we are accountable, first and foremost, to the sole Head of the body, Jesus Christ, Son of God and Savior, as we hear that Word of God in the Scriptures.[2] This theological preamble also echoed another refrain of Barmen not often remembered, the resource role of a hard-won *tradition* (all the Confessions in force among us)[3] by declaring that the UCC claims as its own the faith of the historic church expressed in the ancient creeds and the basic insights of the Protestant Reformers.[4] Therefore, committed as we in the UCC are to a contextual Christianity, a today gospel, it is *this faith* —"the historic faith of the Church with its one 'Word of God in the Scriptures' that each generation is called to make its own." The text defines the context and not the other way around.

While our charters and our mentors had it right, too often we get it wrong. Back in the 1970s, a study of what the UCC seeks in its clergy reported that the United Church of Christ is noteworthy in how little interest its members displayed concerning a pastor's religiosity, biblical faith and evangelism, piety, or explicit emphasis on spiritual renewal and liturgy.[5] What we wanted instead was to keep in step with the times, and to help people make a better world. A case can be made that this concern for both relevance and good works is very much part of our Reformed legacy—*semper reformanda!*—and Christ transforming culture.[6] But those who wrote the always reforming on their banners, and from Geneva forward tried to change the world, *always* grounded their efforts in the one Word of Scripture and historic faith, the very things muted or missing in the 1970s profile of the UCC. In the church of that decade, the culture appeared to be transforming Christ, not the other way around. Something had to be said and done. What follows is an account of movements to restore the "confessing Christ" to its place alongside the "today."

The Witness of the Craigville Colloquys

It was the last day of the first Craigville Theological Colloquy, May 14, 1984, called by a grassroots group to mark the fiftieth anniversary of the Barmen Declaration. A witness statement summing up the conversation was read to the 160 participants. A runner from the conference center office rushed the document page by page into the hands of convener Frederick Trost. Grace and peace! began the sonorous voice known so well to so many:

> On the fiftieth anniversary of the Barmen Declaration . . . we have come together at Craigville to listen for God's Word. . . . Loyal to our founder's faith, we acknowledge Jesus Christ as our sole Head, Son of God and Savior (Preamble, Para 2, *Constitution of the United Church of Christ*). With Barmen we confess fidelity to the one Word of God which we have to hear and which we have to trust and obey in life and in death (*Barmen*, II, 1). Christ is the Center to whom we turn in the midst of the clamors, uncertainties, and temptations of the hour.[7]

Memorable moments. Not only because of the need to hear a clear and bold word midst the clamors, uncertainties and temptations of the time, but because of the coherence between speaker and words spoken. Christ as the one Word. . . . the Center . . . the sole Head are affirmations that reflect who Frederick Trost is and what he does.

To understand this occasion, for many of us a turning point in the life of the UCC, we must go back a few years behind it, then forward from this first colloquy to the present day. The Craigville theological colloquies—held annually now for seventeen years and counting, and widely judged to be the denomination's major forum for theological exchange—had forebears and produced some children. In all cases, Pastor Trost served as mid-wife.

Festivals and Convocations

In 1977 Fred organized a festival at the congregation he then served, St. Pauls, Chicago, to celebrate the anniversary of the nineteenth century founding of the Evangelical Synod of North America.[8] The event was important for retrieving a too-often ignored UCC tradition. Yet a meal and conversation in the parsonage during the festival began the theological trajectory we are tracing. Out of the discussion came a plan to hold a convocation on the Lord's Supper at St. Pauls the following year, and to form an organization that continued to explore key theological themes. Thus was born the Biblical-Theological-Liturgical Group, affectionately known as the BTL Club to contrast its commitments to Tammy and Jimmie Baker's then famous PTL (Praise the Lord) Club. The BTL's convener was Frederick Trost.

At its 1979 meeting in East Petersburg, Pennsylvania, on authority in the church, in the shadow of the recent Three Mile Island debacle, BTL's commitments came crystal clear in its "Call to Faithfulness":

> Our deliberations have made us profoundly aware of the forces that today seek to contest our loyalty to Jesus Christ:
>
> - the civil religion that tempts us to mute the uncivil Word of truth
> - the techniques of management and manipulation . . . that have elbowed aside biblical preaching, sound theological teaching, living worship and sacrament
> - the latest wisdom of this world that beguiles us from our fundamental norms of Scripture and tradition
> - timid and temporizing leadership that cries out for bold proclamation and fearless deed . . .
> - our captivity to the comforts and idolatries of a bourgeois Protestantism that shuts our eyes and closes our mouths before misery, tyranny and untruth
>
> Sisters and brothers this bondage must not be. . . . On Golgotha and Easter morning Jesus Christ has freed us. . . . Let us be who we are! As pastors and teachers in this faith community, we own again our common covenant: to listen for the one Word, Jesus Christ; to tell only this Story of the liberating and reconciling deeds of the triune God.[9]

Sound like Fred? Yes, he set the tone for the meeting and shaped the affirmations and admonitions reflected in the text.

At a 1983 gathering of BTL on the significance of WCC s *Baptism, Eucharist and Ministry* study, yet another effort was mounted to underscore the "confessing Christ" linked to the "today." In the living room of the president of New Brunswick Theological Seminary, Frederick Trost presiding, the christological heritage of John Williamson Nevin and Phillip Schaff was reaffirmed with the formation of the Mercersburg Society, holding yearly convocations since and publishing its important journal, *The New Mercersburg Review.*

In 1984, BTL and the Mercersburg Society co-sponsored the first Craigville Colloquy earlier described. From that point forward, yearly Craigville dialogues took place, with their concluding witness statements, on such subjects as "The Authority of Scripture," "Who is Jesus Christ for Us Today?," " Baptism in the United Church of Christ," "The Holy Spirit in Creation, Truth and Power," " Resurrection and Christian Burial," "How Can We Be Both Catholic and Prophetic?" "Justification and Justice," "How is Christ Formed in Us Today?"

A Resounding Call to Faithfulness

Craigville Colloquy X, with its topic "Theological Standards for Ministry in the United Church of Christ" was the occasion for another confessional birthing. At its final session, note was taken of the strong affirmations made by UCC pastors in the ordination service of the *Book of Worship,* as in the pledge to uphold the Preamble to the UCC Constitution. One group report, however, questioned whether these formal declarations were borne out in current preaching, teaching and denominational accents.[10] It proposed a national UCC gathering to address the issue. Plenary response was enthusiastic and some of the participants volunteered to take the next steps.

Following the colloquy, I phoned Fred to get his counsel. He not only agreed that it was a right moment for such but came up with a better plan: Hold meetings in three different sections of the country with a resounding call to recover the UCC's christological charter for its life and witness. An organizing committee of pastors, teachers and Conference Ministers was formed that sent out an invitational letter to 450 folk who had attended previous colloquies. It began:

> We believe that the future of our Church depends on faithfulness to the one Word of the triune God, Jesus Christ, which we are "to hear and which we have to trust and obey in life and in death."

Again Barmen. And with it the letter's call to listen for God's Word in Scripture and the honoring of our rich heritage that is often neglected in our Church. To address this threat to the gospel, the letter asserted that

> The time has come . . . for thoughtful, joyous and imaginative theological work that underlines our defining commitments . . . to reaffirm this faith, reclaim its biblical roots, retrieve its historic resources, and think together about our Church and its culture in the light of this reaffirmation.

The response was notable. Four hundred pastors took part in day-long meetings in Pennsylvania, Wisconsin and Massachusetts, Frederick Trost presiding. The movement, soon named Confessing Christ, has grown to include a national Steering Committee chaired by Fred, with eight centers across the country that have held 40 consultations on theological and ethical issues ranging from confessing Christ in a time of religious pluralism, violence, post–Christianity, re–imagination, genetic engineering, and same-sex unions through investigations of the significance of the cross, the atonement, the baptismal formula, Bonhoeffer, Barmen, Lutheran-Reformed full communion, the Roman-Catholic joint declaration on justification, the new Presbyterian catechism, Reformed resources for the Christian life, hymnody and preaching in Advent and Lent, to assessments of tradition and traditionalism, the Jesus Seminar, *The New Century Hymnal*, thriving congregations, new trends in worship, and has undertaken a long-term catechism project. The movement has its own website and two Internet meetings with fifty thousand entries since 1993, James Gorman, host. Confessing Christ has published three books and sundry occasional papers, produces a newsletter, *Joy in the Word*! and a daily prayer discipline sent out to its mailing list of 1500, all edited by Frederick Trost with the assistance of colleague Jacki Mitchell.

At the heart of Confessing Christ are the themes anticipated in all the foregoing, set forth in its Statement of Principles:

Confessing Christ affirms faithfulness to the one Word of the triune God, Jesus Christ, which we are to hear and which we have to trust and obey in life and in death. . . . [It] is committed to listen for God's Word in the Holy Scriptures of the Old and New Testaments and in our rich theological heritage. Central to the United Church of Christ, which baptizes in the name of the Father, Son, and Holy Spirit, is its faith in Jesus Christ as Lord and Savior. This faith is grounded in the authority of Scripture and is expressed in the ecumenical creeds, in the confessions and covenants of our Reformation traditions, in the Preamble and in the prayers, worship and public witness of the Church. . . . [It] embraces the responsibility of every generation to make this faith its own.[11]

The UCC has been our ecclesial context in this small saga of confessing Christ today. A church united cannot be what it is without also being a church uniting with its reach toward the wider Christian community. Again, Fred has pointed us this way, with his own long history of ecumenical involvement from his key role in the *Kirchengemeinschaft* with the EKU and the Lutheran-Reformed Formula of Agreement through publications that go to the wider church as well as the UCC, *No Other Foundation* and *On the Way*, his role in founding the Mission House Center at Lakeland College, and his collegiality with Roman Catholic leaders in both Wisconsin and Latin America in the struggle for both doctrinal integrity and justice.

Bonhoeffer spoke often of the necessity of a *disciplina arcani*, the hidden discipline of biblical faith, prayer, sacrament and sound doctrine from which our public witness in deeds of justice and mercy must rise. Without this solid grounding in the Christ of yesterday and tomorrow, our best efforts in contemporaneity collapse into a culture-Christianity. Of such is our struggle to resist the powers by confessing *Christ* today.

Notes

1. *Theological Declaration of Barmen*, Article 1.

2. Preamble, *The Constitution of the United Church of Christ*.

3. *Theological Declaration of Barmen*, Article II.

4. Preamble, *The Constitution of the United Church of Christ*.

5. A Pallid but Personable Faith? *Time* (29 September 1980): 85.

6. See the writer's section in Gabriel Fackre and Michael Root, *Affirmations and Admonitions: Lutheran Decision and Dialogue with Reformed, Episcopal and Roman Catholic Churches* (Grand Rapids: Wm. B. Eerdmans, 1998).

7. The Craigville Colloquy Letter to our Brothers and Sisters in the United Church of Christ, May, 1984.

8. The papers presented by Walter Brueggemann, Barbara Brown Zikmund, Arthur Gray, Avery Post and Gabriel Fackre were published as *Fesitval of the Church* (St. Louis: Office of Church Life and Leadership, 1978).

9. Biblical-Theological-Liturgical Fellowship, East Petersburg Declaration, East Petersburg, PA, 1979.

10. The members of the group were Gilbert Bartholomew, Leslie Ziegler, Willis Elliott, and the writer.

11. Adopted by the Steering Committee in 1995 and used in its Guidelines for its Centers.

The Great Facilitator Meets Herr Pastor Trost

John T. McFadden

I was socialized into my initial understanding of the pastoral vocation at the worst possible time in the worst possible place: the early 1970s in a suburb of New York City.

Understand that in matters relating to church and ministry I was essentially clueless. Raised nominally Roman Catholic, I lost the church completely before rediscovering it during the heady days of the anti-war movement, keeping company with Berrigan-style radical priests and earnest Quaker activists. Local churches were where we staged pot-luck suppers before climbing onto buses to visit imprisoned conscientious objectors. Local churches were the buildings whose former coal bins had been converted into coffee houses, where we listened to Dylan and Guthrie with little thought for the congregations whose hospitality we enjoyed. The minister was the poor soul who had to keep the church members upstairs happy while we pursued God's real agenda of Peace and Love in the church basement; the ministry of reconciliation expressed as shuttle diplomacy.

Remarkably, I identified sufficiently with the role of reconciler to enroll in theology school. (Having the draft board breathing down my neck provided additional incentive.) My noble goal, like that of many of my peers, was to radicalize the church into "relevance." When Rosemary Reuther was asked why she remained within a church that she clearly detested, she snapped back, "Because that's where the copying machines are!" It made perfect sense to me at the time. We dutifully sat through classes in theology and church history, but it never occurred to us that the authentic agenda of the church was far more radical than the one we sought to impose upon it.

After graduation I was called to serve as senior minister of a large church located in an affluent, educated, and thoroughly protean bedroom community twelve miles from downtown Manhattan and the national offices of the United Church of Christ. I was a "young man of promise" who soon found himself visiting those offices frequently, participating in the gossip, intrigue, and power politics that defined the church in that era. I befriended national staffers who had access to mysterious pots of money that could be directed to funding pet projects. I cultivated relationships with those perceived as having "clout." We dreamed and schemed over three-hour lunches charged to expense accounts. "The national," I learned, was where the Real Action was, and pastoring a congregation that funneled large quantities of OCWM dollars into the structure admitted me to the club.

Within my own congregation I assumed the pastoral role for which I had been prepared. I was the great facilitator, the friendly accomodationist, the resident psychotherapist. I preached thoughtful sermons on social concerns and the quest for self-actualization. My weddings reflected the beliefs (or lack of same) held by the couple; my funerals celebrated human achievement rather than God's grace and glory. I attempted to exemplify the word that most thoroughly defined what I understood to be the vocation of pastor in that time and place; I attempted to be Helpful.

Along the way I served a term on the Central Atlantic Conference Board of Directors. Our Conference Minister was a good and faithful man from whom I learned a great deal, but his job was an impossible one. Almost all the churches of the Conference were of Congregational heritage, clinging fiercely to their autonomy. The Conference staff was a collection of colorful personalities spread over five states and the District of Columbia; leading that staff must have been equivalent to herding cats. The board of directors itself operated very much in keeping with Congregational polity: endless discussion and debate, frequent consulting of Robert's Rules, small caucuses discussing strategies during breaks. It was abundantly clear that the Conference Minister reported to the board and enacted its directives. His thoughts and suggestions were always welcome, but if the board instructed him to jump, the expected response was "how high?"

Needless to say, I was poorly prepared for meeting Frederick Trost. In truth, I was poorly prepared for experiencing the entire Wisconsin Conference, with its deep and living roots in the rich traditions of the Evangelical and Reformed Church. When I agreed to serve on a Conference committee, I quickly learned that the United Church of Christ is more than Congregationalism given a new name, and that there are styles of pastoral leadership other than facilitation.

It was the budget committee. Fred greeted everyone warmly, prayed earnestly, and outlined the difficult issues associated with balancing a budget in a year where funds were tight. Then, in a cordial but firm tone of voice, he identified the items in the proposed budget that were not open to discussion or debate!

Having been trained in Puritan self-control, I succeeded in choking back my outrage. Who does this man think he is? What is the point in serving on a committee of the Conference if the Conference Minister makes unilateral decisions? The word "arrogant" was one of the more printable I assigned to him, and I determined to maintain a certain distance. I am certain that for the next year or two he saw me as cool and aloof. The Great Facilitator had met Herr Pastor Trost, and the distance between the two appeared to be unbridgeable.

I can now look back and chuckle at how badly I misunderstood Fred and his motives in that early encounter. What I then perceived as arrogance I now appreciate as conviction; what I then heard as "this cannot be debated!" I now know was "let us debate this with real passion!" I was so deeply schooled in the ways of power that I failed to recognize genuine authority when I encountered it.

Frederick Trost stands first among the mentors who have taught me that the integrity of the pastoral vocation grows from daring to claim the spiritual authority vested in us by the church. True spiritual authority begins only when we reject the sinful temptation to embrace the ways of power. Power is self-centered and self-serving; its clarion cry is "my will be done!" Power is measured in dollars, in clout, in control. It is brokered by fear and intimidation. Its goal is always to win and in winning to create losers. Power builds fiefdoms and empires. Power always believes in its own wisdom, its own strength, its own purpose. Power answers to nothing beyond itself, not even to God.

Authority is temporarily entrusted to our stewardship by that which is greater than us and to which we are accountable. Spiritual authority must answer to scripture, to tradition, and to the living community of the church, from which it never stands apart or above. Spiritual authority grows from the humility born of knowing we are creatures, utterly beholden to our Creator. As such, we can never possess absolute certainty that our thoughts are wise, our actions righteous, so the authority invested in us must often be discharged in Kierkegaardian fear and trembling. Yet, paradoxically, spiritual authority also grows from the confidence born of knowing that where our wisdom and righteousness end, God's begin, and that through the actions of the Holy Spirit these frail, earthen vessels may convey deeper truth and work greater deeds than our own limited abilities would permit. Spiritual authority acts most boldly when it first prays most humbly; it speaks with the greatest strength when it first listens most carefully. Spiritual authority seeks to empty itself of the conceit of possessing its own wisdom, so that it may say not "my will be done," but "Thy will be done."

True spiritual authority may reside in either a Great Facilitator or a Herr Pastor. It often leads us to a place somewhere between the two. When a Great Facilitator understands the truth of spiritual authority, he or she seeks to help the saints discern the prompting of the Holy Spirit in their discussion and debate. The goal is not to build consensus or resolve an issue by taking a vote. Rather, it is to discover together how the living Spirit is working and speaking through the gathered community of the church.

When a Herr Pastor understands the truth of spiritual authority, that person spends years in coming to know the saints of the church, deeply grieving with them in times of pain and loss, celebrating with them in their joys and new beginnings, until the pastor can no longer say with certainty where his or her own life ends and the life of the congregation begins. When the line between "I" and "we" becomes sufficiently blurred, Herr Pastor can speak with a clear, authoritative voice that is no longer tainted by the presumption of personal power.

Both the Great Facilitator and Herr Pastor must return frequently to the sources of their spiritual authority. They must study God's word in Holy Scripture, preferably in fellowship with other Christians. They must pray, both in the stillness of their own hearts and in settings of Christian community. They must read the thoughts of the saints who preceded them, so that they can dialogue with the wisdom of the ages. They must worship God frequently, so that they never forget who they are and whose they are. They must immerse themselves in Christian theology until it becomes second nature to experience the world through God's eyes, rather than their own.

Frederick Trost has not only fostered my growth in understanding spiritual authority, he has somehow succeeded in awakening my inner Herr Pastor. I came to Wisconsin for what I assumed would be a limited number of years as a part of my "career" in Christian ministry. I no longer have a career, I have a vocation. Unless God's will should change drastically, that vocational calling will keep me in the same church community with which I have now laughed, cried, and worshiped God for seventeen years. If I speak more boldly now, I would like to think that I also speak more faithfully. If I trust party politics less, it is because I trust God more. If I have less passion for social movements, it is because I have more passion for Christ's church. If I increasingly speak as one having authority, it is because I have attempted to abandon the sinful conceit of personal power, a lifelong process that demands daily discipline. I have mentors like Fred to thank for guiding me in this vocational journey.

Frederick Trost has ambled through our midst all these years like a great bear of God, dispensing both bear growls and bear hugs as needed. Herr Bear; Herr Trost. We have never had cause to doubt that he is both our bear and God's bear, and the berry patch called the Wisconsin Conference will seem an emptier one without his looming, loving presence. God bless you, dear friend.

Companion in Faith

Robert Bock

For nearly twenty years, I have known Frederick Trost as a pastor and friend. His ministry as President of the Wisconsin Conference of the United Church of Christ dates to July 1, 1981, when he accepted a call to leave his parish in Chicago to begin a challenging task as spiritual guide and theological companion to the more than 260 congregations that composed our Conference. He brought a theology to the Wisconsin Conference that emphasized a teaching ministry based on the centrality of Christ in disciplined conversation with the scriptures and the world. Pastor Trost developed this theology through diaconic ministries, international ministries, ecumenical partnerships and collegial work with his pastoral colleagues. This emphasis on pastoral ministry has sought to celebrate and honor the role of the pastors and teachers of the Conference. It is a firm foundation that will provide a base for the United Church of Christ in Wisconsin for years to come.

The regional and international ministries that developed from this theology are widely known around the country. The focus on ecumenical partnerships in Europe, the United Kingdom, Latin America, and elsewhere has offered opportunities for laity and pastors in the Conference to experience the life of the church as it is confessed around the world. These partnerships have helped many discover how their own faith is nurtured by the faith and courage of others whose brave witness to the gospel, often in painful settings, has strengthened their own.

The first of these remarkable ecumenical partnerships was established with the Evangelical Church of the Union (EKU) in the Church Province of Goerlitz, Germany, in the early 1980s. *Kirchengemeinschaft* (or "full communion") has led to many visits back and forth over the years where theological work and its importance to the public witness of the church has been uppermost to the clergy and laity who have participated. From this came Association ecumenical partnerships with the Evangelical Church in the District of Moers (Rhineland) and with the Evangelical Church in Prenzlau (in the former German Democratic Republic). For the past ten years, "full communion" has included the Conference in theological dialogue with Haus Villigst (a continuing education center of the Evangelical Church of Westphalia), with the church in Honduras, and with faculty and students at Lakeland College.

The second ecumenical partnership founded by the Conference dates from the early 1980s, and is with the South Western Synod of the

United Reformed Church in the United Kingdom. Youth exchanges have marked this relationship for more than a decade, and annual pastoral exchanges between the Conference and the URC have benefitted pastors and congregations alike.

The third ecumenical partnership of the Conference is with the Evangelical and Reformed Synod of Honduras. In more recent years, the Southeast Association of the Wisconsin Conference has developed an ecumenical partnership with the National Spiritual Council of Churches of Haiti, to the spiritual benefit of all who have participated.

A unique ecumenical partnership, developed originally by the Southwest Association of the Conference and in recent years adopted by the entire Conference, is with the Roman Catholic Diocese of San Cristobal de las Casas in Chiapas, Mexico. In this partnership, humanitarian and spiritual concerns have been foremost. The Conference was credited by Samuel Ruiz Garcia, recently retired Bishop of the Diocese and Nobel Peace Prize nominee, with being one of the first Conferences in the United Church of Christ to join him in the non-violent struggle of the church to improve the conditions of the indigenous people of Chiapas. That struggle, still on-going, has led to the creation of hope among the people and some viable economic alternatives for many within the Diocese. Delegations of laity and clergy have been inspired by the faithful pastoral leadership of Bishop Ruiz and other brave Christians who live in humble surroundings, yet are steadfast in their faith.

Other partnerships include those of the Southwest Association of the Conference (with the Coptic Orthodox Diocese of Beni-Soef in Egypt and with the Presbyterian Church of East Africa) as well as the Northeast Association's partnership (with the Synod of Malagasy Protestant Church in France). Through each of these partnerships, we have come to see more clearly what it is like to be part of communities of faith.

It is impossible to describe all the mission trips that have occurred in the nurturing of these ministries. It is even more impossible to itemize the "results," except to say the humanitarian purposes (including medical assistance, housing development, teaching and sharing the Word, learning from the witness of others) have encouraged many of us. In return for any assistance we have given to others, those who went on these missions would be the first to say they were nurtured in their own faith and understanding to a degree they regard as beyond measure.

Within the Wisconsin Conference itself, the past twenty years have been a period in which a wide variety of ministries have been affirmed. An example is the United Church Camps (UCCI). Faced with increasing deficits in outdoor ministries, a committee was formed to assess the situation. Comprised of Conference and UCCI representatives, as well as staff, the committee examined the future of our two outdoor ministry sites. Decisions were made on the location of these ministries, on necessary budgetary support and on financial coordination. Through the *With One Accord* capital campaign, the outdoor ministry facilities were renewed as part of a strategic plan. At both Moon Beach in northern Wisconsin and at the Pilgrim Conference and Retreat Center on Green Lake, we are now blessed with modern, attractive, functional facilities, at the same time budgets have been brought into balance.

Outstanding pastoral leadership among those serving in the Conference together with the faith present in our congregations, has resulted in an unusual period of financial prosperity in the Wisconsin Conference. This continued even in difficult economic periods in large part because giving to "Our Church's Wider Mission" (OCWM), has consistently increased over the past twenty years.

This reflects the good spirit that generally has pervaded the life of the Conference and a trust of the Conference staff by pastors and laity. It is due in no small way to the unanimity that was so often produced in the Associations and congregations by early and thorough consultation on budget, ministry, and stewardship. As a matter of policy, the churches of the Wisconsin Conference have been able to offer over fifty percent of giving to OCWM and "special offerings" to ministries beyond themselves. This has included support for diaconic work, to UCC seminaries and church related colleges, to campus and urban ministries and to the Wisconsin Council of Churches which is considered by many to be one of the strongest ecumenical expressions of the church in the United States.

The pattern of dialogue with pastors and congregations of the Conference and careful coordination with the four Associations of the Conference, was applied ten years ago to the dramatically successful capital funds campaign, *With One Accord*, in which almost all the churches of the Conference participated. Over $6 million was contributed to the campaign and distributed to the United Church Camps, to Sunburst Youth Homes (for the renovation of campus facilities at Neillsville and to assist with the enormous expense of caring for neglected children), to the establishment of a Rural and Urban Endowment (to offer financial assistance to congregations seeking help in maintaining or expanding their ministries) and to the Conference (for the completion of the new Conference Center in DeForest). That success was followed by another capital campaign, *Forward in Faith*, which is still underway and which has already resulted in commitments from the congregations of more than $4 million. *Forward in Faith* includes the encouragement and support of pastors serving congregations in rural and small town settings, in an effort to strengthen those churches and their unique ministries. It also encourages new church initiatives in Wisconsin (and resources to attract devoted and committed pastoral leadership to such settings). There is additional help envisioned for outdoor ministries and for theological education through the establishment of a chair in Christian Theology and Ethics at Lakeland College. This chair will not only encourage students at the college to study the Christian faith, but offer opportunities for the continuing theological education of laity and clergy in our Conference and ecumenically, including the training of licensed and commissioned ministers willing to serve in fragile settings.

Another aspect of the life of the United Church of Christ in Wisconsin, encouraged by Frederick Trost and the staff of the Conference, has been theological conversation, exploring the content of the Christian faith in small groups, seminars, colloquia, and publications, for the sake of understanding and for the public work of the church. The theological journals, *No Other Foundation, On the Way, Koinonia*, and *In the Tradition* (published by the Southwest Association), are unique in the UCC and express the Conference's commitment to theological reflection and dialogue as a crucial element in shaping the church's mission.

In many and diverse ways, there has been a theology of hope and communication present among us that reflects the scholarship and theological commitment of the staff of the Conference and of our companion in faith, Frederick Trost. He has sought to be a servant of the Word among us and in so doing has helped guide the Wisconsin Conference, its pastors and congregations through times exciting and heart-warming during the last twenty years.

"O God, We Lift This Book"

O God, we lift this book before you as a celebration of Christ's mission in the world through the church. At the heart of this book is our trust in your Holy Presence. We are your children, who have learned to love you with our minds as well as with our hearts and souls. We confess that we have been created for learning, for wisdom, and for gentle strength. And for this we are most thankful.

Through this collection and its celebration of the ministry of Frederick Richard Trost, we seek your blessing, an infusion of creativity and prophetic clarity, of authentic hope and wisdom, so that the ministry of all Christians will be transformed. We seek a birthing of servant leadership, of critical thought, and of love, kindness, and compassion.

We yearn for informed, discriminating, morally alert, and spiritually sensitive persons who are prepared to live in a global community. And, lest we become grim and intensely sour, may all those in ministry be given the gift of playfulness.

It is in the name of Jesus Christ that we pray.

David J. Lawson

Letter from a Friend
in the Former German Democratic Republic

July 27, 1994

Dear Frederick,

When people are close to each other, they look for ways to remember each other and they find them. Years ago, you came to know and love us. You came over and over again to visit us. And so you brought together people, parishes, and churches. You took our communion in Jesus Christ over borders and over the great waters.

Nearly the same was said of Saint Christopherus, who is known as patron of travelers. In many German churches you can see him today in a picture or a figure.

There is a fable that tells about Christopherus and it goes like this:

As a Roman officer, he was a tall and strong man. His birth name was "Opherus," which means "Carrier" (*Träger*). He wanted to work for the strongest and bravest ruler in the world. But the most powerful king he found was afraid of the devil. So Opherus began to serve the devil until he recognized that the devil was frightened of a cross he beheld at the side of a road.

And so Opherus began looking for the Lord, whose symbol is the cross.

On the advice of a hermit, Opherus carried travelers over a big river, which had no bridge. One night, a child came to him with the request that Opherus should carry him over the river. He thought, "Sure, nothing could be easier than that!"

But in the middle of the river, the child became so heavy that Opherus sank under the water. "Child, why are you so heavy? It is as if I am carrying the whole world!"

"You are right. You do carry the whole world, for I am Jesus Christ, the one you have been looking for, and I carry all the burdens and sins of the world. Because you carried me, your name shall be Christopherus" (which means "Carrier of Christ").

Dear Frederick! You are also such a "Christopherus" because you are a bridge in the name of the Lord, between us.

Norbert Kruppke †

Osterburg/Altmark, Germany

Norbert Kruppke, a pastor of the Evangelical Church in the Altmark, in the former German Democratic Republic, was an especially close and faithful friend of Frederick Trost until Pastor Kruppke was called to the "ecclesia triumphans" in June 2000. Frederick Trost considered Pastor Kruppke an illustration of pastoral integrity; modest, unassuming, a genuine servant of the Word, whose biblical preaching Pastor Trost greatly admired. Norbert Kruppke's ministry spanned the life of the former German Democratic Republic.

Message of Friendship and Weg–Geleit

Dear Frederick,

You are approaching the door of a great and eventful span of your life; soon you will enter into a new and important time in life's journey. I appreciate the opportunity to express to you my cordial greetings, assuring you of the spiritual fellowship that has been so meaningful and enriching during years past.

Three prayers give expression to this communion. They symbolize your close connection with Christianity and the churches in this country. The first expresses a personal and a family tradition; the second offers strength of faith out of the German middle ages; and, as for the third: may it accompany you in your ongoing ministry:

Speise ist	Berklart Erde
Hilf HERR	Daß sie in uns werde
Guter Geist	Und gute Kraft,
Die DICH preist,	Uns baut und schafft.

Dear Lord, help me, that may I seek Thee with all my strength, in all things. And as I seek Thee, let me also find Thee, and let me grow in joy, because of Thy love which makes me happy. Help me, that I may be united with Thy will according to Thy loving kindness.

Mechthild of Magdeburg

O Almighty God, who sittest upon the throne, make all things within us new this day. Renew our faith, and hope, and love; renew our wills, that we may serve Thee gladly and watchfully with all our powers; renew our delight in Thy truth and in Thy worship; renew our joy in Thee, our longing that all may know Thee, our desires and labors to serve others. And so take care of us Thy people, who embrace the cross of Thy Son and desire to walk in the light and power of Thy Spirit, now and evermore.

Lothar Schreiner
Wuppertal, Rhineland

Contributors

Hans-Jürgen Abromeit is a member of the faculty at Haus Villigst, a continuing education center for pastors and laity in the Evangelical Church of Westphalia, Germany.

Raymond P. Adams is Moderator of the Synod of the South Western Province of the United Reformed Church, United Kingdom.

Victoria J. Barnett is a scholar of the German church struggle, and editor of the new revised edition of Eberhard Bethge's *Dietrich Bonhoeffer: A Biography.*

Browne Barr is retired Dean of the San Francisco Theological Seminary, California and former minister of First Congregational United Church of Christ, Berkeley, California.

Lee C. Barrett III is the Mary B. and Henry P. Staeger Professor of Theology, Lancaster Theological Seminary, Pennsylvania.

Joseph Alden Bassett is Pastor of The First Church in ChestnutHill, Massachusetts.

Martha Ann Baumer is Visiting Professor of Pastoral Studies, Eden Theological Seminary, St. Louis, Missouri.

Edwin E. Beers is a retired United Church of Christ pastor currently serving as a retreat leader and spiritual director.

Thomas O. Bentz is Association Minister of the Southeast Association, Wisconsin Conference, United Church of Christ.

Hans Berthold is the retired Director of Haus Villigst, a continuing education center for pastors and laity in the Evangelical Church of Westphalia, Germany.

Dale L. Bishop is Executive Minister for Wider Church Ministries of the United Church of Christ, Cleveland, Ohio.

Donald G. Bloesch is Professor Emeritus of Theology, Dubuque Theological Seminary, Dubuque, Iowa.

Robert Bock is former Dean of the School of Business, University of Wisconsin, Madison, and Treasurer of the Wisconsin Conference, United Church of Christ.

Theodore A. Braun served on the staff of the National Council of Churches of Christ in the USA as liaison with the Peace Corps, and edits *Grass Roots*, a newsletter of socio-theological commentary.

Walter Brueggemann is Professor of Old Testament at Columbia Theological Seminary, Decatur, Georgia.

John E. Burkhart is Professor Emeritus of Theology, McCormick Theological Seminary, Chicago, Illinois.

Mark S. Burrows is Professor of The History of Christianity, Andover Newton Theological School, Newton Centre, Massachusetts.

W. Sterling Cary is retired Conference Minister of the Illinois Conference, United Church of Christ.

David C. Chevrier is Pastor of the Wellington Avenue United Church of Christ, Chicago, Illinois.

Richard L. Christensen is Associate Professor of Religion, Lakeland College, Sheboygan, Wisconsin.

Deborah Rahn Clemens is Pastor of Friedens United Church of Christ, Sumneytown, Pennsylvania, and teaches at the Moravian Theological Seminary, Bethlehem.

Jake Close is Senior Minister at First Congregational United Church of Christ, Wisconsin Rapids, Wisconsin.

Denise J. Cole is Senior Minister at Olivet United Church of Christ, Columbus, Wisconsin.

Charles A. Copenhaver (†August 1982) was an ordained minister of the United Church of Christ. He served as Senior Minister of the Reformed Church of Bronxville, Bronxville, New York and other congregations.

Richard D. Crane is Pastor of Union Christian Church, Tuskegee, Alabama and teaches at Auburn University.

Herbert R. Davis is retired Minister of Eliot United Church of Christ, Newton Centre, Massachusetts.

Barbara de Souza is a Missionary of the United Church of Christ in Rio de Janeiro, Brazil.

Thomas E. Dipko is retired Executive Vice President of the United Church Board for Homeland Ministries.

Uwe Dittmer is a retired Pastor of the Evangelical Church in Berlin-Brandenburg, Germany.

Thomas A. Duff practiced as a neuro-surgeon for 25 years and is now devoted to writing and painting.

James D. Eckblad is Senior Pastor at Immanuel United Church of Christ, West Bend, Wisconsin.

Jon S. Enslin is Bishop of the South-Central Synod of Wisconsin, Evangelical Lutheran Church in America.

Gabriel Fackre is Abbot Professor of Christian Theology Emeritus, Andover Newton Theological School, Newton Centre, Massachusetts.

Beth Ann Faeth is Associate Minister at First Congregational United Church of Christ, River Falls, Wisconsin.

James Fellowes is Chief Executive Officer of Fellowes Manufacturing Company, Itasca, Illinois.

Jerry Folk is Executive Director of the Wisconsin Council of Churches, Sun Prairie, Wisconsin.

Hans Wilhelm Fricke-Hein is a pastor in the Central Office *Landeskirchenamt*), Evangelical Church in the Rhineland, Düsseldorf, Germany.

Mary Gafner is Pastor of the Washington Reformation United Church of Christ, Monticello, Wisconsin.

James R. Gorman is Senior Pastor of Faith United Church of Christ, Milwaukee, Wisconsin.

Katherine Greene-McCreight is Lecturer in the Religion and Biblical Literature Department, Smith College, Northampton, Massachusetts.

Christa Grengel is Director of the Overseas Department of the Evangelical Church in Germany (EKD).

Wells B. Grogan is retired Senior Minister of First Congregational United Church of Christ, Madison, Wisconsin.

Reinhard Groscurth served for 25 years as Ecumenical Officer of the Evangelical Church of the Union, Berlin, and is now retired.

Henry A. Gustafson is Professor Emeritus of New Testament Theology, United Theological Seminary, New Brighton, Minnesota.

Douglas J. Hall is Professor Emeritus of Christian Theology, McGill University, Montreal, Quebec, Canada.

Paul L. Hammer is retired Professor of New Testament Interpretation, Colgate Rochester Divinity School, Rochester, New York.

John C. Helt is Senior Minister of First Congregational United Church of Christ, Fort Atkinson, Wisconsin.

Thomas R. Henry is Senior Pastor of St. Pauls United Church of Christ, Chicago, Illinois.

Kristin Herzog is an independent scholar in the fields of American literature, theology, women's studies, and the religion and culture of Peru.

Michael F. Hubbard is retired Moderator of the Synod of the South Western Province, United Reformed Church, United Kingdom.

John Huebscher is Executive Director of the Wisconsin Catholic Conference, which is the public policy voice of Wisconsin's Roman Catholic Bishops.

Wilhelm Hüffmeier is President of the *Kirchenkanzlei* of the Evangelical Church of the Union, Berlin, Germany.

Robert G. Hunsicker is Pastor of St. Andrew Church of the United Church of Christ, Lancaster, Pennsylvania.

George Hunsinger is Director of the Center for Barth Studies, Princeton Theological Seminary, Princeton, New Jersey.

Teruo Kawata is retired General Secretary and Conference Minister of the Hawaii Conference, United Church of Christ.

Christoph Keienburg is Pastor of the Lukas parish of the Lutheran Congregation of Paderborn, Westphalia, Germany.

Joanne Kollasch, O.S.B., is a founding member of Saint Benedict Center, an ecumenical monastic community in Madison, Wisconsin.

Gerhard Koslowsky is a retired Pastor of the Evangelical Church in the Rhineland, Germany, where he served for a number of years as Ecumenical Officer.

Norbert Kruppke (†June, 2000) served as Pastor of the historic Nikolaikirche in Osterburg, Altmark, in the former German Democratic Republic.

Karl A. Kuhn is Assistant Professor of Religion at Lakeland College, Sheboygan, Wisconsin.

David J. Lawson is a Bishop of the United Methodist Church, living in Franklin, Indiana.

Gerhard Linn served as Ecumenical Officer of the Evangelical Church of the Union, Berlin, until his retirement in 2000.

John W. Lynes is a Conference Minister of the New Hampshire Conference, United Church of Christ.

Daniel Maguire is a member of the faculty of the Department of Theology, Marquette University, Milwaukee, Wisconsin.

J. Clinton McCann, Jr. is the Evangelical Professor of Biblical Interpretation at Eden Theological Seminary, St. Louis, Missouri.

Charles McCollough is a sculptor, recently retired from the Office for Church in Society of the United Church of Christ.

Michael McConnell is Regional Director of the American Friends Service Committee, Chicago, Illinois.

John T. McFadden is Senior Minister of First Congregational United Church of Christ, Appleton, Wisconsin.

M. Douglas Meeks is the Cal Turner Chancellor Professor of Theology and Wesleyan Studies in the Divinity School of Vanderbilt University, Nashville, Tennessee.

Dorothy Heckner Mendonca is Pastor and Teacher, First Congregational United Church of Christ, Redgranite, Wisconsin.

David J. Michael is Senior Pastor of Lake Edge United Church of Christ, Madison, Wisconsin.

Mark H. Miller is Conference Minister of the South Central Conference, United Church of Christ, Austin, Texas.

F. Russell Mitman is Conference Minister of the Pennsylvania Southeast Conference, United Church of Christ.

Charles E. Mize is Senior Minister of Union Congregational United Church of Christ, Green Bay, Wisconsin.

Ute Molitor is Pastor of Community of Hope United Church of Christ, Madison, Wisconsin.

Robert F. Morneau is Auxiliary Bishop of the Roman Catholic Diocese of Green Bay, Wisconsin.

David S. Moyer is Association Minister of the Northwest Association, Wisconsin Conference, United Church of Christ.

Robert D. Mutton is Association Minister of the Southwest Association, Wisconsin Conference, United Church of Christ.

Mary Ann Neevel is Senior Minister of Plymouth United Church of Christ, Milwaukee, Wisconsin.

Thomas S. Neilsen is Senior Pastor of Swiss United Church of Christ, New Glarus, Wisconsin.

F. Burton Nelson is Research Professor of Christian Ethics, North Park Theological Seminary, Chicago, Illinois and Senior Associate at Oxford University Centre for Hebrew and Jewish Studies in the United Kingdom.

Donald G. Nelson is Pastor of Zwingli United Church of Christ, Paoli, Wisconsin.

Gaylord Noyce is retired Professor of Pastoral Theology, Yale Divinity School, New Haven, Connecticut.

Gail R. O'Day is the A. H. Shatford Professor of Preaching and New Testament at the Candler School of Theology, Emory University, Atlanta, Georgia.

Richard Olmsted is Senior Minister of Acton Congregational Church, United Church of Christ, Acton, Massachusetts.

Walter J. Olsen is retired Pastor of St. Mark United Church of Christ, Milwaukee, Wisconsin.

Gail A. O'Neal is an Associate Conference Minister of the Wisconsin Conference, United Church of Christ.

David Ostendorf is Executive Director of the Center for New Community, Chicago, Illinois.

Dorothy A. Palmer is pastor of the Congregational United Church of Christ, Edgerton, Wisconsin.

Stephen J. Patterson is Professor of New Testament, Eden Theological Seminary, St. Louis, Missouri.

Erwin H. Pegel is retired Pastor of Zwingli United Church of Christ, Monticello, Wisconsin.

Douglas M. Pierce is an Associate Conference Minister of the Wisconsin Conference, United Church of Christ.

Mark X. Pirazzini is Senior Minister of First Congregational United Church of Christ, Eau Claire, Wisconsin.

Carmen Porco is President of Carmen Porco Consulting Services and Director of Housing and Community Learning Centers for the American Baptist Homes of the Midwest.

Shari Prestemon is Executive Director of the Back Bay Mission, United Church of Christ, Biloxi, Mississippi.

Paul A. Quackenbush is Pastor of McFarland United Church of Christ, McFarland, Wisconsin.

William Rader is retired Pastor of the Shared Ministry, the United Methodist Church and the United Church of Christ, Harrisburg, Pennsylvania.

Carl J. Rasmussen is an attorney and a partner of the Boardman Law Firm, Madison, Wisconsin.

Max J. Rigert is Pastor of the Congregational United Church of Christ, Delavan, Wisconsin.

Joachim Rogge (†June, 2000) served as Bishop of the Evangelische Kirche der schlesischen Oberlausitz, Görlitz, Germany.

Barbara Rudolph is a Pastor and Acting Superintendent in the Moers District of the Evangelical Church in the Rhineland, Germany.

Samuel Ruiz Garcia is retired Bishop of the Roman Catholic Diocese of San Cristóbal de las Casas, Chiapas, Mexico.

Stephen P. Savides is Minister of First Congregational United Church of Christ, Watertown, Wisconsin.

Nikolaus Schneider is Vice-president of the Evangelical Church in the Rhineland, Düsseldorf, Germany.

Susan R. Schneider-Adams is an Associate Conference Minister of the Wisconsin Conference, United Church of Christ.

Lothar Schreiner is Professor Emeritus of Missiology and the History of Religions at the Theologische Hochschule, Wuppertal, Germany.

Barbara Kline Seamon is Minister of Central Congregational Church, United Church of Christ, Orange, Massachusetts.

Bryan C. Sirchio is a church musician, retreat leader, and founder of Crosswind Music Ministries, Madison, Wisconsin.

Lynne Smith, O.S.B, is a founding member of Saint Benedict Center, an ecumenical monastic community in Madison, Wisconsin.

Max L. Stackhouse is the Stephen Colwell Professor of Christian Ethics, Princeton Theological Seminary, Princeton, New Jersey.

Jack Stotts is retired President of Austin Presbyterian Theological Seminary, Austin, Texas.

Jane Suddendorf teaches art at Port Washington High School in Port Washington, Wisconsin.

Jeffrey S. Suddendorf is Pastor of First Congregational United Church of Christ, Port Washington, Wisconsin.

Iris Susen-Pilger is a Superintendent of the Evangelische Kirche der schlesischen Oberlausitz, Miesky, Germany.

John H. Thomas is General Minister and President of the United Church of Christ, Cleveland, Ohio.

Joanne Thomson is an ordained Minister of the United Church of Christ, living in Madison, Wisconsin.

Christine M. Trost is Academic Coordinator of the American History and Institutions Office, and teaches American Politics and Government, University of California, Berkeley.

Paul Gerhardt Trost is an artist living in Sonoma, California.

Theodore Louis Trost teaches in the Religious Studies department and the New College at the University of Alabama, Tuscaloosa.

Reinhard Ulrich is Professor of Philosophy and Religion at Lakeland College, Sheboygan, Wisconsin.

Bonnie B. Van Overbeke is Pastor at Memorial United Church of Christ, Fitchburg, Wisconsin.

Mary David Walgenbach, O.S.B., is a founding member of Saint Benedict Center, an ecumenical monastic community in Madison, Wisconsin.

Rembert G. Weakland, O.S.B., is Roman Catholic Archbishop of the Archdiocese of Milwaukee, Wisconsin, and has served in Rome as the Abbot Primate of the Benedictine order.

Eugene S. Wehrli (†February, 2000) served as Professor of New Testament, and as President, Eden Theological Seminary, St. Louis, Missouri.

Paul Westermeyer is Professor of Church Music at Luther Seminary, St. Paul, Minnesota.

Bennie E. Whiten, Jr. is retired Conference Minister and President of the Massachusetts Conference, United Church of Christ.

Richard S. Williams recently retired as Pastor of Dane Immanuel United Church of Christ, Dane, Wisconsin.

Charles A. Wolfe is Pastor of Plymouth Congregational United Church of Christ, Madison, Wisconsin.

Mark E. Yurs is Pastor of Salem United Church Christ, Verona, Wisconsin.

Kenneth R. Ziebell is retired Area Executive for Europe, Global Ministries, United Church of Christ and the Christian Church (Disciples of Christ).

Barbara Brown Zikmund has served as President of Hartford Seminary, Hartford, Connecticut, and has been called to the faculty of the Doshisha University in Kyoto, Japan.

*In Essentials unity
in non-essentials liberty
in all things charity*